Contemporary Cultures, Global Connections

—— ANTHROPOLOGY FOR THE 21ST CENTURY ——

Revised First Edition

Edited by Victoria Bernal

SAN DIEGO

Bassim Hamadeh, CEO and Publisher
Jess Estrella, Senior Graphic Designer
Natalie Piccotti, Director of Marketing
Kassie Graves, Senior Vice President, Editorial
Jamie Giganti, Director of Academic Publishing

Printed in the United States of America.

3970 Sorrento Valley Blvd., Ste. 500, San Diego, CA 92121

Contents

Introduction

Victoria Bernal

Cultural anthropology is often misunderstood as an arcane and antiquated field concerned with documenting isolated tribes or making sense of hunting and gathering as a way of life. Surprisingly, anthropologists themselves sometimes unwittingly perpetuate these stereotypes in the materials they present to undergraduate students. Too often the textbooks and ethnographies selected for teaching rely on classic studies that reinforce students' impressions that the study of culture is about people whose tradition-bound existence stands in contrast to modern living and scientific knowledge. There is a growing gap between the kinds of research now being conducted by anthropologists and the anthropology that is currently taught to undergraduates. The goal of this anthology is to bridge that gap by presenting students with readings that reflect the state of the art in anthropology and provide an overview of the complexity and variety of present-day life around the world. The readings selected reflect the fact that anthropologists today focus on cities, science and technology, media, consumer culture, government policies, corporations, migration, and other institutions and processes shaping life around the globe. Anthropologists no longer approach cultures as worlds unto themselves, but rather from the assumption that we are all local and global at the same time. We study communities and organizations in the United States and Europe as well as rural communities in the Global South, and we study the relationships that connect them. The readings cover essential and enduring themes of anthropology—including politics, economy, belief systems, and kinship, as they are addressed by cultural anthropologists who are engaged in the study of contemporary life. The collection includes chapters on fair trade, NGOs, world music, cyberspace, environmental conservation, and microcredit among other contemporary global trends and public concerns. The anthology is designed with undergraduate anthropology students in mind, but scholars and students across disciplines may find the readings interesting in their own right. The readings demonstrate the significance of culture in all realms of human experience and activity and put to rest the idea that cultural anthropology is about exotic people living in a separate time and place from the rest of the world. The research included here makes clear the relevance of ethnographic approaches and anthropological insights for understanding life in the 21st century.

Globalization is a central theme of anthropology today. The various chapters provide examples of how globalization gives rise to connections, relationships, and processes that cross regions and cultural boundaries, producing differences as well as similarities. The contents were selected to be accessible and geographically diverse, and to explore cultural diversity and consider the ways that people right next to us as well as others far away inhabit different lifeworlds. Readings examine the global relationships that shape people's everyday lives and that link us together across cultural and geographic boundaries.

Anthropology develops our understanding of the conditions that give rise to particular cultural practices, values, and institutions in our own society as well as in other societies and uncovers processes of change. Cultural anthropology challenges us to think critically about our commonsense assumptions about society and human nature. The readings reveal the dynamics and significance of culture in a range of diverse settings including a high school in Silicon Valley, restaurants in Kathmandu, a village in New Guinea, and a mental health center in Tokyo. Most chapters are empirically rich, full of details about people's lives and perspectives. At the same time, the chapters expose readers to theoretically sophisticated analyses and to key concepts and terminology used by anthropologists. Through these compelling accounts of specific conditions and contexts, a broader picture of the relevance of anthropology for explaining world events and solving contemporary human problems emerges.

While some of the contributors are well-known anthropologists, others are among the many lesser-known anthropologists doing exciting work. All of the selections come from peer-reviewed publications, many from the discipline's leading journals, and therefore each chapter has been screened by fellow anthropologists. Most of the work included here first appeared in print after 2000, presenting an overview of emerging trends in cultural anthropology.

If anthropology can no longer be described as the study of primitive tribes or small-scale societies, what defines anthropology today? What most distinguishes cultural anthropology now is not where anthropologists conduct their studies, but the way we look at the world. The anthropological perspective is a creative engagement with the world through which we produce knowledge and think critically about the ways that understandings, facts, and representations are produced. Learning to observe closely, to listen carefully, to read between the lines, to suspend judgment, to perceive the absurdity of our own social conventions as well as those of others, to become attuned to nuance and ambiguity, to see not black and white, but all the many shades of variation in between, to see oneself through others' eyes, and to be able to shift along a range of perspectives from which to view the world—*all are part of seeing like an anthropologist*. The anthropological perspective enriches our understandings of ourselves and the world we live in and opens up conceptual space for imagining new ways of living and new solutions to human problems.

The book is organized so that the opening chapters reflect on the politics of knowledge and raise issues about the ways we think and talk about cultural difference. These readings draw attention to the connections between knowledge production, issues of representation, and relations of inequality. The selections by Said and Piot do this through a focus on Western ideas about the Middle East and Africa, respectively. The essays by Morgan on Ecuadorian ideas about prenatal existence and Cohen on old age in India and the West reveal the significance of culture as a lens through which everyone sees reality, including scientists. The chapters by

Hecht and Emoff explore the meaning of culture through the authors' vivid, firsthand accounts of their fieldwork experiences and the relationships they developed with particular individuals in Brazil and Madagascar. Both essays examine the connection between the anthropologist and their "informant" in ways that reveal the wider circuits of knowledge production, resources, and power within which scholars and their subjects are located. In each case, it is significant that, however isolated or marginalized the informants may be or appear to be, they, too, understand themselves in a global context. The next three articles, written by Weaver, Lyon, and Bernal, present various aspects of globalization and the processes and relationships that connect the contemporary world. Weaver uses concepts from ecology to explain the consequences of global interconnectedness as revealed in the 2008 financial crisis. Lyon discusses world markets and fair-trade initiatives through the experience of coffee farmers in Nicaragua. Bernal focuses on transnationalism and the internet, exploring the ways relationships and identities transcend national borders as revealed through the activities of Eritreans in diaspora. Readings 10, 11, 12, and 13 explore constructions of identity, social categories, and racialization. Shankar looks at ethnic encounters among high school students in Silicon Valley, CA. Gaudio discusses ideas about homosexuality among Nigerian Muslims. Wright analyzes the mismatch between an NGO's Western categories of sexual orientation and those of the Bolivian men it seeks to serve, and Bright examines lowriding and the changing experience of Chicano identity in the southwestern United States. The chapters by Newcomb, Penglase, and Lutz focus on politics, revealing the ways power is experienced and exercised in daily life through the behavior of ordinary people as well as through institutions and authorities. Newcomb explores how new spaces like fitness clubs are giving rise to a new social order of gender and space in Morocco. Penglase examines how drug traffickers gain power and legitimacy in a poor neighborhood in Brazil, and Lutz provides an analysis of the rise of militarism in the United States before and after 9/11.

Many of the chapters throughout the book address globalization and capitalism in some way because these relationships and processes underlie so many current circumstances and conditions. Readings 17–21 were selected to explore distinct aspects of present-day economic life. Freeman's research on women high-tech workers in the Caribbean presents the idea of the global assembly line and provides perspectives on gender and class. Liechty's research in Nepal reveals the process of commodification as food and sex become new objects of commercial exchange in Kathmandu. Karim's study of Grameen Bank addresses the trend of microlending as a solution to poverty and reveals the hidden, gendered, and sometimes unintended effects of interventions. Allison's work on Japanese consumer maladies explores what it means to define ourselves through what we buy, and thus sheds light on consumer capitalism. The contribution by Skoczen examines tourism, economic development, and foreign investment in the Dominican Republic and the local struggles and transformations ensuing from their relationships.

The chapters by Krause on Italy and Adrian on Taiwan address the family from anthropological perspectives. Their studies show that familial relationships, marriage, and childbearing cannot be understood as products of biology, matters of individual choice, or in terms of a private sphere of personal life separate from society. These essays reveal the ways desires and behaviors are enjoined and constrained by wider sets of relationships and institutions. Readings 24 and 25 deal with belief systems and religion. Langford examines encounters of emigrants from Laos and Cambodia with American hospitals and funeral homes, where the understanding and management of death is shaped by cultural beliefs very different from their own. Wesch explores a contemporary incident involving witchcraft in New Guinea. His analysis calls into question the seeming exoticness of the beliefs and practices he observed, placing them in the context of colonization, missionary activity, and the exercise of state power. Wesch addresses questions of anthropological knowledge production that resonate with the issues raised by Said and Piot earlier in this anthology. The final two readings, by Borovoy on Japan and Nygren on Nicaragua, provide anthropological perspectives on science. Borovoy's article reveals how the therapeutic concept "codependence" is premised on Western notions of individuality that run counter to Japanese familial roles. Nygren's study questions assumptions of scientific rationalism as she examines the conflicts involving scientists, development experts, and Nicaraguan peasants in an environmental protection zone.

Taken together, the readings collected here demonstrate the relevance of anthropology for understanding local and global dilemmas of contemporary life. The readings also showcase the methods and concepts that anthropologists today employ in their research. The anthology reveals the enduring promise of ethnography to answer big questions through close analysis of detailed ethnographic data. The anthropologists whose work is featured here examine everyday life and local institutions in the context of global relationships. Far from eclipsing the need for anthropological research, globalization, advances in science and technology, and the increasing mobility and migration of people raise questions about the meaning and conduct of life. They are fundamentally cultural questions, and thus, questions that anthropology is well-suited to answer.

1

Orientalism

Edward Said

I have begun with the assumption that the Orient is not an inert fact of nature. It is not merely *there*, just as the Occident itself is not just *there* either. We must take seriously Vico's great observation that men make their own history, that what they can know Is what they have made, and extend it to geography: as both geographical and cultural entities—to say nothing of historical entities—such locales, regions, geographical sectors as "Orient" and "Occident" are man-made. Therefore as much as the West itself, the Orient is an idea that has a history and a tradition of thought, imagery, and vocabulary that have given it reality and presence in and for the West. The two geographical entities thus support and to an extent reflect each other.

Having said that, one must go on to state a number of reasonable qualifications. In the first place, it would be wrong to conclude that the Orient was *essentially* an idea, or a creation with no corresponding reality. When Disraeli said in his novel *Tancred* that the East was a career, he meant that to be interested in the East was something bright young Westerners would find to be an all-consuming passion; he should not be interpreted as saying that the East was *only* a career for Westerners. There were—and are—cultures and nations whose location is in the East, and their lives, histories, and customs have a brute reality obviously greater than anything that could be said about them in the West. About that fact this study of Orientalism has very little to contribute, except to acknowledge it tacitly. But the phenomenon of Orientalism as I study it here deals principally, not with a correspondence between Orientalism and Orient, but with the internal consistency of Orientalism and its ideas about the Orient (the East as career) despite or beyond any correspondence, or lack thereof, with a "real" Orient. My point is that Disraeli's statement about the East refers mainly to that created consistency, that regular constellation of ideas as the pre-eminent thing about the Orient, and not to its mere being, as Wallace Stevens's phrase has it.

A second qualification is that ideas, cultures, and histories cannot seriously be understood or studied without their force, or snore precisely their configurations of power, also being studied. To believe that the Orient was created—or, as I call it, "Orientalized"—and to believe that such things happen simply as a necessity of the imagination, is to be disingenuous. The relationship between Occident and Orient is a relationship of power, of domination, of varying degrees of a complex hegemony, and is quite accurately indicated in the title of K. M. Panikkar's classic *Asia and Western Dominance.* The Orient was Orientalized not only because it was discovered to be "Oriental" in all those ways considered commonplace by an average nineteenth-century European, but also because it *could be*—that is, submitted to being—*made* Oriental. There is very little consent to be found, for example, in the fact that Flaubert's encounter with an Egyptian courtesan produced a widely influential model of the Oriental woman; she never spoke of herself, she never represented her emotions, presence, or history. *He* spoke for and represented her. He was foreign, comparatively wealthy, male, and these were historical facts of domination that allowed him not only to possess Kuchuk Hanem physically but to speak for her and tell his readers in what way she was "typically Oriental." My argument is that Flaubert's situation of strength in relation to Kuchuk Hanem was not an isolated instance. It fairly stands for the pattern of relative strength between East and West, and the discourse about the Orient that it enabled.

This brings us to a third qualification. One ought never to assume that the structure of Orientalism is nothing more than a structure of lies or of myths which, were the truth about them to be told, would simply blow away. I myself believe that Orientalism is more particularly valuable as a sign of European-Atlantic power over the Orient than it is as a veridic discourse about the Orient (which is what, in its academic or scholarly form, it claims to be). Nevertheless, what we must respect and try to grasp is the sheer knitted-together strength of Orientalist discourse, its very close ties to the enabling socio-economic and political institutions, and its redoubtable durability. After all, any system of ideas that can remain unchanged as teachable wisdom (in academies, books, congresses, universities, foreign-service institutes) from the period of Ernest Renan in the late 1840s until the present in the United States must be something more formidable than a mere collection of lies. Orientalism, therefore, is not an airy European fantasy about the Orient, but a created body of theory and practice in which, for many generations, there has been a considerable material investment. Continued investment made Orientalism, as a system of knowledge about the Orient, an accepted grid for filtering through the Orient into Western consciousness, just as that same investment multiplied—indeed, made truly productive—the statements proliferating out from Orientalism into the general culture.

Gramsci has made the useful analytic distinction between civil and political society in which the former is made up of voluntary (or at least rational and noncoercive) affiliations like schools, families, and unions, the latter of state institutions (the army, the police, the central bureaucracy) whose role in the polity is direct domination. Culture, of course, is to be found operating within civil society, where the influence of ideas, of institutions, and of other persons works not through domination but by what Gramsci calls consent. In any society not totalitarian, then, certain cultural forms predominate over others, just as certain ideas are more influential than others; the form of this cultural leadership is what Gramsci has identified as *hegemony*, an indispensable concept for any understanding of cultural life in the industrial West. It is hegemony, or rather the result of cultural hegemony at work, that gives Orientalism the durability and the strength I have been speaking about so far. Orientalism is never far from what Denys Hay has called the idea of Europe, a collective notion identifying "us" Europeans as against all "those" non-Europeans, and indeed it can be argued that the major component in European culture is precisely what made that culture hegemonic both in and outside Europe: the idea of European identity as a superior one in comparison with all the non-European peoples and cultures. There is in addition the hegemony of European ideas about the Orient, themselves reiterating European superiority over Oriental backwardness, usually overriding the possibility that a more independent, or more skeptical, thinker might have had different views on the matter.

In a quite constant way, Orientalism depends for its strategy on this flexible *positional* superiority, which puts the Westerner in a whole series of possible relationships with the Orient without ever losing him the relative upper hand. And why should it have been otherwise, especially during the period of extraordinary European ascendancy from the late Renaissance to the present? The scientist, the scholar, the missionary, the trader, or the soldier was in, or thought about, the Orient because he *could be there,* or could think about it, with very little resistance on the Orient's part. Under the general heading of knowledge of the Orient, and within the umbrella of Western hegemony over the Orient during the period from the end of the eighteenth century, there emerged a complex Orient suitable for study in the academy, for display in the museum, for reconstruction in the colonial office, for theoretical illustration in anthropological, biological, linguistic, racial, and historical theses about mankind and the universe, for instances of economic and sociological theories of development, revolution, cultural personality, national or religious character. Additionally, the imaginative examination of things Oriental was based more or less exclusively upon a sovereign Western consciousness out of whose unchallenged centrality an Oriental world emerged, first according to general ideas about who or what was an Oriental, then according to a detailed logic governed not simply by empirical reality but by a battery of desires, repressions, investments, and projections. If we can point to great Orientalist works of genuine scholarship like Silvestre de Sacy's *Chrestomathie arabe* or Edward William Lane's *Account of the Manners and Customs of the Modern Egyptians,* we need also to note that Renan's and Gobineau's racial ideas came out of the same impulse, as did a great many Victorian pornographic novels (see the analysis by Steven Marcus of "The Lustful Turk").

And yet, one must repeatedly ask oneself whether what matters in Orientalism is the general group of ideas overriding the mass of material—about which who could deny that they were shot through with doctrines of European superiority, various kinds of racism, imperialism, and the like, dogmatic views of "the Oriental" as a kind of ideal and unchanging abstraction?—or the much more varied work produced by almost uncountable individual writers, whom one would take up as individual instances of authors dealing with the Orient. In a sense the two alternatives, general and particular, are really two perspectives on the same material: in both instances one would have to deal with pioneers in the field like William Jones, with great artists like Nerval or Flaubert. And why would it not be possible to employ both perspectives together, or one after the other? Isn't there an obvious danger of distortion (of precisely the kind that academic Orientalism has always been prone to) if either too general or too specific a level of description is maintained systematically?

My two fears are distortion and inaccuracy, or rather the kind of inaccuracy produced by too dogmatic a generality and too positivistic a localized focus. In trying to deal with these problems I have tried to deal with three main aspects of my own contemporary reality that seem to me to point the way out of the methodological or perspectival difficulties I have been discussing, difficulties that might force one, in the first instance, into writing a coarse polemic on so unacceptably general a level of description as not to be worth the effort, or in the second instance, into writing so detailed and atomistic a series of analyses as to lose all track of the general lines of force informing the field, giving it its special cogency. How then to recognize individuality and to reconcile it with its intelligent, and by no means passive or merely dictatorial, general and hegemonic context?

2

Remotely Global
Village Modernity in West Africa
Charles Piot

IMAGES AND POWER

This study is an attempt to retheorize a classic out-of-the-way place (Tsing 1993)—a society in the savanna region of West Africa where Meyer Fortes, Jack Goody, and Marcel Griaule conducted their ethnographic research. These scholars analyzed Tallensi, LoDagaa, and Dogon societies as if they were timeless and bounded, located beyond the space-time of the colonial and the modern. By contrast, my own analysis of a society in this savanna region—the Kabre of northern Togo—will argue that this place has long been globalized and is better conceptualized as existing within modernity. To claim as much is to argue against appearances, however, for this is a place that has all the earmarks of a still pristine African culture: subsistence farming, gift exchange, straw-roofed houses, rituals to the spirits and ancestors. Moreover, many of these elements of "tradition"—the ritual system, the domain of gift exchange—have flourished and intensified over the last thirty years. And this during a time when the president of the country, who hails from this remote ethnic group, has vigorously pursued a modernizing mission.

I want to suggest that these apparently traditional features of Kabre society are in fact "modernities" (Dirks 1990,1992; Comaroff and Comaroff 1993)—that they were forged during the long encounter with Europe over the last three hundred years and thus owe their meaning and shape to that encounter as much as to anything "indigenous." Moreover, it is in terms of these features that Kabre comfortably, if not always seamlessly, inhabit today's world. I thus join other scholars of Africa (S. Moore 1986, 1994; Mudimbe 1988; Ferguson 1990; Comaroff and Comaroff 1991, 1993, 1997; Appiah 1992; Apter 1992; Cohen and Odhiambo 1992; Gable 1995; Hutchinson 1996; Weiss 1996; Barber 1997; Shaw 1997) whose work seeks to unsettle the orientalizing binarism—and conceit—that associates Europe with "modernity" and Africa with "tradition" and has long informed scholarship about Africa and other places non-Western.

There is more than mere scholarly debate here, however. Demonizing images of Africa circulate in the press these days with startling frequency. In a rash of recent articles in leading U.S. newspapers and journals, under headlines that invite the sort of prurient voyeurism that has long accompanied Western interest in places Other—"The Coming Anarchy," "Our Africa Problem," "Tribal Ritual on Trial," "Persecution by Circumcision"—Africa, and especially West Africa, is portrayed as a place where democracy and development have failed, where drought and disease run rampant, where nepotistic ethnic politics is the norm with genocide right around the corner, and where "traditional" cultural practices such as polygyny, spirit worship ("animism," as the popular press refers to it), and clitoridectomy (often referred to as "female genital mutilation") still hold sway. In short, it is represented as a place where modernity's signature institutions and beliefs—democracy and development, monogamous marriage, individualism and secularism—have failed to take root. Moreover, in many of these articles the blame for this failure is placed on the tenacity of "traditional culture." Such an explanation—striking for its inattention to history—resembles the refrain I repeatedly heard from people working in development in Togo during the 1980s when yet another project of theirs had failed—namely, that it was the local "culture" that had prevented the group in question from changing its ways. Here, of course, the contrast is particularly sharply drawn: "traditional" (anti- or non-modern) culture retards the embrace of modernity.

I sat eating lunch with a high official from the American Embassy on the patio at Marox, a German-owned restaurant that was a popular hangout among expatriates in Lomé. Beyond the railing of the patio, the pock marked street was flush with pedestrians and taxis dodging huge puddles left by a drenching dawn rain—smartly dressed women heading to the Grand Marché; food vendors with piles of fish, fruit, and vegetables on platters on their heads; peddlers selling watches, sandals, and cigarettes.

A large man with a wad of money in his hand and deep scars on his cheeks—a Yoruba from Nigeria—stopped at the railing and asked if we wanted to change money. "Marks? Dollars? I can give you a better price than the banks."

I had just returned to Togo in the summer of 1996 for a short trip to the north and had met the official in a hallway at the embassy while I was "registering" before heading upcountry. When he found out I was an anthropologist who worked among Kabre (Kabiyé), the minority group from the north that has held power since 1967, he proposed lunch—to talk, he said, about Togolese "cultural politics" (a phrase oddly reminiscent of leftist academics describing the struggles of subaltern groups against dominant cultural and political-economic orders; yet here—employed by an embassy official surveilling a troubled post-colonial context—it seemed to have a disturbingly different sense). "I've read some of your work," he said. "Got it off the Internet. But it doesn't address the current conflict between Kabre and Ewe and I'd like to hear your take on it."

He was a slight man who seemed cut from the same cloth as many of my (white, middle-class) students at Duke—clean-cut, smart, easy to talk to, conservative. His job at the embassy was to advise the ambassador and the State Department on local politics. It was he who monitored Togolese elections and who kept tabs on the simmering conflict between Kabre and Ewe, the country's two most powerful ethnic groups—a situation he kept describing, mantra-like, as "another potential Rwanda." He was also in charge of gathering information about the case of a Togolese woman seeking asylum in the States. The case had flashed across the pages of U.S. newspapers during the spring and fall of 1996, and had become a cause célèbre in American feminist circles. The woman, Fausiya Kasinga, originally from a small village in the north, had fled Togo—first to Germany, then to the United States—because she was in danger of being forced by her family to undergo clitoridectomy at the time of her marriage to a businessman in the south.

I myself had become keenly interested in the case when it was first reported in the press that spring, and had used a *New York Times* article on it in a class I was teaching to point out once again how orientalizing the press was whenever it wrote about Africa. The background images that framed the *Times* piece—images of Togo as poor, patriarchal, oppressive, illiterate—dominated and overwhelmed the story of Kasinga herself. It seemed more an article about Africa's Otherness than about either the plight of a woman caught in a nasty local dispute or a difficult and complex issue that defies easy resolution. Demonization all over again.

"Why," I asked, "was the embassy involved in Kasinga's case?"

"Because it's a high publicity case that could affect U.S. policy not only in Togo but also throughout Africa. There are proposals in Congress to tie development money to the eradication of FGM [female genital mutilation]. There's a big debate going on in the State Department right now over precisely this issue. And, it's not all one-sided: there are strong advocates of noninterference in 'cultural' matters, people who are arguing that it's wrong—a type of imperialism—to impose our values on others. The U.S. courts also worry that if they grant asylum in a case like this, the floodgates will open and anyone claiming cultural persecution of any kind will be granted asylum. This is a very sensitive case. We need to make sure we've got our ducks in a row."

Our discussion of the Kasinga case ended (the official wanted to move on to other issues) with his relating a strange twist that had emerged from his undercover work: one of his local sources—a woman in the Togolese government—had told him that Kasinga's claim was almost certainly a cover for the fact that she was a member of an international prostitution ring that worked the Togo-Germany-United States triangle. "Whenever these women get caught," he had been told by this woman, "they use this as their alibi."

Sipping a strong German ale, my companion switched the subject, probing to find out more about my work. He wanted to know how much time I'd spent in the north, where I lived, whether I spoke the language. But he was especially interested in those aspects of northern culture that bore on the current political situation. He wanted to know how much support Eyadéma, Togo's Mobutuesque president, had in his home region and seemed surprised when

I said that it was decidedly mixed. He also wanted to know more about the young men from the north whom Eyadéma recruited into the military and police force. As the most visible arm of the state—clad in olive-green uniforms, brandishing AK-47s, they work the many checkpoints throughout Lomé and along the national highway that stretches to the northern border, often harassing drivers who seem suspicious or whose papers aren't "in order"—they had been the target of intense criticism in the Togolese press during the early 1990s. They were also widely assumed to have "disappeared" members of Eyadéma's political opposition. The press portrayed them as thugs who knew nothing but blind loyalty to the president and the power of the gun—and who were the product, it was suggested, of a "culture of violence" that festered in the rude backward regions of the north.

I calmly but persistently tried to disrupt the stereotype, pointing out how those youths I knew in the north are not the thugs portrayed in the southern media, that Kabre are markedly nonviolent (and indeed always struck me as more so than any people I'd ever known), that Kabre and Ewe, the two groups at odds during the 1990s, have lived side by side in southern Togo since the early colonial period and there get along extremely well. I also suggested that the current conflict between the two groups was explained less by primordialist assumptions about ethnic groups—what the press was fond of calling "tribalism"—than by understanding the volatile mix of processes of underdevelopment with post-colonial power configurations, and that the international community was as responsible for this mix as anyone else.

It was the totalizing, essentializing cultural categories—the "Kabre" and their "culture of violence"—within which this official operated that I found particularly troubling. While he seemed well-meaning, he was the victim of a State Department policy of extraordinary hubris that rotates officers from one country to the next every two years. He thus had had little time to learn much about Togolese and their history, and by default fell back on ethnic stereotype. Most sobering of all was the fact that he wielded enormous power: at his suggestion—by the circulation of a single memo suggesting that Togolese were unwilling to engage in the electoral process or to eradicate clitoridectomy—millions of dollars in aid money, money a country like Togo relies on just to stay afloat, could be cut off overnight.

This encounter underscores the insidious and volatile way in which image and power feed off one another in this postcolonial context, and the enormous stakes involved. It also calls attention to the types of global processes and interconnections that seem ever more commonplace as the century draws to a close—processes that draw into the same tight circle a hill people living in a remote corner of French West Africa, a civil servant from the world's most powerful country, and a Western anthropologist whose work can be downloaded off the Internet at the click of a mouse (and put to use in ways that are beyond his/her control). Clearly, the need is as pressing now as ever to write against power and against the images it deploys in legitimating imperialist agendas.

3

Imagining the Unborn in the Ecuadoran Andes

Lynn Morgan

Fetal personhood is not a "property" that can or will be "discovered" with greater scientific knowledge or increased technological capabilities, but it is produced in and through the very practices that claim merely to "reveal" it.

—Valerie Hartouni, "Fetal Exposures: Abortion Politics and the Optics of Allusion," *Camera Obscura*, May 1992

F etuses are rapidly being granted the status of cultural icons, present not only in the industrialized West but also as actors on the international reproductive rights scene.[1] It is useful, then, for feminists to attend to the diverse cultural, national, and political contexts within which persons are brought into social being. In the above epigraph, Valerie Hartouni argues that "fetal persons" are produced through social practices which themselves constitute and reify the category. This article looks at how women in highland Ecuador imagine and talk about the unborn and how their social practices might illuminate the processes through which fetuses are "naturalized" in the United States.

"Fetal persons" have for several years now been the subject of vigorous public debate in the United States, as physicians disagree over the wisdom of treating fetal "patients," lawyers struggle over the status of embryos fertilized in vitro and other fetal "plaintiffs" not recognized by the Constitution as legal persons, policymakers dispute the wisdom of mandatory pre-natal testing and appropriate custody arrangements for offspring of multiple "parents," and the general public argues over whether fetuses can or should be treated as social subjects.[2] The discourses themselves are constitutive; in other words, the more we puzzle over fetuses,

Lynn Morgan, "Imagining the Unborn in the Ecuadoran Andes," *Feminist Studies*, vol. 23, no. 2, pp. 323–350. Copyright © 1997 by Feminist Studies, Inc. Reprinted with permission. Provided by ProQuest LLC. All rights reserved.

the more we legitimate the subject, and, by extension, the subjectivity, of the "fetal person." What is particularly striking about many of the U.S. debates is the extent to which popular appropriations of science help to constitute fetal subjects. Prolife activists in the United States often call upon the authority of science to support biologically deterministic models of when and how life begins. Rarely, however, do we recognize the extent to which the popularization of science is manipulated to support a personification of fetuses, and rarely do we recognize how unique this is to American culture.

This article reflects on the uniqueness of U.S. abortion discourse by juxtaposing it against a landscape in which fetuses are generally *not* considered persons. In the Ecuadoran highlands where I have conducted anthropological fieldwork, women and men employ a variety of social practices that obscure and impede the possibility that fetuses will be granted personhood. This results not simply from differential access to sophisticated scientific or technological knowledge or equipment but also from a constellation of embedded social practices that render the contents of the womb as ambiguous and uncertain. In Ecuador, the course of pregnancy is governed by women themselves, who use overlapping and sometimes competing discourses to make sense of their own circumstances and the will of God. Even when the highland women use ultrasound screening, they do not personify or individualize fetuses the way people do in the United States; in fact, the women I interviewed rarely used the word *feto,* preferring *criatura* (creature) or *venidero* (the one to come). By looking more closely at constructions of pregnancy and the unborn in Ecuador, I hope to interrogate and destabilize certain scientized suppositions about what people take as the biological "nature" of fetuses in the United States.[3]

THE EMERGENCE OF FETAL PERSONS

In the United States today, the right-to-life movement and right-wing cultural critics use popular understandings of science to invent and reinforce a unified "fetal subject" at multiple sites and at several levels of analysis: historical, rhetorical, visual, and cultural. They rely on the popular interpretation and widespread utilization of ultrasonography, intrauterine electron microscopy, and new reproductive technologies, for example, to support their contention that "life begins at conception" and that "the fetus" is a gradually emerging person endowed with genetic uniqueness and biological facticity. To phrase the social relationship between the born and the unborn in biological terms, as they do, is "in effect an ideological mechanism to turn social facts into natural and therefore immutable facts."[4] The social practices that hitch scientific authority to the prolife cause have worked to keep the abortion debate focused on fetuses by emphasizing (and often literally illustrating) that "the fetus" is a miraculously complex biological entity. The success of this prolife political strategy, however, should not keep us from noticing that the practices that contribute to the social construction of the fetal subject are multiple, omnipresent, overlapping, and culturally particular.

Examples of the social practices that constitute fetuses come from the fields of medicine, ethics, religion, journalism, law, technology, entertainment, politics, and the academy. Some of them have global ambitions, as manifested, for example, in the work of the internationally oriented prolife organization, Human Life International. Some social practices associated with fetal personhood are nationally specific; for example, in Ireland where the contents of women's wombs have become implicated in debates over membership in the European community.[5] Some of the practices are large, public assertions of fetal personhood, such as Operation Rescue demonstrations (broadcast throughout the world on CNN) or anti-abortion billboards featuring ten-foot photographs of disembodied fetuses. Other constitutive practices occur in private: a pregnant woman thumbs through *What to Expect When You're Expecting* looking for a drawing that corresponds to the gestational age of the fetus she carries, so she can fit a visual image to the fluttering in her womb. Simple conversations among coworkers or friends can create fetal personhood, such as discussions among members of a medical team debating the ethics of intervening surgically given a diagnosis of fetal abnormality.[6] When physicians and midwives use ultrasound or fetal monitoring, for example, they enact the importance of fetal well-being. When pregnant women and their partners ascertain fetal sex and use that knowledge to name and personify an unborn child, they construct the fetus as a valued member of the family. When entertainment magazines print stories about unborn "celebrity children," they contribute to the personification of fetuses.[7] Over the past ten years, "fetal persons" have emerged from the realm of obstetricians' and ethicists' offices into popular culture, where they feature in film, print, and advertising.[8] Fetuses are depicted so regularly in everyday U.S. culture that their presence—outside the context of pregnant women's bodies—is scarcely remarkable anymore. Their presence has come to be accepted, by many as natural.[9] The social value attributed to fetuses is accentuated in the United States by low fertility rates, which make each pregnancy and child seem more precious, and by access to contraception which insures that many U.S. women have less experience with unchecked fertility (and pregnancy losses) than their Ecuadoran counterparts.

The cumulative effect of these social circumstances is that North Americans have begun—in historically unprecedented ways—to individualize, personify, and sometimes even glorify and prize fetuses as "super-subjects."[10] Of course, the personification of the fetal subject is not uncritically endorsed by all segments of the U.S. population, and there is considerable disagreement about the status of fetal subjects, pregnancy, parenthood, and reproduction. U.S. reproductive ethics debates are too complex, diverse, and cross-cutting to be reduced to some monolithic "cultural norms." Nonetheless, the recent historical trend toward reification of the fetal subject is striking if the United States is compared even with other Western societies. It is my hope that the cross-cultural comparison I offer here can help us to realize the many ways in which "the fetus we know" is historically and culturally unique.

This study was motivated by my conviction that a comparative anthropological perspective on abortion and fetal personhood in non-Western societies might point out the culture-bound nature of U.S. reproductive rights debates. In particular, I was motivated by the obsession in my own country with the relationship between ideas about fetal personhood and the morality of abortion. But of course this link proved to be too tight, and too tightly American, because "abortion" is the end product of a long chain of social circumstances. In 1988 I spent two months in the Andean town of San Gabriel (pop. 10,000), Carchi Province, Ecuador, about four hours by car north of Quito, the capital. In San Gabriel and surrounding hamlets, I conducted semistructured interviews (tape-recorded, of one to two hours in duration) with thirty mestizo women. Interviews were arranged by my research assistant, Blanca, a twenty-year-old woman who had grown up in this blustery, potato-growing region (where people referred to themselves as *borregos,* or sheep, because they have a reputation as followers rather than leaders, and because warm woolen clothes help people to stay warm at 10,000 feet). Blanca and I ventured out each morning, sometimes trudging up and down the hills of town on foot, and sometimes hitching a ride into surrounding hamlets, to interview women in their homes. We took advantage of the mid-morning lull in a woman's workday to ask her, indirectly, about her perceptions of the unborn by asking about her own fertility history; experience with pregnancy, birth, and child death; and her knowledge of local reproductive ethics. On our way back to the center of town, we would often stop in the cemetery, coffin-maker's shop, vital statistics registry, or health clinic. In 1992 I returned to Ecuador to spend six months in Quito, where I conducted an equal number of interviews with physicians, nurses, midwives and midwifery students, clergy, and members of local women's organizations. The research was designed to investigate the relationship between ideas about fetal identity, development, and personhood, and the morality and practice of induced abortion.

I had initially assumed that a country not polarized by public debate over abortion might endorse a cultural consensus about the moral status of the unborn. Unlike the United States, Ecuador has no history of public controversy over abortion. No public initiatives, past or present, have sought to liberalize church or state positions on abortion. I interpreted the lack of dissent as a reflection of unanimity and looked for the consensus I imagined must exist. My assumption, of course, implied a unified and coherent image of what a fetus is, and this assumption turned out to be highly problematic, as I show throughout this article. In San Gabriel, the fetus was never regarded separately from the pregnant woman, and women's stories about the events of pregnancy and the status of the unborn were as diverse as their experiences. In Quito I found a near-complete void on the subject of abortion and fetuses. I found no pictures of fetuses in magazines or newspapers, only one sensationalist episode of a television talk show focusing on women who had had abortions and the trauma and shame they had experienced. This focus highlighted the woman's ethical standing but not that of the fetus. There were no locally made movies about abortion or intrauterine development (although a dubbed version of *The Silent Scream* was occasionally aired on television). What I found, and what is described below, is that pregnant women are fused with and inseparable from the creatures they gestate. Consequently, responses to my questions about fetuses generated a great deal of incertitude and ambivalence. People often did not hold ready-formed opinions on these subjects, and they frequently disagreed among themselves. I quickly abandoned the search for a cultural consensus, even among the relatively homogeneous Catholic mestizo women in San Gabriel. The emphasis on consistency, I realized, was of course particular to the United States, where we privilege philosophies and narratives that can boast moral consistency. In the push to find consistency, scientific observations of fetal development are mustered to create representations of "the fetus" as a coherent biological "thing."

The focus on consistency is evident when anti-abortion activists who favor capital punishment—and prochoice proponents who oppose it—are criticized as hypocrites. Meanwhile, the moral high road is claimed by advocates of a "seamless web" philosophy, who preach respect for the right to life of all living things, including animals, murderers, and the unborn. In contrast, many of the Ecuadorans I spoke with did not attempt to construct a consistent response in answer to my probing questions about fetal status. Their social and political milieu does not require that they strive for confident or coherent answers to such complex and vexing issues. Several people patiently explained that ambiguity and uncertainty made perfect sense when confronted with life's most profound mysteries. It led me to wonder why, in my country, we insist on erasing the mysterious, on knowing what is, perhaps, ultimately unknowable.

ECUADOR AND THE LIMINAL UNBORN

There are many reasons why North Americans might assume that Latin Americans respect the unborn. *Clandestine Abortion: A Latin American Reality* states that in "every country but Cuba, legal abortion is rarely available except for the strictest medical reasons."[11] The region has been dominated by Catholicism for 500 years, and the Vatican has become an increasingly ardent proponent of fetal personhood over the past twenty years.[12] Loyal Latin American Catholics are sometimes heard to say that they will bear "as many children as God will send" (*los que Dios me mande*). It would be a mistake, however, to conclude on the basis of these stereotypes that Latin Americans subscribe to the notion that fetuses are persons. Because "the fetus" is a culturally specific conceptual entity and not a biological "thing," and because "the fetus" is created in particular cultural circumstances, I realized that I would have to stop thinking and speaking about "the fetus" if I was to understand how the unborn are imagined in Ecuador.

In the rural highlands of northern Ecuador, the unborn are imagined as liminal, unripe, and unfinished creatures. Nascent persons are brought into being slowly, through processes rife with uncertainty and moral ambiguity. Adults are slow to assign individual identity and personhood to the not-yet-born and the newly born. These *criaturas,* as they are often called, bear little resemblance to disembodied, technologized, visualized, personified, and revered

U.S. fetuses. These unknown, unknowable *criaturas* may teeter on the cusp of personhood for months before being fully welcomed into a human community. I will argue that in Ecuador social practices reinforce and perpetuate fetal liminality, insuring that personhood will not be easily attributed to the unborn. This article describes several of the social practices that encode, reaffirm, and perpetuate the notion that the unborn are not persons, that they remain ambiguous and liminal.

First, although abortion is illegal and rhetorically condemned by both church and state, there is little enforcement of anti-abortion laws (although the full extent of reliance on induced abortion is unknown). Second, there seems to be a large dose of social ambiguity built into determining "who counts" as the unborn come into social being. All Ecuadoran women do not count their children in the same ways nor employ the same conventions to number their babies. The civil registry does not have well-established or well-enforced procedures for count-ing live births, fetal deaths, or infant deaths. Third, there is no apparent social consensus for determining how to handle fetal death, including, for example, the baptismal, naming, and burial rites appropriate to miscarried, aborted, or stillborn fetuses. Indeed, a special category of liminal quasi-person (the *auca*) exists in the rural highlands to encompass unbaptized souls and other not-quite-persons. Fourth, induced abortion is characterized by many as a sin, but it is a sin of self-mutilation rather than murder. At issue is the mutilation of the pregnant woman's own body, not the personhood of the fetus. Fifth, beliefs about the course of fetal development range across a wide spectrum. Women contradict each other about when the fetus is "formed" and whether and how formation might affect the morality of abortion. The indeterminacy of the beginnings of life extend to the postpartum period; newborns are often described as still in the process of becoming, not yet fully human. Sixth, it seems that the work of "building personhood" at the beginnings of life is largely a female responsibility; women are predominantly responsible for bringing persons into being. As in the United States, each of these social practices has a particular context in which it is invoked, but the frames of discourse invariably overlap and reinforce each other. The cumulative effect of these social practices in Ecuador is that the unborn remain predominantly blurred, inchoate, and incipient.

AN OPEN SECRET: ILLEGAL ABORTION

Un secreto a voces (an open secret) is how many people in Ecuador describe the availability of abortion. Abortion is officially illegal but nonetheless widely available. Estimates of abortion rates are unreliable in Ecuador, as elsewhere in Latin America, for at least two reasons. First, most estimates are based on numbers of women hospitalized with complications resulting from a combination of both spontaneous and induced abortions. Of abortions registered by hospitals surveyed in Quito, 98 to 99 percent were classified as "type unspecified [i.e., spontaneous vs. induced] and others."[13] Second, hospital-based figures can capture only those women with access to health services, thus excluding much of the rural population, and do not reflect the numbers of women whose abortions are successful and safe. The few existing studies of abortion rates in Ecuador have concentrated on data collection and analysis techniques and do not attempt to estimate the rates per se.[14]

The Ecuadoran Constitution (Article 25) was changed in 1978 to specify that "a child will be protected from conception onward." Similarly, the Civil Code (Article 61) specifies that "the law protects the life of the unborn" *(del que está por nacer),* and the Penal Code (Articles 441 through 447) specifies the penalties for abortion. Ecuadoran law allows abortion under only two circumstances: to save the life of a woman, or when pregnancy is the result of the rape of a mentally ill woman *(mujer idiota o demente).*[15] In what seems a vestige from a more chivalrous era, the penalty for induced abortion can be reduced if a judge determines that the abortion was performed "to protect a woman's honor" *(aborto honoris causa).* The fact that abortion providers and clients are infrequently prosecuted in Ecuador suggests that the practice of abortion is tolerated by a state apparatus that protects the unborn only at the level of rhetoric.

Ecuadorans might continue to have abortion both illegal and widely available as long as the issue remains below the surface of public discourse.[16] Occasionally a newspaper article or television talk show will give journalists, politicians, or clergy an opportunity to condemn abortion, but their bluster is generally treated as requisite occupational rhetoric rather than a realistic recipe for action. (One thoughtful priest, for example, told me that Vatican doctrine is too rigid to apply to the complex circumstances faced by his parishioners,) Occasionally I noted an oblique reference to abortion in the sardonic, ephemeral graffiti found around Quito (such as *crece, crece, hombrecito, hay un aborto esperando por ti,* "grow, grow, little man, there's an abortion waiting for you"). Apart from these quixotic commentaries, however, there is no public debate over abortion in Ecuador. No one calls for more rigorous enforcement of anti-abortion laws, and only a few Ecuadoran women's rights activists argue that abortion should be "decriminalized" *(descriminalizado* or *despenalizado,* as distinct from "legalized").Those who do point out that decriminalization would stop people from profiting from women's misfortunes, prevent the complications that result from clandestine abortion, and reduce the maternal mortality rate and the hospital costs associated with treating abortion complications.[17] Once again, their focus is not on the fetus. Their views, however, are not representative of the public stance taken by many other Ecuadoran women's rights activists. The activists I spoke with in Quito said that the women's movement could not be advanced by making a public issue of abortion at this time. Such a strategy could easily backfire, they said, leaving women worse off than they currently are.

For the purposes of this article, the public and legal domains are significant for what they omit. Abortion is an issue in Ecuador, however covert; but fetal personhood is not. Fetuses are notoriously absent from the *sotto voce* conversations I had with Ecuadorans about abortion. There is virtually no mention of maternal-fetal conflict, nor of "fetal rights." The state's tacit acceptance of clandestine abortion could be viewed as society's pragmatic way of acknowledging that circumstances sometimes compel women to terminate their pregnancies despite the legal and social stigma. The law purports to value and protect fetal life and personhood, but lack of enforcement of anti-abortion laws belies the state's commitment. Fetuses may be theoretical persons by Ecuadoran law, but in social practice there are no fetal persons.

NUMBERING THE BABIES

One way to ascertain the social importance granted to fetuses and infants is to look at whether and how they are enumerated. In this section I argue that the distinction between fetuses and infants is blurred and imprecise in Ecuador, as manifested by how women in San Gabriel enumerate their own offspring and by how civil registration procedures both perpetuate and reinforce this uncertainty.

The women I interviewed in San Gabriel did not share among themselves a common method for enumerating their offspring. When I asked, ¿Cuántos hijos tiene usted? ("How many children do you have?"), some women interpreted hijos to mean "pregnancies," in which case all pregnancies—including miscarriages—figured among a woman's "children." But to others hijos meant "children born alive" or "living children." The point always required clarification during an interview. When Doña Gabriela said, "Ten children, six living," I initially thought she meant that four children had died in childhood, until she explained that one of her ten pregnancies had resulted in a miscarriage at approximately two months' gestation. Similarly, Doña Maria, a seventy-year-old widow in San Gabriel, answered me by saying she had sixteen children. "Living?" I asked. "No," she said, "only five are living." The sixteen included four miscarriages (arrojos, literally "shedding blood"), four children who died in infancy, and three who died later in life.

The differences were significant to me because U.S. conventions mandate that people should distinguish among the hijos socially erased by miscarriage or induced abortion, the miscarried hijos who do not live to be born, the hijos born dead, and those born alive. Ecuadoran women make similar distinctions, of course, cognitively and at the level of lived experience, but in numbering their offspring they have a great deal of latitude in deciding how to classify and represent the differences among living, stillborn, live-born, miscarried, adopted, and deceased children.

The fact that women can count their hijos in so many different yet equally acceptable ways suggests two things. First, it suggests that every pregnancy can be—but is not necessarily—socially significant, no matter the result. The focus here is not on the baby, the "product," but on the woman's pregnancy and her social responsibility to reproduce. (This is a marked contrast to the U.S. "tentative pregnancy" in which some women postpone an announcement until they have completed the first trimester or until after receiving the results of amniocentesis.)[18] Second, it acknowledges that children emerge through a lengthy, gradual process that spans gestation and infancy and that any divisions imposed on the process (such as "trimesters," or "viability") are somewhat arbitrary.

The arbitrary nature of life-cycle divisions is evident, too, in national vital statistics and the registration standards as understood by the civil servant in San Gabriel. Birthrates and infant mortality rates are unreliable in Ecuador, in part because the state began to emphasize the importance of registering births and deaths only in the mid-1980s. For example, in 1982 only 4,627 live births were registered in the country of more than 9 million inhabitants, while by 1986 the number of live births registered was 205,797. "Live birth" figures are an inherently imprecise category as long as they continue to include all children registered that year, including older children. Underreporting continues to be a problem, in part because relatively few births are attended by professionals. In 1986, 85 percent of the 1,406 registered live births in urban areas of Carchi Province (which includes San Gabriel) were attended by a professional, but in the rural areas only 50 percent of the 1,699 registered live births were attended by a professional.[19] The reported infant mortality rate for the country as a whole in 1986 was 50.4/1,000 live births, while in Carchi Province it was 54.4/1,000. Actual rates are undoubtedly much higher, because parents have no particular incentive to register infant births or deaths, especially outside the cities.

Ecuador follows the World Health Organization in defining fetal death as "death prior to the complete expulsion or extraction from its mother of a product of conception, irrespective of the duration of the pregnancy; the death is indicated by the fact that after such separation the fetus does not breathe or show any other evidence of life, such as beating of the heart, pulsation of the umbilical cord, or definite movement of voluntary muscles."[20] The 1986 Vital Statistics Report makes it clear that the Ecuadoran state does not even try to enumerate fetal death or miscarriage:

> Fetal deaths: In Ecuador there is no special registry for reporting fetal deaths; when they occur and interested parties report them, an official of the Civil Registry should fill out a statistical report in duplicate, filing the original and sending the copy to the National Institute of Statistics and Census. In 1986 4,265 fetal deaths were registered [58 of which were in Carchi Province].[21]

Even if the state were more aggressive about collecting these vital statistics, compliance in the hinterlands could not be guaranteed. The law specifies that all live births must be registered, but when I spoke with the civil servant in San Gabriel, he was quite casual about the regulations. In his opinion, if an infant died within the first "four or six hours, or the first day" after birth, the parents did not need to register the birth, although they could if they wanted to. Although the lax registration standards could be regarded as a sign of bureaucratic inefficiency, they could also be interpreted as a codification of the imprecision described above. This particular official was reaffirming the liminality and arbitrariness that characterize the beginnings of life in the Ecuadoran Andes.

The persistence of faith in the *auca* is perhaps the best evidence of the inherent ambiguity of the unborn in the rural highlands of Ecuador. The *auca* has long been a part of Andean ethnography, functioning as a master metaphor for the uncivilized and for several categories of quasi-person. Elsie Clews Parsons reported in 1945 that "[a]n infant (or anyone) dying unbaptized is called *auca* ... and becomes a night-wandering spirit."[22] In Quito, said Parsons, any unbaptized person was referred to as *auca,* including all the indigenous, non-Christian residents of the Amazonian lowlands. The Ecuadoran *auca* includes savages, heathens, and other liminal beings. A celebrated national soccer team embodies fierceness and invincibility, calling itself "Los Aucas," and *Auca* is still in use as a pejorative name for the Huaorani Indians of the Amazonian lowlands (*oriente*). Michael Taussig explains:

> Several modern Ecuadorian Quechua dictionaries clearly bring the various meanings together-savage, seditious, rebel, enemy—and in the Colombian Putumayo today *auca* also connotes, to my friends at least and with varying intensities, the unrepentantly "other" world of savagery down there in the jungles of the *oriente,* a world quintessentially pagan, without Christ, Spanish words, or salt, inhabited by naked, incestuous, violent, magical, and monstrous people. ...[23]

The infant *aucas* described to me in San Gabriel, like the savage Indian *aucas* described to Taussig, were frightening and potentially dangerous; they could, by some accounts, turn themselves into ghosts or cannibals. As one woman told me, "An *auca* comes looking for its mother, to punish her for being irresponsible, for having sinned by not baptizing him." Yet when I repeated this interpretation to another woman, she rejected it as *falso, falso, falso.* Rather, she said, the *auca* makes itself into a big ghost, as tall as a tree, and looks for children to kill by eating their hearts. A third woman ridiculed this account, saying the *auca* does not pursue children, and no one can see it anyway, because it is just smoke. If there was any agreement about the nature of the *auca* in San Gabriel, most women agreed that it is the spirit of an aborted fetus, or stillborn or murdered baby, which cries pitifully at night in sorrow *(por remordimiento)* at not having been baptized. The cries emanate from the site where its body was supposedly discarded *(botado)* or thrown away without benefit of burial (*tirado no más, donde sea).* Four or five women told me of having heard the *auca* themselves, crying outside at night, and of their terror and prayers.

The existence of *aucas* was fairly widely recognized, but there was considerable disagreement about how properly to dispose of an unbaptized fetus or child to prevent it from becoming an *auca.* Luz Maria said that the *auca* can be prevented by baptizing a fetus or neonate even if it is dead; the mother or midwife can sprinkle holy water over its head and say, "In the name of Jesus Christ I baptize you, giving you the name of Jesus [for a boy] or Maria [for a girl]." But other women insisted that only living babies could receive baptism; the rite could not be posthumously conferred. Similar controversy arose over how and where to dispose of fetal remains.

The symbolism of burial space revealed a great deal about the ambiguous, wandering *auca*. Many women disapproved of discarding infant or fetal bodies without ceremony; however, some favored burial outside the cemetery for souls not destined to enter heaven. Others insisted that inside the cemetery was safer for both the living and the dead. Some suggested that fetal remains could be placed, above ground, along the inside of the cemetery fence, literally a liminal position on the outer margins of sacred ground. Another woman rejected burial altogether for the unbaptized: "To bury is bad (*enterrar es malo*). That child (*niño*) has been known to grow up by itself, to make itself into a ghost (*fantasma*). To keep it from becoming a ghost, it is better to put it in any little box and throw it into the river [because this is how Christ was baptized]. The priest said that way it can't do any harm." Although the river is a powerful salvation metaphor in Christian ideology, only one of the women I interviewed mentioned this method. There was little consensus about where the bodies belonged, where their souls would reside, or what their fate would be. The *auca* embodies uncertainty.

The inconsistent practice of other rituals that accompany birth and death, including naming, baptizing, and sitting with the body through a wake, further illustrate this ambiguity. I asked a sixty-five-year-old woman with six children to tell me, hypothetically, how a woman might feel and what she might do if she miscarried at six months' gestation.

> Well, she would feel a little sad [*un poco de pena*] because she lost the child, without having known it, without having seen it, no? Then she would take it, because it is an object born of her [*como es un objecto que nace de uno*], with blood and everything, right? She would put it in a little box and bury it. Without a wake, they don't wake it [*no lo velan*]. Nor does she name it or baptize it.

Another woman had suffered two miscarriages: one at two months' gestation, another at eight months. The eight-month miscarriage was baptized, named, and buried in the cemetery. When the callous anthropologist inquired whether the fetus miscarried at two months would become an *auca* if deprived of baptism, I received a practical, if somewhat distressed, response: "But there's no way [to baptize it], it's just blood, how would you baptize it?" Unformed tissue cannot be properly baptized. But the women I interviewed seemed puzzled when I asked whether unformed tissue would, or could, become an *auca;* neither religion nor social practice offered any ready answer to this question. Thus the *auca* remains a relatively inchoate, subsocial being, a manifestation of discomfort with the prospect of unbaptized souls unable to gain entry into heaven. Its very iconography invokes murkiness: the *auca* is often described as cloudy or smoky or dark; as an *auca*, an unbaptized child "does not see the light [of heaven]" (*no ve la claridad*). The women of San Gabriel don't agree among themselves who becomes an *auca*, or under what circumstances, or what powers the *auca* might possess. Furthermore, they assert, there can be no satisfactory answer to these questions.

In Ecuadoran narratives of pregnancy, childbirth, and child death, the *auca* is invoked to signify the ever-present and inevitable ambiguity that accompanies the transitions into personhood. Interpreted in light of U.S. abortion debates, it appears that U.S. polemics have reduced, indeed virtually eliminated, the space that might be allotted to not-yet-persons.[24] The *auca*, then, can be seen as an affirmation of a place for quasi-persons within the local cosmology. The *auca* accommodates those anomalous, liminal beings who exist somewhere between nothingness and full human personhood, and it reinforces the notion that mortal humans do not exercise complete control over the spiritual agency of the unborn. The *auca,* as part of the local practice of personhood, functions to remind Andean residents of the fragility and spiritual ambiguity of young human life and of the importance of baptism. The *auca* shapes the meanings attributed to the unborn and to babies who die prematurely or without church protection, and it wields a coercive power over those who believe in it by forcing them to think and act in accordance with local practices. To this extent, the *auca* could be considered a political actor with a bit part, influencing local reproductive ethics.

Because the social practices surrounding fetal and infant burial provided such insights into their status, I was interested to compare burial practices for fetal remains in San Gabriel with those in Quito. I asked the chief of perinatology at a Quito hospital what happens to the remains when a woman miscarries in his hospital. Do the parents ever claim the remains for burial?

> Of the abortions [*de los abortos*], the parents never claim the remains. Yes, if it's a stillbirth, or if it dies of some disease, but even with these children many times parents don't claim [*reclamar*]. But with abortions, never, ever. And we don't give them the remains. Never. When it's a formed fetus, when it's already a child, then yes [*cuando ya es un feto ya formado, cuando ya es un niño allí sí*].

His response was telling: in urban areas miscarried fetal tissue is not claimed or socially valued. But his response also complicates matters. He used the word *aborto* to refer to early miscarriages and induced abortions, apparently not distinguishing between them. But then he used *feto* and *niño* seemingly interchangeably to refer to the formed fetus/baby at a later stage of gestation. He thus made a distinction between "formed" and "unformed" tissue and granted to the former a moral and social identity (in death as in life?) not extended to the latter. The same physician went on to tell me about the difficulty encountered by his staff in obtaining permission to perform autopsies on fetuses and babies. Many parents, he says, would rather pay a private physician to sign the death certificate than sign the hospital-issued death certificate which automatically authorizes autopsy. Parents are opposed, he said, to having autopsies performed, although he purported not to understand their reasoning: "I really don't understand them in this sense. The only thing I can think of is that they don't want the child dismembered (*despedazado*). But we don't dismember during an autopsy. And even if we *did* take the heart for study, the parents would never know because we stitch up the chest cavity."

The traffic in body parts he seemed to condone[25] was probably as clear to bereaved parents as it was to me. His words, however, revealed something more than his willingness to deceive. Physical integrity and wholeness is important to the parents, because bodily mutilation is a sin.

ABORTION: SELF- VS. OTHER-MUTILATION

Most rural women answered my query with, "Yes, the fetus is a person from conception." By this they meant that God creates pregnancies and brings babies into being and that at some unspecifiable point during gestation God gives the fetus a soul. Because mortals do not know precisely when this happens, it is better to err on the generous side. Fetuses are "persons" from conception, then, because God made them but not because the community yet accepts them as such.

The women were equally adamant that it is (usually) wrong to induce abortion but not because abortion is "murder." They explained that induced abortion is a sin of self-mutilation. The horror of inducing abortion, I was told, was the blasphemous presumptuousness implied in taking one's bodily fate into one's own hands (*siendo rey de su propia sangre*). God calls pregnancy into existence, they said, and we are not authorized to interfere with His divine plans. Abortion, then, is not about the mutilation or destruction of a person but about presuming to know God's will. The link between the personhood of the fetus and the morality of abortion—so omnipresent in contemporary North American culture—is largely absent in Ecuador. Furthermore, several women told me that a decision to terminate a pregnancy could sometimes be morally defensible if women were in desperate straits. Moral justifications for abortion included abandonment by or abuse at the hands of a partner or husband; desperate poverty, hunger, or homelessness; life-threatening contraceptive failure (such as conceiving with an IUD in place); or the need to protect a family's honor. Even if the fetus is a person, I was told, this does not mean that abortion is *necessarily* wrong in all circumstances. Discussions about the morality of abortion tended to center around the social, economic, and health circumstances facing pregnant women, who were portrayed as the final moral arbiters in reproductive decisions. These discussions tended not to invoke church doctrine; nor were they framed in terms of fetal rights, fetal personhood, or maternal-fetal conflict. The rhetoric around abortion in Ecuador emphasizes the centrality of pregnant women's moral integrity and life circumstances, rather than fetal rights or personification of the unborn.

GESTATIONAL DEVELOPMENT

Pregnant women in the United States have access to books, posters in physicians' offices, and even plastic models depicting an inexorable and cumulative process of gestational development through which an embryo turns into a fetus and then a baby. These visual models and books are part of a cultural iconography that helps to fix an image and create the meanings attached to particular gestational stages.[26] In the rural highlands of Ecuador there is no equivalent to this visual or technologically based information. Women learn about intrauterine fetal development from their own experiences, talking with other women, viewing their own or other women's miscarriages, and feeling fetal movement. The terminology the women use is revealing because it blurs the distinction between the unborn and the born: *criatura* (creature) or its diminutive, *criaturita*; also *nene* or *guagua* (baby), *niño* (child), or *venidero* (one to come), or, rarely, *bebe*. The unborn are not referred to in gendered terms, although, as we see below, the process of intrauterine development is considered different for girls and for boys. The most significant marker of gestational development, women told me, is *formación*. In this context the word refers to the time when the fetus assumes a recognizably human form, but the word *formación* also, interestingly, means "education," drawing a parallel between gestational development and the socialization of children. When does *formación* happen? Accounts varied widely, implying that there is no cultural consensus or ready response apart from the gender differentiation many said was inherent in the process: males develop earlier than females. Doña Blanca washed her laundry while we talked. Thirty-three years old, she had six living children and one daughter who had died at age two. She explained, "Males, they say, form at one month [gestation]. In contrast, females still aren't formed at two months. Females form later *(la mujer se forma de más meses)*." Doña Teresa, a forty-nine-year-old illiterate woman with eight living and three deceased children, answered my question about *formación* by talking about quickening: "I usually felt them move at three months. And when it's female, around six months, it seems, no?" She smiled slyly and explained, "They say girls are lazy *(vaga)*." A fifty-nine- year-old mother of twenty-two, Doña Ileana said that boys begin to form at two weeks' gestational age, and girls begin to form at six months. Doña Maria, aged seventy, explained what her son looked like when she suffered a miscarriage at three months' gestation, because she had witnessed a woman slaughter a pig.

> I arrived home. I began shivering and drooling. That night I started bleeding profusely. The little boy *(varoncito)* was born perfect. He was about this big [indicating about three inches]. He was born completely formed, with all the boy's parts. The miscarried female *(hembrita)* has nothing, she is just a chunk of flesh *(trozo de sangre)*, and in the middle of the chunk of flesh there is a single eye. That's the female. Females form at six months. Males form by the first month. Females, no. The female comes out with a chicken's eye. Nothing more.

Doña Josefina, age sixty-two with six children, explained that *formación* took place at two months in boys, "just like Christ," and that girls remained "like chunks of meat" for a "long time." Observation and personal experience of miscarriage seemed not to affect the social perception that girls form more slowly than boys. The common wisdom about gender differentiation had little practical value, because a pregnant woman in the Ecuadoran highlands does not profess to know whether the fetus she carries is destined to be female or male. But *formación* can affect the morality of abortion, according to Doña Josefina, because an unformed conceptus can, if necessary, be aborted:

> Here abortion is a crime. It's not a crime, though, when the child (*niño*) is not yet in flesh (*cuando todavía no esté en sangre*), when it is not yet formed with the blood of the mother, no? It's still just a few days [from conception], no? Then they say that it's made up of sex substances *(la naturaleza)*—from both sides—and that it's still in water *(todavía está en agua),* no? It's still not formed, nor is it made of flesh. Then they say that it [abortion] is permitted, that it is not a sin. But once it's formed, once it's formed of one's blood, then it [abortion] is a crime.

The "unformed fetus" might be the Ecuadoran equivalent of saying that a woman can be "a little bit pregnant." Because *formación* could happen so early, a woman who wants to terminate a pregnancy should do so as early as possible. Doña Teresa told me: "Of course earlier is better. Preferred, for example, in the case of unmarried women who find themselves pregnant, to do it at one month. At one month. That's like 'bringing down the period' (*bajando la regla*). There is not yet any fetus *(feto)*, no one, nothing."[27] The importance of *formación* was not shared by all the women I interviewed. Some said that abortion was always wrong, whenever it occurred. Doña Ileana disagreed about the emphasis on *formación,* explaining that the unborn "has a right to life" (*tiene derecho a la uida*; she was unique among the women I interviewed in San Gabriel in using this language) "by virtue of the fact that it is in the womb, even if it is only one or two months old it is already alive." This disagreement recalls debates ongoing elsewhere about the sanctity of life versus the social significance of personhood. Here, however, the disagreement occurs within a cultural repertoire that can accommodate a wide degree of variability on the question of when personhood might coalesce.

Not only does *formación* not happen all at once, but the physical and spiritual characteristics of newborns are still fluid and changing up until birth and well into the postpartum period. Newborns, like fetuses, were referred to by terms that indicated their unfinished quality: *tierno* means young or unripe, and is used also to describe green fruit.[28] Doña Josefina told me, "A newborn child (*guagua recién nacido*) is like a child of clay." She explained that the mother should carefully and frequently mold and shape its face and nose, its head and shoulders and legs to make them assume the desired shape. Women swaddle their babies, she said, to make their legs grow straight. Just as their bodies are unfinished and malleable, the spirits and souls of newborns are not yet firmly tethered to the social world. Babies are described as particularly vulnerable to collective social and supernatural forces that older children are toughened against. For example, babies are susceptible to fright (*susto*), evil eye (*mal ojo*), dew, night air, rainbows, inauspicious hours (*mala hora*), and traditionally dangerous places such as ravines. For this reason, said Doña Maria, it used to be the custom for new mothers to stay inside with their babies for forty days after birth (the traditional Latin American *cuarentena,* called the *dieta* in San Gabriel). Until recently, a postpartum mother would be enshrouded by a *toldo,* or screen, over the bed. "The *toldita* was a sheet that was put over the bed so that wind (*viento*) would not get in, is what they used to say. Only this little tiny opening would be left so you could get into the bed, nothing more." The *toldo* prevented dangerous airs from reaching the child. It also served as the Ecuadoran variant of the "social womb" familiar to anthropologists. The social womb extends the physiological womb symbolically into social space, thus rendering biological birth as a necessary but insufficient condition for granting personhood. The infant and mother live inside the "social womb" for a time, until the infant is deemed "person enough," ripe enough or tough enough, to emerge. Sometimes the social womb was the bed where mother and newborn lay enshrouded, whereas sometimes the social womb was the entire house. Doña Maria said she kept her baby in the house for two months after it was born, to prevent harm from befalling the child. "Sometimes," she explained, "I would have to pass through a ravine (*quebra-da*) or overgrown area (*monte*). The child's spirit could get lost, stay behind in those places" (*que se queda el espíritu*). If she had to go out, she would leave the child behind in the house, where it would be safe even if unattended.

BUILDING PERSONS IS A WOMAN'S RESPONSIBILITY

The physical separation of the fetus from the mother at birth is one important step in the process of acquiring personhood, but newborns continue to be dependent on their parents to provide spiritual sustenance and physical strength. Fathers, as well as mothers, are held accountable for safeguarding fetuses and newborns in several ways. They must respond immediately to pregnant women's cravings (*antojos*), abstain from sexual relations for the forty-day postpartum period (*dieta*), and remain faithful to their wives (especially while children are at the breast). One of the most feared infant diseases in San Gabriel is *colerín,* which results when a father upsets his wife. Her anger or rage (*cólera*), passed immediately to the child through breastmilk, results in *colerín,* an acute, incurable disease which kills rapidly. "Don't you see that they're unripe (*tierni-tos*), and they can't take it (*no aguantan*), they can't withstand *colerín.*" Because the consequences of rage can be so grave, the prospect of rage might well give pregnant women and nursing mothers some degree of control over inappropriate male behavior.[29] Apart from these rather limited responsibilities, however, men absent themselves from the sufferings of birth, miscarriage, and infant death. Here a Quito pathologist gradually reveals his conscious insensitivity to the death of his firstborn.

> When a newborn dies, the most affected person is not the father, it's the mother. The person with whom you have to work—to console—is the mother, not the father. The father comes to accept his responsibilities gradually, as the child develops. I'm not the least bit afraid to say this, and I've always said it to my family, in my home. My first son died. I *did not feel* [his emphasis] what my wife felt. I think if the same

thing happened right now to one of my [older] children, the calamity would fall hardest on me.

His honest confession illustrates a point made by Laurie Price in her discussion of Ecuadoran ideologies of the family. She writes that women are encouraged "to feel fully the anguish of a calamity that befalls a family member but [the ideologies do] not prepare men either psychologically or socially to acknowledge that kind of anguish."[30] For the purposes of our discussion, this gendered distinction illustrates the extent to which women are primarily responsible for the reproduction of the social order, for bringing children into social being.

Andie L. Knutson once concluded, with respect to the United States, that "people are made by people."[31] In the highlands of Ecuador, the work of making people, of constructing social persons, is specifically considered women's work. Women "serve as cultural mediators between the living and the dead"[32] but also between the world of the not-yet and the existing social community. Men do not feel the same degree of responsibility for ushering children into social existence, although, as noted above, women want their partners' support and work hard to recruit them to the task of bringing babies into being. When women attempt to control men's behavior through devices such as *pena* (emotional pain and suffering)[33] and the prospect of children dying from *colerín,* they do so knowing that men would otherwise not readily concern themselves with assisting quasi-persons on the margins of life.[34]

PRACTICING PERSONHOOD

The ideologies and actions practiced by women in highland Ecuador militate against the radical individualization of fetuses currently underway in the United States. Yet much to the chagrin and consternation of U.S. feminists and prochoice activists, the abortion debate continues to revolve around the question of whether the fetus is a person. Devised by prolife activists to direct attention to their cause, the question is a trope in an era where definitions of personhood are increasingly based on popular appropriations of biology and genetics.[35] In other words, the answer must always be "yes" where personhood is defined with recourse to unified biological or genetic descriptions alleged to lie outside or prior to social attributes. The question reinforces the absolutist conviction that science can identify biological markers (such as the onset of brain stem activity) or invent medical interventions (such as lung surfactants to enable very premature babies to survive) that will influence decisions about when fetuses should be regarded as persons. Scientific investigation of this sort reinforces the presumption that biomedical insights are attainable, relevant, and consensual, even while the popular appropriations of science divert attention from the processes through which science is imbued with meaning and signification.

A focus on the onset of fetal personhood both presupposes and reasserts that the morality of abortion is and should be contingent on the status of the fetus. Of course many North

Americans, including most feminists, reject the logic that links abortion to fetal personhood. Yet for the purposes of this article, it is useful to point out that even prochoice ideologies in the United States resist the notion of quasi-persons, semipersons, or incipient persons. U.S. ideologies favor a strict distinction between persons and nonpersons, with nothing in-between.[36] In this sense the Ecuadoran example presents an alternative view of the unborn and raises a series of questions about the U.S. context. What is the cultural basis for the absolutist assertion that fetuses must always be either full persons or nonpersons? When did this absolutist imperative emerge? Did the social and political effacement of pregnant women predate the introduction and widespread use of reproductive imaging technologies? Might some pregnancies involve fetal "persons" (if pregnant women and others involved grant them this status), but other pregnancies might not? Perhaps some pregnancies involve incipient or quasi-persons of indeterminate moral, spiritual, and physical status. Certainly the Ecuadoran women I interviewed would not suggest that any society could accurately or confidently pinpoint the beginning of the miraculous, mysterious process of social becoming.

Much of the U.S. debate over abortion has centered around identifying the most defensible moment at which personhood can or should be assigned. People often presume that personhood accrues cumulatively; fetuses and babies gradually acquire additional degrees of personhood, but persons generally do not come undone. Personhood is easily extended but rarely rescinded. It is thus difficult for North Americans to understand that the practices of personhood in the Ecuadoran highlands sometimes allow a degree of ebb and flow over the duration of pregnancy and infancy.[37] Women told me that the gradual process of intrauterine *formación*, for example, may be arrested or even reversed if a pregnant woman knowingly continues to breastfeed an older child. By showing inappropriate favoritism and diverting energy essential for fetal growth, she may "undo" the nascent personhood of the unborn. A *criatura* said to be formed (and thus *una persona*) by six months' gestation may be said at birth to be "little more than an animal" until it is baptized. The trajectory of personhood need not necessarily be linear, because people cannot predict the many influences that bring each person into being. "God keeps certain secrets," people told me, and these things He does not tell us. Incipient personhood is understood as openly ambiguous and variable, its character perennially liminal, amorphous, and irresolvable.

Persons are everywhere the products of social action. In Ecuador at the early margins of life, social practices do not focus on personification of the unborn or reification of fetal subjects. The women I interviewed in San Gabriel have not been schooled, as I have, to imagine individualized, disembodied, animate, technicolor fetuses brought to consciousness through the popularization of science. Nor do their journalists constantly remind them, as mine do me, how contentious and violent abortion politics have become. The women I interviewed in San Gabriel were perplexed that I, or my compatriots, would expect to find a single or satisfactory answer to the question of when fetuses become persons. Why, they wondered, would we press so hard to know the unknowable? Through their eyes, I began to see their ways as sensible and my own as strange. These women imagine the unborn in a variety of ways, including as amorphous quasi-human entities with strong links to spiritual and social (as well as biological) domains. They bring the unborn into social being slowly and carefully, not by medical or legal fiat, but through a combination of overlapping personal, social, and religious actions. These include taking good care of pregnant women, baptizing children, respecting God's will and authority, working and hoping for prosperity, behaving responsibly and working together, protecting the incipient person from natural and supernatural threats and evil influences, and a good bit of luck. Women's stories about their miscarriages and children (both alive and dead) were interspersed with stories of *aucas* and cautionary remarks about the dangers of wind and night air, and the hardships posed by infidelity and poverty. All these examples serve to emphasize the radical disjunctures between their liminal unborn and "my fetus," the fetus I inadvertently reify myself, steeped as I am in my country's scientific images linked to abortion debates. This comparison thus denaturalizes the iconographic fetal subject in the United States and raises a question. Wouldn't U.S. feminists do well to attend to the diverse social practices through which people create people, including the ways in which scientific images are mobilized politically to mask women's authority, responsibility, and moral integrity?

NOTES

Research for this essay was funded by a grant from the Joint Committee on Latin American Studies of the Social Science Research Council and the American Council of Learned Societies with funds provided by the National Endowment for the Humanities, and by a faculty fellowship from Mount Holyoke College. I gratefully acknowledge the assistance and support of my colleagues at FLACSO (Facultad Latinoamericana de Ciencias Sociales, Sede Quito). Special thanks to Blanca, my capable research assistant in San Gabriel, and to Monica Casper, Linda Layne, Rachel Roth, and the reviewers for their comments on an earlier draft of this article.

1.   Jodi L. Jacobson, The Global Politics of Abortion (Washington, D.C.: Worldwatch Paper no. 97, July 1990), 53; Faye D. Ginsburg and Rayna Rapp, eds., Conceiving the New World Order: The Global Politics of Reproduction (Berkeley: University of California Press, 1995).
2.   Monica J. Casper, "Reframing and Grounding Nonhuman Agency: What Makes a Fetus an Agent?" American Behavioral Scientist 37 (May 1994): 839–56; Rosalind Pollack Petchesky, "Fetal Images: The Power of Visual Culture in the Politics of Reproduction," in Feminist Studies 13 (summer 1987): 263–92, reprinted in Reproductive Technologies, ed. Michelle Stanworth (Minneapolis: University of Minnesota Press, 1987), 57–80; Janet Gallagher, "Collective Bad Faith: 'Protecting' the Fetus," in Reproduction, Ethics, and the Law, ed. Joan C. Callahan (Bloomington: Indiana University Press, 1995), 343–79; Carol A. Stabile, Feminism and the Technological Fix (New York: St. Martin's Press, 1994).
3.   A few caveats are warranted at the outset. Cross-cultural comparison can be a useful heuristic tool, but it carries certain risks. One is the danger of reifying "culture," of representing as uniform the views of "a people" which are more accurately depicted as divergent and highly contested. Another pitfall is a tendency to overemphasize similarities within groups while exaggerating contrasts between them. If I contrast "us" and "them" in this essay, I do so deliberately, aware of the representational problems I invoke, but equally convinced that comparison can be a powerful pedagogical and theoretical tool.
4.   Verena Stolcke, "Women's Labours: The Naturalisation of Social Inequality and Women's Subordination," in Of Marriage and the Market, ed. Kate Young, Carol Wolkowitz, and Roslyn McCullagh (London: Routledge & Kegan Paul, 1981), 167.
5.   Laury Oaks, "Irish Trans/National Politics and Locating Fetuses," in Fetal Positions/Feminist Practices, ed. Lynn Morgan and Meredith Michaels (Philadelphia: University of Pennsylvania Press, forthcoming). See also Barbara Duden, Disembodying Women: Perspectives on Pregnancy and the Unborn (Cambridge: Harvard University Press, 1993).
6.   Casper.

7. In March 1996, New York Magazine (11 Mar. 1996, p. 12) carried news of the wedding of Nicole Miller and Kim Taipale, noting, in a striking example of the personification of the fetal subject, "The couple is expecting a son, Palmer Taipale, in March." I thank Rachel Roth for bringing the clipping to my attention.

8. See Janelle S. Taylor, "The Public Fetus and the Family Car: From Abortion Politics to a Volvo Advertisement," Public Culture 4 (winter 1992): 67–79. Also Janelle S. Taylor, "Image of Contradiction: Obstetrical Ultrasound in American Culture," in Reproducing Reproduction, ed. Sarah Franklin and Helena Ragone (Philadelphia: University of Pennsylvania Press, forthcoming).

9. I might add that the multiple venues through which fetuses are created include the rhetoric that feminist scholars employ to remark on and to contest the emergence of fetal subjects.

10. Susan Bordo, Unbearable Weight: Feminism, Western Culture, and the Body (Berkeley: University of California Press, 1993), 80.

11. Alan Guttmacher Institute, Clandestine Abortion: A Latin American Reality (New York: Alan Guttmacher Institute, 1994), 3.

12. See Ana Maria Portugal, ed., Mujeres e Iglesia: Sexualidad y Aborto en America Latina (Washington, D.C.: Catholics for a Free Choice/Mexico City: Distribuciones Fontamara, 1989), 114.

13. Centro de Estudios y Asesoria en Salud (CEAS), "La crisis, la mujer, y el aborto" (Quito, Ecuador: Centro de Estudios y Asesoria en Salud, 1985). See also Alan Guttmacher Institute.

14. See Didier Fassin, "El aborto en el Ecuador (1964-1988)," Bulletin de l'Institut Frangais d'Etudes Andines 19, no. 1 (1990): 215–31.

15. Ximena Costales P., "El aborto: Repercusiones sociales de una drama individual" (Quito: Centro de Investigaciones y Apoyo a la Mujer, unpublished ms).

16. Elsewhere I argue that the beginnings of an internationalization of the U.S. abortion debate are evident in Ecuador. See Lynn M. Morgan, "Ambiguities Lost: Fashioning the Fetus into a Child in Ecuador and the United States," in Small Wars: The Cultural Politics of Childhood, ed. Nancy Scheper-Hughes and Carolyn Sargent (Berkeley: University of California Press, in press).

17. Lilia Rodriguez, "Taller: Mujer y derechos reproductivos" (Quito: Casa Para la Mujer/United Nations Fund for Population Activities, 1989), 20. In May of 1992 I attended a seminar sponsored by the Corporation de Investigaciones Sociales y en Salud (COINSOS), International Projects Assistance Services, and the Prevention of Maternal Mortality Program at the Center for Population and Family Health at Columbia University entitled, "Impacto del aborto en el sistema de salud ecuatoriano" (Impact of abortion on the Ecuadorian health system) in Quito.

18. See Barbara Katz Rothman, The Tentative Pregnancy (New York: Penguin, 1986).

19. Instituto Nacional de Estadistica y Censo, Anuario de Estadisticas Vitales (Quito, Ecuador: 1986), 3.

20. English version found in M.L. Chiswick, "Commentary on Current World Health Organization Definitions Used in Perinatal Statistics," British Journal of Obstetrics and Gynaecology 93 (December 1986): 236-38. Spanish version found in Anuario de Estadisticas Vitales, v.

21. See Anuario de Estadisticas Vitales, iv.

22. Elsie Clews Parsons, Peguche: Canton of Otavalo, Province of Imbabura, Ecuador (Chicago: University of Chicago Press, 1945), 44.

23. Michael Taussig, Shamanism, Colonialism, and the Wild Man: A Study in Terror and Healing (Chicago: University of Chicago Press, 1987), 97. A physician in Quito reported that some people on the coast of Ecuador refer to unbaptized babies as moritos, or Moors, from the colonial Spanish equivalent for "heathen."

24. Perhaps the "not-yet-person" exists in the realm of infertility in the United States, where images abound of "our child" who is not yet conceived. See Margarete Sandelowski, With Child in Mind: Studies of the Personal Encounter with Infertility (Philadelphia: University of Pennsylvania Press, 1993).

25. See Nancy Scheper-Hughes, "Theft of Life: Organ Stealing Rumors," Anthropology Today 12 (June 1996): 3–11.

26. Barbara Duden, Disembodying Women: Perspectives on Pregnancy and the Unborn (Cambridge: Harvard University Press, 1993).

27. See also Susan C.M. Scrimshaw, "Bringing the Period Down: Government and Squatter Settlement Confront Induced Abortion in Ecuador," in Micro- and Macro-Levels of Analysis in Anthropology: Issues in Theory and Research, ed. Billie DeWalt and Pertti J. Pelto (Boulder: Westview Press, 1985), 121–46.

28. See Lauris A. McKee, "Los cuerpos tiernos: Simbolismo y magia en las practicas post-parto en Ecuador," America Indigena 42 (October-December 1982): 615–28.

29. Thanks to Rayna Rapp for suggesting this interpretation.

30. Laurie Price, "Ecuadorian Illness Stories: Cultural Knowledge in Natural Discourse," in Cultural Models in Language and Thought, ed. Dorothy Holland and Naomi Quinn (Cambridge: Cambridge University Press, 1987), 320.

31. Andie L. Knutson, "The Definition and Value of a New Human Life," Social Science and Medicine 1 (1967): 7–29.

32. Mary M. Crain, "Poetics and Politics in the Ecuadorean Andes: Women's Narratives of Death and Devil Possession," *American Ethnologist* 18 (February 1991): 85.

33. Michel Tousignant, "Pena in the Ecuadorian Sierra: A Psychoanthropological Analysis of Sadness," *Culture, Medicine, and Psychiatry* 8 (December 1984): 381–98.

34. That the work of creating persons is stratified according to gender can also explain why aucas weigh so heavily on a mother's conscience, because mothers hold themselves principally responsible for having their children baptized. Women often said that newborns are not full persons prior to baptism: "Not children of God," said one Ecuadoran woman; "More like puppies than persons," said another. A newborn baby, the women told me, does not become a full person until it is welcomed into the Christian community through baptism.

35. Celeste Michelle Condit, *Decoding Abortion Rhetoric* (Urbana: University of Illinois Press, 1991); Sarah Franklin, "Fetal Fascinations: New Dimensions to the Medical-Scientific Construction of Fetal Personhood," in *Off-Centre: Feminism and Cultural Studies*, ed. Sarah Franklin, Celia Lury, and Jackie Stacey (New York: HarperCollins, 1991), 190–205; Clifford Grobstein, *Science and the Unborn: Choosing Human Futures* (New York: Basic Books, 1988).

36. For an alternative view, see Linda Layne, "'I Remember the Day I Shopped for Your Layette': Consumer Goods, Fetuses, and Feminism in the Context of Pregnancy," in *Fetal Positions/Feminist Practices*.

37. See Beth A. Conklin and Lynn M. Morgan, "Babies, Bodies, and the Production of Personhood in North America and a Native Amazonian Society," *Ethos* 24 (December 1996): 657–94.

4

Orientations

Lawrence Cohen

THE ZAGREB TAMASHA

Who is it that can tell me who I am?
—*KING LEAR* I. IV. 230

Tamasha in Hindi is a commotion, a performance—song and dance, tragedy, burlesque, and romance strung together with lots of noise—as in its heir, the modern Hindi film. In 1988 anthropologists from around the world convened in Zagreb for a global conference. Several sessions were devoted to old age. At one, an anthropologist from India presented a paper speculating on the long lives of elders in a hill tribe in northeastern India. Afterward, the floor was opened for questions.

An American anthropologist asked the speaker about the prevalence of dementia among the elders. Dementia is a clinical term, which in 1988 signified progressive and long-term cognitive losses. Most of the anthropologists in the room were from North America, and they knew that dementia was more prevalent among the oldest old, persons in their eighties and nineties, like those of the superannuated hill tribe just described. The question seemed reasonable.

But the speaker did not follow it. There was a pause, and the American repeated the question, varying the key word: *senile dementia? Alzheimer's disease?* The speaker did not seem familiar with the terms. The room became still. The speaker's scholarship was not in question—he had presented a careful ethnography and had addressed questions of deep concern to Indian anthropology and to the emerging field of Indian gerontology—but Alzheimer's disease was not central to his frame of reference. Yet what had been a lackluster session on a hot afternoon suddenly grew focused and then animated as the audience, mostly from the United

States, Canada, and western Europe, struggled to explain what to many of them seemed utterly obvious. Terms flew across the dais.

I was sitting in the back row, en route to India to begin the fieldwork for this book. I sensed in the sudden impasse between audience and speaker a soupçon of tamasha, of what the anthropologist Victor Turner might have called a "social drama." Turner counseled paying attention to such moments of disruption, chaos, and conflict, as much as to more everyday things, in the study of social processes and structures. I had been trained as an anthropologist, to do *fieldwork,* and had romantic visions of writing field notes, of that moment when my life would cease to be just a more or less enjoyable middle-class existence and would become an instrument of knowledge. At that moment in Zagreb I had my own little "breakdown," my own collapse of expectation into a sense of possibility and confusion. I remember deciding that fieldwork had officially begun; I started to write. That the scholars I was writing about might not be so easily reducible to separate "American" and "Indian" camps, and that they were far more subtle and sophisticated in their work than the momentary tamasha I was able to exploit might indicate, did not occur to me at that moment. I was learning one of my first lessons about anthropological desire: it offered Archimedean possibilities, totalities out there for the taking. Everything, everywhere, all the time, was grist for one's interpretive mill: one had only to pretend a stance of complete innocence—life as Holden Caulfield, Harriet the Spy, Candide.

The various words offered by the audience to the speaker did not clarify the original question for him. People kept trying to explain the obvious, until one exuberant participant shouted out "Crazy old people!" The audience's attention shifted quickly to the newcomer. That was not what was meant, they assured the speaker, not at all. They were gerontologists; they were not ageist. They were referring only to specific biological diseases. The efforts to explain Alzheimer's resumed.

I began to wonder, Candide in the back with notebook cocked, whether the anxiety around this challenge to gerontological aesthetics might carry greater significance. In calling into question the translatability of the medical language of dementia, the speaker seemed to have pushed his interlocutors down a slippery slope culminating in an admission (instantly resisted) that these medical terms pointed to the aberrant behavior of elderly persons, to old crazies. And not only was a link between disease and difficult old people being both offered and resisted, but it was being framed as a moral imperative, that *to ask about the minds of old people is essential and expected.*

The obviousness of Alzheimer's for the majority of the Zagreb participants mirrored its social and clinical construction in much of North America and Europe as a discrete, virulent, and unambiguous form of pathology. In rethinking the events of the Zagreb conference some years later, I was reminded of the format of family support groups sponsored by the Alzheimer's Association in the United States. I attended several meetings of such groups in the Boston area from 1990 to 1992. In most sessions, family members were encouraged by a facilitator to acknowledge—openly, to other group members—that their relative had a brain disease. The repeated exhortations to *acknowledge* Alzheimer's were performative; that is, they conveyed meaning as much in the act as in the content of speech. Obviously, group members already knew their relatives were demented: this knowledge had brought them to the group in the first place. But the communal acknowledgment of Alzheimer's, through this adaptation of the confessional rhetoric of the American self-help movement, was framed as a critical first step toward "gaining control of our lives." There is much at stake, whether in self-help sessions or at international conferences, in the confessional naming and renaming of Alzheimer's. The aggressive and iterative obviousness of dementia discloses its structure as a *moral* discourse.

Against this particular normative content, the Zagreb session offered a contrasting and equally normative construction, that of the speaker. "What we mean," another participant told him, "is senility." "Ah, senility …," the Indian anthropologist noted, and the audience relaxed, the hermeneutic circle finally having collapsed. "But you see," the speaker explained patiently, "there is no senility in this tribe." To him this truth was redundant. The point of his lecture had been to describe an isolated society in which the traditional Indian joint family was not yet threatened. Old people in such a society were well-cared for and did not become senile.

The speaker's invocation of the joint family as the sole criterion for assessing the well-being of old people is an important feature of post-Independence Indian literature on old age. Indian gerontology is built around a narrative of the inevitable decline of the universal joint family secondary to the four horsemen of contemporary apocalypse: modernization, industrialization, urbanization, and Westernization. The status and health of old people is consequently declining; solutions must be looked for in the highly developed technologies of Western gerontology and geriatrics. The West occupies a split role in this narrative, as the source of both the problem and the solution. For the speaker, "senility" was counterposed to the "joint family," the latter an index of Indianness and the former, in consequence, of Westernization. He seemed to suggest that it is only meaningful to speak of senile old bodies in the context of fragmented or nonexistent—and thus "Western"—families.

Those audience members not from India did not appear convinced of either the lack of "senility" among this tribe or of the speaker's explanation for it as an index of Westernization. The American who had asked the original question regarding the prevalence of dementia remarked to me later over dinner at a Croatian castle that, assuming that the proportion of tribal elders over the age of seventy was as high as the speaker had suggested, dementia was in all likelihood a more significant problem. Most of the audience, given the zest with which they took up the effort to translate the term, would probably have agreed. Two distinct and seamless narratives emerged: for many of the Americans and Europeans, senile pathology was located in specific and isolatable disease processes; for many of the Indians, senile pathology was located in family dynamics and cultural crisis.

5

Globalization from Way Below
Brazilian Streets, a Youth, and World Society
Tobias Hecht

S treet children probably lead lives more like modern-day hunters and gatherers—sub-stituting the fruits of nature with a precarious economy of scavenging, theft, the oldest profession, and the largess of passersby—than like denizens of a supposedly globalized and postfordist world. What, then, is the relevance of globalization to the lives of such children, children who do not travel in airplanes, use computers, enter shopping malls, work in foreign-owned factories, or produce any goods for the international market?

Based on research conducted at various times between 1992 and 2002, this chapter exam-ines how one individual—Bruna Veríssimo, who grew up in the streets of the Brazilian city of Recife—lives this era of globalization and how she seems to imagine a place for herself in world society. The chapter also discusses experimental methods of research as tools for understanding the individual within processes of global change; it makes the analytical link between the indi-vidual and the global by means of the notion of commodity chains. Through an examination of Bruna's life story and the decade-long process of getting at that story, I argue that concern over, talk about, and advocacy in behalf of street children are related to much larger economic and cultural processes.

In the countries south of the Rio Grande, one cannot really conceive of globalization as a new force; the very name for the region—*Latin America*—would make little sense if the place it described had not been born of something like a global process. In other parts of the world, similar problems arise with the concept.

In considering the place of globalization in the study of Africa, Frederick Cooper (2001:189) argues that there are two problems with the concept, "first the 'global' and second the 'iza-tion.'" The first problem, Cooper argues, is that what passes for global is often just wishful thinking on the part of neoliberal economists or else the alarmism of those who fear market tyranny. Capital does not go everywhere, markets are not as open as advocates of free trade

Tobias Hecht; Jennifer Cole and Deborah Durham, eds., "Globalization from Way Below: Brazilian Streets, A Youth, and World Society," In *Figuring the Future: Globalization and the Temporalities of Children and Youth*, pp. 223–243. Copyright © 2008 by School for Advanced Research. Reprinted with permission.

would like, and the nation-state is hardly irrelevant. The suffix *ization* suggests a phenomenon that is not only new but also arrant, a force that is reconfiguring our social and economic lives at this particular moment in history.

Like any scholar of empires, Cooper has seen it all before: Southeast Asians enslaved by Dutchmen and sent to the southern tip of Africa; West Africans kidnapped by Portuguese, British, and French traders and made to work plantations in the Americas that, in turn, enriched Europe; mass migrations; intercontinental plagues; transoceanic mercantile conglomerates. "For all the growth in international trade in recent decades, as a percentage of world GDP it has only barely regained levels found before the First World War" (Cooper 2001:194). Cooper's larger point is not that nothing is changing but that globalization may not be a useful analytical tool for understanding what is.

Is the new buzzword *globalization* merely déjà vu all over again? In *The Anthropology of Globalization,* Ted Lewellen summarizes other reasons why scholars have dismissed the putative newness and challenged the reach of globalization:

> Long-term migration—often considered a key element of globalization—affects only about 1% or 2% of the world's population and … earlier mass movements, say of the Irish, Italian, and Chinese to the New World in the 19th century, proportionately exceeded anything that is going on today when Western countries have imposed tight restrictions on immigration. The formation of political, economic, and military alliances, such as the European Community, NATO, and the ASEAN, represent more a regionalization than a globalization. … If homogenization of culture is a criterion of globalization, as many in the media claim, then how do we explain the explosive increase in ethnic politics, religious fundamentalism, and local organizing? In most larger countries, 80% or more of production is still for domestic consumption. [Lewellen 2002:9]

Lewellen suggests that a globalized economy has been emerging gradually over the past five or so centuries and that advances in communications have long been making the planet feel smaller. Yet, he argues, and here I agree, that something qualitatively new was born at the opening of the twentieth century's final decade: with the demise of the Soviet Union, large parts of the third world came to embrace neoliberalism. Even where this was not the case, the International Monetary Fund and the World Bank could virtually dictate the economic policies of poor countries (Lewellen 2002:16).

Although I would agree with Cooper that globalization is ineffectual as a tool of analysis, I do consider it useful as a name for something that is qualitatively different about the world since about 1990. Moreover, I suggest that some of the economic changes implied by globalization are linked to international concern about the plight of children, including street children. Globalization brings to mind the macro-effects of liberal trade policies, the communications revolution, capital flows, and the mass movement of people and ideas, but it is also about that now familiar idea of an imagined community. Benedict Anderson (1983) wrote of imagined communities mostly with reference to nationalism, but the idea could easily be applied to the notion of a global community. To see ourselves as part of a global system is not simply a matter of acknowledging the extent of economic integration around the world; it is also a matter of imagination. Talk of the "world's children" and of the collective and custodial responsibility of adults to protect them is one manifestation of that imagination, an assertion of our common humanity.

If globalization is about enormous and rapidly increasing flows of goods, information, and labor across international borders, the lowering of trade barriers, and a revolution in communications, then Latin American street children may have become involved in an analogous and, as I will argue, not entirely unrelated process at about the time the Berlin Wall fell.

Consider the international flow of information about Latin American street children. By the late 1980s, they had become the subjects of films (most notably, Hector Babenco's 1980 feature *Pixote*, until recently the third most commercially successful Brazilian film [Levine 1997]) and numerous television documentaries. They were featured in women's home magazines, in-flight publications, tabloids, and broadsheets. Just as children can be a sign of value, a font of "latent potential" (Anagnost, chapter 3, this volume), their mistreatment can be taken as a reflection of the ill health of the nation. Latin American politicians campaigned on promises to improve the conditions of street children, whose plight was even the subject of hearings in the European Parliament and the US Congress. Meanwhile, UNICEF identified street children as an important priority, and Amnesty International (1990a, 1990b) and Human Rights Watch (1994) released damning reports about their treatment, accusing governments of tolerating death squad killings of youth. At the same time that a number of international and multilateral institutions declared street children to be of great concern and a new focus of their work, specialist nongovernmental organizations burgeoned, with the appearance of such first-world organizations as Childhope and Covenant House and a rapidly growing and changing array of NGOs based in developing countries and dedicated to helping street children. Brazil became host to a vibrant array of nongovernmental activist organizations and service providers. In Rio, one study counted thirty-nine institutions that catered exclusively to street children in that city (Valladares and Impelizieri 1991:9). The survey noted that all these programs had been created around or after the mid-1980s and that their numbers changed rapidly: in the course of the five months it took to complete the study, four new programs were created. In Recife, the setting for my research, a gamut of projects had emerged, with government, civil, and religious organizations all vying for a role. Elsewhere (Hecht 1998), I have suggested that in Recife there was approximately one adult working full-time in behalf of street children for every child living and sleeping in the street.

The first time I saw Bruna Veríssimo was at one of the weekly meetings of the National Movement of Street Children. At the time, 1992, the organization was perhaps Brazil's most spirited social movement, the focus of much local and international attention. The Movimento, as activists referred to it, had championed Brazil's new Statute on Children and Adolescents and, through a well-organized media and human rights campaign, helped to make the murders of poor urban youth a national bane. I began attending the meetings in June of that year in Recife, a port city of some two million in Brazil's northeast.

Boisterous affairs, the meetings brought together representatives from neighborhood base cells (*núcleos de base*) who reported on violence and other matters of concern in their respective areas and discussed the movement's municipal, regional, and national activities. The young activists, invariably from very poor families, were not street children in any strict sense; nearly all resided with their families, and most did not work in the street either. Rather, like most urban children in Brazil, they led lives of quiet hardship in crowded shantytowns and slums. But some homeless children from the city center did belong to the movement.

A few minutes into the second or third meeting I attended, a tall adolescent in a miniskirt and skimpy halter top sashayed across the room and sat on a table. Bruna Veríssimo's bare feet, unexpectedly large, were rough with calluses and poorly healed wounds and hung from the edge of the table, above the heads of the other children, mostly younger and smaller, who sat on the floor. Her feet were so weathered because she was one of the rare members of the movement who actually lived in the street. Biologically male, Bruna cross-dressed and used female adjectives when speaking of herself.

Discussed that day were a police operation to round up children in the street, the contents of a newsletter, an upcoming regional meeting, and a report about violence against street children. Bruna spoke her mind a number of times, demanding to know at one point what difference the report about violence would actually make.

Several months later, I came across Bruna sitting on the warm pavement of a blind alley behind a church in central Recife, embroidering. By then, I had seen her a number of times, but we had never spoken. She sat concentrating on the movements of the needle, her long hair containing her gaze. I greeted her, introduced myself, and was offered a muffled hello in return.

By that point in my research, I had devised a semistructured survey, a loose set of questions I put to the children in the form of a conversation, each question leading to a series of other subjects, which I would ask about in a more or less unpredictable fashion. With the church bells peeling four-thirty, it was that pre-dusk hour when Recife's mangrove mosquitoes (*maruins*) are especially active. Resolved to interview Bruna at some other time, perhaps once we got to know each other better, I sat there in awkward silence, scratching at my legs. Then Bruna, without looking up, told me, "Go ahead. Ask the questions. I know how to answer."

Unsettled, I took out my tape recorder, inserted a blank cassette, and before the bell tolled five, heard her recite how she had been raped by her stepfather at the age of nine, gone to live in the street with other children, stolen, sold her body, longed for her mother's love, known hunger, slashed her wrists, ridden on the back bumpers of buses, sniffed glue, swallowed pills, eaten from the trash, witnessed murders, and come to hate those passersby too afraid not to steer a wide berth. In the same tone of restive ennui, she told of how she had been featured on the radio, in the newspapers, even in a video about street children. "In a place like Italy, a film about street children is worth more than a porn flick," she concluded, looking up for the first time.

Figure 10.1

Bruna's self-portrait and cityscape.

What Bruna had realized, of course, is that street children were of interest to people thousands of miles beyond the narrowly circumscribed tangle of streets where she and other youths spend their days and nights and also that many researchers, journalists, and international advocates were speaking about them, even mentioning their names. Their plight, it seemed to Bruna, was something that could be packaged (say, in the form of a video) and easily transported to places like Italy (by plane) and might benefit the purveyor far more than the subjects. She might not have called street children a commodity, but this seems to have been the general thrust of her quiet accusation.

Anthropologists have used commodity chain analysis to study the social relations that accompany the voyage of exchangeable goods from producer to consumer, say, of diamonds collected in Angola, cut in Antwerp, and sold in Tokyo. Of importance is not the long-distance travel itself but the economic relations and their reverberations at each stage of production, distribution, and consumption. To use the example of diamonds, one might ask how, in Japan, the demand for diamond engagement rings was created in the absence of such a tradition. Might the use of diamond engagement rings be suggestive of changing notions of status, social class, and even love? At the other extreme in the commodity chain, in Angola, one might ask who is collecting the diamonds, how, and who is profiting. What is happening with the money? Not long ago, the profits were fueling a war. How many land mines can be purchased with the money earned from the sale of a single diamond? How many limbs are lost during the lifespan of a dozen mines?[1]

Can such a form of analysis, commodity chains, be applied to Latin American street children, and, if so, would it tell us anything useful? For a number of reasons, the analogy is murky. First, street children are, of course, not being exported, and they likewise produce nothing that is traded internationally. Second, a commodity such as diamonds has existed, to all intents and purposes, forever, but what of street children? Might talk about street children in the early 1990s not have reflected the emergence of a new or at least suddenly acute problem, one that warranted swift attention? Third, although money is moved in the name of street children, it would be cynical to say that the organizations helping them form anything like an industry. Yet as the vignette in the preceding section suggests, street children themselves realize that their image and ideas about them do cross borders and have an exchange value; representations of street children can, in short, be commodified. As these images travel, much information and a certain amount of money are being moved.

Historical records suggest that there is nothing new about children living on their own in urban Latin America. Already in colonial times, many Latin American cities, such as Bogotá, had street urchins (Röggenbuck 1996). The early 1990s was likewise not the first time that children had been a subject of international debate and action in Latin America. By the second decade of the twentieth century, experts in the fields of medicine, education, and criminology gathered at the Pan American Child Congresses to examine the situation of abandoned, destitute, and ill children and to reform laws and institutions with an eye to helping children and infants (Guy 1998). What was new by the last decade of the twentieth century was the degree of prominence children had attained in the international imagination about Latin America, particularly Brazil and Colombia. Street children and their violent deaths came to be two of the most widely known features of these countries.

If diamonds are transported by plane, then how did the images of Latin American street children reach Europe and North America? The simple answer is that these children travel through the advocacy of non-governmental organizations and multilateral institutions such as UNICEF and the writing and images produced by journalists, filmmakers, researchers, and advocates. For Southern African diamonds to be purchased by consumers in Japan or anywhere else, however, it is not enough for the diamonds to exist and for their transport to be possible. There must, of course, be a demand for their consumption. Demand can be invented where it did not once exist, as with diamonds.

The idea of a commodity chain, and globalization more generally, may have useful applications when it comes to understanding the sudden attention to street children in the late 1980s and early 1990s. First, the idea of the chain draws attention to the myriad players and mediators between the diamond and the consumer, between the child who lives in the street and the middle-class individual in the first world who might, say, make a donation to a charity based on a direct-mail appeal (in one year, the US-based Covenant House raised more than $28 million in this way [Walton 1991:25]). Second, just as the mine worker may benefit less than all others involved in the process of moving diamonds from mine to consumer, the consultants for UNICEF doubtless live much better than, say, the adult facilitators of Brazil's National Movement of Street Children, people working on the front lines of an effort to help impoverished children.

The northern interest in Latin American street children required a sort of breaking down of barriers, a kind of universalism, that advocates minimum standards in the treatment of children. If the UN Convention on the Rights of the Child, adopted in 1989 and ratified subsequently by all countries except the United States and Somalia, was the world's most important expression that such standards exist, then street children were held up as one of the most obvious signs that the conditions of third-world children were indeed dismal. In Brazil, the National Movement of Street Children campaigned in behalf of poor children generally; the organization's name and the centrality of street children to its identity, however, served as a way of galvanizing local and international support for a far larger problem. One adult activist suggested to me in an interview, "If we were called the National Movement of Children, no one would listen."[2]

Cultural relativism was of no use in explaining away the problem of street children, and this worked to the advantage of advocates: a practice such as female circumcision, widely condemned in most of the world, tends to be defended by some on the grounds of respecting different, competing cultural norms. When it came to street children, however, public opinion in Latin America may have been divided on just how to contend with them—from calls to help them and their families, to suggestions that they should all be rounded up and incarcerated, or worse—but no one could be heard advocating that the street is a suitable place for children to grow up. Street children became one of the only publicly acknowledged points of worldwide consensus about children. People everywhere are apt to be against children dying of malaria, but no prominent social movements have taken up this cause—which is surprising, given that the number of children killed daily by malaria is roughly the number of adults who died in the 2001 terrorist attack on the Twin Towers.

Just as globalization is about a single world of linked producers and consumers, attention to street children raises questions and facilitates consensus about the treatment that children deserve regardless of borders, national traditions, and regional ideologies. If globalization is introducing any degree of homogeneity into patterns of popular culture, nowhere is this happening in a more dramatic way than in relation to children and youth. Today, Mickey Mouse doubtless has better name recognition among ten-year-olds across the planet than does any single living human being. Meanwhile, movies, television programming, computer software, and the marketing and distribution of toys and children's literature are mostly controlled by a handful of companies; with minor adaptations, multinational corporations can now peddle the same products to children anywhere in the world. For this to be possible, children must be seen as legitimate consumers in the market economy. And it is hard to argue that this is not the case. According to an undated letter sent in 2002 as part of a direct-mail campaign by *Harper's Magazine,* consumers across the planet—children and their obliging parents—have spent four and a half billion dollars on licensed Star Wars merchandise since 1977. Even street children have taken consumer fads to extremes: one anthropologist argues that boys in Caracas are more likely to murder for a pair of Nikes than for food to fill their empty stomachs (Márquez 1998).

Despite some of their consumerist practices, street children turn notions about youth and globalization on their head. They violate most every aspect of increasingly global notions about how childhood should be lived: in the protective realm of school and home, in training as future workers and citizens. Street children live independently of adults, they are visible and often violent, and most of them, in the harshest of cities, do not survive to adulthood. Street children offend a modern awareness of the vulnerability and rights of children while also raising alarm over public safety.

BACK TO THE ALLEY

Seven years after carrying out my initial research, I returned to Northeast Brazil and, following a chance reencounter with Bruna, decided to see whether we might work together to write a book about her life and about her generation of street children, so many of whom, in just a fraction of a generation, had died.

Her life story, as she tells it, begins not so much with her birth but at the age of nine, when her stepfather sexually abused her: the day the street became home and her body a means of livelihood, the day he decided to be she. From that point, her descriptions move both backward, to vague memories of life as a boy in a violent home, and forward, to numbing years of fear, prostitution, drug use, and unrelenting discrimination in the streets, years that defy narration as the discrete incidents typical of biographies.

For a number of reasons, Bruna Veríssimo's life might seem an unlikely point of departure for attempting to understand social groups in Brazil, much less global society. For a start, even the modern consumer choices offered by globalization are inaccessible. But more to the point, Bruna hardly fits easily into any recognizable unit of anthropological analysis. As a young child at home, she was amid the legions of Recife's destitute families. Her mother, a sometimes prostitute, would also beg and worked for a time in a motel, cleaning rooms. The family lived at first in a shack perched along the banks of the Beberibe River, but in a slum clearance scheme, they were resettled to a new community in the Atlantic rain forest, far from the center of Recife. Initially, there was no running water or electricity. None of the hardships Bruna, then known as José Edson, endured were unusual for Recife's underclass. At the age of six or seven, she would hitchhike with her mother to the city's wholesale produce market, where they scavenged for discarded vegetables or offered to carry around crates of produce. Soon, she discovered a more lucrative means of earning money for the family: men would pay her to go off into the forest with them to be fondled and kissed. She became a sex worker at a time when other children were learning the alphabet. She (he)—the pronouns are a matter of confusion here—began to favor playing with dolls and dressing in her older sister's clothing. These feminine tendencies ("My mother's sperm was stronger than my father's," as Bruna explained it) did not go unnoticed by her stepfather, a violent binge drinker.

Raped at the age of nine, Bruna ran away to the streets of the city center. There she joined up with a group of girls who had formed a sort of informal gang. Together, the Pá da Galega,[3] or Blond Girl's Band, roamed, slept, sniffed glue, and stole under the tutelage of Safira, who was a bit older and more experienced than the others. Yet not only was Bruna the sole member who was biologically male, but also she soon rejected her age-mates' means of subsistence:

> With a boy on one side and a girl on the other, whoever passed between us had no way out, old ladies, pregnant women, crippled people. With crippled people, I had this way of kicking away the crutch to stick my hand in the person's bag, which made me feel very sorry later. I never wanted to do it again. That was when I started to be different. I was different from the rest of them, not only from the boys but also from the girls. Like my friend Safira, who thought I was going soft because I no longer wanted to rob pregnant women. I didn't want to mess with crippled people. I was afraid to rob old ladies because they might have a heart attack and I'd feel guilty. … So I started to distance myself from theft.

Eventually making a promise to a saint never to steal again, Bruna moved formally into the sex trade at the age of about eleven. Never a typical street child, she was likewise not a typical transvestite prostitute. For one thing, there was her age:

> Twenty-four hours a day, I was in the middle of the street dressed up in drag like a woman. I showed up so many times in the newspapers. … Sometimes the photographers would stop me in the middle of the street to take my picture. I thought it was because I was sniffing glue in the street, but no, it was because I was so young at that time, cross-dressing as a woman and not hiding my homosexuality.

Bruna was an anomaly as such a young transvestite, and in other regards as well. Transvestites, not an uncommon sight in the poor neighborhoods of Recife, generally say that they are accepted in their communities. "People see us every day, and they are used to us," I was told by a number of them. In the city center, however, transvestites—who probably make up the majority of sex workers in that area—are plentiful at night but can almost never be seen in the street during the day, and certainly not living in the street. The fact that Bruna slept in the street resulted in rejection from the transvestite community as well, who look down on such people. Also, whereas transvestite prostitutes usually claim that they enjoy having sex with clients (see Kulick 1998), Bruna is impotent and speaks of her encounters with johns as a dreaded means of survival. A sense of great loneliness emerges from her narrative, a sort of economy of the emotions in which she says that she has never and will never fall in love, that she loves, only the mother who stood by and did nothing to protect her from an abusive stepfather.

Despite never having attended school, Bruna had learned to read and write by studying street signs and sometimes culled the garbage for newspapers, magazines, and books. I taught her to keep an ethnographic journal, in which she wrote about her daily activities, her encounters with people in the street—housewives who would give her food, fellow homeless people, rag pickers, people walking their dogs in the park. I also lent her a tape recorder so that she could begin conducting interviews on her own.

Our work together consisted of recording our conversations, discussing her journal entries, speaking with people who had known her at different times during her life—friends from childhood, her mother, social workers, and others. We held group interviews with other transvestite sex workers, and Bruna did many interviews on her own, sometimes with questions I gave her but always complemented by her own questions and informed by her peculiar way of interviewing. In addition, Bruna was provided with pastels, watercolors, sequins, glue, drafting paper, and other art supplies. Her pictures represented idealized versions of herself, goddesses, life on the streets, and more abstract representations. In one pastel drawing, a scantily clad prostitute walks along a street. In the background figure a policeman—tiny in proportion—and his car. The self would seem to be large, but the threat of authority is pervasive. In another drawing, a mother and child lie on the pavement outside a department store. As if Bruna had been studying the theories of Philippe Ariès, she depicted the child as at once a pacifier-sucking toddler and a miniature adult, complete with a halter top and makeup.

In exchange for meeting with me a couple times a week, writing in her journal, and conducting interviews, Bruna received a salary, the minimum monthly wage in Brazil. She was also given emergency payments when necessary and various sorts of assistance in kind. My hope was to forge a different sort of research relationship this time, one in which the "trade barriers" between researcher and subject were lowered, where ethnography need not be likened to pornography. Later, during a final period of research and writing in 2002 and 2003, Bruna was paid a regular salary under a grant from the H. F. Guggenheim Foundation. I was also able to sell her drawings and paintings, remitting a sum that was to have paid for a house. What I had not counted on was just how Bruna wanted to organize her relationship, through this collaboration, to a wider global society beyond the streets of Recife.

IMAGINING THE GLOBAL

The anecdote about my first interview with Bruna suggests a troubling nexus between globalization and street children. Street children can come to feel that their image and their intensely private anguish are sought by people from near and far who go to extraordinary lengths to get at them—and with practically nothing to offer in return. Yet my own subsequent ideas of what might constitute fairer and more collaborative research strategies failed to take into account how my co-researcher would interpret and act on these strategies. Here is an example of what I mean.

In late September 1999, Bruna began to conduct interviews on her own for our research about her life story. On the first of October, we met on the grounds of the Law Faculty in the center of Recife. We took a seat on one of the ornate benches in the garden. I handed her a set of three bottles of nail polish and a copy of *Marie Claire* (she is fond of women's magazines). Bruna examined the nail polish and then picked up the magazine and began to leaf through the pages. The pictures were what captured her attention: advertisements for makeup, soap, jewelry, lingerie.

"Were you able to do any interviews?"
"Yes," she said, without looking up.
"Can we listen to them?"
"All right."

Bruna pressed the play button. There was a lot of white noise on the tape. Wind? Breathing? A muffled conversation in the background. Bruna turned the page and looked at an advertisement for eye shadow. Every imaginable hue from peach to lime green.

"What is this?"

"Mascara."

"I mean, on the tape."

"An encounter, last night."

"With whom?"

"Last night, I was out on Mário Melo, walking around, looking at the city, when a man came up to me. He said, 'Someone wants to talk to you.' It was Mônica, a transvestite who is new to Mário Melo, who was looking for me. She said, 'Bruna, this man wants a *suruba a três* … a ménage à trois. Do you want to participate?' I didn't have any money and I was hungry, so I said all right. The man said he would pay me ten and pay Mônica fifteen. I said I wanted fifteen too, but Mônica said she was the one who had found the man. The man said that he was going to pay us twenty-five because that was all that he had, we could divide it up however we wanted. Since he didn't have any money for a motel, we went down to the edge of the river. I had the tape recorder in my bag and turned it on."

There was an elderly lady on the next bench, straining in our direction. I wanted to lower the volume so that she would not hear, but also to raise it to know whether I was actually hearing what Bruna claimed was on the tape. I raised it. The old lady scooted slightly toward the end of her bench nearer us.

"You taped a session with a client?"

"I had the machine in my bag. This is the sort of thing you want to know about, isn't it?"

The man on the tape was muttering a plea.

"He wanted to have sex without a condom," Bruna intoned. "So I said, 'If you are going to penetrate me, put this on.'"

"You taped this?"

"Yes."

"Did he know you were taping him?"

"Of course not."

"You didn't ask for permission?"

"No." She looked up, suddenly impatient. "I wanted it to be very spontaneous. Isn't that what you want?"

"That's dangerous. You can't do that."

"I know. I never have sex without a condom."

"I mean, you can't just record people without telling them."

"Who would guess they were being taped at a time like that?"

It was difficult to disagree with that point, but I still said, "If he had found out, he might have hurt you."

"He didn't find out."

"All right, he didn't. But he could have. Besides, you didn't have his permission. It isn't right."

"Did I give permission to the men who took me inside their cars when I was eleven?"

Other problems surfaced too. Bruna began complaining about rejection by other transvestites on the avenue where she worked. Believing that Bruna was about to publish a book, they protested her presence there. I cringed at this, knowing that if the book was ever to be published, it would be unlikely to make her much money. In any case, the rejection was coming from people who were a part of her everyday life. Still, Bruna suggested that we begin working (to use her words) "like paparazzi," secretly photographing prostitutes at night as they solicited clients.

Something had changed in the research dynamic and within Bruna's life on the street. Although she was sensitive to and hurt by the verbal abuse she regularly received from strangers in the city center, it was something she had lived with most of her life, and it did not happen all the time. In fact, it seemed to occur more when we were together than when she was a short distance away, on her own. I began to notice that, when she would go off alone, say, to a nearby kiosk to buy cigarettes, her presence hardly attracted any attention. When people stared, it was generally when the two of us were together. The combination of the foreigner and the local transvestite attracted attention more than either of us by ourselves. On my own, I was merely a visiting foreigner; on her own, from a distance, Bruna would generally be taken for a woman, and her provocative style of dress was nothing unusual to women in Recife. Yet I drew attention to her, and she to me.

My presence in Bruna's life doubtless changed the life we were studying, altering her relationship with her peers and eventually making both of us the subject of vague threats from transvestite sex workers apparently jealous over Bruna's prospects of being the subject of a book. In Bruna's interviews with her peers, the same questions were asked of her that had been put to me years before when I had done my dissertation research, questions I had hoped, in vain, would not arise in a collaborative project such as this. Those interviewed by Bruna wanted to know how she stood to benefit by collecting their stories and how she might profit by, in effect, peddling their image. What was different this time around was that, instead of being perceived as the perpetrator of this sort of work, I had become a mere accomplice, delegating the most difficult questions about ethnographic authority to Bruna. Seven years after my first maladroit interview with her, Bruna was being asked what she had once—through her guarded gaze, her studied indifference—asked me: what do you stand to gain by trading in my image?

A final period of research on this project was undertaken during three months in 2002. By that time, Bruna and I had interviews spanning a decade. That was when something became disquietingly evident: though much of what Bruna had been telling me could be verified, a good amount was patently untrue. In one of her recorded interviews, she spoke with a young prostitute named Michele. Michele talked about why she had decided to leave home to live in the street, what led her to become a prostitute, what it was like to go out with johns she did not know, and what she did with the money. At one point in the exchange between Bruna and Michele, the improbably high voice of this "girl" suddenly became Bruna's. The interviewer and the interviewed were one and the same. Other characters and events in Michele's life were likewise invented—a "sister" who died of dengue fever never existed, and a murder that had taken the life of a fellow sex worker in 1999 was in every detail the same murder that took the life of a sex worker in 2002. Bruna, despite always maintaining that what she most wanted in life was to leave the street, spurned real opportunities to do so. I had become a client—not the sort she normally dealt with, to be sure, but someone to second-guess, someone with a fantasy to satisfy. Despite my hopes to carry out collaborative research in an egalitarian fashion, a series of imprecise patron-client ties seemed to guide everything. I was a patron in the sense that I was sponsoring the research and offering a measure of economic security. But I was also a client who was seeking something from her and depending on her collaboration.

In telling her life story, in telling stories about her life, Bruna was constanty trying to situate her subjective experience in relation to what she saw as an audience, not only to what she believed I wanted to hear but also to what an imagined readership might want to read. When I asked her why avowedly heterosexual men made up the bulk of the transvestite sex workers' clientele, she would say that those men were looking for what they could not get at home, what ordinary women could not give them. The telling of her own life story was something analogous: the imagined readers were after what contrasted most starkly with the routine events in their own lives. As she seemed to see it, what people wanted to know about, what she had to offer a readership, were tales of sex and violence. And who could say that she had miscalculated?

THE INDIVIDUAL AND THE IMAGINATION OF GLOBAL SOCIETY

The individual is generally seen as an idiosyncratic, unpredictable point of departure for grasping the collective. For Durkheim, individualism was merely indicative of failed social integration. But some have championed the study of the individual as a means of understanding social systems; biographies by Oscar Lewis (1961), Sidney Mintz (1960), and Paul Radin (1926), among others, pushed anthropology in new and contested directions. In this era of great movement of labor, capital, and cultural experience, the notion of a bounded community holds little sway. Michael Herzfeld suggests in his *Portrait of a Greek Imagination* (1997) that the ethnographic biography, an apparent oxymoron, may provide a way of delving into the interlocking social worlds all members of humanity have to negotiate. I believe that the approach is a fruitful one for understanding a life that does not fit easily into any community but that is lived somewhere on the periphery of many different worlds.

It would be difficult to find a more certain target of discrimination in Brazil than a dark-skinned, destitute, homosexual transvestite who practices prostitution and sleeps in the street. But Bruna Veríssimo also associates with concerned housewives, human rights lawyers, artists, proselytizers, and fellow homeless people and prostitutes. Day in and day out, she observes Recife's police, petty merchants, and politicians (she sleeps outside an important government building). Yet she maintains that her only friends are the stray dogs she adopts and that she would not feel comfortable sleeping in a home so long as there are children who must sleep in the street.

Bruna Veríssimo's life offers vistas onto Brazilian urban existence and raises questions about world society. Her lived experience has taken her through *favelas* (shantytowns) and into the street, to reformatories and jails, but also into boyhood and the life of a transgendered prostitute. She has lived as a child, as an adult, and as a black Brazilian. As one of Recife's few surviving members of her generation in the street, Bruna's short but frighteningly eventful life is our only source of knowledge about the scores of murdered children she has known. Her life also intersects with a far wider world in which children and childhood are vital to any consensus that has emerged or might emerge about the nature, terms, and limits of global society. If globalization is anything more than an abstract idea, it can be understood only through subjective experience. Through Bruna's sense of herself as a sort of commodity—one that is photographed and written about, in whose name money is raised and social movements galvanized— she seems to have come to imagine herself into a far larger picture, one in which she rightfully belongs. In 1999, the government of Fernando Henrique Cardoso was actively selling off state assets, often to foreign interests. This irked public opinion because the enterprises were frequently being sold on the cheap, workers were being laid off, and ownership of the companies was shifting to foreign investors. This was the side of globalization most discussed in Recife at the time. A man in the park where Bruna and I would meet joked, "The next thing you know, we're all going to be foreigners," by which he meant that Brazilians themselves would soon be foreign owned. In the second half of the 1990s, the Brazilian press was awash with stories about foreigners coming to Brazil for inexpensive illicit sex, often with minors. Notwithstanding that there was no lack of Brazilian clients for sex workers and that in a city like Recife there are few foreign tourists at all, let alone sex tourists, transactional sex functions as a sort of metaphorical link in the commodity chain between the Brazilian local and the global.

In *Modernity at Large: Cultural Dimensions of Globalization,* Arjun Appadurai distinguishes between fantasy and imagination:

> The idea of fantasy carries with it the inescapable connotation of thought divorced from projects and actions, and it also has a private, even individualistic sound to it. The imagination, on the other hand, has a projective sense about it, the sense of being a prelude to some sort of expression. … Fantasy can dissipate (because its logic is so often autotelic), but the imagination, especially when collective, can become fuel for action. [Appadurai 1996:7]

Bruna was in the business of guessing the very private fantasies of her clients and bringing those fantasies to life. Gender was one realm in which she had already reinvented herself, in this case, as a putative woman—through dress, demeanor, the pitch of her voice, her peculiar sashay, the use of feminine adjectives in self-reference, and the assumption of what Brazilians call the "passive," or receptive, role in sex.[4] She was inventing not only her gender but also her nature, as if she herself were a character in multiple and concurrent scripts, accommodating the fantasies of others. On one hand, for concerned housewives who served her meals or gave her food for her dogs, Bruna was the tame object of charity: a representative of the deserving poor, a Catholic (who never mentioned her devotion to the saints of the Afro-Brazilian pantheon), someone who did not steal, drink, or use drugs. On the other hand, when I first met her in 1992 and she belonged to the National Movement of Street Children, Bruna was a member of an excluded underclass whose lot could be improved only through political organizing.

Bruna maneuvered through, observed, and reflected on several layers of Brazilian society. Although her life had been lived within a narrowly circumscribed mesh of city streets, her imagination—or, to follow the distinction made by Appadurai, her fantasies—had a far wider spatial dimension, taking her to what she referred to as "the other world," by which she meant somewhere beyond Brazil, somewhere richer, where her image (in a film, in a book) could be sold. She was not what you would call "future oriented." The fantasies that she occasionally spoke of formed no part of a project. She was not saving money to travel to Italy, where so many Brazilian transvestites who do manage to leave the country go. There was little to save. In any case, she always found an immediate reason to spend whatever money she had. Bruna was haunted by the fact of still being alive, always aware that she was one of the few survivors from her generation of street children. "I never imagined I would be celebrating my twenty-fourth birthday," she said on that occasion. Her fantasies seemed to be rooted more in the spatial than in any relationship to the future, as if the better life were a parallel existence that would be hers if only she could find it. "Bruna, slave of reality, freed by her dreams," she announced one afternoon as we walked across the city center. She asked me to write it down for my book.

Being hopeful implies imagining beyond the here and now. But there is a painful side to hope because it evidences precisely what is lacking in the present. In Bruna's case, knowing more about the "other world"—be it San Francisco, where she believed that homosexuals could marry (this was before any time when they could), or Rome, where transvestite sex workers like her make much more money—made her immediate reality appear all the more dismal.

In the end, Bruna's autonomy, ironically, depended on her success in marketing herself. Whereas contemporary childhood can rightly be seen as representing a reprieve from the market (Fass, chapter 2, this volume), Bruna bet on the benefits a global market might offer her. Reluctantly, she sold her body, a local enterprise that brought her tremendous suffering, but she was eager to sell her story, a prospect she hoped would allow her to transcend her status quo. As a plane flew overhead one day, she lamented the fact that she would probably never be able to travel in that way. Yet she clearly imagined herself as a protagonist on something like a global stage, an individual with a story to tell or to invent, yearning to satisfy the imagined expectations of a readership not yet extant. We were standing not far from the mangrove swamp where she took her clients who were too poor to pay for a motel room.

NOTES

1. For a detailed example of the use of commodity chains in anthropology, see Collins 2000.
2. In a similar way, AIDS orphans and mother-to-child transmission of HIV have been at the heart of a much larger debate about the use of anti-retrovirals in Southern Africa. See Bray 2003.
3. In Brazil, the word galega (galego in the masculine; literally, "Galician") refers to people who have light-colored hair or skin. Pá is a shortened version of the word patota, a band or informal grouping. The galega here was Safira, whose hair was bleached from the sun and the salt air.
4. Unlike the case of Madagascar (see Cole, chapter 5, this volume), clothing in itself does not have such transformative powers. It is not the clothing that makes the man womanly in Brazil. Heterosexual men dress up as women during carnival, for instance. The most important feminizing activity is receptive sexual intercourse. In Brazil, men who practice only the penetrative role in sex with other men are not necessarily considered homosexuals. But taking the receptive role is said to make a man into a woman. For two points of departure on this subject, see Kulick 1998 and Parker 1991.

6

Wildness in the Heart of Town

Ron Emoff

A pervasive odor enshrouds the streets of Antananarivo, the capital of Madagascar—a combination of lead gasoline combustion, burning hardwood (which Malagasy people use for cooking), and rotting human defecation. This odor is at first both repugnant and engaging, such a powerful olfactory sensation, even a slight burn in the back of the throat, that one can almost imagine it into being much later. At the muddy *taxi-brousse* station in Antananarivo, a light early-morning rain was concentrating this odor and drizzling it onto the bodies of Malagasy people waiting to spend long cramped hours in travel. One young Malagasy man had a stringed instrument in one hand. He stood patiently waiting for his ride, unconcerned that droplets of rain were settling on his rather unusual-looking instrument.

The instrument's wooden body had been carved delicately into the form of a portable radio—cassette player, detailed with carrying handle; fast forward, reverse, and play buttons; radio frequency and volume control knobs; frequency band display; condenser microphone; and speaker—a striking image of aural empowerment. Radio transmissions in Madagascar often originate from the Malagasy National Radio Station. Was this musician empowering himself iconically with the broadcast of his own playing over the national radio frequency, imagining himself into national musical recognition? Perhaps this instrument's mimetic form had been designed to convey criticism over the *unlikelihood* that one's own music would ever be nationally recognized, or over the (in)accessibility in Madagascar of actual radio-cassette players, which are often prohibitively expensive.

I had been in Antananarivo for the past three and a half weeks, waiting to be issued a long-term research visa. I was finally heading for Tamatave, a bustling port town on the east coast of the island, where I would spend most of the next two years. Previously I had only dreamed of the Indian Ocean—an eternal expanse of blue green, with a swollen moon perched on the horizon and reflecting erratically below on yellow bobbing crests. Yet any of my delight with finally arriving in Madagascar was necessarily tinged with ambivalence. For one, very young Malagasy children swathed in filthy rags were always begging for change from *vazaha* (white outsiders) in the dirty, bumper-to-bumper Antananarivo streets. And there was talk everywhere of the environmental devastation widespread throughout Madagascar, which leaves considerably less arable land each year on which to grow rice. Then there were the dire national economic problems and the powerlessness of the current president to do much about them. This was a strange, inequitable, disturbing awakening. I was intensely charged by this world of difference—as if I were learning all over again how food tastes, colors radiate, music sounds—while Malagasy people themselves had to maneuver so tenaciously to survive in this same world.

The man with the stringed instrument seemed to notice my visual fascination with it, though he said nothing to me. Another Malagasy man leaned toward me and said in French that this musician was Antandroy, from the south of the island. To my puzzlement he added, shaking a finger at me, "Faites attention!" The instrument man, who apparently spoke no French, smiled placidly in my direction. Our respective *taxi-brousse* trucks arrived, and the Antandrov man left Antananarivo to return south to his homeland. Heading out of Antananarivo toward the east coast, I wondered why I had been warned to beware of this musician (and "his kind"?).

There are eighteen to twenty different groups of Malagasy people that are usually recognized in Madagascar. Merina are predominant in the central Haut Plateau region, which includes Antananarivo. The man at the *taxi-brousse* station who had warned me about Antandroy was Merina. In the Tamatave region on the east coast, the most populous group is called Betsimisaraka. This name means literally "the many who don't separate," though Betsimisaraka are also recognized in Madagascar as comprising two distinct groups, Northern and Southern Betsimisaraka, each reportedly distinct from the other in temperament, custom, even language. Among some of the other, varied groups in Madagascar, Antandroy (from the south) in particular are sometimes construed to be fierce and contentious in temperament, even to be murderous "savages," as people to be shunned and avoided at any cost. In my yet limited Malagasy, I asked the others on the *taxi-brousse*, mostly Betsimisaraka and a few Merina, if there were any Antandroy in Tamatave. Echoing the earlier admonition, an elder Malagasy man responded, "Iah, misy maro izany. Fa tandremo!" (Yes, there are many. But beware of them!)

Numerous Merina have resettled in Tamatave, attracted commonly by the business opportunities there. Indeed, some of the largest commercial enterprises in Tamatave are owned and run by Merina residents. Antandroy have often come to Tamatave to search for wage labor, which is scarce in their more remote southern homeland. Many Antandroy actually end up being employed by Merina bosses, as night guardians for their businesses. I began to hear more specific tales of Antandroy terror in Tamatave, often told by Merina residents. Stories about Antandroy were always extreme, almost panicked: "Antandroy are fiercely argumentative, confrontational, violent"; "an Antandroy will kill you just to get 1000 Malagasy francs (the equivalent of about 25 cents) from you"; "don't ever go into an Antandroy *quartier*— Antandroy will cut off the head of a stranger who goes foolishly onto their turf." And then gendered dehumanizing slurs: "Antandroy women don't cleanse themselves"; "they are rough, even violent sexual partners"; "they like to bite"; "they carry disease." With some frequency, other Malagasy thus would describe Antandroy as sub- or pre-human "primitives" who are driven by aggressive instinct rather than by reason.

Antandroy are recognized throughout Madagascar, often apprehensively, as staunch adherents to their ancestral customs, and they are often characterized by other Malagasy by their strongly felt connections to Antandroy ancestral land in the south. There is a history of tenacious Antandroy resistance against French colonial occupation of their southern homeland. Often a harsh, drought-stricken region, this area was one parcel of Madagascar that French colonials were unable to subdue. Antandroy reportedly repelled French rifles with just their silver-tipped spears and their maniacal desire to protect their ancestors' land. Yet somehow this valorous past had ceded to, or devolved into, consistently disparaging tales of Antandroy terror.

In Tamatave there are Antandroy encampments throughout the market, or *bazary be*. In particular I noticed two large such encampments on the main road which formed one perimeter of the market. Whole families, ranging from the elderly to infants, all live in these two roadside encampments, barely shielded from the nearly constant passing of trucks, autos, and small motorcycles. These Antandroy shelters are pieced together from fragments of sheet plastic, cardboard, and corrugated sheet metal, all tented between deteriorated colonial-style cement buildings and the sidewalk below. In the daytime Antandroy sell fruit, cigarettes, peanuts, and bread from makeshift stands in their places on the side of this busy road. Throughout the evening, Antandroy men are employed by Indian merchants, whose shops provide the only vertical walls of the Antandroy encampments. These Indian shopowners are often called *karana* in Malagasy—a term, likely derived from the word, "Koran," which sometimes carries a derogatory inflection. Antandroy are paid, only minimally, to sit from sundown to sunrise as guardians of these Indian shops. Since Antandroy evoke such apprehension, even terror—they are also said to kill unrestrainedly anyone who steals from them—Antandroy presence itself is enough to deter most any notion of thievery. In my early days in Tamatave, I often noticed Antandroy men, barefoot and clothed in garments soiled and torn from this constant street existence, sitting calmly on the ground in their encampments, contemplative, silver-tipped spears poised against their bodies. They sat straight-backed and intent, gazing out into the Tamatave streets, projecting an aura of personal and collective dignity as well as of loyalty to their *karana* bosses. These Antandroy guardians were seemingly disinterested in my presence, however—they certainly were not about to kill me over pocket change (or what I considered pocket change, yet 1000 Malagasy francs might buy enough rice to make a meal for two or three people).

It can be the rainy season most any time of year in Tamatave. A fond saying among Malagasy is that Tamatave has two seasons: the rainy season, and the season in which it rains. The humidity is often so thick here that stainless steel will oxidize into rust, and a dense fuzzy blue-green patina will grow overnight on leather. Yet Malagasy don't complain about the rain—indeed rain is often a sign with which ancestral spirits, or *razana,* express their pleasure or goodwill to the living. One afternoon during a sunny break in the weather, I was walking past one of the Antandroy encampments on Tamatave's main thoroughfare. From the camp arose the sound of an accordion, played so rapidly, with such intensity and gripping beauty, that I was frozen in place. This was music so complex, so inspired, that it was actually disturbing to hear, as though being cut through or stripped bare with sound. This seemed more than could humanly be culled from a relatively small button accordion, a performance virtually not possible.

The accordionist stopped playing to tend to some Malagasy customers who had approached to buy bananas. At that time I could speak no Antandroy, which linguistically is quite distinct, for instance, from the Betsimisaraka spoken more frequently on the east coast. I felt an urgency to communicate something, unsure of exactly what, to this Antandroy man. At least some expression of heightened musical appreciation. At this moment a teenage Merina boy I had befriended a few days earlier and who spoke both French and Malagasy auspiciously appeared. I experienced "coincidences" such as this quite regularly in Madagascar; Malagasy friends later explained such occurrences to be indications of ancestral spirit approval and assistance, for I was there after all to learn about *tromba,* a Malagasy ancestral spirit possession practice.

This boy, Thierry, was from Antananarivo and was on vacation in Tamatave visiting an aunt. He had seemed delighted to find a *vazaha* friend with whom to spend time and to practice speaking French. He cheerfully agreed to speak to the Antandroy musician for me. I asked Thierry to inquire only if the Antandroy man would resume playing his accordion. Thierry seemed nervous, though, upon actually approaching the Antandroy encampment. He also seemed to have difficulty communicating with the Antandroy accordionist. Thierry turned to me and told me in French that the accordionist, whose name was Magnampy Soa, simply asked if I had a *magnéto,* a tape recorder, and instructed that I return with it the next day at this same time. Later that evening, overwhelmed with excitement—I'd not only be able to listen again to Magnampy Soa, but I'd also be allowed to record his performance—I recalled the Antandroy man at the Antananarivo *taxi-brousse* station, with his radio—cassette stringed instrument. Again, a tape-recording device or its image was being designated by an Antandroy as a significant medium in or for musical production. Specifically, Magnampy Soa was clearly concerned in part with the preservation of his show for me the next day.

By morning the rain had resumed, quite heavily. Research grants had afforded me the latest not only in field sound-recording components, but also outdoor camping equipment, so transporting my electrical devices in the rain posed no threat to their well-being. I again recalled the Antandroy man in Antananarivo, seemingly unconcerned that the rain was dampening his intricately carved stringed instrument. I felt foolish, excessive, remorseful. Why should my equipment, devices only of replication, be spared from the elements, while Malagasy musical instruments themselves, on which such exquisite sounds are created, must face rapid deterioration? Indeed, Magnampy Soa's accordion was caked with street dirt and age, its cardboard bellows frayed in spots, its once white buttons yellow-gray and worn. Accordions and materials with which to build other instruments are difficult, and in many cases impossible, to obtain in

Madagascar. Another among many irreconcilable inequities, amidst these masterful Antandroy musicians and instrument builders, it was only my strange, distant possessions which were privileged to protection from the humidity, heat, dust, and wind. An agonizing (and likely realistic) image has continued to haunt me, in which I return to Madagascar in the near future to find that Magnampy Soa and others no longer even have instruments on which to perform. Yet I'll still have my collection of well-protected tapes, documenting what once was. Perhaps by instructing me to bring my tape recorder, Magnampy Soa was expressing his own vision of loss, similar to mine. And how could I even begin to give back to Malagasy people, who, among other things, were essentially building an academic future for me?

Upon my arrival at his encampment, Magnampy Soa had his children construct a small corner vestibule out of plastic sheets to keep out the wind and rain during our session—this small hemmed-in space would be our recording studio. I became very fond in particular of Magnampy Soa's children, taking two or even three of them at a time for rides on my one-speed bicycle up and down the streets of Tamatave, to the cheers of onlookers who weren't accustomed to seeing *vazaha* spend fun time with Malagasy. Or accompanying the children to the bakery across the street for sweets, and then taking long walks on the Indian Ocean beach (which was only two blocks away), giggling and splashing together in the surf while speaking in Antandroy.

In the cramped corner space I began to set up my recording equipment, which included microphone stands, numerous wires, microphone preamps, the recorder itself, headphones—an excess of machines and connections, especially in contrast to the *magnéto* more familiar to Antandroy, a small portable self-contained device. Magnampy Soa sat back watching me set up, with perhaps a glint of pleasure over my entanglement of things in this tiny space. He brought his accordion and sat down next to me, his body up against mine. A few awkward moments— possibly for us both—passed. Magnampy Soa said nothing to me, and I ventured only "Misaotra" (Thank you). He took a small bottle of clear liquid, poured some into a glass, and then, while speaking heatedly and rapidly, apparently to no one in particular, he poured the fluid (rum) on the ground in the corner of our recording studio. He was giving a *tsodrano,* a verbalized benediction and offering to his *razana,* his ancestral spirits. So musical performance even in this apparently secular setting was still connected in some way to sacred ancestral spirits. Magnampy Soa continued his rapid recitation for several minutes, then poured himself a drink of rum, and then one for me. Everyone—including his wife, his numerous children, and several neighbors who had come for the session—laughed and applauded when I drank (the rum was extremely strong—I'm certain I winced). I believe I had just honored Antandroy ancestral spirits. Magnampy Soa still had not spoken to me—of course, we had no language in common. He simply pointed to the tape recorder and made a circular motion with his hand. The wind and rain became still as he drew the first sounds from his accordion.

Again Magnampy Soa played with incredible intensity, speed, dexterity, and variation. Sometimes he would coax soft tones from the instrument, pushing and pulling the bellows slowly and delicately; then he would shift into a forceful playing, overworking the bellows in a maniacal fervor. Sometimes he twisted the bellows on his push in and draw out of the accordion, creating a slapping percussion that seemed to intensify certain rhythmic pulses. He whistled and hissed sporadically though excitedly as he played, cigarette dangling from the corner of his mouth, all in sync with his accordion playing. His powerful body would bounce, jerk, throb, and slap the pavement, also in time with the accordion. I felt these motions as his body remained in contact with and even pounded against mine in this small space. He would occasionally yell something over his shoulder to the women present. At moments of particularly heightened musical intensity, the women present would fervently begin to clap several different rhythms simultaneously, or to yell out excited, lyrical verbal phrases.

Sometimes Magnampy Soa was smiling while he played, either looking directly into my eyes or with his eyes closed. At other times his face would reshape into an expression of painful heaviness or longing. Magnampy Soa was clearly absorbing into his own body the sounds he produced, yet he reciprocally seemed to be giving up his body to some musical/spiritual experience that was beyond my grasp. He was there with me in this moment, yet not there as well, carried in part by sound toward some recollection, imagination, communion with his ancestral spirits. Magnampy Soa played without pause through both sides of a ninety-minute cassette tape, and with the click of the end of side two, he abruptly brought his performance to a close. Again we were faced with an incommunicative awkwardness. All I could say was "Tsara be izany!" (That was great!) By this time it was only drizzling slightly. Magnampy Soa got up and went about his business with his fruit stand.

I wasn't certain how to compensate Magnampy Soa for this session. Another impasse—most people I knew in Madagascar were in constant need of material essentials. Yet play-for-pay sessions might only mean contrived performance settings. I was apprehensive that such sessions would likely impede the establishment of more personal relationships with Malagasy people—I didn't want to become known as some culture broker who would simply pay to obtain a good video or audio recording. My work also depended upon experiencing things as best I could as they usually occur in Madagascar (my own presence at most ceremonial events of course was quite unusual or unnatural). In Antananarivo stories were told in particular about Japanese film crews who had gravely taken advantage of Malagasy generosity. I was fond of Malagasy people and felt a loyalty and perhaps even a protectiveness toward them and their practices. So how to help out yet not commodify in the process? (Or was this even possible? Perhaps there really was no way to equitably do what I had come to Tamatave to do.)

I went into the store Magnampy Soa was paid to guard and I bought him a pack of cigarettes and a half-litre of rum. Along with these I gave him a constrained sum of Malagasy francs. I felt extremely close-fisted. That evening I made him a copy of the tape we had made together. When I brought it to him the next day he seemed surprised by the gift, and said, "Tsisy vola" (There's no money). He must have thought that I wanted him to pay for the tape. Magnampy Soa was unaccustomed to being given things by *vazaha*. Indeed, I later learned that he rarely if ever had any contact at all with them. There was another story I occasionally heard among

Merina or Betsimisaraka, a recollection of the practices of earlier Protestant missionaries in Madagascar, who offered gifts to Malagasy as an enticement to convert.

I thereafter regularly visited Magnampy Soa and his family, each time bringing food items—kilos of rice and meat, sometimes fish, beans, or cheese—or medications if anyone was ill. I refrained from giving cash on each visit or later for the *tromba* ceremonies I would attend with Magnampy Soa (except for the customary offering of perhaps rum and some coins to the ancestral spirits). He seemed content with this arrangement. He never asked me for money, nor for much else. In fact, once it was clear to him that I would be a long-term resident in Tamatave, that I truly liked him and his family, that I would continually be coming back just to visit, to eat rice on the ground with him, to play music with him, Magnampy Soa even told me not to bring food each time, that it was Antandroy custom to feed a guest, not the other way around. He only asked that someday when I would no longer need it, I give him my bicycle.

I was establishing strong connections with other Antandroy in Tamatave as well. I spent long hours playing *valiha,* another Malagasy stringed instrument, with Velontsoa, a brilliant and imaginative musician. Velontsoa's determination in building his instruments, in showing me how to play them, in performing many straight hours in cramped *tromba* houses, was unflagging. His wife, Mendoe, would sit through the night at a small stand near Magnampy Soa's encampment selling peanuts and cigarettes to *pousse-pousse* (a rickshaw-like vehicle) drivers, prostitutes, and drunken military men. Her young children often fell asleep in my lap as I sat with her chatting throughout the night. In the daytime, with one of her children on each shoulder, we would go gleefully to the market, or I might take the children to the beach so that Mendoe could have a rare moment for herself.

I spent the most time with Vinelo, an Antandroy man about my age. Vinelo and I would take long walks through Tamatave, joking and laughing heartily, stopping to drink some *divay* (wine, from the French *du vin),* and returning to his encampment to play music together and sit all night under the huge Tamatave sky talking as though we were two childhood friends. Vinelo was intent on having me experience with him as much as possible of Antandroy life. He was known to be one of the most powerful younger Antandroy healers in Tamatave, and he would have me sit beside him through numerous ancestral ceremonies. To heal, Vinelo would become possessed by varied royal Malagasy ancestral spirits. It was highly emotional to sit next to my friend as he transformed, often painfully, into revered royal Malagasy personalities from the distant past. Vinelo wouldn't remember the moments during which he was possessed by spirits, so he would always want me to recount for him, and to tell especially what had happened between the spirits and myself. Generally these Antandroy spirits as well were quite kind and welcoming to me.

Underlying the myth of the Antandroy savage in Madagascar is an acknowledgment among most Malagasy of the exceptional spiritual prowess of Antandroy. Numerous times I was approached by members of other Malagasy groups, who asked to be taken to an Antandroy healer for some sort of assistance, even though there might have been an abundance of healers within their own groups or communities. While most Malagasy believe in one way or another in the *razana,* the collective of ancestral spirits, it seems that too much spirit power in the wrong hands is often feared to be a bad thing, even a manifestation of evil. This sentiment among Merina in particular, many of whom are Protestant, likely reflects a Christian-inspired disdain for any spirit(s) other than the One. Indeed, if Merina were not the ones telling tales of Antandroy terror, it was usually other Christian Malagasy. Among Betsimisaraka in Tamatave, Catholicism tends to be more prevalent than Protestantism; *tromba* spirit possession, however, is also widely practiced among non-Christian Betsimisaraka.

Merina can lead an existence *entre-deux.* They often practice Christianity while at the same time performing ancestral customs such as *famadihana,* in which the bones of ancestors are unearthed and honored as material mediums of departed loved ones. Whereas this *entre-deux* mode of experience can be a cause for anxiety among Merina, Antandroy can exist perhaps more effectively *entre-deux* in a different sense—between the world of the living and the world of the dead—without feeling the inherent obstacles to their beliefs and practices that Christian doctrine imposes. Antandroy bring into the present a past from which some Merina have in ways disconnected themselves—for instance, *tromba* spirit possession itself is often shunned by Merina, especially those more economically privileged. The past with which Antandroy connect so effectively is a past Merina must filter through ever-present reservation (to put it mildly) emanating in part from their experience as Protestants. Among Merina, then, Antandroy are often an ambivalent force. Antandroy evoke fear and apprehension. Yet as their compulsion to tell tales of savagery and terror makes evident, Merina are also fascinated with Antandroy.

And qualities of sound production also play into such an ambivalence. Merina and other Christian Malagasy commonly complain fervently that they find Antandroy music to be distasteful, that it is incomprehensible to them, even demonic. This last evaluation perhaps brings to mind more widespread tales of musical virtuosity so pronounced that it is feared to have been acquired only through making some pact with the devil. Indeed, I've described my own reaction of being even disturbed by the intensity of Magnampy Soa's playing in particular, although this reaction has always seemed primarily an invigorating experience for me, a "disturbance" of what seems humanly possible; yet perhaps voices from my own past impede an unfettered feelingfulness for this extra-human quality. Through their expertise in musical improvisation, in manipulating (what might be thought of as) a somewhat constraining diatonically tuned instrument, in composing and remembering such intricate music, Antandroy are able to create what others often hear as an excess of sound, which then signifies in part a dangerous excess of spirit connection and power.

Magnampy Soa's ancestral spirits would not take human form in *tromba* possession ceremonies unless they were coaxed and appeased with the proper mode of musical performance. It is primarily sound that allows spirit to become embodied. And once spirits do take human form in the present, it is musical performance that often directs their actions and feelings, to which these spirits cede much control. Likewise, the *magnéto*—in its ability to project, reproduce, and indeed symbolically nationalize local practices—itself signifies power among Antandroy, as it represents a heightened sound-dependent capacity not only to please ancestral spirits, but also to enter into contractual rapport with them so as to affect a variety of transformations in the present (healing is such a primary transformative process).

Displaying the *magnéto* or its image also involves incorporation—of a *foreign* mechanical device. Antandroy recognize that their *magnétos* are manufactured *ampitany,* which means unspecifically "out there," or outside of Madagascar. Here Other ways of producing and manipulating sound can be taken and absorbed into Antandroy ancestral practice, thus intensifying Antandroy spirit power. I later learned that processes of incorporation even play a vital role in a Malagasy performative aesthetic. Magnampy Soa told me that the very presence of my foreign recording equipment had been appreciated by his ancestral spirits. So he had not requested the recording session to somehow profit with or from the resulting cassette tape (indeed, he was surprised when I gave him a copy). Rather, Magnampy Soa was creating a powerful foreign and electronic aura becoming to his own revered ancestral spirits. Such incorporated presences inevitably heighten Antandroy (as well as other Malagasy) ceremonial efficacy.

Some Malagasy were clearly expressing a desire to have a say in constructing a particular ethnographic Self. Christian Merina and Betsimisaraka wanted to influence the path of my (or really their) ethnography, castigating Antandroy *as even more* Other, and placing themselves, in even another sense, somewhere *entre-deux.* In constructing this Antandroy Other in such a derisive light, Christian Malagasy were also trying to construct themselves as *not* Antandroy, as *not* "primitives." Karen Tranberg Hansen in this volume also describes an occasion in which an ethnographic "subject" himself attempts to determine the field of study, indeed to create the (other) Other. And I've often thought about how we construct ourselves, as authors, as authorities, as scholars, as musicians (rarely out of earshot of some mode of World Beat groove) in our own world of difference. Back in the United States, I've since felt another sort of musical disturbance (not at all invigorating) over sound bits and musical nuances so frequently borrowed from our own ampitany, an often faceless and voiceless "out there" in music's big business. "Home" has come as well with numerous other disturbing facets—for instance, its inescapable consumer excess and waste, these in the face of vivid recollections of starvation and environmental devastation which continue to haunt me. As Christian Malagasy had constructed some of their own "field" parameters for me, perhaps Malagasy people and Madagascar itself had also effectively reconstructed me, so well that I would no longer fit comfortably into an often painfully familiar scheme of things back home.

After nearly two years in Madagascar it was agonizing to prepare to leave. There were strong connections with many Malagasy people—our farewells were emotional, on both ends. Furthermore, I knew that soon I'd virtually never even see or talk with my neighbors, that my friends would be too busy to spend much time socializing, that children would be too well overprotected to ever walk and joke with a stranger. I'd barely even spoken English in the past two years.

Vinelo insisted on accompanying me at six in the morning to the *taxi-brousse* station and on carrying some of my numerous bags. After all the experiences we had together in Madagascar, after all Vinelo had given me, he had asked the day before if I would buy him a four-dollar pair of leather sandals he had his eye on in one of the *karana* shops. On the way to the *taxi-brousse* station, Vinelo said, choking back emotion, "Tsara be andeho hody" (It's good to get to go home). I think he was trying to ease an anxiety we both felt, that it would be a long time before we'd see each other again.

7

The Ecology of Globalization: The Wolf at the Global Door

Thomas Weaver

PROLOGUE

Walking to the university library on a windy day, I saw fast-food paper sacks, gum, and candy wrappers filling curb gutters and clinging to bushes. There were empty soft drink and beer cartons, drifting papers, and plastic bags under the stadium ramps. I knew it was the day after homecoming. Still, it reminded me of fieldwork in developing countries stumbling over unrepaired sidewalks and deep pot-holed roads. Will cities everywhere look like this? Will it be because of the 2008 world subprime mortgage crisis? I thought of the "wolf" in Yellowstone Park and at the global door:

> I'll huff and I'll puff until I blow your house down, he said.
> Grandma, what big ears you have! The better to hear you with, my child.
> Grandma, what a big nose you have! The better to smell you with, my child.
> Grandma, what big teeth you have! The better to eat you with, my child, he said.

INTRODUCTION

The stimulus for this essay came from readings on the wolf (McNamee 1997; Mech 1981; Robbins 2005; Smith and Ferguson 2005).[1] The derived hypothesis is that the ecology of the wolf might inform our understanding of the connections, and inter-causalities among elements in the mortgage crisis, and those found in globalization. Models are useful representations of one system that may help us understand another by providing analogy, stimuli, and hypotheses.[2] Before discussing the wolf ecology model, however, I need to introduce some ecology constructs that I shall be relying on.

Ecology is the study of the interrelationship among organisms within the given environment of a natural ecosystem such as the Yellowstone National Park. The most useful ecological concepts for my analysis are the balance of nature and related concepts of resilience, adaptability, adaptation, ecosystem, ecological niche, and deep ecology. Others include evolution, the eradication or displacement of a species, and superorganism. The last named is addressed where appropriate. The balance of nature comes from the Darwinian notion of nature as a web of interdependence among all forms of life resulting in a tendency toward relative stabilization in the environment. Stability arises from ecological processes occurring "naturally" among interacting species (Pimm 1991). "Nature" has an intrinsic value in that species co-exist in consonance with each other and with the natural resources available in that ecosystem.

Balance of nature, with the concepts resilience, adaptability, and adaptation, provide the most important principles for this essay—the inter-connectivity and inter-causativeness among units. Charting connections among units builds on the concept of "deep" ecology, which suggests articulation, interdependence, and inter-causation among units that at first appear disconnected and independent. The distinction between "deep" ecology and "shallow" ecology suggests connectedness rather than isolation. It advocates a system of ethics and responsibility not the anthropocentric view of "shallow" ecology which maintains a human right to use and dominate nature (Capra 1995). Other ecological principles include energy flow and the cycling of matter. "Sunlight energy is transferred in decreasing amounts to growing things. Only plants can capture it and turn it to food that other organisms must obtain in order to survive. In natural systems, we know there is a limited amount of oxygen, water, carbon, nitrogen, etc., and as organisms use them, they must be returned to the air, water, and soil over and over again" (Mayer 2009, e-mail communication).

A further word about the balance of nature concept: it seems that after change in any system a return to a prior "balance" is expected. Unchallenged, this implies the functional premise that ultimately a state of equilibrium—more appropriately, "stasis"—either can be, or ought to be, achieved, whereas to a function theorist the phrase denotes the directional dynamic of energy in whatever system is at issue. In ecology, our concern is that it is more appropriate to perceive balance and imbalance as constant processes, each engaging the other. There is never equilibrium or a balance in anything. Certainly there is no equilibrium in global climate and may never have been. Fluctuations and catastrophes exist; examples include volcanic eruptions, falling meteorites, floods, and hurricanes that force new adaptation. And this is proved by geologic and climatic records.

Resilience, on the other hand, is the capacity of a system to absorb disturbance and undergo change while retaining identity. Adaptability is "the capacity of actors in a system to manage resilience, either by moving the system toward or away from a threshold that would fundamentally alter the properties of the system, or by altering the underlying features of the stability landscape" (http://www.resilience.org). Adaptability is different from adaptation, which is an evolutionary change in a system or a population.[3] For example, one prominent adaptation is for small bodied species to produce more offspring per year giving them a better chance to survive (Pimm 1991:44ff). Adaptation and adaptability occur whether the system is in or out of balance. A biological anthropologist clarifies the distinction between adaptability and adaptation as follows:

> Adaptability is the capacity of individuals in populations to adjust to or accommodate to the environment. For example, when people migrate to high altitudes, their breathing adjusts and other physiological changes occur. I think that is what your definition of adaptability implies. Small body size as an adaptation by some species is a population phenomenon and the result of natural selection. To me, the distinction should be between individuals in populations adjusting or "adapting," which is adaptability, and adaptation, which is a population concept, as in populations undergo natural selection and populations adapt. The word adaptation is used more loosely in the social and behavioral sciences, but if you are going to be dealing with ecologic principles, perhaps the distinction I make is more appropriate. (John Meaney, e-mail to author, March 23, 2009)

Ecosystems are larger than, but similar to, ecological niches in that they comprise a biotic or biological community and all physical processes, such as weather, soil, nutrients, energy flow, and disasters such as tornados, floods, volcanic action, etc. Within the natural ecosystem or ecological niche, each species adapts to the needs and demands of other species without threatening their existence. This will prove not to be the case when we apply these two concepts to the global system or parts of it. Ecologists often use the two concepts interchangeably, but I find it more useful for our purposes to make a distinction with the ecological niche referring to a smaller or specialized part of ecosystem (Gunderson, Holling, and Light 1995).

THE ECOLOGY OF THE WOLF IN YELLOWSTONE

With these constructs in hand, we can turn our attention to the ecology of the wolf in Yellowstone. Yellowstone National Park covers over 2 million acres mostly in Wyoming and parts of Montana and Idaho of mostly high, forested, volcanic plateaus with an average elevation of 8,000 feet. The Park includes all organisms—animals, plants, and humans that occupy that environment. Humans are part of a natural ecosystem because we pass laws and regulations, kill or restore wolves, create hunting seasons, and intervene as tourists. The ecosystem in Yellowstone Park is delimited by a certain altitude, mountain ranges, open plains, and a river that runs through it. It constitutes a natural environment unlimited by political boundaries such as parks, national forests, nations, states, and towns. This means, in effect, that some species in the Yellowstone ecosystem, such as the wolf and buffalo, may range up to 600 miles outside of the Park, much to the consternation of neighboring ranchers, farmers, and townspeople. It is for this reason that ecologists on the ground developed the concept of a Greater Yellowstone Ecosystem, which extends into surrounding states and reservations. A focus on the role of the wolf or buffalo represents an ecological niche.

By the 1920s, wolves in Yellowstone were exterminated, creating an *imbalance* in the ecosystem which allowed the elk to become dominant. *Balance* was restored, however, when the wolf was reintroduced in 1995 and 1996. In the next 10 years, the number of wolves increased to 130 animals, dispersed in 13 packs. The wolf in Yellowstone is protected as an endangered species and, until recently, also in surrounding states. The wolf is a key species or "apex predator," whose arrival actuated ripples throughout the natural ecosystem. Of these, the major impact was on the habitat of the once dominant elk. This resulted not because the elk is a primary food source nor the wolf its primary predator, but because of conditions accompanying the wolf's return. A survey by the United States Geological Survey and the University of Minnesota discovered that 53 percent of elk killed were killed by grizzly bears, 11 percent by coyotes, and only 13 percent by wolves, and with drought playing a large part in their survival (Smith and Ferguson 2005). The number of elk declined from 19,000 to 11,000, and the herds moved from that habitat to open spaces on higher ground.

Elk in Yellowstone, also a key species, once fed on vegetation on river banks. The river environment rejuvenated after the introduction of the wolf and the movement of the elk to higher, open ground. With this change, willows, cottonwoods, and aspen trees on the river banks gained new life; their increased shade encouraged trout in the river to grow bigger in size and number; songbirds, such as the yellow warbler and Lincoln sparrow, returned to the river banks; Magpie ravens and other scavengers multiplied because more carcasses were left by predators; the availability of more twigs and branches encouraged beavers, with only one dam in 1996, to construct nine more in the next decade. The primary food source for coyotes of voles, mice, and other rodents doubled. In turn, red foxes and raptors enhanced their numbers.

Here is a word more about the "imbalance" of nature referred to above. Viewed broadly, imbalance occurs when an ecosystem is destabilized by one or more intervening variables. Drought, climate change, and flooding are natural causes, whereas species-dominance may be impacted by removal, or infections, such as parvovirus and brucellosis. In addition to these "naturals," a host of human interventions are possible. These include hunting, introducing foreign plants or animal species, creating laws to establish parks and hunting seasons and to protect species, all of which contribute to imbalance in an ecosystem. Dominance of the elk fashioned an imbalance in the Park, especially in the river environment. The elk and its co-species of animals and plants adapted to the absence of the wolf and began a new cycle of adaptation with its reintroduction. The return of the wolf caused the elk to move to higher, open, safer ground and restored the new river ecology, allowing other species to return to their rejuvenated habitat and a new balance.

It is important to note that, even as apex predator, the wolf does not live in a safe, always balanced haven. In the year 2005, for example, the Yellowstone wolf population decreased because of parvovirus introduced by domestic dogs, others were killed by automobiles, and still others by fighting with other wolves. In the same year, we saw the largest number of births since the reintroduction of the wolf, but 22 of the 69 pups died from parvovirus (The Associated Press 2006; Robbins 2005).

Though our focus has been on the wolf, a few words are in order about the buffalo which has long shared Yellowstone Park, and which, like the wolf, has felt the sting of park outsiders who must deal with its presence. Cattle ranchers, for example, have long, and constantly, expressed fear that buffalo wandering from the Park will infect their cows with brucellosis, a disease that causes cows to abort. That this climate of fear worked was attested by the bison herd's decline in the early 1900s to 30 head. This decline, however, set in motion several decades of restoration effort, and the numbers climbed to nearly 5,000. This increase caused Montana in the 1980s to allow hunters to shoot buffalo that strayed outside the park, and in 2006 to legalize hunting. Sixty-two hundred hunters applied via lottery and 50 licenses were awarded. A hunter observed, "[It was] … just another park-like hunt. … Buffalo often gather around a fallen animal … [that resembles] mourning. Several hunters … saw bison walking over to the bloody bodies and prodding them, as if trying to revive the animals, before hunters shooed them off." In a sidebar, the New York Times, intruding as part of the natural ecosystem, supplied a guide for the modern Buffalo Bill with subtitles: getting a license, outfitters and operators, how to get there, where to stay, and more information (Kurlantzik 2006).

Since the Yellowstone Park buffalo are truly not wild, and spend most of the year within park boundaries interacting closely with tourists, some people object to the hunt as an "unfair slaughter." As one conservationist pointed out, it is incongruous of the state to want the buffalo "to walk outside Yellowstone for three months and to be fair chase [the term used for unmanaged hunting], then walk into Yellowstone and be docile for the tourists." The wolf and buffalo in Yellowstone National Park represent managed ecology that exists mostly for tourism. Every year hundreds of thousands of people from all over the world stay in park lodges to see life in the "wild," an irony since introduction of the buffalo and wolf was made to perpetuate species in danger of extinction (Kurlantzik 2006).

It is worth noting that the wolf and the buffalo have both been extensively symbolized in myth. Early Romans claimed that a female wolf fed and reared the twin founders of Rome. Later in medieval times, the wolf represented a predator of people as well as livestock; and in modern times, it is analogized as a predator in business and in love, as a rogue hiding in sheep's clothing, is slang for woman chaser, and as a dissonant chord in music. Then there are teenagers traveling together like wolves in a pack. The buffalo, on the other hand, is generally perceived as a positive part of Western lore, and, as conveyed by its presence, with Cheyenne Chief Wolf Robe, on the Buffalo Indian Head nickel, symbolically non-separable from the indigenous peoples who populated our Great Plains. It is important to note that a wolf is just a wolf living in a natural ecosystem and was actually eliminated in Yellowstone before 1920 by humans who continue to prey.

Before assessing the ecology of the subprime mortgage crisis, we must explain its origins. Antecedents to the subprime mortgage crisis had been prepared in the 1960s by the creation of an economic super-bubble that began with Senator Goldwater's run for the presidency. The subsequent Reagan administration began what came to be called neo-conservatism involving free market principles that powered the national economic ecosystem through the presidency of the second George Bush.[3] Borrowing, spending, and allowing corporations to self-regulate were the guidelines of this philosophy. Even the crisis caused by savings and loan business in the 1980s did not alert us to the problem with the neo-conservative driven financial system. Good regulatory laws and enforced regulations would have prevented much of the wild investment that brought the economic ecosystem down in 2008 with bursting of the super-bubble.

The economic boom in the United States began when corporations divided production and service sectors into exportable units in a process called deindustrialization. They did this to take advantage of "right to work" states with low wages and benefits, and with relocation inducements such as tax incentives. Less costly construction of plants at new sites made better sense than costly maintenance of older buildings and machines. Manufacturing units in the Northeastern United States relocated to the Southern and Southwestern states resulting in the loss of jobs and unionism. A continuation of this principle was the outsourcing of manufacturing or information units from the United States to Southeast Asia, Mexico, and Central America. Mexico offered savings in transportation and labor, and poor government enforcement of labor and environmental laws (Weaver 1988, 2001; Weaver et al. 2008). In time, workers demand better pay, benefits, and working conditions, and organize unions. This leads owners to move plants to places with more favorable working conditions or to import labor from developing countries. These transitions also generated population movement to new job sites. The latter process I refer to as in-sourcing, which describes better than "undocumented workers or illegal aliens" what happens when nations depend on the importation of labor.

THE SUBPRIME MORTGAGE CRISIS

We turn now to explore how ecological concepts and principles useful in Yellowstone Park will assist in understanding the subprime mortgage crisis and globalization. Whereas the wolf and other organisms are units that operate within the Yellowstone natural ecosystem, the Crisis, at first operated within a national economic ecosystem, then spread to a global economic ecosystem. When viewed as ecosystems, these larger units share common concepts such as "the balance of nature," defined as a web of interdependence, interaction, and inter-causation among all forms of life. Other ecological principles such as energy flow and the cycling of matter assist in the same manner. Plants capture energy from sunlight that turns into food for the survival of other organisms found in the natural ecosystem. A limited amount of oxygen, water, carbon, nitrogen, etc., used by organisms in the natural system get recycled repeatedly to enrich air, water, and soil. Energy flow and cycling of matter in the economic ecosystem is the recycling of money, the restructuring of corporations, innovations, new technology, and dealing with business cycles.

The energy-recycling involves elements in the national economic ecosystem, such as corporations, banks, brokers, federal agencies, politicians, and risk management firms. Important agency organizations on the domestic side include the Federal Deposit Insurance Corporation (FDIC), the United States Securities and Exchange Commission (SEC), and Congressional banking and regulatory commissions, committees, subcommittees, and Congressional staffs, as well as the judicial and executive branches. As business expands to a global ecosystem, it involves similar entities, and adds governments, overseas corporations and branches, aid agencies in most nations, the World Bank, the International Monetary Fund (IMF), and the Group of Eight (G-8), to mention only the most obvious. Recognizing the fluidity of the economic-political situation, our point here and throughout the essay is not to cling too literally to ecological concepts but to use them to identify connections and inter-causation among units that change the ecosystem environment and the behavior of other units. These energy recycling processes led to the creation of instruments that led to the subprime mortgage crisis.

The Housing Boom. The subprime mortgage crisis had its origin in a housing boom fed by the overselling of subprime mortgages. The finance industry could make more money by selling mortgage paper at initial low interest rates. These low interest rates enticed buyers with poor or no credit records and were assisted by dishonest lenders. A common feature of many of these loans is a time-based, interest-escalating provision. Home prices increased between 2001 and 2005 and lenders, believing that this would continue, made more and more loans. Borrowers anticipated that rising equity would enable them to refinance to make higher home payments, purchase cars, furniture, remodeling, and more expensive houses. Interest rates escalated, catching unprepared or unwary borrowers. Warnings came between 2004 and 2006 from some bank employees and a few federal agency officials of the danger of the prime interest lending program and the ailing banking system. However, there was neither voluntary action by corporations nor oversight action by government agencies.

As the housing bubble heated up, banks heavily vested in subprime loans were unaware or did not care about the increased heat. In a process called securitization, they had been pooling good and bad loans into financial units called derivatives or credit-default swaps that were contracts that insured debt holders against default. These financial instruments, intended to reduce risk by spreading it among investors, seemed to be working. For example, in early 2007, with the housing-bubble implosion still on the horizon, $800 billion of the bond market was backed by subprime loans. Private ratings agencies, such as Moody's, Fitch, and Standard and Poor's, cooperated by awarding favorable investment grade ratings, in return receiving fees allowing them to share in the profit that seemed to be never-ending. The mortgage contracts were vulnerable because they existed outside of regulatory laws and lacked transparency, making it difficult to trace their content. The packages sold fast and in large quantities to investors worldwide. Collateralized Debt Organizations (CDO) holders were now obligated to pay once the original mortgage holders defaulted. The Subprime Mortgage industry began to collapse when owners of the securitizations found themselves without sufficient collateral to meet obligations and as long as subprime mortgages were hidden under the housing bubble (Lewis 2009; Norris 2009; Zandi 2009).

What we have just described in the global ecosystem is analogous to the introduction of foreign species into natural ecosystems that had unanticipated consequences. For example, the introduction of a normative buffelgrass intended as cattle fodder and to control erosion along highways turned into a menace in the United States. It grows fast excluding native species and its dry plumes and leaves present a fire hazard. Can we say that the subprime mortgage program and derivatives became hazardous to the economy, or toxic, as they came to be called? The collateralized derivative packages became toxic loans when banks and insurance companies could not cover losses. Lenders, through aggressive mortgage salespeople, took advantage of borrowers who in the long run could not comply with escalating payment schedules. The impact of derivatives on globalization is like the effect of parvovirus on wolf puppies, and buffalo brucellosis that causes cows to abort.

Earlier we spoke of the imbalance of nature. The sale of derivatives established a huge imbalance in the nature of business locally, nationally, and globally. The use of derivatives had a cascading effect that coursed through the economy. I should point out that derivatives and the packaging of investment instruments have existed for a long time. Finance companies, for example, packaged small mortgage and other financing into packages to sell to larger corporations as early as the 1950s. However, it is the nature of contemporary derivatives—their stealth, secretiveness, power, and savageness—that we have come to consider instruments used by predators. Predators are busy even now taking advantage of people trying to refinance mortgages or file for bankruptcy. Perpetrators of fraud and corruption are not confined to what we read about Third World countries or faraway places. They are our neighbors.

By mid-year 2007, there were indications of the impending subprime mortgage crisis. The $800 billion bond market backed by subprime loans dropped by 40 percent, and the largest investors in CDOs, such as Bear-Stearns, were looking for a strategy for survival. Paul Krugman (2007: A-24) wrote in an op-ed piece for the New York Times:

> Seriously, it's starting to look as if CDOs were to this decade's housing bubble what Enron-style accounting was to the stock bubble of the 1990s. Both made investors think they were getting a much better deal than they really were. And the new scandal raises two obvious questions: why were the bond-rating agencies taken in (again), and where were the regulators?

The answer came with the failure in mid-2008 of Lehman Brothers, a global bank heavily vested in securitizing commercial property loans and selling CDOs aggressively to willing buyers. The United States government refused to provide funds to prevent bankruptcy, and realizing its mistake, it made available billions of dollars to rescue Bear-Stearns, Fannie Mae, Freddie Mac, and AIG, the largest insurance carrier in the world and a major player in credit default swaps.

Before the end of the Bush administration in 2008, a rescue plan was installed based on knowledge of prior recessions and the Great Depression of 1929. The depression of 1929 was driven by President Roosevelt's New Deal policies known as Keynesian economics (Cohen 2008). According to the British economist Maynard Keynes, the solution to economic downturns like the 1929 event and the one caused by the subprime mortgage crisis is for governments to inject capital to start credit flowing and buttress financial markets. Hopefully, implementation of Keynesian economics would stimulate consumer spending, important because it represents about 70 percent of GDP. Central banks also became involved trying to keep the economy on an even keel by cutting prime interest rates to almost zero percent. This is the rate of interest charged on loans that banks pay for funds from other banks (Blinder 1998; Holmes 2009). However, government bailout funds did not lead to an immediate solution; instead, financial institutions receiving funds, tightened lending standards, cut back on credit and loans, and this, in turn, placed debilitating pressure on all aspects of the economy (Krugman 2009).

The Crisis, because of its inter-connection and inter-causal nature, had a cascading effect on the whole economy. This state of affairs reduced GDP and lowered tax revenues, resulting in cutbacks in public works and to local and state services for the poor and unemployed. Reduced wages and benefits and high unemployment resulted in defaults on automobile loans, credit card debt, student loans, and curtailed spending. Without credit and strong financial markets, banks lack sufficient capital to extend loans for short-term operating expenses, retail stores close, asset values fall, and larger businesses begin to fail. By mid-2008, the number of failed banks was at 117 and climbing. Other businesses, such as autos and airlines were stressed. The automobile industry had become noncompetitive with the Japanese and Korean small automobiles with better mileage. Much earlier, there were ballooning oil prices, poor oil reserves, and insufficient gasoline processing plants in the United States. This put a stricture on travel and the transportation industry. Dealers closed businesses as sales plummeted. Auto makers began to look for rescue funds in late 2008. Airlines eliminated routes, stepped up lay-offs, and charged extra for luggage, snacks, and other services. Manufacturing and exporting dropped drastically; adding to the downturn is the simultaneous drop in availability of building materials such as wood, metals, and copper.

On September 15, 2008 the market tumbled below 11,000 for the first time since 2001, and by March 2009 it continued to fall to below 7,000 on the Dow. The FDIC, which guarantees deposits up to 100,000 dollars, increased its maximum payout to $250,000. This was an attempt to calm depositors, many of whom were withdrawing savings, and cashing stocks and bonds. But none of this seemed to help, and by the time the United States elections were held in November, the economy dominated all discussion, and for good reason. The country was on its way to a recession very likely to morph into a depression. Also in the fall of 2008, the IMF reported that the global economy had faded by 5 percent, Japan's economy by 2.4 percent, and Germany's by 2 percent. And by late August, because of reduced spending, our imports were declining. As this happened, China, India, Japan, and other Southeast Asian countries, all major exporters, reported a drop in their economies, and this weakened our sale of farming and construction equipment. Our stock market declined more than during the depression of 1929. Unemployment reached the level of the 1974 recession and continued to increase to over 9 percent in 2009. By the end of 2008, the world was in a major crisis.

GLOBALIZATION

Earlier, we provided a working definition of globalization, or more to the point, the global economic ecosystem. Globalization is a connected world through economic, informational, organizational, and political forces. Globalization made the world seem smaller with the Internet and cell phones connecting to the most remote villages in developing countries, and gave a voice to those without a voice in matters reserved to those in established institutions. Before the Crisis, United States hegemony was moderated by louder political voices from other nations and as a result of growing economies of such nations as India and China. For example, China increased manufacturing and exports to the United States, accumulated currency reserves, and amassed excess capital with which they purchased treasury bonds. United States sale of bonds to other governments accrued more external debt, making it the world's top debtor with a budget deficit equal to more than 6 percent of GDP (Romero and Barrionuevo 2009; Soros 2008a; Talev 2009; Zandi 2009). For the world as a whole, the unintended consequences of globalization have been environmental degradation, inequality, and poverty among the working, lower, and middle classes.

The task at hand now is to illuminate the global economic ecosystem through the use of ecological concepts examined in the wolf and subprime sections. These concepts and principles allow us to take a different perspective on the global economy, especially when we view globalization through the ecological lenses of inter-causality and inter-connectivity. For example, if we examine social, political, cultural, economic, or material issues in a global context, we find that the issue-areas most likely to arise include media, transportation, environment, poverty, racism, justice, labor, migration, class, and wealth distribution.

The concept of balance of nature, used in assessment of the wolf ecosystem, can enlighten the global economic ecosystem. Earlier in the context of the wolf, we spoke that some change there seemed to be an expectation of return to a prior "balance." Yet, natural and social systems move in and out of balance constantly.

Some elements in the "balance of business" are connected and inter-causative within that ecosystem. For example, to use the market as a case in point—when the economy is doing well, interest increases and the price of Treasury bonds decreases. When the economy is not doing well, the opposite occurs: interest rates decrease and bond market prices increase. Stocks reflect the same trend. As corporate profit rises and the company's stock rise, and when corporate profits decline, stock prices decline. Corporations also reflect inter-connective trends. For example, changes up or down in market activity and profit or loss in a large corporation can impact the stock market as a whole. A case in point is when Goldman Sachs, longtime leader among banks, demonstrated a remarkable comeback in 2009 that impacted the market as a whole. Gross National Product (GNP) is the most important economic indicator with its components of consumer consumption, investment, government, and exports minus imports (Baumohl 2008; Carnes and Slifer 1991). From another perspective, balance in business requires sufficient capital, risk assessment and management, investors, profit, collateral, supplies, cheap resources, plants, offices, buildings (physical infrastructure), appropriate and sympathetic laws and regulations, lobbyists and connections with useful politicians, a certain level of unemployment to maintain an adequate labor force, little or no inflation, no deflation, and so on. These are necessary interdependent and inter-causative variables for business to succeed. Like the wolf in Yellowstone, these variables must balance, that is, exist in a state of interdependence and activity necessary to promote profit or survival.

Imbalance in capitalism is caused by climate change, drought, and flooding. Drought impacts manufacturing and sales of farming equipment, and related businesses such as feed stores. Periods of drought in farmlands reduce food stores and have a cascading impact on local business and community. Periodic change is caused by business cycles, availability of financing and sales, and the presence of corruption, fraud, and illegal activity such as the drug trade. Natural catastrophes or events such as hurricane Katrina and Southeast Asia tsunamis affect capitalism. Imbalance is also present as world manufacturing increases or decreases and is reflected in increases or decreases in environmental degradation, unequal distribution of wealth, and world poverty (Sklair 2001; Stiglitz 2006; Wolfe 1963, 1977[4]).

Business imbalance and balance are related to the concept of resilience and may apply to multinational corporations that survive in bad times or to populations in developing countries that suffer from poverty, disease, and the diseases of underdevelopment and find a means of survival (Orzech and Nichter 2008:267–282). Resilience is reflected in the adaptability of small family businesses both on the domestic and global fronts. There are over seven million businesses in the United States of which 20 percent with 100 or fewer employees are operated as small family businesses (Birnbaum 2009). Family businesses have existed longer and experienced ups and downs in the economy and adapt better with a network of relatives than large corporations. Family members will more readily defer compensation and lengthen working hours. The poor find alternate means for survival such as participation in the informal economy or illegal activities. Persons in this situation prove the importance of the unity of the domestic unit that places every member including children to work. Undocumented workers in the United States establish informal businesses in landscaping, construction, and house cleaning with family members (Weaver 2001; Weaver and Downing 1971). These observations apply equally to the global economic ecosystem.

Ecological niche and ecosystem are suggestive concepts for understanding globalization. Ecologists often use the two concepts interchangeably as I do in this essay. It may be useful for our purposes to make a distinction with the ecological niche as being smaller than ecosystem. Ecologists in Yellowstone point out that difference by referring to the Greater Yellowstone Ecosystem. Niche activities in domestic and global business, as in the natural world, include specialized activities such as market products, a division selling derivatives, or a delimited business such as manufacturing, financing, banking, and selling of automobiles. The sale of packaged derivatives to multinational investors is an example of expanding the trading niche to the global economic ecosystem. A business that ranges outside its place of origin becomes part of a global economic ecosystem and involves connectivity of entities involved in business transactions however small or wherever located.

Inter-connection and inter-causality are demonstrated in economic events on a global scale such as the cascading or domino effect during decline and growth. Three examples show the domino effect. Failure in the technology industry in the 1980s instigated a down-cycle in the United States economy, with effects felt in Germany, France, Britain and Central and South America. Similarly the failure of the Thai banking system in late 1997 was caused by overvaluation of its currency that increased its ability to borrow. The Thai economy at the time was one of the dynamic growth centers of the world. The Thai currency fell sharply against the dollar, causing investors to withdraw support for a failing economy. The drop in the value of Thai currency affected the price of oil, gold, copper, and aluminum—commodities being consumed by growing neighboring economies. The result was the collapse of an entire regional economic system and expanding to an unbalanced Russian economy that was over-dependent on oil exports for revenue. The impact was felt globally to a lesser extent (Krugman 1999).

The concepts of balance and imbalance are appropriate in considering the international migration of workers. Migration exemplifies inter-connectivity and inter-causality of workers and economies in the United States, Europe, and Southeast Asia, to mention the most obvious examples. In the United States, it highlights a continuous regional economic ecosystem that joins Mexico and the United States (Weaver 2001, 1983). Migrants in the United States led to problems in labor relations by lowering wages and benefits for American workers in similar occupations. The arrival of migrants at any time causes an imbalance in the status quo. In time, a balance is achieved as migrants become integrated or semi-integrated into the American way. The commoditization of labor in Southeast Asia and Europe created problems similar to those in the United States such as pressure on public services in health, welfare, prisons, education, legal, and police. In Europe as in the United States, it led to repressive attitudes and legislation; they restricted the religious expressions of migrants. Prejudice and racism led to calls for "English Only (or German or French only)" laws and restricted access to services by non-citizens.

The importance of the concept of evolution for ecology, conservation, and business is captured in the following observation:

First, all parts of an animal and all stages of its life cycle are affected by evolutionary change; second, some parts of a body [referring to a natural ecosystem] may change very rapidly over a short time, while others will stay unchanged—a form of mosaic evolution. (Drury 1998:113)

We can carry the analogy to business and globalization in terms of stages of institutional change and variation. Evidence for the transformation or evolution over time of a corporation is found in an extensive literature on organizational theory (Carroll 1988; Frost 1985; Hannan and Freeman 1990; Singh 1990). Earlier we commented on the resilience of small family businesses. Small firms may become larger corporations and eventually multinationals. Evolutionary change is also reflected in the development of investment instruments such as deindustrialization and outsourcing with origins in temp labor and the dismemberment and movement of manufacturing and service units to places with more profitable locations.

Superorganism is a concept that offers a different perspective on the global ecosystem. It refers to colonies of ants, bees, and termites with a division of labor that is based on biology and genetics. The superorganism is intermediate between an organism and a natural ecosystem. Its members differentiate according to required tasks to maintain life without overt direction or a command structure. Workers, reproducers, controllers of reproduction, garbage dump workers, hunters-gather[er]s, mushroom growers, soldiers, guards, morticians, enforcers, and pheromone communication—are all apparently controlled by biological force without question and with good results for the life of the unit (Flannery 2009; Holldobler and Wilson 2009). The concept is reminiscent of multinational corporations that appear to function as super-societies. Corporations appear to act in consonance without communication to accomplish goals that seem to be coordinated and clandestine. The reason may be lack of transparency or that they share common values, training, goals, and actions. We referred earlier to the spread of the wolf and buffalo out of the confines of the Yellowstone National Park to what ecologists call the Greater Yellowstone Ecozone. In this sense, capitalism's spread on a global scale into a greater economic ecosystem, or "ecozone" is similar to a natural superorganism. This concept bears exploration.

CONCLUSIONS

Several problems arose as I reflected on writing this essay, such as my use of ecology or the place of culture. Other problems are addressed under recommendations and future research where we describe opportunities for social scientists in the investigation of ecology as explanation. Inter-connections and inter-causality played a large factor in our analysis and the problem remains of measuring the relative influence of [them] among units in the natural and the economic ecosystems. Finally, there is the need to confront the importance of social balance in its relation to capitalism and the free market as enduring paradigms. First, we review the task set forth in this essay that began with examination of the ecology of the wolf.

The reintroduction of the wolf into Yellowstone National Park offered an example of the workings of ecology and inspired the idea that it could serve as a model for the study of globalization. It gave us an opportunity to evaluate whether using a natural-system-based ecology can assist in understanding a social-based economic system. The subprime mortgage crisis bestowed an opportunity to explore the application of ecology concepts and principles to the national and global scenes. It led to such questions as: what in the mortgage crisis is comparable to the ecology of the wolf, and which concepts and principles help understand globalization? Is it the wolf's place as key species with its ripple impact on other species and organisms, its stealth, power, or all of the above? The wolf, as a key species or predator, had a ripple effect on the life of other organisms demonstrated during its absence and again on its reintroduction. Perhaps the word "predator" is too strong for characterizing both the behavior of the wolf and of some business unit, although there is an element of predatory behavior in both instances. The wolf is a noble creature, and business is a noble endeavor. Still, some bankers, some stock brokers, some traders, some mortgage salespersons, and some media purveyors were "key species" or keys to change in the economic ecosystem.

It is clear that the media played a part in the current crisis by creating a climate of panic. The public hears summaries and abbreviated television reports, but behind the voice behind the curtain stand the voices of special business and political interests. Although journalists monopolize reports on the crisis, it is corporations, with the help of lobbyists, which select the media agenda to be read and heard by most people. The hand-in-hand action of corporations and politicians was evident throughout the Crisis and afterwards when searching for solutions. For example, as early as 2001, Senator Phil Gramm (Rep., Tex.) helped pass legislation supporting deregulation. And much later in 2009, politics again asserted its clout when Senator Thomas Dodd (Dem., Conn.) placed a last minute provision in a law that allowed AIG to hand out bonuses from the bailout funds granted by taxpayers. Those receiving bonuses were the very persons who created the Crisis. Eisenhower was correct about the danger of the military-industrial complex, and to this we must change it to the media-military-industrial complex (Barstow 2008; Walsh 2008). This complex cannot be defined as a culture or a subculture, but the units have much in common, but common values, connections, causative factors, and activities aimed at the same goal are not sufficient to make a culture.

Then, where is culture, the old standby of anthropology, the nebulous conglomeration that is much examined, of values, traditions, activities that distinguish one society or sub-society from another? The concept of culture should move from its micro-focus on community and ethnography to a macro-focus of corporation, region, nation state, and world. Institutional, agency, and corporate culture go beyond the narrow recognition of the concept of culture as originally used by anthropology in referring to exotic small scale society. Corporate culture, for example, is the distinguishing manner a particular corporation is structured, handles policy, activity, bonuses, hiring, socializing, compensation, and its leadership. Merrill Lynch, as a case in point, differs from Citigroup, AIG, and other corporations in many ways, although there is a commonality, even if CEOs, presidents, and other top officers differ in approach and philosophy. There are subcultures within the cultures as characterized in the uniqueness of trading units within corporations. The development of these cultures was described in the section on building the super-bubble. Thus, business cultures, acting with the assistance of politicians and poor regulations, used derivatives without monetary reserves to create the current world economic crisis. And from the looks of the situation in mid-2009, the same old game is back in play in terms of risky investments, lobbying against regulations, and granting bonuses for high ranking corporate leaders aided by government rescue funds; this is done even in the face of an uncertain economy.

RECOMMENDATIONS AND FUTURE RESEARCH

Here we suggest opportunities for social scientists in the investigation of various unaddressed issues such as ecology as explanation. Others include measuring the relative influence of inter-connections and inter-causality among units in the natural and the economic ecosystems. Finally, there is the need to confront the importance of inequity and social balance in the relationship of humans to capitalism and of the free market as an enduring economic paradigm.

An important issue not addressed in this essay is the use of ecology by social science and its potential for applied problems. Ecology was used as an explanatory framework in the 19th century by Darwinian evolutionism's misapplication to business as the "survival of the fittest." Later, it was adopted by urban sociologists, and even later in the 20th century by political scientists, urban ecologists, economists, and linguists (Shoaps 2009). Political ecology in anthropology developed out of these perspectives, but as with the other social sciences, it utilizes a limited range of ecological concepts and principles. This essay suggests expanding political ecology in anthropology by a more extensive use of ecological concepts. However, we must remember not to cling too literally to ecological concepts. Finally, how can ecology concepts help policy makers eradicate poverty and inequality, and to generate a better paradigm for capitalism? The plight of the wolf as an endangered species led to corrective legislation in the form of the endangered species act. This was a policy that made people aware of the balance of nature and how humans could take corrective action. Will we eventually establish the idea of "endangered humans" and act to "balance the imbalance" in the global human environment? The concepts and principles explored in this essay, hopefully, add clarity to our understanding of the impact of the global economy As we have time to ponder the meanings of ecology in this sense, we must suggest pertinent policy suggestions for solving social problems.

Another problem that arose is the measurement of inter-connection and inter-causation among units in economic and natural systems. But not all connections have the same value or impact on other units. How do we measure the power of these values? Clearly, an algorithm or mathematical formula must be devised to depict the strength of connections. This is necessary whether they concern the relative impact of the presence of the wolf on the elk and other organisms in Yellowstone, or the inter-connections within the domestic and global economic ecosystems. There was a strong impact from the wolf's presence and absence, but the question remains of which organisms were impacted more and which less. Are there organisms that can be ignored because of their minor affect, or must we measure the impact of the wolf down to the smallest bacterium? This task is one worth pondering. A related problem to inter-connection along the same lines of inquiry is the one of inter-causation. Which units have greater or lesser impact on which units? It would seem that the solution of one of these problems can assist us in resolving the second.

We addressed the concept of balance of nature in the cases of the wolf, the Crisis, and globalization. Can we now speak of a need for social balance between human and business activity? Capitalism generated an imbalance in society by generating inequities in wealth distribution. Those who control business institutions produce profit or suffer loss and encourage consumerism—actions that produce unlimited growth as opposed to a "steady state" that is ecologically and equitably balanced. Systems of justice and business speak reluctantly of social inequality. In board rooms and cocktail parties, the large gap is ignored that exists between the haves and the have-nots, between the developed and developing countries, and between indigenous people of the world and those in power everywhere. The disregard of social inequity translates into a negative consequence for the future of capitalism, the environment, and for life on earth. There is a feeling of entitlement among people of power. Living in a cocoon of luxury, plenty, and protected by cultural, economic, and political insularity, thought is rarely given to these matters. Many economists call them non-economic variables, but others, especially behavioral economists, include them as social and ecological resilience, and as investor psychology (Adger 2000; Akerlof and Shiller 2009).

The conundrum faced by capitalism today is how to best exploit natural resources, make a profit, and at the same time avoid long-term deleterious effects on the environment and people. As it stands now, society pays the social costs of environmental damage and the social problems and inequities of poor or endangered people. Lessons learned from the Crisis make clear that capitalism cannot operate on strict free market principles. Much literature suggests that it is time to re-examine the free market economy and to develop a new paradigm for capitalism (Melman 2001; also see Note 1). Certainly, the weight of the current world economic crisis mandates serious thought on the matter. Soros (2008b), for example, maintains that misunderstanding the current free market is what led to the subprime mortgage crisis. He observes that market movements take on a life of their own. Negative or positive trends are reflected in investor cognition, and their actions, in turn, set up instability in the market system. The booms and busts that follow are manifestations of this change in observation and understanding by the investor. Market economists see these fluctuations as normal and self-correcting trade cycles.

NOTES

1. The paper is based on readings on globalization, ecology, the wolf, and the mortgage crisis written by economists, journalists, and business writers. The *New York Times,* the *Wall Street Journal, Barron's,* the *Financial Times,* the *New York Review of Books,* the Internet, and local newspapers were consulted as well as documentary sites such as *Charlie Rose, Frontline,* and *Nova.* Additionally, the paper draws on notes and manuscripts on globalization, neoliberalism, urban anthropology, and theory courses taught. Books on the crisis were by Bitner, Cooper, Ferguson, Fleckenstein, Morris, Muolo and Padilla, Phillips, Shiller, Krugman (2009), and Zandi. Some writers present case studies on the recessions of the last half of the 20th century.

2. The first reaction to my speech was one of enthusiasm and many said that they could better understand the mortgage crisis and globalization with the ecology of the wolf as a model. This view was shared by most of those who commented on the written version of the presentation. One reader questioned the use of the ecology model; I assume they meant the imposition of a model on a body of data in an attempt to extract meaning. A model or a set of concepts must provide guiding principles for the examination of other bodies of data. Models have always been at the forefront of science. In and around the 1500s, Copernicus and Galileo struggled with the relationship of the earth to the sun, a task that was encumbered by models replete with religious notions. Through the use of new technology, the telescope, and mathematics, they and subsequent scientists were able to bring a better understanding of the planetary system and the place of humans in it. In this sense, physical and social scientists have been struggling with the ecology model as a potential for better understanding not only natural but also human ecosystems.

3. Much blame for the current crisis goes to the Bush doctrinaire policy favoring business and laissez faire neo-conservative economic policies compounded by the wars in Iraq and Afghanistan. The doctrinaire conservative movement began with the Plans for Progress for the 21st Century instigated by Cheney, Rumsfeld, Wolfowitz, and their journalistic cohorts Kristol and others. However, there were important antecedents in its development. Friedrich A. Hayek (1994) is the economist who laid the ground for the theory behind the 1980s conservative governments of Reagan and Thatcher. The major economic paradigm was developed in the early 1950s at the University of Chicago by Milton Friedman, Eugene Fama, and Robert Lucas. The term "Chicago boys" was applied to economists who introduced free market principles to other parts of the world. The major premises behind conservative policy feature giving free play to economic forces, rejecting central planning, and the John Maynard Keynes' theory that recommends government intervention in the economy by injecting money during recessions (Lewis 2009).

4. Wolfe (1963, 1977) has been for many years calling attention to supranational levels of organization in what has come to be called globalization.

5. I am grateful to the Malinowski Committee for this award, to the Society for Applied Anthropology for giving me a hook on which to hang my work, and for the friends and colleagues who have shared their work over many years. I especially treasure the friendship of the many with whom I have served on committees, in offices, and sessions. In recent years, I have received encouragement from Tom May, SfAA President Susan Andreata, and Jim Greenberg. I am thankful to many people for comments and suggestions that improved the final product. A short list includes William L. Alexander, Robert Alvarez, Anne Browning-Aiken, James B. Greenberg, Mike Mayer, John Meaney, Douglas White, Scott Whiteford, and Alvin Wolfe. Mayer and Meaney were especially helpful in clarifying ecology concepts. Art Gallaher, Jr., a close friend throughout my professional career, was helpful in clarifying the organization and writing of this essay, and nominated me for the Malinowski Award. Encouragement and suggestions were received from my wife Dora Edith Weaver, son, Thomas B. Weaver, daughters, Kathy Pippin and Denise Witte, daughter-in-law Janet Lewis, and son-in-law Wesley Witte.

REFERENCES

Adger, W. Neil. 2000. Social and Ecological Resilience: Are they Related? Progress in Human Geography 24(3):347–364.

Akerlof, George A., and Robert J. Shiller. 2009. Animal Spirits: How Human Psychology Drives the Economy and Why it Matters for Global Capitalism. Princeton, N.J.: Princeton University Press.

The Associated Press. 2006. Wolf Pups Dying in Yellowstone. The Arizona Daily Star (Tucson), January 1:A5.

Barstow, David. 2008. One Man's Military-Industrial-Media Complex. New York Times, November 30:A24.

Baumohl, Bernard. The Secrets of Economic Indicators. 2nd ed. Upper Saddle River, N.J.: Wharton School Publishing.

Birnbaum, Jane. Resilient in Tough Times: Running a Business Together Teaches a Family Survival Skill. New York Times, February 5 :B5.

Blinder, Alan S. 1998. Central Banking in Theory and Practice. Cambridge, Mass.: The MIT Press.

Capra, Fritjof. 1995. Deep Ecology: A New Paradigm. *In* Deep Ecology for the 21st Century: Readings on the Philosophy and Practice of the New Environmentalism. George Sessions, ed. Pp. 19–25. Boston, Mass.: Shambhala.

Carnes, W. Stansbury, and Stephen D. Slifer. 1991. The Atlas of Economic Indicators: A Visual Guide to Market Forces and the Federal Reserve. New York: HarperBusiness.

Carroll, Glenn R., ed. 1988. Ecological Models of Organizations. Cambridge, Mass.: Ballinger Publishing Company.

Cohen, Adam. Nothing to Fear: FDR's Inner Circle and the Hundred Days that Created Modern America. New York: Penguin Books.

Drury, William Howard, Jr. 1998. Chance and Change: Ecology for Conservationists. Berkeley: University of California Press.

Flannery, Tim. The Superior Civilization. The New York Review of Books. February 26:23–25.

Frost, Peter J., Larry F. Moore, Meryl Reis Louis, Craig C. Lundberg, and Joanne Martin. 1985. Organizational Culture. Beverly Hills, Calif.: Sage Publications.

Gunderson, Lance H., Crawford S. Holling, and Stephen S. Light, eds. 1995. Barriers and Bridges to the Renewal of Ecosystems and Institutions. New York: Columbia University Press.

Hannan, Michael T., and John Freeman. Organizational Ecology. Cambridge, Mass.: Harvard University Press.

Hayek, Friedrich A. [1944] 1994. The Road to Serfdom. 50th Anniversary ed. Chicago, Ill.: University of Chicago Press.

Holldobler, Bert, and Edward O. Wilson. 2009. The Superorganism: The Beauty, Elegance, and Strangeness of Insect Societies. New York: Norton.

Holmes, Douglas R. 2009. Economy of Words. Cultural Anthropology 24(3):381–419.

Krugman, Paul R. 1999. The Return of Depression Economics. New York: W.W. Norton and Company, Inc.

2007. Just Say AAA. New York Times, July 2, Pp. A22.

2009. The Return of Depression Economics and the Crisis of 2008. New York: W.W. Norton and Company, Inc.

Kurlantzik, Joshua. 2006. American Buffalo: The Hunt is On. New York Times, January 27:D1,D5.

Lewis, Michael. 2009. Panic: The Story of Modern Financial Insanity. New York: W.W. Norton and Company.

Mayer, Michael. 2009. Personal communications by email. Copies in the author's possession.

McNamee, Thomas. 1997. The Return of the Wolf to Yellowstone. New York: Henry Holt and Company.

Mech, L. David. [1970] 1981. The Wolf: The Ecology and Behavior of an Endangered Species. Minneapolis: University of Minnesota Press.

Melman, Seymour. 2001. After Capitalism: From Managerialism to Workplace Democracy. New York: Alfred A. Knoff.

Norris, Floyd. 2009. The Deal that Fueled Subprime. New York Times, March 6:B1,B4.

Orzech, Kathryn, and Mark Nichter. 2008. From Resilience to Resistance: Political Ecological Lessons from Antibiotic and Pesticide Resistance. Annual Review of Anthropology 37(l):267–282.

Pimm, Stuart L. 1991. The Balance of Nature? Ecological Issues in the Conservation of Species and Communities. Chicago, Ill.: University of Chicago Press.

Robbins, Jim. 2005. Hunting Habits of Yellowstone Wolves Change Ecological Balance in Park. New York Times, October 18:D3.

Romero, Simon, and Alexei Barrionuevo. 2009. Deals Help China Expand its Sway in Latin America. New York Times, April 16:A1, A8.

Shoaps, Robin Ann. 2009. Ritual and (Im)moral Voices: Locating the Testament of Judas in Sakapultek Communicative Ecology. American Anthropologist 36(3):459–477.

Singh, Jitendra V. 1990. Organizational Evolution: New Directions. Newbury Park, Calif.: Sage Publications.

Sklair, Leslie. 2001. The Transnational Capitalism Class. Maiden, Mass.: Blackwell Publishers.

Smith, Douglas W., and Gary Ferguson. 2005. Decade of the Wolf: Returning the Wild to Yellowstone.

Soros, George. 2008a. On Globalization. New York: Public Affairs.

2008b. The New Paradigm for Financial Markets: The Credit Crisis of 2008 and What it Means. New York: Public Affairs.

Stiglitz, Joseph E. 2006. Making Globalization Work. New York: W.W. Norton and Company.

Talev, Margaret. 2009. White House Quickly Taps Array of Media. New York Times, March 29:A16.

Walsh, Mary Williams. 2008. Senators Ask Who Got Money From AIG. New York Times, March 6:B1, B6.

Weaver, Thomas. 1983. The Social Effects of the Ecology and Development of the United States-Mexico Border. *In* Ecology and Development of the Border Region. Stanley Ross, ed. Pp. 233–270. Mexico City: ANUIES.

1988. The Human Rights of Undocumented Workers in the United States-Mexico Border Region. *In* The Anthropology and Human Rights. Theodore E. Downing and Gilbert Kushner, eds. Boston, Mass.: Cultural Survival.

2001. Space, Time, and Articulation in the Economic Development of the United States-Mexico Border Region: 1940–2000. Human Organization 60:105–120.

Weaver, Thomas, and Theodore E. Downing, eds. 1971. Mexican Migration. Final Report, National Science Foundation, Grant 01 P74–21168. Tucson: Bureau of Ethnic Research, University of Arizona.

Weaver, Thomas, James B. Greenberg, Anne Browning-Aiken, and William Lee Alexander, eds. 2008. The Impact of Neoliberalism and Commodity Production in Mexico. Tucson: University of Arizona Press.

Wolfe, Alvin W. 1963. The African Mineral Industry: Evolution of a Supranational Level of Integration. Social Problems 11(2):153–164.

1977. The Supranational Organization of Production. Current Anthropology 18(4):615–636.

Zandi, Mark. 2009. Financial Shock: A 360° Look at the Subprime Mortgage Implosion, and How to Avoid the Next Financial Crisis. Upper Saddle River, N.J.: FT Press.

8

Maya Coffee Farmers and Fair Trade

Assessing the Benefits and Limitations of Alternative Markets

Sarah Lyon

F air trade is a form of alternative trade that seeks to improve the position of disempowered producers through trade as a means of development. It has also been celebrated as a contemporary social movement that contests the conventional agrofood system and its exploitative social and environmental relations of production (Murray and Raynolds 2000). In this article, I employ the results of 20 months of ethnographic research (conducted between 2001 and 2003 in Guatemala and the United States) on fair-trade coffee production and market exchange to evaluate fair trade's potential as a form of alternative development. The research demonstrates that fair-trade market participation can offer a variety of potential benefits to producers, including higher prices, stable market access, organizational capacity building, market information, and access to credit. However, I also identify several key limitations of fair-trade markets, such as increasing debt burdens, insufficient compensation, the potential for growing inequality, and a lack of cooperative member participation in the fair-trade movement's international decision making and agenda setting.

BACKGROUND

The researched cooperative is located in a Tz'utujil Maya community on the shores of Lake Atitlán in the department of Sololá. The municipality has approximately 5,200 residents and the rural villages surrounding the community have a combined population of approximately 4,100. The community is accessible by water taxi from Panajachel and Santiago Atitlán and has regular bus and pick-up service to neighboring communities. It is five hours from Guatemala

Sarah Lyon, "Maya Coffee Farmers and Fair Trade: Assessing the Benefits and Limitations of Alternative Markets," *Culture & Agriculture*, vol. 29, pp. 100-112. Copyright © 2007 by American Anthropological Association. Reprinted with permission.

City and three hours from Quezaltenango, Guatemala's second largest city. Although the majority of inhabitants sustain themselves and their families through subsistence agriculture, horticultural farming, coffee production, and weaving, there is also an emerging small-scale tourism industry. Community members in their thirties and younger speak fluent Spanish. However, middle-aged women often are monolingual as are the majority of elder community members. Although there are five evangelical churches in the community, the majority of community members continue to self-define as Catholic even if they do not regularly attend mass (87 percent of the surveyed cooperative members are Catholic).

As Tz'utujil Maya, community members form part of one of Latin America's largest and poorest indigenous populations. Between 40 and 60 percent of Guatemala's 12 million inhabitants are Maya who speak one of 21 distinct indigenous languages (Fischer 2001). According to Fischer, 80 percent of Maya live in rural areas, such as the research site, which are inadequately served by public services. However, whereas 60 percent of Maya Guatemalans live in conditions of extreme poverty (Fischer 2001:5–6), some community members enjoy a relatively prosperous lifestyle as a result of their successful participation in the coffee market during previous profitable years.

During the research period, the cooperative had 116 members. In recent years, the membership has expanded to include 160 coffee producers, a testament to the cooperative's strong and long-standing market connections and guaranteed fair-trade price. Although the membership may seem small in comparison to the local population, it maintains a high profile. This is primarily because of three circumstances. First, the tight-knit, extended family relationships permeating the community mean that virtually every resident has a family member in the group. Second, the cooperative is one of the longest-running organizations within the community. Third, although not every community member belongs to the cooperative, the organizational activities of the group benefit nonmembers through (1) the local multiplier effects of the extra income earned through fair-trade consumer markets and (2) development projects initiated by the cooperative and funded with fair-trade coffee market proceeds in the areas of environmental conservation, infrastructural improvements, and emergency relief. For example, the cooperative played a leading role in the municipal government's 2002 successful effort to organize a weekly trash collection effort in the community. The cooperative is also engaged in an ongoing reforestation project in which seedlings are donated to cooperative members and their extended family members to plant in the agricultural plots surrounding the community (see Lyon 2007 for a thorough discussion of these efforts).

Roseberry (1996) named coffee the "beverage of postmodernism," not to suggest that coffee exists in a unique relationship with capitalism, but that it provides a window through which we can view a range of relationships and social transformations. Coffee's introduction to Latin America intensified existing transnational links and transformed the lives of individuals and the shape of landscapes. By the late 1800s, coffee had become Guatemala's primary export, the foundation of wealth, the determinant of social status, and the arbiter of political power among the economic and political elite. In later years, coffee cultivation, and the exploitative political and social structures that supported it, contributed to the unrest that resulted in the nation's civil war and continues to shape its political, economic, and cultural reality in the present (Paige 1997; Williams 1994).

Despite coffee's turbulent history within Guatemala, it became an increasingly attractive agricultural commodity for smallholders because it is easy to store and handle, its value has historically surpassed that of comparable agricultural products, it can be grown on steep slopes, and if neglected by producers it can be fairly easily rejuvenated (Sick 1999). In the research site the introduction of coffee cultivation is referred to as "the bomb" that exploded in the community, bringing the cash revenues that enabled families to end their decades-long pattern of seasonal migration, build cement block houses, and educate their children. Beginning in the late 1960s and concurrent with coffee's growing attraction for smallholders, the USAID mission to Guatemala and other lenders began prioritizing rural development. In 1970, USAID approved a $23 million rural development sector loan for the development of cooperatives and by the fall of 1975, nearly 20 percent of Highland Maya participated in some form of cooperatives (Handy 1984:240). After the 1976 earthquake and the influx of additional international lenders, Guatemala boasted 510 cooperatives, 57 percent of them in the Highlands with more than 132,000 members (Brockett 1998:112). The cooperative movement remains strong in Guatemala where today there are 1,620 registered cooperatives (729 of which are agricultural) with 579,705 members (64,410 belonging to agricultural cooperatives; Instituto Nacional de Cooperativas Guatemala C. A. [INACOP] 2007).

The researched coffee cooperative was founded with the encouragement and aid of a micro-credit lending institution located in Santiago Atitlán and operated by the Catholic development organization Caritas. In the late 1970s, this organization became the first provider of small, low-interest loans to Lake Atitlán area (located in Sololá, Guatemala) residents for community projects and the purchase of agricultural inputs. The director, Don Diego, reportedly urged a group of community members to form a cooperative in order to establish their own revolving credit fund because at that time it was difficult for the disenfranchised indigenous farmers to secure personal loans from banks. Over 70 community members attended the first meeting and in 1979, 25 male community members founded the cooperative, inscribing several younger brothers and wives to reach the minimum membership of 30 required by INACOP, the National Cooperative Registry. The cooperative grew to 160 members and began exporting fair-trade and organic-certified coffee in 1991. In recent years, the group has maintained a multiyear secure market contract with fair-trade coffee roasters in the United States.

The remarkable growth in agricultural cooperatives across Guatemala coincided with the increasing violence of the nation's erupting civil war and eventual genocide. Between 1950 and the mid-1980s the Guatemalan population grew from 2.8 to 8.5 million and per capita access to land steadily declined (McCreery 2003). Although recent studies do not portray the coffee fields as breeding grounds for revolutionaries (Topik and Clarence-Smith 2003), the unequal distribution of land and the legacy of racism fostered by the nation's coffee economy did fuel the swelling ranks of guerrilla combatants. Individuals who participated in successful community projects and organizations, such as the researched cooperative, consistently faced accusations that they were engaging in subversive or guerrilla activities (Sanford 2003) as villages with autonomous local organizations were specifically targeted by government military forces.

In the aftermath of the civil war the extent of the human rights abuses was exposed. In 1999, the Report of the Commission for Historical Clarification published evidence of massacres in 626 villages and placed the number murdered during the civil war at close to 200 thousand (Comision para el Esclarecimiento Historico [CEH] 1999). Among the victims, 83 percent were Maya, and 93 percent of the human rights violations were attributed to the army (CEH 1999; Sanford 2003). Although the researched cooperative successfully weathered the civil war, the organization's community store was robbed by soldiers and the agricultural monitor was imprisoned at the military base in nearby Santiago Atitlan for several days after he was denounced as a guerrilla. As a result of the war, the village and surrounding communities were plagued by ongoing fear and mistrust, which partially constrains community organizing and development efforts into the present.

RESEARCH METHODOLOGY

In this article, I evaluate the benefits and limitations of fair trade as a form of alternative development. This research question forms part of a larger ethnographic research project conducted over 20 months in Guatemala and the United States (September 2001–March 2003, June 2006). The Guatemala-based research I discuss in this article focused on the 116 members and the administrators of the fair-trade coffee cooperative. The research included ongoing participant-observation at community events, at the wet mill during the harvest (December-March), and at internal cooperative meetings and meetings with external market participants, such as coffee importers, roasters, and certifiers. Participant-observation was also conducted during the visits made by agronomists and certifiers to members' coffee fields to observe production practices and better understand certification requirements.

Data were gathered through semistructured interviews with the majority of the cooperative's remaining 19 founding members and the collection of life histories from 18 community elders to illustrate the community's past and recent transformations. Semistructured interviews were conducted with 53 of the cooperative's 116 members and nearly 30 employees of development agencies, coffee importers, and roasters assisting the cooperative and coffee certifiers. Further data were gathered during participant-observation at the Guatemalan National Coffee Association's annual conference (2000, 2002) and visits to several fair-trade coffee cooperatives located in the Western Highlands (where informal interviews were conducted with cooperative administrators and board members).

The benefits and limitations of fair-trade coffee market participation were assessed according to five primary criteria: (1) coffee prices and market size, (2) trade relationships, (3) organizational capacity, (4) access to credit, and (5) gender. Although I discuss the research results at length, Table 1 summarizes the findings.

Table 1. Summary of Fair Trade's Impacts

Category	Benefits	Limitations
Prices & Market Size	• **Higher: $1.41/pound**	• **83% say prices are not high enough**
	• **More Secure due to long-term contracts**	• **Fair trade markets are not large enough to accommodate total production of worldwide small coffee producers**
	• **40% identify higher prices as primary benefit**	
	• **Corollary benefits: land tenure security & increased education rates**	• **Established fair trade certified cooperatives may limit the market access of younger groups**
Trade Relationships	• **Long-term contracts and ongoing producer/ roaster contact result in: Improved product quality Increased market information**	• **Lack of producer participation in the international decision-making and agenda setting of the fair trade movement**
		• **Membership at large unfamiliar with fair trade, its goals, and its requirements**
Organizational Capacity	• **Required democratic structure: Builds organizational capacity Increases accountability Encourages cooperative service (77%)**	
Access to Credit	• **Cooperative offers short and long-term small loans**	• **High rates of insolvency may: Reduce member income**
	• **54% say credit is primary benefit**	Weaken group's organizational capacity Threaten market success
Gender	• **FLO certification requirements prioritize gender equality**	• **Requirements and goals need clarification**
		• **Little empirical evidence of significant impact on gender equality among producer groups**

PRICES AND MARKET SIZE

The most direct benefit to individual producers is the guaranteed price of $1.21 per pound paid by northern buyers. Dual-certified organic and fair-trade coffee earns a price premium of $0.15 per pound. In addition to the guaranteed price, producers receive a social premium ($0.05) to be used for community development. When market prices rise above the guaranteed floor price, an additional premium is paid. The guaranteed price helps to sustain rural communities and households and, when invested in land and education, supports effective local development.

As stated above, in recent years, international coffee prices, which are established on the New York Coffee, Sugar, and Cocoa Exchange, and the London International Futures Exchange, have declined to a hundred-year low when adjusted for inflation (Lewin *et al.* 2004). At the height of this crisis, during the 2001–02 coffee harvest, members of the cooperative were paid a price of $0.16 per pound (for unprocessed coffee) after taxes and the cooperative's operating costs were deducted. This price was double that paid to noncooperative members by the representatives of local coffee processors who in turn sell the coffee through conventional commodity exchanges. The higher income enabled cooperative members to continue repaying their debts, maintain their standard of living, retain their landholdings, and pay for their children's education during a period in which many of their less fortunate neighbors were forced to sell their land and withdraw their children from school.

Land Ownership

The security of the cooperative members' landholdings is a significant benefit of their higher fair-trade incomes. The significance of land ownership in Maya communities has both economic and cultural dimensions. Access to land is a critical component of total income in rural Latin America (De Janvry and Sadoulet 2000:400). However, to be an effective economic strategy, controlling one's means of production through land ownership must be linked to secure market access. Although this is an increasingly relevant issue in light of contemporary global economic integration, for many Guatemalan Maya communities, including the research site, land ownership was also a critically determinant historical factor. During the 1930s and 1940s, many highland communities and coastal plantations formed an interdependent, and yet highly uneven, economic system dictated by the seasonal migration of low-paid Maya workers. Cooperative members, their parents, and grandparents reported that during this period of seasonal migration the streets of the community were silent as poverty and lack of land forced the majority of inhabitants to leave in search of work. However, beginning in the late 1960s with the introduction of cash crops, including vegetables such as onions and tomatoes in addition to coffee, cooperative members were able to increase their land holdings (by buying back land previously sold to residents of neighboring communities to raise cash) and access new commodity markets, thereby avoiding the arduous cycles of seasonal migration.

The stable fair-trade prices earned by cooperative members enabled them to continue their subsistence agricultural production. Although today they produce significantly more coffee than corn, many cooperative members agreed that producing at least a portion of the corn consumed by the family is a critical part of the yearly agricultural cycle. Cooperative member households own on average 12 *cuerdas* of organic coffee, eight cuerdas of transition coffee, four and a third cuerdas of milpa (a Mesoamerican crop growing system combining maize, beans, and squash in single plots), and two and a third cuerdas of vegetables (such as onions and tomatoes). Of the surveyed cooperative members, 64 percent reported that their milpa and vegetable crops were consumed solely within the household while the remainder reported selling the surplus to regional buyers who resold the products in Guatemala City. In addition to providing additional cash income and cultural continuity, the continued production of milpa represents a livelihood strategy that better enables small producers to cope with uncertain prospects. Furthermore, cooperative members do not interpret coffee and corn as diametrically opposed spheres of production. Instead, they are intimately linked: fair-trade coffee sales supplement subsistence agricultural production and help secure land ownership, allowing members to maintain their agrarian traditions.

Education

The guaranteed prices earned by cooperative members also enable them to educate more of their children for longer periods of time. Nineteen percent of the surveyed cooperative members never attended school and 42 percent completed only three or fewer years, meaning many possess only basic literacy, mathematical and Spanish language skills. On average, cooperative members have six children each and 42 percent of members have at least one child who has completed secondary school and works in an office, as opposed to pursuing traditional agricultural pursuits or caring for the home. Although the fees and supplies for primary school education are minimal, the financial expenses increase incrementally as a student enters junior high. In 2003, the community's only high school graduated its first class of accountants. However, the school is private and, therefore, inaccessible to many potential students. In addition, students pursuing degrees in teaching or other occupations are forced to leave the community and must pay board and lodging expenses in addition to tuition and fees.

Although cooperative members are currently able to sustain their families through fair-trade and organic-coffee production, it is unlikely that the coffee market will expand to the extent that each of their children will be able to successfully follow in their footsteps. In fact, the fair-trade model of alternative development is criticized as being a stopgap measure in the eventual need for agricultural diversification among the world's millions of small coffee farmers. Although cooperative members are not diversifying their production, they are ensuring that at least a segment of the future generation will have a wider variety of occupational opportunities. Seventy-four percent of the surveyed members expressed the hope that their children would become professionals (as opposed to farmers). However, although many cooperative members invest their coffee profits and loans in their children's education with the belief that this will provide the key to secure, high-paying jobs in the formal sector (cf. Sick 1999:17), parents also hope their children's higher wages will at least partially be reinvested in the family farm and help provide for their own needs in old age.

Therefore, the investment in education should not be interpreted as an abandonment of the community's traditional agrarian-based identity. Seventy-six percent of surveyed cooperative members agreed future generations will continue to farm and nearly a quarter of respondents said they hoped their own children would combine professional careers with their agricultural pursuits. In an attempt to reconcile the conflicting demands of professional and agrarian livelihoods, one cooperative member expressed his hope that his children will be successful professionals who hire day laborers to farm their land for them. He explained during an interview, "Land is an investment, and I hope my children invest their money in buying land. The best thing would be to be a professional and buy land and hire workers." He went on to say he planned to teach his children's (hypothetical) future employees all the complicated aspects of organic production, so that his children can join him as cooperative members.

In conclusion, despite higher rates of education among cooperative members' children, the importance of agriculture within the community is unlikely to significantly diminish in the near future. This sentiment is well-expressed by a cooperative member who, when asked about the future of farming in the community in light of the growing number of well-educated youth, responded, "A good percentage are going to continue with this tradition—as *indigenas* we have always dedicated ourselves to our fields, this isn't going to disappear."

Insufficient Compensation and Market Size

Interviewed cooperative members primarily understood fair trade as a market transaction paying slightly higher prices than conventional coffee markets. During interviews and casual conversations cooperative members repeatedly stated that their earnings enabled them to maintain their families but not necessarily get ahead. When asked the farm-gate price they ideally would like to receive for their coffee, 83 percent of the 53 surveyed members named a price greater than the roughly $16.50 per hundred pounds that they were paid during the 2001–02 harvest for green coffee. However, the average of their stated ideal price was a relatively low $20.00.

There is a significant gap in fair-trade markets between the price paid to producers and the price paid by consumers. Interviewed coffee roasters are quick to point out the numerous costs associated with transporting, roasting, packaging, and marketing specialty coffee in the United States. However, some critics question the "fairness" of the fair price. The fair-trade coffee floor price was agreed on in 1988 after field research into production and living costs in coffee producing countries around the world. Despite the fact that 16 years later, producers have widely disparate production and living costs and that many nations' economies have been ravaged by inflation, this price has been raised only once (Rice and McLean 1999:57).

The researched cooperative has enjoyed long-term access to fair-trade coffee markets and in multiple studies, market access is identified as a key producer benefit (Shreck 2002; Paul 2005). However, one of the most frequently voiced criticisms of fair trade relates to the relatively small market for fair-trade products. For example, the market for fair-trade coffee, currently the largest among certified commodities, remains insufficient: although nearly 30 percent of the world's small-scale coffee producers now supply the fair-trade market, the Fairtrade Labelling Organizations International (FLO) estimates that the capacity of producers worldwide who could meet certification standards is roughly seven times the current volume exported via fair-trade channels (Murray *et al.* 2006).

TRADE RELATIONSHIPS

As demonstrated above, the guaranteed price paid to fair-trade-certified producers helps to sustain rural communities and households and, when invested in land and education, can support effective, local development. In addition, and perhaps more importantly, the cooperative has formed long-term, stable trade relationships with northern importers and roasters through its participation in fair-trade networks. The highly volatile international coffee market cyclically rewards small producers with high prices (e.g., when there is a frost in Brazil, prices historically rise dramatically). In fact, it is precisely the possibility of high prices that initially attracts small producers to the commodity. However, the market stability enjoyed by small producers in fair-trade networks helps buffer the conventional coffee market's cyclical crises, enabling members to make long-term plans and investments in their operations, their organizational infrastructure, or their children's education.

Fair trade's focus on supporting smallholder access to new markets facilitates a wider distribution of benefits to small producers (Taylor 2004). Fair-trade buyers and the development agencies that endorse the market are able to assist specific groups rather than offer blanket aid. These direct trade relationships allow fair-trade producers to bypass the often exploitative local buyers and enable groups to bargain more effectively with large buyers such as Starbucks or Wal-Mart (Taylor 2002). Furthermore, the market information they obtain through fair-trade contracts may make producers more confident in dealing with non-fair-trade buyers as well (Ronchi 2002).

Improving Product Quality

The desire to maintain long-term relationships with buyers can provide an incentive for cooperatives to improve their product quality by investing in infrastructural and production improvements. The cooperative is visited on a bimonthly basis by representatives from its long-term Vermont-based buyers, Green Mountain Coffee Roasters. Through this steady contact, cooperative members hone their communication skills, enhance their business practices, and learn valuable information about quality and certification demands. The fair-trade model offers the cooperative a competitive advantage by actively fostering ongoing close contact with their buyers and enabling them to learn international standards for price, quality, and the delivery of export products. Ninety-eight percent of surveyed cooperative members believed that they produce a higher quality coffee than producers who are not cooperative members. The agricultural monitor explained during an interview that the group is "in contact with the foreigners that bring us information about coffee and new techniques. They are teaching us for example how to improve the quality for the consumers."

Producer Participation in the International Fair-Trade Movement

Fair trade is predicated on the formation of equitable economic partnerships between producers and consumers. However, because of the low level of producer participation in the international realm of decision making and standard setting, it has yet to radically transform trade relationships themselves into vehicles for social justice. The members of the researched cooperative have sold fair-trade certified coffee directly to northern markets for more than a decade. On the one hand, although several interviewed cooperative members could articulately analyze the inequities they faced in global agricultural commodity markets, only three out of 53 surveyed members were familiar with the term *fair trade*. On the other hand, 35 knew the name of Elan Organic Coffees, the cooperative's long-term importer (see Lyon 2007 for a more thorough exploration of the strength of producer-roaster relationships in fair-trade coffee networks). This lack of awareness regarding the role they play in the fair-trade movement is symptomatic of the international fair-trade structure in which producers have limited decision-making power and administrative control.

This finding is supported by research in diverse locales indicating that producers understand fair trade in terms of market access (Tallontire 2000:175) or international aid (Shreck 2002) and not as an equitable trade relationship in which they are actively participating. Still other researchers maintain that fair-trade producer groups are "passive suppliers of product" dependent on higher-order groups (Utting-Chamorro 2005), that fair trade is an "intervention" rather than a partnership and that producers do not fully understand the market's benefits (Paul 2005:135). Because of the lack of producer participation in the formation of fair-trade strategies and market operations, it is unable to fully identify and represent the values and priorities of its intended beneficiaries.

To successfully foster equitable international trading partnerships, producers must contribute to the formation of standards, certification requirements, and agreed on levels of just compensation as well as the establishment of future collective goals (Blowfield 2004; Daviron and Ponte 2005). In response to recent criticism, FLO has added four producer representatives to its 12 member board of directors (FLO 2003) and established a producer business unit in 2005 to assist producer groups. In addition, the Latin American Coordinating Committee of fair-trade producer organizations was recently created to negotiate participation and specific demands. However, time will determine whether these accommodations are sufficient.

Fair-trade certified coffee producers must be organized into independent democratic associations. This requirement strengthens the organizational capacity of small producers, one of fair trade's most durable benefits. The strength of a producer association's internal organization, its group identity, and leadership skills have been identified as critical components of fair-trade success. In turn, the security of fair-trade prices and markets enhances a cooperative's general financial and organizational stability because buyers demand a certain degree of accountability and monitoring (Raynolds *et al.* 2004; Daviron and Ponte 2005). In addition, the growth of the fair-trade market has contributed to the promotion of cooperative social development in regions where historically such organizations have not been prominent, such as the Caribbean (Moberg 2005).

Fair-trade consumption in the North is predicated on consumers' access to information regarding the conditions of production and increasingly the social circumstances and cultural traditions of producers themselves (Lyon 2006). Therefore, participation in international fair-trade markets can lend legitimacy and protection to democratic producer associations, which in turn are able to create safe opportunities for members to work together and reproduce long-term traditions of horizontal cooperation, reciprocity, and mutual aid. Impact studies indicate that this organizational capacity building can be translated into enhanced external civic engagement. For example, Taylor (2002) found that many Mexican fair-trade cooperatives are involved in national coffee, credit, and small business associations. Ronchi (2002) demonstrated that the producer organization allows fair-trade farmers to voice their opinions collectively, thereby increasing their power at the national government level.

In regions with a history of targeted rural violence, such as Guatemala, the international nature of fair-trade networks buttresses the strength of cooperatives and the secure civic spaces they foster. Although many Guatemalans see democratic organizations as essential to confronting poverty and precarious economic circumstances, because of the fact that any social organization not under army control during the war was criminalized, fear remains a significant obstacle to rural organization (REMHI 1999).

Cooperative Service

Of the 53 surveyed cooperative members, 77 percent have served on the cooperative's 16 member board of directors at least once over the course of their membership. Of these 77 percent, on average they have fulfilled two terms of service, each lasting either one or two years. Only seven members of the 116 are female. To date, none of these women have served positions on the board of directors and cooperative service largely remains a male pursuit. Despite this high rate of participation, maintaining accountability and democracy is frequently a challenge faced by associations and many fair-trade cooperatives experience difficulties balancing the interests of an increasingly strong management, the elected leadership, and the membership at large.

The varying service records of cooperative members demonstrate that not everyone eagerly jumps at the opportunity to serve. In fact, at times, it has been difficult to recruit board members within the cooperative. Some individuals serve repeatedly whereas others provide excuses for why they cannot fulfill their elected *cargo* (or service position that cooperative members consider similar to the cargos served in the community's religious hierarchy). For example, many of the long-term members of the cooperative feel they have fulfilled their responsibilities and should not be required to provide future service. In addition, those already serving cargos in Catholic Action (generally two-year posts) or religious brotherhoods (one-year posts) are excused from cooperative service obligations because of time constraints. The fact that nearly 60 percent of the surveyed cooperative members attended three years or fewer of school and may be illiterate or have poor Spanish skills also contributes to their reluctance to serve cargos in the cooperative, which to fulfill market demands for certification and quality increasingly resembles a business association. Ironically, some of those best prepared for service, members who are educated and relatively comfortable negotiating cross-cultural social relations and business transactions, are not disposed to accept positions because they are "professionals" as opposed to farmers and cannot miss work to attend the frequent meetings. One member who is a teacher in a local school explained, "They have nominated me but thankfully they understand that I don't have the time. I can't … one can't send his *mozo* (day laborer) to fulfill the cargo and because of my job I'm always going to meetings at the school."

Despite variability in the service records of individual members, the ethos of service and mutual aid remains a highly potent symbolic component of cooperative membership, one that helps to mitigate tensions among members. In interviews, members frequently reiterated the importance of mutual aid, explaining how, "The cooperative helps you at the same time that you have to help it." This experience is supported by similar studies (Bebbington 1996; Hernández Castillo and Nigh 1998; Nigh 1997) indicating that Latin American cooperatives that combine cultural norms of reciprocity and service with contemporary business activities are often more accountable to the needs of their communities and better grounded in local social processes.

On the basis of a longitudinal study in Zinacantan, Mexico, Cancian (1965, 1992) argues that changes in macrolevel systems, including state politics and the global economy, have contributed to decentralized political and social relations in Maya communities and the slow erosion of the traditional bases of community identity. Although this case study does not contradict this finding, it does illustrate that alternative models of engagement with the global economy, such as fair-trade markets, can actually serve to increase solidarity among participating members, rather than threaten it. However, not every resident is a member of the cooperative and there is little empirical research demonstrating that fair trade reinforces political and social relations or the traditional bases of identity at the community-wide level.

De Janvry and Sadoulet (2000:396) argue that access to credit is minimal among the rural poor in Latin America and this lowers the "income generating capacity of the meager asset endowments that the poor possess." Therefore, in countries such as Guatemala, microloan programs can be the key components of local, agricultural development in impoverished highland communities. Historically, it has been difficult for rural indigenous farmers with little education to solicit loans directly from banks and large lending institutions because they do not have the proper guarantees, do not have an existing credit history, do not understand the extensive paperwork that is required, are ashamed of their Spanish language skills, or simply do not relate well with Ladino professionals. During an interview, one member explained the importance of cooperative credit, stating "The cooperative helps associates … it's not like in the banks where they don't give us anything." However, participation in fair-trade markets can enhance the legitimacy of producer organizations, thereby granting them access to national banks and international lenders, a key benefit for small producers who were often historically excluded from formal lending institutions.

Producer Debt

Many fair-trade producer organizations use loans from external institutions to establish microlending programs to help members improve their production quality and quantity, thereby strengthening the organization's market potential. However, these loans must be carefully managed by both the cooperative and the members who borrow. Beginning in 1989, the researched cooperative received several long-term loans through the USAID Small Coffee Farmer Improvement Program. These loans enabled the cooperative to establish an internal microlending program, which has proven critical to the group's ongoing success. In fact, 54 percent of surveyed cooperative members named access to credit as the primary benefit of cooperative membership, compared to the 40 percent who named higher prices. Members apply for both short- and long-term loans that they pay back with their annual coffee profits. Loans are officially designated for improvements on members' coffee plots and the purchase of organic fertilizer. The microlending program provides a means for members to improve the quality and quantity of their coffee production, thereby strengthening the organization's market potential.

Many cooperative members find it difficult to repay their loans to the cooperative, in turn making it difficult for the group to repay its bank loans. Varangis and colleagues (2003) report problems with loan repayments among coffee producers in all Central American countries and the debts held by cooperatives and their members significantly reduce the income generating potential of fair-trade markets. An analysis of the cooperative's microlending program reveals seven principal factors contributing to high rates of insolvency among members:

- Harvest is December-March, however members must wait until June or July for full payment
- High interest rates: 85 percent of surveyed members reported the rate was exorbitant
- Allegations of loan mismanagement by administration and borrowers
- Poor harvests owing to hurricanes Mitch (1998) and Stan (2005)
- Loans used for unproductive purposes (such as education or medical bills)
- Loans are larger than capacity to repay
- Members borrow from multiple lending institutions, exceeding repayment capacity

Large, unpaid loans lower a group's profits and members' income. In addition to lowering profits, large numbers of defaulted loans can weaken the group's organizational capacity and hamper its market success. This can also encumber the group's morale and sense of unity as solvent members begin to feel they are being taken advantage of and indebted members begin to feel the group's management is unresponsive to their needs. Additionally, members deeply in debt to their association may actually begin to have a vested interest in the group's failure because it would potentially erase their own debts (Lyon 2007).

GENDER

Fair trade has prioritized gender equality; however in practice this mandate is underdeveloped. To comply with certification standards, most producer groups have initiated projects and activities designed to address gender issues; however their effectiveness remains to be empirically documented. Although fair-trade publicity materials highlight the steps producer groups have taken to foster women's equality, a review of FLO-certified producer profiles reveals that women's projects are largely focused on activities outside the export agricultural sector and instead on health or subsistence farming. In the case of the researched cooperative, several female members and wives of cooperative members recently formed a weaving group to produce naturally dyed products to sell as part of the cooperative's new coffee tour. Although research on the group is ongoing, preliminary results from June 2006 indicate that the project does not currently generate significant income for participants. They are working to find a foreign buyer for their products. However, several women explained during interviews that their organizational efforts are hampered by their lack of business training. Because of transitions within the cooperative's management, the women have not received significant support from the group and this is perhaps contributing to their desire for separate but equal status. As the leader explained during a focus group interview, "We have to separate the money because this money is ours—it's from our products. It's better that we manage it ourselves so that we can do something with the money. We want to be equal to them."

The ability to improve the opportunities for women in producer associations may be conditioned by cultural tradition. For example, research in Guatemala indicates that well-established cooperatives emerging from older generations may not adequately answer the needs of female members. However, newer cooperatives, by contrast, appear more willing to provide opportunities for women to participate not only as producers but also as cooperative leaders and managers. In summary, although fostering gender equality has been a priority for fair trade, women's current limited participation in producer associations may perpetuate, rather than overcome, the traditional gender bias in Latin America's agricultural sector (Murray *et al.* 2006). Additional in-depth research is required to fully assess the impact of fair trade on gender relations in producer communities and identify specific avenues for improvement.

CONCLUSIONS

One outcome of structural adjustments has been a move toward market-friendly approaches to development (Desai and Imrie 1998; Fowler 2000) as the poor are increasingly seen as those who are not effectively integrated into the market economy (Hulme and Shepherd 2003). This growing focus on poverty reduction has led some aid organizations to direct their efforts toward more functionally oriented peasant groups, such as commodity specific producer associations (Bebbington 2005). By facilitating the incorporation of "marginal" populations into market economies, this shifting development focus may indirectly serve neoliberal-state goals (Ferguson 1994; Fisher 1997; Wilson 2003). With its hallmark slogan "trade not aid," the recent growth of the fair-trade market reflects these shifting priorities and the increasingly popular notion that northern consumption should be channeled into progressive movements to transform the international economy into a form of empowerment for its historically less powerful participants. However, fair trade's contradictory emphasis on the transformation of conventional markets from within differentiates it from development programs that are not rooted in explicit social and economic justice goals.

The research discussed above demonstrates that increased rates of fair-trade coffee consumption in North America and Europe present an opportunity for small producers in less developed nations as they are increasingly integrated into transnational markets on different terms than previous trade relations. Fair trade offers a variety of potential benefits to producers, including higher prices, stable market access, organizational capacity building, market information, and access to credit. However, this international market participation is accompanied by several potentially harmful impacts within the communities and producer households, including increasing debt burdens, insufficient compensation, the potential for growing inequality, and a lack of cooperative member participation in the fair-trade movement's international decision making and agenda setting. Analyzing fair-trade participation as a creative mixture of resources and actions contributes to a more realistic perspective on neoliberalism, one that moves beyond simple market compliance or resistance (Bebbington 2000; Chase 2002) to further our understanding of how neoliberalism and the oppositional strategies it engenders are mutually constitutive.

REFERENCES CITED

This research was generously funded by the Wenner-Gren Foundation for Anthropological Research, Fulbright-Hayes, the Emory Fund for Internationalization, and the University of Kentucky Summer Faculty Research Fellowship. I would like to thank anonymous reviewers for their helpful suggestions.

Bebbington, Anthony. 1996. Organizations and Intensifications: Campesino Federations, Rural Livelihoods and Agricultural Technology in the Andes and Amazonia. World Development 24(7):1161–1177.

———2000 Reencountering Development: Livelihood Transitions and Place Transformations in the Andes. Annals of the Association of American Geographers 90:495–520.

———2005 Donor-NGO Relations and Representations of Livelihood in Nongovernmental Aid Chains. World Development 33:937–950.

Blowfield, M. 2004. Implementation Deficits of Ethical Trade Systems. Journal of Consumer Culture 13:77–90.

Brockett, C. D. 1998. Land, Power, and Poverty: Agrarian Transformation and Political Conflict in Central America. Boulder, CO: Westview Press.

Chase, J., ed. 2002. The Spaces of Neoliberalism: Land, Place and Family in Latin America. Bloomfield, CT: Kumarian Press.

Cancian, Frank. 1965. Economics and Prestige in a Maya Community: The Religious Cargo System in Zinacantan. Stanford: Stanford University Press.

———1992. The Decline of Community in Zinacantan: Economy, Public Life, and Social Stratification, 1960–1987. Stanford: Stanford University Press.

Comision para el Esclarecimiento Historico (CEH).1999. Guatemala Memoria del Silencio. Conclusions and Recommendations. Guatemala City: United Nations.

Daviron, Benoit, and Stefano Ponte. 2005. The Coffee Paradox: Global Markets, Commodity Trade and the Elusive Promise of Development. London: Zed Books.

De Janvry, Alain, and Elisabeth Sadoulet. 2000. Rural Poverty in Latin America Determinants and Exit Paths. Food Policy 25:389–409.

Desai, V., and R. Imrie. 1998. The New Managerialism in Local Governance: North-South Dimensions. Third World Quarterly 19:635–650.

Fairtrade Labelling Organizations International (FLO). 2003. Fairtrade Labelling Organizations International. Electronic document, http://www.fairtrade.net/byproducts.html, accessed September 11, 2007.

Ferguson, J. 1994. The Anti-Politics Machine: "Development," Depoliticization, and Bureaucratic Power in Lesotho. Minneapolis: University of Minnesota Press.

Fischer, Edward F. 2001. Cultural Logics and Global Economies: Maya Identity in Thought and Practice. Austin: University of Texas Press.

Fisher, E. 1997. Beekeepers in the Global "Fair Trade" Market: A Case from Tabora Region, Tanzania. International Journal of Sociology of Agriculture and Food 6:109–259.

Fowler, A. 2000. NGDOs as a Movement in History: Beyond Aid to Social Entrepreneurship or Civic Innovation. Third World Quarterly 21:637–654.

Handy, J. 1984. Gift of the Devil: A History of Guatemala. Boston:South End Press.

Hernandez Castillo, Rosalva Aida, and Ronald Nigh. 1998. Global Processes and Local Identity among Mayan Coffee Growers in Chiapas, Mexico. American Anthropologist 100(1):136–147.

Hulme, D., and A. Shepherd. 2003. Conceptualizing Chronic Poverty. World Development 31:403–424.

Instituto Nacional de Cooperativas Guatemala C. A. (INACOP). 2007. Estadisticas al 28 de Febrero del 2007. Electronic document, http://www.inacop.org, accessed March 27.

Lewin, B., D. Giovannucci, and P. Varangis. 2004. Coffee Markets: New Paradigms in Global Supply and Demand. Agriculture and Rural Development Discussion Paper 3. Electronic document, http:// lnweb18.worldbank.org/ESSD/ardext.nsf/11ByDo cName/PublicationsCoffeeMarketsNewParadigmsinGlobalSupplyandDemand, accessed September 11, 2001.

Lyon, S. 2006. Evaluating Fair Trade Consumption: Politics, Defetishization and Producer Participation. International Journal of Consumer Studies 30:452–464.

———2007 Fair Trade Coffee and Human Rights in Guatemala. Journal of Consumer Policy. 30(3):241–261.

McCreery, D. 2003. Coffee and Indigenous Labor in Guatemala, 1871–1980. In The Global Coffee Economy in Africa, Asia and Latin America 1500–1989. W. G. Clarence-Smith and S. Topik, eds. Pp. 191–208. Cambridge: Cambridge University Press.

Moberg, Mark. 2005. Fair Trade and Eastern Caribbean Banana Farmers: Rhetoric and Reality in the Anti-Globalization Movement. Human Organization 64(1):4–16.

Murray, Douglas L., and Laura T. Raynolds. 2000. Alternative Trade in Bananas: Obstacles and Opportunities for Progressive Social Change in the Global Economy. Agriculture and Human Values 17:65–74.

Murray, Douglas L., Laura T. Raynolds, and Peter L. Taylor. 2006. The Future of Fair Trade Coffee: Dilemmas Facing Latin America's Small-Scale Producers. Development in Practice 16:179–192.

Nigh, Ronald. 1997. Organic Agriculture and Globalization: A Maya Associative Corporation in Chiapas, Mexico. Human Organization 56(4):427–436.

Paige, Jeffrey M. 1997. Coffee and Power: Revolution and the Rise of Democracy in Central America. Cambridge, MA: Harvard University Press.

Paul, Elisabeth. 2005. Evaluating Fair Trade as a Development Project. Development in Practice 15(2):134–150.

Raynolds, Laura T., Douglas L. Murray, and Peter L. Taylor. 2004. Fair Trade Coffee: Building Producer Capacity via Global Networks. Journal of International Development 16(8):1109–1121.

Recovery of Historical Memory Project (REMHI). 1999. Guatemala Never Again! Maryknoll, NY: Orbis Books.

Rice, R. A., and J. A. McLean. 1999. Sustainable Coffee at the Crossroads. Washington, DC: Consumers Choice Council.

Ronchi, L. 2002. The Impact of Fair Trade Producers and their Organizations: A Case Study with Coocafe in Costa Rica. Brighton, UK: University of Sussex.

Roseberry, W. 1996. The Rise of Yuppie Coffees and the Reimagination of Class in the United States. American Anthropologist 98(4):762–775.

Sanford, V. 2003. Buried Secrets: Truth and Human Rights in Guatemala. New York: Palgrave Macmillan.

Shreck, Aimee. 2002. Just Bananas? Fair Trade Banana Production in the Dominican Republic. International Journal of Sociology of Food and Agriculture 10(2):25–52.

Sick, Deborah. 1999. Farmers of the Golden Bean: Costa Rican Households and the Global Coffee Economy. Dekalb: Northern Illinois University Press.

Tallontire, A. 2000. Partnerships in Fair Trade: Reflections from a Case Study of Cafedirect. Development in Practice 10:166–177.

Taylor, P. 2002. Poverty Alleviation through Participation in Fair Trade Coffee Networks: Synthesis of Case Study Research Question Findings. Fort Collins: Colorado State University, Department of Sociology.

——2004. In the Market but Not of It: Fair Trade Coffee and Forest Stewardship Council Certification as Market-Based Social Change. World Development 33(1): 129–147.

Topik, S., and W. G. Clarence-Smith. 2003. Conclusion: New Propositions and a Research Agenda. In The Global Coffee Economy in Africa, Asia, and Latin America 1500–1989. W. G. Clarence-Smith and S. Topik, eds. Pp. 201–225. Cambridge: Cambridge University Press.

Utting-Chamorro, K. 2005. Does Fair Trade Make a Difference? The Case of Small Coffee Producers in Nicaragua. Development in Practice 15(3–4):584–601.

Varangis, P., P. Siegel, D. Giovannucci, and B. Lewin. 2003. Dealing with the Coffee Crisis in Central America: Impacts and Strategies. Washington, DC: World Bank.

Williams, Robert G. 1994. States and Social Evolution: Coffee and the Rise of National Governments in Central America. Chapel Hill: University of North Carolina Press.

Wilson, P. C. 2003. Ethnographic Museums and Cultural Commodification: Indigenous Organizations, NGOs and Culture as a Resource in Amazonian Ecuador. Latin American Perspectives 30:162–180.

9

Eritrea Goes Global

Reflections on Nationalism in a Transnational Era

Victoria Bernal

The May 1998 outbreak of war with Ethiopia over a disputed border generated an immediate outpouring of nationalist sentiment and money from Eritreans around the globe. In June 1998, for example, Eritreans met in Copenhagen and pledged $1,000 per household; in Riyadh they pledged one month's salary each; in Edmonton, Canada $26,000 was raised on the spot at a single meeting. Jubilant reports of these and other meetings circulated via the Internet on the U.S.-based Eritrean website, www.dehai.org. A message reporting on a meeting held in St. Louis on June 14 where $55,000 was pledged in two hours stated, "St. Louis resident Eritreans made history and a lesson to share with other brothers and sisters. This is something that all Eritreans need to emulate." The author signed off, saying "Proud to be Eritrean!!!" and "Awet n hizbi Eritrea. Zikri nswat Ahwatnan Ahatnan" (transliterated Tigrinya phrases that translate as "Victory to the Eritrean people" and "Remember our martyred brothers and sisters"). In response to these efforts, the Eritrean government promptly set up a national defense bank account and the donations flowed in. It is worth noting, moreover, that these donations were not earmarked as humanitarian aid to alleviate the suffering caused by war but were aimed at bolstering the Eritrean state's capacity to wage war. Tekie Beyene, governor of the Bank of Eritrea, described the contributions from the diaspora as "beyond anybody's imagination" (Voice of America, June 24, 1998). As these activities suggest, nationalism remains a burning passion for Eritreans and one that is not dimmed by their transnational mobility or participation in global circuits.

While globalization is thought to render borders meaningless, transnationalism to render nationhood passé, and the Internet to have ushered in a new era of openness and connectivity, the activities of the Eritrean diaspora and the Eritrean state point to the ways that nations not only continue to matter, but how nations can be constructed and strengthened through

Victora Bernal, "Eritrea Goes Global: Reflections on Nationalism in a Transnational Era," *Cultural Anthropology*, vol. 19, no. 1, pp. 3–25. Copyright © 2004 by American Anthropological Association. Reprinted with permission.

transnational flows and the technologies of globalization. For Eritreans, nationalism and trans-nationalism do not oppose each other but intertwine in complex ways in the globalized spaces of diaspora, in cyberspace, and in new definitions of citizenship and state-citizen relations advanced by the Eritrean state.

The Eritrean experience runs counter to common assumptions about the decline of nationalism and the decreasing importance of nation-states. Hannerz (1996), for example, argues that the rise of transnational connections is causing the nation to decline in importance. Appadurai contends that we are at the dawn of a "postnational era," in which "the nation-state, as a complex modern political form, is on its last legs" (1999:19) and that "globalization [is] a definite marker of a new crisis for the sovereignty of nation-states" (2000:4).

This article explores the relation between nationalism and transnational-ism in construc-tions of Eritrean nationhood. It seeks to reveal how and why nationalism and the nation-state remain significant for Eritreans not only despite global linkages but because of them. Situating this study of nationalism in the realm of the transnational has required me to shift frequently between a consideration of the ways in which Eritreans located in Eritrea, particularly members of the nationalist movement and the emergent Eritrean state, use and even construct transna-tional relations to achieve nationalist ends and a consideration of the ways in which Eritreans in diaspora construct nationalism and participate in Eritrean affairs from their transnational locations.

TRANSNATIONALISM, GLOBALIZATION, AND NATIONALISM

The concept of nation draws together various ideas including identity, community, sovereignty, and territory. As Verdery (1996:226-227) has pointed out, nation "names the relations be-tween states and their subjects and between states and other states." As a symbolic community, nation also refers to a collective identity of its members. As Verdery (1996:226) observes, "Nation is therefore an aspect of the political and symbolic/ideological order and also of the world of social interaction and feeling." She defines nationalism as "the political utilization of the symbol nation through discourse and political activity, as well as the sentiment that draws people into responding to this symbol's use" (Verdery 1996:227). In all of its meanings, nation is about boundaries, about inclusions and exclusions, about members and outsiders, about where one sovereignty ends and another begins.

Two influential formulations of transnationalism are those advanced by Appadurai (1999) and by Basch (1994). Appadurai sees transnationalism largely in terms of capital, ideas, and images flowing across national boundaries. Trans- nationalism, in this approach, is an abstract process of circulation that tells little about the actual lives and experiences of people. Such an approach dominates much of the literature on globalization that focuses on flows of capital, technology, and communications networks. In contrast, Basch (1994) defines transnational-ism as a social field created by people who live their lives by participating in more than one nation. This approach has the advantage of making people central and drawing attention to the agency of ordinary individuals in these global processes. But its emphasis on migration and on the activities of migrants in sustaining transnational social fields does not completely capture the sense in which we all live in a transnational era now whether we choose to or not, whether we migrate or remain where we are. The circulation of ideas, capital, and people shapes the character of life even for those who are relatively immobile.

Transnationalism, as I use the term, is not simply another way of talking about diaspora, or one's possession of deep ties to more than one nation, or one's membership in a family that spans more than one nation (though it includes all those things). Transnationalism refers to the fact of living a life that is not in any real sense circumscribed by a nation. As Ong (1999:4) observes, "*Trans* denotes both moving through space or across lines, as well as changing the nature of something." Transnationalism means our frames of reference for our own lives are not constructed on a national basis but in terms of standards, experiences, and concepts that include a larger world. Thus, I see transnationalism in such things as the consumption of foreign media and goods, in dependence on remittances from abroad, in the experience, desire, or expectation of international migration as part of one's life course, as well as in the reliance of local civil society initiatives on foreign donors and international aid. I see transnationalism in the fact that ideas about citizenship, rights, and entitlements, as well as visions of the good life more generally are not constructed wholly in local terms but rather constructed on a broader scale with reference to international standards, concepts, and comparisons, such that any local discussion of such things automatically implies this larger context.

In a literal sense, the term "trans/nationalism" as a description of our contemporary era draws attention to border crossings through evoking national borders. Globalization, on the other hand, suggests borderlessness, a unifying process in which distance and location no longer matter because everything and everyone on our planet are so tightly linked. Globalization was first used to refer to the worldwide integration of finance capital into a single system, but it was soon taken up by scholars in various disciplines as a shorthand reference to the ways that new technologies of information, communication, production, and transportation were transforming not only economic life but all spheres of life through what Harvey (1989) describes as the compression of time and space.

Nations, as systems linking identity, economy, and political order to specific geographical territories, seem to stand in logical opposition to transnationalism and globalization. It is thus not surprising that much scholarly attention has focused on the ways in which transnationalism and globalization undermine the nation and may be bringing about the demise of the nation-state. Yet already the early predictions of the end of nationalism seem simplistic and not particularly useful as guides to understanding the diverse kinds of cultural and economic transformations associated with transnationalism and globalization. Eritrean nationalism is useful as a guide to rethinking these complex relationships precisely because it appears to draw strength from the very processes of globalization and transnationalism that are often thought to undermine nation-states.

Research on Eritrea presents a number of challenges. During three decades of war little research of any kind was conducted by scholars and very little official data were recorded by governmental or international agencies. There are as yet no systematic, comprehensive accounts of the nationalist struggle, the EPLF (Eritrean People's Liberation Front) as a movement, or life in Eritrea during the independence struggle. Similarly, little data or research are available on the Eritrean diaspora. The decades of nationalist mobilization and war, moreover, have politicized knowledge about Eritrea. Scholars who focus on Eritrea usually have done so either because they are Eritrean or because they were inspired by the dedication and self-sacrifice of EPLF fighters. Thus, whether produced by Eritreans or outsiders, scholarship on Eritrea generally has been written from a position closer to advocacy than to critical analysis. Ethiopianist scholars and Eritreanist scholars, moreover, have fought their own battles on intellectual terrain. Unfortunately, in the absence of opportunities to conduct primary research, these scholarly arguments have largely been conducted in terms of legalistic intellectual arguments that have added little empirical knowledge.

The study of nationalism, transnationalism, the Internet, and diasporas raises additional methodological challenges in terms of how best to locate and demarcate one's object of study. I have worked to piece together a broad picture of the development of Eritrean nationalism as well as to focus in on particular vignettes, conversations, and Internet postings that shed led light on the relationships between nationalism and transnationalism in the Eritrean experience and to present this while developing an analytical framework for understanding the Eritrean experience in relation to scholarship on nationalism and transnationalism more generally.

My analysis of Eritrean nationalism derives from a diverse array of sources. I have been fortunate to have visited Eritrea three times: first, in 1981 under Ethiopian rule, followed by two research trips after independence, one in the winter of 1995-96 and another in the summer of 2001. I have conducted archival research using EPLF publications, published accounts of firsthand observers of the nationalist struggle, and the reports of international agencies. I have also been a participant observer of life in the Eritrean diaspora. I first became interested in Eritrea through meeting Eritreans in Europe in the mid- 1970s. When I returned to the United States for graduate school I got to know Eritreans in the Chicago area and have circulated on the periphery of the Eritrean diaspora for over twenty years. Although I am most familiar with the experiences of Eritreans in the United States, I have visited Eritrean homes in Canada, Germany, England, Italy, the Sudan, Tanzania, and Ethiopia. I have also met with Eritreans who live in Saudi Arabia, Sweden, and the Netherlands when they were visiting the United States or Eritrea. I have interviewed Eritreans from various walks of life both in Eritrea and in diaspora as well as Eritreans who resettled in Eritrea after many years abroad. I have followed postings and discussions in Eritrean cyberspace, particularly on Dehai.

The future of Eritrea continues to unfold in fascinating ways. However, I have limited this article to an analysis of Eritrean nationalism up to the end of the 1998-2000 border war with

Ethiopia, with particular attention to the 1990s when Eritrea achieved independence and national policies and practices began to be established by the new state.

The following section considers Eritrea's struggle for independence that gave rise to the particular forms of nationalism and transnationalism in which Eritreans are active. The article then focuses on the Eritrean diaspora, exploring their involvement in the nationalist struggle and the ways in which the Eritrean nation is built transnationally. Why was nationhood such a compelling goal for Eritreans and what is the significance of nationhood in the context of globalization and transnationalism? The section entitled "Nationalism in a Transnational Era" takes up these questions, arguing that Eritreans benefit from nationhood not because the nation is a world unto itself but because the nation is a key actor in the global arena. In the subsequent section, I explore the ways in which Eritreans located in Eritrea and in diaspora have appealed to international authorities and global audiences for support of their nationalist causes. Finally, I look at the ways in which the Eritrean state has taken legal measures to enfranchise the Eritrean diaspora and has created an institutional basis for nationhood that extends beyond national borders.

ERITREANS' STRUGGLE FOR NATIONHOOD

Eritrea achieved nationhood in the era of globalization, and its nationalist struggle was rooted in unprecedented ways: in international ideologies and discourses of nationhood, rights, and social justice, as well as in the transnational social fields created by Eritreans in diaspora and by the Eritrean People's Liberation Front.

Eritrea came into being as a political entity when Italy carved out a colonial territory along the western shores of the Red Sea. As Trevaskis (1960:10-11) puts it, "Italy created Eritrea by an act of surgery: by severing its different peoples from those with whom their past had been linked and by grafting the amputated remnants to each other under the title of Eritrean." The Italians ruled Eritrea from 1886 until 1941. In 1942, Eritrea passed from the Italians into the hands of the British who administered it as a trusteeship until 1952. Eritrea was then federated to Ethiopia under an arrangement that left considerable local autonomy. In 1962, Ethiopia violated the terms of federation and annexed Eritrea, which then remained officially a province of Ethiopia until, after three decades of war, Eritrea formally achieved independence and nationhood in 1993. The despotic rulers of Ethiopia, first Haile Selassie and, following his overthrow in 1974, the Dergue (the central committee of the military government) led by Colonel Mengistu Hailemariam pursued policies that made it appear that Eritrea could not thrive in unity with Ethiopia. For Eritreans, nationhood came to mean self-determination as opposed to domination by Ethiopia.

Eritrea's first major independence movement, the Eritrean Liberation Front (ELF), began the armed struggle in 1961. The Eritrean People's Liberation Front (EPLF), which ultimately succeeded in winning independence for Eritrea, first emerged as a splinter group that broke away from the ELF in 1971. While the ELF had the goal of independence from Ethiopia, the EPLF's vision was revolutionary; it sought to transform Eritrea from within as well as to free it from Ethiopian rule. Through the early 1970s, the ELF and the EPLF fought their own civil war from which the EPLF emerged as the primary liberation movement in Eritrea (Pateman 1990). From 1974 until the definitive military victory over the Dergue's forces in 1991, the EPLF led Eritrea's struggle for nationhood.

Eritreans' experience of the Italian colonial period laid the groundwork for forging a national identity separate from that of Ethiopia, despite much common cultural and religious heritage. Eritreans are neither homogeneous nor seamlessly united as a nation. In fact, the EPLF's construction of Eritrean nationhood sought to contain and control potential lines of internal conflict by formalizing Eritrean cultural diversity into nine officially recognized ethnic groups.[1] Eritrea is also divided almost evenly between Muslims and Christians, although Christians have historically dominated its political economy and continue to do so. The EPLF's emphasis on linguistic and cultural diversity served to divert attention from the potentially more volatile Muslim-Christian split. The EPLF and, subsequently, the government of Eritrea thus have sought to depoliticize diversity by incorporating it into the fabric of Eritrean national identity, defining Eritrea as a nation comprised of nine ethnic groups. In effect, Eritrea is a nation because Eritreans say they are and because they were able to take over the territory called Eritrea through military force and have, subsequently, gained international recognition.

In their nationalist struggle, Eritreans drew on transnational literatures, ideologies, and experiences of socialism and revolution. Nationalist rebels in Eritrea were deeply influenced by Marxist scholarship and by revolutionary struggles elsewhere. The ELF modeled its internal organization after that of Algeria's FLN (Markakis 1988). The EPLF translated key works of Marx, Engels, Lenin, and Mao into Tigrinya (Eritrea's major language), and EPLF communiqués and publications draw heavily from such sources. Some of the top cadres of EPLF, including its leader and Eritrea's current president, Isaias Afewerki, received training in China. Mao's book of sayings was popular among Eritrean student radicals and EPLF's use of slogans to sum up key policies was apparently modeled on Maoist practice (Markakis 1990). When I asked Saba, a woman ex-fighter about her experience as an EPLF guerilla in the field, she told me to read *Wild Swans* (Chang 1991), an account of women in the Cultural Revolution of China, saying "It was just like that." Saba is one of the Eritreans who left the United States to return to Eritrea and join the ranks of EPLF fighters in the field. Chang's book resonated with her own experience of being reprimanded for "bourgeois attitudes" and of having to serve under illiterate peasants.

During the war, tens of thousands of Eritreans joined the forces of the EPLF as fighters. Many others lived as civilians in "liberated areas" of Eritrea under EPLF control. Other civilians, like those in the capital city Asmara, continued to live directly under Ethiopian rule. The struggle against the Ethiopian forces was so protracted and so bitter that by the early 1980s when I first visited Eritrea, the Ethiopians had clearly become an occupying army in the eyes of most Eritreans. Indeed at the time of my visit, Ethiopia was preparing an offensive against the rebels, and the streets of Asmara were filled with vehicles moving troops. Sandbag bunkers and checkpoints outside of important buildings made palpable the sense of Asmara as an occupied city and the feeling of being under siege. Over the course of the long war many Eritreans migrated out of the country as refugees, were displaced within the country by the war, or left their homes in Ethiopia proper and within Eritrea to join the liberation struggle.

Thirty years of armed struggle ended in 1991 with the EPLF's military victory. Official independence was declared in 1993 after an internationally supervised national referendum, in which Eritreans voted overwhelmingly in favor of independence. Today the EPLF calls itself the PFDJ (People's Front for Democracy and Justice) and is in effect the ruling party of a one-party state.[2] Once independence was achieved, the fact that Eritrea's President, Isaias Afewerki, and his ruling party had been the victors who defeated the Ethiopian forces militarily lent the regime considerable legitimacy. Isaias Afewerki came to power, moreover, not simply as another African military leader but as the head of a popular mass movement. By the end of the war, the ranks of EPLF fighters numbered roughly 95,000 (Iyob 1997). It is estimated that more than 65,000 EPLF fighters died in the war (Woldegabriel 1993).

The history of nationalist mobilization by the EPLF and the protracted struggle against Ethiopian domination both gave rise to, and was made possible by, powerful nationalist sentiments among Eritreans. The struggle for independence did not simply liberate Eritrea from Ethiopian rule; it was also a process that created Eritrean nationhood from the ground up. Even as the EPLF claimed de jure nationhood based on Eritrea's colonial boundaries, the Front was engaged in constructing de facto nationhood through grassroots mobilization and political education. In the areas under its control, the EPLF operated like a proto-state, providing public services such as health care and carrying out a program of land reform among other things. Thus, well before the EPLF had established sovereignty over all of the territory of Eritrea militarily, thus legitimating its claim to nationhood by defeating the Ethiopian army, it had already constructed a proto-nation within Eritrea, with the Front acting not simply as an army or a guerilla movement but as an emergent national government performing administrative and public service functions.

The independence movement and the incipient nation developed by the EPLF were sustained in part by transnational linkages to the Eritrean diaspora. Thus, in some sense, Eritrean nationhood itself was built out of Eritreans' connections to one another (across borders) rather than on their connections to Eritrean soil (or to resources and livelihoods located within Eritrea). The Eritrean diaspora was an outgrowth of the nationalist struggle and at the same time a contributing factor to the survival of Eritrean nationalism.

THE ERITREAN DIASPORA: NATIONALIZING THE TRANSNATIONAL

While Anderson (1983) developed the concept of an "imagined community" as a way of talking about nationhood, it is immediately clear that this notion also lends itself to conceptualizing transnational, de-territorialized communities and identities. If nations do not naturally grow out of the soil but are products of cultural imagination, there is no reason why imaginations cannot jump oceans, political borders, and other barriers in creating community. The technological advances of globalization, rather than eroding Eritreans' ties to their place of origin, make it all the more feasible for them to participate in Eritrean nationhood across political boundaries and geographical barriers.

UNICEF (1994) estimates that one million Eritreans fled their country, which amounted to nearly one out of every three Eritreans at the time of independence. As with most things concerning Eritrea, data on the diaspora are hard to come by. Prior to Eritrea's official independence in 1993, for example, the United States recorded information on Eritrean refugees under the Ethiopian category, so there is no official record of Eritreans in the United States as a group over the course of the independence struggle. The number of "Ethiopians" living in the United States was estimated at between 50,000 and 75,000 in 1991 (Woldemikael 1996). The Sudan was the country most accessible to Eritreans, since the two countries share a border. There, too, the United Nations High Commissioner for Refugees (UNHCR) figures do not distinguish Eritreans from Ethiopians. In 1984 there were 465,000 "Ethiopian" refugees in Sudan (Kibreab 1984:72), the majority of whom were Eritreans. The Sudan also served as a way station, since many Eritreans who fled to the Sudan were eventually able to gain admittance to the countries of North America and Europe as refugees, political asylees, or immigrants. Some Eritreans, particularly Muslims, were able to find employment in Saudi Arabia and the Gulf states. After Sudan, the next greatest concentration of Eritreans outside of Eritrea is in the United States.

The earliest group of Eritreans to come to the United States did not come as refugees but as students who came to study and ended up stranded in exile in the United States. After the Dergue came to power in 1974, Mengistu took Haile Selassie's battle against Eritrean nationalism to new extremes, regarding anyone of Eritrean descent as suspect. The Eritrean students generally came from among the more well-to-do urban segments of the Eritrean population. The selection practices used by the United States to screen refugees also gave preference to those with education and skills and therefore the Eritreans who came to the United States as refugees also tend to be more educated than the average Eritrean. Both the students and the refugees were predominantly male, since Eritrean women had less access to education. It would be a distortion, however, to describe the majority of the Eritrean diaspora in the United States as coming from elite backgrounds. They more commonly come from what could be seen as African middle-class or petit-bourgeois backgrounds. In terms of their class positions in the United States, the majority are far from privileged. Very few Eritreans hold professional jobs. Eritreans are concentrated in the service sector and are often underemployed (Woldemikael 1996). They typically work as parking lot attendants, taxi drivers, and hotel staff.

Even though Eritreans are relatively few in number, they have clustered in several urban areas, most notably Washington, D.C. By means of residential clustering, long-distance telephone contact, and later through the Internet, Eritreans have been able to maintain close social links to other Eritreans. Political organizations, meetings, and rallies, as well as social ceremonial occasions such as weddings, have served to bring larger numbers of Eritreans together periodically and have fostered communal networks.

Eritreans in diaspora, while physically removed from the battlefront, played vital roles in the liberation struggle. Eritreans around the world (particularly Eritreans in North America, Europe, and the Gulf states) contributed to the nationalist struggle through the resources they collected and donated and through the public relations campaigns they waged (Clapham 2000; Cliffe 1988; Woldemikael 1991). Eritreans in diaspora organized themselves politically wherever they were, sent their own money to the Front, organized fun- draising campaigns, and sought to educate the world about the Eritrean cause. Social networks and nationalist organizations linked Eritreans to each other and to the EPLF. Exiled Eritreans, moreover, were expected to pay a yearly tax of 2 percent of their gross income to the Front.[3] During the war, Eritreans held annual festivals in Bologna, Italy, which brought together EPLF representatives and exiles from around the world. The EPLF was extremely successful in mobilizing the diaspora and harnessing their skills and resources for the nationalist cause. While solidly based within Eritrea, the EPLF extended far beyond Eritrea's borders and maintained a transnational network of communication with Eritreans in many countries. For Eritreans living abroad, their connections to the nationalist movement served as an organizing force in the experience of diaspora and facilitated their contact with other Eritreans, helping to create a sense of community and purpose.

Perhaps the significance of the nation becomes more clear in its absence: the experiences of the many Eritreans who lived as refugees, exiles, and undocumented immigrants during the three decades of war provide a sobering picture of the vulnerability of those who occupy interstitial positions in the nation-state system. The conditions experienced by Eritreans in diaspora are diverse. Among the most miserable were those trapped in refugee camps in the Sudan (Kibreab 1984, 1997), some of whom I met while conducting fieldwork in Sudan in the early 1980s. Those living without proper documents in the West suffered in less extreme ways. Even Eritreans fortunate enough to be accepted legally as refugees in Canada and wealthy northern European states with generous social welfare programs suffered. For example, I think of the family I visited in Germany in 1982 whose lack of material want only seemed to highlight the intangible losses of community, belonging, and culture that they deeply felt. The isolation, discrimination, and disenfranchisement experienced by Eritrean refugees suggest the dystopic underside of transnationalism, one in which mobility means displacement and alienation, when the nation is not so much a "cage" to be broken out of, to use Nairn's (1996) metaphor, but a space of belonging and entitlement. Some of the experiences of Eritreans in diaspora have thus fostered Eritrean nationalist sentiment because of the racism and exclusionary practices Eritreans encountered and continue to encounter in other countries. In fact, many of the most ardent Eritrean nationalists grew up in Ethiopia proper. National identity and nationalist sentiments in the case of Eritreans must clearly be seen in processual and relational terms. Conditions of exile fostered Eritreans' identification with other Eritreans and with their nation even as they adopted other legal nationalities, made new lives for themselves, and sometimes intermarried with non-Eritreans. Exile also served to make the cultural divisions among Eritreans pale beside all they have in common with each other in contrast to the host societies in which they live. Thus, it seems at times that Eritrean identity makes all Eritreans kin, so that nationalism is as much a social identity as a political one.

For many of the Eritreans in diaspora to whom I have spoken, the Eritrean nationalist cause and Eritrea's survival as a nation have deep personal and emotional meaning. Their connection to Eritrea goes beyond any pragmatic concerns such as personal intentions to return to Eritrea permanently or the well-being of their kin who remain in Eritrea. Their passion for Eritrean nationalism and Eritrean politics is evidenced by, among other things, the time and resources they devoted to the nationalist struggle and, more recently, to the 1998-2000 war. The importance of Eritrean identity in their lives is shown in the efforts Eritreans make to sustain social and political networks across vast distances and to build some sense of community with other Eritreans wherever they find themselves.

The first major Eritrean website, Dehai (www.dehai.org), was initiated by Eritreans in the Washington, D.C., area in 1992 and remained for many years the predominant Internet link for Eritreans in diaspora around the world. Eritreans within Eritrea, however, could not get online until 2000. Dehai is subtitled "Eritrea Online" and has two main components: news that consists of postings of published news related to Eritrea from diverse sources and a message board devoted to political discussion. Both of these are also archived. Postings on the message board include simple statements of opinion, complex political analyses, debates, witty repartee, and poetry, as well as announcements of Eritrea-related activities or holidays. Although many messages are ardent, sincere statements, there is also a liberal use of irony, satire, and hyperbole to ridicule the views of opponents in debates. This, aside from its informative nature, is what makes Dehai entertaining for readers. For active posters, discussions and debates offer a chance to display their wit, expert wordplay, political astuteness, historical knowledge, mastery of folklore and proverbs, and more. As is general with such discussion sites, the number of passive readers is believed to be far greater than the number of posters. According to some of its founders, Dehai averaged 37 postings per day from its inception in 1992 to 2001 (Bushra 2001). The Dehai charter posted in 1995 states: "The main objective is to provide a forum for interested Eritreans and non-Eritreans to engage in solving Eritrea's problems by sharing information, discussing issues, publicizing and participating in existing projects and proposing ideas for future projects."

It is telling that Eritreans in diaspora established the Dehai website and subsequently other websites and discussion lists to discuss and disseminate news about Eritrean politics rather than to share information and ideas about the many issues that confront them in their daily lives in North America and Europe. Through their activities on behalf of Eritrea and their use of cyberspace, Eritreans in diaspora nationalize the transnational, creating national spaces and pursuing nationalist goals within and across transnational space.

If nations are declining in significance as globalization erodes their sovereignty and transnationalism transcends their borders, then how do we explain why Eritreans are willing to give so much and even to die for this idea of nation? In our post-Marxist era we cannot simply resort to labels of "false consciousness." We therefore have to take nationalism seriously and account for the fact that nationhood still holds a great appeal for many people. A conversation I had over 20 years ago with some Eritreans has stayed in my mind. At the time I was a student in Europe and had been struck by the ardent nationalism expressed by various Eritreans I encountered there. The Eritreans I met were eager to enlighten anyone who would listen about the Eritrean struggle for independence. Often they had flyers and posters celebrating and explaining their cause. One day I finally said to a group of Eritreans who, as I now remember it, were passing out leaflets in Copenhagen, "I don't get it. *Why* do you want a nation so badly?" One quickly replied, "You don't understand why *we* want a nation so badly, because *you* already have one."

Now Eritreans have a nation. It would be a cruel irony if, just as they finally realized their goal, nationhood as a global political currency were devalued. But has it been? The fragmentation of larger political units such as the Soviet Union (and in the Eritrean context, Ethiopia) may not signal the demise of the nation but, on the contrary, indicate that nations are so key to jockeying for position in the global arena that everyone wants to have one of their own. Eritreans attacked Ethiopia's nationhood, but they did so even as they reaffirmed nationhood as the most desirable form of political organization. And while critics tried to point out the absurdity of Eritrean nationhood (due to its lack of linguistic, cultural, or religious homogeneity, and a very small territory), they stopped short of recognizing the absurdity (or at least arbitrariness) of all nations. African nations are perhaps exceptionally arbitrary since they were carved out by European powers without reference to local linguistic or ethnic boundaries. Within that context, Eritrea's internal diversity is nothing out of the ordinary. Africa, moreover, abounds with stateless ethnicities, and there is no widespread assumption on that continent that every "people" should have its own nation-state. In fact, I would argue that Eritreans' claim to nationhood stands apart from some of the other movements also seeking to break away from Ethiopia precisely because Eritreans did not simply mobilize around an ethnicity as did the Oromo, for example, but mobilized around the cause of an Eritrean nation that does not define itself on the basis of ethnic homogeneity.

Nationhood is valued by Eritreans, not because a nation constitutes a community unto itself but, on the contrary, precisely because the nation is a key actor in the global arena (cf. Brenner 1997). In this respect, nations may be even more important for poor countries, such as Eritrea, than for countries whose nationals are part of the global capitalist elite. The Secretary-General of the United Nations, Boutros Boutros-Ghali, has stated:

> With its transition from de facto to legally recognized independence, Eritrea has gained formal access to direct international lending by the World Bank and other

intergovernmental institutions, *as only States are eligible for such assistance....* The international community has provided essential political and material backing for Eritrea's emergence from war. ... It should sustain this effort with similar commitment as Eritrean nation-building enters a new and decisive phase. [Boutros-Ghali 1996:37, emphasis added]

The nation-state system is such that even the government of a small, poor, and fairly powerless nation can use its status as a sovereign power to advantage. Eritrea has refused to be a passive "beneficiary" of Western largesse and has shown a willingness to forgo aid if it comes at the expense of local sovereignty. After independence, the government of Eritrea quickly earned a reputation in international circles for being an absolutely tough negotiator that is willing to forgo any aid or project over which it does not exercise control. For example, as one UN worker based in Eritrea told me, agencies arrive in Eritrea with "terms of reference" that are general guidelines they are accustomed to applying unilaterally. "The Eritreans categorically reject those; they come to meetings prepared with their own terms of reference."

Dr. Isaak Woldab, president of Asmara University, echoed sentiments expressed by other Eritreans with whom I talked when he told me, "We don't want a donor-recipient relationship. People are not used to this from a Third World country. But we want to make our own decisions and administer things ourselves. So, anything we do must be done on an equal footing" (interview, January 14, 1996). Of course, Eritrea is not truly on equal footing—its per capita income is half the average of sub-Saharan Africa, for example. The only leg Eritrea has to stand on to claim equal footing at all is that it *is* a nation.

No one who visited Eritrea under Ethiopian rule and again after independence could doubt that, overall, Eritreans will benefit from having a nation of their own. By 1996 (three years after independence), when I traveled to independent Eritrea for the first time, there were already many new schools, new health clinics, and more running water throughout the country. And, whatever their feelings, none of the Eritreans I have met want fewer schools.

The nation of Eritrea allows Eritreans to negotiate some aspects of their position in the world. As a nation, Eritrea certainly participates in a global political economy dominated by more powerful nations and therefore operates under great constraints. Nonetheless, the fact that Eritreans as a nation can make their own development plans and negotiate their own deals with the World Bank and with foreign investors and donors appears to be greatly advantageous when compared to their historical experience as a region of Ethiopia. Roberts (1998) has written about "the New Global Manager" being promoted as the model for leadership in U.S. corporations and business schools. The hallmarks of the global manager—flexibility and a global perspective—suggest another way of thinking about the nation-state and transnationalism. The Eritrean state itself acts like a global manager. Rather than linking itself as a satellite or client to any one economic or political patron, as many postcolonial states did in the early days of neocolonialism, the Eritrean state has a flexible global vision. Its managers attempt to promote Eritrea's interests by skillfully maneuvering everything: from Korean investment to Finnish aid to Kuwaiti loans. At a 1998 "Meeting of Eritrea's Development Partners" that included the World Bank, the IMF, the International Finance Corporation, the European Union, and UN agencies, President Isaias Afewerki stated:

> We are limiting the role of government to creating a conducive environment for development. ... It will undertake critical investments in strategic sectors of the economy only when private investors are either unwilling or unable. ... I would like to emphasize here that our policy is to treat foreign investors exactly in the same manner as we treat domestic investors. [1998:21]

The president's statement highlights the model of the nation with open borders in which the government's role is to facilitate transnational economic flows. Eritrea's leaders have not fully embraced neoliberal logics of development, however. In real terms, the Eritrean state lacks sufficient resources to function as a developmentalist state, so it must court investors and exercise its economic leadership through skillful management of these external relations.

The notion of Eritrea and the World Bank as "partners" is not mere rhetoric from the Eritrean perspective, moreover, but consistent with Eritreans' refusal to accept external domination despite the small size of their economy, territory, and population. As one report on Eritrea's foreign investment climate notes, "A primary tenet of the government is that Eritrea is for Eritreans. Projects will be examined to ensure that the plans include training Eritrean staff to replace expatriate workers and that the projects will not negatively effect the environment or local conditions" (www.countrywatch.com, 2000). While courting foreign investment, President Isaias has been an outspoken critic of aid as "disabling, dehumanizing, and very restrictive" and of donors who he says seek to "substitute themselves for the government" (Euromoney 1998).

Eritreans developed self-reliance as a strategy and a virtue when the EPLF had to survive largely without foreign support. But that stance, like that of the Eritrean state today, was made possible in part due to the resources channeled into Eritrea by Eritreans in diaspora. Even as the Eritrean state seeks to avoid dependence upon foreign powers, its ability to do so is sustained to a considerable extent by transnational flows of resources from Eritreans abroad.

OLIVER STONE'S NEXT MOVIE?: ERITREA AND THE GLOBAL AUDIENCE

Anderson's (1983) analysis of the role of print capitalism (particularly newspapers and novels) in constructing national communities suggests that nations are, among other things, stories we tell ourselves. But he dealt largely with the imagining of the national community as an internal cultural process rather than as a political struggle involving contestants and participants in diverse transnational locations. By contrast, in the case of Eritrea, nationhood developed through a long 30-year war of independence in contest with Ethiopian claims to the same territory.

Eritreans had to articulate a story of Eritrean nationhood not only to themselves but to a global audience. The United States, the Soviet Union (which backed Ethiopia), and international bodies such as the UN and the OAU (Organization of African Unity) were crucial participants and observers of Eritreans' struggle for independence (Habte Selassie 1989; United Nations 1996). Eritreans developed their claims to nationhood in an international context, moreover, that (until the break-up of the Soviet Union) regarded existing national boundaries as sacrosanct. The OAU tended to dismiss the Eritrean movement as secessionist because the OAU honored colonial boundaries at the time of independence as the basis of African nations (Mbembe 2000; Pool 1983). The narratives Eritreans construct about Eritrea as a nation are thus more complicated and problematic than Anderson's notion of imagined community and are much more clearly addressed to international audiences as well as to fellow Eritreans.

The EPLF recognized early on that to succeed fully they had to construct a narrative of Eritrean nationalism that appealed to global audiences. The account of how Eritreans achieved national sovereignty over the course of 30 years is thus not simply one of war. It is also an account of how the EPLF successfully waged a war of words on the international scene, learning how to express their claims to nationhood in ways that would be recognized as legitimate by the UN, the World Court, and the OAU (Habte Selassie 1989; Iyob 1995). Parallel to their military struggle, Eritreans conducted information campaigns asserting the legitimacy of the Eritrean cause to various audiences, from the men or women in the streets of North America and Europe to governments, international organizations, and scholarly circles.

There is a revealing parody in a zine produced by an Eritrean in diaspora in the United States with the title, "Oliver Stone's Next Movie" (Eritrean Exponent 1993). The premise of the piece is the author pitching the story of Eritrea's struggle for independence to Oliver Stone as a movie project. At one point in the text, Stone asks "Is it imperialist whites against native blacks?" [No.] "Moslems against Christians?" [No.] "So, what's the hook, babe?" The author attempts to interest Stone by describing the incredible military odds the Eritreans were up against, the unique role that women played in combat, and so on. But, Stone's response is: "Boring, boring, boring! Darling, I think we are wasting each other's time ... How could this possibly interest my audience? ... A bunch of black Africans kill another bunch of black Africans ... Can we possibly tie this with white people, somehow?"

The parody points up the fact that Eritreans know they have to play to a global audience that is dominated by Western concerns and categories. Part of being an Eritrean is having to explain yourself and doing so in terms of categories imposed by others. The parody works as a piece of humor in the diaspora not least because it echoes the questions Eritreans are so often asked. Ultimately, the parody pokes fun at the painful indifference of the West to Eritrean experience and suffering or, for that matter, to Eritrean existence at all.

The 1998 outbreak of war with Ethiopia once again moved Eritreans to mobilize transnationally and to appeal to global audiences. Ethiopia and Eritrea both waged public relations campaigns in the international media that served as a second battle front as each one accused the other of being the aggressor and of lying about victories and losses. Dehai devoted considerable space to the conflict, including a link titled simply "Ethiopian lies." One message posted on Dehai expressed typical sentiments of outrage at Ethiopia and described the special role of Eritreans in diaspora:

> Today Eritreans in the diaspora have recommitted ourselves to shoulder the responsibility of defending the motherland by assuming ambassadorial responsibilities which include exposing TPLF crimes over Eritreans residing in Ethiopia.[4] If there is anything that the successive Ethiopian governments have mastered, it is deceiving the world community through absolute lies! ... Ethiopia keeps on spending an astronomical amount of money to disseminate false information. [Dehai, posted August 4, 1998]

On June 16, 2000, Eritreans organized a demonstration in front of UN headquarters in New York to protest the UN's "silence and inaction" on behalf of Eritrea (Dehai, posted June 14, 2000). One Dehai participant went so far as to argue that Eritreans should "sue the UN ... in a court of law for gross negligence and breach of contract" for failing to intervene on Eritrea's behalf. The writer went on to speculate as to whether a U.S. court could hear the case, since UN headquarters are located in the United States, or if the case would have to go to "the International Court of Justice" and whether Eritreans in North America could bring the case to court if the Eritrean government did not do so (De- hai, posted June 9, 2000). The author's mixture of savvy and naivete seems to capture something of how Eritreans continue to explore new means of using international institutions and reaching global audiences on behalf of their nationalist goals. Eritreans, it would seem, have reversed the 1980s saying, "think globally, act locally." As Eritrean nationalists, they think in terms of national interests but act globally in terms of the strategies and discourses they employ to achieve nationalist ends. Moreover, whereas in the original phrase, locality referred to a concrete place while globality was an abstract imaginary, in the 21st century we now experience the global on a daily basis, while local loyalties and identities are often both imagined and deterritorialized.

THE TRANSNATIONALIZATION OF THE NATION: NEW FORMS OF CITIZENSHIP ACROSS BORDERS

Like the EPLF before it, the Eritrean state is active in promoting transnational nationalist networks and maintaining links to Eritreans in diaspora. The transnationalization of Eritrean nationhood therefore cannot simply be equated with the existence of an Eritrean diaspora that dreams of "home." It must also be seen as stemming from the character of the EPLF/PFDJ as a nationalist organization that developed a global reach and a global strategy for promoting Eritrea's national interests.

The Eritrean state has, for example, created new legal frameworks and institutional practices to incorporate members of the diaspora into the Eritrean nation. One of the first decrees of the provisional Government of Eritrea after independence was a law defining citizenship that stated that "any person born to a father or a mother of Eritrean origin in Eritrea or abroad is an Eritrean national by birth" (Referendum Commissioner of Eritrea 1993). The Eritrean state thus constructed a new definition of citizenship to encompass a wide range of people of Eritrean descent who reside outside of Eritrea and hold other national identities. The new citizenship law, moreover, did not seek to compel Eritreans settled overseas to choose between Eritrean citizenship and their current legal national identities. Eritreans in diaspora were entitled to national I.D. cards issued by the Eritrean government without having to renounce any other passports they held. The problem of dual citizenship was thus neatly finessed since the Eritrean I.D. card recognizes the individual as an Eritrean citizen for national purposes but has no effect on their other status. For Eritreans in diaspora, this means that in Eritrean matters they are recognized as Eritreans but for other purposes they can continue to enjoy the benefits of U.S., Canadian, or whatever citizenship they hold.

Since independence, the Eritrean government has also recruited numerous Eritreans from the diaspora to fill key government positions. Eritreans from the diaspora thus make up part of the Eritrean state machinery. Perhaps even more noteworthy is that Eritreans in Southern California (where I live) and throughout the diaspora participate officially in national politics. For example, in 1993, polls were set up in Los Angeles so that Eritreans here could vote in the national referendum on independence. In fact, Eritreans cast their referendum votes in North America, Europe, the Middle East, and Africa as well as in Australia, New Zealand, India, and Russia (United Nations 1996). The Eritrean government routinely sends representatives abroad to brief Eritreans overseas on what the government is doing and to cultivate their continued political and financial support. In 1994 and 1995, the Constitution Commission of Eritrea, which is the official body charged with drafting Eritrea's new constitution, held civic education seminars not only in each of Eritrea's 9 provinces[5] but in 11 U.S. cities, 14 European cities, and 4 Middle Eastern cities, as well as in Kenya and the Sudan (Constitution Committee of Eritrea 1995). In May 1997, following the ratification of the constitution, a Transitional National Assembly was formed to serve as the legislative body until countrywide elections to the National Assembly could be held. The Transitional National Assembly included 15 representatives of Eritreans living abroad (CIA 2002).

It is estimated that Eritreans in diaspora remit between US$250 and US$350 million each year (Nelson 2000), while Eritrea's GDP is pegged at about US$650 million (World Bank 1999). (By comparison, diasporic Jews remit around US$400 million each year to Israel [letter to author, May 20, 1998]). When one considers the poor economic position of most Eritreans and their relatively small numbers, these figures are impressive. No one knows the full extent of transnational transfers from the diaspora to Eritrea. As became clear from U.S. investigations into resource transfers by Islamic organizations in the aftermath of September 11, there are various means of channeling funds across international borders outside of any regulatory institutions. Through personal networks and the telephone, large sums can be transferred quite easily, quickly, and inexpensively.[6] Such transactions could be seen as undermining the Eritrean state since they bypass state authority and possible taxation. But ultimately the resource transfers to Eritrea help sustain the local economy. Thus far, the government of Eritrea has therefore made little attempt to control these flows.

The nation of Eritrea has thus developed novel institutional practices and new legal frameworks to encompass diasporas, developments that at some level can be seen as constructing a "deterritorialized nationality" or transnational nation. Eritrea's definition of citizenship is based on descent rather than residence or place of birth, and it is not exclusive. It therefore enfranchises as citizens people who reside in other nations, including those who hold citizenship in other nations and including people of Eritrean descent who have never lived in independent Eritrea and may never do so. The Eritrean nation is thus in various ways organizing itself around transnational linkages, resource flows, and globalizing technologies rather than being broken up by them.

CONCLUSION

The relationship between nations and transnationalism has been recently addressed by a number of scholars who are moving beyond the simple question of whether transnationalism means a decline of the nation to theorizing the complex relationship between transnational phenomena and nationhood. Glick-Schiller argues that transnational migration does not reflect the decline of the nation-state, "On the contrary, transmigrants helped construct nation- states in many regions of the world in the past and are active participants in the constitution of transnational nation-states" (1999a:99). Glick-Schiller's use of the term transnational nation-states draws attention to the ways that nations and nationalism can operate across borders. She gives the example of Haiti, where official discourse seeks to construct Haitians who have emigrated as part of an overseas *departement* of Haiti proper (Glick-Schiller 1999b). Fandy's (1999) study of Saudi opposition in exile and cyberspace is an example of how citizens who live outside their national territory continue to participate in significant ways in national economies and politics. This Saudi example points up the fact that diasporas can also contest national governments, but they generally do so as nationalists seeking to dismantle particular regimes, not the nation itself. Although war may have served to unite Eritreans in diaspora in the effort to assure Eritrea's emergence and survival as a nation, diasporas may be rent by profound political divisions. It is not the homogeneity of their political views, however, that constitute some diasporas as national or nationalist and as significant transnational actors in national politics. Even politically divided diasporas are engaged in national politics to the extent that they are entangled with one another in debates and conflict over diverging visions regarding the future of their common nation.

On the other side of things, states also seek to control and discipline nationals beyond their geographical borders. The old model of a nation was that of a territory inhabited by citizens and administered by a national government that provided services to those citizens—each layer fitting neatly over the next. Globalization and transnationalism have uprooted these relations, creating looser arrangements of relationships in process (Ong 1999).

Sassen has helpfully pointed out that the global and the national are not discrete, mutually exclusive conditions, but rather they "overlap and interact in ways that distinguish our contemporary moment" (2000:215). While Sassen argues that assumptions of "the nation-state as a container, representing a unified spatiotemporality" were never quite accurate, she suggests that a process of "incipient and partial denationalization of domains" is underway (2000: 215-216). Sassen is particularly concerned here with the insertion of global projects into national space, whereas I am equally concerned with the projection of nationalism across transnational space. Thus, while Sassen sees a process of "denationalization" of national space, I see a simultaneous process of nationalizing transnational spaces in that transnational movements of people, resources, and communications are being used to further various nationalist projects.

Several interrelated themes emerge from this analysis of Eritrean nationalism. One theme is the transnational terrain of nationhood or the ways in which nationhood is constructed and sustained by Eritreans' relations to one another across borders. A second theme is the nationalization of the transnational or the ways in which certain transnational phenomena can serve to reinforce the national. Here, the activities of the Eritrean diaspora and their use of cyberspace for nationalist purposes stand out, as well as the ways the nationalist movement within Eritrea and subsequently the Eritrean state organized transnational networks of Eritreans. A third theme is the transnationalization of the nation-state or the ways in which new legal frameworks, institutional practices, and state-citizen relations are emerging in response to transnational relations and global processes.

The Eritrean experience suggests that as transnationalism and globalization reconfigure state-society relations, the nation becomes at once larger, including many citizens who reside outside its borders as active participants in national political and economic life, and smaller, in the sense that the national government is less determinant of the conditions in which its citizens live, whether inside or outside its borders, because transnational capital, media, culture, consumer goods, and ideologies operate in ways that cannot be controlled by any one nation or stopped at the border. In this sense, the nation has become more diffuse, more flexible, more porous. It has changed form but it has not necessarily been diminished. The national government's key role now may be that of managing transnational capital and international relations.

The case of Eritrea is more than simply how the global story plays out in a remote location. It can help us think about processes of globalization and the relation between nations and transnationalism in a productive way. As the example of Dehai illustrates, even the transnational and deterritorialized space of cyberspace is, among other things, a ground on which can be projected national imaginaries. Globalization and transnationalism have not replaced nationalism but have opened up new spaces in which nationalisms can be expressed, contested, and transformed.

Constructions of globalization, transnationalism, and the wired world that emphasize their un-boundedness and their unifying and universalizing effects are overlooking the very powerful ways in which people reinscribe difference and belonging, imagine boundaries, and construct territorial loyalties and identities, even as they engage in global processes and inhabit transnational spaces.

Perhaps this article has focused on what can be seen as a surprising set of circumstances that have allowed Eritrean nationalism to feed off of transnationalism and these historical circumstances will change. That should serve, nonetheless, to bring home the lesson that even huge global processes such as globalization and transnationalism do not stand outside of history and create the world we inhabit but are themselves socially produced and must be localized and historicized to be understood.

Therefore, rather than seeking to generalize about globalization and trans- nationalism as global phenomena, we need to study various transnational experiences and communities in order to elucidate what the new potentialities of space-time compression actually mean for different populations in various contexts. We also need to attend to the shifting terrains of nations and nationalism within processes of globalization. We need to approach nations and nationalism as something much more fluid, contextual, and relational, recognizing the porosity of borders and the shifting goals and capacities of states. It seems that transnationalism and globalization have not rendered nations and nationalism obsolete, but perhaps they have rendered some of our ways of thinking about nations obsolete.

NOTES

I am grateful to the Program in Global Peace and Conflict Studies at University of California, Irvine, for grants that supported my research in Eritrea in the winter of 1996 and the summer of 2001 and to the University of California's Institute on Global Conflict and Cooperation for their support of my research in Eritrea in summer 2001. My heartfelt thanks to Tekle Woldemikael for his generosity in sharing his wealth of knowledge and his extensive archive on Eritrean nationalist movements with me. Many thanks to Nina Glick-Schiller and Susan Coutin who read and commented on earlier versions of this article. Thanks to the many Eritreans in Eritrea and in diaspora whose hospitality over the years has made my research possible and enjoyable.

1. The EPLF's adoption of the Soviet practice of using "nationality" to refer to cultural diversity within the nation can be a source of confusion for some observers. These lines of division among Eritreans would be more commonly understood as ethnicities in contemporary terms, while Nadel (1943) in his work for the British colonial administration in Eritrea called them "tribes."
2. The PFDJ explicitly calls itself a Front and not a party. In that sense, and perhaps only in that sense, it can be asserted that Eritrea is not a one-party state.
3. Specific information on compliance is scant. There is no doubt, however, that large numbers of Eritreans abroad gave money to the EPLF.
4. TPLF stands for the Tigrean People's Liberation Front, which was the Ethiopian movement allied with the EPLF. The TPLF toppled the dictatorship of Mengistu in Ethiopia and took power there following the definitive military defeat of Ethiopian forces in Eritrea by the EPLF. The writer who posted this is probably well aware that the ruling party in Ethiopia now calls itself the Ethiopian People's Revolutionary Democratic Front.
5. The internal regional administrative divisions have since been changed.
6. One method used by Eritreans to transfer funds from the United States is simple. I give money or a check to your relative here and your relative in Eritrea (most likely a merchant or someone else with cash on hand) gives funds to my relative there. The hard currency in the United States might then be used to purchase goods overseas for the merchant's business in Eritrea.

REFERENCES CITED

Afwerki, Isaias. 1998. "Recent Developments in the Eritrean Economy and the Challenges and Prospects for Long-Term Growth." Opening Remarks to the Meeting of Eritrea's Development Partners, Asmara, Eritrea, November 2.

Anderson, Benedict. Imagined Communities: Reflections on the Origin and Spread of Nationalism. London: Verso, 1983.

Appadurai, Arjun. 1999. Modernity at Large: Cultural Dimensions of Globalization. Minneapolis: University of Minnesota Press.

———"Grassroots Globalization and the Research Imagination." Public Culture 12(1):1-20.

Basch, Linda, with Nina Glick-Schiller and Cristina Szanton Blanc. 1994. Nations Unbound: Transnational Projects, Postcolonial Predicaments, and Deterritorialized Nation-States. London: Routledge.

Boutros-Ghali, Boutros, 1996. Conclusion. In The United Nations and the Independence of Eritrea. United Nations Blue Book Series, 12. Pp. 36-37. New York: United Nations, Department of Public Information.

Brenner, Neil. 1997. Global, Fragmented, Hierarchical: Henri Lefebvre's Geographies of Globalization. PublicCulture 10(1):135-167.

Bushra, Ibrahim, with Ephrem Tekle, Ghidewon Asmerom, and Mengis Samuel. 2001. "The Internet and Computing Environment in Eritrean Cyberspace: Past Experiences and Future Directions." Paper presented at the 1st International Conference of the Eritrean Studies Association, Asmara, Eritrea, July 22-26.

CCE (Constitutional Commission of Eritrea). 1995. "Information on Strategy, Plans, and Activities." Asmara, Eritrea: CCE.

CIA (Central Intelligence Agency), "The World Factbook: Eritrea." 2002. Electronic document, http://www.cia.gov/cia/publications/factbook/geos/er.html, accessed February 15.

Chang, Jung. Wild Swans. New York: Simon and Schuster, 1991.

Clapham, Christopher. "War and State Formation in Ethiopia and Eritrea." Paper presented at the CERI Colloquium: La guerre entre le local et le global—Societes, Etats, Systemes, Paris, May 29-30, 2000.

Cliffe, Lionel. "The Eritrean Liberation Struggle in Comparative Perspective," in The Long Struggle of Eritrea, Lionel Cliffe and Basil Davidson, eds. Pp. 87-103. Trenton, NJ: Red Sea Press, 1988.

Countrywatch.com. "Eritrea." Electronic document, http://www.countrywatch.com/em, accessed February 15, 2002.

Eritrean Exponent (zine). "Eritrean Exponent," May/June. Cupertino, CA: self-published, 1993.

Euromoney. 1998. "Africa: Leaders of Africa's New Deal." Electronic document, http://www. emwl.com, accessed July 9.

Fandy, Mamoun. "CyberResistance: Saudi Opposition between Globalization and Localization." 1999. Comparative Studies in Society and History 41(1):124-147.

Glick-Schiller, Nina. "Transmigrants and Nation-States: Something Old and Something New in the U.S. Immigrant Experience," The Handbook of International Migration. Charles Hirschmann, Philip Kasinitz, and Josh Dewind, eds. Pp. 94-119. New York: Russel Sage, 1999.

———"Who Are These Guys? A Transnational Perspective on National Identities," Identities on the Move: Transnational Processes in North America and the Caribbean Basin. Liliana Goldin, ed. Pp. 18-32. Austin: University of Texas Press and the Institute for Mesoamerican Studies, SUNY Albany, 1999.

Habte Selassie Bereket, Eritrea and the United Nations. 1989. Trenton, NJ: Red Sea Press.

Hannerz, Ulf. 1996. Transnational Connections. London: Routledge.

Harvey, David. 1989. Condition of Postmodernity. London: Oxford University Press.

Iyob, Ruth. The Eritrean Struggle for Independence. Cambridge: Cambridge University Press, 1995.

———1997. "The Eritrean Experiment: Inherent Conflicts in the Pursuit of Democracy." Paper presented to the African Studies Program, UCLA, Los Angeles, October 24.

Kibreab, Gaim. African Refugees: Reflections on the African Refugee Problem. London: Africa World Press, 1984.

———1997. People on the Edge in the Horn: Displacement, Land Use and the Environment in the Gedaref Region, Sudan. Trenton, NJ: Red Sea Press.

Markakis, John. "The Nationalist Revolution in Eritrea." Journal of Modern African Studies 26(1):51-70, 1988.

———1990. National and Class Conflict in the Horn of Africa. London: Zed Press.

Mbembe, Achille. "At the Edge of the World: Boundaries, Territoriality, and Sovereignty in Africa." Public Culture 12(1):259-284, 2000.

Nadel, S.F. "Races and Tribes of Eritrea. Asmara," Eritrea: British Military Administration, 1943.

Nairn, Tom. "Internationalism and the Second Coming," Mapping the Nation. Gopal Balakrishnan, ed. Pp. 267-280. London: Verso, 1996.

Nelson, Craig. "War Endangering Eritrea's Self-Reliance," San Antonio Express-News, June 5: 7A, 2000.

Ong, Aihwa. 1999. Flexible Citizenship: The Cultural Logics of Transnationality. Durham, NC: Duke University Press.

Pateman, Roy. Eritrea: Even the Stones are Burning. Trenton, NJ: Red Sea Press, 1990.

Pool, David. "Eritrean Nationalism," Nationalism and Self-Determination in the Horn of Africa. I. M. Lewis, ed. Pp. 175-194. London: Ithaca Press, 1983.

Referendum Commissioner of Eritrea (Dr. Amare Tekle), Referendum '93: "The Eritrean People Determine Their Destiny," Trenton, NJ: Red Sea Press, 1993.

Roberts, Sue. 1998. "Global Strategic Vision: Managing the World," Paper presented at the Conference on New World Orders? Contested Local Terrains in an Era of Globalization, University of California, Irvine, January 17-19.

Sassen, Saskia. 2000. "Spatialities and Temporalities of the Global: Elements for a Theorization," Public Culture 12(1):215-232.

Trevaskis, Gerald Kennedy Nicholas. Eritrea: A Colony in Transition, 1941-52. Westport, CT: Greenwood Press, 1960.

UNICEF. 1994. "Children and Women in Eritrea" (Situation Report). UNICEF.

United Nations. "The United Nations and the Independence of Eritrea." United Nations Blue Book Series, 12. New York: United Nations, Department of Public Information, 1996.

Verdery, Katherine. "Whither 'Nation' and 'Nationalism'?," Mapping the Nation. Gopal Balakrishnan, ed. Pp. 226-234. London: Verso, 1996.

Voice of America, Carol Pineau reporting from Asmara, Eritrea, June 24. 1998. Electronic document, http://www.voa.gov, accessed July 24.

Woldegabriel, Berhane. "Demobilising Eritrea's Army." Review of African Political Economy 58:134-135, 1993.

Woldemikael, Tekle. "Political Mobilization and Nationalist Movements: The Case of the Eritrean People's Liberation Front." Africa Today 38(2):31-42, 1991.

——"Ethiopians and Eritreans," Case Studies in Diversity: Refugees in America in the 1990s. David Haines, ed. Pp. 265-287. Westport, CT: Praeger, 1996.

World Bank. "Eritrea at a Glance," Electronic document, http://www.worldbank.org, accessed June 15, 2000.

10

Speaking Like a Model Minority

"FOB" Styles, Gender, and Racial Meanings Among Desi Teens in Silicon Valley

Shalini Shankar

In 1966, both the *US News and World Report* and *New York Times* lauded Asian Americans as a "model minority" for their high level of education, economic self-sufficiency, low crime rates, and positive social contributions. This characterization has become a stereotype that has enabled post-1965 Asian immigrants and their families relatively easy integration into upper middle-class white society (Prashad 2000). Although recent scholarly work has argued that the model minority stereotype exaggerates the citizenry and scholarly capabilities of Asians in America (Bucholtz 2004; Ima 1995; Inkelas 2006; Kim and Yeh 2002; Lee 2005; Lee and Zhou 2004; Lew 2004), its strength has not diminished in the everyday lives of Asian Americans in Silicon Valley. Indeed, the prominence of Asian Americans in the high-tech industry has created an exceedingly high standard for Asian American youth in ways that not only obscure issues of racism and class inequality in schools, but also create normative expectations for teenagers with little room for variation (Shankar 2008). In this context, what does it sound like to be a model minority?

In this article I examine how everyday performances of teenage linguistic style interact with broader meanings of class, race, and gender. Beginning with the media-ascribed category of the model minority, I examine the specifics of how it shapes meanings of race for Desi (South Asian Americans) teens in a Silicon Valley high school. Ideologies of multilingualism that prevail in South Asia travel with their speakers to an increasingly monolingual California, and such an ideological clash is managed differently by upwardly mobile, well-educated Desis and by middle-class families who have prospered from the tech boom but remain in assembly line jobs. Differences in the ways Desi teens conceive of and manage these ideologies are linked

Shalini Shankar, "Speaking like a Model Minority: 'FOB' Styles, Gender, and Racial Meanings among Desi Teens in Silicon Valley," *Journal of Linguistic Anthropology*, vol. 18, no. 2, pp. 268–289. Copyright © 2008 by American Anthropological Association. Reprinted with permission.

to how they regard their high school, their place in it, and the ways in which school spaces are understood to be public or private. I contrast two distinct Desi teen high school styles that embody these differences: the mainstream style of teens referred to as "popular"; and a marginalized style called "FOB," or "Fresh off the Boat." I focus primarily on FOB styles to examine how FOBs are judged by Desi peers as nonnormative, how they vary according to gender, and the ways they are received at school. In so doing, I analyze how racial meaning is constructed through language use, as well as how gender differently shapes linguistic norms for these speakers.

FOB styles index class-based values that divide the seemingly homogenous category of "Desi" into "model" and "nonmodel" speakers. In this sense, FOB styles are not simply nonnormative; rather they are central to how Desis are ascribed racial status in Silicon Valley. Metapragmatic awareness of normative appropriateness raises the question of whether FOB styles can be understood as "stylistic variables" that teens selectively employ, or "status variables" that are habitual and more difficult to regulate (Irvine 1974). Metapragmatic assessments by teens as well as school faculty inform how model ways of speaking may contrast with FOB styles. Asif Agha (1998) argues that metapragmatic stereotypes about pragmatic phenomena not only essentialize and categorize difference, but also make the stereotypes themselves reportable and subject to contention. Along these lines, FOB styles are far more complex and nuanced than speech generally associated with those "Fresh off the Boat," but nonetheless index nonnormative ways of speaking at school. Michael Silverstein (2003) has termed such interconnected levels of meaning "indexical orders." I examine how the everyday meanings indexed by FOB styles create linguistic stereotypes that form the basis for categorizing teens by race and ethnicity.[1]

HETEROGLOSSIA AND FOB STYLE

While English and Punjabi form the foundation for FOB styles, teen uses of language varieties, accents, registers, voices, and genres can be better analyzed by applying Mikhail Bakhtin's (1981) "heteroglossia" than simply understanding their speech as bilingual. The concept of bilingualism has undergone several useful reformulations to take into account multiple ways of speaking used to construct utterances. Kathryn Woolard (1999) asserts that "bivalency" is preferable to "bilingualism" or "code switching" because the first takes into account the multiple modes and voices available to speakers. Speakers are able to draw on and deploy linguistic resources that index particular social meanings. Like Woolard, Benjamin Bailey (2007) also draws on Bakhtin's heteroglossia as a way to link language use and racial identity for bilingual speakers. Both Bailey's and Woolard's formulations complicate the notion of a pure standard and an impure variation, as well as that speakers make clear-cut choices between languages. In a similar vein, Monica Heller (2007) advocates for an understanding of bilingualism in which language is a resource that speakers negotiate in ideologically charged ways. Speakers manipulate boundaries but do so under particular social constraints and historical conditions.

Style is instrumental to marking group-specific ways of speaking. Judith Irvine (2001) identifies style as the use of linguistic resources from a number of varieties of language toward a socially recognizable end (see also Irvine and Gal 2000). Because style is both actively produced or coproduced by individuals or groups and is habitual and routine (Mendoza-Denton 1999), it is always mediated by speakers and in particular contexts. Penelope Eckert (1989, 2000), for example, has documented how students' affiliation with the social categories of "jocks" and "burnouts" is reflected in their lexical, grammatical, and stylistic use of English, in both conscious and unconscious ways. Although marginalized burnouts intentionally use particular greetings and phrases, their pronunciation of particular vowels unintentionally indexes their neighborhood and other socioeconomic variables. An analogous process of social category formation occurs through racially marked styles of speaking and dressing among Desi teens (cf. Bucholtz 2001; Rymes 2001).

In their multiracial, multiethnic school environment, teens who are called FOBs by popular teens for their style of speaking, dressing, and socializing are not actually brand new arrivals to the United States. Rather, FOB (pronounced as a word, not as individual letters) is a term that upper middle-class, popular Desi teens use to label second- and third-generation middle-class teens whose parents are nonskilled workers.[2] So-called FOBs are middle-class Sikh Punjabis that popular teens marginalize and distance themselves from based on their ways of dressing, speaking, and comportment in school. To emphasize the connection between producers of particular ideological projects and their objects, Susan Gal (2007) has offered the term "clasp" as a way of relating how discourses are produced and linked to categories of individuals. She defines interdiscursive clasps as "speech registers (or registers of semiotic practice) that link those who create the category of a person-type and produce justifications for its indexical signs with those who are recruited to that person-type" (Gal 2007:6). FOB styles—the stereotypical ways in which FOBs are thought to speak—act as clasps between FOBby (FOB-like) and popular Desi teens.

Desi teens in Silicon Valley are not the first to locally define and use term FOB. While the term is not unique to Asian Americans, it is widely used in Asian diasporas, especially in the context of post-1965 Asian migration, to differentiate new arrivals from those who have learned requisite cultural and linguistic codes (Chiang-Hom 2004; Hwang 1979; Reyes 2007). FOB is commonly used by second-generation Asian American youth to distance themselves from the perceived negative attributes of first-generation or 1.5 generation youth (Jeon 2001; Loomis 1990; Rumbaut 2002; Talmy 2004; Zhou 2004). In the Desi context, FOB attributes include not adequately following fashion trends, having oily hair, speaking Punjabi at school, and speaking Desi Accented English (which I explain in detail below). Notably, these codes do not involve distancing oneself from everything South Asian. Cosmopolitan signs of being Desi— including wearing South Asian clothing to the prom, blasting Bollywood soundtracks from luxury automobiles, and incorporating South Asian elements into school performances—are not considered FOBby. Such choices do not mark popular teens as "whitewashed" (Pyke and Dang 2003); rather, these teens are knowledgeable and strategic about when and how they deploy aspects of their ethnicity and speak their heritage language. Such "model" ways of speaking stand in contrast to FOB styles. In these ways, FOB styles act as clasps between marginalized Desi teens and popular Desi teens as well as those school faculty who indicate that marginalized youth embody nonnormative attributes.

Although FOB styles of speaking include the use of Punjabi, English, Bollywood dialogue and song lyrics, hip-hop lyrics and lexicon, Desi Accented English, California slang, and Spanish, the stereotype that FOBs simply code switch loudly in Punjabi is what elicits negative judgment and enables popular teens to appear more model. In a school context, such practices of status making and exclusion are commonplace through talk and social activity (Goodwin 2006). Although I will discuss the numerous ways in which FOB styles are far more differentiated and nuanced than this, the racializing effect of the stereotype is ultimately what prevails (Roth-Gordon 2007; see also McElhinny 2001). For this reason, I use the terms *FOB* and *FOB style* to refer to the middle-class, marginalized Sikh Punjabi youth who engage in these marked language practices. *FOB style* is my analytical term, and I use it to contextualize their identity and style-making practices in the institutional setting of school and in the class-based inequities of the South Asian diaspora.

LANGUAGE IDEOLOGIES AND LANGUAGE USE IN SILICON VALLEY

The model minority stereotype is so prevalent in Silicon Valley that its normative standards pervade everyday life. For teens, this includes excelling academically as well as performing linguistically according to the monolingual standards of high school. Being a speaker of a particular language or being a member of a particular group, however, does not make these labels transparent, strictly referential, or even stable. Susan Gal (2004) has remarked that there is no simple indexical relationship between what the census or other research suggests speakers of a particular ethnicity should speak and their actual affiliations with their heritage language. Rather, "they are likely to be performatives in the following second-order sense: the very use of them in particular contexts marks the user as a certain kind of person within the social group" (Gal 2004:339). Such a distinction is crucial to understanding how Desi teens are predisposed to particular styles of speaking in their schools and communities.

Language ideologies are useful to illustrate diasporic speakers' predispositions toward language use in homelands versus places of settlement. Language ideologies are cultural representations of language in the social world (Irvine and Gal 2000; Kroskrity 2000; Schieffelin, Woolard, and Kroskrity 1998) and guide uses of and values associated with particular languages. Since the colonial period in India, the British offered English-medium schools alongside local-language-medium schools, a dichotomous system that still exists today (Cohn 1985; Khubchandani 1983; see also LaDousa 2006). In this multilingual ideology, different languages are appropriate modes of communication for different interactions and domains. South Asia currently has 15 official languages and more than 1,500 others that are spoken (Jacobsen and Kumar 2004:ix–xxiv). Speakers are socialized to use a variety of languages as well as registers for different contexts. This approach to language ideology and practice, in which multilingualism is a routine part of everyday life, has not collapsed among South Asians in the United States, where English monolingualism is the ideological norm (Crawford 1992, 2000; Silverstein 1996). If anything, using multiple languages and at least registers and lexical elements from several language varieties has strengthened among Desi populations in Silicon Valley.[3]

The specific class, ethnicity, and language-based formations of Silicon Valley Desi communities have engendered different types of relationships between teens and their heritage languages. To better understand these judgments, some discussion of the status of English and Punjabi in Silicon Valley is necessary.[4] English is ideologically favored in both South Asia and Silicon Valley, though varieties, accents, and norms of usage predictably vary between and within these locations. As the language of empire, globalization, and of diasporic locales such as the United Kingdom, Canada, Australia, and the United States, English is imbued with more power and status than other Desi languages (Kachru 2000), although its specific value differs with regard to its status vis-à-vis local South Asian languages (Bhatt 2001; Pennycook 2007). Recent work on Asian American language use advocates for deeper study of English use in favor of documenting a linear retention or loss of heritage language (Lo and Reyes 2004). English is a valued tool in identity-making practices for Desi teens, and they tend to use several different kinds of English, which are exemplified in transcripts below. Despite English's elevated status, heritage language use plays a crucial, if not straightforward, role in shaping diasporic identity (Eisenlohr 2006). As a heritage language, Punjabi is highly valued in Silicon Valley communities. In addition to being widely spoken at family and community gatherings, Punjabi language instruction is offered at *gurdwaras* (Sikh temples) during weekend and intensive summer sessions. Many Sikh youth go to the San Jose gurdwara on a weekly or biweekly basis and participate in casual conversation in Punjabi as they wait in line for *langar*, the meal offered after prayer. This practice, along with the large and prominent Punjabi population in this area, makes Punjabi one of the most widely spoken South Asian languages in Silicon Valley.[5] How and when it is used, however, can vary according to class.

Class is central to shaping linguistic dispositions. In these Desi communities, wealth is a topic of intense focus of conversation, but class categories are not (see Shankar 2006). Many Desi families who moved to Silicon Valley in the late 1970s and 1980s went on to experience unusually high job security until the 2001 stock market crash and can still rely on the equity of their well-appreciated homes. Adults in unskilled jobs have been able to buy property and prosper economically, but the type of cultural capital (Bourdieu 1985) they are able to instill in their children is not on par with that of upper middle-class parents. Such a rift, I argue, is important to understanding how teens regard school as a place to speak their heritage language.

At Greene High School, the diverse, overenrolled public high school where I conducted fieldwork for eighteen months, during the period of September 1999 through May 2001, Desi teens were one of several racial and ethnic groups. Of the approximately 2,200 students during the 1999–2000 school year, nearly 50 percent were Asian American (about 30 percent Desi), 25 percent Latino, 12 percent white, 6 percent African American, and less than 1 percent Native American. Here, upper middle-class students are primarily Sikh Punjabi, Hindu Punjabi, and Hindu Gujaratis. They are children of well-educated, post-1965 immigrants. Their parents have upwardly mobile careers and live in wealthy areas of Silicon Valley. Upper middle-class parents who were educated in English-medium schools, whether in South Asia or elsewhere, tend to speak English far more at home. In these families, parents speak to one another and their children in their heritage language as well as in English. Their children by and large reply in English and speak English among themselves. Teens may speak their heritage language at community gatherings or with elderly relatives who are not fluent in English, but otherwise speak in English. This English-speaking norm, as well as their sophisticated understanding of school fostered through extensive parental involvement, makes English ubiquitous at home and the norm at school.

Middle-class teens are predominantly from Sikh Punjabi families. Their parents did not immigrate as professionals, and while they may have profited financially from the high-tech industry, they rarely gained more cultural capital from this windfall. Middle-class Desi teens display higher levels of spoken and comprehensive fluency in Punjabi than do upper middle-class teens. This is so because at least one middle-class teen's parents or live-in relative does not speak English fluently. Even among adults who attended high school in Yuba City or elsewhere in California, the strength of their community networks and the continuous arrival of Sikhs relatives and spouses from South Asia keep their Punjabi in constant use, so much so that they seldom speak English to one another at home. While their children feel equally comfortable in both languages, they choose to speak Punjabi far more often than teens whose parents did not speak it at home.

Such distinctions map onto the spaces of the school campus and shape Desi teen styles. Greene's sprawling campus is filled with numerous small, one-story buildings that create multiple distinct spaces. Such a layout creates spaces to travel between buildings as well as places to socialize and "kick it," or spend routine time with friends, during morning break and lunch. Here, the seemingly private periods of social time with friends is in the same open, visible locations as other activities. Susan Gal (2002), among others, has remarked that notions of public and private are not clearly demarcated, but can be understood as a continuum that is marked by distinct ideologies. Although there is little that may be considered private about public high school—as student lockers, notebooks, bags, and other seemingly private spaces are all subject to seizure and search—students nonetheless territorialize the school campus during lunch and break and demarcate it into proprietary spaces that blur public and private distinctions.

The "quad" is the grassy, central, ideologically normative space of the school (Gibson 1988; Mendoza-Denton 2007; Perry 2002) where popular teens claim space, and the outlying regions are inhabited by socially and linguistically marginalized students. Eckert (1989) has described the ways in which popular jocks naturally claim and value school spaces as their own, while marginalized burnouts maintain that the school is not truly theirs and that school property may be used in unintended ways for illicit activities. Such differences in orientation are akin to ways in which populars and FOBs differently treat the school. In back areas of the school campus, especially behind the library and the "C" building, FOB cliques claim spaces in which they construct their own styles.

FOB STYLES OF SPEAKING

FOB styles draw on English, Punjabi, Desi Accented English, hip-hop lexicon and lyrics, as well as Spanish and California slang. The following examples are drawn from tape recordings made by students featuring teens (M = male, F = female) speaking among themselves in my absence during March-April 2001. They exemplify that what may be overheard as simply code switching between English and Punjabi is, upon closer examination, a much more complex style. FOB styles include local California slang, such as *hella* (very), and *tight* (very cool), *dude*, and *bro*. Similar to "FOB accents" (Reyes 2007), "Mock Asian" (Chun 2001), and "Stylized Asian English" (Rampton 1995), which all refer to ways of speaking that ridicule the nonstandard English associated with recent Asian immigrants, "Desi Accented English" (DAE) is a language variety I have identified through which teens index insider humor. DAE (formatted in boldface type below) is not simply an accent; rather, it is a way of speaking that indexes a lack of cultural knowledge about common aspects of American life and contains atypical grammatical constructions and lexical elements that may not be shared by other speakers of South Asian English. It may seem ironic that those called FOBs are performing a "FOBby" accent, but their sophistication in doing so is a reminder that FOB styles can indeed be seen in many instances as a stylistic variable. In the following example recorded during a morning break period, Manpreet (F) offers her friend Harbans (F) some of her Pop-Tart pastry. Munching on the snack while the conversation ensues, Harbans interrupts to inquire about the Pop-Tart's flavor, and Avinash (M) offers an explanation.

Example 1: S'mores
1. Harbans: Hey this is good; what is it?
2. Manpreet: S'mores.
3. Harbans: S'mores?
4. Avinash: You know that thing with marshmallows and chocolate? **Maarrsh-**
5. **mallow**, that little white thing?

By using DAE (formatted in boldface) to respond to Harbans's confusion about a flavor inspired by an American campfire treat, Avinash indexes the lack of social knowledge generally associated with FOBs. His emphatic maarrsh-mallow especially elicits laughter, because it is not a foodstuff available in South Asia, and makes this ordinary American flavor seem exotic to the uninitiated. Like Avinash, FOB teens readily use DAE for humorous emphasis in the midst of California accented English. In a conversation where Manpreet disclosed to Ranvir (M) that she was taping their conversation for my research, Ranvir jokingly suggested that this amounted to "sexual harassment." Manpreet smilingly replied, "**It is very-very bad!**" Ranvir laughed and echoed, "**Very-very?**" Here, not just the accent but also the construction very-very, a common expression in South Asian English, index their knowledge of stereotypical ways in which actual FOBs speak, and indicate that they consider themselves to be far enough from this stereotype to use it humorously.

FOB style draws heavily on Punjabi (formatted in italic type below). This can include the use of expressions such as *Oh balle, balle!*, a multipurpose cheer uttered when dancing, as a rallying cry, and for surprise or exasperation, as well as *chak de fatte!* which teens translate as "let's go!" "raise the roof!" or "let's kick ass!"[6] While sometimes used literally, they are also used sarcastically, as in this exchange between Jett (M) and KB (M).

Example 2: "Chak de fatte!" [Kick ass!].
1. Jett: Bend down, pick that up! All yous ready?
2. KB: Whaaaat?
3. Jett: *Chak de fatte*! [Kick ass!].
4. KB: [sarcastically]: Thanks, bro.

In this exchange, the Punjabi phrase is used as a double entendre. In line 1, Jett tries to direct KB to pick up his bag and move along, but when KB takes his time doing so, Jett shouts, "*Chak de fatte!*" (line 3) as KB lackadaisically bends over to collect his belongings. The phrase is not just a rallying cry, but also a humorous suggestion that KB may require a swift kick in order to get moving.

Alongside Punjabi, California slang, and DAE, Spanish is also a resource for FOB style. San Jose's predominantly working-class Chicano population has exerted a visible influence on FOB styles. Latino and Latina styles of clothing and makeup, especially when markers of gang membership (Mendoza-Denton 2007), can also shape FOB styles of comportment and speaking. Spanish phrases can be quite humorous when inserted into conversational exchanges. In the following excerpt from a lunchtime conversation, Kuldeep (M) uses Spanish (formatted in an underlined typeface) in an exchange with Uday (M) and Simran (F).

Example 3: "__No Habla Inglés__" [I (sic) don't speak English]
1. Uday: *Saleya eh garbage can vai?* [Is this a garbage can, stupid?].
2. Kuldeep: <u>No habla Inglés</u> [I (*sic*) don't speak English]. [loud round of
3. laughter]
4. Kuldeep: **Don't know what you say ...**

5. Simran: Throw that fuckin' shit out!
6. Kuldeep: *Oh balle! Hon boleya!* [Oh wow! At least you're talking to me now!].

While Uday attempts to be discreet about Kuldeep's refusal to properly dispose of trash and reprimands him in Punjabi, Kuldeep rebuffs him with two different performances of misrecognition. In the first, he feigns ignorance by saying in Spanish that he does not speak English. This is met with a round of laughter in part because it is a clever retort to Uday's directive, and in part because Uday's statement in Punjabi does not require him to know English. Kuldeep's utterance could be read as an example of what Jane Hill (1995) has called "mock Spanish," but perhaps a more apt name for this would be "mocking Spanish." By occasionally speaking in Spanish in a school environment where they are routinely mistaken for Latinos, FOB boys use Spanish as a way to mock faculty who cannot easily differentiate between them and Latinos. Ridiculing this misrecognition is a continual source of humor for FOBby teens. The conversation continues when Kuldeep, encouraged by the laughter of his friends, chooses DAE (formatted in bold) to tell Uday that he does not understand him. Again, it is ironic that he uses a FOBby accent to communicate this, as a true FOB would have no trouble understanding Uday's Punjabi remark. When Simran reprimands him in English, Kuldeep responds to her sarcastically in Punjabi, and the joke has ended. While these teens studied Spanish in school and live alongside Mexican Americans in their neighborhoods, they rarely speak Spanish outside of these joking exchanges.

Similarly, FOB styles incorporate lexical elements from hip-hop without any political or social interests in black people. Blacks are concentrated in Oakland and other parts of the Bay Area but are a relatively minor presence San Jose. Desi teens listen to commercial hip-hop but do not express interest in becoming hip-hop artists or forming social alliances with blacks. In the following example, the hip-hop shout out "West Siiiiide" is used by both KB (M) and Jett (M) to mollify a tense dynamic that develops between Uday and Kuldeep about the latter's neighbor.

*Example 4: "**Dimag kharab hai, yaar** " [He is crazy, dude].*
1. Uday: Oh man, listen to the bullshit.
2. Kuldeep: *Dimag kharab hai, yaar. Mera neighbor, yaar* [He is crazy, dude. My
3. neighbor, dude].
4. Uday: What has led you to this conclusion?
5. Kuldeep: *Dimag kharab hai!* [He is crazy!].
6. Uday: How do you know people don't say this about you?
7. Kuldeep: He is crazy, fool! Everybody says that, this fool really is crazy,
8. though.
9. Uday: Takes one to know one?
10. Kuldeep: Shut up!
11. Uday: *Main te ude hi karda* [I'm just kidding].

12. Jett: West siiiiide!
13. Kuldeep: *Aha ki karan lag peyan tu?* [What have you started doing?]. Ain't no
14. fuckin' California love, California thug. …
15. KB: West Siiiiide!

When Kuldeep seems genuinely annoyed at Uday's needling, Jett steps in and offers a shout out that indexes the unified front of West Coast hip-hop. Kuldeep is hardly amused and snaps at Jett with a clever use of hip-hop lyrics from the then-popular song "The Next Episode" (line 13–14). KB reiterates Jett's shout out for unity, and the tension begins to diffuse. While such a use of hip-hop could be read as an attempt to "pass" for black or "cross" into this group (Bucholtz 1999; Cutler 2003; Lo 1999; Rampton 1995; Reyes 2005), Desi teens I observed did not use hip-hop lexicon for these purposes. FOB teens' overwhelming use of Punjabi and DAE, compared to their relatively infrequent use of hip-hop lexicon, underscores this point.

FOB styles, as I have illustrated, draw on a wide range of linguistic resources that a recent arrival could not begin to access. Some linguistic practices, including FOBs' use of California slang and ironic use of DAE, do not differ from those of popular Desi teens. What is most marked, however, is their use of Punjabi. It is significant that these teens do not use Punjabi in the classroom unless they believe they cannot be heard. They understand classroom time to be public and are careful there to maintain the monolingual school code. Lunch and break times in their corner of the school campus, however, are considered private. Indeed, the places they call their own are expected to be truly free spaces where they can say and do what they please, however loudly they please. For this reason, they are easily labeled FOBs by the rest of their Desi peers, who try to distance themselves. In turn, FOBs do not have positive opinions of popular teens—Desi and those of other ethnicities—and express their views in Punjabi to one another. As a group of popular Chinese American girls walked by, KB remarked loudly to Simran (F), "*Saliyan Cheeniya … enadi neet bahut pehri ya*" [Stupid Chinese girls … they are very stingy and mean]. Likewise, when a popular Desi boy strutted by them, Jett commented about him to Simran.

Example 5: "**Oh balle, ballee**" *[Oh, wow].*
1. Jett [sarcastically]: *Oh balle, balle* [Oh, wow].
2. Simran: Are you talking about that guy? Are you talking about that guy?
3. Jett: *Onu kera Punjabi andi vai!* [It's not as if he knows Punjabi!].

In such exchanges, it is evident that FOBs are well aware that popular teens ignore them or treat them with disdain. In line 1, Jett speaks caustically at a boy who is perhaps not all he thinks he is by delivering the usually upbeat chant *Oh balle, balle!* in a flat, sardonic way. Simran is curious to know if Jett is bold enough to speak about the boy in such close proximity, which Jett confirms to be the case because he does not believe he will be understood. While this boy may well understand Punjabi, Jett's assumption is that as a popular boy, he would neither understand Jett nor pay any attention to him even if he did. In this way, FOBs are able to maintain a sense of private conversation in what is otherwise a public space where they would be heard. Girls and boys differently regard the school as public and private spaces, and this shapes how they differently construct FOB styles.

GENDERED WAYS OF SPEAKING

FOB styles, like other teenage language use, have been shown to not only to affirm clique boundaries, but also to test the limits of gendered expectations (Mendoza-Denton 2007; Woolard 1994). Following the work of Penelope Eckert and Sally McConnell-Ginet (2003), I examine how these styles vary according to their "communities of practice" (see also Lave and Wenger 1991). While popular styles of speaking do not vary significantly according to gender, FOB language use is gendered according to topic, styles of speaking, and lexical choice. What is significant about this type of gender differentiation is that it reflects other standards of comportment that are prevalent in the lives of FOBby Desi teens. Elinor Ochs (1992) has called the linkage of conversational practices and gendered stances "collocational indexicality," and such a concept draws attention to the broader significance of gendered differences in speaking. Especially for FOB girls, maintaining a good reputation, or *izzat*, encourages them to minimize transgressions—be they sexual, behavioral, or disciplinary (Gillespie 1995; Hall 2002; Maira 2002). While some girls push this boundary further than others, they rarely do so to the extent that boys do.

Middle-class Sikh Punjabi girls attend Greene High School with many teens from their large community network. Here, gossip is rampant and teens are likely to spread rumors in their communities about things they witness at school. Although they can be somewhat more lax at school, girls rarely consider social time at school to occur in a private space. Even here, they are concerned about maintaining their reputation and avoiding school disciplinary measures, both things that could harm their familial and community standing.[7] By contrast, Sikh Punjabi boys are subject to fewer social rules and tend to regard the social space of school as far more private. Treating their place in the school campus as a private space for jokes, humor, gossip, and confrontation, they criticize or choose to ignore school rules when they impede on their language styles.

Instead of quoting hip-hop lyrics, girls gravitate more toward Bollywood as their pop culture source for marking style, and elsewhere I discuss how girls quote *filmi* (filmlike) dialogue and songs (Shankar 2004b). Although these teens are not fluent in Hindi, they nonetheless can quote from films in limited ways. Increased access to English subtitles and the long-standing dominance of Hindu Punjabis in Bollywood films have imbued film dialogue and songs with Punjabi lexical items, phrases, festivals, and kinship terms. When girls speak Punjabi in school, it is generally limited to quoting reported speech, constructing imagined utterances, and using phrases or terms, though their Punjabi speaking ability is as fluent as that of their male peers.[8]

When, for example, Raminder (F) grew tired of her friends telling her how attractive her brother is, she squealed, "Dude! He's my brother!" and recalled a humorous incident that had occurred at the gurdwara in the presence of her friends: "Remember those *budiyan* [older ladies]? There was somebody, like, at the gurdwara yesterday, some *budiya* [older lady], *keh diya, 'Meriyan bhanjiyan nursa da course kar diyan paiyan hain. Tera pra kine salan da hega? Asi Jattan da munda labdiyan hain'*" [she said to me, "My nieces are doing a nursing course. How old is your brother? We're looking for a *Jatt* (a Punjabi caste) boy]. "And [their brother is] a farmer!" added Janvi (F) and Mandeep (F) at the same time, shrieking with laughter that the prospective brides were doing a nursing course but their brother was a farmer. For effect, Raminder reiterated, "She was, like, '*Oho, nursa da course kar diyan*!'" [Oh look, they are doing a nursing course!]. I was like, 'puh-leeez!'" While Raminder could have as easily relayed the content of the older woman's utterance in English, using Punjabi enabled a much more amusing retelling.

While they are less likely to directly speak Punjabi to one another, girls create imagined utterances in Punjabi to embellish conversations. When Manpreet told her friends that her aunts had a suitable boy in mind for her, they loudly shouted "No!" on her behalf. "No, for, like, later on," Manpreet tried to explain as Jaswinder (F) cut her off and said, "The *budi's* like, '*Tu to honiya veeyan, iqiyan salan di*'" [The old lady's like, "You must be about 20, 21 years old"]. Jaswinder's remark caused the rest of the girls to explode with laughter while 15-year-old Manpreet could not hold back a smile. The point that Manpreet was too young to even consider a prospective groom was most effectively made in Punjabi, even though her friends tried to make this clear in English. Here, Punjabi did the work of delivering a sensitive message in a less didactic way than simply shouting "No!" at Manpreet.

Most FOBby girls have close female friends but socialize in co-ed groups. When girls are a majority, they marginalize boys who attempt to enter and derail their conversations. Girls play a large role in community events such as weddings and enjoy discussing participants and technical terms, even when their male peers have little interest in doing so. In the following excerpt, Jaspreet (F), Harbans, and Janvi, discuss a dance that a friend's mother had recently performed at a wedding function while Avinash and Kuldeep attempt to guide the conversation toward their own topics of interest.[9]

Example 6: "We call 'em 'weird.'"
1. Jaspreet: Rammi's mom did a dance! That's so nasty!
2. Harbans: Like on a song?
3. Janvi and Jaspreet [in unison]: No! *On Jago kaad de* [a song from a ladies'
4. *sangeet* (wedding event) during which they performed]
5. Harbans: Oh.
6. Avinash: Is Rammi right there? Rammi's mom did a dance?
7. Harbans: What are those people called? Rajasthani? [people from the Indian

8. state of Rajasthan]
9. Janvi: That's my *mamiji*! [mother's brother's wife]
10. Harbans: What's that called?
11. Janvi: *Gidde wale.* [Punjabi folk dancers]
12. Avinash: *Khusra?* [a transvestite]
13. Kuldeep: She was wearing green, huh? She was wearing a green top with
14. uh … I was like "Oh shit! Who's that?"
15. Jaspreet: I thought she looked hella nice.
16. Harbans: They are called a *gaddi wale*? [truck drivers]
17. Avinash: *Khusre?* [transvestites, plural]
18. Harbans: What's a *gaddian wale*? [truck drivers]
19. Kuldeep: *Gad- gade wale?* … Like truck drivers?
20. Janvi: No, you know how they used to, you know those people that come to
21. your *pind* [village] and they have their little teepees and stuff. They're not
22. *khusre.*
23. Avinash: All right.
24. Harbans: Khusre means half man and half girl, right? *Gaddian wale*? I've
25. never heard that.
26. Avinash: Yo, do they marry *khusre*?
27. Janvi [to Harbans, ignoring Avinash]: You know how you guys call them
28. *paau*? [one who performs a dance]
29. Harbans: Yeah.
30. Janvi: We call them *kale kacheyan wale*. [a type of dancer]
31. Avinash [laughing loudly]: I don't know what the fuck, I don't know what
32. the fuck that is!
33. Kuldeep: Whatever, we understand you.
34. Avinash: If they're weird, we call 'em "weird."

In this conversation, Janvi is very invested in helping Harbans learn the names of dances, types of dancers, and that these dancers are not transvestites. By contrast, Avinash and Kuldeep continually insert themselves into in the conversation, both in hopes of hearing gossip and to offer their brand of humor. As Janvi attempts to explain to Harbans the differences between specific dancers and Harbans tries to say them properly, Avinash repeatedly interjects by asking whether she means transvestites (lines 12, 17, and 26) while Kuldeep is equally unhelpful by mocking Harbans for her confusion between dancers (*gidde wale*) and truck drivers (*gadde wale*), and attempts to further mislead her (line 19). Janvi altogether ignores the boys and tries to explain her family village's name for such a dancer (line 30), which makes Avinash and Kuldeep laugh loudly and tell Janvi what they really think.

While girls spend much of their time gossiping and discussing events like this one, they also use their fair share of profanity. They do not, however, stray from the "standard" English words that would elicit an FCC fine.[10] They steer clear of racial slurs and references to genitalia; the most rancorous expression I witnessed was a girl calling a boy a "bitch." Girls can get away with some linguistic transgressions if they are careful to do so only in the company of close friends. Even speaking on tape worried some girls. Raminder jokingly suggested what would happen if her friend's mother heard the recording of their conversation: "Yeah, right, you know your mom's fuckin' gonna come over here and be, like, 'what the fuck?'" Uttering such things in jest to a small group of friends is very different than shouting them in the school campus, which FOB boys do with abandon. When they "cuss" in English or even speak Punjabi, girls fear being caught by school faculty or overheard by gossiping peers, and restrain themselves.

Unlike FOB boys, FOB girls as well as other Desi girls are cautious about their language practices because using good language is part of a larger code of propriety to which girls are especially subject. Although using good language does not automatically make them good girls, using bad language can quickly earn them a bad reputation. For Desi teenage girls, using profane language is linked to improper comportment and even being sexually active in a cultural context where chastity is valued. They are subject to scrutiny from school faculty as well as peer policing. Tanya Hill, a vice principal, remarked about Desi girls who have violated normative expectations, "These girls, if they knew the tough language they used, their parents would be absolutely floored that their kids even know these words, let alone have them come out of their mouths! In lot of cultures, girls are supposed to be more reserved. The parents would be surprised to see how uninhibited they are with the opposite sex." As Ms. Hill's comment implies, bad language is linked to what must be bad behavior. As Desi girls are expected to display levels of chastity not demanded of girls of other ethnicities, using profane language is a potentially dangerous way of tainting one's reputation. A popular girl, Avneet, explained about the FOBs, "The girls are nice, but some of the boys are kind of weird and can act sort of rowdy." Even girls who sometimes speak in FOB styles remark about boys they know from their gurdwara: "At first the boys start out in proper Punjabi, [but] then they end up swearing and causing trouble." Boys, however, are unconcerned with such judgment, for they operate according to a different set of community-based standards.

HYPERMASCULINE FOB STYLE

While FOB style can be effectively used to articulate many things, for boys it centers on joking, insulting, and fighting. The use of blatantly sexist and homophobic language by young men as they socialize among themselves is not unusual (Cameron 1998; Kiesling 2001), and terms such as *behenchod* (sister-fucker), *gaandu* (gay; pejorative, like "faggot"), *tatti* (shit), and *tuttay* (testicles) are commonplace in boy's FOB styles. Sikh culture in San Jose, like elsewhere, is one in which Sikh boys especially take great pride. From drawing the Sikh *khanda* (religious symbol featuring the *kirpan*, or sword) on notebooks to displaying bumper stickers that say "*Jatt* do it," these boys believe that being Sikh Punjabi is more desirable than being from any other ethnicity. In their communities, Sikh boys socialize with men at events and sit with them at the gurdwara. While Sikhism officially prohibits drinking, in families where it occurs, only males imbibe. Overall, boys are far less monitored and are not discouraged from roaming unsupervised in ways that girls are. In such a religious and social context, expressions of heightened masculinity are not uncommon. While they are not explicitly taught to be hypermasculine, many Sikh boys adopt this stance in the company of other Sikhs, especially other males. Such a cultural context is relevant to understanding how FOB styles become racially coded.[11]

Boys use Punjabi when physically joking with one another. When Uday put KB in a headlock during morning break, KB had to shout, *"Chad de!! Oh bas kar*!"* [Let me go! Oh, stop it!] over the roar of laughter to be released. Using distinct registers, such as villainous ones from Bollywood, also indexes masculinity. When, for example, Simran told Jett that only I would hear the conversation she was taping for me, he deployed evil *filmi* register to reply, *"Nahin! Main tera khoon kar dungaa*!"* [No! I'm going to murder you!]. DAE is also used to index the speech and attitudes of older Desis from a youth perspective. In the following conversation between Harminder (M) and Ranvir (M), the boys create a hypothetical exchange (the hypothetical dialogue is formatted in quotation marks) that might occur between an Indian liquor store owner and an Indian patron.

Example 7: "You Punjabi?"
1. Harminder: "Are you 21?"
2. Ranvir: "No I'm Indian!"
3. Harminder: Seriously, if you go to an Indian liquor store, dude, they will just
4. hook you up with liquor. They don't care about your ID. …
5. Ranvir: Naw, fool. "**You Punjabi?**"
6. Harminder: "**Of course!**"
7. Ranvir: "It's free, fool!"
8. Harminder: "*A le putra … pila*!" [Here son … drink it!].

Here, Harminder and Ranvir effectively enact an imagined encounter between a Desi liquor store owner and a young Desi patron. The joke progresses well until Ranvir speaks out of character (line 7), nearly derailing the intended effect. Harminder steps in and compensates amply by using Punjabi, and the joke is saved.

FOBby boys also enjoy using Punjabi to swear in ways that are not recognizable as transgressions by school administrators but communicate solidarity, humorous insult, and rancor among friends. By now it should come as no surprise that cussing is a cornerstone of boy's FOB style. Insults and discussions of women that could be deemed sexist usually take place out of earshot of girls. In this cultural context, it is not a norm to speak openly about such topics in the presence of the opposite sex.

On numerous occasions, boys strongly advised their female friends to leave their group as conversations headed in more illicit directions. When Simran decided to stay with her male friends after she was asked to leave, Harry (M) quipped, "*Tenu kene jamya? Jamke galti kitti*" [Who gave birth to you? She made a big mistake by giving birth to you]. Simran was so taken aback that her voice crackled when she responded in Punjabi, "*Mere bare gal kardan?*" [Are you talking about me?]. When Jett confirmed in English, "Yes. You is bad," Simran decided it was time for her to find her other friends.[12] For the most part, insults are traded and boys cuss at one another, as in the following exchange in which tension arises when Kuldeep suggests that Uday might be scared to support him in an upcoming fight.

Example 8: "Am I cussing?"
1. Kuldeep: Damn, I don't give a fuck. Why you all scared, fool?
2. Uday: *Behenchod, tu galaan kad da*? [Sisterfucker, are you cussing at me?].
3. Kuldeep: Yeah, that's what really happens. *Tu galaan kad da, saleya*? [Are you
4. cussing at me stupid?]. Uday's cussing at me!
5. Uday: *Mere dandi baad hoy jandi vai* [I might bite my tongue later].

Here, Kuldeep and Uday engage in a metapragmatic exchange about their own language practices. When Kuldeep implies that Uday is afraid of fighting with someone (line 1), Uday asks if Kuldeep is cussing at him to insult him (line 2). Kuldeep taunts him until Uday admits that he may indeed be cussing, and he uses an idiomatic expression (line 5) that indicates that he might feel bad about it later.

As their conversation indicates, Punjabi is the language of choice for talk about fighting, threats, and other illicit activity. When making a threat, like this one that KB jokingly made at Uday during a morning break—"*Uday nu mardena aaj! Uday nu mardena aaj*!!" [I'm going to kill Uday today! I'm going to kill Uday today!]—to recalling details of past fights, boys speak in Punjabi not only to avoid being overheard discussing illicit activity in English by school faculty, but also to convey details more graphically. As he recalled a recent fight he witnessed, Uday described the general setting and participants in English, but switched to Punjabi to remark, "*Frances nu bechari nu pehlan kut kut maraya*" [Poor Frances got beaten very badly first]. *Kut kut* is an onomatopoetic way of describing the violent beating that Uday witnessed, while *bechari* conveys his general sympathy for Frances without seeming too emotionally invested. Indeed, use of Punjabi signals a level of seriousness about fighting that English does not. In the following excerpt, Uday and Kuldeep observe a fight that has just erupted in close proximity to their spot in the back of the school campus.

Example 9: Our Paully Vu
1. Uday: What the hell? There's a fight over there. Someone got popped in the
2. head! Oh that's Paul, isn't it? And that's our Paully Vu!
3. Kuldeep: No it ain't.
4. Uday: That's Paully Vu!
5. Kuldeep: It is?

6. Uday: Yeah, that's our Paully Vu!
7. Kuldeep: Well I can't see any glasses. …
8. Uday: That's Paully Vu, dude!
9. Kuldeep: That's not Paully Vu.
10. Uday: *Oy! dekh tan!* [Oh! Look at that!].
11. Kuldeep: Oh! It is him!
12. Uday: Oh, whuuut?
13. Kuldeep: He got popped?
14. Uday: Daaamn. He got popped.
15. Kuldeep: Well, that's embarrassing, dude.
16. Uday: That's fucked up!
17. Kuldeep: *Paul ne unu bariyan layan si* [Paul gave him a big beating].
18. Uday: He fought Paul Michaels—he's in our neighborhood and shit. What
19. the fuck is going on?
20. Kuldeep: Neighbors fucked him up?
21. Uday: They probably backed him up.
22. Kuldeep: I want to fight that Mexican [referring to Paul].
23. Uday: *Oh dekh lagiyan! Oh dekh vaal kiddan khilare paya vai*! [Oh look! Oh look
24. how his hair has been mussed up!].

During this rapid-fire exchange, Kuldeep does not even look closely at the fight until Uday signals to him to do so in Punjabi. Utterances that deal with the physicality of the fight, such as those pertaining to Paul's beating (line 17) and the postfight state of Paully (line 23), are conveyed in Punjabi. Also important here is the alliance between these FOBby boys and others from their racially diverse neighborhood. Uday repeatedly refers to Paully Vu, a Vietnamese boy, as "our" Paully, because they are from the same neighborhood. Likewise, they are surprised that Paul, a Mexican American boy also from their neighborhood, would fight with one of their own. Alliances made in neighborhoods carry over into school, especially for boys who spend time roaming around outside of school (see Eckert 1989). Such alliances are central to how FOBby boys conceive of their masculinity, and where they may fit in among lower middle-class Vietnamese Americans and Mexican Americans in San Jose. Furthermore, their interest in this fight and fighting in general can be understood as a way of asserting masculinity in the hostile company of popular students, school faculty, and the school in general.

FOB STYLES AND SCHOOL ORIENTATIONS

Using FOB styles is a source of humor and solidarity for boys and girls in an otherwise dull and alienating school environment. Unlike popular, "model" teens, FOBs do not believe that the school is working to their benefit. When discussing a report card received in the mail,

Uday lamented that the school had recorded far more absences than he actually had. KB remarked, "[The] system fucked up." Kuldeep quickly added, "System is always fucking *you* up." That the system is rarely, if ever, on their side is a widespread sentiment among FOB teens. This opposition toward the school and popular teens' affinity toward it echo seminal studies of youth social categories, such as Eckert's jocks and burnouts (1989), or Paul Willis's (1977) "lads" and "earoles." In both these studies, the nonnormative group's rejection of the institutional environment makes them marginal, while the normative group's acceptance of the same fuels their popularity. The Desi situation, however, contains a third, vital element that shapes social action: their community. Both popular and FOB teens are deeply invested in their familial social circles, their reputation, and participating in these contexts. Thus, their styles in school are not performed according to the social dynamics of school alone; rather, the types of gendered identities teens construct in school are necessarily informed by those they construct in their community, and vice versa.

What is valued in their community and the dominant values of the schools can differ significantly for FOBs; it is the former that take precedence for girls and boys, in varying ways. While these youth rarely if ever have open confrontations with teachers or speak badly about them in English when they are in earshot, talking about them in Punjabi is commonplace. Boys avoid interaction with teachers outside of class while girls at the very least greet them, a move that is avoided by FOB boys. One day during lunch, Simran, Kuldeep, Uday, and Jett were perched on the railing of the library's handicap ramp when the sound of walkie-talkies grew louder. As the teacher Ms. Marie Subal approached, she announced, "Coming through, thanks!" Simran greeted her with a cheerful, "Hi Miss Subal!" Ms. Subal responded by saying "Hi" to the group and kept walking, looking at the boys who failed to greet her. As she passed, KB scowled, "**Marie** *pehri yaar. Bahut pehri yaar*" [Marie is mean, dude. She is really mean, dude]. Although Miss Subal was in earshot, KB's use of a South Asian pronunciation of her name as "MAH-ree" rather than American version "muh-REE" camouflaged the fact that she is the subject of his remark. Jett confirmed as she was walking away, "You see these teachers who are hella mean to you in class and you see them outside and they're all nice." Uday echoed this sentiment by saying "She's hella mean fool, hella fucked up." In this interaction, only Simran interacted with Ms. Subal, albeit in a brief way. By commenting about Ms. Subal in Punjabi and using DAE to pronounce her name, the boys were able to claim a private moment in an encounter that girls and faculty would regard as decidedly public.

As their use of Punjabi and English profanity illustrates, boys regard school to be a far more private space than girls do. Girls regard the school as consisting of a number of semiprivate opportunities but ultimately as a public space in which they must carefully self-regulate their speech and comportment. Girls rarely cross limits set by their communities and schools. Thus, their use of FOB style can be a stylistic variable that they control, but a status one when compared to normative standards set by popular Desi teens. Boys likewise control FOB style as a status variable, but their different conception of what is public and private makes their language use a status variable as well. Sikh Punjabi boys, who are under few constraints in community settings, are still subject to school rules. Because their reputations are not at stake, they can make any space private by using Punjabi and assuming that they will not be understood. In these ways, gendered differences in language use play an important role not only in how FOB boys express themselves differently than girls do, but also in how their language use is regarded by school faculty.

METALINGUISTIC AWARENESS AND RACIALIZING CONSEQUENCES

FOBby boys may appear to evade punishment by speaking Punjabi when few understand it but are in fact subject to judgment. Silverstein (1993) argues that metapragmatic discourse is underpinned by particular cultural values and beliefs that appear naturalized through ideologies. In U.S. schools, as well as in other institutional settings, the ideal of English monolingualism prevails. In California schools, where bilingual education has long been a point of contention, even social uses of languages other than English have met with negative reception. Rosina Lippi-Green (1997) illustrates how "standard" ways of speaking are unmarked, normalizing, and powerful in their ability to relegate other varieties as unpreferred (see also Hill 1998; Woolard 1989). While switches in code may be unmarked and integral to constructions of identity, switching frequently is marked in a monolingual U.S. context, and it is against this norm that difference is constructed (Bailey 2007:268; see also Urciuoli 1999; Zentella 1997). In this indexical order, FOB styles index a nonnormative linguistic practice that conflicts with the dominant monolingual value. Although it may seem that multilingualism has no place in these schools, ideologies of multiculturalism complicate this message. Since the early 1990s, multiculturalism has encouraged the celebration of diverse cultures and has framed language as an important part of heritage.[13] The unspoken caveat, however, is that such expressions are limited to designated times and spaces, such as multicultural day performances and curricular events.

Metapragmatic discourse about monolingual English standards underscores how FOB styles stand in stark contrast to this norm. For school faculty, such displays are immediate markers of otherness and cause for further investigation. Hearing loud displays of Punjabi is how Mr. Lopez, a Greene High School administrator, initially noticed FOBby teens. He recalled his surprise when he realized this group is not Latino: "Where did they come from? Our population is so brown. And you were colorblind, let's say. East Indians look like Hispanics. Some of them are real dark, they may look like Afro-Americans. They come here, and it's not like they have a big flag saying 'I'm East Indian.'" Mr. Lopez explained that in the veritable sea of brown faces at Greene, he initially mistook some Desi students for Latinos. This racial ambiguity, which is less a problem for East Asian or Southeast Asian students, was quickly clarified when he heard them speaking in "Indian" (i.e., Punjabi) as he patrolled the schoolyard. As the faculty member in charge of ESL, Mr. Lopez is privy to assessments of each student's language abilities. As we sat in his office one morning, Mr. Lopez scanned his list for Desi students in

ELL "English Language Learners" classes as well as ESL, "English as a Second Language." The associations between his list, ELL and ESL students, and youth who code switch but speak English fluently, are loose at best. When he sees groups of Desi teens not speaking English, they potentially became Desi teens who may not be able to speak English well.

The monolingual ideology that values English alone conflicts with FOB styles that follow a South Asian multilingual ideology of using different varieties and registers for different purposes. On a typically sunny California morning, Mr. Lopez offered to show me how he makes such connections and invited me to accompany him on his surveillance rounds. Gesturing toward the FOBs, Mr. Lopez remarked, "Because of their English, they pretty much stay by themselves, which hurts, because they speak their own language and they don't speak in English and they don't get any better." Whether accurate or not, this association between being Limited English Proficient and being bilingual can be quite detrimental to FOBs. While a handful of youth actually need ESL classes, the vast majority of FOBs speak English fluently and with an American accent; many actually speak it better than Punjabi. Being called FOBs when they are second- and third-generation teens predictably does not improve this situation.

CONCLUSION

Language practices contribute to how some Desis remain model minorities and continue to integrate into upper middle-class white America while others share more economic, academic, and professional similarities with Latinos and other local populations. Being children of adults who hold nonskilled jobs and have far more extensive contact with extended family and new arrivals from South Asia influences linguistic aspects of FOB style in ways that marginalize them at school. While Silicon Valley offered atypical job and wealth accumulation opportunities to these nonskilled workers who became middle class, such economic prosperity has not led to equal increases in social prestige for their children in schools. Differences in cultural capital address how parents may not be able to instill in their children the type of cultural and linguistic knowledge about school codes that would lead them to refrain from using FOB styles at school. On the other hand, FOBby teen use of Punjabi, DAE, and the other language varieties discussed here privileges community language ideologies of multilingualism over school values of monolingualism. Their repertoire of stylistic resources varies from their parents', but their use of distinct varieties, accents, and registers for different types of speech mirrors their parents' ways of speaking. FOBby teens are aware of school codes of profanity and the punitive consequences of violating them, but are less aware of the racializing consequences of not following English monolingualism when they perform FOB styles.

FOB styles contribute to the creation of racialized meanings in the school context by disrupting the homogeneity of the model minority stereotype and playing a key role in racial formation (Omi and Winant 1994). In the struggle over who is and is not to be considered white, Desis, like other immigrant groups, have been consistently left in the blind spot of racial definition or fall subject to its aberrant nature. Scholars note the racial ambiguity that surrounds the category of Asian Americans (Okihiro 1994), and South Asians in particular (Prashad 2004; Radhakrishnan 2003; Visweswaran 1993). It has been suggested that as a model minority, Desis are poised to join white America (Prashad 2000). By engaging in normative uses of language that include speaking in English and minimizing profanity, popular Desi teens are rarely reprimanded by faculty for their styles of speaking and easily live up to the model minority stereotype. They distance themselves from FOB styles by meeting a normative standard and remaining linguistically unmarked, despite being racially marked as Asian American and brown. Popular styles can be understood as an ethnic variation on whiteness, in which a cosmopolitan, Bollywood-influenced style is showcased in performative contexts. Popular identity in school remains model in every way, including linguistically, and leaves these youth well positioned to integrate into wealthy white Californian communities.

Nonnormative use of language, combined with other unpopular speech practices such as quoting Bollywood, exchanging insults, and talking about fights codes FOBby teens as brown rather than white. FOBs distance themselves from popular Desis and instead align with Mexican American, Vietnamese American, and other teens with whom they feel an affinity in their neighborhoods. In Silicon Valley, these populations, like Desis, are not uniformly upwardly mobile and are subject to similar types of racializing judgments. Because boys and girls differently regard the school as more or less private based on the gendered standards of propriety they are expected to achieve in their communities, boys are far less self-censoring than girls in their language use. Both are marginalized by peers, but boys tend to be more conspicuous violators of school codes. The "brownness" of Indians, as Mr. Lopez calls it, suggests that if Desis are not acting in model ways, they should be grouped with those who require reform. These social processes affect the positioning of South Asian Americans vis-à-vis other racial groups in the United States and underscore the role of language use in shaping racial meaning in diasporic communities.

NOTES

Support for this research and writing was generously provided by the Social Science Research Council International Migration Program, Spencer Foundation for Research Related to Education, and New York University. I am grateful to Paul Manning for his insightful comments and detailed editorial assistance, and the two anonymous reviewers for their constructive suggestions for revision, as well as to Bambi Schieffelin, Micaela di Leonardo, Katherine Hoffman, Jillian Cavanaugh, Ana Aparicio, and Nitasha Sharma for reading and commenting on drafts of this article. I am deeply indebted to Amrit, Simran, Mandeep, and other teens for their recording, translation, and transliteration assistance, as well as to Himanshu Aggarwal and Ekta Ohri for additional translation help. Any remaining errors are my own.

1. I use the term *race* to refer to broader classifications such as Asian American, African American, white, and Latino, and the term *ethnicity* to refer to differences in language, religion, and regional specificities within these groups.
2. I use the youth orthography *FOBby*, as evidenced in their own use of this term in its adjectival form. Angela Reyes (2007) reports that Southeast Asian American youth use the acronym *F.O.B.* by pronouncing each letter, as well as the word *FOB*; in my study, only the latter is used.
3. According to the 1990 census, over 70 percent of Desis in the United States are bilingual in their heritage language and English (Garcia 1997:4), and the 2000 census confirms these trends. About 95 percent of the youth in my study understand their heritage language; about 75 percent are conversationally fluent in it. Whereas parents educated in

South Asia learned at least three languages, their children raised in the United States usually only speak their heritage language and English.

4. Arguably Hindi, India's postindependence language; Urdu, the national language of Pakistan; and Hindi-Urdu, a hybrid dialect that is prevalent in Bollywood films all hold both nationalist and popular value in diasporic communities. Yet, because some regions of South India eschew Hindi as a national standard and because of a fraught relationship between India and Pakistan and their languages, debates over whether English should be India's national language persist (LaDousa 2005). I found this contest to be less pronounced in Silicon Valley Desi communities. Although some adults value Hindi as a lingua franca, and using it helped me communicate with speakers who otherwise preferred Punjabi, most adults prefer their heritage language or English over Hindi.

5. Earlier studies about early Sikh farmers who intermarried with Mexican Americans (Leonard 1992) as well as Sikh communities during the 1980s (Gibson 1988) provide important background and context for this discussion of Sikh teenagers. See Shankar (2008) for discussions of similarities with and differences between earlier populations and those discussed here with regard to community values, schools, and youth culture.

6. All Punjabi-to-English translations and transliterations were done with the assistance of teenagers who made recordings and, more recently, with the assistance of a young woman in her mid-twenties whom I have known since she was a teenager in a Silicon Valley high school. My knowledge of Hindi and passive competence in Punjabi enabled me to follow much of the unspecialized conversation. Still, I relied on teens to understand specific terms as well as their norms of usage, which can vary from practices of Punjabi speakers elsewhere, as well as from those of their parents. I use their translations, as they were able to provide the contextual information about utterances as well as local, teen-specific glosses about certain terms and phrases, and have not noted deviances from "standard" Punjabi.

7. Elsewhere I discuss in detail the types of gender norms to which boys and girls are differently subject (see Shankar 2008, chapter 7).

8. Although this study did not track language shift, it has benefited greatly from the work of Don Kulick (1992) as well as other recent work on gender and language shift (Cavanaugh 2006; Hoffman 2006) as well as linguistic syncretism (Fader 2007).

9. Translations of specific terms in this transcript were provided by Janvi, but there appears to be some inconsistency between her translations and those of other Punjabi speakers I consulted later. For example, Janvi insisted that *gaddian wale, paau* and *kale kacheyan wale* are names for dancers in their Sikh Punjabi community, and I have included them as such, but other Punjabi speakers could not confirm these translations. The less common or possibly incorrect usage of these terms appears to contribute to the misrecognition and humor surrounding them in this conversation.

10. Current FCC (Federal Communications Commission) banned words still conform to George Carlin's "The Seven Words you Can't Say on Television"—*shit, piss, fuck, cunt, cock-sucker, motherfucker,* and *tits,* although occasional exceptions are made, and girls tended to use the first three the most. Greene High School shares this list and also discourages the use of words such as *hell, goddamn,* and *asshole* in school contexts, which girls also used.

11. While a comparison between Sikhs and other South Asian ethnic groups is beyond the scope of this paper, the hypermasculine stance of some FOB boys echoes the ways in which the British constructed Sikhs as masculine in comparison to other ethnic groups such as Bengalis (see Metcalf 1997). I am not here suggesting that Sikhs in Silicon Valley should be considered a "martial race," but rather, that this South Asian ideology may have some relevance to the hypermasculine stance expressed by some Sikh boys. I am grateful to Paul Manning for drawing my attention to this point.

12. Jett's comment, "Yes. You is bad" is not in DAE but is similar to other nonstandard English utterances I heard FOB teens use with one another.

13. Elsewhere (Shankar 2004a) I discuss the complicated inception and execution of multiculturalism and the ways in which it often exacerbates the very racial and ethnic inequalities it addresses (see also Labrador 2004).

REFERENCES CITED

Agha, Asif, 1998. Stereotypes and Registers of Honorific Language. Language in Society 27:151–193.
Bailey, Benjamin. 2007. Heteroglossia and Boundaries: Processes of Linguistic and Social Distinction. In Bilingualism: A Social Approach. Monica Heller, ed. Pp. 257–274. New York: Palgrave Macmillan.
Bakhtin, Mikhail. 1981. The Dialogic Imagination: Four Essays. Austin: University of Texas Press.

Bhatt, Rakesh. 2001. World Englishes. Annual Review of Anthropology 30:527–550.

Bourdieu, Perre. 1985. The Forms of Capital. In The Handbook of Theory and Research for the Sociology of Education. J. Richardson, ed. Pp. 241–258. New York: Greenwood.

Bucholtz, Mary. 1999. You da Man: Narrating the Racial Other in the Linguistic Production of White Masculinity. Journal of Sociolinguistics 3(4):443–460.

——2001 The Whiteness of Nerds: Superstandard English and Racial Markedness.

——2004 Journal of Linguistic Anthropology 11(1):84–100. 2004 Styles and Stereotypes: The Linguistic Negotiation of Identity among Laotian American Youth. Pragmatics 14(2–3):127–147.

Cameron, Deborah. 1998. Performing Gender and Identity. In Language and Gender: A Reader. Jennifer Coates, ed. Pp. 270–284. Malden, MA: Blackwell.

Cavanaugh, Jillian. 2006. Little Women and Vital Champions: Gendered Shift in a Northern Italian Town. Journal of Linguistic Anthropology 16(2):194–210.

Chiang-Hom, Christy. 2004. Transnational Cultural Practices of Chinese Immigrant Youth and Parachute Kids. In Asian American Youth: Culture, Identity, and Ethnicity. Min Zhou and Jennifer Lee, eds. Pp. 143–158. New York: Routledge.

Chun, Elaine. 2001. The Construction of White, Black, and Korean American Identities through African American Vernacular English. Journal of Linguistic Anthropology 11(1):52–64.

Cohn, Bernard. 1985. The Command of Language and the Language of Command. Subaltern Studies 4:276329.

Crawford, James. 1992 Language Loyalties: A Source Book on the Official English Controversy. Chicago: University of Chicago Press.

——2000 At War with Diversity: U.S. Language Policy in an Age of Anxiety. Clevedon, UK: Multilingual Matters.

Cutler, Cecelia. 2003. "Keepin' It Real": White Hip-Hoppers' Discourses of Language, Race, and Authenticity. Journal of Linguistic Anthropology 13(2):211–233.

Eckert, Penelope. 1989. Jocks and Burnouts: Social Categories and Identity in High School. New York: Teachers College Press.

——2000 Linguistic Variation as Social Practice: The Linguistic Construction of Identity in Belten High. Oxford, UK: Blackwell Publishers.

Eckert, Penelope, and Sally McConnell-Ginet. 2003. Language and Gender. Cambridge, UK: Cambridge University Press.

Eisenlohr, Patrick. 2006. Little India: Diaspora, Time and Ethnolinguistic Belonging in Hindu Mauritius. Berkeley: University of California Press.

Fader, Ayala. 2007. Reclaiming Sacred Sparks: Linguistic Syncretism and Gendered Language Shift among Hasidic Jews in New York. Journal of Linguistic Anthropology 12(1):1–22.

Gal, Susan. 2002 A Semiotics of the Public/Private Distinction. Differences: A Journal of Feminist Cultural Studies 15(1):77–95.

——2004 Commentary: Perspective and the Politics of Representation. Pragmatics 14(2–3):337–339.

——2007 Circulation in the "New" Economy: Clasps and Copies. Paper presented at the 106th Meeting of the American Anthropological Association, Washington, November 29–December 2.

Garcia, Ofelia. 1997 New York's Multilingualism: World Languages and their Role in a U.S. City. In The Multilingual Apple: Languages in New York City. Ofelia Garcia and Joshua Fishman, eds. Pp. 3–52. New York: Mouton de Gruyer.

Gibson, Margaret. 1988. Accommodation without Assimilation: Sikh Immigrants in an American High School. Ithaca, NY: Cornell University Press.

Gillespie, Marie. 1995. Television, Ethnicity, and Cultural Change. London: Routledge.

Goodwin, Marjorie. 2006. The Hidden Life of Girls: Games of Stance, Status, and Exclusion. Oxford, UK: Blackwell.

Hall, Kathleen. 2002. Lives in Translation: Sikh Youth as British Citizens. Philadelphia: University of Pennsylvania Press.

Heller, Monica. 2007. Bilingualism as Ideology and Practice. In Bilingualism: A Social Approach. Monica Heller, ed. Pp. 1–22. New York: Palgrave Macmillan.

Hill, Jane. 1995. Junk Spanish, Covert Racism and the (Leaky) Boundary between Public and Private Spheres. Pragmatics 5(2):197–212.

——1998 Language, Race, and White Public Space. American Anthropologist 100(3):680– 689.

Hoffman, Katherine. 2006. Berber Language Ideologies, Maintenance, and Contraction: Gendered Variation in the Indigenous Margins of Morocco. Language & Communication 26:144–167.

Hwang, Henry David. 1979. FOB. New York: Theater Communication Group Inc.'s Plays in Process.

Ima, Kenji. 1995. Testing the American Dream: At-Risk Southeast Asian Refugee Students in Secondary Schools. In California's Immigrant Children: Theory, Research, and Implications for Educational Policy. Ruben Rumbaut and Wayne Cornelius, eds. Pp. 191–209. San Diego: University of California, Center for US-Mexican Studies.

Inkelas, Karen. 2006. Racial Attitudes and Asian Pacific Americans: Demystifying the Model Minority. New York: Routledge.

Irvine, Judith. 1974. Strategies of Status Manipulation in the Wolof Greeting. In Explorations in the Ethnography of Speaking. Richard Bauman and Joel Sherzer, eds. Pp. 167–191. London: Cambridge University Press.

——2001 "Style" as Distinctiveness: The Culture and Ideology of Linguistic Differentiation. In Style and Sociolinguistic Variation. Penelope Eckert and John R. Rickford, eds. Pp. 21–43. Cambridge, UK: Cambridge University Press.

Irvine, Judith, and Gal Susan. 2000. Language Ideology and Linguistic Differentiation. In Regimes of Language: Ideologies, Polities, and Identities. Paul Kroskrity, ed. Pp. 35–83. Santa Fe, NM: School of American Research Press.

Jacobsen, Knut, and P. Pratap Kumar. 2004. Introduction. In South Asians in the Diaspora: Histories and Religious Traditions. Knut Jacobsen and P. Pratap Kumar, eds. Pp. ix–xxiv. Boston: Brill.

Jeon, Mihyon. 2001. Avoiding FOBs: An Account of a Journey. Working Papers in Educational Linguistics 17(1–2):83–106.

Kachru, Braj. 2000. The Alchemy of English. In The Language and Cultural Theory Reader. Lucy Burke, Tony Crowley, and Alain Girvin, eds. Pp. 29–31. London: Routledge.

Khubchandani, Lachman. 1983. Plural Languages, Plural Cultures: Communication, Identity and Sociopolitical Change in Contemporary India. Honolulu: University of Hawaii Press.

Kiesling, Scott. 2001. Stances of Whiteness and Hegemony in Fraternity Men's Discourse. Journal of Linguistic Anthropology 11(1):101–115.

Kim, Angela, and Christine Yeh. 2002. Stereotypes of Asian American Students. Eric Digest 172:1–7.

Kroskrity, Paul. 2000. Identity. Journal of Linguistic Anthropology 9:111–114.

Kulick, Don. 1992. Language Shift and Cultural Reproduction: Socialization, Self and Syncretism in a Papua New Guinea Village. Cambridge, UK: Cambridge University Press.

Labrador, Roderick. 2004. "We Can Laugh at Ourselves: Hawai'i Ethnic Humor, Local Identity, and the Myth of Multiculturalism. Pragmatics 14(2–3):291–316.

LaDousa, Chaise. 2005. Disparate Markets: Language, Nation, and Education in North India. American Ethnologist 32(3):460–478.

——2006. The Discursive Malleability of an Identity: A Dialogic Approach to Language "Medium" Schooling in North India. Journal of Linguistic Anthropology 16(1):36– 57.

Lave, Jean, and Etienne Wenger. 1991. Situated Learning in Communities of Practice. Washington, DC: American Psychological Association.

Lee, Stacey. 2005. Up against Whiteness: Race, School, and Immigrant Youth. New York: Teacher's College Press.

Lee, Jennifer, and Min Zhou. 2004. Introduction: The Making of Culture, Identity, and Ethnicity among Asian American Youth. In Asian American Youth: Culture, Identity, and Ethnicity. Jennifer Lee and Min Zhou, eds. Pp. 1–30. New York: Routledge.

Leonard, Karen. 1992. Making Ethnic Choices: California's Punjabi Mexican Americans. Philadelphia: Temple University Press.

Lew, Jamie. 2004. The "Other" Story of Model Minorities: Korean American High School Dropouts in an Urban Context. Anthropology and Education Quarterly 35(3):303–323.

Lippi-Green, Rosina. 1997. English with an Accent. London: Routledge.

Lo, Adrienne. 1999. Codeswitching, Speech Community Membership, and the Construction of Ethnic Identity. Journal of Sociolinguistics 3–4:461–479.

Lo, Adrienne, and Angela Reyes. 2004. Language, Identity, and Relationality in Asian Pacific America: An Introduction. Pragmatics 14(2–3):115–126.

Loomis, Terrence, 1990. Pacific Migrant Labour, Class, and Racism in New Zealand. Alershot, UK: Avebury Publishing Ltd.

Maira, Sunaina, 2002. Desis in the House: Indian American Youth Culture in New York City. Philadelphia: Temple University Press.

McElhinny, Bonnie, 2001. See No Evil, Speak No Evil: White Police Officers' Talk about Race and Affirmative Action. Journal of Linguistic Anthropology 11(1):65–78.

Mendoza-Denton, Norma.1999. Style. Journal of Linguistic Anthropology 9(1–2): 238–240.

——2007 Homegirls: Language and Cultural Practice among Latina Youth Gangs. Malden, MA: Blackwell.

Metcalf, Thomas. 1997. Ideologies of the Raj. Cambridge, UK: Cambridge University Press.

Ochs, Elinor. 1992. Indexing Gender. In Rethinking Context: Language as Interactive Phenomenon. A. Duranti and C. Goodwin, eds. Pp. 335–358. Cambridge, UK: Cambridge University Press.

Okihiro, Gary. 1994. Margins and Mainstreams: Asians in American History and Culture. Seattle: University of Washington Press.

Omi, Michael, and Howard Winant. 1994. Racial Formation in the United States. New York: Routledge.

Pennycook, Alistair. 2007. Global Englishes and Transcultural Flows. London: Routledge.

Perry, Pamela. 2002. Shades of White: White Kids and Racial Identities in High School. Durham, NC: Duke University Press.

Prashad, Vijay. 2000. The Karma of Brown Folk. Minneapolis: University of Minnesota Press.

———2004. Everybody was Kung-Fu Fighting: Afro-Asian Connections and the Myth of Cultural Purity. Boston: Beacon Press.

Pyke, Karen, and Tran Dang. 2003. "FOB" and "Whitewashed": Identity and Internalized Racism among Second Generation Asian Americans. Qualitative Sociology 26(2):147–172.

Radhakrishnan, R.. 2003. Ethnicity in an Age of Diaspora. In Theorizing Diaspora: A Reader. J. Braziel and A. Mannur, eds. Pp. 119–131. Malden, MA: Blackwell Publishers.

Rampton, Ben. 1995. Crossing: Language and Ethnicity among Adolescents. New York: Longman.

Reyes, Angela. 2005. Appropriation of African American Slang by Asian American Youth. Journal of Sociolinguistics 9(4):510–533.

———2007. Language, Identity, and Stereotype among Southeast Asian American Youth. Mahwah, NJ: Lawrence Erlbaum Associates.

Roth-Gordon, Jennifer. 2007. Racing and Erasing the Playboy: Slang, Transnational Youth Subculture, and Racial Discourse in Brazil. Journal of Linguistic Anthropology 17(2):246–265.

Rumbaut, Ruben. 2002. Severed or Sustained Attachments? Language, Identity, and Imagined Communities in the Post-Immigrant Generation. In The Changing Face of Home: The Transnational Lives of the Second Generation. P. Levitt and M. Waters, eds. Pp. 43–95. New York: Russell Sage.

Rymes, Betsy. 2001. Conversational Borderlands: Language and Identity in an Alternative Urban High School. New York: Teachers College Press.

Schieffelin, Bambi, Kathryn Woolard, and Paul Kroskrity, eds. 1998. Language Ideology: Practice and Theory. New York: Oxford University Press.

Shankar, Shalini. 2004a. FOBby or Tight?: "Multicultural Day" and Other Struggles at Two Silicon Valley High Schools. In Local Actions: Cultural Activism, Power and Public Life. M. Checker and M. Fishman, eds. Pp. 184–207. New York: Columbia University Press.

———2004b. Reel to Real: Desi Teens' Linguistic Engagements with Bollywood. Pragmatics 14(2–3):317–336.

———2006. Metaconsumptive Practices and the Circulation of Objectifications. Journal of Material Culture 11(3):293–317.

———2008. Desi Land: Teen Culture, Class, and Success in Silicon Valley. Durham, NC: Duke University Press.

Silverstein, Michael. 1993. Metapragmatic Discourse and Metapragmatic Function. In Reflexive Language: Reported Speech and Metapragmatics. John Lucy, ed. Pp. 33–58. Cambridge, UK: Cambridge University Press.

———1996. Monoglot "Standard" in America: Standardization and Metaphors of Linguistic Hegemony. In The Matrix of Language: Contemporary Linguistic Anthropology. D. Brennis and R. Macauley, eds. Pp. 284–306. Boulder, CO: Westview Press.

———2003. Indexical Order and the Dialectics of Sociolinguistic Life. Language and Communication 23:193–229.

Talmy, Steven. 2004. Forever FOB: The Cultural Production of ESL in a High School. Pragmatics 14(2–3):149–172.

Urciuoli, Bonnie. 1999. Exposing Prejudice: Puerto Rican Experiences of Language, Race, and Class. Boulder, CO: Westview Press.

Visweswaran, Kamala. 1993. Diaspora by Design: Flexible Citizenship and South Asians in U.S. Racial Formations. Diaspora 6:5–29.

Willis, Paul. 1977. Learning to Labor: How Working Class Kids Get Working Class Jobs. New York: Columbia University Press.

Woolard, Kathryn. 1989. Sentences in the Language Prison: The Rhetorical Structuring of an American Language Policy Debate. American Ethnologist 16(2):268–278.

———1994. Gendered Peer Groups and the Bilingual Repertoire in Catalonia. SALSA II, Proceedings of the Symposium about Language and Society. Pp 200–220. Austin: University of Texas.

———1999. Simultaneity and Bivalency as Strategies in Bilingualism. Journal of Linguistic Anthropology 8(1):3–29.

Zentella, Ana Celia. 1997. Growing up Bilingual. Malden, MA: Blackwell.

Zhou, Min. 2004. Coming of Age at the Turn of the Twenty-First Century: A Demographic Profile of Asian American Youth. In Asian American Youth: Culture, Identity, and Ethnicity. Jennifer Lee and Min Zhou, eds. Pp. 33–50. New York: Routledge.

11

Who Are 'Yan Daudu?

Rudolf Gaudio

When I describe 'yan daudu as 'feminine men' to people from the USA and other Western societies, I am often asked, "Are they gay?" The answer is not straightforward. In the earliest days of my research, when all I knew about 'yan daudu was what other people had written or said about them, I imagined I might, as a gay man, be able to become involved in their largely hidden social world. I was intrigued the first few times that I saw 'yan daudu strolling and dancing at nightclubs and outdoor parties, and could not help but compare these images to gay life at home. Although subsequent events forced me to reconsider, but not to reject outright, the naive idea that 'yan daudu were men with whom I could communicate on the basis of a shared sexuality, my interactions with them introduced me to a thriving social world of men who acknowledged and acted upon their sexual attraction to other men. These men comprise what could arguably be called a Hausa homosexual community, though their social life differs in important ways from gay life in the West.

One comparison that seemed apt in the 1990s was that, as drag queens and 'fairies' did for straight-acting gays in mid-twentieth-century New York City, 'yan daudus visibility and social proximity to karuwai attracted conventionally masculine 'men who seek men' [*maza masu neman maza*] and permitted them to meet without blowing their cover. 'Yan daudu often call these men 'civilians' [*fararen-hula*], 'yan aras (an in-group term with no independent meaning), or simply 'men' [*maza*]. The men typically identify themselves as *masu harka* ['people who do the deed'], a 'secret' code term that embraces both 'yan daudu and 'civilians' and is preferred over the standard Hausa term, 'yan ludu ['sodomite,' literally 'people of Lot']. Many masu harka, including those who speak little English, also describe themselves as *homos*, especially when talking to outsiders like me. (The word *gay* tends to be used only by more educated urbanites.) Some 'civilians' secretly self-identify as 'yan daudu—talking and acting 'like women' in private, while maintaining a masculine occupation and appearance in public. Such men are called *'yan daudun riga* ['shirted 'yan daudu'], meaning they treat *daudu*—the practice of men acting 'like women'—like a shirt that can be put on or taken off at will. Unless otherwise noted, in this book *'yan daudu* refers to 'men who act like women' openly and are publicly recognized as such.

Unlike most Western men who describe themselves as gay, masu harka do not see homosexuality as incompatible with heterosexual marriage or parenthood, or vice versa. At some point in their lives most masu harka, including a majority of 'yan daudu, marry women and have biological children. I have chosen not to use the term *bisexual* to refer to married masu harka because I understand bisexuality to refer to an individuals capacity to be sexually attracted to both women and men, and to pursue that attraction socially and physically; this implies a degree of choice regarding sex and kinship which is not widely recognized in Hausa society. Specifically, most Hausa people do not see marriage as a choice, but rather as a moral and social obligation; my own refusal to marry based on my lack of sexual desire for women typically did not follow the cultural logic of my homo acquaintances, who did not see a necessary connection between marriage and heterosexual desire. 'Bisexuality' is thus expected of all masu harka, whether or not they actually desire or enjoy sex with women. Although many masu harka say they enjoy sex with women, these men do not constitute a distinct subgroup, since men who do not desire women sexually are unlikely to admit this except to their closest friends.

I have also chosen not to refer to 'yan daudu as 'transgendered' or 'trans.' Although some writers and activists define *transgender* broadly, I generally hear it used to refer either to people who choose or feel compelled to embrace a gender identity 'opposite' or merely different from their ascribed biological sex (e.g., biological men who live as or become women). With the exception of a male 'transvestite' in Kano whose story circulated on the internet in 2004, I have never met or heard about a 'yan daudu who tried to pass as a woman socially. All the 'yan daudu I have known—even those who were consistently referred to by feminine names—saw themselves as 'real' men and enjoyed the privileges that come from that identity, even while they were stigmatized for being 'feminine.'

Another question I am often asked about 'yan daudu is, "Are they accepted?" Many Westerners, it seems, have heard that there are some non-Western societies in which feminine men, or gender and sexual minorities in general, are supposedly treated with more tolerance and respect than such individuals have historically found in 'the West.' The example of the *berdache*, an outmoded, colonial term for transgendered people in certain Native North American societies, is sometimes mentioned in this regard. Another is the *hijra,* a term used in Hindi and other South Asian languages to refer to eunuchs and intersexed people who live as women. Without making explicit comparisons with such groups (whose histories are too complex to be easily summarized), I generally answer that 'yan daudu's presence is universally acknowledged —no one denies they exist—but that their degree of social acceptance has varied according to time, place and situation. To make my explanation more concrete and up-to-date, I sometimes add that in recent years, Islamic reform movements have grown more powerful in

Northern Nigeria, and this has made life more difficult for many 'yan daudu. "Oh," I am then likely to hear, "Northern Nigeria is Islamic?!" At this point in the conversation I often feel as if the pendulum of cultural assumption has swung to the other extreme, for if some societies are presumed to be more open and tolerant than 'the West,' others have the opposite reputation; and Islamic and African societies usually top that unfortunate list, especially when it comes to gender and sexuality.

Literary scholar Edward Said has described Europeans' long-standing fascination with gender and sexuality in the Muslim Middle East as *Orientalism*. In his book by that title and other works, Said argues that stereotyped images of belly-dancers, veiled women, sheikhs and terrorists, whether they appear in novels, travel writing or television news programs, have led people of European descent to imagine that they are part of a distinct culture—'the West'—that is superior to the cultures of the Middle East; these images have been used to justify the efforts of Western governments and corporations to colonize Middle Eastern lands and exploit their resources. In a similar vein, Leila Ahmed has examined the ways British government officials used reports about the supposedly subordinate status of Egyptian women to justify colonial rule in the late nineteenth and early twentieth centuries; yet many of those same (male) British officials opposed the granting of equal civil rights to women in their own country. More recently, the US government used reports about the Taliban's mistreatment of women to justify the bombing of Afghanistan after the World Trade Center attacks in 2001; under US and allied 'protection' however, the fate of most Afghan women has remained largely unchanged, and unnoticed.

US media coverage of Shari'a in Northern Nigeria shares many of the same Orientalist features. After the first Nigerian state (Zamfara) announced its intention to adopt Shari'a in late 1999, the *New York Times* published a photograph of a taxi with the image of a covered Muslim woman painted on its passenger door, indicating that the taxi was reserved for women only. The *Times* ran this photograph not once, but twice, reinforcing the equation of Shari'a with gender segregation. Neither photograph was accompanied by a story documenting the difficulties women and other Nigerians face in finding adequate, safe and affordable transport of any kind. US media also gave prominent attention to the violence that erupted in Kaduna, a northern city with an ethnically and religiously mixed population, when Shari'a was introduced in early 2000, and again in 2002 when Nigeria hosted the Miss World beauty pageant in its capital, Abuja. In response to Muslim clerics who complained that the pageant objectified women's bodies, a non-Muslim journalist from southern Nigeria wrote, as a kind of joke, that the Prophet Muhammad himself would probably have enjoyed the show and might have taken one of the contestants to be his wife. More than 200 people died in the ensuing clashes between Kaduna's Muslims and Christians, the journalist received death threats and went into hiding, and the pageant was relocated to London. A few months later, the US magazine *Vanity Fair* ran a feature story detailing the events, with a focus on the experiences of the pageants non-African contestants, though the rioting had occurred over 100 miles away from their Abuja hotels.

Perhaps the most infamous story about Shari'a in Northern Nigeria was that of Amina Lawal, a divorced Hausa Muslim woman who was convicted of adultery by an Islamic court in her home state of Katsina and sentenced to death by stoning. The international attention generated by this case went well beyond press coverage to include a segment on *The Oprah Winfrey Show* and several petitions circulated on the internet, before Ms. Lawal was acquitted on a technicality in 2003. (The adultery trials of two other Northern Nigerian women also made headlines in the West, but not to the same extent. Both women were acquitted.) Another international controversy erupted in August 2007 when 18 men were arrested at a hotel in the city of Bauchi for allegedly cross-dressing at a same-sex 'wedding.' Local protesters demanded that the men be prosecuted for sodomy (which, like adultery, carries the death penalty), while international gay-rights organizations sent representatives to assist in the men's defense.

These stories are important, for they highlight the degree to which gender and sexuality have become important and controversial sites of cultural citizenship in Northern Nigeria and in much of the contemporary world at large. At the same time, because they tend to focus on spectacular, exotic or horrifying events, stories like these construct a distorted image of Northern Nigerian social life—not because the details aren't true (though they sometimes aren't), but because they tend to leave out the more common challenges and pleasures that Northern Nigerians experience on a day-to-day basis, as well as the social and historical factors that have led to these experiences and make them meaningful.

Because of their wide circulation, such images, along with other exoticizing portrayals of Islam and of Africa, have the potential to influence the way people interpret my accounts of Northern Nigerian life. This makes it challenging for me to talk about my research in nonacademic settings, such as when I'm socializing with family or friends who don't use words like *exoticizing* on a regular basis. I face similar challenges in writing this book. In both cases my audience is similar: people educated in Western societies who are interested in other places and cultures, but who may have little or no scholarly training in African or Islamic studies, anthropology or linguistics. Whatever your background, in reading my stories about 'yan daudu and others, you will undoubtedly be reminded of things you have heard elsewhere about gender and sexuality, language and culture, Africa and Islam. Some of my stories might sound similar to what you've heard; some will clash. Keep track of these reactions. My aim is not simply to debunk or confirm what you've previously been told or believed to be true. Rather, my hope is that you will rethink those ideas, and reconsider their implications: Where do they come from? Who told you about them, and why? How can you know if they're true or false? And what difference does it make?

ENCOUNTERING 'YAN DAUDU

Gender and sexual diversity were not on my professional agenda when I first traveled to Nigeria in 1991 to take a Hausa-language summer course at Bayero University, Kano (BUK), and to do preliminary research for a doctoral dissertation on the language practices of *mala- mai* (singular: *malam*), Hausa Islamic scholars and teachers. Yet even before I arrived in Kano I knew that local ideologies of gender and sexuality would figure prominently in my day-to-day experiences there. The directors of the language program sent out a letter advising me and my fellow students (14 Americans and one Dutch) that we would be living in the *birni* (also called 'Old City' or just. 'City') inside Kano's ancient walls, whose residents are known for their commitment to Islamic social norms. We were therefore instructed to show respect to our hosts by dressing modestly when we went outside—headscarves for women; no shorts or tank-tops for anybody—and to refrain from mixed-sex socializing. The women in our group were encouraged to get to know our female neighbors, most of whom were in seclusion [*auren kulle*, literally 'locked-up marriage'] but could invite female guests into their homes. My female colleagues were also told that while they could greet our male neighbors, it would not be appropriate to shake hands. The men in our group were likewise encouraged to socialize with our male neighbors, but to refrain from greeting our female neighbors even in passing.

Outside the Old City these rules applied with varying consistency, depending on the religious, ethnic and generational affiliations of the people we met and the activities they were engaged in. At BUK, for instance, a predominantly Muslim campus on the outskirts of Kano, the majority of women (most of whom were students) wore colorful head-scarves and perhaps a shawl draped loosely over the head and shoulders; a small number wore their hair uncovered, sometimes with shape-revealing blouses and jeans; others wore a plain-colored headscarf pinned under the chin—a contemporary version of the Islamic *hijab* or 'covering.' (By the early 2000s, this kind of covering had become more prevalent.) Men at BUK displayed a similarly diverse array of clothing, head-coverings and facial hair (or lack thereof). And students of both sexes mingled, or refrained from mingling, in ways that did not correlate with dress in any obvious way.

I returned to Kano in 1992 to embark on my fieldwork with malamai. With the help of scholars and staff at BUK (where I taught one course) and the Kano State History and Culture Bureau, I set out to establish contacts with malamai throughout the city, whom I interviewed on the relative value of Islamic and Western-style education and on the pedagogical use of Arabic, Hausa and English. All these contacts were with men, but it did not occur to me at first to question the gender arrangements of my fieldwork or of Hausa society in general. Various experiences, however, led me to reconsider both the methodological approach and substantive focus of my research.

Some of the malamai I interviewed brought up the subject of women even though I had not asked about it directly Many of my questions dealt with what is often described as a gap in educational achievement between northern and southern Nigeria: northern Nigerians are said to lag behind southerners in the federal, English-medium school system, and this makes it hard for northerners to find salaried jobs in the civil service and private sector. The gap is usually attributed to northerners' traditional preference for Islamic education and their historical distrust of Western schooling, known in Hausa as *boko* (from English 'book'). When I asked one malam to explain the reasons for this distrust, he offered the following illustration. If you go to a business office or government agency here in Kano, he said, you will find southern women working as secretaries and the like, because they have more *karatu* ['reading,' from Arabic *qara'a*], by which he meant *boko*. But in the south, he continued, you won't find northern women working in offices, even if they've had some *karatu*. Why? Because northern women have *ilirni* ['knowledge,' from Arabic *'ilm*], by which he meant knowledge of Islamic scripture. According to this malam, Western schooling might yield practical, economically useful skills, but Islamic education was crucial to the maintenance of a moral social order; and gender segregation—keeping unrelated men and women separate—was a key symbol of that morality.

The prevailing practice of gender segregation affected my informal social interactions as well. Whereas, in the USA, I often spent time with women friends, in Kano, I initially found myself socializing almost exclusively with men, most of whom were, as I was, in their twenties and unmarried. I began to take notice of the ways these men talked about women. Speaking about marriage, for example, many of my acquaintances focused intensely on the issue of control. A man needs to 'control' his wife, they said; at the very least he must be made to feel as if he were in control. This notion of control, especially the controllability of a potential wife, lay behind many young men's preferences for the type of woman they said they wanted to marry: village girls are more controllable than city girls, uneducated girls are more controllable than educated ones, and so on.

Conversations about courtship and marriage were challenging for me in a number of ways. Though I had lived more-or-less openly as a gay man in the USA since my late teens, when I went to Nigeria for my fieldwork, I retreated into what I had learned to call 'the closet': I got a short, conservative haircut, removed my earrings, and answered presumptuous questions—like why I wasn't married and whether I had a girlfriend—with evasive headshakes and shrugs. Most ethnographers, it seems, develop doubts about the feasibility of their projects when they go out of the library and into the field. When I began to have doubts, I thought first about how I might be able to bridge the religious and cultural differences between me and the people I was working with; but I also felt a growing desire to do research that would not require me to suppress the philosophical and political commitments I had embraced as an out gay man. My experience was similar in many ways to the challenges faced by other researchers, especially feminists, lesbians and gay men, who have sought to maintain respect for the people and communities they were working with, even when some of those people said or did things that offended the researchers' own beliefs and values.

As my circle of acquaintances grew and my relationships deepened over time, I made friends with whom I felt comfortable discussing culturally sensitive matters, and who helped me see that northern Nigerian society was far more diverse with respect to gender and sexuality than I had initially recognized. I was especially surprised to find out that Hausa society, and the city of Kano in particular, have a reputation for homosexuality. Many southern Nigerians, for example, deny that there might be men or women in their region who engage in homosexual behavior, and say it's only 'those Muslims' up north (along with decadent Westerners and

Arabs) who do that sort of thing. For their part, Hausa people are less inclined to deny the existence of homosexuality in their society than they are to gossip about it, often but not always in disparaging terms. Living in Kano, I heard rumors about the homosexual proclivities of prominent local men, read sensationalistic newspaper stories about homosexual scandals in boarding schools, and heard reports of police raids on bars and nightclubs frequented by homosexuals.

These social experiences led me back to the scholarly literature on Hausa history, society and culture, where I found tantalizing references to 'yan daudu in relation to 'prostitution' *[karuwanci]* and *Bori,* the Hausa cult of spirit-possession whose practitioners are widely condemned by orthodox Muslims as 'pagan' *[arna]* or 'heathen' *[kafir]*. In most of these texts the term *'yan daudu* was translated as 'homosexuals,' 'transvestites' or 'pimps,' none of which turned out to be truly accurate, though they all convey a partial sense of 'yan daudu's activities and social identities. The most helpful source I found—and the only monograph devoted to 'yan daudu—was a master's thesis written by Salisu Abdullahi, a student of sociology at Bayero University, Kano, who later became a lecturer in that department. With his encouragement and advice, I began to consider the possibility of changing the focus of my research from malamai to 'yan daudu.

Academic references and personal contacts thus pointed me to places and events that were far removed, socially if not spatially, from Kano's Old City, where I lived, and the largely conservative, scholarly circles I had been traveling in. I asked to be taken to Bori gatherings, which usually took place late at night in the outskirts of town; and I made my way to other parts of Kano, such as Sabon Gari, where 'prostitution' and mixed-sex socializing, along with alcohol and gambling, were more-or-less tolerated. These wanderings taught me a great deal about Hausa social and cultural geography—the ways people, institutions and activities were distributed in space, and the ways people talked about those places. From my previous visits and readings, I was already familiar with the basic distinction between Kano's *birni,* the area inside its ancient city walls, and the rest of the city, often called simply *waje* ['outside']. A more basic distinction is drawn throughout Hausaland between *gari,* a city or town of any size, and *kauye* ['village, countryside']. (A territory with few or no human inhabitants is called *daji* ['forest, bush'].) These distinctions carry great moral weight, for it was in cities where Islam first established itself in Hausaland hundreds of years ago, while so-called 'traditional' *[garga-jiya]* and 'pagan' *[arna]* customs continued to dominate in rural areas well into the twentieth century. In Arabic-Islamic terms, the city represents *dar al-Islam,* the abode of Islam, an oasis of restraint surrounded by *dar al-kufr,* the abode of unbelief, where wild, immoral practices prevail. The moral and aesthetic prestige of the city is also expressed in the lexical distinction between people who are said to be *nagari* ['urbane, sophisticated'; literally, 'of town'], while *kanyanci* ['countryness'] denotes poor manners and a lack of sophistication.

While the city is seen as the cradle of Islamic civilization, cities also bring people and things together in ways that can undermine that exalted image. As we will discuss in Chapter 2, for hundreds of years, Muslim leaders in Kano and other Hausa cities have periodically sought to cast out individuals and practices that they define as contrary to Islam. After the British imperial conquest in the early 1900s, activities like drinking, mixed-sex socializing, and spirit- possession [*Bori*] came to be tolerated in newly constructed 'outside' areas such as Sabon Gari [literally, 'New Town'], a residential neighborhood for poor men who were brought from various parts of British West Africa to work in factories, railway yards and other wage- earning occupations. As happened in other colonial African cities, these areas—known in Hausa as *bariki* [from English 'barracks']—also attracted young rural women whose prospects for work and marriage were derailed by colonial policies that made traditional forms of farming, trade and family life difficult or impossible. 'Prostitution' (a term that often referred to concubinage or other long-term intimate relationships) was one way these women could support themselves and their families of origin; it was also a way to meet potential husbands.

Sabon Gari was originally built in a rural, sparsely settled area east of the Old City, but as Kano continued to grow over the course of the twentieth century, its location became more geographically central. Only a few kilometers away from the Emir's Palace and the main Friday mosque, Sabon Gari today is adjacent to Kano's most commercially vibrant market and its busiest transportation hub. In addition to a diverse population of Muslim and Christian northerners, the area is home to a large community of migrants from neighboring countries and other parts of Nigeria, many of whom operate video stores, restaurants, barber shops (known in Nigerian English as *barbing saloons*), and auto-parts kiosks. The number of churches rivals that of mosques, and the sounds of Hausa commingle with those of Igbo, Yoruba, Pidgin English, French, Arabic and other languages; and it is not uncommon—even after the adoption of Shari'a—to see men walking outside in shorts or women with their heads uncovered. (Bariki areas in other cities and towns have become less free-wheeling.)

In spite of its association with cultural 'Others,' the bariki is a quintessentially Hausa construct, defined both spatially and socially in opposition to more respectable and homogeneous urban neighborhoods. In day-to-day Hausa discourse, a neighborhoods degree of moral respectability is often expressed in terms of the marital status of the women who live there. In Zakawa, for example, a roadside community on the outskirts of Kano with a high concentration of bars, hotels and women's houses, I was told many times that the number of married women (as opposed to 'prostitutes') was no greater than ten out of a population of several hundred. This improbable claim reflected the town's reputation, similar to Sabon Gari's, as a kind of sin city, where men could go to indulge in alcohol and drugs, attend performances of traditional music and Bori, or meet women, 'yan daudu or other men for companionship and sex. Barikis are said to be home to 'worthless people' [*mutanen banza*]—including karuwai, 'yan daudu, drug-dealers and thieves—while 'honorable people' [*mutanen kirki*], that is, married men and their families, live in areas where 'women's houses' are prohibited. If a married man is forced by poverty or other circumstances to set up his household in a bariki area, he may try to protect his own and his family's honor by painting the words *MATAN AURE – BA'A SHIGA* ['Married Women—Do Not Enter'] on the wall outside his home.

After my first personal contacts with 'yan daudu in the spring of 1993, I spent 12 months over the next year and a half visiting women's houses, nightclubs and restaurants in Kano. I also took periodic trips outside the city to attend *bikis,* festivities hosted by 'yan daudu and independent women that are modeled after the parties organized by married Hausa women to celebrate weddings and the naming of babies. All these places and events were open to the (male) public. Over time I established friendly relations with 'yan daudu in several locations that I began to visit on a regular basis. In addition to several spots in Sabon Gari, these locations included: a restaurant and some 'yan daudu's homes in Rijiyar Kuka, another 'outside' Kano neighborhood; a restaurant in the Old City of Katsina, a smaller but equally ancient Hausa emirate located north of Kano, near Nigeria's border with the Republic of Niger; and the market area of Madari, a small town located approximately 200 km southeast of Kano. The overwhelming majority of 'yan daudu I met were Nigerian Hausa Muslims, though some had other ethnic affiliations, especially Fulani. A small number were Muslim, Arabic-speaking immigrants from Chad or Sudan, or Christians with roots in southern or central Nigeria who had been born, raised or educated in the North. I also became acquainted with masu harka, 'men who do the deed,' whose sense of 'honor' *[kirki]* and 'shame' *[kunya]* sometimes made them hesitant to associate publicly with 'yan daudu. One mai harka who was not so hesitant was Mai Kwabo, a married 'civilian' who had many friends and acquaintances in the bariki areas in and around Kano. Because his regular job required his services only intermittently, and because he enjoyed spending time in the bariki, he agreed to work as my assistant in 1993–94.

Mai Kwabo introduced me to a number of the 'yan daudu who helped me in my research, and was instrumental in orchestrating most of the audiotape recordings that are transcribed and analyzed in Chapters 3–5. The number of recordings I was able to make (eight) was limited by 'yan daudu's sensitivity to outside interference in their affairs, and by my hesitation to arouse their suspicions by forcing the issue. Most of my collaborators had had little or no formal education in either the Islamic or Western *[boko]* school systems, and were therefore unfamiliar with the idea of original academic research, especially on topics that are unrelated either to Islamic scripture or to 'modern' subjects such as English, medicine or engineering, which are seen to have practical applications. The very word *bincike* ['research'] was understood by many people to mean government-sponsored spying. It was thus helpful and accurate to emphasize that my interest in 'yan daudu had to do with their celebrated linguistic expertise. Indeed, the tapes I made with my 'yan daudu friends, along with our many unrecorded conversations, did more than help me improve my ability to speak and understand Hausa; they also helped me learn how to use the language to play with and influence others.

When I started to test the waters with respect to changing my research topic from malamai to 'yan daudu, I was concerned about how my local scholarly contacts would react to a shift of focus from the most respected class of men in Hausa Muslim society to one of the most reviled. The process of changing my topic, therefore, involved not only trying to meet 'yan daudu, but also paying attention to the ways other people reacted to my new-found interest in them. Following the advice of several Nigerian friends (and the examples of men from my

Old City neighborhood whom I occasionally ran into in the bars of Sabon Gari), I was careful not to appear 'too interested' in 'yan daudu, in order to avoid giving the impression that they were fixing me up with female karuwai, or that I was being sexually active with 'yan daudu themselves. In this context, too, it was helpful and appropriate to frame my research interest in linguistic terms—to say, for example, that I hoped to learn more about the Hausa language from listening to the clever ways 'yan daudu are said to use *karin magana* ['proverbs'] and *habaici* ['innuendo'] (see Chapter 4). As it turned out, my status as a foreigner made it relatively easy for me to move back and forth between places and social settings with different moral reputations. My white skin made me conspicuous, of course, but it often seemed to inoculate me from the social judgments that would likely be passed against a 'respectable' Hausa man who socialized openly with 'yan daudu and other 'people of the bariki' *[mutanen bariki]*. (I say 'seemed to inoculate' because my sense of my moral reputation sometimes turned out to be naive. Still, I was repeatedly told by many Nigerian friends that as a white man and foreigner I could get away with morally questionable behaviors that they could not.)

I also became sensitive to the fact that some Hausa Muslims are wary of the interest many Western researchers seem to take in religiously sensitive topics like polygamy and wife-seclusion, or in stigmatized aspects of Hausa culture such as Bori and prostitution. In recent decades, there has been a profusion of research on the lives and experiences of Hausa women; there has also been considerable research on practices and institutions that appear to defy orthodox Islamic norms, such as the occupational choices of independent women, Bori spirit-possession practices; charismatic and ecstatic religious movements; youth gangs; and controversial genres of popular culture, such as romance novels and video-films. Like other researchers, I knew that my questions about Hausa Muslim cultural and religious norms, especially with respect to gender and sexuality, could easily come across as disrespectful—not only towards the society at large, but also towards the people who were helping me learn about it. This generated an ethical tension that lasted throughout my fieldwork and continues even today. While I have by no means resolved it, this tension has been intellectually and spiritually productive, for I came to see that many 'yan daudu (and others) had a similarly contradictory relationship with 'respectable' Hausa Muslim society, adhering to beliefs and practices that conformed to dominant cultural values, while sometimes saying and doing things that appeared to deviate from those values.

After completing my doctoral fieldwork in 1994, I returned to Nigeria four times, in 1997, 2000, 2002 and 2006. These visits ranged from one to two months each, and occurred during northern Nigeria's rainy season *[damina]* between the months of May and August. On each trip, I endeavored to revisit my earlier fieldsites in order to greet my friends and acquaintances, to find out how they were doing and how their lives and circumstances had changed. The changes I observed on these visits made me realize that the artifacts I had gathered in the early 1990s—audiotaped conversations, videotapes of bikis, newspapers, invitation cards, field-notes—were the products of a particular moment in the history of Kano, Northern Nigeria, and the world, and in the lives of particular individuals (including myself). With respect to the ethnographic statements I make in this book, therefore, when I use the present tense, I do so because it is my understanding that they describe Northern Nigerian social life at the moment of this writing. Otherwise, I use the past tense, in order to emphasize that my observations were historically specific, not timeless reflections of an unchanging Hausa Muslim culture. I have also tried to refrain from referring to 'cultures' and 'societies' as naturally existing, monolithic entities ('Hausa culture,' 'yan daudu society,' 'Western culture,' etc.) except as these concepts have been imagined, talked and written about by others. When I do use such expressions, I hope not to overlook the fluid nature of 'societies' and 'cultures' or the diversity and inequality that inevitably exist within and between them.

One of the most important historical developments of the last decade, for 'yan daudu and for all Nigerians, has been the explosion of the HIV/AIDS epidemic. Unlike eastern, central and southern Africa, where HIV/AIDS began decimating communities in the 1980s, West Africa did not experience the ravages of the disease on a wide scale until the following decade. In the early 1990s, the Nigerian government was only beginning to address the epidemic and the topic was rarely discussed in the press or in everyday conversation. Among the 'yan daudu and masu harka whom I met at that time, I knew of only one young man who was said to have died of *kanjamau* ['slimming'], as AIDS is called in Hausa. (The word *AIDS* is also used.) By the time I returned in 1997, however, several of my friends and acquaintances had fallen ill or died with symptoms that seemed to indicate advanced HIV infection, though the cause of death was often described as emaciation [*rama*], tuberculosis [*tarin tibi*] or simply 'lack of health' [*rashin lafiya*].

Also in the last decade, historical developments occurred in two other social fields—politics and popular culture—that had a transformative effect on 'yan daudu and on Northern Nigerian society at large. In the political realm, the sudden death in 1998 of Nigeria's military dictator, Sani Abacha, paved the way for national elections in which Olusegun Obasanjo, an army general and former military ruler, was chosen to become the country's first civilian president since the last one had been overthrown by a coup d'état in 1983. Abacha, like most of Nigeria's previous heads of state, was a Hausa-speaking Muslim (born and raised in Kano), while Obasanjo is a Yoruba Christian. Less than five months after Obasanjo's inauguration in May 1999, the state of Zamfara adopted Shari'a, and within a year and a half, eleven other states had followed suit. Although a number of political leaders and commentators insisted that the adoption of Shari'a violated constitutional provisions against the establishment of a state religion, the Obasanjo administration did not formally challenge it. The federal government thus averted a political crisis that some feared could escalate into civil war.

I arrived in Kano in June 2000 shortly before the state government staged an elaborate public ceremony 'launching' Shari'a. As the largest state in the region, its ceremony attracted hundreds of thousands of people (including several 'yan daudu friends of mine) and a host of dignitaries from as far away as Libya and Saudi Arabia. In preparation for the ceremony the government mobilized police and posses of Shari'a-enforcers known as *hisbas* to go around the state warning bar-owners of the impending ban on alcoholic beverages and admonishing 'prostitutes' [*karuwai*] to get married or to leave the state. 'Yan daudu were also targeted by this moral purification campaign. According to the *New Nigerian*, a government-owned newspaper, ridding the state of 'yan daudu and karuwai would "boost morals" and "check vices," creating the social conditions necessary for the full implementation of Shari'a later that year; and the improvement of public morality along Islamic lines would lead to justice and prosperity for all. A number of 'yan daudu and independent women were evicted from the 'women's houses' where they lived and worked. Some took refuge with family or friends, while others fled to states where Shari'a had not been adopted. Most remained in Kano, where they were vulnerable to harassment, arrest and occasional violence that was sponsored, or at least tolerated, by the state. Similar circumstances befell 'yan daudu and independent women in other Northern states.

When I returned to Nigeria in 2002, I was apprehensive about how Shari'a might have affected my friends who were 'yan daudu or independent women. Would I even be able to find them? In most cases, if they had left their old homes and places of work, I would have no easy way of tracking them down; they didn't have telephones or mailing addresses. As things turned out, I did not manage to find most of my old friends, but Shari'a was not the main reason. HIV/AIDS and other illnesses had killed some of them; others had moved to other parts of Nigeria or to Saudi Arabia, usually for economic reasons. The consequences of Shari'a were uneven and contradictory, and fell harder on independent women than they did on 'yan daudu. Independent women who ran restaurants in Kano and other large cities were generally left alone, while women who were believed to practice 'prostitution' had to get married or find a 'legitimate' occupation—no easy task for women who were poor, uneducated and estranged from their families. Independent women fared even worse in smaller towns like Madari, where they were forced to give up even 'legitimate' businesses.

Recent developments in media technology and popular culture have also proved challenging to the proponents of Shari'a. One such development is the Hausa-language film industry, which has grown exponentially since the late 1990s thanks to the widespread availability of inexpensive video production equipment, videocassette recorders and, most recently, digital video technology. Based in Kano, the Hausa video-film industry has produced hundreds of comedies and dramas and created a new class of film 'stars' [*taurari*] whose lives are a matter of intense public interest. The Haus a film industry's success is one result of the liberalization of Nigeria's economy that has taken place in the past 20 years, largely at the behest of international financial institutions and multinational corporations. In Northern Nigeria, these changes have enhanced the influence of wealthy local businessmen, many of whom subscribe to Islamic reformist ideologies that privilege individual piety, and individual success or failure, as opposed to older Islamic movements, like the Sufi orders, that emphasize group worship and loyalty to traditional hierarchies. Yet capitalist competition requires producers to attract mass audiences through marketing strategies that cultivate consumers' aesthetic and emotional desires, which can clash with the sober norms of reformist Islam. Tellingly, much as their predecessors did with respect to movie houses in previous eras, some Islamic clerics have condemned Hausa films for promoting immorality and have called for the closing of commercial video parlors. For their part, the industry's executives and artists consistently defend their films as socially enlightening and consistent with Islamic principles. These responses highlight some of the cultural contradictions that have surfaced in recent years, complicating efforts by Islamic reformists to construct a Northern Nigerian public unified by its commitment to normative Islam.

12

Gay Organizations, NGOs, and the Globalization of Sexual Identity

The Case of Bolivia

Timothy Wright

From 1993 to 1995 I worked as the regional gay men's outreach coordinator for HIV/ AIDS prevention in Santa Cruz, Bolivia with the Proyecto Contra el SIDA[1] (PCS), funded by the United States Agency for International Development (USAID). During 1992, while doing research in Bolivia unrelated to HIV/AIDS, I lobbied USAID to hire me for the purpose of creating within PCS an outreach component for men-who-have-sex-with-men (MSM). I had met numerous self-identified "homosexual" men in Cochabamba that year, and two of them had confided in me that they were HIV positive. These men had traveled to Brazil specifically to get tested since they distrusted in the "confidential testing" options available in Bolivia at that time. I began to pay more attention to the services available for HIV/AIDS in Bolivia, and discovered that no prevention services existed for men-who-have-sex-with-men. I also learned that the level of concern among MSM was high. As a registered nurse with a master's degree in public health, and as a gay man with an established network of "homosexual" friends in Bolivia, I succeeded in my lobbying efforts.

The prevalence data on HIV infection in Bolivia left little doubt about the need for this component. A USAID project paper (1988) admitted that while, "the greatest reservoir of HIV infection in Bolivia is in gay and bisexual men," accessing this population is "a difficult task." By 1992, the Ministry of Health (MOH; had identified 83 (72 male/11 female) HIV/ AIDS cases nationally. Of the infections attributed to sexual transmission, 66% were reported to be in bi- or homosexuals (Melgar 1992).[2] Still, the MOH had no outreach program targeting this group, and it was not clear how the problem should be addressed. In Bolivia, initiating a gay men's outreach effort for HIV/AIDS prevention meant charting unknown territory. The

Timothy Wright, "Gay Organizations, NGOs, and the Globalization of Sexual Identity: The Case of Bolivia," *Journal of Latin American Anthropology*, vol. 5, no. 2, pp. 89–111. Copyright © 2000 by American Anthropological Association. Reprinted with permission.

decision to contract me was not reached by unanimous agreement among all the decision-makers in USAID, PCS, and the MOH. Rather, it resulted from enthusiastic promotion by some and acquiescence by others. The less-than-robust endorsement for this type of outreach work foreshadowed the controversial nature of the work upon which I was about to embark.[3]

By the 1990s, a "gay men's outreach" component in a sexual health project was standard fare for US government programs. From the Bolivian government perspective, however, it titillated and shocked. If in 1985, "Bolivia launched itself in the global age" then by 1992, for better or for worse, globalization was reaching into the quiet, personal, and taboo corners of human sexuality.

MALE HOMOSEXUALITIES AND SILENCE

Sex and the Tradition of Reserved Talk

Silence can be a powerful tool for coping with the forbidden things that people do or about which they know (Alonso and Koreck 1989). In this light, it should be no surprise that in Bolivia male homosexuality and silence have been inseparable partners. This does not mean that homosexuality is never mentioned. On the contrary, within the confines of prescribed discourses it is part of the standard inventory. Tones of indignation, repulsion, anger, or pity make it a safe topic in a wide range of public and private forums, including nervous and degrading jokes and tabloid articles about immorality and crime. However, the more personal homosexuality gets, the closer to oneself, the less is heard about it. This quietness extends to one's relatives and close friends. The fact that male homosexuality has been shrouded in silence and relegated to humorous or degrading forms of discourse is not unique to Bolivia. However, it gains unique meanings as we consider the abrupt changes introduced into Bolivia by gay men's outreach.

Popular Models of Male Homosexuality in Bolivia

The practicality of silence can be more fully considered in light of the prevailing popular model of male homosexuality in Bolivia. Barry Adam (1979, 1986) has proposed a "fourfold typology of social structuring of homosexuality: (1) age-structured, (2) gender-defined, (3) profession-defined, and (4) egalitarian/'gay' relations," observing that while different structures "may coexist in a society, one of them predominates" (Adam, quoted in Murray, 1995: 5). These academic distinctions allow us to juxtapose and contrast complex realities for easy comprehension, but their use must avoid the risk of essentializing Bolivian homosexualities. My discussion of Bolivia focuses on tensions between what Adam identifies as gender-defined and egalitarian/gay structuring of homosexuality.

I argue that in both rural and urban areas of Bolivia, gender norms structure male homo-erotic behavior to an exceptionally strong extent, although we must recognize that dominant heterosexual norms are interpreted and manipulated in countless quiet ways. In this gender paradigm, the culturally dominant male/female dichotomy is preserved even when two biologi-cal males have sex together. In theory, this concept is quite simple: men penetrate, women get penetrated. This model emphasizes penetration, de-emphasizes anatomy (the orifice—vagina, mouth, or anus—is not determinant), and distributes stigma unequally in sexual encounters between men (Lancaster 1988). In male-male sex, the penetrator preserves his masculinity, while he who is penetrated loses it (and acquires the stigmatized label, "homosexual," meaning a woman-like male). Popularly, the terms *activo* and *pasivo* or *hombre* and *maricón* mark these gender distinctions between two men having sex with each other.

The gender-defined structuring of male homosexuality has been described in numerous Latin American countries. Richard Parker provides an excellent overview of the study of homo-sexuality in Latin America and an up-to-date bibliography in *Beneath the Equator* (Parker 1999) (also see Carrier 1995; Kulick 1997 and 1998; Lancaster 1992; Lumsden 1996). However, I believe that this popular model more vigorously defines male homosexuality in Bolivia than in the region as a whole. In the late 1980s and early 1990s, Adam's "gay/egalitarian model" with its notions of shared gay identity between the participants in male-male sex was either unheard of or seen as "alien" (*estilo americano*) by most men-who-have-sex-with-men in Bolivia. Also, the political understandings of coming out of the closet in order to fight oppression and defend gay rights had not taken root. Rather, these actors took for granted the activo-pasivo model, assuming that it was natural. It is within the context of the strict application of the two-gender social structuring of male homosexuality, and the limited influence of the egalitarian/gay model, that the practicality of silence must be interpreted.

Within the setting described above, we can now clarify key terms to be used in this article. "*El ambiente*" (the environment or atmosphere) is a traditional term used throughout the Spanish speaking world by participants in male-male erotic behavior. For the purposes of this paper it is used to describe the places, social relations, and conditions under which the gender-defined model of male homosexuality is manifest. "*Hombres de ambiente*" (sometimes simply "hombres") refers here to men-who-have-sex-with-men who, operating on the idea that gender equals sexuality, believe that their careful preservation of masculinity through penetration eliminates the "homosexuality" from their role in homoerotic behavior and, indeed, from their identity. I will use the term "homosexual" (or the common vernaculars "*marica*" and "ma-ricón") to refer to men who identify themselves as "homosexual," an identity that carries with it the implication of playing the passive (penetrated) role in man-man sex. The term "gay" is used here to refer to a homosexual identity embraced by individuals of the same biological sex and the same sexual orientation who share their bodies in erotic ways and do not acknowledge a gender distinction based on roles played. It is also charged with the political connotations of pride and human rights. "Gay" identity is associated with the United States and Europe, although it is surely found on every continent. As local and traditional understandings interact with global and (postmodern ones, language changes. It is precisely in deference to this state of flux, and the confusion it creates, that I use cautious qualifiers here.

Silence and Hombres de Ambiente

The role of silence would be hard to overemphasize as the hombre/maricón model is put into practice in Bolivia. Silence here refers to the avoidance of talking about homosexuality when it is used in reference to oneself, whether in the context of sexual practice or as a basis for personal identity. Silence is a valuable and malleable resource in the social and psychological management of male-male sexual practice under Bolivia's dominant gender-defined regime. Three arguments—one focusing on the hombre, one on the maricón, and one on the larger society—defend this assertion. We start by looking at the hombre de ambiente.

The role of the hombre de ambiente seems paradoxical: is it possible to be a non-homosexual man who participates in homosexual sex? Elsewhere in this issue Paulson and Calla analyze the practice of avoiding social analysis of the privileged and the "normal," in order to focus on marginalized "others." Generally speaking, the hombres described here occupy the most privileged position that el ambiente of Bolivia has to offer. This is because they are publicly marked neither as homosexuals nor as bisexuals—labels which stigmatize—but rather as "normal men" ("hombres normales"). It is unusual for such a man to describe himself as de ambiente. Many of these men also have sex with women, are married, and/or have children. This very large group of MSM is ignored by all the AIDS and sexual health projects that I know about in Bolivia.

A man who has sex with another man and yet does not lose his sense of masculinity and "normality," is an embodied expression of ambiente social rules. According to this specific, sub-cultural knowledge, anatomy is selectively ignored as the body of an hombre connects with the body of a faux-woman. In contrast, I have spoken with many Bolivian men outside the ambiente who insist that sex is determined by gross anatomy; to these men, all male-male sex is homosexuality expressed equally by both participants. Thus, hombres de ambiente walk on thin ice in the maintenance of their masculine identity. Where ambiente rules apply, they easily preserve their hombre status by following well-known rules. Beyond el ambiente's borders, it is silence that protects them and what they have at stake: masculine identities, egos, and power related to their social positions. Actors who play the hombre role in the sub-culturally accepted model of male homosexuality generally do not want a marked sexual identity attached to their homoerotic behavior, and do not want to be studied.

Silence and Maricas

Although men who identity themselves as "homosexuals" (pasivos or maricas) often say they dream of a stable relationship with a loyal hombre partner, in practice the romantic fiction of the hombre/marica couple cannot withstand the light of day or the scrutiny of society.

Hombres do, however, have love affairs (*aventuras amorosas*) with "homosexuals." In fact, while different in important ways, these affairs are in many ways similar to the ones described by Albro (this issue) between married *mestizo* men and *cholas* in the valley of Cochabamba. Albro's description of mestizo/chola affairs as "socially invisible relationships … illicit, covert, risky, notorious, unreliable, based on self-interest, and temporary" describes with precision most hombre/"homosexual" relations. On more than one occasion, I have even heard an hombre in a temporary relationship with a marica refer to "her" as *"mi cholita."* This image serves to symbolically distance the hombre from his male partner, here represented as a feminized and indianized other. Silence plays a critical role in these affairs since the general population does not accept the identity distinction that only ambiente "insiders" understand.

Cholas and maricas, at least in some cases, share the role of gratifying the sexual urges of hombres, men they meet, among other places, in the same chicherías in the environs of Quillacollo (Avenida Blanco Galindo). In relation to Albro's article, it is interesting to speculate to what extent maricas, like cholas, serve as "root metaphors" in local culture and to what extent, as traditional maricas become modern "gays," hombres will feel threatened, just as they are by cholas who abandon their polleras for modern dress and more liberated ways. Certainly maricas help make male identity possible by clarifying its boundaries. It is likely that the egalitarian/gay model threatens the comforting reassurance of masculinity upon which so many current participants in male-male sex depend.

Maricas find hombres (and hombres find maricas) in plazas, parks, neighborhood streets, movie theatres, dance halls, and bars. Practicality often requires that the two improvise quick sex in all sorts of semi-private locations: in stairwells, behind bars, in alleyways, or in bushes. These rendezvous can be dangerous, and "homosexuals" in Bolivia pride themselves on being *zorras* (female foxes) with lots of urban smarts; only half-jokingly, they plead for protection to *Santa Putana* ("Saint Whore, the marica goddess"). Clearly, silence plays an important role in the social management of these quick sex experiences; silence is one of the few resources available for making these public or semi-public events at least partially private—a goal generally seen as desirable. Silence here may take the form of denial-in-the-aftermath. While a marica may brag with another marica about "her" sexual conquests, silence is a rarely broken code of conduct in conversation with any "outsider."

Silence and the Accommodation of Homosexuality

It is critical to keep in mind that no man-who-has-sex-with-men, no matter how important the role of sex is in his life, defines himself only in terms of his sexual identity. People have more than one identity and each one may be compartmentalized or called upon, emphasized, or tucked away, depending on the changing circumstances of everyday life (see Paulson and Calla, this issue). Among themselves, individuals who identify themselves as gente de ambiente form social networks to help each other solve such problems as finding employment. *Gente de ambiente* in Bolivia also form alliances with other groups of "social outcasts," broadening the circle. However, my observations strongly suggest that for most gente de ambiente, family is their most important source of affective and material support. I feel confident in arguing that during most hours of any given day, most homoerotically-oriented men in Bolivia see themselves first and foremost as sons, brothers, and cousins. And beyond their family ties, many cherish roles as neighbors, colleagues and employees.

In exchange for broader acceptance in these relationships, most choose to de-emphasize their deviant gente de ambiente identity. It is common for quiet familial accommodations, "conspiracies of silence" (Carrier 1995), to allow sex-the-act to occur easily and frequently, so long as sex-the-deviant-identity is kept hidden. Since the popular understanding of homosexuality in Bolivia equates it with extreme femininity in men, space is open to allow men who meet normative standards of masculinity to quietly have sex with other men. Indeed, while the stereotypes of homosexuality in Bolivia persecute those identified as maricas, they also facilitate strategies of concealment for men who present themselves before the world as "normal guys." The desire for familial and social acceptance is a strong force that binds homosexuality and silence.

In fact, the traditional silence surrounding the sex lives of men-who-have-sex-with-men in Bolivia is so compelling that we need to look more closely at the question: How did the globalization of gay identity and gay organizations reach Bolivia at all? Our attention now turns to this question.

GAY MEN'S IDENTITY AND NOISE

AIDS and a Changing World

AIDS began to disturb the silence around male homosexuality even before the disease officially reached the country in 1985. New forms of discussing sexuality, including male homosexuality, anid particularly in relation to AIDS, arrived from afar via mass media. Between February 1993 and February 1995, I carefully collected all articles on sexuality and/or AIDS from *El Deber*, the major newspaper of Santa Cruz de la Sierra (Wright 1999). Of this collection of 483 articles, a full 246 (51%) were sold to *El Deber* by international wire services (Reuters, Associated Press, EFE, AFP, and ANSA). These articles revealed that issues related to homosexuality were now openly debated in courts, churches, schools, legislatures, medical societies, and in the street (especially in the form of parades) in many countries abroad. Lupton (1994) argues that the texts of newspaper articles "are sensitive barometers of social process and change." I have little doubt that these articles produced at least some confusion in the minds of many Bolivian readers regarding their taken-for-granted understandings of homosexuality. This is especially likely because many middle class and elite urban Bolivians eagerly look overseas for models of "modernity" and the up-to-date standard of "science."

Between 1985 and 1992, scientific considerations of sexuality most certainly increased in the Ministry of Health as the official number of HIV/AIDS cases rose from 1 to 83 (Melgar 1992). Furthermore, AIDS became a new justification for international development assistance in 1988 when USAID awarded the MOH a three year, $500,000 assistance grant to begin HIV/AIDS surveillance work and to provide some basic training for preventative education (USAID 1988). In short, rumblings from overseas arriving via mass media, together with development dollars deposited into the MOH's account for AIDS work began the process by which the traditional silence on homosexuality unraveled.

The Rise and Fall of Ethnography

As mentioned above, the decision to establish a gay men's outreach HIV/AIDS prevention component involved disagreements between USAID and PCS (the financier and the administrator). Since a full consensus was never reached, gay men's outreach was viewed with skepticism by some of the project's authorities from the beginning. And what about the Ministry of Health? It is important to point out that in Bolivia, health-related initiatives that reach the country through foreign aid assistance must be approved by the MOH. And once health projects are begun, they operate under the guidance and supervision of this ministry. Yet, the sharp contrast between Bolivia's poverty and the wealth of the donor countries generally makes this more true in theory than in practice. Nevertheless, a respectful execution of protocol is required. I am not privy to knowledge of the negotiations regarding the initiation of gay men's outreach. However, I suspect that the MOH and I might have been in agreement on the following point: such an endeavor should be kept as quiet as possible. In fact, gay men's outreach was to generate much sound and fury.

According to the conventional development mindset (Paulson and Calla, this issue), the scientist/professional is the agent (or subject), and "the other" is the object of study and action. What happens when the agent and the object are fused in one person? As an openly "homosexual" AIDS expert, an agent/object all at once, I was viewed as a somewhat ambiguous figure by the people who hired me, especially by the PCS national director. As time passed, considerable effort was made by the project leadership to reduce this disturbing duality and re-establish the conventional order; that is, to the extent possible, to make me a scientific/ professional agent with substantial distance from the objects I was to study and help.

In 1993, I was moved from Cochabamba to Santa Cruz, the department most impacted by HIV/AIDS, where PCS had a regional office. Until that time I had been working informally among gente de ambiente via a participant-observer approach. Suddenly, in Santa Cruz, I had a desk in an office, a supervisor, abundant supplies, and a support staff—an ideal stage for "health professional" performances. There was a problem, however: unlike Cochabamba where I knew many gente de ambiente, I had no such contacts in Santa Cruz. Since my job clearly required me to find "homosexuals" in a city with no "gay neighborhood," the fancy office did me little good. However much the project leadership preferred to see me in the "health agent" role, it had little choice but to allow me to carry out ethnographic research. So, once again, I found myself playing the "object" role, being a "homosexual" in that fuzzy place called "the field." This task raised a myriad of ethical questions.[4] I noticed, for example, that my PCS colleagues were embarrassed by my detailed descriptions of what I saw "out there." Subtly, I was trained to provide sanitized, desexualized portrayals of a vague "gay community." Ironically, the discouragement in the office of my ethnographic voice encouraged me to identify more with other "homosexuals," people with whom I could communicate.

I began my field research in Santa Cruz by working with one individual, and things snowballed from there. My contacts in Cochabamba suggested that I look up Miguel (a pseudonym), an underemployed salesman of contraband Brazilian apparel who knew his way around the city and had lots of free time. Through Miguel I made other contacts, and through them, still others. After a mere two months of field research, the basically amorphous and constantly shifting borders of ambiente geography and its cultural roles, relationships, symbols, and gestures were still only partially clear to me when the pressure increased to return to the office and to the agent role.

Based on what I had learned to that date, I produced a two-part document in the form of a cursory ethnographic report (Wright 1993) and a set of policy recommendations. By that time I had learned enough to know that ambiente identities were far from monolithic, and that understanding unspoken codes of conduct guides social coping strategies, integral to the insider's approach.

In the recommendation section of my report I wrote the following:

> The world of men-who-have-sex-with-men, the gente de ambiente, is called el ambiente precisely because it is more an atmosphere than a fixed spot on a map. The ambiente is real to people who understand it and provides opportunities for HIV prevention programming. If its rules are violated, however, swift and stern rejection follows. It is difficult to overstate the extreme concern gente de ambiente in Bolivia have for privacy and discretion. It is recommended that the project imitate the model provided by the local ambiente by NOT trying to establish geographically fixed service centers for the gente de ambiente (Wright 1993).

Rather, I proposed a telephone hotline and a team of outreach workers, selected from among the many gente de ambiente peer groups I had found, and hired at modest wages on short-term contracts. The project would select individuals who expressed an interest to learn about HIV/AIDS, and they would then share their new knowledge with their *amigos de confianza,* that small group of people who talk together frankly about their sex lives. This approach would allow outreach workers to review actual practices and to seek feasible ways for these to be adjusted, if necessary, with HIV prevention in mind. Basically, the idea was to pay individuals to get trained and then return them to their networks. The AIDS literature of the time highlighted the logic of this strategy: "Discussions of targeting messages are full of references to 'risk groups' and 'communities' when, in fact, peer groups may be the social group most relevant for purposes of educating about behavior change" (Petrow 1990). Furthermore, I reasoned that such individuals, better than anyone else, understood their friends' cherished identities, and knew the specific geographies they traversed and the off-hour schedules they kept. Put simply, peers knew how to act and where to go to get outreach work accomplished.

The development agency, however, was perplexed and disturbed by my proposals. On the one hand, I was praised for the report. On the other hand, it was promptly ignored. After I presented my findings on the structure and function of el ambiente in the national PCS office in La Paz, the national director responded by saying: "very interesting, now enough of this ethnographic stuff." The position of the project leadership was clear at this point. My job was to function as the "health professional," the agent, working for the benefit of the target population; as a doctor treats a patient. Activities that could respond to quantifiable process and outcome evaluations would be given priority. A pattern emerged in the flow of approvals and disapprovals of my proposals, and also in the recommendations that came from above, backed by funding. The ethnographic phase of gay men's outreach was over. The Gay Community Center would soon open up.

Doing Development and Making Gays

The pressures to open up a gay community center were considerable. The *Proyecto Contra el SIDA* was institutionally linked to the Centers for Disease Control and Prevention (CDC), whose "Bolivia Team" called for the establishment of a "base of operations" for providing services to "homosexual/bisexual" men. They argued that "the target population for the services needs to be clearly defined. The project will be able to focus on its goals, move ahead, and have a visible impact only after these broad issues are addressed" (Trip Report, April 15, 1993). Funds were made available to hire two full-time outreach workers, to pay the rent of a house, and to purchase a TV and VCR plus furniture for the house. "Visible" was the operational word here and, with that in mind, in early 1994, a gay community center was inaugurated.

As a North American gay man, I have benefited tremendously from identifying with the gay community, so I came to accept the opening of a center even though it seemed unwise in the Bolivian context. I also understood public health criteria and knew that we couldn't adequately address legitimate concerns about project impact if our work was kept entirely invisible and silent. Nevertheless, the value of the gay center was always limited, and its attempts to redefine gente de ambiente as gays produced scant results.

While project personnel increasingly talked about "the gay community," in fact, this was by no means a monolithic or unified group. Two axes of differentiation in particular severely restricted the formation of, and participation in, a gay organization: socio-economic class and gender identity divisions.

The gay organization proved attractive to a specific and rather small population within el ambiente, a group known as *los placeras,* gente de ambiente who socialize in the city's central plaza. This mostly lower-middle class group chose to congregate in the plaza because they lacked the resources for more private settings; the gay center resolved this problem and therefore appealed to them. By contrast, the affluent gente de ambiente had available to them a broader range of meeting locations, and by long standing custom, avoided publicly congregating with individuals of lower socio-economic status. Their appearance in the center was rare. There are also groups of gente de ambiente who are much poorer than los placeros. On more than one occasion they met to find acceptance in the gay center, and even organized themselves into a block during a campaign to elect leaders of an organization that formed in the gay center—bringing social class tensions to the fore. When this group lost the election they sensed injustice and, with great bitterness, split from the organization and formed an alternative, "people's" gay group in the Villa Primero de Mayo, a poor section of town. In short, social class differences excluded most of the ambiente's members from participation in the gay center.

Gender identity divisions also took their toll. Men who identified with the center tended to play the "female" role in their relations. By contrast, the very large number of men who see themselves as "hombres normales" did not show up because their masculine social image and sexual roles as penetrators informed them that they were not "homosexuals." One result of the dominant one-sex two-gender discourse was that half of the dyad of most men-with-men sexual encounters was missing from the gay organization (as it is from the common definition of homosexuality in Bolivia). Hombres define themselves as heterosexual men, so have no reason to join the outreach project or to learn about risks of their particular sexual behavior.

Although most of the men who frequented the gay center engaged in sexual relations as the pasivo or "female" partner, they did not have strongly effeminate mannerisms and did not dress as women. In fact, because they are understood to be "like women" but appear like men, the\ are referred to within el ambiente as *los camuflados* (the camouflaged) (Wright and Wright, 1997). By contrast, the Santa Cruz "homosexuals" who are notably effeminate men and/or transvestites found little welcome in the organization. The placeros who dominated the gay center organization complained that such participants would give the whole group a bad name. Also, these effeminate men do not necessarily find it easy to accept the gay identity; I heard more than one transvestite comment, *"yo no soy gay, yo soy mujer"* ("I'm not gay, I'm a woman").

In short, men-who-have-sex-with-men who were too rich or too poor or too masculine or too effeminate were unlikely to be attracted to the gay center or welcomed as members of the emerging "gay community." While my ethnographic research told me that the participants of the gay organization were not representative of the full gamut of the ambiente world, from the point of view of the institution, it was a success just to get some "homosexuals" to come to the center. With them PCS could "do development" on terms it recognized. Soon after the center opened, psychologists began to appear to talk with the participants about the role of self-esteem in condom negotiation, and other qualities of self-definition. While the two full-time gay outreach workers gradually essentialized their understandings of sexual identity, few participants went along with the idea. Nevertheless, the mere existence of a gay community center drew enormous attention, both from within the ambiente and beyond its borders.

Local Actors Step In

The gay community center drew remarkable public attention almost from the moment it opened. Discussion about who was really behind this center placed the Bolivian Ministry of Health in a real dilemma. While financed by the US government and administered by an international project, as a health initiative, it was technically within the MOH's domain. On the one hand, if the MOH were to fully disown the gay center as the product of PCS that would mean publicly acknowledging its heavy dependency on foreigners for financing, planning, and implementing major projects; clearly an embarrassing affront to national pride and sovereignty. On the other hand, the MOH was not prepared to assume the position of an entity that actively supported a pro-gay community center. And what about this group of people who, for the first time in Bolivia, were being referred to as "los gays"? Were these longstanding Bolivian "homosexuals," suddenly discovering a collective identity? Or were they a product of foreign imaginations, being invented, as it were, in the service of obscure international agendas? The print media had a heyday with the debates that arose around los gays and their center (Wright 1999) as the Church, the municipal government, PCS, USAID, the police, civic organizations, the inter-institutional AIDS committee, and, of course, the public health sector all jockeyed to position themselves through public statements.

Among the most contested immediate questions was, "Just how many gays are there?" Many Bolivians I spoke with over the years were quite confident that the number of male "homosexuals" in their respective cities could be counted on their fingers; in some cases they claimed that they could even name them. It was commonly believed that "one can tell" by the way they look or dress. The "homosexual" was always a man (scant acknowledgement was made of female homosexuals) who was effeminate and at least partially cross-dressed. For many, the notion that a gay community center might exist in Santa Cruz with voluntary participants who were generally unremarkable in appearance, just average-looking guys, turned the world topsy-turvy.

A journalist from *El Deber,* interviewed me about my work as the coordinator of gay men's outreach. Her main interest was how many "homosexuals" there were in the city. I was unsophisticated in working with the press at that time, and unsuccessful in escaping her numbers game by arguing the true complexity of her question. The day after the interview the following headline appeared (*El Deber,* 23 June 1994): *Hay cerca de 17 mil homosexuales en Santa Cruz* (there are approximately 17,000 homosexuals in Santa Cruz).

Two days later Tacuara, a local commentator, responded to that article with a piece entitled, "Gays en Santa Cruz"? (*El Deber,* 25 June 1994). In this article he seemed to equate the apparent increase in homosexuality with modernity—a negative side effect of the otherwise positive advance of development: "Development has its price," he wrote, it improves standards of living but also brings with it "delinquency, prostitution, drug addiction and homosexualism." My sense is that his stance of resignation—a paradoxical blend of disgust with a call for tolerance—expressed the views of many.

Still, the question of the total number of "homosexuals" remained unresolved. My error in speculating with the journalist fed polemics. In the months that followed the startling "announcement" that there were 17,000 homosexuals in Santa Cruz, I heard many opinions about this issue. While I told people over and over that I had never made the claim attributed to my name and that, in fact, I had no idea how many "homosexuals" there were in Santa Cruz or even what that label meant, a debate proceeded based on the journalist's "statement-of-the-facts." For some, the report illustrated the damage being done to the country by foreigners. For others, it was a battle cry and an announcement of freedom. For still others, it was a declaration of the end of the world.

Among the physicians and epidemiologists in the Proyecto Contra el SIDA, skepticism focused on the "bad science" that produced this statistic. Of course, the numbers were based on no science at all, but rather a bad experience with an obsessed journalist bent on sensationalism. Nevertheless, a significant "hard science" faction within PCS began to push for "scientific survey research" to count the homosexuals of Bolivia. Several draft survey questionnaires were eventually elaborated and even pre-tested. According to the reasoning behind this call, the denominator (i.e., the total population) had to be quantified in order to measure HIV incidence and prevalence among los gays (Hennekens, Burning and Mayrent 1987). Development and evaluation discourses also fueled the urge to count up the homosexuals. As this reasoning went, it was important to be able to distinguish the "target population" from non-target units (Rossi and Freeman 1989). Only then could resources be reasonably allocated and effective programs designed. To the "hard science" faction in PCS, project action should be guided by the objective principles of epidemiology, development science, and evaluation methodologies; in practice, their proposed means of implementing these principles boiled down to surveys based on identities of convenience. From my point of view, these proposals drained energy and wasted time in a fruitless and unethical oversimplification of el ambiente.

There was also a "soft science" faction within PCS, made up largely of psychologists. The organizational structure of PCS reflected its two factions: in the medical department were the "hard scientists," while the "soft scientists" were in the IEC (Information, Education, and Communication) department. To the "soft scientists" the emphasis should be more on human relationships, (sub)cultural sensitivity and respecting identities, and less on quantification. At times, inter-faction battles raged between these two sets of priorities.

From these battles between the medical and IEC departments a modus operandus finally emerged for the management of gay men's outreach. As the coordinator of this component in PCS I watched an uneasy consensus slowly develop. Over time, *"la comunidad gay"* was referred to more and more in the project until it became part of the PCS lexicon. It came to be understood as meaning the people who showed up at the gay center, a group that could be both counted and treated sensitively. By defining "the gay community" in this limited way, the

Proyecto Contra el SIDA presented a model that solved the Ministry of Health's dilemma: they could conceptualize the management of a gay center in a purely technical, public health framework, in which medical professionals/agents could guide, care for, and control "homosexual" objects. The center would be more about pathology than liberation.

From the Ministry of Health point of view, "homosexuals" were to be treated like another risk group: prostitutes. And working with prostitutes was nothing new to the MOH. Prostitution is simultaneously legal and illegal in Bolivia; while it is a violation of the penal code (Serrano 1972), state-run health clinics for sex workers operate throughout the country. In these facilities, female sex workers are evaluated and treated for sexually transmitted diseases. Upon receiving a clean bill of health, their *carnets de salubridad* (health cards) are stamped and these "registered" prostitutes are allowed to work in "registered" brothels. Sex workers must pay two fees in these visits—one for the medical care received and another fee to the police, for unspecified services. By 1994, PCS had substantial experience attending these "registered" sex workers in a number of the state-run health clinics. In fact, the project's work with "registered" prostitutes had become quite routine; written guidelines existed for lessons on condom negotiation, communication skills, and identifying the symptoms of diseases; one-on-one counseling sessions with psychologists had become standardized, and project posters hung on the walls.

The majority of sex workers, however, labor outside of the formal, "registered" system. Some prostitutes officialize their status with the state in order to work on a full-time basis in "registered" brothels. For the rest, there is the informal economy of the street. Nationally, PCS did very little work with these "unregistered" prostitutes, referred to by the MOH as "*las clandestinas*" (the clandestines). The Ministry of Health viewed these sex workers as renegades that ought to be captured as criminals and brought into the "registered" system. From the project point of view, they were just too hard to find. But what about los gays? If the "gay community" was to be understood as the men who showed up at the gay center and these were seen by the MOH as prostitute equivalents, the question remained: What kind of prostitutes—"registered" or "unregistered"? The evidence shows that over time los gays came to be treated much like the "registered" sex workers (with some interesting twists), at least within the confines of the gay center of Santa Cruz. Both the MOH and PCS found this to be the most convenient arrangement and importantly, it facilitated harmony between them. With some modifications, it made work possible along already well-established pathways, in a fixed site, and on a Monday through Friday, nine to five schedule.

The modifications included the promotion of a sort of gay liberation-lite by the two gay outreach workers. When I left the country in 1995, outreach activities by these men still aimed at working in the ambiente's natural settings. When I returned to Bolivia for a visit in 1998, I found their work almost entirely restricted to the gay center. Their true outreach activity had been reduced to convincing gente de ambiente to attend center meetings. If they went, they were told, they would be well-received by professionals who would teach classes on sexual health issues. The managerial style control (Zimmerman, this issue) of gay men's outreach had become so complete that it erased its earlier controversial nature. The gay employees now did little more than sweep floors. Just as prostitutes did not run prostitute clinics, gay men did not run the gay center. However, this is more a theoretical depiction of how it was supposed to work. In practice, attendance was low and little education was offered by PCS or MOH professionals. In fact, the gay center was little more than a site where a small number of friends met to socialize. Clearly, it could function neither like a "registered" prostitute clinic nor a center of gay liberation.

To truly promote gay identity is to stimulate political positions and/or acts that challenge authoritarian structures. Even as the PCS/MOH coalition settled on a benign treatment of los gays at the center as "registered" prostitutes, outside the center the police regularly treated them like criminals, along the lines of las *prostitutas* clandestinas. A review of newspaper articles about meetings between public health and police officials in Santa Cruz, and reports in the political section of *El Deber,* combined with personal testimonies from gente de ambiente (especially among the poor and effeminate) revealed a clear picture. In language that conflates "risk groups" with criminals, the police periodically raid the few gay bars that exist and especially the working class drinking establishments frequented by gente de ambiente. These raids lead to detentions and bribe payments. These degrading and emotionally devastating events become headline news in the ambiente circuit for days afterwards. They also inform the gente de ambiente that the PCS/MOH language of gay liberation is not backed by political commitment in the face of human rights abuses.

On various occasions the gente de ambiente turned to PCS for support in the wake of authoritarian abuse. Other than sending psychologists to listen empathetically, the project categorically refused to take action. Some top-rank PCS officials argued that it was doing more good to keep a low profile while promoting sexual health and offering emotional support. I would argue, however, that the option of keeping a low profile was forfeited the day the project insisted on establishing a gay center. In fact, the project's promotion of gay identity—public sexual minorities—was recognized by many gente de ambiente as motivated by bureaucratic considerations which had nothing to do with liberation.

Dennis Altman (1994:24–25) argues that, "the two major variables in the establishment of AIDS organizations appear to be epidemiological and political." Regarding the latter, he suggests that all over the world AIDS projects assume the prevailing organizational patterns characteristic of the country in which they develop. This point appears to be well-illustrated in Santa Cruz, Bolivia with its gay center seen as analogous to a "registered" prostitute health clinic run by the state. Its linkage to USAID further reinforces Altman's point in this development aid dependent country. It should be observed, however, that in the case of gay men's outreach, the continuity of officialdom's organizational pattern vis-à-vis the social management of "homosexuals" took precedence over the organizational pattern of the gente de ambiente. I argue that through the choice of which patterns to follow, important opportunities to carry out significant HIV/AIDS prevention work were squandered.

CONCLUSION

The AIDS epidemic has fostered the sudden foundation of gay organizations in unlikely places. Bolivia is a case in point. To start with, we have seen that gay identity is contrary to the prevalent Bolivian cultural understandings of male homosexuality. Furthermore, the socio-political and economic conditions in this poor country of less than 10 million people lack criteria normally deemed necessary for establishing a powerful community identity and organizing people to challenge authority. Nevertheless, gay organizations have been promoted in Bolivia because of international public health standards. For this reason, Bolivia can be looked at as a case study of the globalization of sexual identity. We have seen, however, that this is no simple instance of hegemony from the core to the periphery. Rather, an array of local actors interact with the suggestion of a global, public health sexuality. In the case looked at here, the results are a gamut of in-progress, globally influenced yet clearly Bolivian male homosexualities.

I expect that my experiences and frustrations as a gay man and a health professional working with HIV/AIDS in Latin America resonate with those of many others, and I hope to stimulate debate in this arena. While pro-gay, I opposed the foundation of a gay organization as I watched it established by gay-indifferent or anti-gay authoritarian structures. As I witnessed the sound and fury generated by the foundation of a gay center, the endless press coverage, the urgent call to count up the "homosexuals," and the ultimate conversion of los gays into a target group parallel to that of "registered" prostitutes, I grew to understand the meaning of silence to the gente de ambiente. AIDS work still needs to be carried out in this group, but it will not be very effective until ethnographic research sensitive to subculture realities is taken into account.

NOTES

I would like to thank the following individuals for their helpful comments, suggestions and support: Susan Paulson, Mary Weismantel, Heather McClure, Jose Luis González Castedo, Remberto Vaco Marco, Beatriz von Poser, the five peer reviewers of this article, and my mentor of many years, Joseph Carrier.

1. Formally, this project's title was, *"Programa Colaborativo de SIDA/ETS"* (The Collaborative AIDS/STD Program); a linkage between CDC and USAID is marked in this title by the word "collaborative." More often, it was known simply as *"El Proyecto Contra el SIDA"* (The AIDS Project).
2. This set of MOH data is difficult to read. The biological sex of the identified individuals with HIV/AIDS is listed in one column, their sexual orientation in another. My experience with Bolivian health officials suggests that the individuals recorded as bisexuals or homosexuals were men.
3. It was difficult for them to believe my assertion that I knew many "homosexual" men in Cochabamba and elsewhere in the country since this population was invisible to them. In a meeting in La Paz on 28 August, 1992, with USAID, CDC, and PCS officials I challenged them to have one person from the project attend my birthday party, scheduled for the following day in Cochabamba. They sent a project psychologist. She was well-received by close to 40 "homosexual" men.
4. As a North American gay man, the ethical dilemmas that came up in the process of doing field research on Latin American homosexualities were many; this topic is beyond the scope of the present paper. However, I strongly recommend Joseph Carrier's 1999 article on this theme.
5. This group was formed more in name, as a momentary protest, than in reality.

REFERENCES CITED

Primary Sources

Center for Disease Control and Prevention/Bolivia Team. 1993. Trip Report (Draft): STD/AIDS Prevention Project in Bolivia. El Deber

——1993a. "Hay Cerca de 17 Mil Homosexuales en Santa Cruz." El Deber, 23 June, 1993.

Santa Cruz: El Deber. 1993b. "Gays en Santa Cruz." El Deber, 25 June, 1993. Santa Cruz: El Deber.

Melgar, Maria Luisa. 1992. Situacion del SIDA en Bolivia, 1985–1992. La Paz: Departamento Nacional de Salud.

Serrano, Servando. 1972. Código Penal. Cochabamba: Editorial Serrano Ltda. United States Agency for International Development Bolivia Project Paper. AIDS Prevention and Control (Project No. 511–0608). Washington DC: USAID

Wright, Timothy. 1993. Male Homosexuality and AIDS in Santa Cruz, Bolivia: Sexual Culture and Public Health Policy. Proyecto Contra el SIDA: Unpublished report submitted to the United States Agency for International Development.

——1999. AIDS and Metaphors in the Bolivian Press. Inter-disciplinary paper submitted in partial satisfaction of the requirements for the degree Master of Arts in Latin American Studies, U.C.L.A. Unpublished manuscript.

Secondary Sources

Adam, Barry. 1979. Reply. Sociologists Gay Caucus Newsletter 18:8

——1986. Age, Structure, and Sexuality. In Journal of Homosexuality 11:19–33.

Alonso, A.M. and Koreck, M.T. 1989. Silences: "Hispanics," AIDS and Sexual Practices. In Differences, 1.1:101–124.

Altman, Dennis. 1994. Power and Community: Organizational and Cultural Responses to AIDS. Bristol, PA: Taylor and Francis, Inc.

Carrier, J.M. 1976. Cultural Factors Affecting Urban Mexican Homosexual Behavior. Archives of Sexual Behavior 5:103–24.

——1989. Sexual Behavior and the Spread of AIDS in Mexico. In The AIDS Pandemic. R. Bolton, ed. Pp. 37–50. New York: Gordon and Breach.

——1995. De Los Otros: Intimacy and Homosexuality among Mexican Men. New York: Columbia University Press.

——1999. Reflections on ethical problems encountered in field research on Mexican male homosexuality: 1968 to present. In Culture, Health, and Sexuality. 1:3, 207–221.

Hennekens, C.H., J.E. Burning, and S. Mayrent. 1987. Epidemiology in Medicine. Boston: Little Brown and Company.

Kulick, Don. 1997. Brazilian Transgendered Prostitutes. American Anthropologist 99 (3):574–585.

——1998. Travesti. Sex, Gender and Culture among Brazilian Transgendered Prostitutes. Chicago: University of Chicago Press.

Lancaster, Roger N. 1988. Subject Honor and Object Shame: The Construction of Male Homosexuality and Stigma in Nicaragua. Ethnology 27:2.

——1992. Life is Hard: Machismo, Danger, and the Intimacy of Power in Nicaragua. Berkeley: University of California Press.

Lumsden, Ian. 1996. Machos, Maricones, and Gays: Cuba and Homosexuality. Philadelphia: Temple University Press.

Lupton, Deborah. 1994. Moral Threats and Dangerous Desires: AIDS in the News Media. Bristol, PA: Taylor and Francis, Inc.

Murray, Stephen O. 1995. Latin American Male Homosexualities. Albuquerque: University of New Mexico Press.

Parker, Richard. 1999. Beneath the Equator: Cultures of Desire, Male Homosexuality and Emerging Gay Communities in Brazil. New York: Routledge.

Petrow, Steven, ed. 1990. Ending the AIDS Epidemic: Community Strategies in Disease Prevention and Health Promotion. Santa Cruz, CA.: Network Publications.

Rossi, Peter, and Howard Freeman. 1989. Evaluation: Systematic Approach. Newbury Park: Sage Publications.

Wright, Timothy, and Richard Wright. 1997. Bolivia: Developing a Gay Community—Homosexuality and AIDS. In Sociolegal Control of Homosexuality: A Multi-Nation Comparison. Donald J. West and Richard Green, eds. New York: Plenum Press.

13

"Heart Like a Car"
Hispano/Chicano Culture in Northern New Mexico
Brenda Bright

In its idiomatic usage in the United States, *bad* means *good,* not as in *nice,* but as in *well-executed. Bad* connotes the paradoxical dangerousness and respectability of minority social actors and oppositional cultural forms. *Badness,* as both desirable and pleasurable, is the product of social tensions. Chicano car customizers highlight these meanings in their creations, their cars, known as "lowriders." Lowriders are beautiful *bad* cars of every make and model, designed to ride "low and slow" and to appear "mean and clean."[1] Throughout the Chicano southwest United States, and increasingly beyond, they sport spectacular paint jobs in pinks, greens, oranges, deep purples, and reds that are highlighted with coatings of metal flake and as many as 18 layers of lacquer. The interiors are elegantly upholstered and detailed. Many are lowered and have hydraulic pumps installed at the wheels to make the cars lift up and down, bounce, and even dance on demand. Small, wide wheels accentuate the low, lean look. As the pictured New Mexico license plate commandingly reads, the cars are "4U2SEE" (see Figure 1). Their owners, also referred to as lowriders, drive these beautiful, luxurious roadway spectacles very slowly, literally taking over the road and forcing other drivers to "deal with" their slow, deliberate driving style.

When interviewed at a car show in Española, New Mexico in the summer of 1990 for a national television special on America's car mania, Dennis Martinez, a Hispano lowrider from nearby Chimayó, explained lowriding in terms of its cultural features: "It's my culture, man. It's like my inheritance. My family all lowride, so I just keep lowriding myself. It's something that's *traditional.* I have a heart that's like a car, you know. My heart is in my wheels" (Lynch Frost Productions 1990). At the same show, Vicky Gutierrez said, "Here in Española we love our cars!" Martinez describes the love of lowriding as *traditional* and Gutierrez the love of cars as *local*—particular to Española (see Figure 2).[2] These assertions of local specificity contain the

Brenda Bright, "'Heart Like a Car': Hispano/Chicano Culture in Northern New Mexico," *American Ethnologist*, vol. 25, no. 4, pp. 583–609. Copyright © 1998 by American Anthropological Association. Reprinted with permission.

kernels of other significant connections being made by Hispano lowriders through the cars, namely to commodities and to ethnopolitical culture. Northern New Mexico Hispanos take the car, a general feature of American culture, and customize it into a lowrider, one of several politicized Chicano cultural forms adapted in the area in the wake of the Chicano Movement. In light of widespread incorporation of cars in the cultures of the United States, the statements of Martinez and Gutierrez indicate a seemingly contradictory aspect of consumer culture that

Car culture in northern New Mexico demonstrates how local culture, as a referenze and as a creation, becomes even more significant as national and global popular cultures create new power configurations, new alliances, and new identities. An examination of Española area lowriders highlights the ways extralocal processes such as mass production and ethnopolitical mobilization are integral in the creation of local tradition in an area marked by tourism, loss of land, and labor outmigration. [ethnic identity, localization, commodification, popular culture, mass culture, Chicanos, New Mexico]

Figure 1. "4U2SEE" (For you to see) vanity plate. Sante Fe. Photograph by author.

is only beginning to be addressed within anthropology—how people experience and create mass-produced culture as a form of local culture. Here Hispanos customize a mass-produced commodity into an ethnic cultural form and subsequently create the car as a form of local culture. Lowriders are evidence of the creation of a simultaneously local and extralocal ethnopolitical identity.

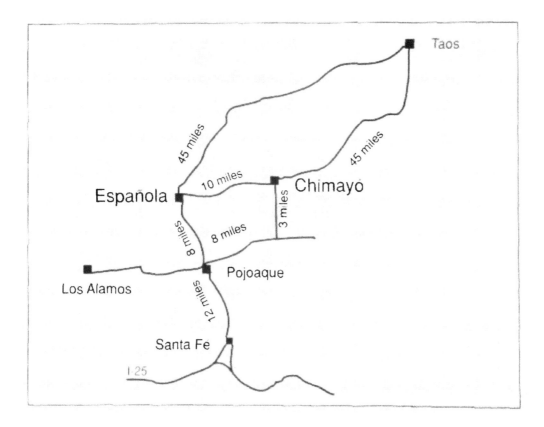

Figure 2. Map of the Española area.

The presence of these elaborately "bad" cars and their linkage to local culture and tradition raise questions about culture, commodities, tradition, and locality important to anthropology. How is local culture constructed in the presence of mass-produced and mass-circulated commodities (Miller 1994)? How "local" is local culture (Appadurai 1995; Bright 1995)? The statements by Martinez and Gutierrez suggest an intermingling of local popular traditions with the collective imaginary in which mass culture is not something external invading the popular from outside but instead develops out of certain potentialities already within the popular itself—noted here as "traditional" or "local" propensities (Rowe and Schelling 1991:8). Given the intermingling of the local with the mass, the potentialities are two-fold, those developing from within local culture and those developing from within mass and mediated culture. An analysis of such cultural productions requires careful attention to both dimensions. Their intermingling in the Española area of northern New Mexico is the subject of this essay.

A growing body of work within anthropology and cultural studies details how the products, practices, and politics of modernity are radically changing the relationships between the imagination and social life (Abu-Lughod 1990; Appadurai 1990, 1991; Fischer 1986; Foster 1991; García-Canclini 1992; Ferguson and Gupta 1992; Marcus 1995; Shank 1994;

Thornton 1988; Urla 1996). Because of translocal and transnational flows in capital, people, ideas, technology, and media, the realms of social life are increasingly disjunctive. In many ways, they have become deterritorialized, or perhaps reterritorialized.[4] At the very least, they are not so resolutely local as anthropologists have historically assumed. Increasingly, media and commodities provide important materials for the creation of social relationships and social identities. Accordingly, Appadurai (1991) identifies the contemporary need within anthropology to interpret how local historical trajectories flow into complicated transnational and translocal structures. The ethnographic study of commodity forms that circulate widely, yet are ultimately localized in some sense, enables us to attend to socially generated cultural meanings. Such a project requires a three-fold approach. First, genealogical research on relevant objects, media, and social movements is necessary to articulate the conditions of generation, adaptation, and circulation within broader meanings. Second, historicized social research on a particular locale details the contexts under which objects and media become part of social life. Third, ethnographic research delineates the work of making mass media and commodities suitable to creating social relationships and social identities (Carrier 1991).

Given the changing relationships between the imagination and social life, it is increasingly important to consider how locality influences cultural production and ethnographic accounts of that production. The ubiquitous presence of mass-produced commodities and localized versions of mass culture challenge single-site ethnography. To ask how local is local culture, paying careful attention to translocal dynamics in their local inflections, is to ask what sorts of ethnographic approaches are appropriate to the conditions of contemporary culture (Ferguson and Gupta 1992; Marcus 1990; Thornton 1988). Marcus (1995) argues that the world-system context has radically changed the grounds of contemporary social life, and with it, the grounds for anthropological accounts. In response to these shifts, he suggests, two key approaches have emerged. While the single-site approach is maintained by many, providing full attention to the local conditions and responses of groups to macroprocesses, a second multisite mode of ethnographic research is emerging. Multisite ethnographies address the disjunctive contexts in which subjects act and are acted upon. As Marcus details, multisite ethnographies develop strategies to follow a set of connections particular to the research topic at hand, and in so doing, they reveal both a particular cultural formation and aspects of the system itself.

Theorizations of social life in the world-system context indicate that locality is never simply a constraint. It is produced through material means, social relationships, and ethnographic accounts.[5] Locality as a staple of social life—as well as the grounding of ethnographic research and writing—is a problematic arena only recently examined by anthropologists. Is it the case that access to mediated images frees people from the constraints of their more circumscribed local lives? If so, then how? With careful attention to locality as a form of cultural production, anthropological approaches can ascertain under what conditions, and how, mediated cultural forms are incorporated into local cultural landscapes. Methods for studying local culture, however, must be crafted carefully and supplemented with complementary translocal approaches to account for the specificities of contemporary cultural formation.

The questions I explore in this essay are the products of a multisite ethnography of a translocal phenomenon, lowriding in the U.S. Southwest. In the broader project, I trace the meanings of lowriding, a form of car customizing associated with Chicanos. I study lowriding in three distinct sites, asking how locality effects the meanings of a mass yet customized cultural form.[6] The sites are Los Angeles, California; Houston, Texas; and Española, New Mexico. In all three sites, there is a significant discourse of local culture: how Houston lowriders differ from Los Angeles lowriders, how Los Angeles lowriders consider themselves years ahead of all other lowriders, and how to tell Chimayosos—New Mexicans of Hispano descent from the village of Chimayó—from other New Mexican lowriders.

Each locality has dimensions that exceed such comparative glosses. In metropolitan areas, forms of lowriding work according to the logics most often ascribed to mass-produced popular culture—they provide alternative communities and potential identities. They also communicate experiences and desires (Lipsitz 1995). In Los Angeles, lowriding activities provide alternatives to strictly local and often limiting forms of identity, such as gang participation. At the same time, lowriding aesthetics construct a style considered unique to Chicano experiences of social relationships and structured marginality (Bright 1995, in press).[7] In its early period in Houston (1977–84), lowriding provided a form of community that integrated newly arrived Chicano migrants with Chicano locals in the context of an expanding economy. In most metropolitan settings, lowriding provides a means of self-identification as well as opportunities for unique community construction. In such settings, lowriders participate in the pleasures of consumer culture through the aesthetics and performances of the cars. They also use their cars and the images on them to challenge and mediate the boundaries of marginality particular to minorities in metropolitan areas of the United States. These boundaries are marked in part by police surveillance, racism, and spatial segregation.

In metropolitan settings, lowriding is primarily associated with the broader concerns and practices of working-class Chicano culture, albeit with local influences and ramifications. In contrast, lowriding in the rural yet semiurban Española area links local Hispano culture and tradition with the ethnopolitical concerns of the Chicano movement. In northern New Mexico, tourism and craft commodification have fostered an intercultural economy that traffics in the cultures of native inhabitants—Hispano and Native American—and in the unique New Mexican landscape (Babcock 1990a, 1990b; Rodriguez 1987). Area Hispanos provide much of the working-class labor force for the area, especially for the state government in Santa Fe, the area tourist industry, and nearby Los Alamos Laboratories. Given these factors, it is not surprising that lowrider aesthetics in northern New Mexico exhibit a concern with boundaries, emphasizing autonomy and locality as the significant factors of identity. I argue that in northern New Mexico, lowriders merge regional ethnicity, working-class ideologies, and Chicano nationalism in a discourse of tradition in order to claim a "place" and a unique identity for themselves. This article explores the interaction between traditional and mass forms in the development of culture, identity, and locality in northern New Mexico. More broadly, it analyzes how commodities are re-created, or customized, in local relationships and webs of significance.

LOWRIDERS

The term *lowrider* was coined in California in the 1960s and lowriding has subsequently become an important part of Chicano popular culture throughout the Southwest.[8] Lowriding's popularity is fueled in part by the publication of *Lowrider Magazine,* based in California. *Lowrider* began regional distribution in the late 1970s, prompting increased lowrider and lowrider car club participation throughout the Southwest, including the Española area.[9] Española is an important regional town and local trading market in northern New Mexico with a population of more than 8,000 that is 84 percent Hispanic. It is located along the Rio Grande River between the tourist towns of Santa Fe and Taos. Seven miles east of Española is Chimayó, with a population of 2,789 (97 percent Hispanic). The Española and Chimayó area is a well-known lowriding haven, often referred to as "the lowriding capital of New Mexico" (see Figures 2 and 3). In Española, the favorite cruising strip is Riverside Drive, also known as Highway 68, the road that links Santa Fe to Taos. It is a major commercial strip, with hotels at either end of town. The town's main strip malls front Riverside Drive as do the major grocery stores, auto parts stores, service stations, and hamburger stands. Most area residents come to Española for shopping, making Riverside Drive the central place in a town that has no real center. Highway 68 is also the road traveled by tourists as they pass through Española on their travels between Santa Fe and Taos. Lowriders are a familiar sight on this road, elaborately decorated automobiles slowly making their way down Riverside with barely visible drivers. This is especially true on Saturday nights, when they cruise a loop from one end of town to the other, sometimes stopping in a frontage parking lot to meet with friends and enjoy the view. Lowriders are one of the few local "sights" that tourists stop to view as they make their way between Santa Fe and Taos.

Less visible than cruising are the ways cars, like other commodities in this area, are constantly repaired and remodeled as they circulate in familial, gifting, and trade networks. Lowriding takes place within these networks, within and across familial and cohort group ties. Cars and trucks have long lives and are often passed from parents to children. Twenty-three auto-body shops in Chimayó alone attest to the amount of repair and customizing work done in the area. Local lowriders constitute roughly ten percent of the area population, although they are an ever shifting group as people move in and out of interest in lowriding practice.

The northern New Mexico region is best known to outsiders as the cultural and geographical center of the "land of enchantment." Its unique landscapes of semiarid mountains, wind-carved sand outcroppings, beautiful forests, and verdant agricultural river valleys are home to long established Native American Pueblos and Hispano villages. Each year thousands of tourists are attracted to the area stretching from Albuquerque north to the Colorado border.

This region, originally settled by Pueblo Indians, was a northern province of New Spain, then Mexico, and later a southwestern territory of the United States. Under Spain and then Mexico (1540–1646), New Mexico's political economy was subject to the frontier modes of governmental and ecclesiastical management that operated at a far distance from Mexico City. As a U.S. territory (1846–1912), it was subject to colonial modes of management that fostered increased social and economic marginality among the area's native residents. New Mexico was late in receiving statehood in 1912.

LOCALE

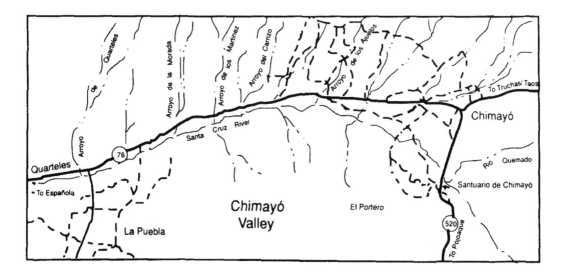

Figure 3. Map of the Chimayó valley.

Throughout the Spanish, Mexican, and U.S. periods, Santa Fe has been an important governing, trading, and ecclesiastical center. Taos is significant for its location at the northern end of the Santa Fe trail. By contrast, the importance of Española is strictly regional, and its ethnic and class composition is in stark contrast with that of Santa Fe and nearby Los Alamos.[10] As mentioned earlier, Española's population of 8,389 is predominantly of Hispanic origin (84 percent), as is Chimayó's population of 2,789 (93 percent). Most of Española's non-Hispanic population is Native American, with the Santa Clara Pueblo just to the south and the San Juan Pueblo just to the north. Los Alamos's population of 11,455 is predominantly white (83 percent white non-Hispanic origin) with 12 percent of Hispanic origin while Santa Fe's population of 55,859 is more mixed with 47 percent of Hispanic origin. The median income in Española is $19,785 per household, and in Chimayó it is $19,858. In contrast, Santa Fe's median income is $30,023, while the Los Alamos median income is the largest in the state at $48,330 (Bureau of the Census 1990).

As the home of the majority of area lowriders, Chimayó is of particular importance to this article.[11] It is located seven miles east of Española. Route 76, which connects them, runs along the Santa Cruz River. The river valley is bounded to the north by a sawtooth line of sand cliffs. People live on either side of Route 76, predominantly along arroyos, or dry creek beds, that drain from the sand cliffs into the river. Over the past 15 years, a series of earthen dams have been built to the north and parallel to the river, between the sand cliffs, to control flooding. Arroyos are the major residential roads and landmarks of the area.

For many, Chimayó is best known as the home of one of northern New Mexico's most famous Hispano landmarks, the Santuario de Chimayó (see Figure 4). The Santuario functions as a spiritual center for many religious and cultural activities (Borhegyi 1956). The chapel is used by both locals and tourists, and the Santuario is the site of a variety of pilgrimages. Perhaps the best known of these is the Easter procession during which pilgrims walk the road from Santa Fe to the Santuario. In the summer, Española's Fiesta de Oriate begins at the Santuario with a convocational Mass and blessing of the Fiesta's King, Queen, and their court. After the blessing, Fiesta runners carry the torch the seven miles from the Santuario to the fiesta grounds in Española. The village fiesta in July honoring patron saint Santiago, or St. James, begins with a procession of church auxiliary groups, locals, ex-residents, and a handful of tourists who carry a small glass case with the *bulto* (statue) of Santiago from the Santuario to the more recently built and much larger Sagra Familia Church a few miles away on Route 76. Tourist buses run regularly from Santa Fe to Taos, stopping in Chimayó at the Santuario, at Ortega's Weaving and Gallery, and at the Rancho de Chimayó Restaurant. Tourism has spawned a supplemental economy for this area.

Local residents often identify the land with one family group or another, as family plots along particular arroyos are often subdivided generation after generation (Crawford 1989; Rodriguez 1987,1992). When Victor Martinez named the owners of body shops for me, he was unsure of the last name of one owner whose shop was near Ortega's Weavers and Gallery. He identified the owner in terms of location: "I think he's Trujillo because the Trujillos live more over there." In the summer of 1990, I lived with my family in the Arroyo de los Martinez, also known as Daniel's Arroyo after the trailer park at its entrance off Route 76. Named tor the deceased son of the trailer park's owners, the site testifies to the importance and presence of family groups in the area.

Historically Catholic, Chimayo's population is now Catholic and Evangelical Protestant. Most lowriders are Catholic and use the symbols of Mexican American Catholicism on their cars. Area Protestants are often critical of these practices as inappropriate, interpreting this usage of religious images as an expression of culture rather than faith. While locally contested, such practices participate in the broader dynamics of representation and cultural objectification of the region.

Over the course of the 20th century, the northern region of New Mexico has developed a tourist and commodity economy that objectifies local landscapes and culture, and in the process produces locality as a form of identity. Changing modes of government and persistently distant relations to the cultural centers of the ruling nation-states have generated long struggles over tradition in this area (Briggs 1980; Briggs and Van Ness 1987; Deutsch 1987; Forrest 1989; Grimes 1976; Rodriguez 1987, 1992; Weigle 1976).

One example of this struggle can be seen in the history of image carving. In this area, wood carvers have long made religious figures for worship. In his study of New Mexican wood carvers, Briggs argues that the history of image carving in New Mexico reveals a process of localization during the Spanish, Mexican, and early U.S. periods (1980). The area was regularly without clergy, due to the remoteness of the region and its small population. In the absence of clergy, area residents adapted their religious practices. Early attempts to imitate the religious iconography of metropolitan artists were transformed over time to an internal adherence to local tradition. This period also saw the transformation of various patron saints according to local cultural patterns. The function of such saints and images in Hispano life has been one of mediation, enabling the symbolic connection of individuals, groups, and social movements.

Processes of localization and mediation continue into the present. The 20th century has featured the large-scale commodification of the cultural goods of Hispano and Native American groups. The area has received large numbers of mass-produced commodities from outside the state. This circulation of goods has contributed to local discourse about culture and the boundaries of goods and practices. For example, New Mexican carved images have increasingly become cultural commodities produced for purchase by outsiders attracted to their imagery and craft, but who rarely use them in spiritual practices.[12] Artists who produce religious objects such as saints and biblical scenes for sale to outsiders or nonpractitioners are faced with the dilemma of how to justify their work. According to carver George Lopez, objects sold to outsiders were not yet blessed and hence did not have the status of full cultural objects (Briggs 1980). Other carvers refuse to sell religious images to nonbelievers. Contemporary carvers combine traditional materials and aesthetics with modern techniques and prototypes while consciously seeking to evade the control that Anglo elites exercise over the form and content of carvings as well as the context for their exhibition and marketing. Such dilemmas are particular to members of a group whose material culture is valued by nonmembers.

Two processes influencing localization in wood carving are particularly noteworthy. In contrast with other historical periods, the contemporary period features the use of writings about the works of local carvers and the local industry, a new kind of prototype used as a resource by a number of carvers (Briggs 1980:187). The second process is the increasing economic integration of local Hispanos since the 1960s, influential for cultural production generally as well as for wood carvers and lowriders. Significantly this change occurred in the context of continued political and economic marginalization along with the heightened risk of loss of language, culture, and history. It is in concert with these developments that New Mexicans draw on symbols of locality—land, water, and New Mexican religion—in order to articulate their existence and their grievances (Briggs 1980:210).

That such cultural and economic trends give rise to an intensified symbolic representation of the area creates important effects and challenges for local residents. Many local residents are involved in producing traditional Spanish colonial arts or tourist crafts for sale, often subsidizing incomes from working-class jobs. They are employed to construct images of their land and cultures in styles that foster tourist consumption, perhaps best exemplified in "Santa Fe style" (Babcock 1990b).[13] For example, several Chimayosos were employed to paint, but not design, a mural for the interior of the La Fonda Hotel on the plaza in Santa Fe. While they are called upon to re-create their culture for others, they also create their own art works and use them to represent themselves—for example, these same people make representations of their culture on their lowriders. For many, religious images are not only mediators, but also icons of identity and resistance.

As in earlier centuries, Hispano lowriders engage in a process of localization, adapting commodities to an internal orientation; however, the isolation of earlier centuries is no longer the dominant constraint on local practices and forms. Lowriders are faced with the dilemma of making extrinsic objects, such as cars, cultural while living in a milieu that features labor outmigration as well as tourist commodification and class difference. Most of the original lowriders in the area spent some of their early work lives in California industries or in regional mines, later returning to set up households near their families. At home, lowriders experience Hispano culture both as their native culture and as it is commodified for non-Hispano tourists while facing the pressures of a growing market for their familial land among outsiders. Under these circumstances, lowrider adaptation strategies are highly inflected by concerns with place, social relationships, and identity.

THE CHICANO MOVEMENT AND MASS COMMUNICATION

In New Mexico, the traffic in culture—and the culture of traffic—between the Chicano Movement and local cultures is multifaceted and linked to mass communication. The popularity of lowriding expanded broadly in the late 1970s with the publication of *Lowrider Magazine,* then produced and distributed in San Jose, California. The magazine itself was greatly influenced by the rhetorics of the Chicano Movement, an important premise of which was to incorporate traditional Mexican American crafts and aesthetics into modern Chicano life (Lujan 1970; Ybarra-Frausto 1991). The movement mobilized people to appreciate Chicano cultural productions, in part through its use of popular symbols. As New Mexico wood carving and lowriding demonstrate, the symbols and forms forged within the movement became important forms for adaptation. Cultural, political, and institutional networks promoted this traffic in culture, linking the imagination, culture, and social life of people of Mexican descent across the United States. Area ethnopolitical movements responded directly to historical experiences of political, economic, and cultural alienation. Reies Tijerina's La Alianza Federal de Mercedes (Federal Alliance of Land Grants) was organized in Rio Arriba County in 1963 to reclaim lands from the Spanish land grants that Hispano residents lost to the U.S. government (Acuña 1981; Nabokov 1969; Rodriguez 1987). Simultaneously, these experiences were accompanied by the development and mass distribution of Chicano culture in the form of music such as War's song "Low Rider," Cheech and Chong movies, Hollywood gang films, and magazines such as *Q-Vo* and *Lowrider*. In New Mexico, the appreciation of these newly politicized traditional Chicano art forms complemented the production of tourist and ethnic arts—both Hispano and Native—in the Rio Grande valley. Hence the loss of land and increased tourism—the very things that threatened to erode Hispano culture—instead created the conditions under which the Chicano Movement strengthened local conceptions of culture.

CARS AND SOCIAL LIFE

Lowrider cars belong to a social life based in large part on gifting, tinkering, and bartering within kinship and friendship networks. Family incomes mostly derive from working-class jobs, craft production, and the waning practice of agriculture. Area households also rely on resources gained from gardening, trading labor, and sharing efforts as in acequia management and wood collecting. Agriculture, especially the growing of chiles, is practiced mainly by older men. Many local women work for the government, either in maintenance or administration for Los Alamos Laboratories or for the state government in Santa Fe. Some run fast-food restaurants in Española. Others take in children, enabling them to stay home with their own. Many men work at construction in Santa Fe, as machinists or contractors for Los Alamos, or in businesses in Española. Prior to the 1970s many young men and their wives left the area to work in industries in California, in mines in Grants and Colorado, or to find work in Utah. Often they returned within ten years with savings to set up their own households. Because of the dangerous nature of their work, man of the area resident have been disabled temporarily or permanently. The plethora of body shop mentioned earlier indicates how cars are part of a large secondhand economy. Cars are used and reused. Dents are repaired. Rust is removed and metal replaced. It a car is beyond use, then it is used for parts. Sometimes the car bodies are used as barriers for flood control in the sandy arroyos (see Figure 5). Parts of old cars are often sold at swap meets.

Many people are involved in the transformation of a car to a lowrider. A car can be handed down or bought from a family member, bought new, bought used, or salvaged. Junior Trujillo bought his father s Impala and fixed it up. Ana Flores inherited her family's Monte Carlo, and with a little help from her father and her boyfriend, renovated and customized it. Herman Herrera salvaged his parents' '37 Chevy from under a collapsed shed and restored it with the help of Eliseo; and Melecio Martinez. Often, some portion of the work is done professionally.

Julian Quintana has an upholstery business and reupholsters many of the local cars; hence, his car is known as "Stitches." Vicky Gutierrez had her '77 Mustang's "girlish look" painted by Marshall Martinez and the upholstery done at Floyd's Upholstery (see Figure 6). Dennis Chavez bought his '73 Ford Ranger used and started customizing it in 1979. Now it belongs to his son who shows it. Victor Martinez s grandfather used to drive Victor's uncle's lowrider and his family called him the "oldest lowrider around."

Customizing transforms a used car, which is often inherited or bought from a family member, into a beautiful "bomb," as cars from the forties and fifties are known. Many local lowriders, like Dennis Martinez, trace the customizing practices back to their fathers and uncles Martinez's father had a '50 Mercury with spinners, white walls, and spinner skirts. His uncle had a '52 white Chevy, "down on the ground." Ana Flores's uncle was one of the first low riders in Española. In this area family members of both sexes are often invoked in customizing. These intergenerational links also become a link to family tradition that provides evidence of the pervasiveness of area lowriding through time.

Figure 5. Car bodies used as drainage control. Photograph by author.

Figure 6. Vicky Gutierrez and family. Photograph by author.

Even though the Española area is predominantly rural, it is subject to the influences of urbanization and industrialization. As mentioned earlier, many of Chimayó's older generation of lowriders, born in the 1940s, moved to California cities for industrial jobs in the sixties and often brought cars back with them when they returned to set up their households. These experiences have influenced their working-class sensibilities and heightened their value of local connections. Eliseo and Melecio Martinez, who live near the western boundary of Chimayó, are brothers who married in the early 1960s and moved with their wives to California to work. Both men were early members of "Los Paisanos," a car club that began around 1 976 and became more official in 1981 when Herman Herrera joined. Eliseo and his wife lived in Compton (in the Los Angeles area) for two years. While there, he worked in an airplane factory and his wife worked assembly for *TV Guide*. In 1967 they returned to Chimayó, and in 1970 Eliseo began work on the truck he currently drives, a modified '38 Ford. The truck rests on a shortened '76 Grand Prix frame. The truck bed is from a '50/'51 and has been shortened and made thinner. The truck has been several colors in its long life but is currently painted orange with red flames. Inside it has black upholstery and an orange ceiling. Melecio has constructed several cars, among them a customized '55 Hillman van that he brought back from California in 1965. The Hillman lasted about ten years; then, he installed a new engine and began customizing it anew. The two brothers have been instrumental in helping others make their cars, especially their nieces Liz and Rene and their friend Herman Herrera.

Dennis Chavez lives near the Santuario on the eastern side of Chimayó. Once owned by his family, the Santuario was sold by Chavez's great-great grandfather to the Archdiocese of Santa Fe in 1926, through the intervention of Mary Austin and others (Kay 2987). Chavez and his wife lived in Los Angeles from 1965 to 1966, in Germany from 1966 to 1968, and back in los Angeles and Oakland from 1968 to 1971. During this time, Dennis had several customized automobiles, including a '47 Studebaker with suicide doors (doors that are hinged at the rear rather than the front) and baby moon rims, a '59 Ford and a '56 Mercury with tuck and roll upholstery. From 1971 to 1979, he was informally involved with friends and family members who also had customized cars. They in turn "hung around" with guys from nearby Nambe who formed one of the valley's first car clubs, the Rod Angels, in 1978. Many of Chavez's group formed the Chimayó Valley Cruisers in 1979.

Dave Jaramillo, owner of "Dave's Dream," conceived of his car as an object that would bring his family closer together. (He worked for several years in the mines of Grants, New Mexico, returning on weekends to work with his cousin Dennis Martinez on the car, a 1969 Ford LTD. Their work on the car began in 1976 and lasted until 1978 when Dave died in a car accident. At the time of his death, the car was unfinished, but since then it has fulfilled his expectations in several ways. Martinez's wife, Irene, and his cousin, Dennis Martinez, have completed it. Dave and Dennis were close friends and members of the same car club. Dennis and Irene commissioned a Santa Fe artist to paint a family portrait, featuring Dave, Irene, and Dave Jr. on each side of the car. Irene showed the finished car at car shows where it was known as "El Gran Chimayoso." The car was purchased in 1990 by the Smithsonian Institution for their transportation collection and for exhibition with "American Encounters." Its purchase was facilitated by Dennis and Irene, who were again active in conceiving and facilitating the car's restoration, including the restoration of the family mural. The car, commonly known as "Dave's Dream," could also be known as "Dennis's Dream" or "Dennis, Irene, and Dave Jr.'s Dream." Such family relations are the foundation for the production of lowriders in this area (Brewer 1990).

Cars are most often communal or familial projects, but the motivations for modifying the cars are often related to local trends in popular culture.[14] For example, while Ana Flores had always loved her family's 1972 Monte Carlo, her interest in lowriders was sparked in high school when she and a girlfriend, Yvonne, began reading *Lowrider Magazine.* Noting how the magazine's emphasis on east L.A. style and lowriders excited them, Ana remarked, "We were east L.A. this and lowrider that!" After she was 1 8 and began working at Los Alamos, Ana started customizing the Monte Carlo Super Sport given to her by her mother. Ana learned about cars, including engines, from her father. At the time of my research, her boyfriend was helping her customize her car.[15] In the summer of 1990, Ana was a member of La Reina's court for the Fiesta de Oñate. Her high school friend, Yvonne, is now married to Chris Sanchez. *Lowrider Magazine* featured the couple's car on the cover of the August 1990 issue (see Figure 4).

To be sure, participation in lowriding has gendered dimensions. Lowriders are important carriers of customary practices *and* expressive vehicles for identity in the Española area. Men's interest in cars often begins as a predominantly—but not exclusively—male adolescent concern with style, personal identity, and mechanical skills. After high school, increased independence in work and familial relations frequently paves the way for men's cohort relationships to develop into car clubs. Women's interests, as such, are similarly constituted, but tend to be initiated later and made manifest during their years of employment prior to marriage. After marriage, women's direct participation wanes dramatically as their activities and priorities shift to their own families. In addition, it is very difficult to open the trunk of a car with "shaved" door handles while trying to juggle children and groceries. While there are women who drive lowriders, men predominate and usually participate in some kind of organized lowrider group. In a few clubs, wives of members are allowed voting status, but for the most part, women do not form or join clubs. When they do join clubs, they tend to be active for a shorter period of time than men do. Women like Ana Flores, who learned to work on cars, meet with some local resistance.

When lowriding is a family activity, it is organized around men's interests and family participation. Moreover, men are more likely than women to claim that their car is a "family" project or that their car connects them to their family. In one case, an Española man claimed that his car was his family—he was divorced from his wife and no longer lived with her or their children. Instead, he "took care" of the car which features a mural of a beautiful blonde on the trunk (see Figure 7). Men's cars function as representations of masculinity and male relationships. In addition, cars are sites of mechanical and aesthetic proficiency. They are material sites for the imagining and construction of men's relationships and responsibilities, and they occupy a central location in the lives of many

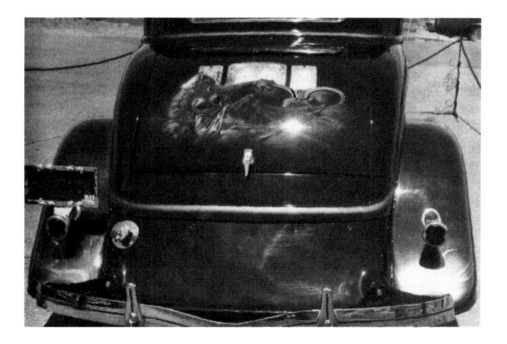

Figure 7. Car as family. Photograph by author.

men. Not surprisingly, they can become the subject of domestic tension. The time, effort, money, and care they require is seen by some wives as in direct conflict with familial responsibilities and relationships. In this rural area, families can feel quite fragmented because members must work away from home in Los Alamos or in Santa Fe. As a result, the meanings of family and of gendered identity become heightened in a culture that values family relationships. When Dennis Martinez says, heart is in my wheels," and adds "I have a heart like a car," he alerts his audiences to the multiple meanings that cars have. Cars carry people and feelings, and car customizing allows a man to express his feelings. Men care tor their cars, they care for their families, and having a nice car is one way of being a man. For some, it is a way of being a man who cares tor his family. The socioeconomic context of these car-related practices— rural area, working-class jobs, employment outmigration, heavy tourism, and cultural appropriations—coupled with a history of marginalization from the land, make the cars themselves an important surface for assertions of personal and cultural identity.

I suggest that we think of tradition as invoked by lowriders as a process of improvisation, a process that reconverts cultural practices for current conditions. Garcia-Canclini defines reconversion as follows: "to reconvert cultural capital means to transfer symbolic patrimony from one site to another in order to conserve it, increase its yield, and better the position of those who practice it" (1992:32).[16] A symbolic process akin to what Garcia-Canclini describes can be seen at work in lowrider aesthetics. In northern New Mexico, where representation is a key economic and cultural practice, lowriders incorporate the emblematic images of their culture their families, their land, their religion, their struggle—onto the many surfaces of their cars.

LOCAL/TRANSLOCAL INSCRIPTIONS

In the aesthetic of Española area lowriders there is one particularly striking indication of the simultaneous localization and translocalization of culture: the pairing of an image with personal meaning, often drawn from local culture, with an image or reference to extralocal identities and processes. Dennis Martinez's statement, "It's something that's *tradition*. I have a heart that's like a car, you know. My heart is in my wheels," links the historical importance of lowriding practice to its affectivity. His statement situates the car within a particular narrative construction that suggests how the car, a mass-produced object, becomes embedded with in a cultural context through relationships, material practices, and textualizations.

A "heart that's like a car" suggests the ways in which the car is an embodiment, enhancing both bodily mobility and affectivity. In this vein, the car is similar to the human body, a site of cultural inscription. In contemporary contexts where most aspects of our lives are disjointed, cars simultaneously isolate us and provide continuity between people and places. Customizing a car enlarges the possibilities of bodily inscription, exhibition, and, for many lowriders, social relations. These activities take place on cars that are in reality mobile canvases. Given the broad range of aesthetic practices and representational forms in this heavily tourised area, cars provide a site relatively free from the potential commodification to which many other forms are subject.

Figure 8. Dennis Martinez and his 1970 Monte Carlo. Photograph by author.

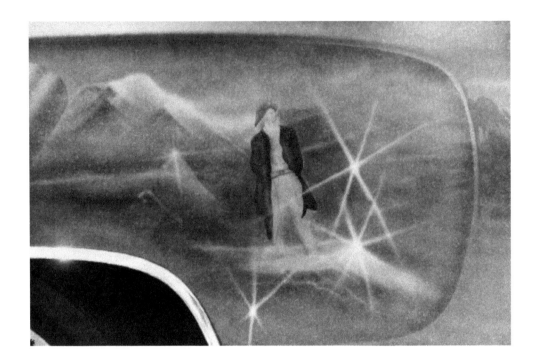

Figure 9. Sangre de Cristo Mountains and pachuco. Photograph by author.

The simultaneous presente of local and translocal symbols is seen in Dennis Martinez's salmon pink 1970 Monte Carlo (see Figure 8). The ghostly painted images on the car ally him with two traditions—one local Hispano and the other Chicano. The mountainous landscapes on the rear panels of the car are reference to the local mountains (see Figure 9). The depiction of the land in this area signifies culture, family, community, continuity, and, importantly, conflict (Rodriguez 1992). The roses between the rear and side windows are a metonymic symbol invoking the owner's Hispano culture as well as his deceased mother and her garden (see Figure 10). The rose also represents *la Virgen* de *Guadalupe,* who provides her believers with a means to know God's love and acts as a sign of God's acknowledgment of the Hispanic New World. In both cases, the rose symbolizes empowerment and tribute, just as Martinez—as a descendant of Mexicans ano his mother's son—has been empowered by the love of these two women.

Figure 10. Rose mural. Photograph by author.

In the foreground of the mountainous landscape stands a third ghostly image—the *pachuco*. An invocation of Chicano consciousness signifying cultural awareness, integrity and self-determination (see Figure 9), pachucos were Mexican American male youths in the 1940s, members of the early generation of U.S -born Mexicans. They too had a style to "deal with" —zoot suits with fingertip-length sleeves, broad shoulders, baggy pants pegged at the ankles, and ankle-length watch chains. During World War II Mexican American zoot suiters in Los Angeles were hunted down and beaten by American soldiers stationed there. For the servicemen, zoot suits symbolized excess—their styling required additional fabric during a time of limited resources when such constructions were outlawed—and lack of proper patriotic feelings (Mazón 1984). In the historical reconstructions of the Chicano Movement, the pachuco represents the first Mexican American to embody Chicano consciousness. Through style, pachucos defiantly express the contradictions of being Mexican American (of being neither Mexican nor American yet suffering violence and discrimination because of cultural difference

For lowriders, the pachuco serves as a powerful symbol for claims to difference made through style. It became one of the symbols adapted and promoted by *Lowrider Magazine* in the late 1970s as lowriding's popularity grew throughout the Southwest (Plascensia 1983). Martinez uses it here as an emblem of empowerment. Concerned with working-class empowerment (in part as a result of an accident he suffered while employed at Los Alamos Laboratories—he lost an eye), and with cultural empowerment for area Hispanos, Martinez sees his car as an opportunity to express his skills and culture (see Figure 11). For him, these two arenas are linked and simultaneously represented in the images on his car. The challenge to viewers is how to contextualize and understand these acts of representation

Arthur Medina's white '75 Cadillac is called "Lowrider Heaven." The front license plate says "little LA," a nickname of Española, tying local experiences to extra local processes and larger identities (see Figure 12).[18] Medina, who aspires to be known for his art work, has painted the head of Jesus on the trunk. He also has painted Jesus on the exterior of his house (see Figure 13). When I asked him it he was a religious man, he replied, "I believe in God a lot." When I pressed him to tell me why it was important to him to have Jesus on his car, he said, "Well, like, he did a lot for us! Like, I could be putting knights or something on my car, but I feel better if I put him on it. I just feel better. It's like he's guiding me." His explanation, while seeming to posit a choice between popular culture and religious culture, actually unites them within a single repetoire, indicating the extent to which religious iconography is a local form of popular culture. As both cases show traditional forms become the popular culture of the area. The car for Arthur Medina is a place where he expresses his feelings. He says, "I put on it what I feel." Since he thinks of his work as art, he prefers that his car be hand painted, a technique that he considers more conducive to expressing feeling. Thus, these lowriders indicate two symbolic trends among lowriders from the Española area. One is the use of tradition as central to the popular culture of the area. The second is the connection of local culture to extralocal processes and identities.

Figure 11. 1970 Monte Carl Photograph by author.

Figure 12. Arthur Medina's 1975 Cadillac. Photograph by author.

Figure 1 3. Cadillac in front of Arthur Medina s home. Photograph by author.

Given the wide range of images that lowriders use on their cars, cars from the Española area are distinguished to the extent that religious images are prevalent. For Chimayó lowriders, the Santuario de Chimayó plays a consolidating role influencing which symbolic forms they choose and circulate (see Figure 4). An important regional landmark and spiritual center, the Santuario symbolizes Chimayó and is the backdrop for many photographs. In addition to those seeking its spiritual powers, people interested in folk art and Hispano folklore are drawn to the Santuario. The carving of Jesus over the altar in the Santuario is well known. The west wing of the Santuario contains the healing dirt, many images of Jesus, la Virgen and saints as well as appeals, *testimonios* (testimonials), and thanks for help received.

Victor Martinez's '50 Ford is customized in the style of a '50s customized car—complete with continental kit extending the support of the rear bumper flame paint job, and original option rims (see Figures 14 and 15). But just above the continental kit is a mural depicting the sacred heart of Jesus, an invocation of cultural authority and a symbol of suffering, sacrifice, and love (see Figure 16). With these two aesthetic devices—the replication of an 'American' cultural style through the '50s motif and the image of Jesus—the owner ties himself to an "American moment" while also invoking local and extralocal cultural authority. The skill with which he makes his vehicle is his particular and very personal claim to self-respect.

Place provides an important context tor the display of cars in addition to being a meaningful reference for images on cars. Victor Martinez and his family attend the Catholic Church in nearby Santa Cruz, but his wife's family owns a hamburger stand directly across from the Santuario. Both Victor and his wife Barbara work there on the weekends. He often parks his car outside the stand in full view of the Santuario and its visitors. Hence, Victor is aware of the symbolic significance of whatever image he puts on his car, and this awareness has influenced his choice to exhibit a religious image instead of another form. Arthur Medina's family also owns a food, folk art, and souvenir stand across from the Santuario. Arthur is an artist in that he not only made his car, the Cadillac described above, but in 1991 was in the process of teaching himself wood carving and trying to define his own craftwork, much of which also carried religious themes. This work was made for sale to tourists visiting Santuario.

These examples provide a sense of the narrative constructions and connections made possible through customizing activities Each car is an individual project, a family project, and a local reference. Each requires structuring a "vehicle" for family togetherness as well as for personal and group narratives. It is a "vehicle" for claiming local and extralocal identity. In this sense, the car is a "cultural vehicle" enabling the reinvention of culture. It is in this creative sense that the lowrider says, "It's my culture, man" while explaining that the best metaphor for the building of a lowrider is "giving new life to an old soul."[19] In New Mexico, customizing aesthetics are influenced by a sense of cultural difference that is rooted in highly localized identities—related to family, land, and local cohorts—but inflected by responses to economic and cultural appropriations in the area that necessitates appeals to a larger-scale, extra-local identity.

Figure 14. Victor Martinez's 1950 Ford. Photograph by author.

Figure 15. Victor Martinez's 1950 Ford rear view. Photograph by author.

Figure 16. Sacred heart of Jesus mural. Photograph by author.

THE SMITHSONIAN

For the 1992 quincentennial, the Smithsonian produced an exhibition entitled "American Encounters" to be on display for roughly ten years (Morrison 1992). They wanted to use the cultures of the Rio Grande valley area of New Mexico to demonstrate a long history of multiculturalism in the United States. In the process of preparing the project, the Smithsonian purchased the previously mentioned lowrider car, "Dave's Dream," from Irene Jamarillo in Española (Brewer 1990). During the course of the Smithsonian's research, lowriders, more than any other group researched, emerged as controversial in New Mexico culture.

In 1990, the Smithsonian lobbied the New Mexico state government to contribute $1,000,000 to the "American Encounters" exhibition. New Mexico residents expressed concern that they were going to be "represented" by the lowly and exotic lowrider car. Given local concerns with autonomy and self-representation, many New Mexican residents saw this as an opportunity to express their views and represent themselves broadly as they found themselves being incorporated into the Smithsonian's imagining of the nation. The Smithsonian responded to editorials in the local papers with assurances that the exhibition was not focusing on lowriders per se, but on the complexities of New Mexican cultures and intercultural relations (Kennedy 1991; Miller 1991).

The message of this discussion was that lowriders play an important symbolic role in the larger discussion of New Mexican "culture," a message not lost on Española lowriders or their audiences. This discussion of cultural representation indicates one of the important controversial features of popular culture: that the objectification of culture disrupts established class and cultural hierarchies. While lowriders see themselves and their cars as positively engaged in representing their culture, this vision is not always shared by others. Some Anglos see them as bothersome troublemakers and are often afraid of them. Some Hispanos likewise think of them as troublemakers and worry that they give all Hispanos a bad name. Others deride them for their attachment to religious symbols in the name of having a good time. The cars are thought by some to be excessively adorned and in bad taste. Tomás Ybarra-Frausto cites lowriders as a key example of *rasquachismo,* a Chicano aesthetic sensibility that turns ruling paradigms upside down and produces "a sort of good taste of bad taste" (1991:155). It is in the context of conflicts over culture and representation that lowriding has the important effect of carving out a niche of pleasure, autonomy, and self-authored and authorizing representation for working-class Chicanos throughout the Southwest.

RECONVERSIONS

Lowriding in New Mexico is at once a historically situated series of social practices and a form of local "Chicanoized" Hispano culture. The customizing techniques that characterize lowriding in the upper Rio Grande valley have been employed since the 1940s among Mexican Americans and Hispanos throughout most of the Southwest. But lowriding as a popular social practice and the clubs and competitions associated with it date from the 1970s. New Mexico adaptations of lowriding are based in part on the development of the form in California, knowledge gained by outmigrating and returning New Mexican workers, and the ideology of ethnic empowerment—communicated through the regionally distributed *Lowrider Magazine* that stresses lowriding as a uniquely "Chicano" form of customizing. Potentialities already within the form made it suitable for translocal adoption. Potentialities at the local level included local conditions (tourist commodification, land appropriation, and work conflicts), local social practices (such as kin-based trading and gifting), as well as local popular cultures (religious images as icons of identity and resistance).

Understanding lowriding as a form of Chicano culture practiced by northern New Mexican Hispanos requires a frame of elaboration for analyzing ethnic identity processes in northern New Mexico. Issues of Hispano identity are most cogently addressed in Sylvia Rodriguez's work on Taos Hispanos and the dynamics of identity processes in northern New Mexico. Rodriguez examines "Hispano ethnicity and its relation to contemporary Mexicano-Chicano ethnopolitical identity and mobilization" (1992:96). She notes that constituencies for Chicano (national-political) and local Hispano forms of ethnopolitical and ethnocultural expression tend to overlap, especially in ritual revivals, Danza Azteca, lowriders, and Cinco de Mayo celebrations. In "The Hispano Homeland Debate Revisited" (1992), she elaborates the contours of the recent debate about Hispano distinctiveness. Certain academics, key among them geographer Richard Nostrand (1984), claim that a significant portion of Hispanos of all classes in northern New Mexico see themselves as related to but distinct from other Mexicanos and Spanish-speaking people. The problem that concerns Rodriguez is that Norstrand and his supporters assume "that any sense of Hispano distinctiveness, whether true or false, will impede the development of a broader, more progressive Chicano (or American or working class) political consciousness and therefore is undesirable or retrograde" (1984:104). But Rodriguez's work suggests that the two forms of identity are in fact not incompatible. The process, as argued by Michael Hannan, proceeds as follows:

> When modern centers penetrate the local community, they undermine the salience of small-scale identities. ... Sustained mobilization in opposition to further penetration by the center must be on a scale commensurate with that of the center. Therefore, successful penetration by the center alters the condition of competition among the various bases of collective action in a direction that favors large-scale identities. [Hannan 1979:255–256, quoted in Rodriguez 1992:105]

Extrapolating the significance of this argument for northern New Mexico, Rodriguez proposes the following:

> Rather than being an impediment to the emergence of a broad-based, extralocal Chicano identity, the traditional, small-scale organization has become the medium through which a larger identity is realized. Rooted in the village community, Hispano identity has become "Chicanoized" through modernization, outmigration and resistance. [1992:105]

Rodriguez asserts that lowriders are among the forms of ethnic cultural resurgence that indicate the "Chicanoizing" of Hispano identity.

The broader question here is the part cars play in modernization, outmigration, and resistance. A further answer to how lowrider cars can be both traditional and a response to processes of development and modernization is found in Donna Haraway's meditation on the relations of bodies and machines in the late 20th century, what she calls the potential politics and myths of cyborgs. The idea of cyborgs—hybrids of machines and organisms—as contemporary reconversions transcends the dualisms that posit what seem to be more clearly bounded, somewhat autonomous relations between people and machines, and people and commodities. These dualisms wrongly promise some ideal state of humans apart from machines. "Cyborg imagery can suggest a way out of the maze of dualisms in which we have explained our bodies and tools to ourselves" (1991:181). Cyborg imagery posits a way of thinking about people and machines in which "intense pleasure in skill, machine skill, ceases to be a sin, but an aspect of embodiment. The machine is not an *it* to be animated, worshipped, and dominated. The machine is us, our processes, an aspect of our embodiment" (1991:180). For Haraway, this meditation is necessary in order to adequately understand, envision, and participate in the ontology of the late 20th century. She defines a cyborg as a creature of social reality, lived social relations, and fiction.

"I have a heart like a car" and "my heart is in my wheels" imply just such a dialectic between body and machine and between person and commodity, as the unique features of the car are being called into the service of local personal and cultural concerns. Machinelike qualities (emulating transportation) are extended to the body as the heart becomes a vehicle of transport for loved ones. This is coupled with the extension of affectivity to the purpose of the machine itself. Haraway's person-machine hybrid is Briggs's mediator, a vehicle for social relations that enables pleasurable textualizing of social reality in a way that allows mobility, social location, and a mobile canvas. Lowriders collapse the seeming dualities between persons and machines and persons and commodities as they engage in reconverting tradition and customizing modernity. If modernity promised products and techniques to free us from the constraints of locally based culture, it did so with the threat of uprooting us from social relationships. In response, lowriders engage in traditionalizing commodities by customizing them with meanings that enable a continuity of relationships. As reconversions, lowriding practices reinterpret and reinscribe local meanings into the surfaces and materials of modern life.

Given this context, Dennis Martinez makes perfect sense when he says, "My heart is in my wheels." His statement stresses the personal dedication expected from any car customizer. It is similar to saying "I love my car" or "Here in Española we love our cars." But indeed it is a more interesting assertion than that. "My heart is in my wheels" claims the car as a lowrider's purpose, empowerment, sacrifice, and joy. It is the expression of aspirations and affections, the execution of vision and skill. To make a lowrider, Chicano customizers must draw upon and simultaneously create culture. These cars are pleasure, the sort that comes through the responsible mastery of circumstance through skills that are both cultural and technological. These cars bring pleasure from performing "culture," disrupting boundaries and derailing expectations.

When Dennis Martinez says, "I have a heart like a car," he implicitly identifies the most dramatic aspects of these cars. Namely, the car is a repository and a carrier—for the owner's "work," his family, and his tradition. Each car is the product of a baroque sensibility. This is demonstrated in the process. The making of a car requires a vision of aesthetics and meaning. Said another way, it requires customizers to link narratives of commodities to cultural and personal histories, thereby implicating themselves in the design of the car. The making of a customized car requires the recreation of tradition from the intermingling of popular traditions and mass culture. Such practices are highly inflected by the horizontal coexistence of a number of symbolic systems that are the products of modernization processes. Traditions are not simply practices passed on from one generation to the next; they are practices that enable cultural continuity and require maintenance. Lowriders intertwine tradition and history with personal vision, deploying cultural and personal symbols to localize commodities. The aesthetic details reveal a dialectical appeal to self-respect and cultural authority (Ross 1989). This appeal plays out in specific ways in New Mexico where tradition becomes a form of improvisation and an important resource for popular culture productions. As Néstor García-Canclini suggests, the separation of tradition from modernity no longer works:

> The traditional and the modern are mixed together all the time. … Modernization is not a matter of replacing traditional high and popular forms but of reformulating their function and meaning. … Instead of the death of traditional cultural forms, we now discover that tradition is in transition, and articulated to modern processes. Reconversion prolongs their existence. [1992:30–31]

As lowriders indicate, local culture is creative, appropriating symbols of modernity to assert autonomy and difference. Commodities are localized in social networks, material practices, and textualizations. Simultaneously, local practices and social relationships are nested within broader translocal processes. Lowriders exemplify contemporary modes for the translocal production of locality, demonstrating how local culture is produced in a globalizing world.

NOTES

This essay has benefited enormously from my discussions in New Mexico with Victor Martinez, Nolan Martinez, Dennis Martinez, Amy Padilla, Ana Flores, Dennis Chavez, Benito Cordova, Annie Sahlin, Gino Romero, Orlando Romero, Lonn Taylor, and Alan Barber. I thank all who have so generously commented upon this article as a work in progress, including Jacqueline Urla, Susan Phillips, Paulla Ebron, and Michael Fischer. I am especially indebted to Thomas Dumm and George Lipsitz. A special thanks to the anonymous *AE* reviewers for their insightful suggestions. An earlier version was delivered at the 1993 American Studies Association meetings in Boston, Massachusetts in the panel, "Imaginary Homelands and Contingent Traditions." My writing was supported by a Luce/ACLS Dissertation Fellowship in American Art as well as a postdoctoral fellowship from the Getty Research Institute for the History of Art and the Humanities.

1. *Hispano* refers to the people of Spanish and Mexican descent in New Mexico. *Chicano* is an ethnopolitical term that refers to Mexican Americans and all people of Mexican descent living in the United States. *Chicano* is used primarily by those who have incorporated an explicitly political component in their group identity. This component stresses culture (heritage, practices, and creations) and the conditions of its production within the United States. While *Chicano* designates an ethnopolitical identity for many, it has been used historically as both a nickname and as a slur. Its politicized usage was adopted in the Chicano Movement of the 1960s. This movement developed among Mexican American activists and students as part of the civil rights struggles in the United States. Important locations of radical political activity were the University of California; Denver, Colorado; Crystal City, Texas; and Tierra Amarilla in Rio Arriba County, New Mexico. See José Limón 1981. See also Anaya and Lomelí 1991; Muñoz 1989; Rodriguez 1992; Saldivar 1990; Ybarro-Frausto 1977.
2. Española is located on the highway between Santa Fe and Taos. Primarily a Hispano town with a population of 8,389 according to the 1990 census, it is the regional trading town and destination for people migrating from the area villages of northern New Mexico in order to participate in the cash economy. Significantly, it is also a town that many tourists pass through on their way to and from the more popular tourist destinations of northern New Mexico.
3. By and large, studies of car culture focus on manufacturing, aesthetics, and subcultures. The greatest shortcoming of automotive and subcultural studies is that they do not adequately investigate the relationships between local cultures, work cultures, and networks of mass production and mass culture. See Gradante 1982, 1985; Moorhouse 1991; Plascencia 1983; Plath 1990; Stone 1990; Watkins 1991; Wolfe 1965.

4. These are Appadurai's finanscapes (money), ethnoscapes (people), ideoscapes (ideas), technoscapes (technology), and mediascapes (media). His argument is for conceptualizing these particularities as part of larger formations with their own particularities and sets of perspectives (1990:6).

5. As Appadurai argues (1995), the ethnographic record can be read as presenting the technologies and teleologies of localization. In short, a rereading of the ethnographic record foregrounding the idea of locality itself can be informative and provide new avenues for ethnographic conceptualization and representation. Other writers on the conditions of modernity and postmodernity call for a rethinking of the intersections of locality and the material and cultural conditions of social life (Battaglia 1995; Ferguson and Gupta 1992; Marcus 1995; Miller 1994) as well as locality and ethnographic accounts (Fischer and Abedi 1990; Marcus and Fischer 1986).

6. The central questions of my project, *Lowrider: Chicano Culture in the Time of the Automobile,* are four-fold (Bright in press). First, how is popular culture utilized in the creation of contemporary communities? Second, how do local cultures and political economies influence the process by which Mexican Americans create and adapt an extralocal ethnopolitical identity in the process of creating and adapting lowrider styles? Third, how is gender constructed in local and extralocal versions of popular culture, sexuality, and ethnicity? Fourth, how do so-called minorities address the challenges of structured inequality, mass media, and commodity culture through their participation in popular culture?

7. While it is true that gangs as corporate entities are not strictly local, gangs are typically comprised of sets that come from a shared geographical area, and for whom a territory based identity is foundational. In Los Angeles, many lowriders narrate their participation as having been decided in a choice between gang membership or car customizing (see Bright 1995). Los Angeles lowriding most nearly resembles Appadurai's suggestion that the presence of multiple mediated forms provides alternatives in culture and identity that are not so resolutely local (1991). The Houston example suggests that migrants also use popular forms to create communities for themselves.

8. The widespread use of the label *Chicano* dates from the 1960s as does the term *lowrider,* although for reasons that are both different and related. Lowriders share customizing techniques with other customizing enthusiasts—especially chopping and channeling. While cars customized by Mexican Americans have primarily emphasized appearance over performance and speed, many Mexican Americans have also wanted fast cars. Before the 1960s, the differences between Mexican American and Anglo cars were subtle and not so clearly identified with any one style of customizing. In fact, early hot rods looked much like today's lowriders, with bodies close to the ground. Three developments during the 1960s distinguished lowriders from hot rods. First was the production of muscle cars (often with "raked" front ends and raised rear ends) and with them the solidifying of Anglo aesthetics emphasizing speed and high performance. Second was the adaptation of hydraulic lifts so that Mexican American cars could be lowered, allowing the owner to have a "low" car with the ability to raise it up to legal associated limits as necessary. Third was the identification of this style with a Mexican American experience and identity, and competitive cruising scenes developed. The most notable was Whittier Boulevard in East Los Angeles. See Bright 1995. See also Rodriguez 1984, Stone 1990, and Wolfe 1965.

9. *Lowrider Magazine* was published from 1977 until 1984 when it went bankrupt. Alberto Lopez bought *Lowrider* and renewed its publication in 1988. Since then, lowriding has increasingly migrated across ethnic and racial lines. Los Angeles has a long history of African American car customizers and lowriders. With the advent of gangster rap out of Los Angeles in the late 1980s and MTV air time for hip hop videos, lowriders have been increasingly known as part of hip hop, with origins in African American and Afro-Caribbean youth culture (Rose 1994). See Bright 1997.

10. The class antagonisms between Española and its wealthy neighbors of Los Alamos and Santa Fe can be seen in a series of jokes known as "Española jokes," similar to Texas Aggie jokes and Pollack jokes. These jokes make fun of Española for its residents' backwardness and lack of intelligence. They ridicule Española as a poor, rural, underdeveloped area populated by social undesirables. Española area residents typically do not tell these jokes (Cordova 1990; Sagel 1993). See Battaglia 1992 for an insightful reading of the ways jokes are located within power relations and serve to displace culture.

11. Around the state, Chimayosos are known as tough, proud, and somewhat countryish in their ways, a characterization many of them accept. I argue that their self-image has developed in part because of their experiences with cultural appropriation and subordination.

12. In New Mexico, the partial transformation from spiritual object to cultural commodity has been influenced by Anglos involved in the study and "preservation" of "native" art and architecture and through their fascination with exotic practices such as interest in penitente practices, which were stimulated in part by Anglo encroachment (Briggs 1980:44; Weigle 1976:75, 90–91). Please see Sylvia Rodriguez's writings on the cultural politics of the Taos area for a full historical examination of these processes (1987, 1992).

13. In a related example, the city of Española, which lies in between the tourist centers of Santa Fe and Taos, is badly in need of more revenue dollars and has instituted an urban development program aimed at attracting what appears to be the area's last untapped resource, the tourist business. The residents are constructing a new town plaza and church. They are simultaneously enacting legislation creating an "Old Town" zone with building code restrictions

similar to those in place in Santa Fe. This will create an identifiable, albeit romanticized, dehistoricized, and rehistoricized image of the town as a picturesque "Spanish" town and the home of Spanish conqueror and colonizer, Don Juan de Oñate. This in a town that, unlike Santa Fe, never had a central plaza.

14. The cars are detailed to be unique. For example, special taillights from a 1959 Cadillac are added to a 1964 Chevrolet Impala. Other special touches include undersized steering wheels, dice knobs on the gearshift, and double "frenched in" antennae. One addition cinches the lowrider's uniqueness among customized cars—hydraulic lifts that allow the car to "hop" front, back, and side to side. This kind of work is done on almost any vehicle, for example, a 1938 Ford truck with a 1950 truck bed placed on a modified 1976 Grand Prix frame and given a flame paint job and double antennas.

15. An early boyfriend insisted that she could not have a nicer car than his.

16. See also Stonequist (1937). He discusses "reviving" and "modernizing" local culture as a way to keep old issues alive and point out new ones. This prevents "accommodation on any particular level from becoming too fixed and crystallized, thereby helping to raise the ultimate status of … [the] group" (1937:174).

17. For a historical analysis of the zoot suit riots, see Mauricio Mazón 1984. The Chicano interpretation of the pachucos as the first Mexican Americans has been promoted in the works of Luis Valdez. His play Zoot Suit, produced as a movie in 1978, depicts the racism and persecution that pachucos experienced and links their distinctive style of dress with their experiences as the first Mexican and American generation that was neither Mexican nor American (Sanchez-Tranquilino 1987; Valdez 1978a and 1978b).

18. Just as Los Angeles is the largest settlement of Mexican migrants outside Mexico city, Española is the regional destination for people migrating from the area villages of northern New Mexico in order to participate in the cash economy.

19. Making a car can be productively compared with making family photo albums. The difference is that cars are quintessentially paternal vehicles when compared to photo albums that are predominantly maternal projects.

REFERENCES CITED

Abu-Lughod, Lila. 1990. The Romance of Resistance: Tracing Transformations of Power through Bedouin Women. American Ethnologist 17:41–55.

Acuña, Rodolfo. 1981. Occupied America: A History of Chicanos. 2nd edition. New York: Harper and Row.

Anaya, Rudolfo, and Francisco Lomeli, eds. 1991. Aztlán: Essays on the Chicano Homeland. Albuquerque: University of New Mexico Press.

Appadurai, Arjun. 1990. Disjuncture and Difference in the Global Cultural Economy. Public Culture 2(2):1–23.

——1991. Global Ethnoscapes: Notes and Queries for a Transnational Anthropology. In Recapturing Anthropology. Working in the Present. Richard G. Fox, ed. Pp.191–210. Santa Fe, NM: School of American Research Press.

——1995. The Production of Locality. In Counterworks: Managing the Diversity of Knowledge. Richard Fardon, ed. Pp. 204–225. New York: Routledge.

Babcock, Barbara. 1990a. "A New Mexican Rebecca": Imaging Pueblo Women. Journal of the Southwest 32(Winter): 400–437.

——1990b. "By Way of Introduction." Journal of the Southwest 32 (Winter):383–399.

Battaglia, Debbora. 1992. Displacing Culture: A Joke of Significance in Urban Papua New Guinea. New Literary History 23(4):1003–1017.

——1995. On Practical Nostalgia: Self-Prospecting among Urban Trobrianders. In Rhetorics of Self-Making. D. Battaglia, ed. Pp. 77–96. Berkeley. University of California Press.

Borhegyi, Stephen F. de. 1956. El Santuario De Chimayo. Santa Fe, NM: Ancient City Press. Brewer, Steve

——1990. Stereotypes Disintegrate in Lowriders. Albuquerque Journal 20 September: C-1.

Briggs, Charles. 1980. The Wood Carvers of Córdova, New Mexico. Albuquerque: University of New Mexico Press.

Briggs, Charles L., and J. R. Van Ness, eds. 1987. Land, Water, and Culture: New Perspectives on Hispanic Land Grants. Albuquerque: University of New Mexico Press.

Bright, Brenda Jo. 1995. Remappings: Los Angeles Low Riders. In Looking High and Low: Art and Cultural Identity. Brenda Jo Bright and Liza Bakewell, eds. Pp. 89–123. Tucson: University of Arizona Press.

——1997. Nightmares in the New Metropolis: The Cinematic Poetics of Lowriders. Journal of Latin American Popular Culture 16:13–29. In press. Lowrider: Chicano Culture in the Time of the Automobile. University of California Press.

Bureau of the Census. 1990. Census of Population and Housing. Washington, DC: U.S. Government Printing Office.

Carrier, James. 1991. Gifts, Commodities, and Social Relations: A Maussian View of Exchange. Sociological Forum 6(1):119–136.

Cordova, Gilberto Benito. 1990. The 3 1/2 Cultures of Española. Albuquerque, NM: El Norte Publications/Academia.

Crawford, Stanley. 1989. Mayordomo: Chronicle of an Acequia in Northern New Mexico. New York: Anchor Books, Doubleday.

Deutsch, Sarah. 1987. No Separate Refuge: Culture, Class and Gender on an Anglo-Hispanic Frontier in the American Southwest, 1880–1940. New York: Oxford University Press.

Ferguson, James, and Akhil Gupta. 1992. Beyond "Culture": Space, Identity, and the Politics of Difference. Cultural Anthropology 7(1):6–23.

Fischer, Michael, M. J. 1986. Ethnicity and the Postmodern Arts of Memory. In Writing Culture: The Poetics and Politics of Ethnography. J. Clifford and G. Marcus, eds. Pp. 194–233. Berkeley: University of California Press.

Fischer, Michael M. J., and Medhi Abedi. 1990. Debating Muslims: Cultural Dialogues in Postmodernity and Tradition. Madison: University of Wisconsin Press.

Forrest, Suzanne. 1989. The Preservation of the Village: New Mexico's Hispanics and the New Deal. Albuquerque: University of New Mexico Press.

Foster, Robert J. 1991. Making National Cultures in the Global Ecumene. Annual Reviews in Anthropology 20:235–60.

García-Canclini, Néstor. 1992. Cultural Reconversion. In On Edge: The Crisis of Contemporary Latin American Culture. G. Yúdice, J. Franco, and Juan Flores, eds. Pp. 29–13. Minneapolis: University of Minnesota Press.

Gradante, William. 1982. Low and Slow, Mean and Clean. Natural History 91 (4):28–39.

——1985. Art among the Lowriders. In Folk Art in Texas. F. E Abernethy, ed. Pp. 70–77. Dallas, TX: Southern Methodist University Press.

Grimes, Ronald. 1976. Symbol and Conquest: Public Ritual and Drama in Santa Fe, New Mexico. Ithaca, NY: Cornell University Press.

Hannan, Michael. 1979. The Dynamics of Ethnic Boundaries in Modern States. In National Development and the World System: Educational, Economic and Political Change, 1950–1970. John Meyer and Michael Hannan, eds. Pp. 253–275. Chicago: University of Chicago Press.

Haraway, Donna J. 1991. A Cyborg Manifesto: Science, Technology and Socialist-Feminism in the Late Twentieth Century. In Simians, Cyborgs, and Women: The Reinvention of Nature. Pp. 149–182. New York: Routledge.

Kay, Elizabeth. 1987. Chimayó Valley Traditions. Santa Fe, NM: Ancient City Press.

Kennedy, Roger. 1991. Museum Director Promises State Quality Exhibition at Smithsonian. Rio Grande Sun, July 25: A4.

Limón, José. 1981. The Folk Performance of "Chicano" and the Cultural Limits of Political Ideology. In and Other Neighborly Names: Social Processes and Cultural Image in Texas Folklore. R. Bauman and R.D. Abrahams, eds. Pp. 197–225. Austin: University of Texas Press.

Lipsitz, George. 1995. Their America, and Ours: Intercultural Communication in the Context of "Our America." Ethnic Studies Department, University of California, San Diego. Unpublished Manuscript.

Lujan, Gilberto Sánchez. 1970. El Arte del Chicano. Con Safos, Winter: 11. Lynch-Frost Productions

——1990. Auto Obsession. American Chronicles. Fox Network. October 4.

Marcus, George E. 1990. Imagining the Whole: Ethnography's Contemporary Efforts to Situate Itself. Critique of Anthropology 9(3):7–30.

——1995. Ethnography in/of the World System: The Emergence of Multi-Sited Ethnography. Annual Review of Anthropology 24:95–117.

Marcus, George E., and Michael M. J. Fischer. 1986. Anthropology as Cultural Critique: An Experimental Moment in the Human Sciences. Chicago: University of Chicago Press.

Mazón, Mauricio. 1984. The Zoot Suit Riots: The Psychology of Symbolic Annihilation. Austin: University of Texas Press.

Miller, Daniel. 1994. Modernity: An Ethnographic Approach. Oxford: Berg.

Miller, Jay. 1991. Inside the Capitol. Rio Grande Sun, July 1 1:A5.

Moorhouse, H. F. 1991. Driving Ambitions: An Analysis of the American Hot Enthusiasm. Manchester. Manchester University Press.

Morrison, Howard. 1992. American Encounters: A Companion to the Exhibition at the National Museum of American History, Smithsonian Insitution. Washington, DC: Smithsonian Institution.

Muñoz, Carlos. 1989. Youth, Identity, Power: The Chicano Movement. London: Verso.

Nabokov, Peter. 1969. Tijerina and the Courthouse Raid. Albuquerque: University of New Mexico Press.

Nostrand, Richard. 1984 .Hispano Cultural Distinctiveness: A Reply. Annals of the Association of American Geographers 74(1):164–169.

Plascensia, Luis F. B. 1983. Low Riding in the Southwest: Cultural Symbols in the Mexican Community. In History, Culture and Society: Chicano Studies in the 1980s. Mario T. Garcia et al., eds. Pp. 141–175. Ypsilanti, Ml: Bilingual Press.

Plath, David W. 1990. My-Car-isma: Motorizing the Showa Self. Daedalus 119(3):229–244.

Rodriguez, Roberto. 1984. Assault with a Deadly Weapon: About an Incident in E.L.A. and the Closing of Whittier Boulevard. Los Angeles: Rainbow Press.

Rodriguez, Sylvia. 1987. Land, Water, and Ethnic Identity in Taos. In Land, Water, and Culture: New Perspectives on Hispanic Land Grants. C. L. Briggs and J. R. Van Ness, eds. Pp. 313–403. Albuquerque: University of New Mexico Press.

———1992. The Hispano Homeland Debate Revisited. In Perspectives in Mexican American Studies 3(1992):95–116.

Rose, Tricia. 1994. Black Noise: Rap Music and Black Culture in Contemporary America. Hanover, NH: Weslayan University Press.

Ross, Andrew. 1989. No Respect: Intellectuals and Popular Culture. New York: Routledge.

Rowe, William, and Vivian Schelling. 1991. Memory and Modernity: Popular Culture in Latin America. London: Verso.

Sagel, Jim

———1993. Lowdown Laughs: The Española Joke. In Dancing to Pay the Light Bill. Pp. 55–58. Santa Fe: Red Crane Books.

Saldívar, Ramón. 1990. Chicano Narrative: The Dialectics of Difference. Madison: University of Wisconsin Press.

Sanchez-Tranquilino, Marcos. 1987. Mano a Mano: An Essay on the Representation of the Zoot Suit and Its Misrepresentation by Octavio Paz. Journal: A Contemporary Art Magazine Winter:34–42.

Shank, Barry. 1994. Dissonant Identities: The Rock'n'roll Scene in Austin, Texas. Hanover, NH: Weslayan University Press.

Stone, Michael C. 1990. "Bajito y Suavecito": Low Riding and the "Class" of Class. Journal of Latin American Popular Culture 9:85–126.

Stonequist, Edmond. 1937. The Marginal Man: A Study in Personality and Culture Conflict. New York: Scribner's Sons.

Thornton, Robert. 1988. The Rhetoric of Ethnographic Holism. Cultural Anthropology 3:285–303. Urla, Jacqueline

———1996. Outlaw Language: Creating Aternative Public Spheres in Basque Free Radio. In The Politics of Culture in the Shadow of Capital. Lisa Lowe and David Lloyd, eds. Pp. 280–300. Durham, NC: Duke University Press.

Valdez, Luis. 1978a. Zoot Suit. Los Angeles, CA: Center for Theatre Groups, Mark Taper Forum.

———1978b. Once Again, Meet the Zoot Suiters. Los Angeles Times, August 27: V:54.

Watkins, Evan. 1991. "For the Time Being, Forever": Social Position and the Art of Automobile Maintenance. Boundary 2 18(2):150–165.

Weigle, Marta. 1976. Brothers of Light, Brothers of Blood: The Penitentes of the Southwest. Albuquerque: University of New Mexico Press.

Wolfe, Tom. 1965. The Kandy-Kolored Tangerine-Flake Streamline Baby. In The Kandy-Kolored Flake Streamline Baby. Pp. 62–89. New York: Pocket Books.

Ybarra-Frausto, Tomás. 1977. The Chicano Movement and the Emergence of a Chicano Poetic Consciousness. New Scholar 6:81–109.

———1991. Rasquachismo: A Chicano Sensibility. In Chicano Art: Resistance and Affirmation. Richard Griswald del Castillo et al., eds. Pp. 155–162. Exhibition Catalog, Wight Art Gallery, UCLA, Los Angeles. Tucson: University of Arizona Press.

14

Gendering the City, Gendering the Nation

Contesting Urban Space in Fes, Morocco
Rachel Newcomb

He who takes his wife out in public divorces her.

—Moroccan proverb[1]

What a woman sees of the sky is only that which passes over the circle [the open roof over a household].

—Moroccan proverb

Over the past fifteen years, the appearance of new spaces for social interaction in urban Morocco suggests that an analytical division of Muslim social spaces into "public/male" and "private/female" is inadequate for comprehending the ways city dwellers actively construct gendered social space.[2] During fieldwork conducted in Fes, Morocco in 2001-02, I noticed that arguments over how women should occupy particular social spaces often prompted discussions over the appropriate place of women in Moroccan society at large. In local disputes concerning how to regulate interactions between unrelated men and women in spaces that often seem designed to facilitate their interactions, more was often at stake than a single place. Debates over the possibilities and limitations that delineate gendered urban space speak to larger contestations over the position of women in modern Muslim nation states like Morocco.

Rachel Newcomb, "Gendering the City, Gendering the Nation: Contesting Urban Space in Fes, Morocco," *City & Society*, vol. 18, no. 2, pp. 288–311. Copyright © 2006 by American Anthropological Association. Reprinted with permission.

Divisions of space such as "public" and "private" are frequently mapped out onto gendered space, with the assumption that one gender's entry into another's space constitutes a social transgression. However, as women and men in the Middle East and North Africa increasingly occupy the same public spaces for social and economic reasons, women's presence and movement through public space must be reexamined. Urban spaces, in particular, offer an opportunity to examine how discourses of modernity are accepted, contested, or transformed by their users. In this paper, I examine women's disputes over social space in the city of Fes to show how people navigate competing ideologies to test the limits of gender. In the Moroccan context, two particularly prominent ideologies are represented by gender-focused discourses of the nation-state and its Islamist critics. The nation-state characterizes the Moroccan female citizen as simultaneously modern, secular, and Islamic, while an oppositional religious discourse frames the nationalist vision as hopelessly enslaved to Western secularism, suggesting that the Moroccan woman needs to "return" to an authentic, "traditional" Muslim identity, modeled after the imagined example of the Prophet.[3] The spread of both discourses has been influenced by the constant flow of Moroccan migrant populations between Morocco and Europe, North America and the Middle East, and the proliferation of new communication technologies like satellite dishes, internet, and cell phones.

Responding to both positions, Fassi[4] Moroccans often draw on local meanings to create identities for themselves that resist and transcend these ideologies. These include notions of what it means to be Fassi and female, shame as a positive attribute, and hospitality. I use Michel de Certeau's concept of "everyday practices" to show how practitioners of culture regain their agency as they manipulate competing ideologies and turn them to their own ends (1984:xiv). Whether Moroccan women are arguing over the divisions of space in an exercise club or over how to respond to an invisible suitor met over the internet, their everyday practices illustrate how users appropriate social space, articulate conflicts, and respond to ideologies in locally meaningful ways.

The Ville Nouvelle[5] of Fes offers a unique opportunity to observe these processes in urban areas of the Muslim world that are not considered central to political and economic operations of power. An examination of provincial cities complements existing anthropological studies of urban areas of the Middle East and North Africa that have focused on cities that are loci of government and political power, such as Cairo or Casablanca (e.g. Ossman 1994; Singerman 1996; Hoodfar 1997; Ghannam 2002; Salamandra 2004). The provincial characteristics of a city like Fes, with a population of over a million residents, make it an interesting area for inquiry. Recent studies that focus on the lived experience of individuals in Moroccan urban environments have focused on the hegemonic effects of media, modernity and globalization, and on the hybridity of women's expressive discourses in the marketplace (e.g. Ossman 1994; Kapchan 1996; Cohen 2005). In *Picturing Casablanca*, for example, Susan Ossman characterizes Casablanca as a postcolonial space predicated on representation and colonial planning, governed by abstract media images that lead to a fragmented existence. In part this reflects a trend in anthropological studies of urban space since the 1980s to focus on representation and on the city as text (Jacobs 1993:827). This article, while indirectly concerned with similar issues, seeks to revive the specificity of a lived city, examining how discourses from outside are received and interpreted by individuals.

Academic research in Fes has largely ignored the Ville Nouvelle in favor of studies of the ancient *medina* as a site for religious learning and where "traditional" trades and professions are still practiced. Yet Fes, like other Moroccan cities affected by French colonization, is divided. The Ville Nouvelle, constructed during the French Protectorate (1912-56), with its substantial population of modern city dwellers remains on the margins of academic debates. How do individuals in Fes, particularly women, situate themselves in the built environment? How do local and global discourses interact in the gendering of this modern Muslim city? More importantly, which discourses are most salient to women as they determine the rules for occupying new urban spaces? These questions shed light on the ways in which national and global processes articulate themselves in a specific local setting.

The focus on everyday practices and individual efforts to contest or manipulate discourses of power, enables a shift away from framing this inquiry as a study of the ways "traditional" people deal with "modern" spaces and ideologies. The reified nature of this construction is limiting, as it continues to associate tradition with all that is "native," while modernity implies something imposed from above, usually from the West. Moving away from considering colonial and postcolonial space solely in terms of issues of representation and reception, De Certeau's emphasis on individual tactics that insinuate, manipulate, and finally reappropriate social space is better suited to highlight human agency in response to powerful ideologies. Everyday practices consist of those small, sometimes fragmentary tactics that represent "the ingenious ways in which the weak make use of the strong" (de Certeau 1984:xvii). In Fes, women give meaning to social spaces by using their own cultural categories to shape space in a way that reflects the construction of a female, Moroccan and Fassi identity.

However, this is not a neutral process. Individuals' contestations of urban social space transcend the creation of individual identities. In defining the meanings and uses of new spaces, individuals make claims for collective visions of gendered identity and relationships. Everyday practices, rather than being mere individual tactics, are profoundly social. In this case, gendered everyday practices assert individuals' ideas of the proper place for women while simultaneously responding to and transforming various discourses about the position of women in Moroccan society.

FES: REPRESENTATIONS OF AN "ISLAMIC" CITY

Historically, the city of Fes was renowned for its merchants and artisans, and for its reputation as a center of Islamic learning. The area referred to today as the *medina* was constructed in 808 by Sultan Idriss II, shortly after the Islamic conquest of Morocco. Fes served as the capital under various dynasties and in the 15th century received waves of Muslim and Jewish immigrants expelled from Muslim Spain. However, by the 16th century, Fes had begun to decline in national importance, and under the French Protectorate in 1912, the capital was moved to Rabat, where it remains to this day. One of the great imperial cities of Morocco, the *medina* of Fes has long been a favorite topic for Orientalist historians, who asserted that Fes embodied the essence of the "Islamic city" but paid little attention to actual social organization (Abu-Lughod 1987:157). French colonial historian, Roger Le Tourneau (1949) characterized Fes as the preeminent Islamic city in Morocco, asserting that longstanding residents of the city evinced a moral, religious, and civilized temperament that was unlike that of other Moroccans, particularly those from the countryside. Early Orientalist scholarship set the tone for later interpretations by focusing on themes (e.g. Islam as an urban religion, centrality of urban institutions like the bazaar, mosque, public bath; lack of municipal organization) said to be characteristic of the "Islamic City," which continued to dominate scholarship. Conceptions of space rigidly associated with public/male and private/female also accompanied these characterizations. This repetition of the same themes and descriptions illustrates what Edward Said has described as the Orientalist tendency toward citationary practices, whereby new representations were built upon old ones and "the actualities of the modern Orient were systematically excluded" (Said 1978:177).

The French built the Ville Nouvelle of Fes after the Protectorate began in 1912. Their practice of separating *medinas* from Villes Nouvelles in Morocco, which Janet Abu-Lughod (1981) has called "urban apartheid," was a new strategy befitting Morocco's status as a protectorate, designed to protect native customs and simultaneously to create a modern city of order and administration. In colonial administrations, power became dispersed through the social system to operate internally and productively, producing institutions characteristic of the modern nation-state but also individual modern subjects (Mitchell i988:xi). After Independence in 1956, Moroccans with the economic means moved into the Ville Nouvelle, as the French had neglected the *medina*'s infrastructure. The Ville Nouvelle provided better sanitation, transportation, and electricity, and most of the city's business opportunities and bureaucratic services (Porter 2003:130). Today, the medina has become overpopulated due to rural to urban migration, with a population density of more than i,000 inhabitants per hectare. Although UNESCO declared the city a world heritage site in 1980, little has been accomplished in the way of renovations. The economies of both the Ville Nouvelle and *medina* remain largely unindustrialized, with the majority of workers employed in artisanal, commerce, and civil service positions. The official unemployment rate for Fes is 20% (Guerraoui 1996:161).[6]

Moving beyond a focus on the *medina*, on Fes as an "Islamic city" or on representations of the city's colonial past, this study seeks to examine individuals in the Ville Nouvelle and their concrete ways of transforming urban space according to distinctive local conceptualizations. This analysis of everyday practices in Fes looks not only at how power is dispersed through space but also at how people appropriate, manipulate, or transform discourses of power. Accounts that privilege the old medina as characteristic of a timeless, essentialized Fes, and the Ville Nouvelle as a place that has been corrupted by colonialism and other imported modernities are misleading. As a space of Moroccan social life, the Ville Nouvelle is important for an understanding of contemporary social processes.

For the middle class Ville Nouvelle residents among whom I conducted my fieldwork, the *medina* serves as an object of nostalgia, as a symbol of the former apogee of Moroccan civilization, and as a place over which they feel proprietary even if they no longer own property there. The rural/urban divide long noted by scholars working in Morocco is echoed in opinions of Ville Nouvelle residents about the residents of the *medina*, as the latter are referred to disparagingly as uncivilized people from the countryside *('arubf)* who are held responsible for the deterioration of the old city (Porter 2003). Many Ville Nouvelle Fassis trace their family origins back hundreds of years. Fassis have an reputation in Morocco for being influential; they are assumed to be working hand-in-hand with the government, receiving favors, and occupying prominent positions in business and politics. My informants bore the same prominent names and origins of those who had moved on to achieve success in the economic and political centers of the country, Casablanca and Rabat, but most came from middle class families who enjoyed only limited local political and social influence. Some had inherited family businesses or civil service positions, but others were unemployed and had no immediate prospects. The wealth of a great-grandfather who once had the ear of a sultan was now considerably dissipated among heirs, and in some cases remained a nostalgic memory.

These middle and middle-upper class Ville Nouvelle residents were ambivalent about the *medina* and rarely went there, except to shop for jewelry or household goods (e.g wool, traditional wooden furniture). Bewildered by the tourists' preference for what they saw as a dirty, overcrowded space overrun with rural migrants, informants frequently talked about the Ville Nouvelle's cleanliness and order.[7] They were proud of its tall high rises, wide boulevards, cafes, and modern administrative buildings. While in Casablanca there have been some attempts to preserve the city's 1920s art deco architecture, in Fes many of the original French structures have been demolished in the past decade to make way for new high rises. In the central Ville Nouvelle neighborhood where I conducted my fieldwork, gleaming white apartment buildings had begun to tower over the old French-built arcade where many of my informants lived. Known as "Lux" for the old Cinema Lux that was torn down in the mid-1990s, this neighborhood had originally been a Jewish quarter, and there were still a few older Jewish residents left who had not emigrated to Europe, Israel, or North America. Since the late 1990s many of the older French structures had been purchased and torn down by developers. The self-defined "pure" or original Fassis moved further out into newly created suburbs.

For eighteen months in 2001-02, I lived in a new apartment building in the "Lux" quarter and conducted fieldwork among residents of this neighborhood. My husband is a member of an extended family still occupying one of the old French buildings, and this fact gave me access to the everyday lives of people I otherwise would not have met. By participating in meals and other quotidian activities with his family, and being present for special events like weddings, I got to know several local extended families and their networks of friends and professional associates. The broad objectives of my fieldwork were to learn more about new roles for women in Moroccan society in light of agitation for changes to the *mudawana* family codes.[8] My fieldsites included the neighborhood itself, a women's non-governmental organization, a hotel nightclub, the exercise club described in this article, and the local streets, houses, cafes, public baths, schools, shops and offices that my informants frequented. Data was gathered by participant observation, and structured and unstructured interviews, genealogies, surveys and maps.

THE PUBLIC/PRIVATE DICHOTOMY

North African Meanings and Contexts

An examination of Fassi views on women's presence in existing urban spaces provides an interesting window onto tactics used in the gendering of new spaces. In Fes, the mixing of unrelated men and women is an endeavor fraught with tension. In the street, a woman's presence is acknowledged by catcalls and stares. What are the rules in a Moroccan city for women's behavior in new public spaces?[9] These "rules" are constantly discussed, challenged, and negotiated. Social scientists working in the Middle East and North Africa have long noted the culturally idealized orientation of women toward the home and men toward the street. "The most important rule in the code of movement," writes Willie Jansen about Algeria, "is that one should remain within the space reserved for one's own gender … The feminine space is directed inwards, toward the courtyard; the masculine space is directed toward the outside, the streets. The difference in available space reflects the social hierarchy between the genders" (Jansen 1987:183). Other analytical representations of the public/private dichotomy locate this divide within Islam and the idea that mixing between the sexes will lead to social chaos (Mernissi 1987). The street has been described as a place of reason, as opposed to the irrational, emotional world of women and the home (e.g. Eickelman 1976). More recent work has challenged the public/private dichotomy, arguing that much like Orientalist writings about the "Islamic city," the public/private dichotomy reflects Western secular biases and a tendency toward binarisms (Gole 1997; Bier 2006). Other studies demonstrate a more nuanced analysis of the meaning of the public/private. For example, Kapchan (1996) documents women's roles in the marketplace while Deeb (2006) describes their roles as political and religious activists. Holmer-Eber (2003) analyzes women as transformers of social networks.

Spatial seclusion of women was a feature of urban Moroccan society until the 1940s (Mernissi 1994). In 1943, King Mohammed V presented his daughter in public without a veil, and around the same time, Moroccan nationalists instituted programs promoting education for girls (Mernissi 1987:155). After Independence, particularly in the 1970s with the government's creation of civil service positions, numerous women entered school and the workforce. In the 1960s alone, female employment increased by 75%. The large majority of female workers during this period held jobs either as low status domestics or higher status government civil servants; others worked in agriculture and textiles.

Despite the fact that spatial seclusion of women, particularly among the urban elite, was a feature of Moroccan life prior to the 1940s, it should not be assumed that women had no place in public life. Describing the seclusion of urban elite women, colonial officials and historians of the region imposed Eurocentric interpretations of public and domestic space onto local contexts, which meant that women's activities often went undocumented. In North Africa, women always played a significant role in regional economies, although they were underrepresented in French colonial statistics because work was only counted in terms of observable markets and not domestic economic production (Clancy-Smith 1999:28). Yet, the spaces in which women moved depended upon environment, economics, and social class, and were not easily reducible to a set of rules or prescriptions.

Because the visible range of movement for women has expanded in the past forty years in response to changing political and socio-economic conditions, examining specific ethnographic performances can provide a useful view of how women conceive of their presence in different spaces. As urban women increasingly come to occupy previously "male" spaces, a breach in territorial distribution and domination opens up, limits are crossed, and the separation between "male" and "female" space is called into question. Navez-Bouchanine suggested that while traditional spaces in urban Morocco often demarcate public and private space, the structure of the Villes Nouvelles lends itself to space that is neither public nor private, but often simultaneously both (1991:135).

Through discussions about place, Fassis attempt to negotiate and sometimes delineate space and the rules for inhabiting it. Whoever defines a space assumes that he or she refers to a set of rules all can agree upon. However, often individuals contest both the space and the rules for its occupation, particularly in the case of new spaces. At times, women extend principles for conduct in the home to a public space. The code of conduct for women requires that women "t'hasham," which literally means "to be ashamed," though my informants explained that "t'hasham" meant being polite, obedient, pleasant, and demure, particularly in front of elders, men, and non- kin. All my Ville Nouvelle informants agreed that t'hashaming was a positive attribute best demonstrated by Fassi middle-class women, in contrast to the conduct of medina women, whose country origins led them to be loud, ill-mannered and uncouth.

Other principles of conduct are more nebulous. Some Fassis stated their belief that women should not be seen by unrelated men without being fully covered. This belief extends to the idea that unrelated men and women should not share the same space, which was disputed by women who frequented cafes, claiming that ignoring the men who shared the same space was sufficient. Being associated with a particular family is also thought to guarantee a good reputation, particularly in cafes. Public spaces contain conflicting resonances, encouraging women to be both visible and invisible, simultaneously acting in the public realm yet out of reach. The threat of incurring social judgment, circulated by "gossip," the *klam dtyal* nas, is always present. As a bewildering array of new social spaces open up, whether to label them as public or private becomes less important than comprehending why Fassi Moroccans contest those spaces, and in which instances a particular viewpoint will prevail.

Moroccan society remains gendered, with many social activities limited to interactions with persons of the same sex. Examining the complex tactics of women's everyday practices sheds light on the logic of gendered social urban spaces. Through these tactics, women not only define their presence in physical and metaphorical spaces (the cyber world) but assert divisions according to social class, age, employment status, education, and religion. Many still associate women with domestic space, so that women's occupation of public space is often inflected with attempts to redefine such spaces as partly domestic or private, hence suitable for female presence. Frequently, men and women are present in the same places but are associating solely with their own gender. In cases where the inevitable mixing of unrelated men and women takes place, Fassi women borrow from available rules for interaction, such as attempting to remain unseen or ignoring the presence of men entirely. In case of conflict, the concept of "shame" (hshuma) may be invoked to trump an opponent, suggesting that the other has strayed too far and is in danger of losing all morals. In new spaces people quarrel fiercely over how men and women should relate to one another and how women are to occupy the space. I never witnessed similar debates concerning the presence of men. Most of the debates I heard were between women. Only when prompted, men made statements about women and space.

COMMON DOMAINS: STREET AND CAFE

The complex "rules" for occupying the mixed spaces of cafes and streets involve successfully balancing appearances with actions, with the threat of being perceived as sexually promiscuous as the punishment for transgressions.[10] Women were more likely to be present in the Ville Nouvelle cafes than in the cafes of the medina. Among my middle class Ville Nouvelle informants, younger professional women and students (ages 20-45) went to cafes. Yet older women and those who did not work or attend university never visited them.[11] Professional women who visit cafes rarely sit with men, although they often greet co-workers at other tables before sitting at their own. Female university students noted that they went to cafes to study, but also to talk and flirt with the male students.

Although men claimed they had no problems with women's presence in cafes, they also qualified that there are certain cafes where women might not feel comfortable. "Some of the cafes just aren't clean (naqj)," Karim, an unemployed man in his thirties, said.[12] "A place should be clean if it is for women. Women would not like the popular (sha'abi) cafes because they are so dirty (musikh)." In the Ville Nouvelle, sha'abi cafes are often places that were built by the French, with decor that seems not to have changed since. Describing a cafe as "dirty" (musikh) also conveys class differences. Middle class residents of Ville Nouvelle frequently refer to cafes in poorer neighborhoods or the medina as musikh. A cafe that is musikh might also be filled with smoke and men who are zufriya, types who are inclined to bother women, drink alcohol, and start fights. There are also upscale cafes that, while physically very clean, are known meeting spots for prostitutes. These have attracted the label of musikh, illustrating that in this context, cleanliness is a social category associated with morality.

The level of comfort professional women expressed about particular cafes often related to whether proprietors were cognizant of women's places in familial, professional, and social networks. Association with a particular family guarantees that cafe owners will be hospitable and that women will not be harassed. The guarantee of hospitality here transfers principles from the private domain into the public, as a householder would never allow guests to feel uncomfortable. "Everybody here knows me," Naima, a lawyer, said of the cafe near the courthouse where she worked. "I work with all these people, and the waiters will not let anyone bother me." This tactic applies rules of hospitality and respect for guests to a world that was once solely the domain of men.

For women, streets, unlike cafes, do not encourage lingering. The street is a pathway between destinations: market, school, work, or home. While women are always in motion, men lounge on corners or outside cafes. For men, the street outside one's building is an extension of the home, and a place to hang out with friends or relatives. However, men also tend to remain in the street closest to their own homes unless they are visiting friends elsewhere. Streets in unfamiliar neighborhoods possess an unwelcoming quality that encourages men to keep moving. During the daytime, women run errands or take walks with other women, but at night (except during Ramadan), women do not go out. My informants noted that Fassi women distinguish themselves by their demeanor, and that they should not be too aggressive, loud, or forward. Girls must conduct themselves unobtrusively, and those who do not fall in line are scolded that they "have no shame." Young, unmarried women are at a dangerous, vulnerable age, and they should do everything possible to avoid gossip. Yet at the same time, they need to dress stylishly, wear make-up, and be visible to attract potential husbands, who might see them in public and then ask around the neighborhood about the girl's family and marriageability. Street harassment is an issue, and the severity of harassment varies with tightness of clothes, facial expression, and the time of day; all potential indicators of sexual availability. In fact, the most common explanation Fassis of all ages gave for harassment was that it was a way of determining who might be a prostitute.

"Men just talk to see who might go with them," a middle-aged woman, Fatima, explained, "and if the woman answers, it means she is fair game. A good girl (bint an-nas) is ashamed and will never answer them." Women's presence in the streets is fraught with more tension than inside cafes. Fassi women in their twenties spoke of the social pressure they felt to be seen in public wearing the latest clothes, yet they walked a fine line in trying not to accrue negative judgment. This constant balancing act often results in a split in women's self-image. Fassi culture insists on an acceptance of some parts of a modern, Western-oriented image and a rejection of others. Yet which parts are to be accepted and rejected is uncertain.

Media images contribute to this confusion, and satellite television, now accessible to all middle class Fassis, provides provocative images from MTV, European and American movies, and soap operas. Simultaneously, satellite programs from the Middle East convey the contradictory message that the acceptance of Western fashions represents the Muslim world's dependency and enslavement by the Christians. Some Fassi women have adopted a more Islamic style of dress in response. The practice of veiling (that is a headscarf or *hijab*) is one tactic that many younger women have begun to employ in public spaces. Whether they do this to avoid harassment or demonstrate their piety, this concealment has variously been interpreted as extending the private space into the public, or as signaling the wearer's intentions not to engage the public.[13]

TACTICS IN NEW SPACES: EXERCISE CLUBS AND CYBER CLUBS

As the preceding section demonstrates, in public spaces women must maintain a careful balance between visibility and propriety, advertising their beauty while creating a sense of separation between themselves and the words and gazes of unrelated men. But what are the rules for spaces that are neither exclusively public nor private, such as a mixed exercise club or a cyber cafe? Located in a new apartment building close to the old French racetracks and a former army barracks, "American Steel Fitness"[14] was the first club in Fes to have separate floors for men and women, so that middle and upper class Fassis could exercise every day, rather than on a rotating schedule, as in other clubs. Female customers (between 20 and 50 years old) could pass through the men's space on the ground floor, but men were not allowed to come upstairs. Yet the club was poorly designed, and the women's aerobics space was visible to the men by a balcony that could be clearly seen in the slanted mirrors that reflected down into the men's space. When the owners realized this oversight, they installed curtains to appease their female customers.

However, the heavy velvet curtains presented an added problem. By late spring of 2002, the weather had grown quite hot, and when the curtains were closed, the air did not circulate. Women began to quarrel about whether the curtains should remain open or closed, even when there were no men below. Most of the grumbling went on among women in their late twenties, the older women rarely participated. Almost always the demands to close the curtain were obliged. On one particularly hot day, Amina, who exercised in a headscarf and a tight leotard, arrived late to find the class already in session and the curtains wide open. Visibly angry, she shut the curtains with a flourish. Another woman, a perfectly made-up beauty who often went down to the men's floor for "weightlifting demonstrations," decided to challenge her.

"Come on," Miriam pleaded. "I'll stand there where they can see me if you care so much."

"Shame (*hshuma*) on you!" Amina snapped back. "It's haram (forbidden) for the men to be able to leer at us while we exercise."

"There's nobody down there to see us!" Miriam said.

"Do you have no shame? The curtains stay closed, or else I am leaving the club!" she threatened. The instructor continued to teach the class, the two women glaring at one another in the mirror. Afterwards, in the dressing room, the drama continued. "Who does she think she is?" said Miriam. Amina was out of sight, but Miriam spoke loudly. "She's no prize. Does she think the men want to look at her anyway?"

"And in this heat!" her friend chimed in.

"She acts like she's so pious, but it must come from the heart, it's not how you dress or whether the men can see you!" insisted Miriam. "Those fundamentalists (ikhwaniym), they are impossible to understand. They wear tight clothes; they cover their heads. She's crazy. This gym is not for fundamentalists. If she doesn't like it, she should stay in her house." Miriam grabbed her shampoo bottle and stormed off to the showers.

A second scene, which I witnessed late one afternoon in a Ville Nouvelle cyber cafe, revolved around similar issues. Qur'anic recitations blaring from one computer competed for attention with American hip-hop from another, and with the din from the cafe below us, filled with people. At this time of day, high school or university students occupied most of the twenty computers. As usual, most were engaged in Internet chats, and next to me, three teenaged girls whom I knew from my neighborhood wrote to a boy in Tangier. Zahra in particular was interested in him, and on his request that she sent him her photo. "You are beautiful, and I want to meet you," he typed back in French, as the three girls laughed, the main one blushing and covering her face with her hands. "Wait, look, he asked you something else," one of the girls said, pointing at the screen. The girl read his question out loud. "'Are you a virgin?' Eh, of course! What does he think I am? Shame on him!" she said indignantly, and then typed in "*Hshuma*. Of course!" She looked at both of her friends. "*Hshuma!*" she announced again. The mood for flirtation having passed, she looked at her watch and closed the computer screen, announcing that it was time to go.

When American Steel Fitness opened up in the winter of 2001-02, it was very popular among affluent Fassis. I joined ASF shortly after it opened, and over the next several months I developed acquaintances with some of the other members. Founded by a Moroccan-American and his American business partner, ASF advertised itself as an American club. Equipment was imported at great cost from the United States, classes were to start on time and with a high level of professionalism, and in the future, the male and female floors would be mixed. At first, middle-upper class Fassis responded enthusiastically, and the club was always packed with women. In locker room conversations, women bragged about their travels overseas—summers on the Costa Del Sol in Spain, and the exercise clubs they had experienced in France, where men and women exercised together. A few women even trickled down into the men's section to observe "weightlifting demonstrations." For a while, the club was a symbol of a new cosmopolitanism that well-to-do Fassis previously had to go outside of the city to find.

Yet gradually the novelty began to wear off. The aerobics instructors complained about their low, "un-American" wages. The showers were often broken. These were American prices for Moroccan quality, people grumbled. But the most contentious issue became the fact that men and women were sharing the same space, albeit on different floors, and that men could gaze up into the women's space from the mirrors. Amina was the most vocal in pointing this out, and before every aerobics class, I heard women comment whether one of the "fundamentalists" would show up and insist on the curtains being closed.[15] Amina complained that the men might one day try to sneak up to the women's section. Initially most of the customers had accepted the premise of the owners that Fes was ready for a Western-style club in which men and women would eventually exercise together. But with the increasingly strident voices of the "fundamentalists," the other women became more hesitant. Many ceased asserting their opinions that the club should be mixed. Soon the only women speaking were the ones who insisted on the closing of the curtains.

In the scene I described earlier, tensions that had been simmering finally came to the surface. Miriam, who wanted the curtains open because of the heat, described her opponent as being attentive only to the surface appearances of piety. Those who desired a strict separation of men and women ought to stay at home where no one could see them. But Amina, whom I interviewed about her views on the club, did want the convenience of belonging to an exercise club that was open to both sexes every day. "I know in America this is how you do things," she told me. "But this is Fes. We're Muslims. It's *haram* (forbidden) the way some of the women act here." Amina, who was in her early forties, had recently started wearing the *hijab* and seemed interested in pointing out to other women that they were, as she said, "not acting like Muslims." She stated that it was important to remind people of the proper distance between men and women. Creating this distance was the issue, particularly due to the problematic placement of the mirror, which revealed what the separation of floors should have concealed.

Miriam, who argued with Amina but did not criticize her to her face, did not seem cowed until Amina had accused her of having no shame. Her religion was her business, she said, and Amina had no right to judge her. Shortly after this argument, she stopped coming to the club, and membership as a whole dropped. Eventually the two owners returned to the United States, leaving the management of the club in the hands of the Moroccan-American owner's family. The owners expressed their disappointment that Fassis "were not ready" for such a club. Miriam agreed, distancing herself from the women who wanted the curtain and calling them "typical Fassis." Although she was born and raised in Fes, she was not interested in claiming to be a Fassi, and instead called attention to her Meknes roots. When I spoke to her about the fact that she had stopped coming to ASF, she told me in French, "I can't stand to be around hypocrites. It's because of people like them that this city does not progress." She distinguished between her own open-mindedness and Fassi obsessions with decorum, which she felt were entirely on the surface. Again, concerns with appearance and not reality were what Miriam felt the "fundamentalists" were focusing on, but she also emphasized that her differences with Amina related to categories of identity and not religion. Although many middle-class Fassis were decidedly non-judgmental about religious matters, they did distinguish subtly between their own moral behavior and that of Moroccans from elsewhere, a distinction that Miriam used to emphasize not morality but hypocrisy.

The exercise club was not easily classifiable as public or private, male or female, and thus, women argued over the physical separation of male and female space within the club, even when no men were present. Arguments in favor of the curtain posited the culturally valued attribute of shame over the cosmopolitanism and class- bound distinctions that the club origi-nally carried. Assumptions that middle-upper class Fassis would accept "American" ideas about the appropriateness of mixed exercise clubs proved not to be true, and in this case, neither social class nor age were significant predictors of how women would respond to the issue of the curtains. While women who shared Amina's view on the curtains did not manage to convince the others of the correctness of their position, once the concept of "shame" was invoked, many simply left the club.

Cyber cafes are another new setting where men and women occupy a mixed space, both literally and metaphorically, as they browse the internet. Diverse groups of people share the cyber cafe for multiple purposes, ranging from job hunting and game playing to looking for a spouse, or listening to Qur'anic recitations. In 2002, Fes seemed to have a cyber cafe on every block of the Ville Nouvelle. Over time, the fees had gradually decreased to around 50-70 cents per hour, which has made internet use more widely available to middle class Fassis. Most of the customers are under the age of 50, with the majority under 30. Young people have colonized the cyber cafes in Fes, both in the medina and the Ville Nouvelle. Chat programs, conducted in French or English, are popular with unmarried men and women, especially high school and university students. For women in particular, having a boyfriend in cyber space can mean escaping the watchful eyes of parents and communities. A few unmarried professional women in their 20s and 30s even forged relationships with Moroccans in other cities that occasionally resulted in clandestine meetings, others conducted forbidden relationships with foreign men.[16] Fassi men use the internet to meet foreign women, and some marriages (and emigrations) are facilitated as a result. There is a marriage service for the very religious, where devout Muslims all over the world post personals.

Undoubtedly the internet has assisted in the widening of social boundaries, offering in-creased opportunities for interaction between men and women (Skalli 2006). The internet also provides safety for those who wish to hide behind its anonymity. Yet certain Fassi values, such as the honor of maintaining female virginity prior to marriage, are emphasized, as revealed by the conversation between the young women and their faceless male interlocutor. In the episode described earlier, Zahra was quick to send her photo to her chat partner. When he inquired about her virginity, she accused him of "having no shame," not because this was an embarrassing question, but because she was offended that he did not automatically assume her purity and good intentions.

The cyber cafes and the metaphoric space of the internet are new sites in which interactions between men and women are not strictly regulated. As in the regular cafes, in the cyber cafes men and women sit at neighboring computers but largely do not interact with one another. In cyberspace, however, gender mixed conversations are the order of the day. Women control to whom they will speak and what they will reveal, and whether to arrange physical meetings or limit their encounters to the printed word.

The narrator in Algerian novelist Assia Djebar's *Fantasia* writes, "When I write and read the foreign language, my body travels far in subversive space, in spite of the neighbours and suspicious matrons; it would not need much for it to take wing and fly away!" (Djebar 1993:184) Writing in French in internet chat programs, Moroccan women are like the three Algerian sisters in Djebar's novel Fantasia, who created a "secret spirit of subversion" by conducting pen-pal relationships with men all over the world (ibid:i2). That French was the language of colonialism was not an issue for the young women I described in this incident. They usually spoke Moroccan Arabic but conducted their chats entirely in French. "It's just easier," Zahra claimed. "I don't know how to type on the Arabic keyboard." She admitted that her parents would not have approved that she was chatting with boys, but she said, "the people you meet [on the internet] are not in the same room with you. There's no danger. I haven't done anything wrong." As for the people who shared the physical space of the cyber cafe with Zahra, she never talked to them, and she almost always came with her girlfriends. The presence of her friends as witnesses to her online relationships may have served as proof that Zahra was not doing anything wrong, but Zahra simply said she liked to go to the cyber cafe with her girlfriends because it was fun. Other young women, however, use the internet alone.

The world of the internet allows Fassi women to create new relationships that might transgress community standards of morality while simultaneously upholding personal moral codes. Using programs designed in other countries for use in languages that are not their native tongue, young Fassi women nonetheless appropriate the cyber space as their own. Demonstrating agency in manipulating the technologies and languages of others for their own purposes, they exhibit a strong sense of adherence to local values. Such instances demonstrate that while rules for women's behavior in new spaces are not always clear, women themselves navigate among competing ideologies to occupy those spaces according to their own standards.

CONCLUSION

These debates resonate well beyond the individual cases that I provide, as they speak to a larger vision of the role of women in the Moroccan nation-state. Images of how women should occupy public space are abundant, in magazines, newspapers, television media, and government discourse. On the one hand, the Moroccan government promotes a unitary vision of the "Moroccan woman" as "the guardian of Moroccan cultural values at home and the proponent of modernity outside her house" (Moroccan Government 2005). Meanwhile the Islamist position represented by nationally known figures such as Nadia Yassine and Abdelilah Benkirane, leader of the religiously oriented Party of Justice and Development, argues that women's entry into the public sphere and demands for equality threaten the integrity of the Moroccan family and, in fact, the strength of the entire nation.

These representations of the ideal Moroccan woman respond to other issues in Moroccan society, most notably the 2000-03 conflict over legal reform of the Moroccan personal status code governing a woman's rights in marriage and divorce. The media tended to dichotomize these debates, representing positions over women's status as falling either into the more secular government camp (which nonetheless claims a religious basis for its formulations) or the more explicitly religious one. However, an interpretation of Moroccan women's presence in urban spaces indicates that women themselves do not fall neatly into these two categories. Small-scale disputes over space reveal how women engage with and resist competing ideologies that might circumscribe their movement or force them to compromise their sense of morality.

Imbuing public spaces with aspects of the domestic sphere is one tactic by which Fassi women make their presence in urban public spaces more acceptable. But they are also acting in ways that are new and unique, creating a bricolage among available rules for conduct and improvising where necessary. The concept of shame proves to be socially significant, and Fassis invoke it when situations are muddied by the presence of competing ideologies (Guessous 1984). "Shame" is a tactic used to control the terms of interactions in new social spaces: the American-style exercise club or the internet. Although some lower and middle class Fassis often assume that the elite follows an imported, Europeanized moral codein their behavior, the conflicts over men's visual access to women in the club reveal that this is not always the case. Even elite women have conflicting ideas about how men and women should occupy a shared space. Similarly, the incident in the cyber cafe demonstrates how women in cyber space subvert community controls while simultaneously adhering to the local values.

When subject to analysis, situations in which the gendered quality of a space is challenged reveal the current fault lines within Moroccan culture, and the issues that are contested. Controlling the dynamics of women's movement and its meanings is an activity in which disparate groups in Fassi society have multiple political stakes. High levels of unemployment for men, the circulation of new discourses over women's rights and empowerment, and efforts to define Moroccan relationships to Islam are some of the issues that complicate the presence of women in new, mixed spaces.

As Fassis negotiate the terms of their engagement with each other in new public arenas, the loss of shame is not the only threat to cultural integrity. People seem uncertain whether signs of the changing position of women in Moroccan society reveal a positive or negative future. Some grumble that educated women take jobs away from men, while others claim that giving women more rights in marriage will lead to more divorces. Disagreements about women and space reveal profound uncertainties as to the future of the Moroccan nation state, and as gendered territories are metaphorically defended or conquered, disputes reveal that more is at stake than the matter over which women are arguing. These are not merely debates about the degree of interaction between men and women in an exercise or a cyber club, but arguments over the interpretation of culture, and over conflicting views on how women should behave in an increasingly mixed society. Women in new, mixed spaces are, after all, doing other things besides exercising and searching the internet. They are making economic contributions to the welfare of their families, receiving university degrees at a rate comparable to that of men, participating in the public sphere through non-governmental organizations, demonstrations, and even parliament, and demanding to be accepted on their own terms.

Women's tactics shape urban spaces in unique ways, not only affecting the character of the Ville Nouvelle of Fes but also revealing the ways discourses about the position of women in the Moroccan nation state are rejected or appropriated by users. Visions of nation are not crafted solely in the media, economic and political capitals but in provincial cities, towns, and rural areas, where the processes through which individuals define and make use of space are no less significant. Although the gendered character of new urban spaces often remains ambiguous or unresolved, the debates themselves are interesting for what they reveal about local efforts to negotiate competing ideologies in gendering new urban spaces, and by extension, the nation.

NOTES

This article is based on fieldwork conducted in Fes, Morocco from 2001-02, enabled by funding from Princeton University and a Fulbright grant. I am grateful to my Fassi informants for contributing to my research, and to Lawrence Rosen, Abdellah Hammoudi, Haley Duschinski and Lisa Wynn for reading and commenting on earlier versions of this article. In addition, many thanks to the three anonymous reviewers who assisted in revising this article.

1. "Alli da mrato li jamaa, taytlaqha" and "Ma t-tshuf min al-sma ghayr duz al-halqa" These two proverbs were known to older Fassis, many younger people were unfamiliar with them.
2. The public/private dichotomy remains a much-debated framework of analysis in anthropology and Middle East Studies, criticized for being more of a reflection of Euro-American constructs than of the societies studied. See, e.g. Lamphere 1993; Nelson 1974; Pateman 1983; Afsaruddin 1999; Bekkar 1997; Abu-Lughod 1986.
3. A website published by the Moroccan government from 2000-03 best represents the government's position. Slightly altered since the revision of the personal status codes governing a woman's rights in marriage and divorce, the website continues to promote the same ideologies concerning the ideal Moroccan woman. For the opposing religious discourse, see Benkirane (2002).
4. Name given to residents of the city of Fes.
5. "Ville Nouvelle" refers to those districts of the city built by the French protectorate (1912-56) and since. While numerous studies have been conducted in the medina, little attention has been given to how Fassis interact with the French-built environment, and build over and around the original French buildings.
6. As of 2002, urban unemployment nationwide was at 18.3%, rural at 3.9%, averaging 11.6% for the whole country (El Aoufi and Bensaid 2005).
7. Middle and upper class Fassis blame rural migrants for the deterioration of the medina. Yet Megzari (1984) shows that many property owners in Moroccan medinas are themselves middle and upper class Moroccans who rent to rural migrants but refuse to maintain the structures.
8. Changes included the increase of grounds on which women can petition for divorce, raised the age of marriage, and placed some restrictions upon polygamy while not outlawing it altogether.
9. I use the term "public space" as a place of free assembly where individuals do not have to pay to gain admission. Because access to the exercise club and cyber cafe is restricted to those who can pay, this limits participation there to middle and middle-upper class Fassis. "Public space" is distinguished from "public sphere," for which I follow Habermas' definition of a public sphere as a space "where private people come together as a public" (1991: 27) to form opinions and mediate between family and state.
10. Women spoke of not wanting to be taken for a "prostitute," but this did not literally mean being confused for one. Rather, this term was used along with a few others loosely meant to identify a woman who engages in illicit sexual activity.
11. "Regular socializing outside the home for the middle class Ville Nouvelle women who did not spend time in cafes took place in the public bath (hammam). In the neighborhood of Cinema Lux, women of all ages go to the hammam once a week and stay for hours. But many younger professional women have foregone this practice and dislike the hammam because it "takes too much time" and is too "traditional," an activity they associate with their mothers' generation. See also Buitelaar (1998).
12. All personal names are pseudonyms.
13. I thank one of the anonymous reviewers for offering the latter observation. For debates on veiling, see Chebel 1988; El Guindi 1999; Hessini 1994; MacLeod 1991; Mernissi 1987 and Zuhur 1992.
14. I did not change the name of the club.

15. "Fundamentalist" was used disparagingly by the young professional women at the exercise club. I am certain that the women who wore a hijab would have objected to being called "ikhwaniyyin," as it had certain class (rural migrants who had fallen into extremist groups) and cultural connotations (the Egyptian brotherhood, the Taliban) and was a term that many religious Fassis did not wish to be identified with.
16. According to Islamic law, a Muslim man may marry a Christian or Jewish woman, but a Muslim woman cannot marry outside her faith unless her husband converts. It is less acceptable for Moroccan women to marry foreigners, while relationships between foreign women and Moroccan men are widely accepted.

REFERENCES CITED

Abu-Lughod, Janet. 1987. The Islamic City—Historic Myth, Islamic Essence, and Contemporary Relevance. International Journal of Middle East Studies 19:155-176. Abu-Lughod, Lila

——1986. Veiled Sentiments: Honor and Poetry in a Bedouin Society. Berkeley and Los Angeles: University of California Press. Afsaruddin, Asma

——1999. Hermeneutics and Honor: Negotiating Female 'Public' Space in Islamic Societies. Cambridge: Middle Eastern Monographs.

Benkirane, Abdelilah. 2002. Interview. Femmes du Maroc, no. 83, November.

Bekkar, Rabia. Statut social des femmes, acces a l'espace et a la parole pub- lique. In Espaces Publics, Paroles Publiques Au Maghreb et Au Machrek, eds. H.D. Tai'eb, R. Bekkar, J.C. David. Pp.81-96. Paris: Harmattan.

Bier, Laura. 2006. A Working Bibliography on Public Spheres in Comparative Context. www.ssrc.org/programs/mena/ publications/ Public_ Spheres_Bibliography.pdf . Accessed 12 June 2006.

Buitellar, Majro. Public Baths as Private Places. In Women and Islamization: Contemporary Dimensions of Discourse on Gender Relations. Pp. 103-123. Oxford and New York: Berg.

Chebel, Malik. 1987. L'esprit de serial: Perversions et Marginalites sexuelles au Maghreb. Casablanca: Lieu Commun.

Clancy-Smith, Julia. A Woman Without her Distaff: Gender, Work, and Handicraft production in Colonial North Africa. In Social History of Women and Gender in the Modern Middle East, eds. Meriwether, M. and Tucker, J. Pp. 25-62. Boulder: Westview Press.

Cohen, Shana. Searching for a Different Future: The Rise of a Global Middle Class in Morocco. Durham: Duke University Press.

de Certeau, Michel. 1984. The Practice of Everyday Life. Steven Randall, trans. Berkeley: University of California Press.

Deeb, Lara. An Enchanted Modern: Gender and Public Piety in Shi'i Lebanon. Princeton: Princeton University Press.

Djebar, Assia. 1993. Fantasia: An Algerian Cavalcade. Portsmouth, NH: Heinemann.

Eickelman, Dale. 1976. Moroccan Islam: Tradition and Society in a Pilgrimage Center. Austin: University of Texas Press.

El Aoufi, Noureddine and Mohammed Bensai'd. 2005. Chomage et employabilite des jeunes au Maroc. Rabat: Cahiers de la strategie de l'emploi.

El Guindi, Fadwa. 1999. Veil: Modesty, Privacy, and Resistance. Oxford: Berg.

Ghannam, Farha. 2002. Remaking the Modern: Space, Relocation, and the Politics of Identity in a Global Cairo. Berkeley: University of California Press.

Gole, Nilufar. 1997. The Gendered Nature of the Public Sphere. Public Culture 10(1).

Guerraoui, Driss. Famille et developpement a Fes. In Culture, Femmes et Famille, R. Bourquia, M. Charrad, and N. Gallagher, eds. Pp. 157-78. Casablanca: Afrique-Orient.

Guessous, Soumaya Naamane. 1984. Au-dela de toute pudeur. Casablanca: Editions Eddif.

Habermas, Jurgen. 1991. The Structural Transformation of the Public Sphere: An Inquiry into a Category of Bourgeois Society. Boston: MIT Press.

Hessini, Leila. Wearing the Hijab in Contemporary Morocco. In Reconstructing Gender in the Middle East: Tradition, Identity, Power. F.M. Gosek and S. Balaghi, eds. Pp. 40-57. Columbia University Press.

Hoodfar, Homa. Between Marriage and Market: Intimate Politics and Survival in Cairo. Berkeley: University of California Press.

Holmes-Eber, Paula. 2003. Daughters of Tunis: Women, Family, and Networks in a Muslim City. Boulder: Westview Press.

Jacobs, Jane. 1993. The City Unbound: Qualitative Approaches to the City. Urban Studies 30: 827-48.

Jansen, Willy. 1987. Women Without Men: Gender and Marginality in an Algerian Town. Leiden: E.J. Brill.

Kapchan, Deborah. Gender on the Market: Moroccan Women and The Revoicing of Tradition. Philadelphia: University of Pennsylvania Press.

Lamphere, Louise. 1993 Domestic Sphere of Women and the Public World of Men: The Strengths and Limitations of an Anthropological Dichotomy. In Gender in Cross-Cultural Perspective, eds. C. Brittell and C.F. Sargent. Pp. 86-95. New York: Prentice-Hall.

Le Tourneau, Roger. 1949 Fes avant le protectorat. Casablanca: SMLE.

MacLeod, Arlene. 1991 Accommodating Protest: Working Women, the New Veiling, and Change in Cairo. New York: Columbia University Press. Megzari M

——1984 La dedensification de la medina de Fes : cadre et moyens juridiques, Memoire INAU, Rabat.

Mernissi, Fatima. Beyond the Veil: Male-Female Dynamics in Modern Muslim Society. Bloomington: University of Indiana Press.

——1993 The Harem Within: Tales of a Moroccan Girlhood. London: Bantam.

Mitchell, Timothy. Colonising Egypt. Berkeley: University of California Press.

Moroccan government website. Moroccan Woman. Electronic document, http://www.mincom.gov.ma/english/generalities/mwoman/women.htm Accessed 15 January 2006. Navez-Bouchanine, Francoise

——L'espace limitrophe, entre le prive et le public, un no man's land? Espaces et Societes 199:135-159.

Nelson, Cynthia. 1974. Public and Private Politics: Women in the Middle Eastern World. American Ethnologist i(3):55i-63. Ossman, Susan

——Picturing Casablanca: Portraits of Power in a Modern City. Berkeley: University of California Press.

Pateman, Carol

——1983. Feminist critiques of the public/private dichotomy. In Public and Private In Social Life, S.I. Benn and G.F. Gaus, eds. Pp. 281-303. London:Croom Helm. Porter, Geoff D.

——Unwitting Actors: The Preservation of Fez's Cultural Heritage. Radical History Review 86:i23-i48.

Said, Edward. 1978. Orientalism. New York: Vintage Books. Salamandra, Christa

——A New Old Damascus: Authenticity and Distinction in Urban Syria. Bloomington: Indiana University Press.

Singerman, Diane. Avenues of Participation. Princeton: Princeton University Press. Skalli, Loubna

——Communicating Gender in the Public Sphere: Women and Information Technologies in the MENA Region. Journal of Middle East Women's Studies 2(2^35-59.

Zuhur, Sherifa. Revealing Reveiling: Islamist Gender Ideology in Contemporary Egypt. Albany: SUNY Press.

15

States of Insecurity

Everyday Emergencies, Public Secrets, and Drug Trafficker Power in a Brazilian *Favela*

Ben Penglase

This article examines how drug traffickers attempt to exert control over residents of a *favela* (squatter neighborhood) in Rio de Janeiro, Brazil. In exploring how drug trafficking organizations produce "ordered disorder," or what I call (in)security, I seek to expand upon previous analyses of the power that traffickers exert over favela residents. Prior analyses have shown how traffickers attempt to legitimate themselves by taking advantage of the Brazilian state's failure to provide public safety in these neighborhoods; in exchange for providing local security and enforcing social norms, traffickers have demanded the complicity and silence of favela residents. Building upon these analyses, and upon my fieldwork in a favela in Rio, I draw on Giorgio Agamben's (2005) notion of states of exception and Michael Taussig's (1999) concept of "public secrets" to show how traffickers also assert their control by alternating between states of security and insecurity and by deliberately manipulating secrecy.

My ethnographic analysis has larger implications for the analysis of how state and nonstate actors construct political orders. First, we can understand the nature of drug trafficker power and its relationship to the state more clearly when we view sovereignty as the ability to institute or suspend "normality," rather than as the possession of exclusive lawmaking authority over a particular territory. Rather than providing parallel structures of self-policing enabled by the state's absence from poor neighborhoods, traffickers depend upon divisions and tensions between various state actors and upon the state's "disruptive presence" in favelas. This allows traffickers to alternately impose their own rules in favela neighborhoods or suspend them and act as the force that institutes the "state of emergency." Thus, the state and nonstate actors are co-participants in the creation of a state of (in)security whose effects shape daily life throughout the city of Rio de Janeiro.

Second, by shifting attention from trafficker "governance" to a Foucauldian-inspired emphasis on "governmentality," we can examine security and governance not as given institutions and norms, but as discourses produced by particular social actors (in this case, drug traffickers).[1] As a result, it becomes clear that attempts by traffickers to legitimate themselves depend upon favela residents' participation in the construction of "public secrecy." In so doing, residents of favelas both shape a larger city and nation-wide state of (in)security, yet also hold out the possibility of transformation.

DRUG TRAFFICKER POWER IN RIO'S FAVELAS

The favela where I conducted my research, which I call Caxambu, is located in the northern part of Rio de Janeiro.[2] It is an old and "stable" favela: families first occupied the hillside that the favela is built upon in the early decades of the twentieth century, and most residents are connected to each other through dense and multistranded relations of kinship and long-term propinquity. Thus Caxambu would seem at first glance to substantiate earlier analysts' explanations for the effects of drug trafficking in Rio's favelas.

Analysts have proposed two models for understanding how favela-based traffickers have attempted to legitimate themselves. The first model emphasizes a reciprocal, if unequal, system of exchange, whereby traffickers provide public security in favelas in exchange for residents' silence about their criminal activities. The second model emphasizes clientelistic networks, arguing that traffickers have built upon and transformed older networks tying favela residents to political and economic elites.

In a pioneering article, Elizabeth Leeds argued that violence in Rio's favelas must be placed within a larger historical context and must be seen as the "visible and tangible form of the violence used by the state" against the poor (1996:50). Favelas such as Caxambu reveal this pattern. These neighborhoods have long occupied an ambiguous grey zone in Rio de Janeiro, at once officially "illegal," since their residents often did not own the land they built their homes upon, and yet also openly tolerated, as they were affordable housing options for the urban poor-which, in turn, helped to guarantee a cheap source of labor. Indeed, from the very beginning of settlement of Rio's favelas, the state played a dual role in organizing the poverty and racialization of neighborhoods such as Caxambu while marginalizing and excluding them.

The explosion of urban violence in Rio's favelas in the 1980s, Leeds argues, must be understood in this context of "the selective presence and absence of the state... and continuous violence and repression against the lower classes" (1996:49). While the state tolerated, or perhaps quietly encouraged, the city's poor and dark-skinned residents to build their own communities, city officials also denied these same neighborhoods access to regular city services. Not only have health, education, and basic sanitation services been inadequate or nonexistent, but the state has also failed to provide public safety. Rather than being a force that upholds the law, Rio's police have, since their inception, been charged with enforcing public order

(Holloway 1993). In a society marked by sharp inequalities, police viewed favela residents (and other poor and dark-skinned residents of the city of Rio) as threats to the city's established social order and as real or potential criminals to be contained and repressed. At the same time, the absence of regular provision of city services has ensured that favela residents have been an attractive target for politicians who promise "improvements" in exchange for votes. Thus, while favelas have been excluded from the provision of basic urban infrastructure and public safety, they have been deeply integrated into patron-client political networks and into the city's economy (Leeds and Leeds 1977).

In the 1980s, as Brazil returned to procedural, if not substantive, democracy, urban violence began a decades-long increase (Pinheiro 2000; Caldeira and Holston 1999). In poor neighborhoods, a new set of political relations emerged as the legacy of dictatorship, especially impunity for police violence, became connected with the growth of the transnational drug trade.

Particularly important was the emergence in the early 1980s of a drug organization called the *Comando Vermelho* (the Red Command, or CV) (Amorim 1993; Penglase 2008). The members of this group realized that the city's favelas provided strategically useful locations for the stockpiling of marijuana and cocaine destined for sale to clients in wealthier parts of the city. Drug dealers associated with the CV also turned antagonism between favela residents and the police to their advantage: in exchange for providing safety and conflict resolution and occasional short-term assistance, the CV demanded that favela residents turn a blind eye to their activities. This arrangement is known throughout Rio's favelas as the *lei do morro* (law of the hillside).

Luiz Eduardo Soares argues that drug trafficker power is especially influenced by favela residents' perceptions of the police. The arbitrariness and violent actions of the police, Soares argues, is contrasted with the order and intelligibility of drug trafficker rule. Violence by drug traffickers is deplored. But unlike the police, drug traffickers are seen as subordinating their "despotic practice to an intelligible and public order" (2000:40).

In her insightful ethnography of gender and humor in a favela in northern Rio, Donna Goldstein argues that favela residents often felt vulnerable in a situation where the police and judicial system were seen as corrupt or abusive. As a result, "the absence of the state in such areas means that these local gangs provide a parallel or alternative rule of law that deals with 'private matters' which the state is unable and unwilling to address" (Goldstein 2003:225). Likewise, Leeds argues that the services offered by the drug groups are valued because the state does not provide them: "the perception by favela residents-indeed, by most of the working class-that the formal justice system does not work for them has led a portion of the population to accept an alternative justice system" (1996:62).

Other analysts have complicated this picture by examining the ties that link drug traffickers and the state, and by arguing that traffickers' claims to providing security should be seen as a rhetorical claim, or a "myth of personal security" (Arias and Rodrigues 2006:54). Recently Desmond Arias (2006) examined how traffickers have consolidated their control over favelas by constructing flexible and horizontal networks that link them to local social movements, politicians and state institutions, and global flows of illegal commodities. Through these networks, drug traffickers can use their expertise in violence and their intimate knowledge of favelas to link themselves to wholesale suppliers of cocaine, corrupt policemen, and politicians and civic groups seeking access to favelas, all the while seeking to legitimate themselves by building support among favela residents.

In a similar vein, Michel Misse has argued that Rio's drug trafficking groups drew upon a pattern of "dangerous liaisons" that connected criminals to agents of the state (2006:179-210). Misse emphasizes, in particular, the links established between markets in illegal goods (such as the illegal lottery, contraband, and prostitution) and markets in political goods (such as protection or selective legal enforcement) offered by agents of the state. Misse argues that the gap between the criminalization of drugs, on the one hand, and demand for this illegal market, on the other, is part of a larger political economy; not only can corrupt police "sell" selective enforcement, but politicians can use their ability to encourage or discourage "crack downs" on crime as political merchandise to be sold for electoral support.

Misse's and Arias's clientelistic and network-driven models emphasize the links between the state and criminal organizations, and Leeds and Goldstein emphasize how nonstate actors provide security in the absence of state efforts to protect populations. Thus all of these approaches tend to emphasize how state and nonstate actors seek to create stability and normative orders. This emphasis on how state and nonstate actors produce order is important, but only captures part of the picture. As Kay Warren (2002) has warned, it is important not to reify stability and see violence as a threat to an otherwise "normal" social order.

To their credit, both Arias and Misse point out how networks and linkages are dynamic, conflictual, and unstable. Ties between traffickers and politicians, or between traffickers and favela residents, Arias (2006) argues, are based on the opportunistic political calculation by the parties involved and are always open to renegotiation or collapse. Arias and Rodrigues (2006) also show how traffickers often exercise their power arbitrarily, favoring more influential favela residents or those with whom they have stronger social ties. But this strategy has its limits: when traffickers undertake actions that are "consistently seen as an abuse of power that affects protected groups of residents ... traffickers risk losing their limited legitimacy" (Arias and Rodrigues 2006:74). Misse likewise argues that ties between criminals and state agents are "dangerous" because they are subject to constant renegotiation, often through violence, and are characterized by a general lack of trust.

Nonetheless, seeing stability as normative and violence as a breakdown of order, as Taussig (1992) has pointed out, often hides how political regimes naturalize their power by producing instabilities and uncertainties in the lives of people that they seek to control. My research in Caxambu reveals the importance of examining violence not as a breakdown of order but the "flipside" of what Taussig has called the "illusions of order congealed by fear" (1992:2). Insecurity and violence are not always the result of the failure of networks or of traffickers pushing their self-interests to the point where they violate their own rules. Sometimes traffickers and state agents co-participate in constructing political authority through the use of disorder, secrecy, and ambiguity.

CAXAMBU AND THE "LAW OF THE HILLSIDE"

At first glance, my ethnographic research in Caxambu substantiates earlier analyses of how drug traffickers attempt to legitimate themselves in Rio's poor neighborhoods. In many ways Caxambu could be seen as an example of a classic CV-run favela, where in the absence of state provision of public security, the residents traded their complicity for "protection" by traffickers.[3] Residents of Caxambu told me that once the CV "took over" the hillside neighborhood in the mid 1980s, they put an end to crime in the favela. For instance, Seu Janio, a man in his sixties, told me:

> Seu Janio: I think that there is no better *morro* [hillside, the locally preferred term for favela] to live in than here.
> Ben: Why is that?
> Seu Janio: Because this is a morro where lots of things that happen elsewhere … they're rare here. So there's peace, dignity. It's a family-based morro *(É um morro familiar)*.[4] I know everyone. Girls here don't get raped, like in other morros. This is a morro that, thank God, despite everything is like a big family. The people have lots of respect. It used to be that the morro was really tough. Really tough. Back then, just to give you an idea of what it's like now. Now you see lots of people out late at night. There was a time when no one would go out after six o'clock at night. [Laughs.]

Echoing the idea that trafficker rule is based upon a system of reciprocal exchange, residents of Caxambu would often state that because the traffickers "protected" them, they respected the drug traffickers. A central component of this relationship of "respect" is the "law of silence": residents would not inform the police about drug-dealing in their neighborhood. It is essential to note that the exchange that underlies the law of silence is highly asymmetrical and is enforced by the willingness of drug traffickers to commit violence to punish real or suspected informants. And, as Arias and Rodrigues (2006) have argued, despite the rhetorical claims by traffickers to impartially uphold local social norms (or "respect"), actual application of the rules varied tremendously depending upon a resident's social ties to traffickers or local position of influence.

The constant anxiety about informants also reveals the fear and ambiguity that are the flipside of the traffickers' "laws"; indeed, the most dangerous accusation that could be leveled at someone in the favela was to accuse that person of being an "X-9," or informant, an accusation that teenagers threw around in arguments, and that, more seriously, would sometimes surface as a threat in local disputes between residents.[5] As this concern reveals, the exchange between drug gangs and favela residents also depends on ambiguity and uncertainty: residents not only feared that they might be "unjustly" accused of being informants, but also sometimes attempted to use the arbitrary nature of trafficker justice to their advantage.

Residents were also aware that relations between residents and the traffickers were heavily influenced by the personality of the local head of the drug trafficking organization. During the late 1990s the drug operation in Caxambu was run by De, who was allied with the CV. The leaders of trafficking organizations in Rio's favelas are often referred to as *o homen* (the man) or as the *dono do morro* (owner of the hillside). Favela residents often compare good donos with bad donos, and most residents stated that De was a good dono. A good dono must appear to be concerned with the community, eschew or seek to minimize violence, and discourage drug use within the community (see Alvito 2001). Many people in Caxambu felt that De fit this bill: he was relatively old for a drug boss (in his mid-30s), pursued a policy of negotiation with the police, he supposedly did not use drugs, and he was said to discourage young boys from entering the drug trade.

The relations between traffickers and residents are also mediated by shared social identity and shared ties to local places (Alvito 2001; Zaluar 1985). A key criterion for determining a good dono, for example, was if that person had grown up in the neighborhood. Residents of Caxambu frequently emphasized that De had grown up in Caxambu, "inheriting" the drug trade from his older brother, and that most of the traffickers in De's organization were locals. Residents often felt that the shared ties to local place brought traffickers and residents together in a common social community that moderated drug traffickers' violence.

CONSTRUCTING (IN)SECURITY AND THE POWER OF THE SECRET

A more detailed ethnographic examination of how local-level drug-trafficking syndicates construct structures of power in Rio's favelas, though, reveals that in addition to trading "security" for complicity, traffickers also deliberately produce disorder, insecurity, and ambiguity. As Weldes et al. (1999) have argued, security and insecurity must be seen as culturally constructed and mutually constituted. Discourses about the production of security must not be taken as givens, but must be examined to reveal how, why, and when particular social actors claim to be providing order. These representations are part of a larger political economy, and are also crucial to the construction of the actors-such as "the state" and the "drug-gangs"-who respond to insecurity.

In the case of Brazilian favelas, the essential question to ask is: who defines security or insecurity? In many societies, state officials are granted the right to speak on behalf of the state, to identify threats and dangers, and to determine the best solution. These discourses are dominant, but are not the only ones: other social actors generate alternative discourses that clash with or appropriate the discourse of state actors (Weldes et al. 1999:19). But in Rio's favelas, and perhaps in poor and working-class communities in Brazil and throughout Latin America, statist definitions of "threat" or "safety" are not the dominant ones. Instead, traffickers and other nonstate actors often participate in generating discourses of safety and danger. Focusing on security as a discourse reveals how traffickers, various state actors, and favela residents all co-participate in the creation of a state of (in)security, a situation where security and insecurity are simultaneously present.

Two concepts, taken from Michael Taussig and Giorgio Agamben, help to understand the complexities of drug trafficker power: first, the idea of a "permanent state of emergency" or what I will call a state of (in)security; and second, the idea of the "public secret."[6] Rather than instituting a predictable, normative order, drug gangs deliberately create (in)security. They do this by abrogating to themselves the power not only to institute normative systems but also to violate the systems that they themselves create. In Agamben's (1995) terms, they are the force that can declare the state of exception. Likewise, this authority is not founded on open discussion and consensus but on the deliberate construction and manipulation of secrecy and ambiguity, which Taussig has called a "public secret" (1999:2).

THE COMANDO VERMELHO AND THE COMANDO AZUL

The authority that traffickers exert is enabled by, and thus dependent upon, the insecurity generated by police violence, crime, and the collapse of the Brazilian judicial and penal systems. Residents of Caxambu would frequently tell me that they felt safer in Caxambu than in the areas that were not under the control of the local drug gang, and that they trusted the traffickers more than the police. For instance, Pedro told me:

> Everyone here likes you and your wife. Everyone here receives you with open arms. You can walk around at will, can leave that tape-recorder right here-"Oh, it's Ben's"- and no one will touch it. Do you understand? Because... the Man here [the head of the drug gang] respects people, and doesn't want anyone to mess with anyone else. You see sometimes … I even leave the door of my house open. I trust them more than I trust the police.

The security provided by local traffickers was also dependent upon the fear generated by the tensions and conflicts within drug-trafficking groups. Residents were particularly fearful that the favela might be "invaded" and taken over by rival drug gangs, who might not be locals and might not respect residents. The threat of invasion and the rhetorical creation of the danger of foreign drug gangs-who were called *alemaes,* or Germans, in local slang-can be seen as objects of exclusion upon which the discourse that constructed drug dealers as locals and protectors depended.

The residents of Caxambu followed news reports about wars between rival gangs and splits within the CV with keen interest, as they worried that rivalries in the drug trade might intensify violence in their neighborhood. For instance, on May 22, 1999, during my period of fieldwork, a leader of the CV and his son were killed in prison. The killing became a major topic of conversation in Caxambu. Some residents openly worried that the killings might disrupt the balance of power and lead to increased conflict as different factions fought for ascendancy.

The residents of Caxambu felt that the current stability in the neighborhoods was due to De's skill in diplomatically navigating rivalries in the drug trade. Yet they were also aware of the fragility of this peace, because they knew that De could be arrested or killed at any moment. For example, I asked Anacleto if he thought the situation in Caxambu could change in the next few years, and told me, "Tomorrow, it could change tomorrow. Who knows if tomorrow it'll be so stable?"

Fears of violent and corrupt police and anxieties about drug-gang rivalry go hand-in-hand: the rise of the drug trade in the late 1970s and early 1980s fed off patterns of corruption and illegality in the police and justice system. Corrupt members of the police force realized that they could turn rivalries within Rio's drug groups to their advantage. Corrupt policemen often supplemented their income by extorting payments from detained traffickers, sometimes threatening to turn dealers or seized weapons over to rival gangs. It was even widely speculated that certain battalions of Rio's military police provided assistance to one or another of the rival drug groups.

This scenario of fear and anxiety, and of widespread concern with state corruption, fits with the argument that traffickers provide a sense of stability and safety where the state is unable or unwilling to do so. But trafficking syndicates also depend upon ongoing and constant insecurity, or at least the threat of insecurity, to legitimate their control. Without the twin threats of rival gangs and abusive police, the bargain that residents made with traffickers would have nothing behind it except brute force. Drug groups, like other forms of organized crime and the state itself, can function as protection rackets: they can produce real or imagined threats in order to "sell" security to their clients (Tilly 2002; Gambetta 1993).

As I have mentioned, recent research has explored how drug-trafficking organizations are part of "destabilizing networks," permeating Rio's political and economic structures, connecting various legal and illegal markets, and perpetuating long-standing patron-client political structures (Arias 2001; Misse 1997). The complementary perspective should also be taken: state actors also often destabilized favelas, and these destabilizing networks co-participated in the perpetuation of local political orders. If the police did not occasionally invade and harass residents, if the threat of "invasion" by rival gangs was not omnipresent, if the fear of crime was not sustained, then the deal that traffickers made with the residents would collapse.

Some Rio state authorities clearly recognized that the structures of power created by favela-based traffickers depended upon the state's disruptive presence. Leeds, for instance, quotes the former head of the military police in Rio, Colonel Carlos Magno Nazareth Cerqueira, as stating that police corruption and involvement in organized crime is the "greatest weapon that organized crime has at its disposal to allow it to operate freely" (Leeds 1996:64). Yet tensions and divisions within the state itself—particularly within the police force—ensure that arbitrary and violent policing works hand-in-hand with favela drug trafficking. Colonel Nazareth Cerqueira himself is a tragic example of the often violent divisions within the Rio de Janeiro state police: an active proponent of human rights and of fighting corruption within the police, he was murdered, under suspicious circumstances, in 1999.

A powerful example of the symbiotic relationship between violent policing and drug- trafficker power was what happened in Caxambu after the police shot and killed a local man known as Ari *o Sorveteiro* (Ari the Ice Cream Seller). On a Sunday morning, the police snuck up the hill on foot and opened fire on De, who was sitting on a chair at the top of the hill. Ari, who had been talking to De, was killed in the cross-fire. After shooting Ari, the police placed several bags of cocaine near Ari to make it seem that he was a drug dealer.

For weeks after the shooting, no one dared to wash the large bloodstain on the sidewalk where Ari had been killed. The local drug dealers spray-painted red circles around the bullet holes that pock-marked the walls and scrawled *Paz* (Peace), near them. The day after the shooting, the local traffickers strung a banner over the road complaining of police violence and accusing the PM (the military police) of being "the real criminals."

Residents were deeply upset by the shooting; not only had Ari been a well-liked person, seen as uninvolved with the drug trade, but the shooting happened during a time when lots of people were walking around the hillside. Several days after the shooting, the policeman who killed Ari drove into the favela, got out of his patrol car, and walked around at the top of the hill with his hand on the trigger of his revolver, seemingly taunting residents to complain about the crime. The shooting was never investigated nor was anyone ever prosecuted.

Because of the state's disruptive presence, the police come to be seen as "just as criminal" as the drug traffickers, and were sometimes described as the *Comando Azul,* or Blue Command, comparing the police's blue uniforms to the red of the *Comando Vermelho* (Red Command). But local drug traffickers drew sharp distinctions between the police and themselves. Although their practices are depicted as similar (both are violent), the fact that drug traffickers claim to abide by an explicit set of rules is held to distinguish them from the police. Without the anchor of the disruptive presence of the state, this discourse would collapse.

TUBARAO (THE SHARK) AND THE POWER OF THE EXCEPTION

As Carl Schmitt notes, the exception is more interesting than the regular case. The later proves nothing; the exception proves everything. The exception does not only confirm the rule; the rule as such lives off the exception alone. [Agamben 1999] Analyzing the "law of the hillside" as a normative order risks examining drug trafficker power from the perspective of the traffickers themselves. Favela residents and traffickers in Caxambu both speak about reciprocal relations, however asymmetrical they may be, and about a normative code that guides their interactions.

But as Arias and Rodrigues (2006) have argued, thinking of trafficker rule as based upon "laws" or "rules" is highly misleading (though both favela residents and some social scientists do this). Far from being founded on consensus, drug trafficker power in Caxambu was founded upon a highly unequal and uneven exchange, built out of fear and the threat of violence as much as upon shared social ties.

Traffickers impose their power not just by generating rules and security, but also by taking two additional steps. First, traffickers deliberately position themselves as the sovereign who is above, or beyond, the law. Second, they also occasionally- sometimes deliberately, sometimes "accidentally"-violate the very rules that they institute. These actions are not exceptions to the laws of the hillside. Instead, the exception to the rule of "mutual respect" is how trafficker rule is instituted and continually reinforced.

Favela residents are highly aware that despite the CV's rules, drug dealers reserve the right to step out of the boundaries whenever it suits them. Though favela residents often stated "if you respect the drug dealers, they'll respect you," they also warned that drug dealers were often unpredictable and should be avoided. A neighbor put it this way: "I grew up in the countryside. There you learn how to deal with snakes. If you pass by one you don't make a lot of noise, you don't bother it and make it angry. You just pass by as quietly as you can." It was indeed hard to mistake how certain members of the drug gang would often deliberately flaunt the local drug gang's own rules by, for instance, firing their guns at random or showing off their weaponry and intimidating favela residents for no apparent reason.

A more significant example occurred one afternoon shortly before I had moved to Caxambu. I was invited to a Saturday afternoon *churrasco* (barbeque) at the home of Seu Lazaro, the head of the local Resident's Association. When I arrived at his house, Seu Lazaro was sitting on his front porch drinking beer and invited me to sit down with him. A short while later a drug dealer nicknamed Tubarao (the Shark) came in through Seu Lazaro's front gate. Tubarao was a wiry black man in his twenties with a clean-shaved head and a twisted broken-tooth sneer, and he always wore mirrored sunglasses. His sinister appearance and his eagerness to use violence accounted for his nickname. Tubarao was respected and feared. He was also often high on cocaine, making him even more erratic.

Seu Lazaro had a large cooler that he kept stocked with beer to sell on hot weekend afternoons. Tubarao sat down next to me and asked if Seu Lazaro had any cold beer to sell. Tubarao wasn't wearing a shirt, and strapped to his bare chest was a leather holster that prominently displayed a 45-caliber revolver. Seu Lazaro looked over at Tubarao and said, "Sure, but come with me." They walked over near the gate and exchanged a few words, and Tubarao stepped outside.

A few minutes later Tubarao returned. He had draped a white t-shirt over the revolver, though it was obvious that the gun was still there. We chatted a bit about a Mike Tyson boxing match that was going to be shown on television, and after a few minutes Danilo, Seu Lazaro's nephew, came by with two bottles of Skol beer. Tubarao took them and walked out the gate.

"You know," Seu Lazaro told me, "I saw that kid grow up. I knew him when he was a little kid, in diapers."

By brazenly revealing his weapon but then pretending to "hide" it, Tubarao was sending a clear message: while he would respect Seu Lazaro, being considerate of Seu Lazaro's desire to create a welcoming atmosphere for his guest, there should be no illusions about who held more power. The larger message was unmistakable: local traffickers enforce the rules, but this does not mean that they will always follow them. A clearer example could not be possible of the status of the sovereign as the social actor who constitutes power precisely because he can stand outside of legitimately constituted normative authority-"the point of indistinction between violence and law, the threshold on which violence passes over into law and law passes into violence" (Agamben 1995:32).

SECRECY AND AMBIGUITY: THE "PUBLIC SECRET"

The fact that traffickers often violate their own rules also points to a second concept that helps to clarify the nature of trafficker power: the "public secret." Taussig defines the public secret as "that which is generally known, but cannot be spoken" (Taussig 1999:50). Following the classic arguments of Simmel and Canetti, Taussig argues that secrecy is central to the constitution of power and social order. The secret simultaneously creates a community, generating social subjects who possess the most important social knowledge, who "know what not to know," and yet instills murk and ambiguity at the center of power. This concealment "has the overt character of a prohibition ('Thou shalt not profess to know X') but whose heart is a dissimulation ('Even when X is generally known, you are enjoined to act and think as if X cannot be known')" (Surin 2001:206).

In Caxambu, the law of silence functions as a public secret; everyone knows that it is prohibited to speak about the activities of drug traffickers, even though everyone knows about the activities of drug traffickers. Particularly revealing is how favela residents use indirection in comments that seem to be talking about no one in particular, but which are, in fact, describing drug traffickers. For instance, one resident told me about how the current drug gang was different than former ones:

> Now this *pessoal...* this *rapaz* who is here is smarter, more cunning. He doesn't let anyone invade anyone else's house. Do you understand? He doesn't let the *pessoal* ... because he already has what he wants from the residents, and the residents need him, so w e ... understand?

This conversation is typical of the use of semantically broad terms-such as *pessoal* (personnel), *rapaz* (guy), and simply *ele* (he)-to talk about individuals who are known to both speakers (in this case the head of the drug group in Caxambu and local traffickers). This semantic ambiguity was not only common in taped inter-views, but was a constant feature of everyday talk, the use of a restricted code among participants who could assume enough shared understanding so that the meanings of deliberately vague utterances can be decoded.

Significantly, the local head of the drug trafficking organization was referred to by his direct name only in utterances where there were no other clear indications that he was, in fact, the head of the local drug gang. In all other cases, he was referred to simply as *o homem* (the man) or *o dono* (the owner). In other words, the use of secrecy ("hiding" De's name), presumed that the listener actually shared in the "secret" knowledge. In this case, the purpose of hiding knowledge that was openly known was not to avoid revealing a secret, but to actively create a community of people who know what they shouldn't know. Participating in knowing the "truth" of the secret was a way of marking oneself as an "insider" who could, it was hoped, count of the protection of drug traffickers.

The anxiety about informants (known locally as X-9s) and about being erroneously or maliciously identified as an X-9 reveals that the constitution of this community was also fraught with anxiety and fear. According to the law of silence, no one spoke to the police. Yet residents knew that this was not always the case: the police sometimes coerced information out of residents through harassment, torture, or extortion; residents who had incurred the hostility of local drug dealers, often because of unpaid drug debts, were sometimes tempted to "turn informant" for revenge. There was also a constant concern that rivalries within the drug group might lead traffickers lower on the hierarchy to use the police to usurp power for themselves. The anxiety and concern generated by secrecy came to be a powerful weapon that residents could use in their own conflicts and disputes, threatening to "unmask" their neighbors as X-9s.

At a deeper level, the public secret is that traffickers do not always provide security or "respect" favela residents. For example, residents of Caxambu often spoke, though in hushed and veiled terms, of cases where local drug traffickers forced people to let them use their homes as hideouts, as drug or weapons stockpiling points, or places for "cutting" and packaging cocaine or marijuana for retail sale. In some cases drug dealers compensate homeowners for this use of their house, and the packaging of cocaine is often subcontracted out to residents for a set fee (Rafael 1998; Misse 2006). Drug trafficker intrusion upon the homes of locals was quietly alluded to, though often openly known. Other cases, where drug traffickers forcibly evict home owners or move into their homes, were rarely mentioned or were discussed openly only if the particular drug dealer responsible for these actions had been killed, imprisoned, or otherwise removed from power. Indeed, one of the most powerful complaints that residents made against traffickers was that they had "unfairly" evicted people from their homes.

Another complaint, though one voiced very cautiously, occurred when the traffickers set up *bocas de fumo* (drug-selling points) near homes. Residents worried that this exposed them to violence from the police, rival drug gangs, or paranoid (and occasionally "coked-up") local drug dealers. In several cases in Caxambu, residents who had new bocas set up near their homes attempted to involve Seu Lazaro, the president of the local Residents Association, as a mediator on their behalf with the drug traffickers. Seu Lazaro's anxiety in taking up such tasks was palpable, and for good reason; as Robert Gay has argued, the increasing power of favela-based drug groups has dealt a harsh, and often deadly blow to the once autonomous and combative favela-based social movements (2005:54—58).[7] More commonly, rather than directly confronting drug dealers, favela residents voiced their concern by talking about their fear of stray bullets.

Other anxieties shrouded by public secret were parents' fears about how to deal with boys in the drug trade who wanted to pursue relationships with their daughters. Thus, while residents of Caxambu would talk about how the hillside drug dealers "respect" local women, these statements often went hand-in-hand with commentary about the dangers that local girls and their families face if the girls turn down the advances of local drug dealers. Cases where this occurred were not unusual but were almost never openly discussed.

In all these cases, the public secret was that, although the traffickers claimed to respect residents-protecting them from outside threats but otherwise not harassing them-relations between traffickers and residents were far more complex and contradictory. Arias and Rodrigues have argued that the inconsistent manner in which traffickers implement the "rules" of the law of the hillside is part of a larger political logic whereby traffickers claim to uphold social norms, but in practice systematically favor influential residents whose support they cultivate (2006:65). Favela residents often acknowledge that rules and decisions made by traffickers vary according to the local status of violators or disputants or according to the whims of particular traffickers. In general this variation is tolerated as long as those who are "favored" by traffickers are locally influential residents. When traffickers are too arbitrary in imposing rules or fail to cultivate the support of influential residents, "the incidents provoke anger and outrage (revolta) among residents" (Arias and Rodrigues 2006:73).

If the often arbitrary and ambiguous nature of trafficker power is examined, however, as a "public secret," then a different picture emerges. The "truth" of trafficker arbitrariness is not simply the revelation of a "hidden" reality, but is integral to how traffickers exert power through their ability to decide the exception. For Taussig, the drive to transgression is integral to the secret-that the traffickers often violated order and acted arbitrarily, and that residents often sought personal exemptions to the rules, does not mean that the public secret had been unmasked. Rather, the power of the public secret of the "law of the hillside" is exactly that everyone acts as if it were true, while knowing that the secret propels its transgression. If it is never clear exactly how and why traffickers will rule in a resident's favor, then residents must simultaneously deny this "secret," in order to maintain the fiction of predictability, while cultivating trafficker support in the hope that the "exception" will be ruled in their favor.

The power of the public secret is not that it conceals a more cynically self-serving political strategy, but that it provides a set of culturally familiar, and convincing, tropes to help people navigate the ordered disorder of their lives. The public secret functions much like the "hidden" truth of complex and conflict-ridden family relationships that are often systematically denied when speaking to non-kin. In this way, the law of the hillside draws upon tropes of family and kinship, ideas of respect based on common social identities, and common ties to a particular space. The point in keeping the secret is not simply denying the "reality" of family conflict, but of marking oneself part of a shared community of people united by "knowing what they shouldn't know."

For many favela residents, this way of conceiving of power and authority-through tropes of kinship and "blood," and based upon the idea that despite the real truth that families are often fraught with jealousy and conflict, when challenged by strangers families should stand united-is more convincing than two other dominant ways of conceiving of authority and legitimate uses of violence: ideas about universal equality and abstract citizenship; or tropes (which are equally familiar) of favela residents as threats to the stability of the rest of Rio who "require" violent policing. Indeed, trafficker rhetoric about favelas being families united against the brutality of the state and the neglect of wider society is deliberately created as a counter-discourse to the old images of favelas as "savage" and "barbaric" (Abreu 1987).

CONCLUSION

The "old school" Comando Vermelho favelas, such as the one where I did my research, are now very much an exception and probably a relic of what, in the ever accelerating chronology of the rapidly mutating drug trade, counts as the dark and distant past (the late 1990s). Nonetheless, precisely because it more closely approximated the classic model of drug trafficker control, Caxambu serves as a useful ethnographic case; it demonstrates how traffickers attempt to consolidate their control over favela residents by both instituting and suspending "normality," and by deliberately manipulating truth and secrecy to create a state of (in)security.

The type of power exercised by drug traffickers, it is worth emphasizing, does not occupy a vacuum left by the state, nor does it necessarily challenge or oppose itself to state power. Rather, the ability of drug traffickers in Rio's favelas to institute the "state of the exception" can exist alongside the state's role as the ultimate source of a normative social order. Traffickers appear to be content to allow the state to perform most of its functions, as long as they do not inordinately challenge traffickers' interests. When this does occur, as I have argued elsewhere (Penglase 2005), traffickers have demonstrated their ability to suspend "normality" not only in favelas, but throughout the city of Rio as a whole.

The ultimate irony is that both traffickers and the state attempt to legitimize themselves by casting themselves as the purveyors of "impartial justice" and their opponents as the source of "arbitrary violence." Yet both depend upon each other for their discourses and political-economic strategies to be effective. The state needs an illegal criminal market place, both to anchor its claims to provide law and order and, in many cases, as an attractive buyer of "protection." Favela-based traffickers, in turn, need state agents both as purveyors of protection and as destabilizing agents that they can contrast with their own, apparently more "benign," form of control. In this sense, both traffickers and the state co-participate in creation of state of (in) security.

For many favela residents, the "public secret," the knowledge that is openly known and yet not speakable, is that both the state and the traffickers are responsible for creating the "everyday state of emergency" within which they are forced to live. As Agamben has argued, "the state of exception tends increasingly to appear as the dominant paradigm of government in contemporary politics" (Agamben 2005:2). Perhaps residents of Rio's favelas can teach us to pay attention to similar social constructions of (in)security and secrecy in apparently more stable and open societies such as the United States.

NOTES

I would like to thank *PoLAR's* two anonymous reviewers for their comments and, of course, to extend my thanks to the residents of Caxambu, whose names for obvious reasons have been altered. An earlier version of this article was presented on March 17, 2006, as part of a panel on nonstate security communities organized by Kristina Mani for the Latin American Studies Association's annual conference, in San Juan, Puerto Rico, and benefitted tremendously from the comments of Pablo Policzer and the other panelists.

1. By *governmentality* I mean, drawing upon Foucault, the "multiform tactics," practices, discourses, techniques, and forms of knowledge by which selves are fashioned and subjects are governed (Foucault 1991:87-104). What I am highlighting, though, is the production of subjects through strategies of "abnormalization."
2. *Caxambu* is a pseudonym for the favela where I conducted ethnographic research from 1998-1999 and in 2001.
3. By the late 1990s, according to both favela residents and social scientists, conflicts within Rio's main drug-trafficking organizations have produced a turnover in drug- group leadership, with a younger and supposedly more violence-prone generation of drug dealers assuming power.
4. In this context, *familiar* means that the favela is seen as marked by strong social ties, that it's a family-based neighborhood.
5. A popular funk song by Cidinho and Doca, "X-9 Torrado" ("Toasted X-9") that I often heard in Caxambu, described how traffickers sometimes kill informants by placing old tires around them and burning them alive.
6. I am aware of the dangers of deploying concepts that have, at their root, the Nazi Holocaust as their paradigmatic experience (Hesse 2004). I hope, nonetheless, that these analytical tools can illuminate, rather than foreclose, the particularities of a Brazilian context marked by the legacies of European colonialism and the trans-Atlantic slave trade.
7. Gay cites reports that one hundred community leaders in Rio's favelas have been assassinated by drug organizations between 1992 and 2001 (Gay 2005:187).

REFERENCES CITED

Abreu, Maurlcio de A. 1987. Evolucao urbana do Rio de Janeiro. Rio de Janeiro: Jorge Zahar.

Agamben, Giorgio. 1995. Homo Sacre. Palo Alto, CA: Stanford University Press. 1999 Potentialities: Collected Essays in Philosophy. Stanford: Stanford University Press.

——State of Exception. Chicago: University of Chicago Press.

Alvito, Marcos. 2001. As cores de Acari. Rio de Janeiro: FGV Editora.

Amorim, Carlos. 1993. Comando Vermelho. Rio de Janeiro: Editora Record.

Arias, Enrique Desmond. 2006. Drugs and Democracy in Rio de Janeiro. Chapel Hill: University of North Carolina Press.

Arias, Enrique Desmond, and Corinne Davis Rodrigues. 2006 The Myth of Personal Security: Criminal Gangs, Dispute Resolution, and Identity in Rio de Janeiro's Favelas. Latin American Politics and Society, 48(4):53—81.

Caldeira, Teresa P. R., and James Holston. 1999 Democracy and Violence in Brazil. Comparative Studies in Society and History 41(4):691—729.

Foucault, Michel. 1991. The Foucault Effect. Chicago: University of Chicago Press

Gambetta, Diego. 1993. The Sicilian Mafia: the Business of Private Protection. Cambridge, MA: Harvard University Press.

Gay, Robert. 2005. Lucia: Testimonies of a Brazilian Drug Dealer's Woman. Philadelphia: Temple University Press.

Goldstein, Donna. 2003. Laughter Out of Place: Race, Class, Violence and Sexuality in a Brazilian Favela. Berkeley: University of California Press.

Hesse, Barnor. 2004. Im/Plausible Deniability: Racism's Conceptual Double Bind. Social Identities 10(1):9—29.

Holloway, Thomas H. 1993. Policing Rio de Janeiro. Stanford, CA: Stanford University Press.

Leeds, Anthony, and Elizabeth Leeds. 1977. Sociologia do Brasil Urbano. Rio de Janeiro: Zahar.

Leeds, Elizabeth. 1996. Cocaine and Parallel Polities. Latin American Research Review 31(3): 47—83.

Misse, Michel. 1997. As ligacoes perigosas: mercado informal ilegal, narcotrafico e violencia criminal no Rio. Contemporaneidade e Educacao. 2(1):93— 116.

——2006. Crime e violencia no Brasil contemporaneo. Rio de Janeiro: Lumen Juris.

Penglase, Ben. 2005. The Shutdown of Rio de Janeiro. Anthropology Today 21(5):3—6.

——2008. The Bastard Child of the Dictatorship: The Comando Vermelho and the Birth of "Narco-culture" in Rio de Janeiro. Luso-Brazilian Review 45(1):118—145.

Pinheiro, Paulo Sergio. 2000. Democratic Governance, Violence, and the (Un)Rule of Law. Daedalus 129(2):119—143

Rafael, Antonio. 1998. Um abraco para todos os amigos. Niteroi: EDUFF.

Soares, Luiz Eduardo. 2000. Meu casaco de general. Rio de Janeiro: Companhia das Letras.

Surin, Kenneth. 2001. The Sovereign Individual and Michael Taussig's Politics of Defacement. Nepantla 2(1):205-219.

Taussig, Michael. 1992. The Nervous System. New York: Routledge.

——1999. Defacement: Public Secrecy and the Labor of the Negative. Palo Alto, CA: Stanford University Press.

Tilly, Charles. 2002. War Making and State Making as Organized Crime. In Violence: A Reader. Catherine Besteman, ed. Pp. 35-60. New York: New York University Press.

Warren, Kay. 2002. Toward an Anthropology of Fragments. In Ethnography in Unstable Places. Carol Greenhouse, Elizabeth Mertz, and Kay Warren, eds. Pp. 379-392. Durham, NC: Duke University Press.

Weldes, Jutta, Mark Laffey, Hugh Gusterson, and Raymond Duvall, eds. 1999. Introduction: Constructing Insecurity. In Cultures of Insecurity. Minneapolis: University of Minnesota Press. Zaluar, Alba

——1985. A maquina e a revolta. Sao Paulo: Brasiliense.

16

Making War at Home in the United States

Militarization and the Current Crisis

Catherine Lutz

It takes a good deal more courage, work and knowledge to dissolve words like "war" and "peace" into their elements, recovering what has been left out of peace processes that that have been determined by the powerful, and then placing that missing actuality back in the center of things. ... The best corrective is, as Dr. Johnson said, to imagine the person whom you are discussing—in this case the person on whom the bombs will fall—reading you in your presence.

—Edward Said, "The Public Role of Writers and Intellectuals"

I will not begin with the story of a pair of people holding hands as they leapt to their deaths from the Towers on September 11. It has been told, and often sold, a thousand times over. I cannot begin with the story of a man holding his child in Afghanistan later that autumn, listening to the approach of distant U.S. bombers that would soon cut him and his child down like daisies. This one has had far fewer tellings, for it has had little exchange value in the modern economy of war, race, mass media, cultural politics, and oil. Neither story can be told to fully good purpose without first unearthing what they evoke beyond the wailing webs of mourning that ramify from each life extinguished.

That, I will argue, is the long process of militarization and empire building that has re-shaped almost every element of global social life over the 20th century. By militarization, I mean "the contradictory and tense social process in which civil society organizes itself for the production of violence" (Geyer 1989:79). This process involves an intensification of the labor and resources allocated to military purposes, including the shaping of other institutions in synchrony with military goals. Militarization is simultaneously a discursive process, involving a shift in general societal beliefs and values in ways necessary to legitimate the use of force, the organization of large standing armies and their leaders, and the higher taxes or tribute used to pay for them. Militarization is intimately connected not only to the obvious increase in the size of armies and resurgence of militant nationalisms and militant fundamentalisms but also to the less visible deformation of human potentials into the hierarchies of race, class, gender, and sexuality, and to the shaping of national histories in ways that glorify and legitimate military action (Bernstein 1999; Linenthal and Engelhardt 1996). While it is often called by such names as "military strength," or framed as a tool to defend freedom, militarization is a process that helped spawn the violence of September 11 and the violent response of October 7: To understand militarization, so many must hope, is to put some impediment in its deadly path.

While militarization has been shaped within innumerable states, corporations, and localities, the United States is now the largest wellspring for this global process. A nation made by war, the United States was birthed not just by the Revolution of 1776 but also by wars against Native Americans and the violence required to capture and enslave many millions of African people. Twentieth-century U.S. militarization accelerated in three major bursts: with the 1939 loosing of fascist forces in a world never recovered from the First World War,[1] again with the establishment of the national security state in 1947, and now with the events of September 11, 2001.

Bitterly watching the United States charge headlong onto the slaughter fields of Flanders and U.S. intellectuals' enthusiastic drumbeat of acquiescence, Randolph Bourne called war "the health of the state" (1964). He meant that the state's power grows in wartime, accumulating legal powers and public wealth to pursue the battle, and that it often maintains that expanded power far into the putative peacetime that follows. Bourne was certainly proven prescient, as the last century's wars enlarged the government and enriched military corporations, shrank legal controls over both entities, and captured an empire of postconflict markets (e.g., Jensen 1991; Kaplan and Pease 1993; Sherry 1995). And, in 1947, with the institution of the National Security Act and a whole host of other antidemocratic practices, the broad latitude of political elites in what is euphemistically called "statecraft" was to be taken for granted.

While many, particularly progressives and libertarians, see and worry about these changes, the entrenched notion that war is the health of the nation has garnered little attention and no irony. It is instead widely accepted that military spending preserves freedom and produces jobs in factories and in the army. The military is said to prepare young people for life, making men out of boys and an educated workforce out of warriors through college benefits. Virtues like discipline and teamwork are seen as nurtured by military trainers and lavishly exported to society at large. That these contentions are problematic becomes evident in the close ethnographic view of communities shaped by military spending outlined below.

It is true, however, that the capillaries of militarization have fed and molded social institutions seemingly little connected to battle. In other words, the process of militarization has been not simply a matter of weaponry wielded and bodies buried. It has also created what is taken as knowledge, particularly in the fields of physics and psychology, both significantly shaped by military funding and goals (Leslie 1993; Lutz 1997). It has redefined proper masculinity and sexuality, (D'Amico 1997; Enloe 2000), further marginalizing anyone but the male heterosexual—the only category of person seen fit for the full citizenship conferred by combat. Militarization emerges from the images of soldiers in recruitment ads that blast across the popular culture landscape through both the $2 billion annual recruitment budget and Hollywood fare from *The Sands of Iwo Jima* to *Black Hawk Down*. It has rearranged U.S. social geography through internal migrations to the South and West for military work (Markusen et al. 1991) and has accelerated the suburbanization process and the creation of black bantustans in the core of older cities. It created the bulk of both the federal deficit and the resistance to social welfare benefits in a workforce divided into those soldiers and veterans with universal health care, a living wage, and other benefits, and those without them (Hardin 1991). It has contributed to the making of race and gender in the United States through the biases of military spending toward the whiter and more male segments of the workforce.

Much of the history and the physical and symbolic costs of war on the home front and of war itself have been invisible to people both inside and outside the military. This is the outcome of secrecy laws, of an increasingly muzzled or actively complicit corporate media, and of the difficulty of assessing a highly complex and far-flung institution and the not-so-obviously related consequences of its actions. The costs have also been shrouded behind simplified histories, public relations work, or propaganda. Most recently, Tom Brokaw's *The Greatest Generation,* Stephen Spielberg's *Saving Private Ryan,* and the many best-selling paeans to soldiering by Stephen Ambrose are responsible for selling a powerful nostalgia and desire for war in a new generation. These popular culture works assert that war builds character, makes men, and grants freedom to the nation and a kind of supercitizenship to those who wage it. This militarization in the United States is not, of course, what the current crisis is supposedly about. The bookshelves of stores that have a section devoted to our current predicament burst with books on Islam and fundamentalist Islam, the Taliban, and Nostradamus. They are on "the Arab World" and the vectors of danger to the U.S. population in the form of germs and weapons of mass destruction, weapons that are construed as dangerous only in the hands of the immature nations, something Hugh Gusterson has termed "nuclear orientalism" (1999).

September 11 has been treated in the media and by politicians as both a rupture in history and as the next "Good War." From that war, of course, come the constant references to Pearl Harbor and President Bush's imagination of the enemy as the "Axis of Evil." The same people who busily proclaimed the end of history a few years ago now say it has just begun, with September 11 as the starting point. The U.S. involvements in global affairs that may have precipitated these events in some way have been ignored: The people who jumped from those downtown workplace windows flew free of history. Attempts to explain the events through historical contextualization were shouted down as treasonable excuse. Those who died in Afghanistan, by contrast, were historically particularized, each implicated in a prior chain of conspiracy that sent jumbo jets crashing into buildings, each recoded as a Taliban terrorist, and so their deaths were justified.

A number of anthropologists, alongside historians, have written for years against these erasures. They have found or put themselves in the midst of violent whirlwinds: Carolyn Nordstrom (1997), Linda Green (1994), Veena Das (1990), Orin Starn (1999), Begona Aretxaga (1997), Michael Taussig (1987), Liisa Malkki (1995), Allen Feldman (1991), C. Valentine Daniel (1996), Cynthia Mahmood (1996), and a long list of others have shown us that war is about social deformation, silencing, and resilience as much as it is about the body's physical destruction.[2] The anthropologies of immiseration produced by such scholars as Brett Williams (1994), Nancy Scheper-Hughes (1992), Philippe Bourgois (1996), Katherine Newman (1999), June Nash (1979), Gerald Sider (1986), Paul Farmer (1996), Ida Susser (1996), Kim Hopper (1991), and Judith Goode and Jeff Maskovsky (2001) are also important to set alongside the more explicitly war-centered works. They reveal what the epigraph above suggests is often hidden: the indistin-guishability and interdependence of physical and structural violence. This is in contrast to the notion that violence is mere tool or accident en route to the pursuit of a state's political interest, or that there are separate "forms" of power, such as military, political, and economic.[3] These works can be used to illustrate the intertwining of the violence of the 20th century with the widening international and intranational gap between the rich and poor and with the surges of old and new forms of racism. I focus here on the context of the emergence of this violence focusing on the historical and anthropological contexts of war and war preparation in, or involving, the United States.

This article is organized around two central questions: (1) What is the 20th-century history of militarization, and how is it related to the notion of militarism, to the nation-state, to changing modes of warfare, and to broader social changes? and (2) How can we connect global and national histories with specific ethnographically understood places and people involved in the militarization process? I can begin to answer these questions with reference to ethnographic and historical research in a military city, Fayetteville, North Carolina. Its 120,000 people live next to the Army's giant Fort Bragg, and its story tells about the history of U.S. cities more generally (Lutz 2001). In closing, I suggest how this can help us understand the crisis that erupted on September 11.

MILITARISM, MILITARIZATION, AND STATES

The term *militarism* has sometimes been used synonymously with the term *militarization*. It is usually much narrower in scope than the latter, however, identifying a society's emphasis on martial values. It also focuses attention on the political realm and suggests warlike values have an independent ability to drive social change, while *militarization* draws attention to the simultaneously material and discursive nature of military dominance. In addition, North American scholarship has rarely applied the term *militarism* to the United States; it more often projects responsibility onto countries it thereby "others." This makes it hard to identify growing military hegemony in the United States and in other societies in which ideological claims suggest the nation is peaceful by nature, and engages in war only when it is sorely provoked (Engelhardt 1995). Moreover, there is no universal set of "military values" whose rise indexes a process of militarization because cultural forms have intersected with and remade society's military institutions. So, for example, faith in technology has supported a high ratio of arms to soldiers in the U.S. military. While some might assume that this is the natural outcome of U.S. affluence or of high-tech weaponry's superior efficacy as a modality of war, neither is necessarily the case, as the Vietnam War and September 11 both demonstrated. Such technological faith comes through the power of military industrial corporations to shape political discourse and decisions in the United States through lobbying and campaign contributions, via the revolving door between military and military industrial leadership, and military corporate advertising. The faith is also rooted deeply in advertising campaigns for better living through those sciences that brought advances in transportation, food technology, home appliances, and computers.

Military institutional growth and a glorification of war and its values, however culturally defined, have not always developed in tandem: U.S. military spending remained low in the 19th and early 20th centuries while political culture glorified war and the martial spirit. Oliver Wendell Holmes Jr., told students at Harvard in 1895 that: "So long as man dwells upon the globe, his destiny is battle. ... War's ... message is divine" (Karsten 1989:33). William James even argued against war while still assuming a love of battle: "The popular imagination fairly fattens on the thought of wars. ... Militarism is the great preserver of our ideals of hardihood" (Karsten 1989:36). Contemporary American political culture does not tolerate such talk of the merits of violence. Instead, politicians, pundits, and some Fayetteville citizens speak about soldiers as those who are "placed in harm's way," reversing the image of soldiers as warrior-killers and eliding the state's role in their movements. At the same time, substantial resources are allocated to war preparation.

These elisions aside, however, the growth of a behemoth military and of military industrial corporate power have helped make what C. Wright Mills called "a military definition of reality" (1956:191) become the common sense of the nation. That is, it is deeply and widely believed that human beings are by nature aggressive and territorial, that force is the only way to get things done in the world, and that if one weapon creates security, 1,000 weapons create that much more. By this definition, as one soldier told me, "defense is the first need of every organism" (anonymous, conversation with author, June 30, 1999).

Militarization is a *tense process*, that is, it can create conflict between social sectors, and most importantly between those who might benefit from militarization (e.g., corporations interested in expanding international markets for their goods) and those who might not, but who nonetheless may bear some of its costs. This conflict happens on the local level as well. In the 640 U.S. communities with large military bases, realtors and retail owners benefit from the military's presence, unlike lawyers, public sector workers, and retail workers who must cope with the shrunken tax base associated with the military bases' federal land. The structural violence a war economy creates is not the simple equation so often painted of subtracting the government's military spending from its social spending. An example of the more complex factors involved is found in Fayetteville, where retail labor is the main category of work created by the post, as Fort Bragg soldiers take their salary dollars there to shop. Not only do retail jobs pay less than any other type of job, but retail workers also face the reserve army of unemployed military spouses whose in-migration to Fayetteville the military funds. Fayetteville wage rates are lower than in any other North Carolina city as a result.

Militarization also sets *contradictory* processes in motion, for example, it accentuates both localism (as when Fayetteville and other cities compete for huge military contracts or bases) and federalism (as when the fate of dry cleaning businesses in Fayetteville can hinge on Pentagon regulations on putting starch in uniforms or on sudden deployments of large numbers of soldiers). Militarization might seem always to have the latter centralizing tendencies but there has been, in the United States especially, a tradition of what Lotchin (1984) calls the "entrepreneurial city"—competing for interstates, county seats, conventions, prisons, and military bases and contracts. This curbs the state, as does citizens' ability to make more claims on a government in exchange for their mobilization for war.

Charles Tilly has argued that most states are birthed by and wedded to war. He in fact names the state a kind of protection racket, raising armies that safeguard the people from violent threats they pretend to see, provoke themselves, or wreak on their own people. He also, however, leaves open the possibility for legitimate defensive armies to emerge in some contexts. "Someone who produces both the danger and, at a price, the shield against it is a racketeer. Someone who provides a needed shield but has little control over the danger's appearance qualifies as a legitimate protector, especially if his price is no higher than his competitors" (Tilly 1985:170–171). Most of the armies that emerged from the 18th century onward claimed to be the primary tool of the state—or, more grandly, the very enablement of a people. These armies could be defined as virtually the sine qua non of both state and nation.

States that formed earlier in the modern period, such as those in Europe and the United States, were better able to externalize their violence, protecting at least the middle and upper classes from the violence their global extraction of resources required. States that emerged more recently have often been shaped as clients to those earlier and more powerful ones. For this reason, the latter show a much greater disproportion of power between military and civil forces (however much those two categories problematically entail or contain each other). In these client states, the military is favored, as the state strikes bargains more with the foreign patron (who provides military assistance in exchange for commodities, labor pools, and access) than with the people within that state. This has certainly been relevant in the current crisis, as Saudi Arabia's elites, for example, struggle to be seen as defenders of the nation rather than clients of the United States, and as the United States exempted Saudi Arabia from its list of terrorist states, despite the fact that almost all the hijacker-murderers of September 11 were from that country.

Beyond this general relationship between the state and violence, many historians have noted the United States' especially intimate relationship to war, that U.S. violence has centered on the idea of race and, moreover, has contributed to the making of races. The early U.S. Army was defined as a kind of constabulary whose purpose was nation-building through "Indian clearance," rather than defense of national borders (Weigley 1967:27). The Army also built roads and forts to facilitate colonial settlement, an aim so intrinsic to the military that "any difference between soldiering and pioneering escaped the naked eye" (Perret 1989:137). The real and imagined threat of slave insurrection rationalized the raising of local official militias in the 19th century as well, and the military fought the Mexican-American and the Spanish-American Wars with racial rationales. European colonialism was, of course, also rooted in race violence, and the World War, which ran with brief interruption from 1914 to 1945, was fueled by contests over colonial holdings and militant expansionism based in racial supremacism (whether European, American, or Japanese).[4] U.S. military power went global as the 20th century opened, when Filipinos, Puerto Ricans, and Hawaiians were made racial wards of the state.

This long history of race and war is encapsulated in Fayetteville's annual International Folk Festival. It begins with a parade down the city's main street led by a contingent of the Fayetteville Independent Light Infantry, a militia begun in the slave era, and still in existence, though more as social club than armed force. The soldiers in archaic dress costume are followed by a march of war refugee nations from Puerto Ricans and Okinawans to Koreans and Vietnamese who have made the city home.

20TH-CENTURY MODES OF U.S. WARFARE

To understand when, why, and how the militarization process has sped up in the United States and globally in the 20th century, when and how warfare has emerged from it in the contemporary world, and how social relations are reshaped, I begin with the notion of an era's dominant "mode of warfare." While many accounts of warfare remain technocentric, that is, focused on the scientifically and technically advanced tool purportedly at its center (such as the machine gun, the atom bomb, or the computer, e.g., Ellis 1975), this phrase draws our attention beyond the central weapon or strategy of a country or era's military organization to the wider array of social features any type of war making leads to. The mode of warfare that emerged with industrial capitalism and the nation state most extensively by the 19th century was mass industrial warfare. This required raising large armies, whether standing or relatively episodic. War in this mode also centered on manufacturing labor, with many workers required to produce tens of thousands of relatively simple guns, tanks, and ships, and, eventually, airplanes. The advantage of industrial warfare over artisanal warfare was immediately evident in colonial wars in which the European powers captured vast territories. This point can be overemphasized, however; the Belgian Congo represents a case in which simple guns, chains, and severed hands did the work of creating a labor force to extract the colony's wealth (Hochschild 1998) and Maori guerilla warfare in New Zealand was effective for years against the more technically advanced weaponry of the British (Belich 1986).

As or more important than the efficacy of a mode of warfare, however, has been the form of life it has encouraged inside the nation waging it. Industrial modes of warfare, for example, pressed governments to extend civil rights and social benefits to gain the loyalty and labor of those larger segments of the population conscripted into the mass army (Skocpol 1993; Tilly 1985) as well as taxed. For, first of all, mass industrial armies confront the problem of labor, and the symbolic benefits of citizenship have often been exchanged for them. World Wars I and II were fought in this mass industrial mode and helped shape the labor geographies and gender/race/class structures of the societies that waged them. They further entrenched patriarchal authority by excluding women from armies (except as sexual aids to soldier morale) and from high-paying manufacturing jobs (even if they temporarily involved some women and racial minorities during wartime). These wars also helped absorb excess industrial capacity that increasingly threatened capital accumulation. They did so by producing massive numbers of commodities whose function it was to be destroyed. In round numbers, America produced 300,000 planes, 77,000 ships, 20 million small arms, 6 million tons of bombs, 120,000 armored vehicles, and 2.5 million trucks in World War II alone (Adams 1994:71). The wars also prevented crisis within the U.S. economy after the war by requiring retooling of factories for domestic production and by providing new markets, commodities, and desires both overseas and domestically (Baran and Sweezy 1966).

The Cold War's beginning has been variously dated from 1917 to 1947, but after World War II, U.S.-Soviet enmity became associated with a new mode of warfare. Termed "nuclearism," it was initiated in 1945 with the bombing of the U.S. western desert and then Hiroshima and Nagasaki. While technocentrism suggests that the new weapon and its massive destructive power were key to the transformation that began that year, what changed, more importantly, was the perception of danger among the people purportedly protected by nuclear weapons and the new social relations that emerged because of these weapons' manufacture. Nuclearism's economy centered on producing more and more complex forms of the bomb and what are euphemistically called "platforms," such as jet fighters, nuclear submarines, and other forms of war machinery (Kaldor 1981). This mode of warfare allowed nations to keep smaller armies since air-delivered nuclear and other weapons replaced ground forces.[5] As weapons became more elaborate and fewer in number, the number of workers needed to produce them (and the unions associated with manufacturing) declined. Scientific and engineering labor—overwhelmingly white and male both in 1945 and today—became more important than manufacturing labor.

Nuclearism and the military budget undergirding it have not been neutral in their redistributional effects, exacerbating class, gender, and racial disparities in wealth and status. Military industrial jobs migrated to areas of the country with fewer African Americans. When women found work in such industries, they encountered a gender pay gap wider than the one prevailing in the civilian sector (Hardin 1991; Markusen and Yudken 1992). These workers were often nonunionized: Indeed, the Pentagon actively advocated relocation of weapons companies to nonunion areas, sometimes even billing taxpayers for the move. While North Carolina, for example, has numerous military bases, more Department of Defense tax dollars come out of North Carolina than go back into it (Markusen *et al.* 1991; Markusen and Yudken 1992), and the inability of localities to tax federal property has further impoverished the several counties from which Fort Bragg land was taken. One of those, Hoke County, with a heavy African American population, has been near the top of the state's 100 counties in its poverty rate, and the jobs it has been able to attract are mainly in its numerous prisons and poultry processing plants.

This mode of warfare also spawned expanded codes of secrecy to protect the technical knowledge involved in weapons development (as well as to hide the fraud and waste, accidents, and environmental costs entailed): The homosexual, in particular, was seen as a "weak link" who could be blackmailed to give up military secrets. Such fantasies envisioned the Soviets undermining U.S. culture from within (Dolan 1994). This secrecy also fundamentally deformed norms of democratic citizenship already under pressure from consumerist notions of self and eroded civil liberties. Nuclearism also reshaped forms of masculinity and femininity. The physical bravery and male bonding seen necessary for earlier forms of warfare were replaced by technical rationality and individual strength. Middle-class womanhood, too, was reframed: The home a woman kept for her family was newly conceived as a bomb shelter-like haven (May 1988).

While civilians died in large numbers during the first half of the century under industrial regimes of war (primarily in colonial wars but also in the European theatres of war), the nuclear mode of warfare sharply eroded the practical, if not the conceptual, distinction between soldiers and civilians, as each was equally targeted by other nuclear powers. This takes Tilly's (1985) point a step further: The power of governments with nuclear weapons is greatly strengthened, as much against its own people as others', forcing the people of nuclear nations into a more lopsided bargain with their states, trusting them with not only their own future but also with that of the human race. Nuclear empowerment also helped both the Soviet Union and the United States administer their populations by suggesting that the nation's survival depended on subsuming internal conflict to the demands of national unity. It is in this sense that Mary Kaldor (1991) called the nuclearism-based Cold War "the Imaginary War": war that was more scenario than actual battle, its cultural force came from managing internal social divisions (for example, controlling the demands of the civil rights movement in the United States) more than from its defense of the nation (see also Home 1986). So it was in Fayetteville in the 1950s that debates about Communism and Jim Crow were wedded. Segregationists argued that the subversive aims of the Soviets would be advanced through "race mixing" or by race conflict, which Communist propaganda would exploit. A local civil rights leader had to defend the need to integrate schools within the same paradigm: "Our deeds must match our ideals and words concerning the rights of men and their equality before the law, or the two-thirds of the world's population that is not white will turn to the communists for leadership. ... America [would then be] doomed to suffer attacks with atom and hydrogen bombs, leaving millions of us lying in unsegregated graves or interned in integrated prison camps" (Lutz 2001:114–115).

What some nuclear planners discovered, moreover, was that nuclear weapons were unusable, because (as one general observed of war itself) they "ruined a perfectly good army." They were also prone to kill downwinders and to accidents whose consequences were as likely to destroy lives at home or in colonial holdings like Micronesia (Alcalay 1984) as overseas. The 40 major nuclear accidents of the Cold War era contaminated U.S. and Soviet soil and water at their own hands, not the enemy's (Rogers 2000). This recognition occurred even as other planners fully contemplated first strike use to disable enemy nuclear capacities, even though a *single* one of the tens of thousands of extant nuclear weapons in the late 1950s would totally devastate a 500-square-mile area and start fires over an additional 1,500 square miles.

The nuclear mode of warfare also spawned a twin—proxy wars against both nonviolent and violent insurgencies that threatened U.S. and Soviet interests overseas. These movements arose especially in those societies in which class differences were gaping, but the insurgency wars were joined with U.S. and Soviet weapons and training particularly where investment or strategic aims were at stake. In those counterinsurgency wars, 10 million people lost their lives (Rogers 2000:35). Perception is as important as the reality, and official chronologies now speak of the "blessings" of nuclear weapons, ignoring this deflected body count as well as the environmental damage they and their proxy wars caused. Instead, they focus on the lack of a nuclear exchange between the superpowers, and call one party the "victor."[6] Despite the dissolution of the Soviet Union, a nuclear abolitionist movement, and the perception that nuclear weapons are a thing of the past, the United States continued to have 10,500 nuclear weapons in 2000 (Center for Defense Information 2002a). Nearly $65 billion has been spent on the chimerical idea of a nuclear "missile shield," a program that both continues the deterrence dream of nuclear warfare, on the one hand, and is a radically less spectacular (and bombastically masculine) form, "distinguished by stealth, speed, and accuracy ... far less arresting than the bomb and its mushroom cloud" (Lam 2001), on the other. The compression of time and space through these and other military means—the focus on seeing the enemy as tantamount to destroying his "assets"—has led some to call this another and new mode of warfare, the visual or the postmodern (Gray 1997; Virilio 1990).

During this period, the number of countries with substantial middle classes and dropping poverty rates increased, but the extent of structural violence intensified in other, especially African, states. This was the result of a steady decline in the price of raw materials, disinvestment in areas both intra- and internationally seen as "basket cases" or human refuse zones, and the increasing indebtedness of poorer states to wealthier ones and the banking enterprises within them. These factors meant an increasing rate of wealth flow from poorer to wealthier states. The promotion of neoliberalism by the elites of nations rich and poor has meant that whatever legal protections for local markets had been in place have been dismantled; the people who suffer as a result look for the source of their immiseration and find local elites rather than the foreign powers who might have once been so identified.

The post-Cold War period saw the United States emerge as human history's first truly global power. Even before the massive increases of 2002, its military spending was equal to that of the next 12 most significant national militaries combined. By way of comparison, Britain's 19th-century empire appears a weakling; the two next largest navies together equaled the British navy (Mann 2001:58). The reach of the U.S. military that began to widen in World War II remained breathtaking and unprecedented: There are currently 672 U.S. overseas military installations that serve as a far-flung archipelago of what is euphemistically called "forward basing" rather than imperial outposts.[7] "Platforms" such as battleships, nuclear submarines, and jets, as well as spy satellites and other listening posts, go even further toward creating a grid of operations and surveillance that comprehensively covers the globe.

The social and environmental costs of U.S. global military operations, however, include apartheid-like conditions, prostitution, and other retrogressive effects on women in the surrounding communities, and environmental devastation around bases at home and abroad (Armstrong 1999; Enloe 2000; Shulman 1992). Overseas, these costs have been levied in the name of these societies whose people are seen as helpmates to the explicit project of U.S. global patronage and policing. What all these military functions share is the idea of the potential necessity for the violent defense of white and male supremacism, now simply called "civilized values," against those of savagery or barbaric evil (Slotkin 1992).

While many people believe that the Cold War's end shrank the U.S. military substantially, it did not. There was an initial 18 percent drop in military spending, but a groundswell of aggressive lobbying by defense contractors, weapons labs, and the Pentagon mended the losses.[8] Budgets had reached the original Cold War levels of $343 billion even before September 11. The military, however, did restructure in the 1990s as business had in tune with the new tenor of a neoliberal age: It downsized and temped its force (active duty troops dropping from just over 2 million to about 1.4 million, and reserves increasing), outsourced more of its work (training the militaries of other countries to do proxy work for U.S. interests, while retaining plausible deniability when human rights abuses occur), and it privatized some of its otherwise public workforce (as when it gave the contract for guarding Fort Bragg's huge ammunition dump to a private security firm) (Sheppard 1998). With the demise of the Soviet Union, U.S. military industries became not just the source of the state's coercive power but also of its economic power in a more direct sense: It became the largest global merchant of arms, exporting as much as all other arms producing countries combined.[9]

New war-making doctrines were developed, their intention or outcome being to protect the military and its industries from decimation. Christened "Operations Other than War," they included Evacuation Operations, Support to Domestic Civil Authorities, and Disaster Relief, among many others. Some missions gave the military tasks once seen as civilian jobs, such as famine relief. As it took on social and policing jobs that one soldier from Fayetteville described dismissively to me as "babysitting," it could seem that the army was demilitarizing.

Such contradictory effects are also evident in the response to environmental damage found on the military bases that were closed to allow reallocation of funds to military industry purchases. On the one hand, the mess, sometimes of monumental proportions, was cleaned up partially with EPA funds, which could be considered militarized when allocated to that purpose. On the other hand, military funds might be considered demilitarized when they were used to clean and convert bases to civilian uses.

It was in this flurry of new mission development that "humanitarian war" came to be seen, not as oxymoron but as an adjunct to human rights work and democratic aspirations around the world. It emerged as the newest mode of warfare and was distinguished from ordinary modern warfare primarily by its ideological force. This is a powerful and paradoxical combination of social evolutionist and human rights discourse. The reinvigoration of social evolutionism in the United States in the 1980s and 1990s was evident and promoted in books proclaiming a "clash of civilizations" between the Western and advanced, and the barbaric elsewheres, or predicting a "coming anarchy" of clashes between the rich and poor nations, but with an America triumphant because of its superior culture (Huntington 1996; Kaplan 1994). The humanitarian wars that drew on these various and seemingly antithetical discourses did little to prevent or stop such gross human rights violations as the genocide in Rwanda, the 1999 massacres in East Timor, and the rubbling of Chechnya by the Russians; this is an index of the frequent use of the term *humanitarian war* as pretext for other national purposes.

Humanitarian warfare has often been twinned (as was nuclearism with counterinsurgency) with what Mary Kaldor identifies as "the New Wars." Paramilitaries fight these wars without clear lines of command; they target civilians with torture, rape, and terror bombings. Their aim is "to sow fear and discord, to instill unbearable memories of what was once home, to desecrate whatever has social meaning" (Kaldor and Vashee 1997:16).[10] As Carolyn Nordstrom (1997) has noted, their intention to prevent dissent or even discussion is signified by their frequent maiming of eyes, ear, and tongues. These are often civil wars rather than wars between states and they have involved the use of "small" or inexpensive arms that are thereby made widely available, further raising the death toll of civilians that reached 90 percent of all war deaths by the end of the century. In some cases, U.S. arms and training are thrown on one side or the other in line with larger strategic interests, and especially in pursuit of corporate access to resources and labor. Some forms of new warfare need no weapons or soldiers at all, such as the deadly use of sanctions in Iraq. Warfare it is, however, with its intention to coerce regime change through bodily suffering (Arnove 2000).

The United States has increasingly relied on executive order for engagement in war, an antidemocratic practice that became ensconced with the national security state in 1947 (Lens 1987). So did the rise of so-called black budgets in military agencies, which were estimated at $39 billion per year in the late 1980s; these are tax dollars exempt from public knowledge or oversight (Weiner 1990). Antidemocratic effects also accompanied the turn from a conscripted to an all-volunteer force, which came in 1973 in response to active rebellion within the military against the war and played out on Fayetteville's streets and at Fort Bragg (Lutz 2001).

The volunteer army rearranged the exchanges that had taken place between the state and citizens during the era of conscription: Civilians were no longer potential involuntary soldiers or sacrificers of their children, but spectators (Mann 1987). The soldiers recruited became increasingly conservative in their politics, something that has changed the political climate in Fayetteville as well as throughout the nation. While tacitly remembering the Army's rebellion, however, explicit politically molded memories of the Vietnam era suggest a still unreciprocated bargain with veterans of that war that continues to shape both political culture and military strategy (Gibson 1994). These various forms of memory, for example, have lowered tolerance for U.S. battlefield deaths. Together with the longstanding ascendancy of the Air Force and Navy among service branches under the regime of nuclearism in which they specialized, this has meant a sometimes nearly exclusive reliance on aerial bombardment in U.S.-led wars. This is a devastating choice for the people of a host of countries targeted for such attention (Blum 1995), but one that ensured fewer political costs for the United States whose populace could be convinced that there was moral virtue (the bombs were labeled *smart*) and little cost to the nation from warfare so waged.

The people of the United States emerged from the Cold War $16 trillion dollars (Center for Defense Information 2002b:43) poorer, however. If the concept of friendly fire were extended to structural violence, the impoverishment would be much greater. It would include joblessness, attendant human suffering, and premature deaths and hunger that have resulted from the inequalities the military budget exacerbates. It does this by creating fewer jobs per dollar spent than equivalent social spending (Anderson 1982) and by derailing the movement for expanded social welfare benefits, as noted above. In Fayetteville, where the contrast in benefits given soldiers and civilians is most visible (even as some of the lowest rank-enlisted soldiers with families qualify for food stamps), this division plays out rancorously. The upper hand in the debate, however, goes to those who can appeal to the idea of soldiering as a unrecompensable sacrifice for the nation (even as the likelihood of death in battle has been mini-scule over the last 20 years, when a total of 563 American soldiers died from "enemy" fire).[11] With the growing "transnationalism" of corporate operations and the search for cheap labor overseas, that violence has increasingly been from the fist inside the glove of neoliberal trade policies and foreign loans, which together have provided the means and rationale for the flow of resources and wealth from the south to the north, the brown to the white areas of the globe. It remains an entrenched notion among the U.S. population, however—increasingly subject to control of information flows about global realities by media beholden to corporate and state interests—that aid and wealth flows from north to south.[12]

This larger picture of militarization and its history is connected to particular communities and individual lives. The long home front and its future fate hinge on our reconnecting both sides of the fence that separates the Fort Braggs and the Fayettevilles and seeing what militarization has wrought both at home and abroad. The current crisis and the socioeconomic and legal changes that it has already prompted will take their steep toll first in those places like Fayetteville that are most enmeshed in military institutions. An understanding of their past and present predicament can provide transferable insights to other places and help elucidate how the national context has come to have the textures it does. Ethnographic understanding of militarization's shaping of all U.S. places seems an urgent project for anthropology, as it will allow us to see the seams, fissures, and costs in the otherwise seemingly monolithic and beneficent face of state-corporate-media war making.

MILITARIZATION AND THE CURRENT CRISIS

How can the national, historical, and local ethnographic understanding just outlined help us understand the current crisis? There are deep continuities with the past, despite the claim that September 11 represented a major historical rupture both because the United States was attacked and because it announced merely the beginning of a campaign of terrorism that fundamentally threatens global well-being. The attacks on New York and Washington are said to represent a new asymmetric warfare in which a militarily much smaller adversary exploits weaknesses to strike blows at a larger power with minimal costs to itself.[13] Guerrilla warfare, however, has been similarly defined. Forces within the state claimed to require new monies and powers to combat this novel risk. Regardless of the name used, the state was to engage in much business as usual, which is to say purchases of expensive weapon systems such as battleships and nuclear weaponry designed for earlier modes of warfare. While their expensive weaponry and surveillance equipment were completely irrelevant, as we saw, to the box cutters of September 11, military industrial corporations like General Dynamics, Raytheon, and Lockheed Martin experienced a sharp rise in their stock prices in the immediate wake of the September 11 attacks. They were to be the prime beneficiaries of the immediate increase of $48 billion dollars and the five-year increase of $120 billion in the military budget proposed by the Bush administration with the crisis mentality created by September 11.[14] This war, like others of the 20th century, will differentially affect the fortunes of various social sectors in the United States, increasing social inequality nationally and in places like Fayetteville.

Continuities of discursive militarization abound as well: the simple dualisms of Manichean nationalism in which evil empires or terrorist networks confront the Goodness of U.S. freedom; the blurring of the boundary between policing and soldiering, and between the civilian and the military worlds and identities, even as those boundaries have been sharpened in other ways, and especially through the allocation of a kind of supercitizenship to soldiers (Kraska and Kappeler 1997; Lutz 2001); the growth of secrecy and erosion of civil liberties, although with the recent crisis the drop seems especially precipitous; and the melding of state and media pronouncements on the war that has been ongoing as media mergers and corporatization (sometimes with the very companies that have so benefited from militarization) have intensified since deregulation in the 1980s (Bagdikian 2000; MacArthur 1992). In this war, the press has militarized even more dramatically, boosting "America's New War" (this CNN moniker itself a kind of ad or "branding") as a new commodity. The state has used the tools of public relations in modern warfare since early in the 20th century; this process is simply accelerating in the current crisis. A professional firm has been hired to manage information flow and interpretation and the Pentagon's specialists in disinformation have received more funding, new offices, and new names. Their work includes both a careful whitewashing of the extent and "look" of war deaths, particularly of civilians, and collaboration with Hollywood fiction filmmakers.[15]

Moreover, the notion that we have encountered radically new conditions of global and national life draws attention away from the fact that the bombing of Afghanistan (and of other countries that may follow in the days between the writing and your reading of this article) has causes deeper in the past and broader in scope than the planning and carrying out of the terror attacks on New York and Washington. U.S. support for the Taliban in the immediate period leading up to the bombing was fueled by the desire to "normalize" relations in the interest of securing a trans-Afghanistan pipeline to Central Asian oilfields for U.S. corporate and strategic interests (Rashid 2000). In this, the story is similar to many instances where repressive regimes were supplied arms and money in exchange for access to resources (Klare 2001). The list includes Saudi Arabia, Israel, Iran, Iraq, Guatemala, El Salvador, Honduras, Chile, South Korea, Indonesia, South Vietnam, and so on. With their country's food poverty and relative arms wealth, the Afghans in power share characteristics with many regimes around the world, where a generation of war, much of it originally Cold War enflamed, has created the social conditions for militancy.

Sources of hope are available. Pressures for demilitarization have exerted themselves throughout global and U.S. national history. In the United States, an antimilitarist tradition has been a vigorous force at many points from the framing of the Constitution through the anti-ROTC movement of the World War I period to the antiwar novels and films of the 1930s and the 1960s to the current mass movement to combat the democratic losses and intensified militarizations of this most recent period (Ekirch 1956).[16] That tradition has existed within the military as well. Dwight Eisenhower, an important example, expressed his unhappiness with the mushrooming military budget of the 1950s and believed it "would leave the nation a militarized husk, hardly worth defending" (Brands 1999). People around the world have made claims against impunity for repressive government and paramilitary forces from Israel to Colombia to South Africa (Feldman 1998; Gill and Green in press; Hitchens 2001; Said 2001). The international human rights movement helped bring down Eastern European police states, made possible a dramatic rise in international legal mechanisms to control violence, and pressed to define not only physical violence but also structural violence as a human rights violation. The Jubilee and nuclear abolitionist movements gained wide support, and conventions against the use of landmines, chemical and biological weapons, nuclear weapons testing, and State torture have been almost universally accepted.[17] In just one instance, as this article was being completed, a treaty to ban the use of children as soldiers had just come into force, a claim against the current use of an estimated half-million children in militaries and paramilitaries worldwide. Voluminous and immediate sources of information to counter official lies as well as avenues for solidarity and antimilitarization work have opened up with the internet.

CONCLUSION

I vividly remember a day in the early 1980s when the anthropologist Ben Colby began to speak at a small conference on culture and cognition. He had been studying the distinct beauty and richness of mathematical thinking among the Ixil people of Guatemala. He said he could not talk of mathematics and cognition in Guatemala because his friends there were dead or fleeing in panic from the aerial bombardments of the scorched earth campaign viciously perpetrated by the Guatemalan military: Their anticommunism was a front for landowners' anxiety about other Guatemalans' claims for fairness in land allocation, labor conditions, and allowable identities in their own communities. It was an ideology in some synchrony with U.S. anticommunism, and training and arming the Guatemalan military (Schirmer 1998). He brought the war home to us, as a previous group of anthropologists brought the war in Vietnam home to the discipline. As each of these clarion calls grew fainter, with the urge to "normalcy" and to "innocence," anthropological thoughts turned on how to write less imperial ethnographies, but not ethnographies of imperialism.

Our practice of anthropology has not prevented many of the hundreds of thousands of college graduates who have taken our courses from being shocked by the violent opening of the 21st century. Students may have encountered an anthropology that deconstructed the myth of a single modernity and of progress. They may even have learned about the violence that plagues other lands and been taught to seek its sources in inequalities and ideologies. They may have heard about the vast' genocide and enslavements that accompanied the encounter between "Europe and the People without History." Yet too few were shown the tortured bodies and burned landscapes visible behind a Potemkin multicultural village. Too few were confronted with the idea of the U.S. Imperium, of global militarization, and of the cultural politics, that make its wars seem either required of moral persons or simply to be waited out, like bad weather. These missing pieces of anthropological knowledge have only now come home to roost with great urgency. Would that they had not, but because they have, we now are called to address the realistic and unrealistic fears of our students, neighbors and colleagues, and work tirelessly to ensure those fears are redirected to the irrationalities and hidden purposes behind the glittering face of power and its moral claims.

NOTES

1. The usual periodization of the World Wars might more aptly be World Wars Ia and Ib.
2. See Lutz 1999 for a historical account of ethnography's relationship to war.
3. For a fuller account of this relationship and review of the literature that gives it ethnographic depth, see Lutz and Nonini 1999.

4. The race hatred that fueled World War II was evident in the exterminationist aims of many Allied actions against the Japanese; in contrast, the Germans and Italians were sorted into the good and the bad among them (Dower 1986).

5. The U.S. Army's size and budget, for example, shrank by half and the Air Force grew explosively in the early 1950s (Bacevich 1986). This also fundamentally shaped U.S. science and engineering, as its talent went to work in military R and D, which took fully 70 percent of federal research dollars by the mid 1980s (Marullo 1993:145).

6. How this becomes possible has been traced by Gusterson in his important study of U.S. nuclear scientists (1996). The lobbying and educational role of the transnational community of dissident nuclear scientists, however, was one key to the Soviet Union's embarking on a course of denuclearization before its demise (Evangelista 1999).

7. Including national guard, reserve, and minor installations, there were 3,660 global U.S. military sites in 1999 (U.S. Department of Defense 2000).

8. These are among the interests that Marullo (1993) has dubbed the "Iron Pentagon": military contractors (whose profits were double those of other corporations in the 1980s), the Defense Department, weapons laboratories, Congress (with members heavily subsidized by military corporate donations), and military industry labor.

9. The United States had 49 percent of the share of global arms exports in 1999, which totaled $53 billion (International Institute for Security Studies 2001).

10. See Sluka 2000 on the unparalleled contemporary levels of state and extrastate torture and terror.

11. The combat death total is equivalent to the number of people who die every five days on U.S. roads (a number that could count as an indirect war death, as traffic fatalities are much lower in countries that invested in public transportation more than in armies) (National Center for Statistics and Analysis 2001).

12. See Mann 2001 for important distinctions between regions.

13. Some strategists define asymmetric warfare as an indirect approach to affect a counterbalancing of force, and see it as more likely in the world of a single overwhelming hegemony like the United States.

14. This would bring the Department of Defense total to $451 billion in 2007, a figure that excludes many additional billions of military-related costs (such as interest on the debt) found in other budget categories.

15. In October 2001, studio heads announced they would help wage war on terrorism through their products. One of them, *Black Hawk Down,* was made in close consultation with the Pentagon and the White House, which edited the final script (International A.N.S.W.E.R. 2002).

16. On long-standing campaigns to demilitarize U.S. public schools and offer counterrecruitment information see, for example, American Friends Service Committee 2001.

17. The United States often voted alone or with a very small set of states, often those termed "rogue" by the United States itself, against any limits on its military's prerogatives; votes, for example, were 109–1, 95–1, 98–1, and 84–1 on 1980s resolutions to ban the proliferation of chemical and biological weapons, and 116–1 and 125–1 on resolutions prohibiting the development and testing of new weapons of mass destruction (McGowan 2000).

REFERENCES CITED

Adams, Michael C. C. 1994. The Best War Ever: America and World War II. Baltimore: Johns Hopkins University Press.

Alcalay, Glen. 1984. Maelstrom in the Marshall Islands: The Social Impact of Nuclear Weapons Testing. In Micronesia as Strategic Colony: The Impact of U.S. Policy on Micronesian Health and Culture. Catherine Lutz, ed. Pp. 25–36. Cambridge: Cultural Survival Occasional Papers.

American Friends Service Committee. 2001 [1998]. National Youth and Militarism Program. Electronic document, www.afsc.org/youthmil.htm. Accessed May 21.

Anderson, Marion. 1982. The Price of the Pentagon. Lansing, MI: Employment Research Associates.

Aretxaga, Begona. 1997. Shattering Silence: Women, Nationalism, and Political Subjectivity in Northern Ireland. Princeton: Princeton University Press.

Armstrong, David. 1999. The Nation's Dirty, Big Secret. The Boston Globe, November 14: Al.

Arnove, Anthony, ed. 2000. Iraq under Siege: The Deadly Impact of Sanctions and War. Boston: South End Press.

Bacevich, A.J. 1986. The Pentomic Era: The U.S. Army between Korea and Vietnam. Washington, DC: National Defense University Press.

Bagdikian, Ben H. 2000. The Media Monopoly. 6th edition. Boston: Beacon Press.

Baran, Paul, and Paul Sweezy. 1966. Monopoly Capital: An Essay on the American Economic and Social Order. New York: Monthly Review Press.

Belich, James. 1986. The Victorian Interpretation of Racial Conflict: The Maori, The British, and the New Zealand Wars. Montreal: McGill-Queen's University Press.

Bernstein, Barton J. 1999. Reconsidering "Invasion Most Costly": Popular-History Scholarship, Publishing Standards, and the Claim of High U.S. Casualty Estimates to Help Legitimize the Atomic Bombings. Peace and Change 24(2):220–248.

Blum, William. 1995. Killing Hope: U.S. Military and CIA Interventions since World War II. Monroe, ME: Common Courage Press.

Bourgois, Philippe. 1996. In Search of Respect: Selling Crack in El Barrio. Cambridge: Cambridge University Press.

Bourne, Randolph. 1964. War and the Intellectuals: Essays by Randolph S. Bourne, 1915–1919. Carl Resek, ed. New York: Harper Torchbooks. Brands, H. W.

——1999. Review of Destroying the Village: Eisenhower and Thermonuclear War. Journal of American History 86(2):839–840.

Center for Defense Information. 2002a. The World's Nuclear Arsenals. Electronic document, http://www.cdi.org/issues/nukef&f/data-base/nukearsenals.html#United States. Accessed April 1.

——2002b. 2001–2002. Military Almanac. Washington, DC: Center for Defense Information.

D'Amico, Francine. 1997. Policing the U.S. Military's Race and Gender Lines. In Wives and Warriors: Women and the Military in the United States and Canada. Laurie Weinstein and Christie C. White, eds. Pp. 199–234. Westport, CT: Bergin and Garvey.

Daniel, E. Valentine. 1996. Charred Lullabies: Chapters in an Anthropology of Violence. Princeton: Princeton University Press.

Das, Veena. 1990. Mirrors of Violence: Communities, Riots and Survivors in South Asia. Oxford: Oxford University Press.

Dolan, Frederick M. 1994. Allegories of America: Narratives, Metaphysics, Politics. Ithaca: Cornell University Press.

Dower, John W. 1986. War without Mercy. New York: Pantheon Books.

Ekirch, Arthur, Jr. 1956. The Civilian and the Military. New York: Oxford University Press.

Ellis, John. 1975. A Social History of the Machine Gun. New York: Pantheon.

Engelhardt, Tom. 1995. The End of Victory Culture: Cold War America and the Disillusioning of a Generation. New York: Basic Books.

Enloe, Cynthia. 2000. Maneuvers: The International Politics of Militarizing Women's Lives. Berkeley: University of California Press.

Evangelista, Matthew. 1999. Unarmed Forces: The Transnational Movement to End the Cold War. Ithaca: Cornell University Press.

Farmer, Paul. 1996. Infections and Inequalities: The Modern Plague. Berkeley: University of California Press.

Feldman, Allen. 1991. Formations of Violence: The Narrative of the Body and Political Terror in Northern Ireland. Chicago: University of Chicago Press.

——1998. Faux Documentary and the Memory of Realism. American Anthropologist 100(2):494–501.

Geyer, Michael. 1989. The militarization of Europe, 1914–1945. In The Militarization of the Western World. John Gillis ed. Pp. 65–102. New Brunswick, NJ: Rutgers University Press.

Gibson, James William. 1994. Warrior Dreams: Paramilitary Culture in Post-Vietnam America. New York: Hill and Wang.

Gill, Lesley, and Linda Green, eds. In press Biting the Bullet. Santa Fe: School of American Research Press.

Goode, Judith, and Jeff Maskovsky. 2001. The New Poverty Studies: The Ethnography of Politics, Policy and Impoverished People in the U.S. New York: New York University Press.

Gray, Chris Hables. 1997. Postmodern War: The New Politics of Conflict. New York: Guilford Press.

Green, Linda. 1994. Fear as a Way of Life. Cultural Anthropology 9(2):227–256.

Gusterson, Hugh. 1996. Nuclear Rites: A Weapons Laboratory at the End of the Cold War. Berkeley: University of California Press.

——1999. Nuclear Weapons and the Other in the Western Imagination. Cultural Anthropology 14 (1):111–143.

Hardin, Bristow. 1991. The Militarized Social Democracy and Racism: The Relationship between Militarism, Racism and Social Welfare Policy in the United States. Ph.D. dissertation, Department of Sociology, University of California at Santa Cruz.

Hitchens, Christopher. 2001. The Trial of Henry Kissinger. London: Verso.

Hochschild, Adam. 1998. King Leopold's Ghost: A Story of Greed, Terror, and Heroism in Colonial Africa. Boston: Houghton Mifflin.

Hopper, Kim. 1991. A Poor Apart: The Distancing of Homeless Men on New York's History. Social Research 58(1): 107–133.

Horne, Gerald. 1986. Black and Red: W. E. B. Du Bois and the Afro-American Response to the Cold War, 1944–1963. Albany: State University of New York Press.

Huntington, Samuel P. 1996. The Clash of Civilizations and the Remaking of World Order. New York: Simon and Schuster.

International A.N.S.W.E.R. 2002. Protest "Black Hawk Down." Electronic document, www.in-ternationalanswer.org/news/update/011802blackhawkdown.html. Accessed April 1.

International Institute for Security Studies. 2001. The Military Balance 2000–2001. London: Oxford University Press.

Jensen, Joan M. 1991. Army Surveillance in America,177S-1980.NewHaven, CT: Yale University Press.

Kaldor, Mary. 1981. The Baroque Arsenal. New York: Hill and Wang.

——1991. The Imaginary War: Understanding the East-West Conflict. London: Blackwell.

Kaldor, Mary, and Basker Vashee, eds.

1997. Restructuring the Global Military Sector, vol. 1: New Wars. London: Pinter.

Kaplan, Amy, and Donald E. Pease, eds. 1993. Cultures of United States Imperialism. Durham, NC: Duke University Press.

Kaplan, R. D. 1994. The Coming Anarchy. Atlantic Monthly 273(2):44–76.

Karsten, Peter. 1989. Militarization and Rationalization in the United States, 1870–1914. In The Militarization of the Western World. John Gillis, ed. Pp. 30–44. New Brunswick, NJ: Rutgers University Press.

Klare, Michael. 2001. Resource Wars. New York: Metropolitan Books.

Kraska, Peter B., and Victor E. Kappeler. 1997. Militarizing American Police: The Rise and Normalization of Paramilitary Units. Social Problems 44(1):1–18.

Lam, Ilisa. 2001. Turbulent Spaces, Shifting Discourses: Gendered Dimensions of American Militarization in the Western Pacific. Paper presented at the American Ethnological Society annual meetings, Montreal, Canada, May 3–6.

Lens, Sidney. 1987. Permanent War: The Militarization of America. New York: Schocken.

Leslie, Stuart W. 1993. The Cold War and American Science: The Military-Industrial-Academic Complex at MIT and Stanford. New York: Columbia University Press.

Linenthal, Edward T., and Tom Engelhardt, eds. 1996. History Wars: The Enola Gay and Other Battles for the American Past. New York: Metropolitan Books/Henry Holt and Co.

Lotchin, Roger W., ed. 1984. The Martial Metropolis: U.S. Cities in War and Peace. New York: Praeger.

Lutz, Catherine. 1997. The Psychological Ethic and the Spirit of Containment. Public Culture 9:135–159.

——1999. Ethnography at the War Century's End. "Ethnography: Reflections at the Century's End," theme issue, Journal of Contemporary Ethnography 28(6):610–619.

——2001. Homefront: A Military City and the American Twentieth Century. Boston: Beacon Press.

Lutz, Catherine, and Donald Nonini. 1999. The Economies of Violence and the Violence of Economies. In Anthropological Theory Today. Henrietta Moore, ed. Pp. 73–113. London: Polity Press.

MacArthur, John. 1992. SecondFront: Censorship and Propaganda in the Gulf War. New York: Hill and Wang.

Mahmood, Cynthia Keppley. 1996. Fighting for Faith and Nation: Dialogues with Sikh Militants. Philadelphia: University of Pennsylvania Press.

Malkki, Liisa. 1995. Purity and Exile: Violence, Memory, and National Cosmology among Huto Refugees in Tanzania. Chicago: University of Chicago Press.

Mann, Michael. 1987. The Roots and Contradictions of Modern Militarism. New Left Review 162:35–50.

——2001. Globalization and September 11. New Left Review (n.s.) 12:51–72.

Markusen, Ann, Peter Hall, Scott Campbell, and Sabina Deitrick. 1991. The Rise of the Gunbelt: The Military Remapping of Industrial America. New York: Oxford University Press.

Markusen, Ann, and Joel Yudken. 1992. Dismantling the Cold War Economy. New York: Basic Books.

Marullo, Sam. 1993. Ending the Cold War at Home: From Militarism to a More Peaceful World Order. New York: Lexington Books.

May, Elaine Tyler. 1988. Homeward Bound: American Families in the Cold War Era. New York: Basic Books.

McGowan, David. 2000. Derailing Democracy: The America the Media Don't Want You to See. Monroe, ME: Common Courage Press.

Mills, C. Wright. 1956. The Power Elite. New York: Oxford University Press.

Nash, June. 1979. We Eat the Mines and the Mines Eat Us: Dependency and Exploitation in Bolivian Tin Mines. New York: Columbia University Press.

National Center for Statistics and Analysis. 2001. 2000. Annual Assessment of Motor Vehicle Crashes. Electronic document, www-nrd.nhtsa.dot.gov/pdf/nrd-30/NCSA/ Rpts/2001/Assess2K.pdf. Accessed April 1.

Newman, Katherine S. 1999. No Shame in My Game: The Working Poor in the Inner City. New York: Knopf.

Nordstrom, Carolyn. 1997. A Different Kind of War Story. Philadelphia: University of Pennsylvania Press.

Perret, Geoffrey. 1989. A Country Made by War: From the Revolution to Vietnam—The Story of America's Rise to Power. New York: Random House.

Rashid, Ahmed. 2000. Taliban: Militant Islam, Oil and Fundamentalism. New Haven, CT: Yale University Press.

Rogers, Paul. 2000. Losing Control: Global Security in the Twenty-First Century. London: Pluto Press.

Said, Edward. 2001. The Public Role of Writers and Intellectuals. The Nation, September 17: 27–36.

Scheper-Hughes, Nancy. 1992. Death without Weeping: The Violence of Everyday Life in Brazil. Berkeley: University of California Press. Schirmer, Jennifer G.

——1998. The Guatemalan Military Project: A Violence Called Democracy. Philadelphia: University of Pennsylvania Press.

Sheppard, Simon. 1998. Foot Soldiers of the New World Order: The Rise of the Corporate Military. New Left Review 228:128–138.

Sherry, Michael S. 1995. In the Shadow of War: The United States since the 1930s. New Haven, CT: Yale University Press.

Shulman, Seth. 1992. The Threat at Home: Confronting the Toxic Legacy of the U.S. Military. Boston: Beacon Press.

Sider, Gerald M. 1986. Culture and Class in Anthropology and History: A New-foundland Illustration. Cambridge: Cambridge University Press.

Skocpol, Theda. 1993. Protecting Soldiers and Mothers: The Political Origins of Social Policy in the United States. Cambridge: Cambridge University Press.

Slotkin, Richard. 1992. Gunfighter Nation: The Myth of the Frontier in Twentieth-Century America. New York: Harper Perennial.

Sluka, Jeffrey A. ed. 2000. Death Squad: The Anthropology of State Terror. Philadelphia: University of Pennsylvania Press.

Starn, Orin. 1999. Night Watch: The Politics of Protest in Peru. Durham, NC: Duke University Press.

Susser, Ida. 1996. The Construction of Poverty and Homelessness in U.S. Cities. Annual Review of Anthropology 25:411–435.

Taussig, Michael. 1987. Shamanism, Colonialism, and the Wild Man: A Study in Terror and Healing. Chicago: University of Chicago Press.

Tilly, Charles. 1985. War Making and State Making as Organized Crime. In Bringing the State Back In. Peter Evans, Dietrich Rueschemeyer, and Theda Skocpol, eds. Cambridge: Cambridge University Press.

U.S. Department of Defense, Office of the Deputy Under Secretary of Defense (Installations) 2000. Department of Defense Base Structure Report, Fiscal Year 1999. Washington, DC: Government Printing Office.

Virilio, Paul. 1990. War and Cinema: The Logistics of Perception. P. Camiller, trans. London: Verso.

Weigley, Russell F. 1967. History of the United States Army. New York: Macmillan.

Weiner, Tim. 1990. Blank Check: The Pentagon's Black Budget. New York: Warner Books.

Williams, Brett. 1994. Babies and Banks: The "Reproductive Underclass" and the Raced, Gendered Masking of Debt. In Race. Steven Gregory and Roger Sanjek, eds. Pp. 348–365. New Brunswick, NJ: Rutgers University Press.

17

Pink Collar Bajans
Working Class Through Gender and Culture on the Global Assembly Line
Carla Freeman

One hot afternoon at the crowded Lower Green bus stand in Bridgetown, Barbados, schoolchildren in neat uniforms and shoppers laden with heavy parcels hiding from the baking sun found their own hushed conversations punctuated by sudden shouting and defensive retorts. The morning shift at Global Informatics Ltd. had been busy, and most of the data processors had worked overtime the day before, catching up on a heavy batch of credit card receipts from a Canadian client company. Five of the sixty young women workers in the shift emerged from the glass doors of Barbados's newest informatics company, animated as they compared their daily work rates and resultant pay. All were data processors and all but one had achieved the "incentive" bonus earned by fulfilling a ten-thousand-keystroke-per-hour minimum. The bonuses, together with overtime pay, had boosted their wages for the week by roughly 25 percent. At the shift's end, comparing their newly posted production rates, the women had changed from slippers to patent leather or well-polished high heels and now they ambled slowly toward the bus stand. The commotion that erupted there centered on Christine, one of the data processors who was nicely turned out in a bold floral skirt suit and an elaborately braided hair style. Suddenly Paul, her former boyfriend, who had been waiting for her under a shady breadfruit tree, began shouting and motioning wildly for everyone around to look closely. "You see *she?* You *see* she?" he exclaimed. "Don' mind she dress so. When Friday come, she only carryin' home ninety-eight dollar." What his outburst conveyed was, "In case you people might mistake her for a middle-class woman with a good office job, let me tell you, she is really just a village girl with a factory wage." Onlookers shifted their feet. Some showed signs of disdain for the public airing of a domestic dispute; a group of

Carla Freeman, "Pink Collar Bajans: Working Class Through Gender and Culture on the Global Assembly Line," *Carla Freeman High Tech and High Heels in the Global Economy*, pp. 21–65. Copyright © 2000 by Duke University Press. Reprinted with permission.

schoolgirls laughed. The taunts so disturbed another group of data processors at the bus stand that some beckoned a manager to come outside and "stop the palava."

The threat posed by mocking the image of prosperity and professionalism of the data processors is conveyed in a Barbadian adage that warns, "Gold teet don' suit hog mout" and implies that even extravagant adornments can't hide one's true station in life. The adage and the story together reveal a deep tradition of propriety and expectations of conformity between class status and appearance. For "Little England," the once-prized sugar isle of the British empire, conformity and respectability lie at the heart of cultural tradition, and "knowing one's place" is an admonition well known to Bajans of all generations. By exposing the reality of Christine's meager wage in contrast to her impressive appearance, the disgruntled former boyfriend threatened to undermine a powerful set of images conscientiously created and enforced by women workers and the informatics industry that employs them. While dress may seem peripheral or "superstructural" to a study of women workers on the global assembly line, here amid the high-tech glow of computer terminals within this new niche of the "office-factory," dress and appearance become vital embodiments of the informatics sector and of new feminine identities for working women as members of the new pink-collar service class.[1]

This brief story elucidates a convergence between realms of tradition and modernity, gender and class—where transnational capital and production, the Barbadian state, and young Afro-Caribbean women together fashion a new "classification" of woman worker who, as gendered producer and consumer is fully enmeshed in global and local, economic and cultural processes. This new classification of pink-collar worker is made possible by the ambiguous place of informatics within the bounded categories of manufacturing and service sectors of the economy, and between blue-collar as opposed to white-collar labor. The story suggests how problematic these polarities are. Informatics is predicated on some of our most potent icons of modernity—sophisticated computer technologies, new satellite communications, and jet transportation—and the power of these images and symbols contributes significantly to the appeal of these jobs to recent secondary school graduates. Indeed, modernity and traditional notions of Barbadianness are bound up together in this new enclave, as they have been in the very formation of the Caribbean as a region. Eric Williams ([1944] 1994) asserted that the scale and global importance of the region's sugar industry placed it firmly in the forefront of the modern industrial world, and he provocatively argued that the Caribbean was modern even before Europe itself (see also Mintz [1974] 1989; Sutton 1987; Trouillot 1992). This view challenges us to think of modernity, not as a singular benchmark set by Britain or by Europe as a whole, but in a plural form (modernities), and to see the Caribbean, not as a "backward" outpost of the "modern" West, but as an early expression of the economic and cultural complexities of modernity.

Starting from the premise that the Caribbean is quintessentially modern, transnational, and creolized, this book explores the ways in which tradition and modernity and local and global culture and economies inflect the experiential and symbolic dimensions of gender and class in Barbados in the new industry of informatics. This chapter sets the scene by describing the ways in which recent changes in the transnational economy and its restructuring of clerical work affect Afro-Barbadian women and gendered identities associated with particular kinds of work in the Caribbean. I begin by exploring the emergence of the "global assembly line" and its recent incorporation of clerical work as a feminized, proletarianized "pink-collar" sector. In the Anglophone Afro-Caribbean, where women's work has long been integral to the island's economy and to its emphasis on "respectability," what emerges from this global/local conjuncture is that women's identities, as feminine members of the working class, become refashioned through a set of gendered practices encoded in the concept of "professionalism" enacted on the production floor, as well as in modes of consumption associated with the new informatics industry. This observation demands that we look simultaneously at their engagement in production (both formal wage-earning jobs and informal "after hours" income-generating labor) and the importance of new practices of consumption in ways that are seldom brought together in analyses of globalization. In the light of the important recent emphasis on the triangulation of race, class, and gender, especially for Caribbean studies, I note at the outset that race is a less central workplace issue at the local industry level of informatics given the relatively homogeneous Afro-Caribbean racial identities of both management and labor force of the companies studied. It operates more dramatically, however, at the macro level of the international division of labor. The movement of multinational industry has tended to go from "whiter" industrialized nations to "darker" third world countries, and as such we witness a racialized international division of labor.[2] In some territories of the Caribbean, most notably Trinidad, Guyana and Suriname, race and ethnicity are the central divisions of social and political life, and in the region at large, color and class stratification are tightly interconnected. In Barbados, while part of this continuum, the racial and ethnic matrix is somewhat distinct. There remains a small local nonblack population (roughly 5 percent), including (but not limited to) a white corporate elite that owns or controls a significant portion of the island's major industrial sectors (Beckles 1989a), though the public sector is entirely under the control of Afro-Barbadians.[3] Within informatics, race enters the scene less in explicit structural hierarchy than in the form of verbal play and rhetorical styles of reference,[4] and ownership of local informatics companies is both "black" and "white."[5] Black Barbadians own two of the three local firms, and a North American company and a local, historically white company jointly own the third.[6] Management and supervisory positions are held almost entirely by black Barbadians, trained by overseas representatives, with no apparent "color" hierarchy in which phenotypically lighter managers appear higher in the organizational structure than darker ones. Similarly, hiring and promotion practices at all levels show none of the pattern of racial hierarchy that is often described in other parts of the region. I therefore focus on the relationships between gender and class with regard to Barbadian history and culture and the island's embeddedness in the global cultural economy. In my emphasis on the relationships between production and consumption, I take up recent theoretical debates about social class and status by probing the ways in which the gendered emergence of off-shore services as a new arena of work challenges previous conceptualizations of class identity and expectations of class consciousness. I begin with the global picture and move to the local.

GLOBALIZATION AND NEW INTERNATIONAL DIVISIONS OF LABOR

"Globalization" and "transnationalism" can be seen as cliches of the 1990s, conveying the idea that the world is getting smaller through expanding telecommunication networks, ease and affordability of air travel, and the rapid movement across national borders of capital, migrants, travelers, media, consumer goods, and even drugs and disease.[7] Among advertisers and politicians, academics and journalists, we find some extolling the "democratization" of expanding markets of goods and information, others bemoaning the loss of "local" culture, distinctiveness and tradition, and still others decrying the so-called demise of the nation-state.[8] The question at stake, as Robert Foster (1991) frames it, is whether homogenization or heterogenization will win out.

> Has this emergent order taken a single shape—recognizably American, relentlessly commercial—a shape reflective of transnational corporate control over the flow of media goods and services; and if it hasn't, will it? Or does this order contain (if not generate) possibilities for "creolization" and "indigenization," new syntheses of cultural forms that, however derivative or similar, always remain disjunct and different? In other words, are globalization and localization of cultural production two moments of the same total process, a process conditioned by increasing "flexibility" in the structure of capitalist accumulation? (236)

What most studies of globalization and transnationalism share, regardless of theoretical or disciplinary approach, is the sense that something radically new and dramatic is taking place in this era of late-twentieth-century capitalism and a new millennium. Even among those who acknowledge long historical roots to the transnationalism we now witness (e.g., Eric Wolf, Sidney Mintz, Immanuel Wallerstein), there is general agreement that today's global flows are marked by a decisively new scale.

In the broadest sense, globalization arid transnationalization imply an intensification and expansion of capitalism—with all its economic under pinnings and cultural manifestations—across the world. Popular metaphors such as "global village" and "transnational communities" imply that distances and borders shrink and fade as jet travel, mass media and telecommunications technologies, and fast flows of capital and commodities bring even remote areas of the world in contact with metropolitan centers. For David Harvey (1989), the "conditions of postmodernity" of late capitalism are marked by periodic time-space compressions—a speeding up of economic and social processes such that novelty is ever fleeting, whether in arrangements of production or in styles and designs of consumer goods and fashions. Modes of manufacturing and the organization of the global financial landscape manifest these changes most dramatically. Capital's inherent tendency to fluctuate and change is part and parcel of these accelerations.

"Flexibility" lies at the heart of the forces of change embodied in global capitalism. Flexible accumulation derived through flexible production, labor, and specialization, for example, have entailed dramatic reorganizations of work, markets, and finances on both local and global arenas. Scholars have referred to these changes as a new phase of capitalism, "disorganized capitalism," or "post-Fordism" (Lash and Urry 1987; Offe 1985).[9] For Harvey, the regime of "flexible accumulation" emerged out of post-World War II Fordism. Based on Henry Ford's five-dollar, eight-hour day on the automobile assembly line, and grounded in F. W. Taylor's early tract *The Principles of Scientific Management* (1911), Fordism established the basic concept of dividing the labor process into discrete tasks for maximal productivity based on time and motion studies of labor and explicitly tied mass production to mass consumption in its vision for a democratic society. Postwar Fordism, Harvey says, was not merely a system of mass production but a total way of life. "Mass production meant standardization of product as well as mass consumption; and that meant a whole new aesthetic and a commodification of culture" (1989:135). By the 1960s, the postwar recovery and economic rise of Japan and Western European countries, followed by several other newly industrializing countries in Southeast Asia, meant greater competition for the United States. The oil crisis and recession of the early 1970s pushed many corporations to find measures of cost-cutting, rationalization, and control of labor all conceptualized under the rubric of "flexibility."

Flexible specialization and production implies small, decentralized firms oriented toward niche markets in contrast to the large firms under postwar Fordism that were centralized and oriented toward mass production. Flexible accumulation embodies the whole gamut of late-twentieth-century corporate capitalist rationalization strategies, including technological innovation, automation, the creation of new product lines and specialized market niches, the movement of production enclaves to geographical regions with abundant and controllable (cheap and nonunion) labor, and corporate mergers and efforts to accelerate capital turnover (Harvey 1989:145). Some scholars have argued that flexible specialization along with the use of robotics and artificial intelligence have supplanted mass production itself. In this mix, however, mass production has not disappeared; it has been internationalized. Furthermore, the new informatics "open offices" are highly sophisticated realms of work in terms of technology and the organization of labor. Like maquiladoras (the name given to offshore manufacturing plants in Mexico that are subsidiaries of transnational corporations), these operations are the product of corporate restructuring strategies that rely on flexible arrangements of labor and mechanisms of control, as well as changing electronic and telecommunications technologies—both central dimensions of contemporary globalization.

The popular and evocative expression "global assembly line" denotes this fragmented process by which an increasing number of goods and commodities are now produced. When we picture a traditional assembly line, we see workers arranged in a neat row, each performing a distinct piece of the total production of a given commodity. But on the global assembly line, a pair of sneakers or a shirt, for example, may be cut, sewn together, and "finished" in three different countries, possibly three different continents, with the materials originating from a fourth. Even automobiles bearing the logo of American production may similarly be assembled from foreign-made parts. As the new assembly line spans multiple continents, it also hops over language barriers, cultural traditions, and state authorities. Now special terms concerning conditions of employment, environmental restrictions, and rates of taxation and building rentals are set within a given nation but outside of state law in export processing zones, or free trade zones. The new "international division of labor" on which this global assembly line is based represents a shift in the production, distribution, and consumption relationships between countries that began on a mass scale in the 1960s.[10] It has meant a dramatic restructuring of both capital and labor on the world stage (Frobel, Heinrichs, and Kreye 1980; Sanderson 1985).[11] Whereas colonial and, later, "third world" territories have long been the source of raw materials and the powerful "first world" "mother countries" have represented the privileged realm of industrialization and consumption, the new international division of labor signaled a change in the organization of production and ultimately of consumption as well. Third world countries have increasingly become central producers of commodity goods and parts in labor intensive industries,[12] and management and research, the white-collar strata of industrial interests, have increasingly become the preserve of "core" or industrialized nations. This geographical separation of management from production constitutes one of the essential characteristics of what some have called a new "world order."[13]

The proposal and passage of the North American Free Trade Agreement (NAFTA) raised public awareness of these reconfigurations and generated debate among wide-ranging political constituencies in the United States, Canada, and Mexico, as well as the Caribbean. These discussions introduced to the conundrum of the global assembly line a complex set of issues involving the impetus toward protecting "American jobs" and the pressures on the part of developing nations to diversify their economies and generate foreign capital by wooing foreign industry. David Harvey's "new world capitalist order" (1989) and Fredric Jameson's "post-modern global space" (1991) agree that the intensification of globalization has developed unevenly. Some communities and groups are more deeply enmeshed than others in global networks, and some are virtually left out of them. Some nations and some neighborhoods have greater access than others to the fruits of globalization, and some are differentially affected along the demographic lines of gender, race, and class.

Critiques of the globalization of production, the power of multinational corporations, and anxieties over the changing role of nation-states are increasingly echoed in the realm of culture, where charges of cultural imperialism are employed by many who bemoan not just "globalization" but more specifically the Americanization of global flows of culture, media and commodities. Tied to the strong influence of dependency theory in recent decades, the concept of cultural imperialism has been the predominant framework for evaluating globalization (Tomlinson 1991). As such, a growing body of literature now addresses the ways in which transnational capital, labor, and culture have permeated and transformed local cultures and economies, thereby presenting a threat to indigenous cultural traditions. Some have treated various ways third world cultures resist such penetrations or at least incorporate foreign commodities and culture in specific, localized ways. Accounts of tourism, for example, often depict local cultures as synthetic wholes vulnerably positioned in a losing battle against the invasion of white, western culture. On the other hand, attempts to assert the voices and agency of third world peoples who "talk back" to the metropole have challenged the depiction of a unidirectional flow of culture from core to periphery and the image of the third world as passive and powerless. In an insightful commentary on this tension, Akhil Gupta and James Ferguson (1992) have warned against a naive "celebration" of creative consumption within the periphery at the expense of situating these acts within Western global hegemony.[14]

In this ethnography I locate the simultaneous forces of globalization and localization and women's agency within the malleable context of global capitalist hegemony. I say "malleable" here to emphasize that hegemony, in the Gramscian sense I intend, is a relationship through which consent to power is manufactured, and thus mutable. The forces by which the social order and multinational corporate power maintain legitimacy in the Barbadian context of the informatics industry involve not only capitalist discipline but also the flexibility on the part of the corporations and the state to heed women's interests that are grounded in their particular, gendered, Afro-Caribbean, late-twentieth-century culture. In this region, whose colonial and postcolonial history is entirely permeated by transnational movements, both forced and voluntary, economic, political, and social, there is simply no way around the articulation between these spheres of "local" and "global" economy and culture.[15] Such an articulation is not a matter of unidirectional force, but rather takes place in a number of ways—through resistance to global pressures and corporate policies, assertions of traditions (recent or centuries old), and demands for access to a wide array of transnational culture and commodities.[16] The purpose here is not to glorify global production or consumption but rather to emphasize their interconnections and to interpret their meanings for women as key actors in a part of the world where "local" culture has always meant a complex creolization of European, African, and Asian derived traditions and where the economy has always been transnational.

Recent treatments of transnationalism and global culture demonstrate a number of difficulties posed by how to conceptualize and study the unwieldy set of processes bound up in "globalization." As many scholars have pointed out, analyses of globalization have tended to come in two basic packages: the subject of global culture has largely been taken up by the humanities, while the global economy has been the preserve of the social sciences (King 1991:ix), with a further division between ungendered studies of world systems and gendered studies of workers (and, to a lesser extent, consumers) in specific "local" places. Anthropology represents a unique realm for rectifying these divides. With its tool of ethnography, and its central concept, culture, its emphasis on history, and, for Caribbean anthropology, its transnational, modern, and creolized subjects, anthropology provides a useful set of theoretical and methodological ingredients for coming to grips with an increasingly complex set of social phenomena.

Several interesting questions remain to be explored more deeply: How do imported images and goods, tied to notions of modernity and progress, come to be desired and imbued with value, localized in their uses and meanings, and expressive of cultural differences and histories? What meanings (gendered and otherwise) do they come to have in people's everyday lives? And, how are they bound up with new capitalist hegemonies and relations of production broadly speaking? To begin to address these questions within transnational and globalization studies we need to take the workings of culture more seriously as both constituted by global processes and constitutive of them. To date, we have few rich examples of ethnographic analyses of these interrelationships.[17] Some have advocated broadening our conceptualizations of "diasporas" and transnational communities, with an emphasis on "travel" as opposed to the village as the locus of cultural inquiry. Along similar lines, notions of hybridity, creolization, and spatial metaphors of place, locality, and a "third time/space" of transnational experience have been proposed as tools for encompassing these new ways of experiencing daily life through the articulation between local and global forces (Bhabha 1994). For Arjun Appadurai (1990; 1996) the spatial metaphor is expressed in his array of "scapes" (ethnoscapes, finanscapes, technoscapes, ideoscapes), which, in their fluidity, undermine the utility and significance of nation- states as the central arbiters of modernity and transnationalism. Moving beyond those general assertions, I suggest that states, transnational corporations, and local groups of social and economic actors both challenge and support each other as they face new sets of circumstances and contexts for enacting power and identities. Within this dialectic, the specificity of local cultural-political economies is crucial to our understanding of how globalization is configured and how it is experienced by different people across the world.

BARBADOS AND THE CARIBBEAN: SITUATING EXPORT PRODUCTION AND TRANSNATIONALISM

Export-oriented industrialization in the Caribbean, as in many other regions of the developing world, has become the dominant economic model, following a long history of monocrop agricultural extraction under colonialism and unsuccessful attempts following World War II at "import substitution." As early as the 1960s, investment policies of developing countries began to shift from models of import substitution to "export diversification" because of changes in international trade and tariff regulations (Nash 1983). For Barbados, as chapter 3 explores in detail, this shift involved diversification of a sugar-based economy toward a tripartite structure that includes tourism and manufacturing.

Growth and change in sectors of the Barbadian economy in the postwar years falls into three periods: the period of agricultural dominance, between 1946 and 1962; the period of transition, between 1963 and 1970; and the period of export diversification first to manufactured goods and now into services, from 1970 to the present. The dominant economic role played by sugar for more than three hundred years of Barbadian history declined significantly between

1946 and 1980 (in terms of share in domestic output, employment, and foreign exchange earnings). Successful efforts at economic diversification accompanied the decline in the sugar industry itself.[18] Between 1963 and 1970, tourism and light manufacturing surpassed sugar as the primary source of economic growth, and the hope was that one sector might support another in the face of market swings or downturns. The transformation began in the 1950s with the establishment of the island's first Board of Tourism and continued in the decade after with the enactment of the first incentive legislation for enclave manufacturing.[19] The three sectors, however, represented different sorts of economic security. For example, sugar exports continued to yield greater potential value added while manufacturing exports signified perhaps twice the employment gain achieved by an equal advance in the tourism or agricultural sectors.

For Latin America and the Caribbean nations, the debt crisis of the 1980s, rising interest rates and cost of oil, and weakening terms of trade with the United States led to severe balance of payments problems that were soluble only through increasing exports. The United States responded to the crisis with several economic initiatives aimed at promoting political stability in Central American and the Caribbean (Deere *et al.* 1990), and alleviating the economic crisis in these developing countries, as well as insuring a source of cheap labor for U.S. industry in the wake of competition from newly industrializing nations in Asia. In 1983 President Ronald Reagan's Caribbean Basin Initiative enabled approved Caribbean nations to attain one-way duty-free access to U.S. markets for particular goods for twelve years. Indeed, while vigorous resistance from U.S. unions successfully banned textiles and garments from these initiatives, some Caribbean countries were granted special production quotas, limiting garment production to items assembled from fabric made and cut in the United States.[20] Several Caribbean countries, including Barbados, Jamaica, and Trinidad, now marginalized by Mexico's preferential trade conditions under NAFTA and undergoing severe contraction of traditional export commodities (e.g., sugar and bananas), have applied to the United States for parity in trade relations. With export production as the linchpin of Caribbean economies, it is clear why informatics investors are attracted to a small island like Barbados. Among Barbados's many assets according to these investors are its English-speaking tradition, high literacy rate (98 percent), and "orderly" society, and its well-entrenched tourism sector and reputation for "polite service."[21] Government officials and state bureaucrats also see these factors as the bases for the success of this new industry and the promise it represents for future growth and development of the nation.

Export production and high consumption of foreign goods are not the only expressions of transnationalism in Caribbean history and culture. The ties between the West Indies and England, Canada, and the United States reach back to the earliest days of colonialism and permeate most dimensions of life there today. Nearly every West Indian has some family member living abroad, creating enormously significant networks of social, economic, political, cultural, and emotional exchange. Transnational kin networks rely on transatlantic travel and communications for economic support, information, and nurturance in numerous forms (Olwig 1999). While labor migrations have led thousands of Caribbean men and women to jobs in transportation, nursing, and domestic service in cities such as London, New York, and Toronto, children of school age are frequently sent back "home" to the Caribbean, where they are believed to receive stronger discipline, and better care and education without the racism and gang influence that they are likely to encounter in North America or the United Kingdom. Many families in the Caribbean rely on the remittances and goods sent by relatives working abroad, and in turn, many transmigrants depend on family "at home" to maintain properties for them, or to provide a home when they return for holidays or need an emotional base. Transnational political networks figure prominently in both "metropolitan" and Caribbean elections. Jean-Bertrand Aristide's reference to New York as the "Dizyem Depatman-an" or Tenth Department of Haiti is one example of the importance of Caribbean transnationalism in "local" political economy and culture (Basch, Glide-Schiller, and Szanton-Blanc 1994:1).

Early transnational migrations from Barbados took place largely within the region; in the late nineteenth and early twentieth centuries, roughly fifty thousand people worked as seasonal laborers in British Guiana and Trinidad, and between forty-five thousand and sixty thousand went to work on the construction of the Panama Canal. Migrations to Britain and to Canada and the United States ebbed and flowed during the twentieth century, the largest waves occurring between 1955 and 1961, when nearly twenty thousand Barbadians sailed for Britain as part of the Sponsored Workers scheme. In the 1960s Canada and the United States eased their immigration policies just as Britain was tightening hers, and cities such as New York and Toronto were "Caribbeanized" (Sutton 1987).

The growth of export production and major flows of labor migrations accompanied other manifestations of Caribbean transnationalism in the past century. Most striking is travel abroad for pleasure and shopping. In 1993 alone, U.S. Emigration issued nonimmigrant (tourist) visas to twenty-five thousand Bajans, or nearly 10 percent of the entire population (George Gmelch and Sharon Gmelch 1997:185). Bajans' penchant for imported goods and foreign travel is counterbalanced, however, by an equally strong pride in local culture, deep ties to family, and a pull toward home, which Gmelch and Gmelch see reflected in the fact that Bajans have "one of the lowest naturalization rates of any foreign-born immigrant group in the United States" (1997:181).

This tension between "home" and "away," or the local and the transnational, permeates the lives and experiences of the women in this study. Women working in the informatics sector are at once deeply conscious of the place of their new industry in the global economy, taking pride in working for a foreign company and loving to travel abroad, and little interested in making any where else their home. Their work as data processors looks (and feels to them) like modern, high-tech, sophisticated officelike work. Yet their engagement in a "triple shift" of domestic responsibilities, wage work, and numerous informal income-generating activities such as cake baking, sewing, and trading of goods and services resembles the strategies that women of the Caribbean have employed for hundreds of years to make a living. The complexities of this juggling act are discussed in greater detail in chapter 6. It is important to note here, however, that the confluence of new and old, "modern" and "traditional" practices and identities is heightened in the informatics arena because of its strikingly new, global image and structure. A highly valued "perk" of working for Data Air, for example, is the possibility of winning airline travel vouchers (called "thank-you cards") for trips to destinations across the Caribbean, North America, and Europe. In addition to visiting far flung family members abroad, women use these trips to buy foreign goods, some for their own consumption and some to sell at home to supplement their low wages.

Travel opportunities also contribute to these women's emergent sense of themselves as "modern" working women. But, as the public scene between Paul and Christine at the bus stand suggests, there are ambiguities and even dangers bound up with these new appearances and by informatics workers' pursuit of transnational fashion and display. The threat that a "factory girl" might be confused for a "middle-class office worker" and undermine Barbadian respect for social (class) boundaries and their distinguishing appearances is merged with Paul's sense of marginality from the money, status, and time commitment bound up in Christine's employment in informatics. Another key dimension of the emphasis on dress and appearance is its demonstration of the interconnections between local culture and imported, multinational corporate culture. Some scholars writing about global factories present western dress and appearance among the female workers as superficial compensatory practices that mute women's inclination to resist (in an organized manner) the harsh labor conditions they face in their jobs (Elson and Pearson 1981a, 1981b; Grossman, 1979; Fuentes and Ehrenreich 1985) and provide an excuse to enhance local measures of surveillance and discipline over women. This form of consumption becomes equated with sexual promiscuity and a threat to proper femininity and religious decorum (Ong 1987; Fernandez-Kelly 1983). The Anglophone Afro-Caribbean context of Barbados presents both similarities and some striking contrasts to these earlier accounts. In Barbados, European and other Western styles and cultural practices are not necessarily construed as "threats" to local culture.[22] Furthermore, women's ability to dictate their own work identities and practices without the interference or control by male kin places them in remarkably different circumstances than those of many of their Asian and Latin American sisters. While forms of patriarchy certainly underlie some aspects of women's home and work lives in Barbados (Senior 1991), informatics workers' employment is in no way mediated or controlled by their male lcin.[23] Whether married or single, these women control their own labor. Similarly, references to women's "mercenary," "exhibitionist," and acquisitive habits often made in such popular cultural arenas as contemporary calypso and dub music, are not part of any specific campaigns to restrict the movements and sexuality of high-tech workers in Barbados as some have reported elsewhere (Ong 1987). Whereas working in a factory and wearing new kinds of clothes can bring charges of promiscuity and immorality to Malaysian or Mexican women and can threaten their marriageability, Bajan informatics workers have little such concern. They resent these characterizations and at the same time enjoy a sense of prestige from many of their associated practices (e.g. travel abroad). Furthermore, to them and their employers, their special way of dressing is appropriate to their jobs. As such, the meanings pink-collar workers interpret from and ascribe to "femininity" and its associated prescriptions for habits of work act to both challenge and re-formulate both local and transnational conventions.

Global consumption among today's data processors, along with their role as high-tech offshore producers in the information age, are potent examples of the "conditions of post-modernity" to which Harvey refers. Indeed, these women's identities as producers in this new sector are very much bound up in a set of consumption practices that both enable and demand them to look like "professional" office workers. The task for anthropology, as I see it, is to connect the ways in which new modes of consumption together with new modes of production give rise to new meanings of local culture and newly flexible identities.

CONSUMPTION ACROSS "FIRST" AND "THIRD" WORLDS

Extensive debates have emerged in the 1980s and 1990s surrounding the forms and meanings of consumption and consumerism in everyday life (e.g., Appadurai 1986; Breclcenridge 1995; C. Campbell 1990; Fine and Leopold 1993; Friedman 1994a; Howes 1996; Miller 1995a; Wilk 1990). On the one hand, many scholars express interest in and concern about the meanings of new forms of consumption for people in the third world. On the other hand, however, global consumption, when discussed in relation to transnational production, is generally seen as the privilege of those in the "West" afforded by the (exploited) labor of third world workers. These formulations raise two important issues.

First, consumption is often presented as a novel phenomenon for people in the "developing" world when technology and media-hyped goods and symbols are involved. Images are conjured of a nearly naked Masaai warrior sporting Ray Ban sunglasses, a dark-robed Bedouin woman drinking a Coke, or, for that matter, a Caribbean native leaving the languor of palm trees and beaches for the air-conditioned office to work at a computer eight hours a day (Lutz and Collins 1993). What we sometimes miss, however, is the long history of transnational movements that have given rise to the high valuation of these goods and their particular meanings and modes of incorporation into specific cultural contexts. Second, the new anthropology of consumption and consumerism, regardless of perspective, includes a gendered dimension. Consumption in one sense has long been the realm of women standing in necessary counterpoint to production—men produce whereas women shop, or consume—where the former constitutes work and the latter pleasure.[24] Where the "new international division of labor" model presents production and consumption as geographically and hierarchically opposed—the poor and powerless of the third world produce for the rich and powerful first world—Maria Mies (1986) introduced a provocative gendered dimension to this framework. For her, the world economy is predicated on a system of capitalist patriarchy that incorporates women in strategic roles on both "sides" of the international divide: third world women as proletarianized producers and first world women as consumer "housewives." What Mies, more than a decade ago, drew our attention to were the complex mechanisms through which women are mobilized around the world to fuel the expansion of capitalist accumulation and the integral relationship between consumption and production in this process. Her work represents an unusual treatment of the global arena in linking the experience of people of the first and third worlds and also in emphasizing the gendered dimensions of the workings of global capitalism.

More characteristic of the globalization literature is a peculiar divide between apparently ungendered macro analyses and gendered micro analyses. Women as gendered subjects often take center stage in studies of factory production along the global assembly line (Peña 1997; Sklair 1993; Ong 1987, Fernandez-Kelly 1983) or of consumption of particular goods and media in global outposts (Abu-Lughod 1993,1995; and in Breckenridge 1995; Howes 1996; Miller 1995a, 1995b). These studies generally conclude with the implications of global production/consumption for women, households, and gendered ideologies in the given local context. However, in analyses of the wider forces (both cultural and economic) shaping these movements and their implications for nations and local cultures, the role of gender and of women as the central producers and consumers strangely recedes (see works by Appadurai, Feather stone, Hannerz, Harvey, and Robertson). Mies's formulation, limited though it is in its binary portrayal of third/first world women, is a notable exception.

Global assembly lines are as much about the production of people and identities as they are about restructuring labor and capital. In a discussion of third world women workers, Mohanty (1997:5) integrates transnational realms of practice and the ways in which gender and race hierarchies become naturalized by the maneuvers of late capitalism. She argues that "the relation of local to global processes of colonization and exploitation and the specification of a process of cultural and ideological homogenization across national borders, in part through the creation of the consumer as 'the' citizen under advanced capitalism, must be crucial aspects of any comparative feminist project" (1997:5). Her project is to explore the connections between actors on the worker/producer side of the equation, asking, "Who are the workers that make the citizen-consumer possible?" However, while her discussion of the ideologies underlying these constructions of third world women workers is persuasive, she merely hints at her initial provocative connection between "worker-producer" and "citizen-consumer."

What Mies could not anticipate, and what Mohanty underplays in her 1997 analysis, is the significance of women's increasingly simultaneous engagement in both production and consumption on both "sides" of the international division of labor. The informatics workers in Barbados demonstrate through a variety of practices that they are not the passive pawns of multinational capital they have sometimes been depicted to be. Nonetheless, the agency they enact as workers and as new transnational consumers may ultimately have the ironic effect of challenging their sense of class consciousness and of gender-based solidarity. In the following chapters I explore the tensions between hegemony and agency by bridging the realms of production and consumption, economy and culture in this new transnational industry in the Caribbean. In doing so, I address both a new category of work and a newly emergent "class" of worker. By highlighting the culturally specific and locally gendered ways in which new workers in the offshore operations of major multinational corporations experience their incorporation into the global assembly line, this study contributes to a growing body of scholarship on gender, power, and agency in transnational capitalism (Fernandez-Kelly 1983; Kondo 1990; Ong 1987; Pena 1996; Safa 1995; Ward 1990b; Wolf 1992; Yelvington 1995). As such, a brief discussion of this literature is called for to demonstrate where Barbados and informatics fit into the broader picture.

WOMEN AND PRODUCTION ON THE GLOBAL ASSEMBLY LINE

In the 1970s and early 1980s, studies of "women and development" paved the way for explorations of the ways in which an increasingly global economy, and its vast movements of capital, labor, and changing technology, pose radical implications for third world women (e.g., Boserup 1970; Etienne and Leacock 1980; Nash and Safa 1986; Reiter 1975; Rosaldo and Lamphere 1974). Several notable studies from those decades expand on Folker Fröbel, Jürgen Heinrichs, and Otto Kreye's articulation of the new international division of labor by questioning the fact that the massive labor pools that form the crux of international movements are predominantly female and examining ways in which various and sometimes contradictory notions about gender have constituted third world women as ideal workers on this new global assembly line.[25] Despite competing theories about the inherently exploitative or advantageous nature of the global assembly line for economic development in the third world, it has been made clear that the ever- expanding free trade zones have enormous ramifications for local, regional, and global economies and play major roles in transforming communities, households, families, and the lives of individual women who are selectively incorporated to perform these jobs (Wallerstem and Smith 1992:253–62).

Two aspects of this study of Barbadian informatics workers make it important as a point of comparison with the existing literature, in my general assertion that global capitalism is not monolithic. One relates to the cultural context of the Afro-Caribbean and the long and well-recognized tradition of women's waged work as central to the national economy and the survival of households, as well as to women's self-images and identities. Some have described greater gender equality and historically high labor force participation rates for women within the Afro-Caribbean as a vestige of slavery, where despite some divisions of labor based on gender, women worked shoulder to shoulder with men doing the most arduous jobs in the cane fields, proving their physical strength and tenacity (Mathurin 1975). Rosina Wiltshire-Brodber (1988:143) argues simply, "Slavery had the effect of leveling the sexes. Human worth was measured purely in labour terms and women laboured as hard as men. To speak of Caribbean male dominance in the context of slavery is to parody the concepts of power and dominance. ... This Caribbean context provided fertile ground for the reordering of gender relations among slaves. The process was to continue into post-slavery Caribbean society."

The other factor relates to the pink-collar aspect of this new industry itself, and its relationship to assembly work in the garment and electronics industries, which have been the predominant employers of women on the global assembly line. Transnational labor and women workers have been relatively well documented in parts of Asia (Heyzer 1989; Ong 1987; Wolf 1992), Mexico (Fernandez-Kelly 1983; Pena 1997; Sklair 1993; Tiano 1990; Wilson 1991), and the Hispanic Caribbean (Casey 1996; Ortiz 1996; Safa 1983, 1995).[26] Relatively little has been written about transnational labor in the Anglophone Afro-Caribbean, with the exception of Bolles 1983 and 1996 and Pearson 1993 on Jamaica and Kelly 1997 on St. Lucia. One aspect to this focus on Asian and Hispanic women has been a presumed dichotomy between "traditional" culture and modern transnational or global capitalism and a generalized sense that women working in multinational factories are largely new to wage labor and are deliberately drawn from patriarchal societies that have not traditionally seen women as breadwinners or as active in the formal capitalist economy. Several accounts make clear that employment in these sectors has relied heavily on migrant labor from agricultural regions, where women's labor was unremunerated or contained within the domestic realm.[27] Maria Patricia Fernandez-Kelly (1983), Viclci Ruiz and Susan Tiano (1987), Gay Young (1987), and Helen Safa (1995) describe ways in which rationales based on local notions about machismo and conventional gender ideologies about women's so-called natural ties to the domestic realm and family, and their prescribed temperaments of self-sacrifice and nurturance, pervade explanations of female labor on both sides of the Mexican border and between multinationals and the state in the Hispanic Caribbean.[28] Aihwa Ong (1987) demonstrates the complex ways in which traditional village patriarchs and religious leaders mediate between foreign (male) corporate employers and women workers in their recruitment into and experience of factory assembly work in Malaysia. Each account explores the complicated maneuvers and convergences between capitalist and noncapitalist, local and foreign patriarchies, and their manipulations of female workers across the global assembly line. While each takes up the question of women's expressions of agency and modes of resistance to conditions of capitalist discipline and exploitation there emerges an image of multinational capital, as a monolithic force, roaming the world and eagerly tapping into convenient pools of available female labor, ideal because of their position within cultures of "traditional" gender roles and ideologies. This general pattern of "footloose" industry has been dramatic. The forms of women's response to these conditions vary, however, according to the culture, and several accounts demonstrate the way in which these often involve the manipulation of "traditional" feminine predispositions.

Ong describes a convergence between tradition and modernity in the responses of Malay women working in foreign electronics factories. They challenge patriarchal Muslim authority and control at home through their new status as wage earners, and at the same time exercise spontaneous and contagious episodes of spirit possession, in which they effectively shut down their rigid and high tech production line by drawing upon cultural resources deeply embedded in Muslim tradition. In Silicon Valley, Karen Hossfeld (1990:173) describes tactics in which Asian and Hispanic women turn managers' racist and sexist stereo-types to their individual advantage by feigning a language barrier to avoid taking instruction, or by complaining of "female problems" to avoid heavy work. In Ong's account, capitalist discipline is exerted through the combined forces of factory surveillance, public scrutiny, and self-regulation, each weighing the feminine morality of the neophyte workers against the threats posed by capitalist incorporation. Spirit possession, then, according to Ong, became the medium of protest among women caught between capitalist modernity and Muslim tradition. Diane Wolf (1992:256) emphasizes even more explicitly the multiple forms of and interconnections between traditional and capitalist patriarchies and, consequently, the simultaneously exploitative and empowering implications of assembly jobs for the Central Javanese factory daughters she studies.[29] Michael John Watts (1992:6) concludes, "The arrival of global capital, and of industrial work discipline, no more imposes the dead hand of subordination or marginalization on women workers than the patriarchal authority of the 'traditional' Javanese family always produces a passive capitulation by household members to its demands. Globality and locality are inextricably linked, but through complex mediations and reconfigurations of 'traditional' society; the nonlocal processes driving capital mobility are always experienced, constituted, and mediated locally. *An industrial and distinctively gendered working class is made; yet, through Us own use of cultural and symbolic resources, it makes itself*" (italics mine).

In the Caribbean, as in other regions incorporated into the global assembly line, we see women engaging strategies for accommodating or resisting the pressures of capitalist production involving ironic reformulations of "traditional" gender ideologies for rebellious ends. The same gender ideology may be deployed on different occasions for different, perhaps contradicting, ends. Many data processors take excused absences from work to care for children because corporate employers are flexible in accommodating women's expected feminine roles; alternatively, employers cite the tradition of the extended family and involvement by aunties and mothers in raising children as a reason not to provide day care facilities for the workers' children. Simultaneously, we witness various convergences between "traditional" and global capitalist forms of patriarchy in the incorporation and shaping of a new feminine proletariat. For example, women's suitability for low-skilled and monotonous assembly work is often associated with their naturally docile and patient temperaments as secondary wage earners, and women's low wages are explained as appropriate to their status in households with husbands or fathers as the primary wage earners. While several treatments of women's incorporation into transnational factories, such as those mentioned above, shed light on the varied and simultaneous expressions of power, agency, resistance, and accommodation among the feminized workers in these industries, we have generally seen these processes within an apparently monolithic framework of multinational capital. To go beyond this, a transnational perspective demands that we keep specific local contexts in view. In the context of informatics in Barbados we can examine the accommodations and redefinitions performed by transnational corporations in the face of local demands and conditions (by the state as well as women workers). In recruitment practices, the maintenance of a labor force beyond the course of a decade, and in numerous day-to-day ways, foreign-owned corporations attend to the cultural traditions, gender ideologies, and aesthetic values of the Barbadian workers they employ.

Most accounts of multinational industries describe their search for the ideal female worker: single, childless, young, well educated, and without previous work experience. Indeed this profile is echoed around the world as the most "naturally" suited to the labor-intensive assembly work involved in export production. The extent to which this profile draws on specific cultural or uniform multinational corporate gender ideologies (associating femininity with docility, patience, dexterity, and dependency) needs closer scrutiny. In the informatics industry, we need to ask why the same company, Data Air, with the same capitalist agendas in its two Caribbean operations, employs almost all women for its Barbados facility and roughly half men in the Dominican Republic.[30] More generally, how are invocations of "natural" femininity deployed to similar or different ends?

The Afro-Caribbean context of Barbados presents some important differences in women's circumstances of industrial incorporation. Although the "family" becomes a potent metaphor for the paternalistic role played by corporate employers, there is little expectation that women's actual families have any role in their availability or performance as workers.[31] Unlike cases around the world described by Cynthia Enloe (in Fuentes and Ehrenreich 1983), in Barbados, fathers, husbands, and influential female kin and friends exert little control over women's employment decisions. The only involvement of family or friends in women's recruitment into informatics is typically that of providing information by spreading the word of job openings or putting in a good word to an inside contact. Ethnographic accounts of Barbados demonstrate that industrialization, wage work, and a woman's family responsibilities are not seen as antithetical or in competition with each other. Constance Sutton and Susan Malciesky-Barrow (1977:306) observe, "A job or career for a women is never spoken of as an alternative to marriage or maternity. … This reflects not only different expectations and assumptions about a woman's economic and social roles but also the presence of a family and kinship system that acts as a support for women of all ages." Furthermore, and in stark contrast to policies and practices in many parts of Southeast and East Asia, in Barbados not only is there an assumption that women will continue to work after marriage, but also the Barbadian state guarantees (and enforces even within the offshore sector) a three-month maternity leave for all working women.

Women's movement through stages of the life cycle has not precluded their wage earning even within the realm of new and competitive industries like informatics.[32] With regard to fertility patterns and women's work, there is clear evidence that employment in the formal sector corresponds to lower rates of fertility among Caribbean women (Senior 1991:126–27; Yelvington 1995:96).[33] However, the virtual absence (even rejection of) punitive measures imposed by corporate employers on women's desire to work and be mothers[34] and what I show as the increasing longevity of women workers in these industries across stages of the life cycle and well past the short-term employment trends within multinational industries elsewhere in the world together demonstrate important counterpoints to the portraits drawn by both Ong (1987) and Fernandez-Kelly (1983) in their landmark case studies. To ground these distinctions in their particular local context, I discuss at greater length in chapter 3 the history of women's work and the relationship between matrifocal families and divisions of labor in the Afro-Caribbean. For the moment, it is important to reiterate the point made simply and strongly by Joycelin Massiah (1986:177) that "women in the Caribbean have *always* worked" and to add that, in contrast to many other cultural contexts of global production, motherhood and work have always together been central to defining femininity in the Caribbean. The point to be emphasized here is that local cultural traditions and, in particular, the meanings of gender influence the shape of transnational production in specific ways along the global assembly line. Where others have emphasized the central role played by women in the expansion of transnational production, this work specifically aims to unpack the specific gender ideologies (local and global) that have, in complex and sometimes contradictory ways, conceived women as and in turn made them into "ideal" global workers. This emphasis on gender ideologies is important not just in relation to Barbados and the Afro-Caribbean culture but also in relation to informatics as a new realm of work that occupies an ambiguous place between traditional "white"- and "blue"-collar labor.

THE "PINKING" OF WHITE-COLLAR SERVICES

In the past two decades, the "information age" has signaled a dramatic shift in the U.S. economy from manufacturing to service industries. Services now out-rank manufacturing in their share of national output (more than 67 percent of GNP in the "developed" economies and 51 percent of GDP in the "developing" world) (Posthuma 1987:7). One out of every five employees in the United States is a clerical worker and over three-fourths of the entire labor force works in a service industry. In the 1980s, while services accounted for 21 million new jobs, more than 2 million in manufacturing disappeared (9 to 5,1992:8).

The shift to a service-based economy, denoted by the expression "postindustrialism," is integral to the notion of the new world economic order that Harvey (1989) and others describe. This notion implies that, facing the loss of manufacturing industries to the "third world," these advanced or postindustrial nations will retain an expanding service sector, and it includes the broader argument that, the world over, services are increasing in their representative importance in the labor market. Certainly, the Caribbean's emphasis on tourism as the major source of foreign exchange and employment represents a vast expansion in the importance of services compared with the traditional sectors of agriculture and manufacturing. Informatics in Barbados presents an intriguing case for investigating these trends. Its "product" is information, manipulated and produced in electronic form as a service to clients overseas. Its labor process, however, operates on a piece-rate system much like factory-based production, in which systems of monitoring and assuring consistent levels of "quality" more resemble a manufacturing plant than an office.

Before I explore the tensions over these boundaries in the informatics arena it is important to emphasize the extent to which the expansion of services, like the expansion of industrial labor along the global assembly line, is tied to increasing numbers of women workers and to gendered conceptualizations of work itself. The particular form in which white-collar labor is refashioned for a specifically feminine labor force within an unusual "factory" context constitutes the "pink-collar" nature of the setting for this research.

The shift to services, or the so-called second industrial revolution, is in the process of reshaping the industries where women are heavily concentrated, and presents new and complex implications for our analyses of the global economy as well as for the day-to-day lives of thousands of working women and their families. In the United States, several changes are reorganizing the clerical work that has spawned the offshore data entry industry. First, new computer technologies and digital telecommunications systems are capable of generating, handling, and transmitting work that was once labor intensive, highly skilled, and confined to paper transactions. Facsimiles and data communication equipment have drastically cut costs and made possible simultaneous transmission of information regardless of geographical distance. The shift to digitalization, for example, means that whereas a telephone line may transmit 10,000 bits of information per second, satellite transmission can speed the process exponentially, sending 6.3 million bits per second. The current thrust toward privatization and mergers of telecommunications companies is also encouraging increased usage of new services (e.g., electronic voice services, electronic mail, interactive computer networks, high-speed facsimile transmission).

Concomitantly, production in all economic sectors of the United States has become increasingly information intensive, and there has been a proliferation of knowledge-based industries that themselves rely on new labor forces and technologies. Even in 1986 there were roughly three thousand on-line databases, and over 90 percent of these were located in the United States (Posthuma 1987:6). In a competitive marketplace where production and distribution have become increasingly integrated, information technology becomes indispensable in meeting communications demands. And at the same time that more and more data are being generated internally, management requires greater amounts of information for strategic planning and research. On-line information searches by industries are estimated to be growing at over 30 percent a year. The variety and number of new products and services surrounding this proliferation of information is staggering, ranging from data processing operations, software development and evaluation houses, and outfits that update on-line databases to those companies that service and maintain computer equipment and support the telecommunications and technological demands of these changing industries.

The impact of computer automation and the rise of the "paperless office" for clerical work has received increased attention as technological advancements in telecommunications coupled with rapid changes in both local and global economies have presented new labor processes, recruitment patterns, and the reorganization of work itself. Until quite recently, labor studies focused almost exclusively on skilled, heavy industrial work that comprised an essentially male domain. Now, with the expansion of light industries where female labor is typically favored, a new kind of labor study is emerging, with greater exploration of the ways in which gender has historically intersected directly with technological innovations (e.g., typewriters, sewing machines, video display terminals). The feminization of certain job categories is often correlated with lower skills, lower rates of remuneration, lower prestige, and recently, extensive automation, and computer regulation and surveillance.[35] In the sphere of information-based industries, banks, insurance companies, airlines (reservations), and credit card companies are among those arenas of heavily female-centered fields undergoing radical technological restructuring—again, we are witnessing a historical shift in which those arenas undergoing automation, deskilling, and demotion are also feminized.[16] What is at stake is a process by which the concept of skill itself is gendered, and that which is associated with women, devalued.

With the introduction of new office technologies and the accompanying hype by hardware vendors, technical schools, politicians, and the press has been a tendency to raise the expectations of secretaries and clerical workers for new skills, access to better jobs, and, thus, better salaries and greater status (Murphree 1987). The new technology is presented as bringing an end to the traditional boss-secretary relationship, and the paperless office is hailed as a means for paring down the numbers of office workers and transforming those remaining into "all-round communications workers with sophisticated computer skills" (Pringle 1988:97). In theory, the new technology provides the opportunity for secretaries to do a greater variety of tasks that include high-level functions such as planning, managing, developing databases, and preparing financial analyses, but in general the reality is not so rosy. The technology alone does not insure any of the promised rewards, and many studies have noted that the attitudes and agendas of management have played a much more powerful hand in reshaping the conditions of office work than the technology itself. In short, the same technology may have significantly different effects on the labor process in different environments, depending on the context of use, size, and agendas of the workplace managers.[37]

In the realm of information-based services, two major trends have emerged as part of the increased implementation of office automation technologies. First, information-based jobs have become fragmented such that fewer people with lower levels of skills are required to perform the same work. Restructuring most often takes the form of dividing office work into two separate categories, administrative support and typing and data entry. Each category requires limited training and lower levels of skills and subsequently commands a lower rate of remuneration than the original diversified secretarial job. Second, the physical arrangement and geographical location of work are simultaneously being decentralized such that clerical workers are often moved to separate "operations floors" or, even more dramatically, clerical work is housed outside the physical domain of the company, up to thousands of miles away and "offshore." The shift to total operations performing the discrete jobs of data entry, word processing, and claims adjudication, such as those in the Caribbean, has meant that face-to-face relationships between clerical workers and professional and managerial staff is becoming increasingly rare. These offshore workers represent one extreme on a continuum of clerical-work rationalization that also includes part-time, temporary, and home-based clerical workers in the United States.[38]

On a typical shift at Data Air or Multitext, between about fifty and one hundred Barbadian women sit in partitioned computer cubicles of a given production floor from 7:30 in the morning until 3:30 in the afternoon, taking a half-hour break for lunch and sometimes a fifteen-minute stretch in between. Their key-strokes per hour are monitored electronically as they enter data from airline ticket stubs, consumer warranty cards, or the text of a potboiler novel for top U.S. airlines, appliance houses, and publishers. In each case, the surveillance of the computer, the watchful eye of supervisors, and the implementation of double-keying techniques are all aspects of the production process integral to the companies' guarantee of 99 percent accuracy rates.

These trends allow little opportunity for computer operators to learn the more complex capacities of their machines and drastically shorten their career ladders by limiting their tasks and allowing them little or no access to managers and professional associates.[39] Furthermore, the constant monitoring and measuring of productivity and error rates of these operators increases their stress.

Part-time, temporary, home-based, and offshore work are examples of expanding schemes described as "flexible" in the clerical sector. This new pool of workers is characteristically female, and these "flexible" jobs are often presented as ideally suited to women's multiple roles as homemakers, caretakers of dependent children and sick and elderly relatives, and wage earners. Part-time, temporary, and home-based work are often presented as providing a sort of "safety net" for women whose domestic roles make full-time work impossible. Embedded in the corporate rationales are familiar, essentialist notions about women as secondary wage earners whose lower rates of pay and minimal benefits merely supplement those of a primary male breadwinner. As Mohanty (1997) points out, these ideologies about femininity and domesticity situate third world women and women of racial and ethnic minorities in the United States in especially vulnerable and exploited positions in the economy of late capitalism.

The flight of clerical work offshore is explained by multinational managers and company owners with a familiar litany of rationales that are subtly but inextricably bound up in these gendered (racial/national) ideologies of production. They claim that "you simply can't get Americans to do this sort of work anymore" and that attrition levels and wage rates in the United States make back-office costs prohibitive. Some companies have moved step-by-step through alternative labor forces and work arrangements, first trying automation devices in their home offices and cutting back employees from full- to part-time status, then experimenting with other contingent arrangements such as temporary, home-based, or subcontracted clerical work, and finally moving their work out of the United States altogether, either by setting up their own offshore shop or contracting work to an existing vendor. Like corporate investors in other industries, they are drawn to the Caribbean by its proximity and the availability of frequent, inexpensive flights to the United States (this is especially so for East Coast companies) and by its tax incentives, low-waged and well-educated work force, good roads, airport, and custom-designed factory shells, and, as a special lure to traveling executives, its beaches and luxury hotels.

For labor forces in Barbados and other parts of the developing world, offshore clerical work represents new employment opportunities, enhanced by the power and novelty of informatics technology and officelike work setting. Despite the strict disciplinary pressures, other aspects of these jobs make them especially attractive to the hundreds of Barbadian women who apply each year. Considering the exploitative conditions under which thousands of offshore assembly-line operators work across the world, the working environments and benefits offered to offshore pink-collar operators in Barbados may even be better, in some respects, than those provided to their counterparts in the United States. While wages are less than half that of a U.S. worker, strict labor laws established by the Barbadian state ensure that all Barbadian workers are guaranteed certain basic employment benefits, such as maternity and sick leave, severance pay after two consecutive years of employment, and three weeks of paid vacation.[40]

Barbadian, Dominican, and American operators for Data Air, for example, all confront increasing stresses of electronic monitoring devices and measures, such as production quotas and incentive schemes, to further reduce costs and maximize production, as well as the insecurity created by rapidly changing technology. They differ, however, in their specific relationship to these various rationalization measures and in the cultural meanings associated with them. For example, the special meaning of "pink collar" is particularly pronounced for the Barbadian women I interviewed and differs from that of their counterparts in the sister plant of Data Air located in Santo Domingo. There the average length of employment for operators is two years, in marked contrast to the longevity of operators in the Barbadian plant. Male informatics operators in the Dominican Republic describe their jobs as stepping stones toward better, computer-based jobs. Because they are able to work permanent day or night shifts to accommodate class schedules, they see their jobs as means of gaining relevant experience while in school. The Barbadian female operators, however, generally hope for stable, long-term employment and seldom express at the outset the expectation to move up to higher-level computer work. These differences point to some of the ways in which gender ideologies and the structure of the labor market intersect.[41] These differences also demonstrate that even within branches of the same company, local cultural and economic conditions weigh heavily into the recruitment and incorporation of workers, and into the ultimate meanings these jobs have in their lives. Irene Padavic (1992), writing about U.S. workers, asserts that industrial "demand factors" need greater consideration in looking at occupational segregation between the blue- and white-collar realms. She argues that women's preference for clean white-collar jobs, though strong, does not actually determine their occupational choices, and when given the choice between a higher-paying, blue-collar and traditionally masculinized job and a lower-paid but white-collar job, women generally choose the former. In the United States, she concludes, economic reality wins out over comfort and the symbolic status associated with office work.

In Barbados, however, data processors openly acknowledge in their testimonies that they could earn more money in the cane fields but prefer the clean, cool and computer-centered realm of offshore informatics—a powerful illustration of their valuation of this new industry's symbolic capital and physical appeal. This preference is not a matter of false consciousness but a phenomenon grounded in West Indian culture and traditions of "getting by," through which women piece together their livelihoods by engaging in multiple economic activities (in formal and informal sectors) and place great value on cultural as well as economic forms of capital. Before moving ahead to the nuances of this process, however, it is useful to place the discussion of offshore informatics in Barbados within the broader context of labor studies, specifically those that explore the intersections between gender and class.

LABOR STUDIES AND THE CULTURE OF PRODUCTION

Class as a concept for understanding the differential positions of groups within the social structure has undergone numerous challenges in recent years. Several converging phenomena—including the transformation of the manufacturing sector in western industrialized nations, the globalization of production, the restructuring of the service economy and its accompanying technological changes, and the increasing emphasis placed on consumption in defining lifestyles and identities—have led some to argue that the concept of class has reached the end of its usefulness, or at least that the traditional bases for categorizing class groups require rethinking.[42] Such challenges have emerged in discussions of the political and economic "conditions of postmodernity" (Harvey 1989). Heeding many of these cautions, I argue that class, nonetheless, is pertinent to this discussion in two ways. First, simply, workplaces, as the centrally recognized realms of production, continue to be powerful loci for structuring socioeconomic status and identity, as informed by cultural, symbolic, and economic capital As such, this study of informatics and its somewhat ambiguous status as an "industry" or "white-collar" service sector leads us to consider its new producers in relation to class. Simultaneously, we need to rethink the foundations on which class identities are based. Indeed, the exploration of an apparently simple question—Is information processing "factory work" or is it "clerical work"?—underlies much of this book. If we rely on the shape and execution of the labor process itself, we can argue that this is factory work in secretarial clothing. The women workers in informatics are not a bourgeoisie; they own nothing with which they produce; they earn no capital, only wages; they can have no organized effect on the use or organization of either capital or the political order in the society in which they live.[43] Yet, so powerful are the images and appearances (of the computer technology, the officelike setting, and the professional look of the workers), and the desire on the part of workers that these jobs represent, if not in themselves, at least the possibility of future white-collar work, that I argue for a more complex reading of what this new arena represents in the traditional paradigm of "blue"- versus "white"-collar labor. Such a reading demands that we define more broadly our sense of class, in ways that draw from and expand upon the classic theories of Karl Marx and Max Weber.

Classes are broadly understood by both Marx and Weber as groups that emerge in the social structure from their particular relationship to patterns of production, distribution, and exchange. For Marx, the group's relationship to the dominant mode of production was of primary concern, and, as such, the two significant classes bound up with industrialization and the capitalist mode of production in a relationship of dependence and antagonism are the bourgeoisie and the proletariat—capitalists and working classes. The power of Marx's conceptualization of class and capitalism as a mode of production is unmistakable in the emphasis of most labor studies on the occupational structure and people's relationship to the means of production as workers or owners—as the basis for identifying class identity, consciousness, and struggle. For Weber, on the other hand, whose emphasis rests on the workings of the capitalist market and the social differentiation among status groups, the significance of intermediate classes (or what are often called the "new middle classes") situated between the proletariat and the bourgeoisie and fragmentation within and between these class groups are also salient. Weber asserts that status further defines and complicates economic divisions of class, and he acknowledges lifestyles and consumption practices as integral to the demarcation of status groups. This awareness has gained greater analytical appeal as economies are increasingly based on service sectors, and consumption takes on greater importance in people's lives. Following in the tradition of Thorstein Veblen ([1899] 1953), and, in a sense, by marrying Marx and Weber, Pierre Bourdieu's emphasis on status and prestige (1984) in structuring and giving meaning to the lived experiences of class helps us to interpret the multiple factors involved in the creation of informatics as a new category of work lodged between traditional factory production and white-collar services.[44] This exploration attempts to resolve two problems that have been persistent in class analyses and labor studies. The first relates to an older Marxist assumption that labor and capital are generic, that their structural positions are of primary importance, and that culture, therefore, has little bearing on relations of production or on what constitutes class identity. The second problem involves the constraints to understanding women's experience of class when class relations and identity are tied exclusively to production. These two issues, that of culture and gender and their relationship to class, are central to my discussion.

Michael Burawoy's *Manufacturing Consent* (1979) and *The Politics of Production* (1985) contribute to our understanding of workers in the capitalist labor process, moving from economistic structures to the practices of human agency. In particular, he explores the role of games in both legitimating the underpinnings of capital (securing the accumulation of surplus) and in resisting or struggling against these very conditions. Paraphrasing Marx, he says, "We do make history, but not as we please. ... The game metaphor suggests a 'history' with 'laws' of its own, beyond our control and yet the product of our actions" (1979:93). He draws our attention to the multiple dimensions of the labor process and of worker "adaptations" to this labor process, resisting the separation of superstructure (political/ideological) from the base (economic) dimensions of "objective" class analysis by insisting that we take these as integrally connected and mutually defining. "Day to day adaptations of workers," he points out, "create their own ideological effects that become focal elements in the operation of capitalist control. Not only can one not ignore the 'subjective' dimension, but the very distinction between objective and 'subjective' is arbitrary. Any work context involves an economic dimension (production of things), a political dimension (production of social relations), and an ideological dimension (production of an experience of those relations). These three dimensions are inseparable" (1985:39).

It is not only the inseparability of these dimensions that must be emphasized, but also the mutually defining properties they take on, and their relationship to a wider context than the production process alone. To make this leap, it is essential that culture be brought more squarely into the picture. For Burawoy, culture, like other dimensions of "imported consciousness," lies outside the crux of production. Thus, the lived experience or "behavior" of work is grounded essentially in the capitalist organization of production, and, as such, factors that distinguish workers (e.g., race, age, gender, and rank) and experiences they have had outside the workplace have little bearing on the way in which they will experience their work inside. Human nature, Burawoy argues, leads workers throughout the reaches of capitalism to construct games, follow their "instinct to control," and, in accordance with his Marxist framework, assume the power to create the "possibility of an emancipated society" (1979:157). In short, "the organization of work may vary with the social, political and economic context but the behavior of workers is in accordance with the organization of the labor process and largely independent of any precapitalist consciousness they carry with them" (1979:156). I argue, however, that because production is not generic in either its organization of labor or its recruitment and discipline of laborers, we must incorporate into our reading of the labor process the simultaneous processes of the culture of production and the production of culture. That is, we must do more than simply interpret workers' understandings and experience of production from the point of view of culture. We must look at how culture shapes these living structures themselves. As such, informatics production is incomprehensible outside of its particular cultural context.[45]

In a recent critique of the theoretical divide between class and culture, Edward LiPuma and Sarah Keene Meltzoff (1989) argue that class itself "should be treated as an emergent cultural category." Employing the work of Bourdieu (1977,1983,1984) in an ethnography of Galician fishing communities in Spain, they propose that class is constituted by economic capital (e.g., money, wealth, and position in the production process), cultural capital (e.g., lifestyles, tastes, and manners such as speech), and social capital (one's ancestry as well as one's relations with significant social others). Together, these forms of capital constitute class distinction and identity. In contrast to those who base social class on the occupational structure (Goldthorpe 1987; Parkin 1972; Wright 1979) and deny the relevance of status to the essential productive bases of class (Wright 1985:79), Bourdieu in his conceptualization of social class goes beyond the economic base of both Marx and Weber, and he argues that multiple forms of capital are employed in distinguishing between classes. He sees taste and consumption as integral to class identity and steeped in ideologies as well as structures. In turn, these become naturalized and foundational in reproducing broader social inequalities (Miller 1995a). Like gender, then, class, understood to encompass both material and symbolic economies, becomes an expression of social boundaries and cultural limits construed as essences.

Li Puma and Meltzoff use Bourdieu's multiple capitals to demonstrate the intrinsic connections between the so-called objective realm of production and the apparent morass of culture. "Class statuses are the product of the way in which a community objectifies patterns of correspondence between economic, social and cultural capital, ... [and] what we call class identity is the necessary, mediated, and manifest product of the culture/production unity" (1989:322–23). One of the central implications of this class/culture formulation is that individuals and groups may have ambiguous class identities if their embodiment of forms of capital challenge those objectified patterns of their culture.[46] If we look at production, not as a separate domain from culture and nonmarket activities, but as deeply bound up with them, and if we see that class is constituted by multiple and changing forms of capital, which themselves are deeply gendered, then what is dismissed by some as "another electronic sweatshop" or "factory work in a showcase" will be revealed to mean much more to the women inside.

A Caribbean study that also draws on Bourdieu by adapting Li Puma and Meltzoff's culture/production framework is Kevin Yelvington's analysis (1995) of a locally owned Trinidadian factory. He uses the concept of "embodied social capital" to describe ethnicity and gender, denoting their physicality and relatively fixed character. "Certain configurations of embodied social capital, then, both facilitate and preclude the acquisition of other kinds of capital, including various forms of social capital, embodied or generalized" (32). As Yelvington himself acknowledges, the convertibility of one form of capital to another is not always easy (or even possible). His use of embodiment to describe the complex of given and ascribed nature of gender and ethnicity is useful for interpreting the particular case of Barbadian women workers in informatics. Yelvington asserts that ethnicity and gender are commodified identities, but that class is "constituted by the kinds of labor being sold and the kinds of labor doing the selling and ... by the ways in which labor and laborers are appropriated" (38). He demonstrates the multiple ways in which economic and noneconomic capital are employed and exploited in the process of enhancing capitalist power. By structuring identities in particular ways, Yelvington says, owners wielding the power to extract profits define identities that in turn insure their accumulation. While their power is not complete, it is strong enough to "symbolize" and construct ethnicity and gender in ways that situate groups of workers in opposition to each other, and thus to preclude their shared class consciousness. Again, we are reminded of Paul, the angry former boyfriend at the start of the chapter. For him, Christine's new "professional" femininity is a powerful symbol of distinction that he is intent on deflating.

My own study begins where studies independently exploring production (e.g., Yelvington 1995) and consumption (e.g., Miller 1994) have left off. I look at the relationship between class and gender and contextualize their mutually defining properties within both local Barbadian culture and among the multiple forces of globalization. In doing so, I show not only that class identity relies on gendered practices and ideologies but also that gender identity draws on configurations of class. Fundamental to this dialectic are complex relationships between production and consumption.

Contemporary analyses of changing labor conditions, the continuum of restructuring that connects blue- and white-collar work, and the role played by technology in these transformations can hardly be initiated without mention of Harry Braverman's *Labor and Monopoly Capitalism* (1974). Braverman posed a major challenge to the dominant approach in studies of work and technological change that focused on the structural organization of occupations as distinct from the social and economic forces that shape particular divisions of labor. He argues that capitalists used technology to fragment, deskill, and generally weaken the working class, which comes increasingly under the scrutiny of management through its use. Braverman's approach to production has been widely applied by the "critical labor process school" to a variety of industrial work settings. Technology in earlier studies was often seen as unilaterally progressive, enhancing skills and upgrading the skill level of the labor force. This is a view often espoused in business and development literature. Braverman asserts, however, that in order to extract the greatest profits from purchased labor power, capitalists try to maximize control over the labor process and that to achieve this control, capital separates mental from manual work, conception from execution, in restructuring production. In removing conceptual work from the manual producer and putting it into the hands of managers, the production worker is supposedly "freed" from the need to know about the work process and is thereby proletarianized.

The proletarianization argument of the Braverman school asserts that by way of Fordist measures—rationalizing and fragmenting skilled work into lower skilled and repetitive tasks—workers (including white-collar office workers) who were once in control of their labor, become de-skilled and marginalized within the labor process. For example, offices that once performed such duties as data entry or word processing within the context of other more highly skilled tasks have become fragmented into independent divisions in which workers perform more limited jobs. As demonstrated by Barbados's informatics sector, these jobs have been physically separated into spaces that blur the boundaries between factory floors and professional offices. These spaces provide increased structure and allow greater control over production but minimize personal contact between workers and managers and among workers themselves. Additionally, a restructuring of the work hierarchy has squeezed its middle level, leaving a small managerial/professional level of staff in the upper strata and a large production level of workers who perform the lower-skilled jobs in the bottom strata. Braver- man's inclusion of office work in his proletarianization argument was, from the perspective of labor studies, a provocative step, and though he does note that women constitute the actors in these "reservoirs of mass occupations," he does not take up the ways in which gender plays an integral part of the proletarianization process itself (1974:385).

Braverman's inattention to gender as a central component of production relations has inspired several feminist critiques within the critical labor process school. Michael Apple's analysis (1984) of the feminization of teaching provides a useful point of reference here. Apple extends Braverman's model in noting that the decline in the number of jobs with autonomy is closely related to the change in the sexual division of labor, and that de-skilling has had a profound effect on female labor. He notes that there is a close relation between the entry of women into a sector of work and its subsequent downward transformation in pay and skill levels, and he links these trends in the teaching field to those in the clerical sector. Even in such attempts to describe the patterns of a segmented and gendered labor force, we are often still left wondering why and through what mechanisms particular arenas of work simultaneously become rationalized and feminized.

Women's entry into the paid work force has typically been configured so that it does not threaten men's position of authority in instances of technological change and labor market restructuring. The story of Paul and Christine at the start of this chapter, on the other hand, hints at the tensions that can arise when this gendered class hierarchy is put into question. In instances when women appear to be replacing men, Maureen McNeil (1987:192) says, "you can almost always be sure the job has been redesigned and devalued in some way." By the 1930s, women's entry into the clerical arena in the United States coincided with a juncture in which these jobs simultaneously ceased to be the training grounds for managers (Davies 1982). Both teaching and clerical work shifted from largely male occupations in the nineteenth century to largely female enclaves in the twentieth, and reveal drastic reorganizations in their respective labor processes. The changes, Apple says, relate to patriarchal relations in the wider social and economic spheres. Bourgeois ideologies about domesticity and women as nurturing and empathic, with "natural" qualities that make them ideal teachers, coincided with greater bureaucratization in the field, as positions of principal and superintendent were filled more and more by men. As Ken Prandy (1986:147) adds, even when there appears to be parity in the kinds of work men and women perform, there is "typically a difference in the way in which the occupation fits into an overall career pattern. So, for example, male bank clerks are seen as being on the bottom rung of a promotion ladder which will lead through supervisory positions, perhaps to bank manager. The same ladder may in principle exist for women, but in practice is climbed by them much less frequently."

In the realm of the "new office," clerical work, much like garment assembly, "became sex-typed as appropriate for women due to their supposedly greater manual dexterity, patience for repetitive work and attention to detail. The fact that women could be paid less than men was also an obvious advantage" (Carter 1987:206). In these studies, new office arrangements, including word processing and data entry pools, are treated as dressed-up factories, differing predominantly in their clean and professional-looking ambience. The "'sexy secretary' with her 'bourgeois' pretensions is here overtaken by the proletarian figure; (and in Marxist critiques) her gender is subordinated to her changing class position" (Pringle 1988:97). This view of the informatics sector in Barbados has led some critics to describe it as an "electronic sweatshop" and to perceive the officelike environs as an insidious veneer on top of a familiar assembly-line workplace. What emerges, however, from this study of informatics is not strictly a proletarian figure, and certainly not a bourgeois one, but instead a blurry category of feminine worker who is created by corporate prescriptions and who chooses this realm of work much because of possibilities generated by its ambiguous position in the industrial/ services hierarchy. Central to my discussion, then, is the question, How are gendered notions of work connected to these "reclassifications" of labor? That is, how do they become naturalized and incorporated such that they become explanatory justifications for situating women in particular realms of labor with particular prescriptions for demeanor, mindset, and social value? In short, how is work transformed from white- to pink-collar sectors, and how is this transformation experienced? In what ways does the emergence of the pink collar encompass new modes of consumption that are tied to new arenas of production? These questions and perspectives transcend some of the limitations of Braverman's critical labor process school, which tended to suspend the notion of the secretary as a feminine subject in favor of identifying her solely within the category of the proletarianized working class. For Braverman, as for Burawoy, it is the labor process that defines the worker and her/his experience. As Micaela di Leonardo (1985), Cynthia Costello (1985), Louise Lamphere (1985) and Patricia Zavella (1985) have demonstrated, women's particular forms of work culture—embodied in processes of organization, modes of resistance and consent, the formation of networks, and the "double consciousness" of their family and workplace responsibilities—challenge such a generic formulation of work and of people's relationship to it (di Leonardo 1985:494).

Where Braverman privileged the class dimension of proletarianization, Pringle (1988) leans in the opposite direction, asserting that the decline in status among clerical workers is due not simply to their proletarianization but to "shifts in the structure of femininity" whereby secretaries "lost some of their status as ladies' and were thrown into the mass category of 'girls.' This happened via a process of sexualization rather than through loss of control over the means of production" (193). Taking this observation further to explore the relative absence of class consciousness among clerical workers, Margery Davies (1982) argues that the emphasis on femininity and the view of office workers in the early twentieth century as women first and workers second obscured their proletarianization and declining status relative to male office workers of the nineteenth century. "The nineteenth-century clerk had not turned into a proletarian; he had merely turned into a woman" (175).

Despite a voluminous literature on work, economic restructuring, and the implications of new technologies for labor, the experience of clerical workers in increasingly automated environments have fallen between a number of cracks in labor studies. As women workers who are seldom unionized and frequently (if erroneously) viewed as middle-class, pink-collar workers have been the focus of study much less than hard-hatted, blue-collar men in heavy industries, or women on assembly lines in light manufacturing plants (Freeman 1993). What this trend reveals is a perpetuation of the image of office work (and even merely officelike work) as somehow exempt from the critical concerns of industrial labor because of its pleasant surroundings and perhaps its personalized nature. In short, labor studies seem to have accepted the very ideology that perpetuates this mythical but powerful perception. Furthermore, when there have been discussions about the process of proletarianization that include women, they tend to avoid altogether the gender permutations involved in their process of incorporation.

The concepts of gender and class are receiving increasing attention in discussions of power and human experience, from fields as wide ranging as sports and fashion to politics and factory work. Here I define "gender" as the socially imputed meanings associated with maleness and femaleness, or the "social magic" by which females are cast as a certain kind of feminine subject and males as masculine ones (Moi 1991). "Social magic," according to Toril Moi, "is a socially sanctioned act which attributes an essence to individual agents, who then struggle to become what in fact they are already declared to be. In other words: to cast women as women is precisely to *produce* them as women. ... Like all other social categories, the category of woman therefore at once *masquerades* as and *is* an essence" (1036). By unearthing the processes through which sexual difference is socially constructed, we may critically assess the creation and effects of such institutions as the sexual division of labor and traits asserted as "naturally" predisposing women or men to possess particular temperaments or to perform particular jobs. Imprecision over the usage of "gender" in recent years has been reflected in murky conflation of "gender" and "women's" studies within studies of labor in Latin America and the Caribbean. While studies of women have inspired a new focus on gender relations and identities, they are certainly not a privileged realm for such analysis, as demonstrated by several studies of masculinities in the region (e.g., Gutman 1996; Lancaster 1992). Nor do studies of women necessarily portray gender as a fluid and contested category. In short, a discussion of gender, like class, is one about power and both the practice and representation of social identities.

Flexible labor along the global assembly line has routinely been equated with female labor despite a long tradition of masculinized factory work, but the reasons behind the feminine face of global production are far from obvious and indisputably not "natural."[47] Following Simone de Beauvoir's assertion that one is not born a woman but made one, recent literature about women workers in global capitalism makes clear that ideal pools of flexible labor are actively created and not simply found; their creation relies heavily on both local and transnational forces that employ strategies of "gendering" (feminizing) embedded within capitalist production.[48] In fact, what makes the equation of "docile girls," "feminine third world women," and "ideal worker" so insidious is its very taken-for-grantedness. Even explanations that seem to cut to the quick of women's incorporation into the global labor force (e.g., that women are preferred because they can be paid less than men) still fail to probe deeply enough the question "why?" How is women's labor cheapened so that both men and women come to believe that women can be paid less than men? To answer this question, and to explore its specificity in a cultural context that in many ways challenges the presumption that femininity equals docility and domesticity, we must turn to the gender ideologies this presumption reflects and the contexts in which it is articulated—the "pink-collaring" of offshore office work in Barbados.

A recent increase in the literature on gender in the Afro-Caribbean is connected in part to the emergence of Caribbean-based gender studies programs and to a growing number of scholars interested in mapping historical and contemporary expressions of gender ideology and practice as they relate to colonial pasts and transnational futures.[49] These are novel and important discussions building on and often critiquing earlier paradigms in which gender was treated solely in the context of kinship or within the bi-polar framework of "reputation" and "respectability" (Wilson 1969). Locally, Barbadians speak about gender in terms of what behaviors are deemed appropriate for women and for men, and they do so in ways that often naturalize culture through discourses about sexuality and human nature.[50] Childbearing in Barbados is considered an essential element of femininity (superseding and often preceding marriage, for example), and women's bodies are said to be better suited to sedentary factory and office work than are men's bodies, which, as one woman put it, "need to be moving around all the time." Often these values reflect cultural "ideals" that fly in the face of actual practice, as we will see with regard to notions of "respectability" and "reputation." In interpreting these disjunctures, my aim is to read "emic" or locally derived expressions and understandings about gender (and, in particular, women's roles, identities, and experiences and their imagined pasts and futures) against "etic" analyses—those derived through observation and interpretation of the contemporary Barbadian context and its social history.

In particular, changing gender ideologies surrounding women's work and the relationship between women's income earning and their consumption practices are crucial to understanding the meanings of informatics and its status in the hierarchy of occupations. For Afro-Barbadian women, a number of double standards have pervaded social and economic life and power relations. On one hand, female heads of households and women generally have been hailed as the backbone of this matrifocal society. Their strength, creativity, and sheer tenacity in supporting their children and maintaining the social fabric are alluded to across the realms of literary production and popular culture, as well as on political platforms and in historical and sociological treatises. On the other hand, their still limited representation in positions of political and economic power is striking, and it bears repeating that female-headed households remain the poorest of the poor. Women in Barbados are simultaneously revered, as mothers and providers, and ridiculed, as mercenary, manipulative sexual partners. The tension between these two stereotypes lies at the core of the informatics workers' emergent identities and perception within the wider arena of Barbadian social life. An analysis of gender ideologies as they are tied to those of class will help us better understand the contradictions here.

Class analyses and gender analyses have endured a somewhat fraught relationship, and even of late, as the interrelationship of race, class, and gender is increasingly acknowledged as integral to most human experience and expression, the tension persists. In part this residual tension is the legacy of competing approaches of Marxism and socialist feminism. This tension must be mediated in order to adequately analyze women's relationship to the means of production—the base from which they experience gender oppression with regard to the subjugation of women in patriarchy—including male control over women's sexuality. Attempts to bring these dimensions of oppression together have ranged from a "dual systems" approach, according to which capitalism produces the "places for a hierarchy of workers" and "gender and racial hierarchies determine who fills the empty places" (Hartmann 1976:18), to more integrated approaches that view "capitalist-patriarchy," for example, as a mutually reinforcing system of oppression reliant on specific strategies of gendering workers and "classifying" women.[51] A number of studies have demonstrated the dynamic interconnections between women's household-based, informal sector, and formal waged work in ways that challenge us to engage the multiple dimensions of women's lives in our attempts to study the impact of the international economy. Furthermore, women's stage in the life cycle, as daughters, mothers, partners, and wives, together with their relationships to the means of production and household distribution play a significant role in shaping and reworking their class identities.[52] In Caribbean studies, as Sonia Cuales (1988:120) aptly notes, analyses of gender and class have engaged less in a "marriage" than, at best, a "visiting relationship."[53]

Building on these earlier approaches, I demonstrate here, through the experience of women working in the new transnational arena of informatics in Barbados, how class, gender, and culture are integrally connected in shaping individual women's sources of identity and in framing the transnational economic systems in which they live and move.

Feminist critiques have been crucial in reframing class analysis by asking where women fit into the picture of class structure: Are women's class identities defined necessarily by their relationships to husbands and fathers and within households? Can production be understood without consideration of the multiple dimensions of reproductive labor? They ask also how the "life-chances" associated with the same occupation vary according to whether the worker is a man or a woman. These two sets of questions, one from a neo-Marxist position identifying the bases for defining women's class identities and the other, a more neo-Weberian approach, focusing on the gendering of labor itself, resonate strongly within the context of pink-collar workers in Barbados.

As many have already pointed out, if women's class identity is subsumed under the rubric of the household, and if it depends on the occupational position of their husbands as breadwinners, then women present clear contradictions to the presumed configuration of nuclear and patriarchal family/household structure. This is especially true for the majority of the women in this study, whose work is essential to the survival of their households, whether they are heads of households or not. Also, if we rely on women's own relationship to the means of production, or their structural economic position as workers, without examining the particular ways in which their incorporation into the labor force is itself predicated on gendered realities, and relates to their simultaneous positions within a household, we fail to realize that women's entry into wage labor typically weakens and strengthens patriarchal relations—at home and at work (Solcoloff 1980:143). Furthermore, as Christine Delphy and Diana Leonard (1992) demonstrate, the distribution and consumption of resources within a family cannot be assumed to be equal; thus we must question the extent to which individual members, young and old, male and female, share an identical "class situation." Consumption is as an increasingly central arena of not simply survival but also creativity, pleasure, and self-definition among the Caribbean women workers. As such, a consideration of consumption demands that we look closely at these patterns within households and their respective meanings for individual women. Finally, within the sphere of production, the call to question the gendering of labor has particular significance within clerical work, where men and women have faced different manifestations of technological and structural transformations of labor processes.

The feminine identities that become central to the formation of the informatics sector clearly reflect (and serve) corporate prescriptions and agendas in many of the ways that others have asserted, especially in regard to the desire for cheap labor and its translation into natural properties of women workers (see Fernandez-Kelly 1983; Ong 1987; Wolf 1992; Yelvington 1995). Indeed, given the peculiar nature of informatics as somehow (symbolically if not structurally) in between blue-collar industry and white-collar services, class becomes an embodied identity, through particular notions of femininity (proper, respectable, maternal, fashionable, modern, and professional). Cultural orientations not only set the terms through which workers experience their identities but also create the medium for their very definition (and counter-definitions). This places a somewhat different emphasis on the relationship between production and culture. What lies at the crux of this relationship for the Bajan informatics workers is the way in which gender permeates labor and laborers in every market and nonmarket field. Bajan pink-collar identities come to reflect and to refashion those designed by multinational capital, and they do so through local cultural practices. The ways in which these definitions are drawn and reworked rely on dimensions of cultural capital (themselves both "local" and "global" in form). The pursuit and exchange of cultural capital together with economic capital ultimately reconfigure women's class consciousness and its modes of expression. Even though informatics does not present these women with a clear vehicle for actual class mobility, their work status gives them the sense that new identities are nonetheless possible. This sense of possibility is bound up with a host of symbolic elements (appearances of the workplace and the workers, computer technology, new management practices, and so on). These elements, in turn, are integral to refashioning women's class consciousness and in their pointed disinclination to unionize.

Global industrialization and the incorporation of women workers into this process brings our attention back to a basic premise of Marx and Engels, as well as that of Esther Boserup (1970), the mother of "women and development" studies: that the material basis of women's subordination would be challenged through their integration into social as opposed to domestic production (Crompton and Mann 1986:4). For Boserup, women's entry into wage work is a necessary step to their incorporation into the economic development process and is therefore liberating insofar as capital confers power. Although her work has been critiqued for its modernization premise (Beneria and Sen 1986), she paved the way for a significant body of research that has taken up the gendered (and now) international division of labor, and the relationships between women's domestic or "reproductive" labor and their social or "productive" labor. Class figures into this picture in the growing recognition that even when women are incorporated into the formal sector of the economy as wage earners, their position and experience is distinct. Use-value as well as exchange-value production is integral to defining active labor. That this has not historically been emphasized (by colonial administrators or development officials alike) has significantly affected the extent to which women and men have shared a class consciousness. In Barbados, like much of the rest of the Caribbean, despite a strong tradition of trade unionism, in which agricultural and manufacturing workers have won powerful political representation, women are marginal participants in organized labor. Their recruitment into export processing industries has been said to exacerbate this trend, by virtue of the nonunion status of most foreign-owned off-shore plants. Additionally, the patriarchal tradition of the trade union movement and the spirit of competitive individualism inculcated in the high-tech workplace accentuate this situation. Thus, on one hand we witness increasingly proletarianized populations of women and on the other, limited traditional possibilities for their expression of class consciousness.

PRODUCING AND CONSUMING FEMININE IDENTITIES AND CLASS CONSCIOUSNESS

Without taking into account the status-based associations that both workers and the general public ascribe to particular occupations, we cannot begin to predict or interpret the emergence (or rejection) of class identification, consciousness, solidarity, and action. In one of few discussions of the relationship between class and gender in the Caribbean, Cuales (1988:119) argues that women located in the expanding and rationalized "grey" areas of white-collar and commercial services (e.g., clerical workers, nurses, and social workers) are increasingly occupying class situations that resemble the working class but not necessarily adopting working class positions (political side-taking). As Christine and Paul's bus stand episode reveals, images are powerfully linked to notions of appropriateness, status, and, ultimately, class consciousness. Within the broad sweep of capitalist globalization, and the expansion of the global assembly line into new realms of work, local culture and notions of identity enact themselves in significant ways, reshaping the very contours of multinational industries and therefore, even in a small way, of global capitalism itself. The medium through which this "localization" of the global takes place is an array of gendered practices that demand simultaneous consideration of class and status, economy and culture, production and consumption. Though Bourdieu neglects to consider the gendered dimensions of class, he articulates this general aim well:

> The movement from probability to reality, from theoretical class to practical class, is never given: even though they are supported by the "sense of one's place" and by the affinity of habitus, the principles of vision and division of the social world at work in the construction of theoretical classes have to compete, *in reality*, with other principles, ethnic, racial, or national and more concretely still, with principles imposed by the ordinary experience of occupational, communal and local divisions and rivalries. (1987:7, quoted in Crompton 1993:174)

In the offshore informatics sector, we will see that structural and economic underpinnings of class are uneasily bound up with and challenged by elements of status that blur distinctions between wage and salaried workers in the realm of clerical services, in part through the new practices of consumption made possible and encouraged by the operators' status as informatics workers. But keeping up with the styles, as prescribed by corporate dress codes and worker self-fashioning, costs money and takes time, and the emphasis on professional looks merges with expectations of professional work habits, availability, and commitment. For these women the pride of distinction associated with defining themselves in contrast to their factory counterparts in the garment and electronics operations next door is subtly supported by the industry and the state (itself invested in the image of modernity and progress tied to informatics).

This is not to say that by simply wearing imported suits and jewelry, workers are duped into thinking they have the high-level secretarial or white-collar jobs that, indeed, many aim for or that they are blinded to the factorylike nature of both their labor process and their paychecks. A host of "professional" images and practices within the industry have an unmistakably powerful effect on their perceptions of themselves and their work. Their pride in their association with informatics and their link to modernity through their computer-based work are expressed in part by the fact that they are inclined to keep these jobs long beyond the average tenure of offshore production jobs elsewhere in the world.[54]

C. Wright Mills in his classic work *White Collar* (1956) says, "When white-collar people get jobs, they sell not only their time and energy but their personalities as well. They sell by the week or month their smiles and their kindly gestures, and they must practice the prompt repression of resentment and aggression. … Here are the new little Machiavellians, practicing their personable crafts for hire and for the profit of others, according to rules laid down by those above them" (xvii). The "emotional labor" Mills associates with the white-collar workers has oddly permeated the pink-collar realm of offshore informatics, despite the fact that the employees are located thousands of miles away from their customers, linked only through voiceless, faceless computer technology.[55] A particularly intriguing element of this added labor of gentility and "professionalism" is the emphasis on gendered identity and workplace appearance. Bourdieu's modes of "distinction" (1984), which are widely expressed in the medium of clothing, recall the white-collar workers' "claims to prestige" described by Mills. Of the new middle classes he discusses in *White Collar,* Mills says, "Their occupations enable and require them to wear street clothes at work. Although they may be expected to dress somewhat somberly, still, their working attire is not a uniform, or distinct from clothing generally suitable for street wear. … The wage worker may wear standardized street clothes off the job, but the white collar worker wears them on the job as well" (241).[56] Remarkably, neither Mills nor Bourdieu pursues the gendered dimension of these acts and meanings of distinction, though the relevance of their formulations for the informatics enclave and its specific emphasis on a particular brand of femininity is striking. The lengths to which data processors go to set themselves apart, in their own minds and in the eye of the public, from traditional factory workers in neighboring garment and assembly plants is revealing of the importance of what

Mills calls "white collar prestige" (1956:240) and of Weber's concept of closure explored by Parkin (1979) and Yelvington (1995) in which groups exert their power to create exclusionary boundaries around resources and opportunities. Again, by broadening our sense of capital to include cultural, social, and symbolic dimensions, we can better interpret the sense of affront and shock expressed by a group of data processors when their fellow worker quit her job to work in the cigar assembly plant next door, and their multiple efforts to distinguish themselves from their "traditional factory worker" peers. While their wages may not be much better, the cache of informatics and its superior image in the industrial hierarchy make it feel like a "higher class" operation, and not one to leave for the fumes and dust of a factory.

The question of women's class consciousness and its relation to other dimensions of women's identities as workers, members of families, and feminine subjects raises important issues about the extent to which culture and class interact. Helen Safa (1990:95, 1995:88) concludes her discussions about women and industrialization in the Hispanic Caribbean by saying that "women's increasing importance as wage earners should enable them to achieve greater recognition and higher levels of class consciousness as workers in their struggle with unions, management and the state." She says, however, that while in the context of their families women have been remarkably successful in challenging traditional patriarchal gender ideologies, these other institutions have been far more resistant to change. No wonder, then, that women continue to identify themselves proudly as wives and mothers—it is in the arena of the family that they feel themselves most powerful. An outcome of this emphasis on women's domestic identity, Safa argues (along with Gallin 1990:190), is that it simultaneously precludes a woman's identification as a worker and therefore her class consciousness. The Afro-Barbadian women workers of the informatics industry stand in contrast to many of their sisters in the Hispanic Caribbean, and even farther reaches of the global assembly line, in that they do identify themselves proudly as workers, even if their femininity is also a significant locus for corporate control and discipline. The implication here is that women's engagement in "femininity plays"—fashion statements that blur the imagery of class—serves to reconfigure their class consciousness at the same time that it situates these women workers in a complex of transnational and local relations from which they derive pleasure and pride.

If we agree that the working class is not homogeneous, and that data entry operators in Barbados experience class as gendered Afro-Caribbean subjects within a distinctly feminized arena, we might argue that despite the similarities of family background (the vast majority cited the occupational and educational base of their parents as solidly working class), education, and economic means between themselves and traditional factory workers, they occupy a new class fraction whose identity is shaped around a complex of cultural-economic and production/consumption relations.

NOTES

1. See Williams 1991 for a rich ethnographic exploration of the ways in which even the smallest acts, objects, and ideas both contain and enact representations of politics and economic difference. Williams (1991:30) quotes Michael Gilsenan, who says, "English furniture? Well, yes. Furniture, ways of sitting, mores of dress, politeness, photography, table manners and gestures overturn societies, too. Such conventions, techniques, and ways of acting in and on the world are as important as any religion, and changes in them may be as dislocating as changes in belief."

2. The acknowledgment that globalization and technological transformations of work have differential effects not only on women but in particular on women of color is made by Beneria and Roldan (1987), Colclough and Tolbert (1992), and Glenn and Tolbert (1987), who note that minority clerical workers in the United States face greater risks of job losses, while more skilled white workers confront restrictions on mobility out of low-paying jobs.

3. As such, Barriteau argues, black Barbadians "experience little racial discrimination in the areas of health services, education, transportation, housing and public sector employment" (1995:151). The corporate elite are still critiqued for maintaining a tradition of patronage and nepotism, evidenced by the publication of Beckles's book (1989b) on the history of the Barbados Mutual Life Assurance Society, and a series of "race debates" that flared along these lines during the period of my fieldwork.

4. For example, expressions such as "dark" or "clear skinned" for light or "brown skin" or "that girl with fine hair" for straight hair emerged in jokes and casual conversation or in identifying individuals to me. These were similar to other explicit physical descriptors used to call attention to particular people in their graphic directness (e.g., "Mary? Oh she that fat, fat girl") or comments made to me, such as "Carla, you just dipped in bleach!" when I returned to Barbados after a year, or " You looking more and more like a chicken every day … what man will have you now?" when I had lost some weight.

5. These terms are more widely used in Barbados than elsewhere in the Caribbean, though they differ from "black" and "white" in the United States. Furthermore, the "black" ownership of some of these local firms is not limited to "brown-skin" elites, as is more likely in other Caribbean countries and as might have been at an earlier time in Barbados as well.

6. Though Jamaica is historically a Caribbean nation in which the color/class hierarchy is marked, Pearson (1993) notes that the informatics industry there is notable in the fact that local ownership of new firms "come neither from the traditional landowning oligarchy nor the capital-owning elite of Jamaican society. They are the upwardly mobile products of the post-independence expansion of technical and professional education amongst the black middle classes who have been mainly educated at the University of the West Indies" (290).

7. Some recent discussions that theorize in different ways the forces behind and manifestations of the contemporary global and transnational culture and economy are: Appadurai 1996; Bash *et al.* 1994; Bird *et al.* 1993; Cvetkovich and Kellner 1997; Featherstone 1990; Friedman 1994; Giddens 1990; Gilroy 1993; Guarnizo and Smith 1998; Hannerz 1996; Harvey 1989; King 1991; Lash and Ury 1987; Ong and Nonini 1997; Robertson 1992; Swedenberg and Lavie 1996; Wilson and Dissayanake 1996. Where some have attempted to distinguish between these terms (limiting "transnationalism" to those movements explicitly anchored in one or more national territories, and reserving "globalization" to flows that are truly boundaryless), I employ them more broadly here. In either case, the specificity of the producing and consuming cultures is vital to understanding the meanings of these processes.

8. Appadurai (1996) has made this argument of "post-nationalism" whereas Gertler (1997) argues that the nation-state continues to be a key regulatory force, economically and otherwise.

9. "Flexibility" can refer to a number of aspects of production and marketing: "financial flexibility (wages), numerical flexibility (hours, workloads, or numbers of workers) and functional flexibility (multiskilling and broadbanding)" (Henry and Franzway 1993:133).

10. Frobel, Heinrichs, and Kreye (1980) are credited with coining the expression "new international division of labor."

11. The paradigm described by "dependency" theorists set the stage for Frobel's international division of labor (IDL) framework, as they had long identified globalized capital accumulation (through colonialism) as the basis for underdevelopment in the third world (Frank 1967; Amin 1974). Like some proponents of the dependency school, Fröbel, Heinrichs, and Kreye saw that, contrary to persistent dualisms of neoclassical economic frameworks that presented core and periphery as linked, though quintessential separate in their roles in the IDL, losses of decision-making power and labor restructuring occur within both spheres.

12. Other approaches, most notably those adopted by international development agencies, have taken a more neoclassical economic view of world market industrialization. Their premise is that the free flow of capital internationally will gradually lead to a leveling of inequalities in exchange, thereby creating an economic equilibrium. In other words, investment in industry should ultimately help to equalize wages and prices worldwide. Sharing many of these premises is another model that describes a "vertical integration" of global production. Here, first and third world countries are hierarchically organized in an international division of labor where the latter, on the bottom, provide manual labor, and as we move up the production ladder "nationality becomes increasingly

European in the command centers of research, knowledge and management" (Nash 1983:3). Like the neoclassical models, the vertical integration perspective presents relations between "core" and "periphery" as an essential and timeless feature of the global market and lacks any historical discussion of the bases for the hierarchy that now defines them.

13. These industries are "labor intensive" both in the amount of labor required to produce a good and in the quality of the labor process entailed.

14. As part of these new economic geographies we also see the emergence of "global cities" in highly industrialized nations (Cox 1997; Sassen 1991).

15. For a fascinating historical exploration of commodification and consumption that avoids the simplicity Gupta and Ferguson warn of, see Burke 1996.

16. Notably, Miller (1994) makes a similar argument in his treatment of modernity and mass consumption in Trinidad. He asserts that mass consumption of imported goods, far from wiping out distinctive culture, actually enhances and sharpens notions of "Trinidadian-ness." Mintz (1977) and Trouillot (1989) have eloquently discussed anthropology's view of the Caribbean, long ignored and even repudiated for its lack of "purity" of culture and a truly indigenous population of natives. Interestingly for precisely these reasons, the Caribbean now appears to be gaining anthropological currency.

17. Expressions of resistance to globalization often adopt a sense of an "invented primordial" culture defined against these flows/dependencies.

18. Important recent exceptions include Ong and Nonini 1997 and Lowe and Lloyd 1997. See also Bell and Valentine 1997; Breclcenridge 1995; Burke 1996; de Guy *et al.* 1997; Howes 1996; Miller 1995a, 1995b; Mintz 1996b; Watson 1997.

19. See Goddard (1998) for a useful explanation of the decline of the Barbadian sugar industry.

20. It is worth noting here that this legislation did not apply to sugar manufacturing, and, similarly, the national income accounts of Barbados consider sugar milling a separate economic category. These phenomena relate closely to sugar's association with slavery and the conceptualization of agriculture as a separate (different) entity: from "modern" industry. The irony is that investment in sugar factor) machinery and technology has been substantial, but it is not eligible for the tax incentives and exemptions given to other export industries.

21. As Safa (1995:8) points out, the U.S. apparel industry is estimated to have lost roughly three hundred thousand jobs, with half moving to Mexico, Central America, and the Caribbean. The passage of NAFTA between Canada, the United States, and Mexico has intensified these movements, and has posed detrimental effects to non-member Caribbean nations. Already, Jamaica has experienced significant job losses as garment industries have fled to Mexico for preferential trade relations.

22. These descriptions are developed in greater detail in chapter 3. Briefly, the emphasis on order and politeness take shape in numerous cultural stereotypes by and during my fieldwork was quoted in a speech as saying, "Bajans aren't necessarily warm like Jamaicans and Trinidadians, but they can be counted on for politeness." Grounded in Barbados's history as a stable parliamentary democracy, these cultural stereotypes are strategically employed as promotional tools by economic development representatives and state bureaucrats in tourism and industry alike.

23. This point requires greater elaboration and is explored in greater depth in later chapters. On one hand, cultural imperialism is of great concern to social critics within the West Indies. Rex Nettleford, among other local intellectuals, has decried forces of British and U.S. cultural imperialism for the past twenty-five years, in relation to such issues as western (white) ideals of beauty depicted in advertising and beauty pageants (Barnes 1997). Others, such as the former senator Carmeta Fraser, have tied these issues to economic concerns in asserting local production (of food, clothing, and other imports). On the other hand, the belief that many "imported" cultural forms have now become "Bajan" or "Caribbean," such as fashion shows, 1994) is also a widely argued point.

24. Fuentes and Ehrenreich (1983:15) asserted, "The factory system relies upon and reinforces the power of men in the traditional patriarchal family to control women." Quoting Cynthia Enloe, they add, "Even recruitment is a family process. Women don't just go out independently to find jobs; it's a matter of fathers, brothers and husbands making women available after getting reassurances from the companies. Discipline becomes a family matter since, in most cases, women turn their paychecks over to their parents. Factory life is, in general, constrained and defined by the family life cycle."

25. In a fascinating recent work on the British common law practice of coverture in the late eighteenth and early nineteenth centuries, Margot Finn (1996) explores the powerful role consumption practices played in married women's ability to evade these strictures, purchase goods on their husbands' credit, and gain some degree of independence from unsuccessful unions. See also de Grazia 1996 for an exceptional collection of historical essays on gender and consumption.

26. See, for example, Abraham-Van der Mark 1983; Beneria and Roldan 1987; Bolles 1983; Elson and Pearson 1981a, 1981b; Fernandez-Kelly 1983; Kelly 1987; Lim 1985; Mies 1986; Nash and Fernandez-Kelly 1983; Ong 1987; Safa 1981, 1995; Ward 1990a; Warren and Bourque 1991; Wolf 1992.

27. Notable exceptions include Bolles on Jamaica (1983,1996); Kelly on St. Lucia (1987); and, though not about a foreign-owned, export-oriented factory, Yelvington's 1995 study of a Trinidadian small-appliance factory is a relevant addition to this literature.

28. The observation that, despite the hopes of economic planners, free trade zones and export production have not decreased unemployment rates has been related to this point. In short, the argument has been that women had not been counted as part of the labor force, never having worked for wages previously. Therefore, in the light of the recruitment of female labor and the high rates of turnover in these industries, they have both marginalized male labor, and ironically, contributed to rising unemployment figures (Fernandez-Kelly 1983). Tiano (1990) presents a different argument, countering the presumption that female maquila employment is directly tied to male unemployment, by asserting that these women are not largely drawn from families with unemployed male heads of households. Male joblessness is not what led most of these women into taking these jobs, nor is male unemployment necessarily related at all to female selection within these industries. Instead, she argues that women take these jobs either because there is no male supporting the household or because the contributions made by the male of the household are insufficient to support the entire family. These factors, according to Tiano, are related more generally to the broad state of the Mexican economy than to the specific recruitment and employment practices of the maquiladora sector.

29. Peña (1997:16) has also pointed out that women have long been wage workers in Mexico, indicating that the rhetoric of women as "first-time" workers in the free trade zones is contradicted by history. The power of this assumption is great, however, and as the above accounts reveal, it fuels the general feminine stereotype of the Mexican woman as naturally domestic, passive, inexperienced and therefore in need of protection, and so on.

30. This point is made as well in Ong and Nonini 1997 with regard to Chinese capitalism and tradition.

31. Speculating an answer to this question, some say that the more dire economic conditions in the Dominican Republic account for men's employment in this sector. Interestingly, the conception of these jobs as "computer jobs" seems, as well, to be emphasized as a way of compensating men for what otherwise might be construed as "feminine" work (i.e., typing).

32. Diane Wolf (1992:258) also presents evidence from her study of women factory workers in Java to challenge the presumption that women work as part of family- articulated, household strategies for survival. In her study, she says, "These young Javanese women initially seek factory employment to gain new experience and some cash for themselves—not for the family's economic good. Family benefits accrue only later, over time."

33. Intel, which operated a microcomputer chip assembly plant in Barbados prior to the opening of the informatics industry, had attempted to impose a pregnancy test or prospective workers. After a short but strong bout of resistance to this practice, the proposal was dropped. Interestingly, women in the informatics industry reported this to me with horror—asserting that their employer would never have attempted such a repressive policy.

34. This relationship between work and fertility rates is not so for Indo-Caribbean women agricultural workers (Aisha Khan, personal communication, 1997). Richard Stoffle's study (1977) of the impact of industrialization on mating patterns asserts that individuals typically pass through several predictable union stages (visiting, common-law, and legally recognized marriage) and that women's entry into industrial work actually accelerates their progression in the mating process.

35. The most selective industries (traditionally, electronics, in contrast to garments or textiles) are known to take extreme measures in much of the world, requiring, for example, pregnancy tests or sterilization certificates to ensure that their workforce remains childless and therefore available.

36. See Benson 1984; Crompton 1986; Fernandez-Kelly 1983; Hochschild 1983; Mur- phree 1984; Nash and Fernandez-Kelly 1983; Paules 1991; and Pyle 1990 for useful discussions of the gendering of work in various female-centered arenas, from clerical work to that of flight attendant, waitress, and assembly-line producer.

37. It is important to note that deskilling occurs unevenly even within the same industry For example, workers may be laid off by machines, generating a demand for other skilled workers to maintain and repair these machines (Block 1990).

38. For a nuanced ethnography of culture and computerization, see Hakken and Andrews 1993.

39. See Boris and Daniels 1989; Christensen 1988; Hartmann, Kraut, and Tilly 1986–87; and Webster 1996 for both historical and contemporary analyses of home-based and other related restructuring arrangements as they relate to gender and changing technology.

40. See Appelbaum 1987; Carter 1987; 9 to 5,1990; Posthuma 1987; and Samper 1987 for excellent discussions of these processes of technological transformations and the gendering of labor.

41. A good illustration of the appeal of these jobs is the response by two thousand applicants to the announcement of thirty positions in an operation that opened in 1993.

42. The idea that these jobs are stepping stones for the Dominican men is, I should emphasize, their expressed hope, just as many Bajan women hope that their jobs will lead to something better. The fact that in the Dominican Republic, however, workers stay in the jobs for an average of two years does set them dramatically apart from their Barbadian

counterparts. How successful the Dominicans are in achieving their upwardly mobile goal, I do not know. The trajectory of workers who leave these zones is still to be explored.

43. See Skeggs 1998 for a recent critique of these rejections of the significance of class.

44. This is so, with the exception of some women's ownership of sewing machines with which they create garments and household accessories for sale on the informal market. With respect to their capacity as wage workers in informatics, they occupy the position of proletariat from the point of view of Marx's classical model of class structure. It is important to note, as well however, that, historically, women of the bourgeoisie have also lacked such capital and rights. Assigning women to one or another class position, again, relies on a view not only of their labor/occupation or that of their husbands/fathers but also, depending on the particular cultural and historical context, an understanding of all of these factors and their relation to and reliance on multiple forms of capital.

45. For insightful analyses of Bourdieu along these lines, see Jenkins 1992; Knauft 1996; and Skeggs 1998.

46. Interestingly, in his comparative chapter based on ethnography in 'Zambian mines Burawoy resists arguing that culture plays a significant role in the production process, because he sets out to counter arguments of African "primordialisms" (e.g., the myth of the indolent worker). To disprove the "ideological" arguments, he emphasizes structure—specifically the role played by colonial structures that enact cultural idioms (prejudices surrounding racial and ethnic categories) "in which to couch production relations" (1979:215). In fact, he goes so far as to conclude, "Activities of Zambian workers on the shop floor, in the mines and in the office were determined within the narrow limits by the relations in production. … ethnic and racial categories are usually important only when reproduced by the labor process itself" (1979:215). In the end, economic structure supersedes ideological superstructure.

47. See also Olin Wright 1997 for a reformulation of the Marxist concept of social class and a discussion of the ambiguities of class identity.

48. According to Fernandez-Kelly and Sassen 1995, 75 percent of all global assembly workers are reported to be women. See also Cagatay and Ozler 1995; Standing 1989.

49. A good example of this process is the convincing set of ideologies that persuaded thousands of American wives and homemakers during the Second World War that patriotism and factory labor were not antithetical to femininity, and then reversed its tune with a new cult of domesticity when men were available to return to the labor force.

50. The University of the West Indies campuses now offer training in gender and development studies. For recent works by both Caribbean and non-Caribbean scholars on gender ideologies, women's studies, and local feminisms, see Barriteau 1995; Barrow 1997; Bolles 1997; Douglass 1993; Lopez-Springfield 1997; McClaurin 1996; Mohammed 1994; Momsen, 1993; Reddock 1994,1998; Yelvington 1995.

51. Yelvington notes in his ethnography about a factory in Trinidad (1995) that sexuality is often the medium through which workers articulate ideas about gender. For an excellent examination of the relationships between gender, kinship, and sexuality see Yanigasako and Delaney 1995.

52. See, for example, Bennholdt-Thomsen 1988; Mies 1986; Ward and Pyle 1995; Weilhof 1988.

53. Acevedo 1995; Beneria and Roldan 1987; Fernandez-Kelly 1983; and Safa 1990 have each explored the significance of life-cycle stage for the particular meanings of women's wage earning.

54. Cuales (1988:121) attributes this tentative engagement between analyses /politics of class and gender in the Caribbean to "the relative weakness of the left and of class struggle in the region" and to a tendency to take up class or gender as the major locus of struggle. Although she points to the need for greater appreciation of family structures and patterns in developing our understanding of class and gender consciousness, and in particular the implications of "visiting" relationships for class and gender equality, her own discussion does not integrate these theoretical frames with regard to the historical or contemporary contexts of Caribbean societies. Rosina Wiltshire-Brodber (1988:142) argues that because race and class mutually reinforce each other in the Caribbean, with whites predominantly at the top and blacks predominantly at the bottom of the social order, race and class have superseded gender as the "principal organizing forces for resistance and change."

55. While, surely, women's notions of modernity transcend the realm of computers and informatics (e.g., through the media, the tourism sector, the intensity of imported commodity goods) the importance of the computer here is emphasized because this tool is a special modernist icon. It feeds into a long tradition privileging education as the source of upward mobility and heightens this ethic with the hyperbolic sense of technological change—the emergence of a computer fast-track from which passive or unsuspecting nations might find themselves marginalized. For these women, then, the computer is a sign—a symbol laden with meaning and its meaning is the Future— distinct from agriculture and from factories. It is linked to finance, to accounting (the career goal most often cited among the women I interviewed) and to white-collar, professional work in general. Correspondence courses in computer fields (from programming to various sorts of "literacy" courses) are very popular, as are evening and part-time courses at the Community College and Polytechnic.

56. See also Hochschild 1983 for a discussion of the increasing importance of "emotional labor" within services, especially those performed by women workers.

57. In this same passage, Mills continues by noting that the difference (in dress between the wage worker and the white-collar worker or the salaried worker) is "revealed by women. After later adolescence, women working as clerks,

compared with wage-working women of similar income, spend a good deal more on clothes; and the same is true for men, although to a lesser extent" (1956:241). See also Susan Porter Benson's (1986) historical discussion of dress, femininity, and class among department store saleswomen and their customers; and Kathy Peiss's (1986) analysis of the importance of dress among working-class immigrant women in early-twentieth-century New York.

REFERENCES CITED

Abu-Lughod, Lila.1993. "Finding a Place for Islam: Egyptian Television Serials and the National Interest." Public Culture 5, no. 3:493-513.

———1995. "The Objects of Soap Opera: Egyptian Television and the Cultural Politics of Modernity." In Daniel Miller, ed., Worlds Apart: Modernity Through the Prism of the Local. London: Routledge.

Acevedo, Luz del Alba. 1995. Feminist Inroads in the Study of Women's Work and Development." In Christine E. Bose and Edna Acosta-Belen, eds., Women in the Latin American Development Process. Philadelphia: Temple University Press.

Amin, Samir. 1974. Accumulation on a World Scale: A Critique of the Theory of Underdevelopment. New York: Monthly Review Press.

Appadurai, Arjun ed. 1986. The Social Life of Things: Commodities in Cultural Perspective. Cambridge: Cambridge University Press. 1990. "Disjuncture and Difference in the Global Cultural Economy."' Public Culture 2, no. 3:1-24.

———1996. Modernity at Large: Cultural Dimensions of Globalization. Minneapolis: University of Minnesota Press.

"Appelbaum, Eileen. 1987. "Restructuring Work: Temporary, Part-Time, and At-Home Employment" In Heidi Hartmann, Robert E. Kraut, and Louise A. Tilly, eds., Computer Chips and Paper Clips: Technology and Women's Employment, vol 2. Washington, D.C.: National Academy Press.

Barnes, Natasha B. 1997. "Face of the Nation: Race, Nationalisms, and Identities in Jamaican Beauty Pageants." In Consuelo Lopez-Springfield, ed., Daughters of Caliban: Caribbean Women in the Twentieth Century. Bloomington: Indiana University Press.

Barriteau, Eudine. 1995. "Postmodernist Feminist Theorizing and Development Policy and Practice in the Anglophone Caribbean: The Barbados Case." In Marianne H. Marchand and Jane L. Parpart, eds., Feminism/Postmodernism/Development. New York: Routledge.

Basch, Linda, Nina Glick-Schiller, and Cristina Szanton-Blanc. 1994. Nations Unbound: Transnational Projects, Post-colonial Predicaments, and Deterritorialized Nation-States. Langhorn, Pa.: Gordon and Breach.

Beckles,Hilary McD. 1989a. Corporate Power in Barbados: The Mutual Affair: Economic Injustice in a Political Democracy. Bridgetown, Barbados: Caribbean Graphics.

———1989b. Natural Rebels: A Social History of Enslaved Black Women in Barbados. London: Zed Books.

Bell, Daniel, and Gill Valentine. 1997. Consuming Geographics: We Are Where We Eat. London: Routledge.

Betheria, Lourdes, and Martha Roldan. 1987. The Crossroads of Class and Gender. Chicago: University of Chicago Press.

Bennholdt-Thomsen, Veronika. 1988. " 'Investment in the Poor': An Analysis of World Bank Policy." In Maria Mies, Veronika Bennholdt-Thomsen, and Claudia von Werlhof, eds., Women: The Last Colony. London: Zed Books.

Benson, Susan Porter. 1984. "Women in Retail Sales Work: The Continuing Dilemma of Service." In Karen Sacks and Dorothy Remy, eds., My Troubles Are Going to Have Trouble with Me: Everyday Trials and Triumphs of Women Workers. New Brunswick, N.J : Rutgers University Press.

———1986. Counter Cultures: Saleswomen, Managers, and Customers in American Department Stores, 1890–1940. Urbana: University of Illinois Press.

Bhabha, Homi. 1994. The Location of Culture. London: Routledge.

Bird, John, Barry Curtis, Tim Putnam, George Robertson, and Lisa Tickner. 1993. Mapping the Futures: Local Cultures, Global Change. London: Routledge.

Block, Fred. 1990. Postindustrial Possibilities: A Critique of Economic Discourse. Berkeley and Los Angeles: University of California Press.

Bolles, A. Lynn. 1983. "Kitchens Hit by Priorities: Employed Working Class Jamaican Women Confront the IMF." In June Nash and Maria Patricia Fernandez-Kelly, eds., Women, Men, and the International Division of Labor. Albany: State University of New York Press.

———1996. Sister Jamaica: A Study of Women, Work, and Households in Kingston. Lanham, Md.: University Press of America.

Boserup, Esther. 1970. Women's Role in Economic Development. London: George Allen and Unwin

Bourdieu, Pierre. 1977. Outline of a Theory of Practice. Cambridge: Cambridge University Press.

———1984. Distinction: A Social Critique of the Judgment of Taste. Cambridge, Mass.: Harvard University Press.

Braverman, Harry. 1974. Labor and Monopoly Capitalism. New York: Monthly Review Press.

Breckenridge, Carol A., ed. 1995. Consuming Modernity: Public Culture in a South Asian World. Minneapolis: University of Minnesota Press.

Burawoy, Michael. 1979. Manufacturing Consent: Changes in the Labor Process under Monopoly Capitalism. Chicago: University of Chicago Press.

——1985. The Politics of Production: Factory Regimes under Capitalism and Socialism. London: Verso.

Burke, Timothy. 1996. Lifebouy Men, Lux Women: Commodification, Consumption, and Cleanliness in Modern Zimbabwe. Durham: Duke University Press.

Campbell, Colin. 1990. "Character and Consumption: An Historical Action Theory Approach to the Understanding of Consumer Behavior." Culture and History 7:37–4 8.

Carter, Kenneth L. 1997. Why Workers Won't Work: The Worker in a Developing Economy: A Case Study of Jamaica. London: Macmillan.

Carter, Valerie J. 1987. "Office Technology and Relations of Control in Clerical Work Organizations." In Barbara D. Wright, ed., Women, Work, and Technology: Transformations. Ann Arbor: University of Michigan Press.

Casey, Geraldine. 1996. "New Tappings on the Keys: Changes in Work and Gender Roles for Women Clerical Workers in Puerto Rico." In Altagracia Ortiz, ed., Puerto Rican Women and Work: Bridges in Transnational Labor. Philadelphia: Temple University Press.

Christensen, Kathleen, ed. 1988. The New Era of Home-Based Work: Directions and Policies. London: Westview Press.

Colclough, Glenna, and Charles M. Tolbert II. 1992. Work in the Fast Lane: Flexibility, Divisions of Labor. Albany: State University of New York Press.

Costello, Cynthia B. 1983. " 'WEA're Worth It': Work Culture and Conflict at the Wisconsin Education Association Insurance Trust." Feminist Studies II, no. 3:497–518.

Cox, Kevin, ed. 1997. Spaces of Globalization: Reasserting the Power of the Local. New York: Guilford Press.

Crompton, Rosemary. 1993. Class and Stratification: An Introduction to Current Debates. Cambridge, Mass.: Polity Press.

Crompton, Rosemary, and Michael Mann, eds. 1986. Gender and Stratification. Cambridge, Mass.: Polity Press.

Cuales, Sonia, 1988. "Theoretical Considerations on Class and Gender Consciousness." In Patricia Mohammed and Catherine Shepherd, eds., Gender in Caribbean Development. Mona, Jamaica: Women and Development Project, University of the West Indies.

Cvetkovich, Ann, and Douglas Kellner, eds. 1997. Articulating the Global and the Loca: Globalization and Cultural Studies. Boulder, Colo.: Westview Press, 1997.

Davies, Margery W. 1982. Woman's Place is at the Typewriter: Office Work and Office Workers, 1870–1930. Philadelphia: Temple University Press.

Delphy, Christine, and Diana Leonard. 1992. Familiar Exploitation: A New Analysis of Marriage in Contemporary Western Societies. Cambridge. Mass.: Polity Press.

di Leonardo Micaela. 1985. "Women's Work, Work Culture, and Consciousness: An Introduction." Feminist Studies II, no. 3:491–96.

Douglass, Lisa. 1993. "Jamaican Gender Ideology, Sexuality, and the 'Cult of Masculinity.'" Paper presented at the annual meeting of the American Anthropological Association. Washington, D.C., November.

Elson Diane, and Ruth Pearson. 1981a. "Nimble Fingers Make Cheap Workers: An Analysis of Women's Employment in Third World Export Manufacturing." Feminist Review, spring, 87–107.

——1981b. 'The Subordination of Women and the Internationalisation of Factory Production." In Kate Young, Carol Wolkowitz, and Roslyn McCullagh, eds., Of Marriage and the Market: Women's Subordination Internationally and Its Lessons. London: Routledge and Kegan Paul.

Etienne, Mona, and Eleanor Leacock, eds. 1980. Women and Colonization: Anthropological Perspectives. New York: Praeger.

Featherstone, Mike, ed. 1990. Global Culture, Nationalism, Globalization and Modernity. London: Sage.

Fernandez-Kelly, Maria Patricia. 1983. For We Are Sold, I and My People: Women and Industry in Mexico's Frontier. Albany: State University of New York Press.

Fine, Ben, and Ellen Leopold, eds. 1993. The World of Consumption. New York: Routledge.

Finn, Margot. 1996. "Women, Consumption and Coverture in England, c. 1760–1860." Historical Journal 39, no. 3:703–22.

Foster, Robert J. 1991. "Making National Cultures in the Global Ecumene." Annual Review of Anthropology, 20:235–60.

Frank, Andre G. 1967. Capitalism and Underdevelopment in Latin America. New York: Monthly Review Press.

Freeman, Carla. 1993. "Designing Women: Corporate Discipline and Barbados' Off-Shore Pink Collar Sector." Cultural Anthropology 8, no. 2:169–86.

Friedman, Jonathan, ed. 1994a. Consumption and Identity. New York: Harewood.

Fröbel, Folker, Jürgen Heinrichs, and Otto Kreye. 1980. The New International Division of Labour. Cambridge: Cambridge University Press.

Fuentes, Annette, and Barbara Ehrenreich. 1985. Women in the Global Factory. Boston: South End Press.

Gallin, Rita. 1990. "Women and the Export Industry in Taiwan: The Muting of Class Consciousness." In Kathryn Ward, ed, Women Workers and Global Restructuring. Ithaca, N.Y.: ILR Press.

Giddens, Anthony. 1990. The Consequences of Modernity. Cambridge, Mass: Polity Press.

Gilroy, Paul. 1993. The Black Atlantic: Modernity and Double Consciousness. Cambridge, Mass.: Harvard University Press.

Glenn, Evelyn Nakano, and Charles M. Tolbert II. 1987. "Technology and Emerging Patterns of Stratification for Women of Color: Race and Gender Segregation in Computer Occupations." In Barbara D. Wright, ed.,Women, Work, and Technology Transformations. Ann Arbor: University of Michigan Press.

Gmelch, George, and Sharon Gmelch. 1997. The Parish Behind God's Back: The Changing Culture of Rural Barbados. Ann Arbor: University of Michigan Press.

Goddard, Robert. 1998. "The Decline and Fall of the Barbadian Planter Class: An Interpretation of the 1980s Crisis in the Barbados Sugar Industry." Unpublished manuscript.

Goldthorpe, John. 1987. Social Mobility and Class Structure in Modern Britain. 2d ed. Oxford: Clarendon Press.

Grossman. Rachael. 1979. "Women's Place in the Integrated Circuit." Southeast Asian Chronicle 66 (January–February).

Guarnizo, Luis Eduardo, and Michael Peter Smith, eds. 1998. Transnationalism From Below. New Brunswick, N.J.: Transaction Publishers.

Gupta, Akhil, and James Ferguson. 1992. "Beyond 'Culture': Space, Identity, and the Politics of Difference." Cultural Anthropology 7, no. 1–6–23.

Gutman, Matthew. 1996. The Meanings of Macho: Being a Man in Mexico City. Berkeley and Los Angeles: University of California Press.

Hakken, David, with Barbara Andrews. 1993. Computing Myths, Class Realities: An Ethnography of Technology and Working People in Sheffield, England. Boulder, Colo.: Westview Press.

Hannerz, Ulf. 1996. Transnational Connections: Culture, People, Places. London: Routledge.

Hartmann, Heidi. 1976. "The Historical Roots of Occupational Segregation: Capitalism, Patriarchy, and Job Segregation by Sex." In Martha Blaxall and Barbara Reagan, eds., Women and the Workplace. Chicago: University of Chicago Press.

Hartmann, Heidi I., Robert E. Kraut, and Louise A. Tilly, eds. 1986–87. Computer Chips and Paper Clips: Technology and Women's Employment. 2 vols. Washington, D.C.: National Academy Press.

Harvey, David. 1989. The Conditions of Postmodernity. Oxford: Blackwell.

Henry, Miriam, and Suzanne Franzway. 1993. "Gender, Unions, and the New Workplace: Realizing the Promise?" In Belinda Probert and Bruce W. Wilson, eds., Pink Collar Blues: Gender, and Technology. Melbourne: Melbourne University Press.

Heyzer, Noeleen. 1989. "Asian Women Wage Earners." World Development 17:1109–23.

Hochschild, Arlie R. 1983. The Managed Heart: Commercialization of Human Feeling. Berkeley and Los Angeles: University of California Press.

Hossfeld, Karen. 1990. " 'Their Logic Against Them': Contradictions in Sex, Race, and Class in Silicon Valley." In Kathryn Ward, ed., Women Workers and Global Restructuring. Ithaca, N.Y.: ILR Press.

Howes, David, ed. 1996. Cross-Cultural Consumption: Global Markets, Local Realities. London: Routledge.

Jameson, Frederic. 1991. Postmodernism, or, The Cultural Logic of Late Capitalism. Durham: Duke University Press.

Jenkins, Richard. 1992. Pierre Bourdieu. London: Routledge.

Kelly, Deirdre. 1987. Hard Work, Hard Choices: A Survey of Women in St. Lucia's Export-Oriented Electronics Factories. Occasional paper no. 20, Institute of Social and Economic Research. Cave Hill, Barbados: University of the West Indies.

King, Anthony, ed. 1991. Culture, Globalization, and the World System. Current Debates in Art History, 3. Binghamton: Department of Art and Art History, State University of New York.

Knauft, Bruce M. 1996. Genealogies for the Present in Cultural Anthropology. New York: Routledge.

Kondo, Dorinne K. 1990. Crafting Selves: Power, Gender, and Discourses of Identity in a Japanese Workplace. Chicago: University of Chicago Press.

Lamphere, Louise. 1985. "Bringing the Family to Work: Women's Culture on the Shop Floor." Feminist Studies II, no. 3:519–40.

Lancaster, Roger. 1992. Life Is Hard: Machismo, Danger, and the Intimacy of Power in Nicaragua. Berkeley and Los Angeles: University of California Press.

Lash, Scott, and John Urry. 1987. The End of Organized Capitalism. Cambridge, Mass.: Polity Press.

LiPuma, Edward, and Sarah Keene Meltzoff. 1989. "Toward a Theory of Culture and Class: An Iberian Example." American Ethnologist 16. no. 2:313–34.

Lopez-Springfield, Consuelo, ed., 1997. Daughters of Caliban: Caribbean Women in the Twentieth Century. Bloomington: Indiana University Press.

Lowe, Lisa, and David Lloyd, eds. 1997. The Politics of Culture in the Shadow of Capital. Durham: Duke University Press.

Lutz, Catherine A., and Jane L. Collins. 1993. Reading National Geographic. Chicago: University of Chicago Press.

Massiah, Joycelin. 1986. "Work in the Lives of Caribbean Women." Social and Economic Studies 35, no. 2:177–240.

Mathurin, Lucille Mair. 1975. The Rebel Woman in the British West Indies during Slavery. Kingston: African-Caribbean Publications.

McClaurin, Irma. 1996. Women of Belize: Gender and Change in Central America. New Brunswick, N.J.: Rutgers University Press.

McNeil, Maureen. 1987. Gender and Expertise. London: Free Association Books.

Mies, Maria. 1986. Patriarchy and Accumulation on a World Scale: Women in the International Division of Labor. London: Zed Books.

Miller, Daniel. 1990. "Fashion and Ontology in Trinidad." Culture and History 7:49–77.

——ed. 1995a. Acknowledging Consumption: A Review of New Studies. London: Routledge.

——ed. 1995b. Worlds Apart: Modernity through the Prism of the Local. London: Routledge.

Mills, C. Wright. 1956. White Collar: The American Middle Classes. New York: Oxford University Press.

Mintz, Sidney W. 1974. "The Caribbean Region." Daedalus 103, no. 2:45–71.

——1977. "The So-Called World System: Local Initiatives and Local Response." Dialectical Anthropology 2, no. 4:253–70.

——1989. Caribbean Transformations. New York: Columbia University Press.

Mohammed, Patricia. 1994. "Nuancing the Feminist Discourse in the Caribbean." Social and Economic Studies 43, no. 3:135–67.

Mohanty, Chandra Talpade. 1997. "Women Workers and Capitalist Scripts: Ideologies of Domination, Common Interests, and the Politics of Solidarity." In M. Jacqui Alexander and Chandra Talpade Mohanty, eds., Feminist Genealogies, Colonial Legacies, Democratic Futures. London: Routledge.

Moi, Toril. 1991. "Appropriating Bourdieu: Feminist Theory and Pierre Bourdieu's Sociology of Culture." New Literary History 22:1017–49.

Murphree, Mary C. 1984. "Brave New Office: The Changing Role of the Legal Secretary." In Karen Sacks and Dorothy Remy, eds., My Troubles Are Going to Have Trouble With Me: Everyday Trials and Triumphs of Women Workers. New Brunswick, N.J.: Rutgers University Press.

——1987. "New Technology and Office Tradition: The Not-So-Changing World of the Secretary." In Heidi I. Hartmann, Robert E. Kraut, and Louise A. Tilly, eds., Computer Chips and Paper Clips: Technology and Women's Employment, vol 2. Washington, D.C.: National Academy Press.

Nash, June. 1983. "The Impact of the Changing International Division of Labor on Different Sectors of the Labor Force." In Nash and Maria Patricia Fernandez-Kelly, eds., Women, Men, and the International Division of Labor. Albany: State University of New York Press.

Nash, June, and Helen Safa, eds. 1986. Women and Change in Latin America. New York: Bergin and Garvey.

Offe, Claus. 1985. Disorganized Capitalism: Contemporary Transformations of Work and Politics. Cambridge, Mass.: MIT Press.

Olwig, Karen Fogg. 1999. "Follow the People: Movement, Lives, Family." Paper presented at conference on "Migration and Transnational Theory Re-examined." Santo Domingo, Dominican Republic, April.

Ong, Aihwa. 1987. Spirits of Resistance and Capitalist Discipline: Factory Women in Malaysia. Albany: State University of New York Press.

Ong, Aihwa, and Donald Nonini, eds. 1997. Underground Empires: The Cultural Politics of Modern Chinese Transnationalism. New York: Routledge.

Ortiz, Altagracia, ed. 1996. Puerto Rican Women and Work: Bridges in Transnational Labor. Philadelphia: Temple University.

Padavic, Irene. 1992. "White-Collar Work Values and Women's Interest in Blue-Collar Jobs." Gender and Society 6, no. 2:215–30.

Parkin, Frank. 1972. Class Inequality and Political Order. London: Paladin.

Paules, Greta Foff. 1991. Dishing It Out: Power and Resistance Among Waitresses in a New Jersey Restaurant. Philadelphia: Temple University Press

Pearson, Ruth. 1993. "Gender and New Technology in the Caribbean: New Work for Women?" In Janet Momsen, ed., Women and Change in the Caribbean. Bloomington: Indiana University Press.

Peña, Devon. 1997. 1997. The Terror of the Machine: Technology, Work, Gender, and Ecology on the U.S.-Mexico Border. Austin: University of Texas, CMAS Books.

Posthuma, Annie. 1987. "The Internationalisation of Clerical Work: A Study of Offshore Office Services in the Caribbean." SPRU Occasional Paper Series no. 24. University of Sussex.

Prandy, Ken. 1986. "Similarities of Life-Style and the Occupations of Women." In Rosemary Crompton and Michael Mann, eds., Gender and Stratification. Cambridge, Mass.: Polity Press.

Pringle, Rosemary. 1988. Secretaries Talk: Sexuality, Power, and Work. London: Verso.

Pyle, Jean Larson, 1990. The State and Women in the Economy: Lessons from Sex Discrimination in the Republic of Ireland. Albany: State University of New York Press.

Reddock, Rhoda. 1998. "Contestations over National Culture in Trinidad and Tobago: Considerations of Ethnicity, Class and Gender." In Christine Barrow, ed., Caribbean Portraits: Essays on Gender Ideologies and Identities. Kingston: Ian Randle Publishers.

——1994. Women, Labour, and Politics in Trinidad and Tobago: A History. London: Zed Books.

Reiter, Rayna R., ed. 1975. Toward an Anthropology of Women. New York: Monthly Review Press.

Robertson, Roland. 1992. Globalization: Social Theory and Global Culture. London: Sage.

Rosaldo, Michelle Z, and Louise Lamphere, eds. 1974. Women, Culture, and Society. Stanford: Stanford University Press.

Ruiz, Vicki L. and Susan Tiano, eds. 1987. Women on the U.S.-Mexico Border: Responses to Change. Winchester, England: Allen and Unwin.

Safa, Helen I. 1981. "Runaway Shops and Female Employment: The Search for Cheap Labor." Signs 7, no. 2:418–33.

——1983. Women, Production, and Reproduction in Industrial Capitalism: A Comparison of Brazilian and U.S. Factory Workers." In June Nash and Maria Patricia Feraandez-Kelly, eds., Women, Men, and the International Division of Labor. Albany: State University of New York Press.

——1990. "Women and Industrialization in the Caribbean." In Sharon Stichter and Jane L. Parpart. eds., Women, Employment, and the Family in the International Division of Labour. Philadelphia: Temple University Press.

——1995. The Myth of the Male Breadwinner: Women and Industrialization in the Caribbean. Boulder, Colo.: Westview Press.

Samper, Maria Luz Daza. 1987. "A Comparative Study of Responses to Office Technology in the United States and Western Europe." In Barbara D. Wright, ed,. Women, Work, and Technology Transformation. Ann Arbor: University of Michigan Press.

Sanderson, Steven, ed. 1985. The Americas in the New International Division of Labor. New York: Holmes and Meier.

Sassen, Saskia. 1991. The Global City: New York, London, Tokyo. Princeton, Princeton University Press.

Senior, Olive. 1991. Working Miracles: Women's Lives in the English-Speaking Caribbean. Bloomington: Indiana University Press.

Skeggs, Beverly. 1997. Formations of Class and Gender. London: Sage.

Sklair, Leslie. 1993. Assembling for Development: The Maquila Industry in Mexico and the United States. San Diego: Center for U.S.-Mexican Studies, University of California.

Sokoloff, Natalie. 1980. Between Money and Love. New York: Praeger.

Standing, Guy. 1989. "Global Feminization through Flexible Labor." World Development 17, no. 7:1077–95.

Stoffle, Richard W. 1977. "Industrial Impact on Family Formations in Barbados, West Indies." Ethnology 16, no. 3:253–67.

Sutton, Constance. 1987. "The Caribbeanization of New York City and the Emergence of a Transnational Socio-Cultural System." In Sutton and E. M. Chaney, eds., Caribbean Life in New York: Sociocultural Dimensions. New York: Center for Migration Studies.

Sutton, Constance and Susan Makiesky-Barrow. 1977. "Social Inequality and Sexual Status in Barbados." In Alice Schlegel, ed., Sexual Stratification: A Cross-Cultural View. New York: Columbia University Press.

Swedenburg, Ted, and Smadar Lavie, eds. 1996. Displacement, Diaspora, and Geographies of Identity. Durham: Duke University Press.

Tiano, Susan. 1990. "Maquiladora Women: A New Category of Workers?" In Kathryn Ward, ed., Women Workers and Global Restructuring. Ithaca: ILR Press.

Tomlinson, John. 1991. Cultural Imperialism. Baltimore: Johns Hopkins University Press.

Trollope, Anthony. 1860. The West Indies and the Spanish Main. New York: Harper and Brothers, 1860.

Trouillot, Michel Rolph. 1992. "The Caribbean Region: An Open Frontier in an Anthropological Theory." Annual Review of Anthropology, 21:19–42.

Veblen, Thorstein. 1953. The Theory of the Leisure Class. 1899. Reprint, New York: NAL Penguin.

Ward, Kathryn. 1990a. "Gender, Work, and Development." Annual Review of Sociology, September.

——ed. 1990b. Women Workers and Global Restructuring. Ithaca, N.Y.: ILR Press.

Ward, Kathryn B., and Jean Larson Pyle. 1995. "Gender, Industrialization, Transnational Corporations and Development: An Overview of the Trends." In Christine E. Bose and Edna Acosta-Belen, eds., Women in the Latin American Development Process. Philadelphia: Temple University Press.

Warren, Kay B., and Susan C. Bourque. 1991. "Women, Technology, and International Development Ideologies: Analyzing Feminist Voices." In Micaela di Leonardo, ed., Gender at the Crossroads of Knowledge: Feminist Anthropology in the Postmodern Era. Berkeley and Los Angeles: University of California Press.

Watson, James, ed. 1997. Golden Arches East: McDonald's in East Asia. Stanford: Stanford University Press.

Watts, Michael John. 1992. "Capitalism, Crises, and Cultures I: Notes Toward a Totality of Fragments." In Allen Pred and Michael John Watts, eds., Reworking Modernity. Capitalisms and Symbolic Discontent. New Brunswick, N.J.: Rutgers University Press.

Webster, Juliet. 1996. Shaping Women's Work: Gender, Employment, and Information Technology. London: Longman.

Werlhof, Claudia von. 1988. "Women's Work: The Blind Spot in the Critique of Political Economy." In Maria Mies, Veronika Bennholdt-Thomsen, and Claudia von Werlhof, eds., Women: The Last Colony. London: Zed Books.

Wilk, Richard. 1990. "Consumer Goods as Dialogue about Development." Culture and History 7:70–100.

Williams, Eric. 1970. From Columbus to Castro: The History of the Caribbean, 1492–1969. New York: Harper and Row.

——[1944] 1994. Capitalism and Slavery. Chapel Hill: University of North Carolina Press.

Wilson, Fiona. 1991. Sweaters: Gender, Class, and Workshop-Based Industry in Mexico. New York: St Martin's Press.

Wilson, Peter H. 1969. "Reputation and Respectability: A Suggestion for Caribbean Ethnography." Man 4, no. 1:70–84.

Wilson, Rob, and Wimal Dissanayake, eds. 1996. Global/Local: Cultural Production and the Transnational Imagery. Durham: Duke University Press.

Wiltshire-Brodber, Rosina. 1988. "Gender, Race and Class in the Caribbean." In Patricia Mohammed and Catherine Shepherd, eds., Gender in Caribbean Development. Mona, Jamaica. Women and Development Studies, University of the West Indies.

Wolf, Diane L. 1992. Factory Daughters: Gender, Household Dynamics, and Rural Industrialization in Java. Berkeley and Los Angeles: University of California Press.

Wright, Erik Olin. 1979. Class Structures and Income Determination. New York: Academic Press.

Yanigasako, Sylvia, and Carol Delaney, eds. 1995. Naturalizing Power: Essays in Feminist Cultural Analysis. New York: Routledge.

Yelvington, Kevin. 1995. Producing Power: Ethnicity, Gender, and Class in a Caribbean Workplace. Philadelphia: Temple University Press.

Young, Gay. 1987. "Gender Identification and Working Class Solidarity among Maquila Workers in Cuidad Juarez: Stereotypes and Realities." In Vicki L. Ruiz and Susan Tiano, eds., Women on the U.S.-Mexico Border: Responses to Change. Winchester, England: Allen and Unwin.

Zavella, Patricia. 1985. "'Abnormal Intimacy': The Varying Work of Networks of Chicana Cannery Workers." Feminist Studies II, no. 3:541–57.

18

Carnal Economies

The Commodification of Food and Sex in Kathmandu

Mark Liechty

I n the summer of 2001, people in Kathmandu were in a state of alarm over the country's ever-more-violent Maoist insurgency, despondent over their elected government's almost total ineffectiveness, and traumatized by the gruesome murder of Nepal's royal family. Yet as I wandered Kathmandu streets after several years' absence, what surprised me—perhaps because of their seeming incongruity with those bitter times—were the ubiquitous signs and advertisements for a new kind of restaurant. Establishments billing themselves as "Restaurant with Dance" seemed to be everywhere, from downtown commercial districts to suburban residential neighborhoods. My initial assumption that these must be a new variation on the old disco theme proved unfounded as I visited several venues to discover that it was not the patrons who were doing the dancing. Whether glitzy or seedy, what all of these "dance" restaurants had in common was minimally attired young women performing suggestive dance moves to Hindi and Nepali pop songs as entertainment for patrons who were almost entirely local, male, and middle class. Almost everyone assumed that the young women dancers were also prostitutes and the same assumption applied to other women in attendance, especially if they were unaccompanied by a man. In the evenings, these restaurants seemed to be doing a good business serving groups of men who eyed the girls as they ate snacks such as chicken chili and finger chips and drank local beer and whisky. Outside, the streets were mostly abandoned because of fears generated by a recent spate of Maoist bombings in the capital.

This article is not about Nepal's current political scene,[1] nor is it about these new "dance restaurants,"[2] per se, but about larger cultural trends in the commodification of food and sex. The question of why these new leisure venues were thriving in such a grim sociopolitical context is probably worth a study of its own. However, I am interested in these new "Restaurants with Dance" more as a continuation of an earlier pattern in Kathmandu, namely, the frequent

Mark Liechty, "Carnal Economies: The Commodification of Food and Sex in Kathmandu," *Cultural Anthropology*, vol. 20, no. 1, pp. 1–38. Copyright © 2005 by American Anthropological Association. Reprinted with permission.

link between restaurants and prostitution. Since I first began doing research in the city in the late 1980s, I had been perplexed by the fact that local restaurants were often associated with prostitution. This puzzle launched my inquiry into the commercialization of food and sex in Kathmandu.

Initially, I wondered why these two consumer services—in their modern, market-driven manifestations—should have become so often intertwined on Kathmandu streets and in the imaginations of middle-class patrons. A search for comparative data soon made it clear that a close symbiotic relationship between prostitution and restaurants (and other similar public commercial venues) has, in fact, been a hallmark of emergent capitalist social economies for centuries worldwide (a topic that I consider in more detail later). Yet these same comparative studies often served to highlight, by way of contrast, the very different historical and cultural dynamics at work in the South Asian context. In a society in which food and sex are extraordinarily marked and regulated cultural categories (often through minutely determined rules regulating with whom one may share food and sexual relations), both the history and contemporary cultural experience of sexual and culinary exchange unfold as unique local manifestations of broader patterns of commodification and market formation. This article traces the South Asian cultural themes of commensality and endogamy in their local Nepali variants through the processes of cultural renegotiation that have accompanied the shift in Kathmandu's middle-class culture from a moral economy of caste to a moral economy of class. Kathmandu's new "Restaurants with Dance" are only the most recent development in the process whereby food and sex, commensality and endogamy, are brought in line with a new logic of social value based in new patterns of market-oriented social relations.

CASTE AND CLASS

In Kathmandu, an emerging urban middle class creates itself as a cultural entity, contests its terms of membership, and constructs boundaries between itself and its class others (above and below) by engaging in cultural practices that weave together cultural paradigms with deep roots in Nepali society (such as caste-oriented notions of prestige, orthodoxy, and propriety) and new market-driven, mass-mediated values and desires.[3] From this perspective, "class" is not a thing or a set of characteristics to be defined and measured but a matter of practice and process. Class is not prior to or outside of discourse and performance but an emergent cultural project wherein people attempt to speak and act themselves—and their new socioeconomic existence—into cultural "reality" or coherence. Cultural practices surrounding food and sexuality are among the most fascinating elements of this emerging middle-class culture because the meanings surrounding commensality and endogamy undergo profound shifts as transactions in food and sex are displaced from the realm of caste and kin relations into the public culture of the marketplace and class relations. These new discourses and practices surrounding food and sex are notable because they lay out with exceptional clarity the shifts in cultural logic that accompany the emergence of a new middle-class society.

The emergence of class-based forms of sociality by no means implies the demise of caste society. On the contrary, the moral logic of caste continues to powerfully inflect the everyday lives of people in Kathmandu, not least in the areas of food and sexuality. Yet I argue that the "epistemological styles" (Appadurai 1990) of social life in Kathmandu have shifted, leaving the transactional and moral logic of *class* as the framing principle for everyday experience, whereas the valence of *caste* is increasingly circumscribed within specific cultural settings. In charting this shift, I do not mean to imply some kind of inevitable victory of "modernity" over "tradition."[4] Instead, I am interested in the encounter between different forms of moral and transactional logic. Transactions in food and sex are especially fascinating because these exchanges are where competing "epistemological styles" lay claim to the body itself. Urban Nepalis shift between class bodies and caste bodies as they move through a varied cultural landscape in which different sociomoral logics produce or demand different ways of being. This article traces some of the key transformations in this cultural landscape as a new market-based, class-oriented logic draws transactions in food and sex into its moral orbit.

Although the commercial availability of either food or sex is not entirely new in Kathmandu,[5] what is unprecedented since the 1970s is the scale and nature of this commodification. Along with Kathmandu's rapid integration into global circuits of money, images, goods, and desires have come transformations in the meaning, nature, and experience of sociality. Social transactions (such as those involving sexual and culinary exchange), once largely confined within an intimate, noncommercial domestic economy, have increasingly shifted into the market economy. Market transactions in food and sexual experience come to be mediated not only by money but also by the consumer aesthetics of fantasy and longing that haunt these newly commodified "goods" (Haug 1987).

As commodified forms of culinary and sexual relations, restaurants and prostitution share a set of common cultural dynamics surrounding the meaning and nature of exchange. Contemporary relations between public eating and prostitution in Kathmandu must be seen in light of a class and gender politics of incorporation and transgression. In Kathmandu, restaurants and prostitution are male consumer domains tied up in acts of in*corp*oration, both in their having to do with very physical, bodily functions and with crossing boundaries (transgression), whether of individual or corporate bodies. As such, this article explores a shifting cultural geography in which the terrain of the physical body—with its vulnerable margins—mirrors the social body (of a caste or class group). As the logic of sociality shifts from a moral economy of caste to one of class, so do the experiences of vulnerability and the politics of bodily (and moral) transgression change through a calculus of power and punishment. The processes at work in the commodification of food and sex join together with contemporary projects of negotiating gender identities, caste membership, and new forms of class membership. Therefore, the contemporary intersection of public eating and prostitution is more than simply about shared space: the public "servicing" of appetites for food and sex are bound up with changing patterns of social structure (caste and class), gender relations, domestic economies, and the cultural construction of public and private spheres.

FOOD AND SEX

It is hard to imagine two more intimately interrelated human preoccupations than food and sex. Elspeth Probyn suggests there is a "doubleness of food and sex" (2000:74): both are physical, sensual, and symbolic channels through and between which cultural meanings "naturally" flow; both are simultaneously domains of pleasure and of the production and reproduction of the species; and both are interfaces between the material and the imaginary, the corporeal and the social, and nature and culture. Because food and sex relate to basic biological imperatives—eating is essential to the survival of the individual, as sex is to the survival of the species (Fieldhouse 1986:173)—the two domains serve as primary and overlapping sites for semiotic elaboration.

The fact that humans have "a universal tendency to make ritual and verbal associations between eating and sexual intercourse" (Leach 1964:53) suggests that food and sex offer people everywhere an especially compelling set of symbols and practices through which to naturalize sociocultural constructs such as gender, caste, and class. Experiences of food and sex are inescapably social: as Mary Douglas and Baron Isherwood observe, "In the structure of a culture, consumption, commensality, and cohabitation are forms of sharing; degrees of admission to each are often depicted by analogy with one another" (1996:61). Cultural practices of culinary and sexual consumption and exchange, through their continuous cross-referencing and analogizing, are often among the most important tools in the production of sociality.

Although cultures of food and sex are important means of naturalizing social hierarchies between groups (caste, clan, class, etc.), they also play important roles in the production of gender divisions within communities. For example, the linguistic associations between food and sex often carry a not-so-subtle message of male dominance. Expressions like "meat house" and "meat market" have long been metaphors used to describe brothels (as in French slang *maison d'abattage,* lit. "slaughterhouse" [Corbin 1990:338]) and, more recently, beauty pageants and sorority houses. Speech practices that analogize exchanges of food and sex help to solidify gender hierarchies. Of meat and women, Nick Fiddes notes: "The portrayal of women, by men, as meat is an instance of the wider caricature of women as animal ... and [her] availability as a natural resource for men. ... Women are called meat as if assigned for men's consumption" (1991:160).[6] The language of food and sex merge to mark women as the objects of male control, by justifying the availability on demand of her "services" (whether culinary or sexual) and naturalizing cultures of gender hierarchy. With exchanges of food and sex so inescapably tied to cultures of gender, it is not surprising that the commercialization of culinary and sexual services in Kathmandu parallels important shifts in gender politics. This article considers how gender relations change as transactions in food and sex move increasingly from the private, domestic sphere to the public, commercial sphere. How does the "free trade" in food and sex affect the local politics of gender?

Human preoccupations with food, sex, and sociality are often culturally interlinked and this is undoubtedly tied to the fact that sexual and culinary exchanges both involve passing or crossing frontiers, thresholds, or orifices of the individual as well as the social body. As Arnold van Gennep noted a century ago, such crossings are almost always culturally mediated: the cultural complexities surrounding the biological imperatives of food and sex are, in this sense, "rites of passage" (van Gennep 1960).[7] Many of these rites (in the form of rules, prohibitions, etc.) are to protect the body—whether individual or social—from the danger of defilement that uncontrolled crossings threaten to produce (Douglas 1966:121, 139). To the extent that the body is a social microcosm, protecting the body's boundaries is protecting the boundaries of the community.[8]

There is now a growing body of general social science literature on relations between food and human sexuality,[9] but perhaps nowhere are the cultural links between food and sex stronger than in South Asia.[10] Not only are there strong symbolic and linguistic links but also parallel logics of commensality and endogamy stand as principal structures of caste society.[11] In South Asian caste society, the basic sociocultural logic that determines whom one can marry also determines with whom one can exchange food.[12] Although the boundaries of sexual exchange do not perfectly correspond with the boundaries of food exchange, together the corporate boundaries produced through practices of endogamy and commensality go a long way toward determining the boundaries of caste.

In the South Asian cultural context, the dangers of boundary-crossing, incorporative acts are often especially marked. In a caste society—in which ritual and social rank has traditionally been mediated by (among other things) concepts of purity and pollution (Dumont 1980)—boundaries of the social and corporeal body are perhaps even more minutely policed than in other societies. The boundary crossings associated with food and sex may be almost universally "dangerous," but in South Asian caste societies the corresponding moral principles of commensality and endogamy overtly harness this danger as a means of producing and reproducing social difference. Who one is within caste society has everything to do with those with whom one eats (along with elaborate regulations regarding how foods are prepared, who is doing the preparing, and who can transact what with whom) and those with whom one has sexual relations.[13] The corporate body (caste group) is thereby produced and policed at the margins of the corporeal body. In caste society, policing vulnerable body margins is central to social membership.

If crossing corporate and corporeal boundaries is morally dangerous, it is also potentially empowering. Anthropologists have long noted that cultural danger almost always offers cultural power. The recognition of danger is almost by definition the recognition of power.[14] Perhaps even more explicitly than elsewhere, food and sex have been marked as both dangerous and powerful in South Asia. Those things marked as most dangerous for those at the top of the caste hierarchy (e.g., eating meat and alcohol) are, among lower levels of caste society, the most powerful. In Nepal (as elsewhere in South Asia), popular deities are propitiated with offerings of blood and alcohol (practices abhorrent to high-caste ritual sensibilities), and Tantric forms of both Hinduism and Buddhism famously harness the powers of sexual intercourse to the liberatory quest. Crossing and controlling the boundaries of the social body is clearly bound up with the cultural production (and protection) of power.

To the extent that caste is a historically sedimented system of social privilege, the transgressive implications of commensality and endogamy have long been of special concern to those seeking to preserve the sociopolitical powers inscribed in caste hierarchies. The very fact that Nepal's earliest formal legal codes paid such minute attention to the regulation of exchanges in food and sex (as I discuss in more detail below) illustrates what is at stake in a moral economy of caste when people transgress the boundaries of specific collective bodies. This also illustrates how the moral economy of Nepal's caste society has long been contested and unstable. As such, caste's current encounter with the moral logic of the market is only the most recent development in the historical transformation of Nepali society. By focusing on the emergence of restaurants and prostitution, this article tracks the dangers—and powers—of culinary and sexual transgression as the commodification of food and sex appropriate and transform them.

PROSTITUTION

Much has been written on the history of prostitution, much less on the history of restaurants, and very little on relations between the two. Timothy Gilfoyle's review essay "Prostitutes in History" (1999) is an extremely useful summation and analysis of the huge surge in scholarly publications since 1980 on the modern histories of prostitution in many parts of the world.[15] One of Gilfoyle's main conclusions is that, in spite of its antiquity in many parts of the world, capitalist modernity has generated unique cultures of prostitution.

> Prostitution had a long history in the African, Asian, and Western worlds. Yet commercial sex assumed new forms after 1800. As urban capitalism generated new middle and mobile working classes, men delayed marriage and patronized prostitutes in exceptional numbers. Industrialization and economic transformations created a ready supply of migratory, independent, low-wage-earning women, many of whom viewed prostitution as a viable economic alternative to poverty. Not only were these male and female subcultures unprecedented in scope, but they were embedded in poplar, modern, consumer cultures that countenanced new behaviors of sexual expression and purchase. ... Even while prostitution was ubiquitous in earlier societies, modern capitalism ... generated new cultural patterns. ... In sum, middle-class pursuit of prostitution became a characteristic feature of modern society in Asia, Europe, and America. [1999:135–136]

In Nepal, modern socioeconomic processes (wage labor, industrialization, class formation, etc.) have shaped a new culture of commercial sex.

Among the many themes that connect the histories of prostitution elsewhere with the experience in Kathmandu is the modern association of prostitution with public commercialized leisure venues, in general, and eating establishments, in particular. Because emergent middle-class public spheres have historically been male dominated—drawing women into the new consumer culture only gradually—commercial leisure establishments around the world have "naturally" doubled as markets for male sexual services.[16] In Kathmandu as well, prostitution and commercial eating and drinking establishments come together in a new market-driven, male-dominated, middle-class leisure sphere.

The Geography of Prostitution: Commercial Liminality

In the 1990s, prostitution in Kathmandu was still very much "underground" and shrouded with secrecy in a way that would be unimaginable in most other parts of South Asia. For example, although Indian news media found prostitution a very unremarkable phenomenon (except when it came to issues such as AIDS), in Kathmandu, prostitution was the subject of shocking expose and investigative journalism.[17] It was also illegal.[18] Not surprisingly, finding people who were knowledgeable and willing to talk about prostitution was difficult. In the hundreds of open-ended, informal interviews that my coworkers and I conducted, many people were willing to talk of intensely personal, even sexual, matters, but none spoke firsthand of participation in the local sex market, as either workers or consumers. The material presented here comes from interviews with a number of Kathmandu-based physicians in clinics specializing in sexually transmitted diseases (including AIDS), social workers, and journalists who dealt with prostitutes and their clients as part of their professional investigations. These were people who had acquired over the years significant insights into the local sex market through interactions with sex workers and clients and research into the causes and consequences of prostitution.[19]

Historically, various forms of sex trade never developed in the Kathmandu valley as they did in some other parts of South Asia. Although some kind of fee-for-service sex work must have existed around Kathmandu's barracks and hostels for a very long time, the city never developed the highly visible "red light" zones associated with many colonial and postcolonial cities in India. Neither did the city have the temple-based ritual "prostitution" known to have existed elsewhere on the subcontinent (cf. Marglin 1985). Prior to the 1950s, elites in Kathmandu kept women as concubines (Pradhan 2048 v.s.:22–23), but the more or less customary prostitution practices associated with specific extremely low-ranking occupational caste groups, although not uncommon in the lowland areas of Nepal bordering India,[20] did not exist in Kathmandu. Until quite recently, market-based sex work (i.e., essentially women's sexual wage labor) was a very limited and concealed phenomenon in the Kathmandu valley.

That situation changed dramatically between 1960 and 1980, decades that saw the Kathmandu valley and its hinterlands drawn into a fast-growing cash-wage and consumer economy as the city grew into a modern national capital.[21] New international aid and trade relations produced an enormous surge in cash flow into the valley (Joshi 1997, Tiwari 1992) that in turn fostered a new middle-class consumer culture (Liechty 2003). According to a published source, the first known brothels in Kathmandu appeared in the early 1960s.[22] But the most dramatic rise in the numbers of prostitutes (and their visual public presence) in Kathmandu dates from the late 1970s and early 1980s, a trend that can be linked directly to the parallel rise of public consumer settings such as hotels, restaurants, and lodges. In the early 1990s, a Kathmandu-based journalist noted,

> You know before also there used to be prostitutes. Fifteen, twenty years ago [c. 1970–75] there were four or five pimps who used to hang around by Rani Pokhari, or Ratna Park. If somebody was seen talking with those guys down there, you knew what was going on. And then they had very limited [numbers of] women in from the villages.
>
> But now, I mean it started only about ten years back, around just the beginning of the '80s, you could suddenly find these girls in all the new restaurants. There were even places right in New Road. For 50 bucks [rupees] you could get a girl, and for another 50 a room.[23]

By the early 1990s, there were an estimated 3,500 to 5,000 women working as full- or part-time prostitutes in Kathmandu.[24]

An important reason why prostitution in Kathmandu has increased so rapidly, although remaining relatively discrete, is the emergence of new forms of public space, exemplified by areas such as New Road and Thamel (See Figure 2). New Road was Kathmandu's first modern consumer district, home to the city's first public cinema and shopping center as well as some of its first restaurants, hotels, and high-end retail establishments specializing in tailoring and imported ready-made clothing, consumer electronics, home appliances, photo developing, and video and audio cassettes. For decades, New Road (and adjacent areas) has been the focal point of Indian tourism in Kathmandu. Prior to India's economic "liberalization" in the 1990s, Kathmandu (with its relatively unrestricted import policies) was a favorite shopping destination for middle-class Indians (as well as a popular Hindu pilgrimage site and casino gambling venue). New Road shops, hotels, lodges, and restaurants thrive on Indian tourism. Thamel, by contrast, is synonymous with non-South Asian tourists. Since the 1970s, Thamel has gone from being a sleepy out-of-the-way neighborhood on the edge of town to the hub of a frenetically bustling tourist district jammed with hotels, restaurants, curio shops, travel agencies, and trekking outfitters.

With few permanent residents and a wide variety of commercial settings, these new public spaces offer cover for a variety of shadowy transactions including drug dealing and prostitution. New Road and Thamel are convenient liminal zones, outside of the close social surveillance of the old residential neighborhoods, where drug users and prostitutes can carry out transactions while melting into the urban flow. According to social workers, many of Kathmandu's prostitutes live and work in the New Road and Thamel areas precisely because of the anonymity these transient, chaotic commercial districts offer. Unlike almost anywhere else in the city, prostitutes feel comfortably ignored here and able to carry out their own business in an area created by and for commercial transactions.

Although tourism has played an important role in creating both New Road and Thamel, the relationship between prostitution and foreigners differs in the two places. Prostitution thrives in both areas because of their heavy concentrations of restaurants and lodges, but in the New Road area, Indian tourists (as well as businessmen, travelers, and residents) are its main, although not exclusive, clientele. Although many in Nepal worry that Kathmandu is becoming a sex tourism destination for Indians (Dixit n.d.:13), it is much more likely that Indians who are in Nepal for other reasons (business, shopping, gambling, or pilgrimage) also seek out the services of sex workers. The huge numbers of Nepali women working in Indian brothels (Pradhan 2048 v.s.) mean that Nepal is associated with prostitution in the minds of many Indians. As one Nepali source put it, Nepal seems to attract Indian *ve{sa}y{am} prem{im}* (prostitute lovers).[25] The large volume of Indian tourists, as well as businessmen who often live in Kathmandu without their families and transport workers (truck and taxi drivers), help to maintain an active prostitution business in the New Road area.[26]

Thamel is also well-known as a center of prostitution in Kathmandu, although the links between tourism and sex are less immediate. As in New Road, prostitutes report that a number of Thamel restaurants and hotels serve as pick-up points and/or fronts for organized prostitution. Yet unlike New Road, tourists are not the main customer base for prostitutes in Thamel. Although people in Kathmandu often assume that the relatively wealthy Western and East Asian tourists that frequent Thamel also keep prostitutes in business, all of my sources agreed that instances of non-South Asian tourists soliciting Nepali prostitutes were rare.[27] Of the social workers I interviewed in the early 1990s, none reported having heard of prostitutes who had served *American* or *kuire* (both generic names for non-South Asians) tourists.[28] In fact, most non-South Asian tourists come to Kathmandu looking for an exotic rather than an erotic experience.[29] Local Nepali men form the clientele for prostitution here because they, along with the sex workers themselves, can take advantage of the transient commercial aura of Thamel to transact in commodified sex.

Urban, transient, and commercial zones such as Kathmandu's New Road and Thamel are places where modern prostitution has become "naturalized"—where impersonal transactions in sexual gratification "naturally" take place (and take their place) among countless other impersonal commodity transactions. These liminal commodity zones are also where bodies lose their caste-based moral meanings and become anonymous parts of a "free market" of commercial exchange. The modern market creates spaces in the city where the caste body (and its transactional moral logic) becomes a class body, "free" to transact in a new domain of value: cash.

Fact Versus Fantasy: The Middle-Class Discourse of Prostitution

The sudden surge in prostitution around 1980 seems to stem from a combination of four components: cash, mobility, anonymity, and fantasy. Arguably, the rapid expansion of prostitution in Kathmandu occurred only at the moment when these factors coalesced. As the local economy became increasingly infused with cash (leaving those on the social margins increasingly vulnerable)[30] and as Nepalis and foreigners became more physically mobile (moving out of the morally constraining orbits of kin and community), commercial venues such as restaurants and lodging arose to meet the needs of a mobile population, forming transient, anonymous zones in the city, and the supply and demand for—indeed the possibility of—large-scale prostitution emerged.

Fantasy is a much more difficult element to evaluate. Prostitution and pornographic media consumption are linked consumer trends in Kathmandu (Liechty 1994:439–473). Back-alley video parlors that specialize in "blue films" are well-known pick-up points for prostitutes,[31] and sex workers themselves reported clients combining pornographic videos with sexual encounters. The arrival of video technology and widespread consumption of videos (including pornography) around 1980 occurred at roughly the same time that informants noted a sudden rise in prostitution in Kathmandu. What pornography and prostitution share is the collapsing of sexual desire and gratification into the commodity form. When sexual gratification becomes a leisure commodity, purchasing it in the form of a prostitute is only one step away from purchasing it in the form of a blue film. They are two manifestations of the same consumer desire. Even if it is impossible to prove causal links between the two, it seems reasonable to assume that at least some of the growth of prostitution in Kathmandu is linked to the increased circulation of the sexual fantasies associated with pornographic media.[32] In these media, sexual relations become experiences of individual consumer gratification within a commercial leisure economy.

In commercially mediated contexts such as these, the body of the sexual other is pulled out of a caste-based paradigm that identifies corporeal essences and ranks them in hierarchies of purity, pollution, and power and is reimagined in a new paradigm of pleasure, price, and power. Once the prostitute's body has been commodified, it becomes fertile grounds for commodity aestheticization, alongside an aestheticization of "sex" itself (Haug 1987). Commodified bodies and pleasures become parts of larger "networks of objects" and "object paths" through which meanings move promiscuously, displacing desire from one commodity to another (Baudrillard 1988:31). As commodities, bodies (and bodily pleasures) are easily "infected" by the meanings circulating in the object and image networks in which these bodies move and in which other object bodies are represented (film, magazines, fashion, etc.). In short, part of the story of "modern" prostitution in Kathmandu is the story of the emergence of the "free" body in a "free market." Freed from the sociomoral constraints of the caste body, bodies are free to circulate among the images and fantasies of the commodity market. Clearly, the sudden growth of prostitution in Kathmandu since the 1980s is tied to the emergence of a new economy of sexual-body-commodity fantasy.

Kathmandu's local middle-class moral economy is another key fantasy realm through which "the prostitute" circulates. Rumors, gossip, and accusations of prostitution are central themes in a variety of moral critiques that help define "ideal" middle-class behavior, especially for women. Attributions of sexual impropriety—especially, the sale of sex for money or goods—are one of the most common means by which people seeking to create a middle-class culture in Kathmandu morally critique their class "others." For those claiming Kathmandu's moral middle, prostitution is often associated with the seductive allure of fashion and is always something located socially "below" (because of poverty and immorality) or "above" (because of affluence and immorality). This almost gratuitous talk of prostitution in so much of middle-class discourse makes it nearly impossible to separate the reality from the fantasies of sex work in Kathmandu.[33]

When I first heard tales of women prostituting themselves for fashion, I thought I had come upon a particularly heinous twist in the story of Nepal's capitalist modernization. But as the same story was told to me over and over again ("My former neighbor," "An old classmate of mine," "A secretary at my office," "Some school girls," "Some nurses," "Some waitresses," "Girls from Darjeeling"), I began to see this tale in a different light. I began to wonder if, when people spoke of women who turn to prostitution to satisfy desires for material goods, they were really telling a kind of morality tale—a tale that is less about the morality of the women than about the morality of the goods. This is not to say that no one trades sex for goods. They likely do, at least occasionally. But more importantly, for the people in the middle class telling this tale and imagining this chain of events, the story of the "fashion prostitute" is a way of expressing anxiety over the power of the new world of consumer goods. Through tales such as these, people claiming the moral middle express their fears of a world of alluring but somehow sinister fashion goods: a world that threatens to turn wives, daughters, and sisters into prostitutes. By locating the prostitution "fashion fall" in classes below and above, people "in the middle" can at once claim the moral high ground and abreact their own middle-class nightmares.

The litany of "probable" fashion prostitutes (secretaries, schoolgirls, nurses, waitresses, girls from Darjeeling, etc.) also points to a second form of middle-class moral anxiety: the problems surrounding women's work and women's independence in a patriarchal society. Even though members of Kathmandu's middle class are precisely those people who have used the city's exploding market economy as their vehicle to socioeconomic and cultural independence (free from the "irrational" strictures of the previous caste-based "traditional" society), these same middle-class people are profoundly uneasy with the prospect of women (especially unmarried women) using the market economy as the basis for their own autonomy. Women in the market were the targets of powerful moral condemnation (by women as often as men). I often had the impression that, in the minds of members of Kathmandu's middle class, an unmarried woman who was working and appeared to have money (who "does fashion") was, almost by definition, a prostitute—especially if she had no clear social ties to the community.

For this reason, few people could resist introducing fashion into the already fraught discourse of women and work. One young woman (interviewed by a female coworker) described how office work compelled women into both fashion and moral compromise:

> Some people, they have been compelled to do *fashion* just to feed themselves. Like in the *travel agencies*. I've heard that they tell the girls, "Ordinary isn't enough!" They are obliged to wear *standard* [fancy, expensive] clothing or lose their jobs. They have to look *tip-top*. That's why the girls who work there have to do *fashion* whether they can afford it or not. It's for the *boss,* too, you know. They have to be good looking.[34]

Working in an office, women have no choice but to go beyond acceptable, "ordinary" middle-class attire into the realm of the socially (and sexually) improper. Closing out this woman's remarks is the gratuitous sexual innuendo linking the high-fashion female office worker with "the *boss.*"

With so much sexual stigma surrounding women, labor, and fashion, a great deal of sexual fantasy is projected onto almost any seemingly independent women in the public domain. Travel agency or hotel receptionists ("They also work as 'escorts'"), secretaries ("It's for the *boss* too, you know"), nurses ("They know a lot about contraception"), and waitresses: In the popular imagination, all of them are more or less synonymous with prostitutes. The "Darjeeling girl" is another of these fantasy categories. Because people from Darjeeling are likely to have better English skills (as well as being more outgoing and cosmopolitan) than those from Nepal, they are in considerable demand for private-sector office jobs in Kathmandu.[35] On the basis of this reputation, some local women competing for those jobs also claim to be from Darjeeling. The result is a kind of vicious circle: because "Darjeeling girls" are involved in subordinate wage relations (and because they are outgoing and sophisticated, and they interact with males), they must also be prostitutes. Ironically, according to some informants, this sexually charged reputation results in some local prostitutes claiming to be "Darjeeling girls."

Put simply, in Kathmandu in the early 1990s, almost any form of female wage labor—even in the seemingly reputable upmarket commercial sector—was likely to be shrouded in a haze of sexual innuendo, at least in popular middle-class discourse. Any wage-based relationship between a male superior and a female employee was open to sexual insinuation as though the only possible basis for wage transactions across this power and gender gradient was prostitution. According to this middle-class patriarchal fantasy, the underlying basis for any woman's earnings was some kind of transaction of sexual services: a woman has nothing to offer in the marketplace but sex.[36] At the very least, this condemnation of women's wage labor points to the powerful gendering of the market economy as male. As producers and laborers, women enter this economy only as objects of male consumer desire.

The "rightful" place of the middle-class woman in the market is as a consumer, not as a producer. Significantly, the image of the "fashion prostitute" collapses these two roles, highlighting the contradiction of middle-class women's empowerment and disempowerment in the new market economy. Middle-class women are expected to consume—to bear the burden of presenting the fashioned body—but their labor is immediately suspect. Thus, the woman who sells her body to buy fashions is the ultimate fantasy outcome (and likely real outcome) of the gendered market economy.

Perhaps an even more powerfully charged sexual fantasy category is "the schoolgirl." Like wage-earning women, schoolgirls still seem to be a social anomaly that threatens Kathmandu's middle-class patriarchal sensibilities. Along with office women, schoolgirls are females that exist outside of the "acceptable" male dominated domains of household and kin networks (even if for only a few hours a day). As such, they become the objects of unbridled sexual fantasy.[37] I was repeatedly told of scandals involving schoolgirls and prostitution, most often students from Kathmandu's all-female Padma Kanya (P.K.) College or St. Mary's School in Jawalakel. Some of these stories dated back to the 1970s and most pointed to "fashion" as the compelling culprit.

People that I interviewed said that they did indeed encounter some young women from Kathmandu schools engaged in prostitution, but much more common were women who pretended to be schoolgirls.[38] One social worker told me of how sex workers, hoping to capitalize on male fantasies, will carry around copies of English magazines or novels and even buy school uniforms. "They feel that if they look like a P.K. student, the customers will be willing to pay a lot of money." Another informant spoke of a restaurant in Bhag Bazaar (near the Padma Kanya campus) where she saw women in P.K. uniforms being picked up by clients.

How much schoolgirl impersonation goes on among Kathmandu prostitutes is impossible to say, but there is no denying that when it comes to sexual fantasies, in the words of one male informant, "Boys really go for girls from these [P.K., St. Mary's, etc.] places." It is probably no coincidence that young men in Kathmandu who mentioned pornographic (or blue films) as among their favorite types of film or video (a group that included most urban-born, middle-class males) when asked to name their favorite X-rated film(s) were rarely able to remember any others aside from ones with "school girls" in the title: "Sexy Schoolgirls," "Private Schoolgirls," and so forth (Liechty 1994:439–473).[39]

Clearly, erotic fantasies of "schoolgirls," "Darjeeling girls," and "office girls" help to drive the local sex-work market while also advancing middle-class projects of social distancing and consumer critique and validating patriarchal regulation of women's honor and suitable sexuality. It is because prostitution is embedded in such a complex mixture of erotic, social, and moral enterprises that it is so difficult to separate the "fact" from the "fiction" of sex work in Kathmandu. Indeed, the "fictions" of erotic fantasies clearly help drive the "facts" of the local sex market.

If these media- and market-inflected, paternalistic fictions are one more or less modern frame in which prostitution is imagined, the social logic of caste is another. As noted above, sexual relations and caste are inextricably linked: the logic of caste largely determines which sexual relations (across various caste lines) are permitted and prohibited. Significantly, as the 19th-century rulers of Nepal attempted to codify caste hierarchy and practice in an effort to bring the entire nation into a single ranked caste society, they paid meticulous attention to matters of sexual interaction. According to Andras Hofer, more than one-third of Nepal's first formal national legal code, the *Muluki Ain* of 1854, "deals with sexual relations, both inter-caste and intra-caste. The scrupulous accuracy of the legislator amply confirms the importance these relations have for the maintenance of the [socioreligious] hierarchy" (1979:69). As it sought to protect a national caste hierarchy through the codification of caste practices, the 19th-century Nepali state built an elaborate system of prohibitions around the basic principle that "sexual intercourse is forbidden … between members of pure and impure castes" (1979:69). The state's interest in regulating sexuality was a fundamental part of its interest in protecting the boundaries of caste groups and thereby protecting the social privileges of the upper castes.

In the context of Kathmandu's increasingly class-oriented social ethos, observance of these old social prohibitions is giving way to the logic of the market. As commodified gratification, sexual intercourse is no longer conducted between bearers of caste bodies (with all their attendant sociomoral sensibilities and consequences) but between bodies situated in the strictly "rational" categories of commercial exchange: seller and buyer, worker and consumer. Whereas sex workers tend to be from traditionally "low" castes and communities, their clients come from across the spectrum of caste and ethnic groups in Nepal.[40] Yet what most of these male consumers have in common is a general middle-class status; the kind of disposable income needed to engage in consumer sex means that most patrons are members of Kathmandu's urban middle class (or their Indian counterparts).[41] Considering Kathmandu's middle class is still largely, although not exclusively, upper caste, this means that many, if not most, of these sexual commodity transactions are occurring across the old boundaries of "pure" and "impure" castes.

Among sex workers, this caste disparity, and the moral transgression that it represents, has become something of a joke. As one informant mentioned, "When I've spoken to these women they laugh about how the Brahman boys won't take water from them, but they're willing to 'take a kiss'!" (Here, the English word *kiss* is a euphemism for sexual intercourse.) For these men, the old caste logic of sexual transgression has fallen away, but accepting water from an "impure" person is still defiling. Upper-caste men may retain scruples (or at least deeply ingrained, embodied revulsion) in matters of caste commensality, but in matters of sexual relations, caste-based principles have given way to the pleasures and gratifications the "free" market.

The apparently greater persistence of commensal prohibitions (versus intercaste sexual regulations) in Nepali society has a certain logic. Although it is perhaps counterintuitive to Western ways of thinking, in Nepal the limits of intercaste commensality have traditionally been set even more narrowly than the limits of intercaste sexual relations (Hofer 1979:81). In other words, the rules concerning from whom one can accept different kinds of food and drink have been even more minutely (and restrictively) delineated than those that regulate with whom one can have legitimate sexual relations. For example, Nepal's *Muluki Ain* of 1854 lays out several instances of permissible hypergamous marriage unions,[42] in which the higher-caste husband is prohibited from accepting cooked food from his slightly lower-caste wife or, in other cases, from his own children (1979:81). By this logic, one's caste body—especially those of the highest caste groups—was so susceptible to the dangers of impurity transmitted from the biomoral bodies of others that even one's own wife and children could be defiling! The ultimate social penalty of outcasting (and therefore loss of high-caste privilege) was the price to be paid for daring to allow impurities to transgress the boundaries of (or become incorporated into) one's body, and therefore, one's caste community.[43] For this reason, the emergence of a vibrant restaurant culture in Kathmandu is perhaps even more noteworthy than the parallel growth of large-scale, market-driven prostitution. The commercialization of food exchanges represents an even greater transformation of sociomoral logics than the commodification of sexual intercourse even if both follow a similar trajectory.

RESTAURANTS

Compared to recent historical studies of prostitution, research into the history of public eating remains limited and is almost entirely focused on Europe. Several recent works consider the emergence of restaurants (Spang 2000) and the commercialization of culinary arts in Europe (Trubek 2000).[44] Just as premodern and modern forms of prostitution are distinctly different, Spang and Trubek argue that the restaurant (as opposed to earlier public eating venues such as cafes, inns, and taverns), with its culture of privacy, individuation, gourmandizing, and culinary professionalization, is a distinctly modern form of consumer leisure. Especially relevant to this study are Spang's observations on relations between Parisian restaurants and new forms of middle-class consumer sexuality. According to Spang "among the restaurant's most distinctive features" were *cabinets particuliers* (private rooms), which were widely viewed as spaces for "illicit rendezvous of all descriptions" (2000:117, 208). The commercially available "public privacy" of the restaurant cabinet was "less like that of a family dining room … than that of a bedroom" (2000:213). Spang describes how 19th-century Parisian restaurants, like the prostitution that they were so intimately associated with, were thought to "provide polite male society with one of its necessary safety valves" (2000:213). As in Kathmandu, restaurants serviced the carnal appetites—culinary and sexual—of a middle-class male clientele.

For the purposes of this article, perhaps the most relevant comparisons are not between South Asia and the West but between Nepal and India. Both Nepal and India share a basic set of "Indic" cultural traditions, but different national histories have meant that the commercialization of culinary and sexual services have been underway far longer in India than in Nepal. The emergence of large-scale commercial prostitution during the British colonial era and the relatively early emergence of western-style eating establishments in places like

Bombay (Conlon 1995) put India far ahead of Nepal in terms of commercialization.[45] Nepal's almost total isolation up to 1951,[46] followed by its speedy emergence as a mass-tourist destination, combined with its unusual caste culture,[47] have meant that Nepal has had very different historical experiences with commercial market formation and consumer culture. In fact, the speed with which certain cultural transactions have entered the market makes Kathmandu an ideal place to consider the cultural dynamics of commodification.

Although we have the beginnings of a history of restaurants in the West, the history and cultural practice of public eating in South Asia remains largely unex-amined. Frank Conlon's article "Dining out in Bombay" (1995) is perhaps the only formal study of restaurant culture in South Asia. Conlon focuses mainly on the British colonial roots of Bombay's restaurant culture,[48] but he only briefly discusses how "Hindu ideological concerns for commensality and purity ... contributed to anxiety regarding the provenance and purity of food for consumption ... in places of public dining" (1995:92). Ravindra Khare's work (1976) on Hindu domestic foodways also briefly alludes to the moral perils of restaurant eating. Khare notes that restaurants, with their disregard for "orthodox culinary and *jati* [caste] commensal rules," stand as a "total refutation" of the moral and religious food practices that are taught in (especially high-caste) Hindu homes (1976:246). This "total refutation" of orthodox Hindu foodways is what makes the emergence of a popular restaurant culture in Kathmandu so remarkable, especially considering that the leading patrons of commercial food services are not just middle class but upper caste.

MAKING RESTAURANT CULTURE IN KATHMANDU

As in Europe, where restaurants emerged from centuries-old traditions of cook shops, alehouses, taverns, and eventually coffeehouses and cafes (Mennell 1985, Spang 2000, Trubek 2000), in Kathmandu the modern restaurant was also predated by a variety of establishments providing snacks, meals, and alcohol and serving the needs of transients and travelers (Liechty 2001a). For Stephen Mennell, a restaurant is a place with "a particular combination of style and type of food, social milieu and social function" (1985:136). In Kathmandu, this coalescence of style, menu, and social role occurred gradually in the decades following 1951 with the first restaurants emerging to meet the changing needs of a changing urban population.

The first of Kathmandu's "street-level" restaurants—that is, restaurants outside of two or three high-priced hotels that catered exclusively to expatriates and local elites—were several pie and cake shops located in a neighborhood of untouchables (members of the local butchers caste) near the heart of the old city. Starting in the mid-1960s, these pastry shops were patronized mainly by youthful foreign tourists. Significantly, caste played a key role in this early chapter in local restaurant history. In the mid-1950s, a steadily growing population of USAID personnel set up homes in or near Kathmandu.[49] USAID policy, then as now, aimed to transplant entire American nuclear families, setting up "the wife and kids" in single-family homes near the USAID compound (a converted 19th-century palace southwest of the old city). Along with enormous baggage allowances and "commissary privileges"—access to a warehouse of American food regularly airlifted in—these American households also employed numerous domestic servants. As in the homes of Nepali elites, most of these servants came from low-caste groups (e.g., sweepers and gardeners), but problems arose when attempting to employ cooks. Whereas high-caste Nepali elites employed equally high-caste cooks (to maintain their caste purity), Americans, because they were themselves ritually untouchable, could find no one but the lowest of the low castes willing to take on the grossly defiling task of running a kitchen for beef-eating non-Hindu foreigners.[50]

By the mid-1960s, a number of men from the local Newar butchers caste had worked as cooks in USAID homes where they had learned to make, among other things, excellent American-style pies and cakes. When their American employers left Nepal, several former cooks established bake shops in their homes, which soon became popular with young tourists, American Peace Corps volunteers (PCVs), and expatriates. One Kathmandu resident, who was in his mid-twenties at the time, recalled, "They knew how to make pies! And they were clean so you didn't get sick eating there, so soon they were very popular with the Westerners, the very few young Westerners who were coming at that time. They are all closed now, but this is how it started." Although neat and clean, these shops run by untouchables were ritually out-of-bounds for most Kathmandu residents, especially the upper-caste people who could have afforded them. It is important to see how these pioneering public eating establishments emerged at the historical intersection of Kathmandu's local caste culture and a new transnational consumer culture (i.e., tourism and development). The first Nepalis to break into the restaurant trade were those at the bottom of the caste hierarchy—those with the least to lose from transgressing the rules of purity and danger associated with transactions in food.

Once their moneymaking potential had been demonstrated, before long higher-caste Nepalis began to overcome their scruples by opening (and patronizing) restaurants. By the late 1960s, places like the "Yin Yang Restaurant" and "Aunt Jane's" (opened by Jane Martin, the American wife of the local Peace Corp director [Wheeler 1973:200, McHugh 2001:6–9]) were serving up apple pie, "buff" (water buffalo) burgers, and iodine-soaked salads to young tourists, PCVs, and a handful of adventuresome local Nepali young people. One of those local teenagers—a man who by the 1990s had become one of Nepal's most successful hoteliers—spoke fondly, even nostalgically, about the ambiance and almost magical aura of these early restaurants.

Aunt Jane's? Wasn't that beautiful, Aunt Jane's? Look at the atmosphere there! When you go, that restaurant, every Marine boy used to go there, all these diplomats used to go there, all the rich people used to go there, the rich Nepalese boys used to go there. … [And] restaurants like the "Yin Yang"—that was in Freak Street and that was fantastic! I used to go to those restaurants and hear the songs of these hippies. That was a sudden change in the life—a new kind of restaurant. I mean restaurants with the dim lights, and the music going on, and the discotheques. You know the discos started in the 60s. So that was the attraction. We wanted to enjoy the ambiance of that kind of nightlife. Like, music going on till 10 in the night. And at that time, strange kinds of food, like pancakes, pie, cake and all these things. All those were very new things, so many people like us, we were very attracted by these kinds of new things. [At that time] it was fashionable. But it was *more* than [just] fashion. It was looking for knowledge, a quest for new things.[51]

What so captivated this young man was a combination of food, ambiance, and sociality—the three elements of Mennell's definition of a "restaurant" (1985:136). For Nepalis, this was a "sudden change." These new establishments were about much more than just provisioning food: they were places to be and be seen while eating special foods in an intentionally created ambiance. In this context, the meaning of food was no longer its sociomoral (caste) provenance but its "fashion." As commodified style, food (and eating) had become markers of a new form of prestige based in a logic of class.

By the early 1970s, dozens of Nepalis had set up their own restaurants catering mainly to growing numbers of young tourists. Soon Kathmandu's tourist districts boasted eateries ranging from bakeries and Mexican restaurants to pizza parlors and health-food restaurants. On the growing global youth tourist circuit, Kathmandu was known as the "Alice's Restaurant of the East," a place where "you can get anything you want." Along with cheap hashish, food became one of Kathmandu's prime tourist attractions.

Between 1960 and 1990, the number of public eating establishments in Kathmandu rose from no more than a few dozen to, by one informant's estimate, at least 7,000, including everything from tea shops to five-star restaurants. Although some of these establishments serve expatriate and tourist clientele, few do so exclusively, and most (especially at the lower end) cater almost entirely to local Kathmandu residents. The growth of Kathmandu's restaurant culture has to be seen in light of the new social demands of an increasingly class-based society. In the new class and consumer society—with its changing patterns of labor and social distinction—restaurants, as public consumer spaces, serve as important venues for a new kind of sociality. Class society demands a new public sphere governed by the logic of the market and its enveloping constellation of "modern" values (achievement, progress, and consumer materialism).[52]

In 1960, almost no self-respecting Nepali would have eaten in one of these public eateries, but by the 1990s tens of thousands of local residents of all caste and ethnic backgrounds frequented restaurants on a regular basis. Although the arrival of foreigners and foreign-style restaurants had some impact on local perceptions—surrounding public eating with a new aura of style and desire—other developments in the city were much more important. When I asked a Kathmandu man why so many people went to restaurants today when they would not have 30 years earlier he replied, "Because the people now aren't the same ones as 30 years ago!"

What had happened? A variety of factors, such as population growth, greater cash flow, greater availability of different foods, and new patterns of labor and time use, are important contributors to the rise of public eating in Kathmandu.[53] However, I wish to focus on what may be a more important shift in the cultural logic of eating. The attitudes that kept most Kathmandu residents out of public eating establishments up until the 1960s had little to do with purely socioeconomic matters. In Kathmandu, the surge in demand for restaurant fare since the 1960s accompanies a shift from an earlier caste-based logic of social interaction to an increasingly inescapable class-based cultural dynamic. As caste-based ritual concerns are increasingly confined to private, domestic settings, the new public sphere revolves ever more around the new logic of wage labor, market transaction, and consumerism.[54]

Prior to the 1960s and 1970s (and for many elderly people still), food and eating were extremely important, sensitive, and consequential elements of daily social life. Food—its cooking, eating, giving, and receiving—is one of the principle domains in which social rank and prestige are played out in a caste society.[55] One elderly woman from a high-caste Kathmandu Newar family recalled how for most of her life the matter of food had been tightly bound up in issues of rank, purity, and avoidance. She emulated the behaviors of the Rana elites and, even in the early 1990s, recalled with obvious pride that she used to serve food to Ranas and they would eat it, a sign of ritual and social parity.[56] This woman—like most others of her generation—was constantly attuned to questions of who prepared the foods she ate, how they were prepared, and the ritual status implications of food transactions.

For this elderly woman, the thought of going to a restaurant was still anathema. Her son told of his mother's distress upon hearing that he had eaten in restaurants. Rather than having him leave home to eat, she promised that all he had to do was ask and she would prepare any kind of special food he wanted. Sensitive to her son's "modern" attitudes toward caste, she warned him that eating in a restaurant is dangerous not only in terms of ritual pollution but because food is a particularly conducive substance for the transmission of other kinds of evil.[57] Eating outside opens the door to evil spells, spirits, and witchcraft. This young man noted how his own wife would pick up where his mother left off, discouraging his restaurant-going habit with warnings of unsanitary conditions and possible infections. "Those places cook for money," she told him. "I cook for love."

From ritual pollution, to witches, to germs, the reasons that women use to discourage men from eating commercially prepared foods may have changed, but the implications of restaurant eating for domestic relations between women and men remain. Kathmandu's new middle-class public sphere is by no means limited to men; women control a large part of a family's domestic budget and are a clearly targeted market sector. However, public eating remains a gender-marked consumer activity, and throughout the 1990s, it was still unusual to find women unaccompanied by men in a restaurant, even in groups. In an interview conducted in 1991 by a female coworker, one unmarried women in her mid-twenties—the owner-manager of a small Kathmandu beauty parlor—described her feelings about eating in restaurants.

Do you like to go to restaurants?

Yeah, some. There's one in front of the *beauty parlor*. I just go there and ask them to bring some *chowmein* for me while I'm working. … But I don't go to other restaurants, where I don't know the people.

Why don't you like going to other restaurants?

I don't know, I just feel odd even eating in a restaurant. That's why I just take it and eat it at the *beauty parlor*. I get the feeling that people are probably thinking [when they see a woman sitting in a restaurant] "Hey, what could they be talking about? … If somebody sees me eating in a restaurant, then they'll go and say to my family, "Oh, we saw her sitting in a restaurant!" and I feel that this would be not good for my reputation—it would earn me a bad name. I mean, there could be no bigger loss than this, no?

Especially for urban middle-class women, prestige or *ijjat* (honor) is too precious and precarious a possession to risk losing at a restaurant.

Beyond concerns for their personal reputations, there are other reasons why women remain a relatively underrepresented segment of the restaurant-going public. Culinary practice within the caste paradigm has important implications for domestic gender politics. Because women have traditionally been preparers of food and men have been consumers, women and women's status are that much more tied to, and invested in, the domestic production and consumption of food, whereas men have relatively less to lose by eating outside the home. As preparers and producers of ritually compliant food, women not only "cook for love" but for status. In the logic of food purity and pollution, women protect a family's (and therefore a community's) caste standing, which is a role of no small significance. In effect, a caste-based practice keeps food preparation and consumption within the home and controlled by women. Men eating outside the home may mean less work for women, but it also means less cultural and political authority.

Another reason why restaurant going is a noticeably gendered (male) activity is the "unsavory" associations restaurants have with the consumption of meat and alcohol. Both meat and alcohol have traditionally been marked as vulgar, defiling, and dangerous foods best avoided by women and upper castes (Hofer 1979:53). Changing attitudes toward meat and alcohol, especially among upper-caste men, have contributed enormously to the rise of public eating in Kathmandu. As in other parts of Hindu South Asia, high-caste groups in Nepal have traditionally followed prohibitions on meat and alcohol, although in a somewhat more relaxed manner than among similar caste groups to the south.[58] For example, both Nepali Chetris (Ksatriyas) and Brahmans eat goat meat (unlike most Brahmans, who have purely vegetarian diets), but traditionally neither has consumed alcohol or buffalo meat. Indeed the 18th- and 19th-century Chetri and Brahman rulers of Nepal classified Kathmandu Newars as ritually untouchable on the specific grounds that Newars used "liquor and buffalo meat both for ritual and domestic consumption" (Nepali 1965:148). Many of the people I spoke with agreed that until very recently Chetris or Brahmans in Kathmandu could expect to be ritually outcasted if they were known to consume alcohol or buffalo meat. A Chetri journalist I spoke with noted how, by the early 1990s, it was "normal" for even high-caste Hindus to drink alcohol and eat buffalo meat: "If they had done that just 20 years back, not talking about 50, that guy would have been an outcaste. But now they do it openly."

This easing of prohibitions against alcohol and buffalo meat among upper-caste men seems to be both cause and effect of the growing availability of commercially prepared foods. The lowly "momo"—a Tibetan-style meat dumpling—played an important role in this transformation. In the 1960s, as Tibetans fled to Nepal following the Chinese invasion of Tibet, refugees began selling momos from street side stalls and, soon, in small enclosed restaurants. One middle-aged Kathmandu Brahman explained local responses to these new momo establishments: "Newars have always been eating [momos], but the higher castes didn't. Now they do, but they don't eat openly. They eat only *inside* a momo shop. They won't take it home, but when they go to a restaurant, they do eat." He went on to describe how, before the 1970s, it was very risky for upper-caste people to eat momos: "But when this restaurant culture started, when they started selling momos in a proper restaurant, *then* it really picked up. Because initially people felt it quite difficult to have momos, especially Bahuns [Brahmans] and Chetris, they felt quite uncomfortable eating outside. So when these Tibetan refugees started opening a restaurant—a *closed* restaurant—the business really picked up." Ironically, it was the privacy of these public eating establishments that finally allowed upper-caste men to relax their dietary prohibitions against buffalo meat, ignore the ritual impurities imparted by low-caste cooks, and succumb to the allure of the new "restaurant culture."

The anonymity that allowed upper-castes into restaurants is also an important factor for other patrons. For many Kathmandu residents going to a restaurant, especially the "lower-end" momo and m{am}su parik{am}r (lit., meat-menu) shops, is still a somewhat shameful practice, even for people who are not high caste. Consuming meat, and especially alcohol, outside the home carries the stigma of crudeness, vulgarity, and lack of control. When it comes to meat and alcohol consumption, for many patrons, restaurant-going is a matter of "Luk{im}, luk{im}, j{am}ncha" [Hiding, hiding, one goes], as one middle-aged Newar family man explained. For many men, a primary concern is to avoid being seen by one's {amp}hno m{am}nche (own people), including in-laws and kin (especially seniors). These are the ones that a man tries to avoid when entering or exiting a back-street meat and alcohol restaurant.

One of the crucial changes that draws men into these meat and alcohol restaurants is that increasingly a person's {am}phno m{am}nche are no longer their caste and kin fellows but their class fellows. Unlike in previous generations, when a man would have most likely worked everyday with his {am}phno m{am}nche in various kinds of caste-based craft, farming, or trade occupations, changes in middle-class employment now make it far more likely that a person's work associates—and social acquaintances—come from a range of caste, ethnic, and regional backgrounds. Yet even while work places increasingly become socially integrated, it is still awkward for people to entertain friends and acquaintances from other caste or ethnic backgrounds in their own homes. The logic of caste hierarchies and ritual pollution may have retreated (for the most part) from the new class- and market-dominated public sphere, but its legacy lives on in the domestic setting. Several people explained how, out of deference to their parents (or other elders), they would not bring work colleagues to their homes. But even in many nuclear families—where no one need fear offending the sensibilities of elders—the domestic acts of cooking, serving, and eating food are still inescapably surrounded by an aura of ritual propriety that allows people to be fully at ease only when matters of purity are properly observed. For all of these reasons, restaurants have become more and more important focal points for a new kind of sociability emerging from new conditions of labor and class. Whereas the home continues to preserve the commensality of caste, restaurants offer venues for the commensality of class.

The enormous proliferation of restaurants specializing in alcohol and meat dishes points to the emergence of this new kind of gendered and class-based commensality. Perhaps because of their association with ritual and physical danger,[59] meat and alcohol have become the staples of male restaurant culture in Kathmandu.[60] From *chang* (Tibetan barley beer) and momos in a filthy back street dive, to Johnny Walker and *khas{im}* (goat meat) in a five-star restaurant or bar (and many stages in between), there are meat and alcohol combinations and venues to match almost every income and level of distinction.

To the extent that this kind of consumer sociality depends on commercially provided services, restaurant-going has become a central feature of male sociability. There is a popular saying to the effect that a man who does not drink, eat meat, and smoke has no friends. One man explained how a friend, or group of friends, will come by and say "Let's go to a restaurant!" where it is assumed that each man would pay for himself. Saying "no" not only puts one at risk of being seen as antisocial but, even worse, as unable to afford it, hen-pecked, or not tough enough to handle liquor. In Kathmandu's small, backstreet meat-menu restaurants, a plate of fried meat (buffalo, goat, or pork) and a half glass of *raks{im}* (a clear, potent rice liquor) sold for around 12 to 15 Nepali rupees ([Rs.] in the early 1990s), an amount well within the reach of the mainly Newar small businessmen, drivers, contractors, and skilled tradesmen (electricians, mechanics, etc.)—all wage earners with regular cash flow—who patronized the meat-menu shops. These are men who often have some education but prefer the "traditional feeling" of the undecorated and utilitarian, but intimate, backstreet restaurants where one can slip in and out without attracting much attention. One man described how he liked to meet his friends after work and before going home to the traditional late evening meal prepared by his wife. When I pressed him on why he liked to go to these restaurants, he explained, "Because you can get food there that you can't get at home. I mean, both of these [meat and alcohol] are expensive and, well, if you have meat at home, you have to feed it to the whole family. But if you eat it here, it's just one person. It's cheaper than eating meat at home!"[61] Describing how he chewed cloves and cardamom pods on his way home hoping his wife would not notice the smell of garlic and alcohol on his breath, this man conceded the transgressive implications of his new male consumer pleasures even while claiming his privileges as a wage earner in the male-dominated labor market. Consuming meat and alcohol in the gender-segregated confines of a restaurant allows men to live out new forms of commensality and literally embody their own gendered market power and privilege.

CONCLUSION: CONSUMER TRANSGRESSION

Recent transformations in the economic cultures of food and sex in Kathmandu exhibit several important parallels. First, the emergence of both restaurants and prostitution represent the public commodification of transactions (whether in food or sex) that, until only a generation ago, had been almost exclusively private and domestic. That restaurants and prostitution have been so closely linked in the city underlines the fact that both industries have emerged only as the caste-based transactional logic that once regulated both food and sex has been pushed increasingly into the limited confines of a new "private" sphere. As commodities, both food and sex can now be "publicly traded." Second, both the rise of prostitution and of public eating are manifestations of the new moral economy of the market, an economy of "free trade" that thrives within the anonymity of commodity transactions. The commodity form creates a space of anonymity—the public privacy of the bourgeois public sphere—in which an earlier form of sociality gives way to the market-based sociality of class.[62] These convergences, or parallels, in the rise of prostitution and public eating in Kathmandu point again to the intimate ties between social transactions in food and sex, ties that remain strong even as these transactions move out of the domestic economy of private interpersonal relations into the public economy of impersonal commercial relations.

This move from the interpersonal to the impersonal in the transaction of culinary and sexual services has important implications for gender relations both in the home and in public spaces. The increased commercial availability of (typically male) bodily gratifications (whether of food or sex) graphically illustrates the emergence of a largely male-dominated, middle-class cash and wage economy. In this new economy, not only is paid women's labor often sexually stigmatized, but also women's "services" to men (both culinary and sexual) become matters of public market transaction. Male appetites that were once almost exclusively serviced—but also regulated, manipulated, and mediated—by women within a domestic political and moral economy become increasingly transacted within the moral economy of the cash and commodity market and its modern politics of gender.[63] Women are by no means excluded from the consumer public sphere: an important part of local middle-class culture revolves around women's consumption, especially in realms marked as "fashion" (Liechty 2003). However, because their legitimate participation is as consumers, not producers (or wage earners), women's market participation is typically dependent on men. Furthermore, key parts of the consumer domain—the public consumption of food and sex—are marked off as dangerous, transgressive, and available only to men.

The logic (and power) of transgression informs and impels male consumer acts in several ways. First, the transgressions involved in the recent rise in consumption of meat, alcohol, and sexual services by men in Kathmandu help to solidify and confirm male authority in the new market-driven class culture. The very acts that only a generation ago might have resulted in outcasting (because of transgressing the boundaries of caste endogamy, commensality, and diet) now help to construct a new sociality of both gender and class relations. As we have seen, the new public servicing of male carnal appetites has important implications for the re-creation of patriarchy.[64] When they become "freely traded" leisure commodities, food and sex help to marginalize women in the new commodity culture by eroding their control over these transactions in the domestic sphere, where a very different moral economy pertains. When they enter the market-driven public leisure sphere, the commercial purveyance of culinary and sexual services (and the transgressions entailed in their consumption) help to consolidate male authority. Restaurants (and to a certain extent prostitution) help to produce a new class-based (male-privileging) social practice—what I have referred to as the commensality of class. Commercial transactions in both food and sex (e.g., when prostitution is associated with business negotiations) are among the pillars of a new form of sociality that lays out new class strata even while cutting across old caste divisions.

Here, ultimately, may be the most fundamental link between restaurants and prostitution. When food and sex are commodified—when transactions in food and sex are re-created as commodity transactions—cultural domains and practices that had once been infused with the moral logic of caste take on the value-free "freedoms" of the "free market." The parallel social logics and practices of caste endogamy and commensality show that exchanges of food and sex are clearly linked in the sociality of caste. As commodities, food and sex are also united but in new ways. When institutionalized as commodity transactions, exchanges of food and sex become homologous within the leveling calculus of exchange value. Meat, alcohol, and sex emerge as homologous male consumer pleasures. When consubstantiated as objects of (male leisure) consumption—united under the sign of the commodity—food and sex are "naturally" coinstitutionalized in the modern space of the restaurant.

The three perhaps most highly marked (dangerous) transactional acts or substances in caste society (meat, alcohol, and coitus) are precisely those that have emerged as among the principle commodities of a new male class sociability. Food and sex, when united in the commodity form, seem to harness the dangers of a caste-informed social logic, transforming them into the very stuff of market-based social relations. Restaurants and prostitution become the privileged sites for a new exclusive (and exclusionary) male class sociality. In this way the market structures both class and gender hierarchies. As modern male consumables, alcohol, meat, and sex retain their traditional dangers, but in the context of the capitalist marketplace, the same transgressions that would have once been antisocial (with serious social consequences such as outcasting) now emerge as constitutive elements of a n e w form of sociality. In short, the meaning of consumption changes in the transformation from caste to class society.

To the extent that two transactive logics persist in Kathmandu, consumption produces two different kinds of sociality. An earlier caste-based transactional logic has been increasingly relegated to a limited private domestic sphere while market and class-based rituals of purity and danger increasingly dominate the new public sphere, in effect producing two social bodies. On the one hand, restaurants service the new commensality of class, whereas the middle-class fixation on prostitution as a class discourse (with prostitution always socially above or below) shows how both food and sexual prohibitions are shifting from a caste paradigm and into a class paradigm. In the new middle-class public sphere, the body's margins are those of a new class social body. However, there still remains a caste social body, to the extent that domestic spaces and women's domestic roles retain the ritual logics of caste exchange norms and caste endogamy is still the ideal and the norm in marriages. People's physical bodies remain the same, but as they move from private to public space, the vulnerabilities of their body margins—and the meanings of their transgressions—are transformed as they move from one social body to another, each with its own moral and material economy.

NOTES

My sincere thanks to Yasuko Fujikura, Greg Grieve, Heather Hindman, Laura Hostetler, Genevieve Lakier, Pratyoush Onta, Lazima Onta-Bhatta, Manjushree Thapa, and Amy Trubek for helpful comments on various drafts of this article. Thanks also to discussants and questioners at the University of Illinois at Chicago, the University of Iowa, the University of Chicago, Duke University, Princeton University, and elsewhere where versions of this article were presented. Research for this article was conducted between 1988 and 1991 and in follow-up visits in 1996 and 2001 with the help of the Departments of Anthropology and South Asia Regional Studies of the University of Pennsylvania, a Fulbright-Hays Doctoral Dissertation Research Abroad Fellowship, and faculty travel grants from the University of California at Santa Barbara and the University of Illinois at Chicago. Thanks also to the International Institute for Asian Studies (IIAS) in Leiden, the Netherlands, for a postdoctoral research and write-up grant. Special thanks to Som Raj Ghimire, Krishna and Ganu Pradhan, Ang Tshering Sherpa, and Surendra Bajracharya, coworkers during the research phase of this project.

1. When a small, ultra-leftist party broke away from Nepal's parliamentary system in 1996 and declared a Maoist "People's War" on the state of Nepal, few paid much attention. Yet eight years later, the Maoists control (by some estimates) up to two thirds of Nepal and have brought the government in Kathmandu to a point of crisis (Thapa 2003; Thapa and Sijapati 2003). Maoism in Nepal has no immediate bearing on this article, although it is worth noting that the extreme poverty and exploitation in rural Nepal that fuels the insurgency also played a role in the historic rise of the Kathmandu middle class (Liechty 2003). These conditions have also helped generate the influx of destitute women into Kathmandu that make up the "lower" end of Kathmandu's sex-worker spectrum.
2. For discussions of similar phenomena in India, see Appadurai 1991 and Appadurai and Breckenridge 1991.
3. This article is an extension of a larger project that explores the intersection of consumer culture, mass-media consumption, and class formation (Liechty 2003). Whereas my book focused mainly on the constitution of middle-class practice in Kathmandu, this article looks more directly at the transformation of local caste culture in the face of capitalist commercialization.
4. No one is predicting the demise of caste in South Asia, although it is clear that the meaning of caste and the nature of caste society are constantly evolving (Fuller 1996), as they no doubt always have. The story of caste and class in South Asia is one of historical encounter and mutual transformation not teleological supercession.
5. I deal more with the history of public eating and sex work below, and in more detail elsewhere (Liechty 2001a).
6. The associations between meat eating and patriarchy are enough to have led some to advocate a "Feminist-Vegetarian Critical Theory" (C. Adams 1990)!
7. Van Gennep defines exchanges of food and sex as "equivalent" to the extent that both are "rites of incorporation," whereby people are drawn together in ritual bonds of social solidarity (1960:33–34).
8. This cultural fixation on the body and its margins is by no means limited to "simple" or non-Western societies. Alan Hyde's recent study of the body in official American legal discourse (1997) is an extraordinary illustration of how the

body, and perceived threats to body margins, is used as a metaphor for the nation and the perils posed by illegal immigration, drug trafficking, disease, and degradation. Hyde shows how the language of the body and its vulnerabilities naturalizes ideologies of the state. See especially Part 3, chapters 12–15.

9. See Farquhar 2002, Fiddes 1991, Counihan 1999, Counihan and Kaplan 1998, Probyn 2000, and Fieldhouse 1986.

10. See, for example, Joseph Alter's fascinating study (2000) of the role of sexual and dietary regulation in the biomoral politics of Gandhian nationalism.

11. Sudhir Kakar argues that "in the Indian consciousness, the symbolism of food is more closely or manifestly connected to sexuality than it is in the West. The words for eating and sexual enjoyment ... have the same root, *bhuj*, in Sanskrit, and sexual intercourse is often spoken about as the mutual feeding of male and female" (1990:91).

12. There is a large literature on the transactional basis of caste society in South Asia, much of which focuses on inter- and intracaste exchanges of food and marriage partners. In particular, see Daniel 1984; Marriott 1968, 1976a, 1976b; and McGilvray 1982.

13. See Khare (1976) on the social and ideological intricacies of Hindu foodways and Hofer (1979) on the history of religious regulations concerning sexual relations in Nepal.

14. The cultural empowerment that derives from the movement across dangerous borders is a theme that runs throughout the history of anthropology. Exemplary works include van Gennep's famous study of ritual passages (1960), Joseph Campbell's "hero's journey" (1949), Victor Turner's studies of liminality (1967), Mary Douglas's work on "purity and danger" (1966), Jean Comaroff's work on the body and ritual in southern Africa (1985), Mary Helms's writings on distance and empowerment (1988), and no doubt, many others.

15. Gilfoyle notes that "Few subjects have moved so dramatically from the margins to the center of historical study as prostitution" (1999:140).

16. From Argentina to Kenya to France, modern prostitution has allied with other emergent forms of commercialized entertainment, such as dance halls, amusement parks, cinemas, cabarets, and most commonly, bars, cafes, and restaurants (Gilfoyle 1999). For example, in his study of prostitution in New York City, Gilfoyle notes that from the beginning, brothels were almost always associated with "taverns, inns, or saloons" (1992:163; cf. Peiss 1986). A mid-19th century French lithograph (reproduced in Solomon-Godeau [1996:118]) depicts two elaborately dressed Parisian prostitutes standing on a sidewalk beneath a sign reading "Restaurant et Cabinets," while several men cast lascivious sideways glances. Spang 2000 includes similar images associating restaurants with prostitution. The image conveys a taken-for-granted association between restaurants and prostitution, with the restaurant serving as a meeting point for prostitutes and their clients.

17. See for example, "Dharanko Ve{sa}y{am}vriti Kasar{im} Tikeko Cha?" [How is prostitution in Dharan?], *Suruchi Saptahik* Asar 1, 2048 v.s. (June 15, 1991), and "Kath-manduko Ve{sa}y{am}vritima Sambhr{am}nta Pariv{am}rPani Samlagna: P{am}nc Haj{am}r Sammak{am} Ve{sa}y{am} Sa{du}akm{am}" [Kathmandu's elite families are also involved in prostitution: On the streets, prostitutes for up to Rs. 5000], *Prishtabhum Saptahik* Ashad 6, 2048 v.s. (June 20, 1991).

18. The illegality of prostitution in Nepal is de facto if not de jure. Although sex workers are routinely harassed and arrested, scholars debate whether there are actually any existing legal statutes outlawing prostitution (Y. Fujikura, personal communication, March 2002). For more on public debates on the regulation of prostitution in Nepal, see Fujikura 2003.

19. To protect them and their contacts, in this article I do not cite key informants by name but by profession.

20. For various perspectives on women's sex work among Badi castes in Nepal's Tarai region, see Cox 1992, Cameron 1998, and Pike 1999.

21. See Liechty 2001a for more details including a discussion of hill poverty, labor migration, and the "supply side" of prostitution in Kathmandu.

22. "Yaun Jivan: Kathmandum{am} Ve{sa}y{am}vriti" [Sexual life: Prostitution in Kathmandu], *Saptahik Punarjagaran* (Kathmandu) Asoj 15, 2048 v.s. (Oct. 1, 1991).

23. New Road is the city's central commercial district and is discussed in more detail below.

24. The lower figure appeared in an article on prostitution in *Saptahik Punarjagaran* (Kathmandu) Asoj 15, 2048 v.s. (Oct. 1, 1991). The higher figure is the estimate of a Nepali doctor working with prostitutes in a clinic for sexually transmitted diseases in Kathmandu (cf. Upreti 1992). For a general discussion of factors leading to a growing supply of, and demand for, commercial sexual services, see Liechty 2001a.

25. "Yaun Jivan: Kathmandum{am} Ve{sa}y{am}vriti" [Sexual life: Prostitution in Kathmandu], *Saptahik Punarjagaran* (Kathmandu) Asoj 15, 2048 v.s. (Oct. 1, 1991).

26. This is not to say that local Nepali men do not also frequent New Road prostitutes. Rather, it is the transient Indian population (along with Indian demand) that helps create the liminal urban space within which prostitution can flourish.

27. Although it is impossible to say why tourists from outside South Asia are less likely to use prostitutes than are Indian tourists, one reason may be that the youthful Western and East Asian "adventure tourists" who make up the bulk of Kathmandu's non-South Asian arrivals often travel as couples. More importantly, sex is not part of the "imagined

place" that these trekkers come to Nepal hoping to find (Liechty 1996a). In the First World touristic imagination, Kathmandu is the place for Eastern mysticism and exotic culture, throwback evocations of Hippie culture, and mountain adventure (or at least planning for, and recovering from, such adventures). For these tourists "doing" Nepal means "roughing it." On the international youth tourism circuit, Kathmandu is known for its garbage, hustlers, intestinal parasites, dope dealers, black marketers, and labyrinthine bureaucracy—not for its sex trade.

28. This is not to say that there are no contacts between First World tourists and local prostitutes. Some hotel owners reported that occasionally a foreign tourist, after getting drunk or high, would come and inquire about prostitutes. One hotel manager reported that now and then a small group of tourists would ask whether prostitutes are available before checking in. Finally, one social worker spoke with me about local boys who report occasionally working as male prostitutes for Western clients, although this informant felt that the occurrence was infrequent. Dixit (1990:26–30, n.d.:11) reports similar findings regarding limited male prostitution with tourists in Kathmandu.

29. Sometimes, however, exotic and erotic desires do combine in romantic intimacies between Nepalis (especially, it seems, Sherpas and others with the romantic aura of Tibetan culture) and Westerners (V. Adams 1996:59–60, 103; Ortner 1999; Spano 2001).

30. See Note 20.

31. Citing research by Gertrude Koch, Linda Williams notes that early pornographic films in Europe "were associated mainly with brothels, their major function being economic: to arouse the viewer to the point of purchasing the services of the women of the house" (1989:74).

32. This discussion is in many ways an illustration of Arjun Appadurai and Carol Breckenridge's commentaries on the 1984 Mira Nair documentary film *India Cabaret* (Appadurai 1991; Appadurai and Breckenridge 1991). They discuss how scenes from Hindi cinema provide scripts that turn denizens of suburban Bombay cabarets (dancers and patrons) into characters in their own media-driven self-fabrications. Similarly, ties between pornographic videos and the culture of prostitution in Kathmandu show how "lives are now inextricably linked with [mass-media] representations" (Appadurai 1991:208).

33. Elsewhere (Liechty 2003), I explore in much greater detail the complex interplay between discourses of fashion, prostitution, and gender in the cultural production of middle-class life in Kathmandu. It is clear that "the prostitute" plays a leading role in middle-class imaginations—perhaps especially women's—because the extremes of consumer desire and sexual objectification are collapsed in this figure, making it both a source of intense anxiety and a resource for social critique (Liechty 1996b, 2001b).

34. Italics in quoted material designate English words used in statements otherwise made in Nepali and presented here in translation.

35. Darjeeling is the former British colonial "hill station" or resort area located in India to the east of Nepal. Many people from the Darjeeling region are ethnically Nepali and speak Nepali as a local language.

36. Possible exceptions to the stigma attached to middle-class women's labor include such things as working in beauty parlors or in NGOs working on women's issues. These tend to be gender-segregated work environments where wage transactions are strictly between women.

37. In her recent article on schoolgirls in Meiji Japan, Miyako Inoue (2003) describes similar patterns of sexual fetishization. Inoue points out that modern schoolgirls were "neither producers nor reproducers" but rather "public beings" and as such, "a sign of menace and transgression needing to be tamed because her publicness potentially blurs the boundary that distinguishes 'modern women' from prostitutes" (2003:159–160). The idea of the "public woman" seems to carry an almost universal erotic charge within bourgeois patriarchy, as in the 19th-century French euphemism for prostitute, *filles publique* (Clark 1985:106).

38. Gilfoyle provides a fascinating comparative perspective when he notes that in early 20th-century New York City it was not uncommon for prostitutes to pose as school girls, wearing "juvenile attire" and carrying book satchels (1992:285).

39. That most of this "school girl" video pornography is from the United States, Europe, or Japan suggests that this erotic fantasy is by no means unique to Kathmandu.

40. Elsewhere, I have discussed the demographics of sex workers and clients in Kath-mandu (Liechty 2001a).

41. In the early 1990s, most clients were paying between 300 and 1,000 Nepali Rs. (about US $6 to $20) per encounter. These costs appear low by Western standards, but in a society where a middle-class job as a civil servant pays only about 4,000 Rs. per month, these are sizable sums.

42. Hypergamous unions are those in which a woman of lower caste rank legally marries a man of higher caste rank. Typically, however, the gap between the two caste groups is relatively small.

43. According to the *Muluki Ain,* "The Brahmin, who knowingly accepts *bhat* [cooked rice] or water" from someone of a lower caste "will be degraded to the offerer's status. … And he will be prosecuted, in addition, if he conceals his defilement and transfers it to his fellow caste members by continuing to live in commensality with them" (Hofer 1979:59).

44. See also Mennell 1985, and Habermas 1989.

45. There is now a growing literature on the colonial construction of Indian prostitution. See Banerjee 1989, I. Chatterjee 1990, R. Chatterjee 1993, D'Cunha 1991, Ghosh 1994, Levine 1994, and Pivar 1981. See Dell 1997 and Sleightholme and Sinha 1997, for work on the contemporary period.

46. Throughout the colonial era, Nepal remained (at times nominally) independent of British rule. In part to protect elite privilege, Nepal's ruling Rana family—a line of autocratic hereditary Prime Ministers—followed increasingly isolationist, xenophobic state policies until 1951 when a popular revolution deposed them in favor of a democratic constitutional monarchy. For a cultural history of Nepal's relations to foreigners and foreign goods, see Liechty 1997.

47. For example, Nepali Brahmans have traditionally been allowed to eat some kinds of meat (e.g., goat and chicken), whereas for Indian Brahmans eating any meat is a caste violation. For this reason, "pure-vegetarian" restaurants—run by, and expressly catering to, Brahmans—although ubiquitous in India, are rare in Kathmandu. Those that do exist are treated more like other ethnic or regional restaurants (in this case, typically South Indian) than as having to do with caste imperatives as such.

48. As with Spang, Conlon also contrasts premodern and modern South Asian public eating establishments: from spartan rest houses serving religious or business travelers (1995:94) to modern restaurants serving resident expatriates and Indian middle- and upper-class urbanites. Mainly "a social resort for Bombay's male population," some early restaurants also courted a female and family clientele by providing "family cabins" or glass-partitioned spaces "where genteel, respectable groups could dine without being exposed to public gaze," although others could use the same spaces "for liaisons that required discretion" (1995:100–101).

49. Because of its strategic location between "Red China" and Soviet-leaning independent India, following World War II the United States quickly figured Nepal into its Cold War plans via projects of economic development. In 1947, the United States became only the second nation to establish diplomatic relations with Nepal (following Britain in the early 19th century), and in 1951, the United States was the first foreign country to establish an official aid mission in Nepal (Wood 1987:47).

50. For accounts of Americans in Nepal during the 1950s and 1960s, see Hugh B. Wood's memoir (1987) and especially Heather Hindman's work (2003) on expatriate lifestyles and the cultural politics of foreignness in Kathmandu.

51. The U.S. Embassy's contingent of Marine Guards played its own role in the establishment of new forms of leisure and recreation in Kathmandu. Some of the city's first discos and bars were started by Nepali friends of marines to provide them with places to "hang out" (and spend money) while off duty.

52. In European history, the rise of restaurants (along with literature, theater, and other commodified leisure forms) is seen as an important part of the transition from aristocratic to bourgeois control of the public sphere (Habermas 1989:31 ff.). Although acknowledging the fundamental differences between the moral economies of early modern Europe and modern Nepal, the emergence of restaurants in Kathmandu over the past decades illustrates similar developments in the rise of a new class-based bourgeois public sphere.

53. For a discussion of all of these factors, see Liechty 2001a, 2003.

54. One large and fast-growing segment of Kathmandu's new food service economy that I do not address in this article is food catering. Catering services, although not technically tied to public eating, are nonetheless caught up in many of the same shifts in ritual and status concerns associated with restaurant-going. Kathmandu's catering industry thrives by filling the need to serve food to guests at weddings and other life-cycle rituals, events that represent perhaps the most powerful remaining caste-based imperatives in the city's social life. Yet as these life-cycle events are drawn into the orbit of claiming and negotiating class status, a n e w consumer-based logic of status display propels catering services (in which earlier caste-based concerns for food preparation and transaction are ignored) into the very heart of "traditional" caste rituals. Ironically, many people, who would never dream of allowing a crew of low-caste cooks into their own kitchens to prepare a wedding feast, do not think twice about who is preparing or serving the food for their daughter's catered wedding banquet.

55. See Khare 1976; Khare and Rao 1986; Marriott 1968, 1976a, 1976b; and Daniel 1984.

56. See Note 46.

57. Hofer (1979:53) quotes a passage from the Sanskrit *Grhastharatnakara* according to which: "Food is the filth of men … the evil deeds of men resort to their food. Whoever eats the food of another partakes of that man's sin."

58. See Zimmermann (1987:180 ff.) for a discussion of the moral logic of vegetarianism in Hindu philosophy.

59. One common perception was that drinking liquor requires eating meat and vice versa. Alcohol helps to digest meat, and a person who does not eat meat while drinking alcohol gets drunk easily. Even worse, because alcohol is thought to p{am}knu (cook) meat, failure to eat meat along with alcohol puts the drinker at risk of having their own "meat" (stomach, liver, etc.) "cooked" instead. People I spoke with said that today no one associates these properties of meat and alcohol with any kind of broader South Asian humoral understandings of foods as "heating" or "cooling" (cf. Daniel 1984, Zimmermann 1987), yet still they retain an aura of danger. There is a sense that what gives pleasure or enjoyment (maj{am}) also brings danger. One man likened alcohol to the *kickann{im}* of Nepali folklore (the beautiful female ghosts or spirits who seduce, feed off of, and kill men through copulation; Hedrick and Hedrick 1972:80; cf. Kakar 1982:27–28). Alcohol, too, is thought to provide pleasure while actually consuming the

consumer; the common association of liver disease with alcohol consumption only confirms such a view. By this logic, eating meat is almost an antidote to drinking alcohol.

60. See Fiddes 1991:145–146, for a discussion of the common ethnographic association of meat consumption and maleness. Around the world, "meat is almost ubiquitously put to use as a medium through which men express their 'natural' control, of women as well as of animals" (Fiddes 1991:146).

61. In her study of caste, class, and gender in South India, Karin Kapadia describes similar splits in financial status between married couples and suggests that the "considerable economic inequality" between wage-earning husbands and non-wage earning wives may actually constitute class divisions within families (1995:251).

62. Habermas discusses how the emerging institutions of the European bourgeois public sphere—salons, coffee houses, and literary societies—were open to anyone "in so faras they were propertied and educated." Thus, these new "public institutions" were private, or class segregated, to the extent that they shut out the masses that were "so pauperized that they could not even pay for literature" (1989:37–38).

63. Ironically, a growing number of women—often poor widows or single mothers—use the new economy to transact in sexual commodities as a way of surviving in an increasingly cash-driven world.

64. Habermas's (1989) portrayal of the rise of the bourgeois public sphere in Europe notes the exclusion of lower classes from the new "public institutions" (notably including things like coffee houses and other restaurant-like establishments) but does not recognize the parallel exclusion of women. This double exclusion (in terms of both class and gender) highlights the fact that the emerging 18th- and 19th-century European public sphere represents not simply the persistence of patriarchy but the creation of a new ideology of exclusion aimed at women (Eley 1994; Hansen 1993; Landes 1988; cf. Chatterjee 1989). In Kathmandu, the cultural dynamics are different, but the results—the "classing" and gendering of bourgeois sociability—are similar.

REFERENCES CITED

Adams, Carole. 1990. The Sexual Politics of Meat: Feminist-Vegetarian Critical Theory. New York: Continuum.

Adams, Vincanne. 1996. Tigers of the Snow, and Other Virtual Sherpas: An Ethnography of Himalayan Encounters. Princeton: Princeton University Press.

Alter, Joseph. 2000. Gandhi's Body: Sex, Diet, and the Politics of Nationalism. Philadelphia: University of Pennsylvania Press.

Appadurai, Arjun. 1990. Technology and the Reproduction of Values in Rural Western India. In Dominating Knowledge: Development, Culture, and Resistance. Frédérique A. Marglin and Stephen A. Marglin, eds. Pp. 185–216. Oxford: Clarendon Press.

——1991. Global Ethnoscapes: Notes and Queries for a Transnational Anthropology. In Recapturing Anthropology: Working in the Present. Richard G. Fox, ed. Pp. 191–210. Santa Fe, NM: School of American Research Press.

Appadurai, Arjun, and Carol Breckenridge. 1991. Marriage, Migration, and Money: Mira Nair's Cinema of Displacement. Visual Anthropology 4(1):95–102.

Banerjee, Sumanta. 1989. The Parlour and the Streets: Elite and Popular Culture in Nineteenth Century Calcutta. Calcutta: Seagull Books.

Baudrillard, Jean. 1988. Consumer Culture. In Jean Baudrillard: Selected Writings. Mark Poster, ed. Pp. 29–56. Stanford: Stanford University Press.

Cameron, Mary M. 1998. On the Edge of the Auspicious: Gender and Caste in Nepal. Urbana: University of Illinois Press.

Campbell, Joseph. 1949. The Hero with a Thousand Faces. Bollingen Series XVII. Princeton: Princeton University Press.

Chatterjee, Indrani. 1990. Refracted Reality: The 1935 Calcutta Police Survey of Prostitutes. Manushi 57:26–36.

Chatterjee, Partha. 1989. Colonialism, Nationalism, and Colonialized Women: The Contest in India. American Ethnologist 16(4):622–633.

Chatterjee, Ratnabali. Prostitution in Nineteenth Century Bengal: Construction of Class and Gender. Social Scientist 21(9–11):159–172.

Clark, Timothy J. The Painting of Modern Life: Paris in the Art of Manet and his Followers. New York: Knopf.

Comaroff, Jean. 1985. Body of Power, Spirit of Resistance: The Culture and History of a South African People. Chicago: University of Chicago Press.

Conlon, Frank E. 1995. Dining Out in Bombay. In Consuming Modernity: Public Culture in a South Asian World. Carol A. Breckenridge, ed. Pp. 90–127. Minneapolis: University of Minnesota Press.

Corbin, Alain. 1990. Women for Hire: Prostitution and Sexuality in France after 1850. Cambridge, MA: Harvard University Press.

Counihan, Carole M. 1999. The Anthropology of Food and Body: Gender, Meaning, and Power. New York: Routledge.

Counihan, Carole M., and Steven L. Kaplan, eds. 1998. Food and Gender: Identity and Power. Amsterdam: Harwood Academic.

Cox, Thomas. 1992. The Badi: Prostitution as a Social Norm among an Untouchable Caste of West Nepal. Contributions to Nepalese Studies 19(1):51–71.

Daniel, E. Valentine. 1984. Fluid Signs: Being a Person the Tamil Way. Berkeley: University of California Press.

Dell, Heather. 1997. "English Sex," Middle-Class Wives, and Prostitutes: Sexual Consumption as Deterritorialization in Colonial and Postcolonial India. Paper presented at the 96th Annual Meeting of the American Anthropological Association, Washington, D.C., November 19–23.

D'Cunha, Jean. 1991. The Legalization of Prostitution: A Sociological Inquiry into the Laws Relating to Prostitution in India and the West. Bangalore: Wordmakers.

Dixit, Shanta. 1990. Hear No AIDS, See No AIDS, Speak No AIDS. Himal 3(3):26–30. N.d. Socio-economic Dimensions of HIV/AIDS in Nepal. Unpublished MS.

Douglas, Mary. 1966. Purity and Danger. London: Ark Paperbacks.

Douglas, Mary, and Baron Isherwood. 1996[1979] The World of Goods. New York: Routledge.

Dumont, Louis. 1980. Homo Hierarchicus. Chicago: University of Chicago Press.

Eley, Geoff. 1994. Nations, Publics, and Political Cultures: Placing Habermas in the Nineteenth Century. In Culture/Power/History. Nicholas Dirks, Geoff Eley, and Sherry Ortner, eds. Pp. 297–335. Princeton: Princeton University Press.

Farquhar, Judith. 2002. Appetites: Food and Sex in Post-Socialist China. Durham, NC: Duke University Press.

Fiddes, Nick. 1991. Meat: A Natural Symbol. New York: Routledge.

Fieldhouse, Paul. 1986. Food and Nutrition: Customs and Culture. London: Croom Helm.

Fujikura, Yasuko. 2003. Border and Boundaries in the Era of Aids: Trafficking in Women and Prostitution in Nepal. Studies in Nepali History and Society 8(1):1–35.

Fuller, Chris J., ed. 1996. Caste Today. Delhi: Oxford University Press.

Ghosh, Durba. 1994. Prostitution, Sanitation, and Soldiers: The Contagious Diseases Acts of India, 1864–1888. MA thesis, Department of History, University of Wisconsin, Madison.

Gilfoyle, Timothy. 1992. City of Eros: New York City, Prostitution, and the Commercialization of Sex, 1790–1920. New York: Norton.

——1999. Prostitutes in History: From Parables of Pornography to Metaphors of Modernity. American Historical Review. 104(1):117–141.

Habermas, Jurgen. 1989[1962]. The Structural Transformation of the Public Sphere. Cambridge, MA: MIT Press.

Hansen, Miriam. 1993. Foreword. In Public Sphere and Experience: Toward an Analysis of the Bourgeois and Proletarian Public Sphere. Oskar Negt and Alexander Kluge, authors. Peter Labanyi, Jamie Owen Daniel, and Assenka Oksiloff, trans. Pp. ix-xli. Minneapolis: University of Minnesota Press.

Haug, Wolfgang. 1987. Commodity Aesthetics, Ideology and Culture. New York: International General.

Hedrick, Basil C., and Anne K. Hedrick. 1972. Historical and Cultural Dictionary of Nepal. Metuchen, NJ: Scarecrow Press.

Helms, Mary. 1988. Ulysses' Sail: An Ethnographic Odyssey of Power, Knowledge, and Geographic Distance. Princeton: Princeton University Press.

Hindman, Heather. 2003. Stability in Motion: Expatriate Women in Kathmandu, Nepal. Ph.D. dissertation, Committee on the History of Culture, University of Chicago.

Hofer, Andras. 1979. The Caste Hierarchy and the State in Nepal: A Study of the Muluki Ain of 1854. Innsbruck: Universitatsverlag Wagner.

Hyde, Alan. 1997. Bodies of Law. Princeton: Princeton University Press.

Inoue, Miyako. 2003. The Listening Subject of Japanese Modernity and His Auditory Double: Citing, Sighting, and Siting the Modern Japanese Woman. Cultural Anthropology 18(2):156–93.

Joshi, Bikas. 1997. Foreign Aid in Nepal: What Do the Data Show? Himal South Asia 10(2):70-71.

Kakar, Sudhir. 1982. Shamans, Mystics and Doctors: A Psychological Inquiry into India and its Healing Traditions. Boston: Beacon Press. 1990 Intimate Relations: Exploring Indian Sexuality. Delhi: Viking.

Kapadia, Karin. 1995. Siva and Her Sisters: Gender, Caste and Class in Rural South India. Boulder: Westview.

Khare, Ravindra S. 1976. Hindu Hearth and Home. Delhi: Vikas.

Khare, Ravindra S., and M. S. A. Rao, eds. 1986. Food, Culture and Society: Aspects in South Asian Food Systems. Durham, NC: Carolina Academic Press.

Landes, Joan B. 1988. Women and the Public Sphere in the Age of the French Revolution. Ithaca: Cornell University Press.

Leach, Edmund. 1964. Anthropological Aspects of Language: Animal Categories and Verbal Abuse. In Mythology. 1972 edition. Pierre Maranda, ed. Pp. 39–67. Harmondsworth, UK: Penguin.

Levine, Philippa. 1994. Venereal Disease, Prostitution and the Politics of Empire: The Case of British India. Journal of the History of Sexuality 4(4):579–602.

Liechty, Mark. 1994. Fashioning Modernity in Kathmandu: Mass Media, Consumer Culture, and the Middle Class in Nepal. Ph.D. dissertation, Department of Anthropology, University of Pennsylvania.

——1996a. Kathmandu as Translocality: Multiple Places in a Nepali Space. In Geography of Identity. Patricia Yaeger, ed. Pp. 98–130. Ann Arbor: University of Michigan Press.

——1996b. Paying for Modernity: Women and the Discourse of Freedom in Kathmandu. Studies in Nepali History and Society 1(1):201–230.

——Selective Exclusion: Foreigners, Foreign Goods, and Foreignness in Modern Nepali History. Studies in Nepali History and Society 2(1):5–68.

——2001a. Consumer Transgressions: Notes on the History of Restaurants and Prostitution in Kathmandu. Studies in Nepali History and Society 6(1):57–101.

——2001b. Women and Pornography in Kathmandu: Negotiating the "Modern Woman" in a New Consumer Society. In Images of the "Modern Woman" in Asia: Global Media/Local Meanings. Shoma Munshi, ed. Pp. 34–54. London: Curzon Press.

——2003. Suitably Modern: Making Middle Class Culture in a New Consumer Society. Princeton: Princeton University Press.

Marglin, Frédérique Apffel. 1985. Wives of the God-King: The Rituals of the Devadasis of Puri. Delhi: Oxford University Press.

Marriott, McKim. 1968. Caste Ranking and Food Transactions: A Matrix Analysis. In Structure and Change in Indian Society. Milton Singer and Bernard S. Cohn, eds. Pp. 133–171. Chicago: University of Chicago Press.

——1976a. Hindu Transactions: Diversity without Dualism. In Transactions and Meaning. Bruce Kapferer, ed. Pp. 109–142. Philadelphia: ISHI.

——1976b. Interpreting Indian Society: A Monistic Alternative to Dumont's Dualism. Journal of Asian Studies 36(1):189–195.

McGilvray, Dennis, ed. 1982. Caste Ideology and Interaction. Cambridge: Cambridge University Press.

McHugh, Ernestine. 2001. Love and Honor in the Himalayas: Coming to Know another Culture. Philadelphia: University of Pennsylvania Press.

Mennell, Stephen. 1985. All Manners of Food: Eating and Taste in England and France from the Middle Ages to the Present. Oxford: Basil Blackwell.

Nepali, Gopal Singh. 1965. The Newars: An Ethno-Sociological Study of a Himalayan Community. Bombay: United Asia Publications.

Ortner, Sherry. 1999. Life and Death on Mt. Everest: Sherpas and Himalayan Mountaineering. Princeton: Princeton University Press.

Peiss, Kathy. 1986. Cheap Amusements: Working Women and Leisure in Turn-of-the-Century New York. Philadelphia: Temple University Press.

Pike, Linnet. 1999. Innocence, Danger, and Desire: Representations of Sex Workers in Nepal. Re/productions 2. Electronic document, http://www.hsph.harvard.edu/Organizations/ healthnet/SAsia/ejournals/ejournalsframe.html, accessed July 7, 2004.

Pivar, David J. 1981. The Military, Prostitution, and Colonized Peoples: India and the Philippines, 1885–1917. Journal of Sex Research 17(3):256–269.

Pradhan, Gauri. 2048 v.s Nep{am}lm{am} Cel{im}be{tu}{im}ko Deha By{am}p{am}r. Kathmandu: Nepal Bal Majdur Sarokar Kendra.

Probyn, Elspeth. 2000. Carnal Appetites: Foodsexidentities. London: Routledge.

Sleightholme, Carolyn, and Indrani Sinha. 1997. Guilty Without Trial: Women in the Sex Trade in Calcutta. Piscataway, NJ: Rutgers University Press.

Solomon-Godeau, Abigail. 1996. The Other Side of Venus: The Visual Economy of Feminine Display. In The Sex of Things: Gender and Consumption in Historical Perspective. Victoria de Grazia and Ellen Furlough, eds. Pp. 113–150. Berkeley: University of California Press.

Spang, Rebecca L. 2000. The Invention of the Restaurant: Paris and Modern Gastronomic Culture. Cambridge, MA: Harvard University Press.

Spano, Susan. 2001. Trekking to Cloud Nine in Nepal. Los Angles Times, September 9: A1, A8-A9.

Thapa, Deepak, ed. 2003. Understanding the Maoist Movement of Nepal. Kathmandu: Martin Chautari.

Thapa, Deepak, and Bandita Sijapati. 2003. A Kingdom Under Siege: Nepal's Maoist Insurgency, 1996–2003. Kathmandu: The Printhouse.

Tiwari, Ashutosh. 1992. Planning: Never Without Aid. Himal 5(2):8–10.

Trubek, Amy B. 2000. Haute Cuisine: How the French Invented the Culinary Profession. Philadelphia: University of Pennsylvania Press.

Turner, Victor. 1967. Betwixt and Between: The Liminal Period in Rites of Passage. In The Forest of Symbols. Pp. 93–111. Ithaca: Cornell University Press.

Upreti, Aruna. 1992. There Are at Least 5,000 Prostitutes in Kathmandu. The Independent (Kath-mandu), September 2: 6.

van Gennep, Arnold. 1960[1909]The Rites of Passage. Chicago: University of Chicago Press.

Wheeler, Tony. 1973. West Asia on a Shoestring. Victoria, Australia: Lonely Planet.

Williams, Linda. 1989. Hard Core: Power, Pleasure, and the "Frenzy of the Visible." Berkeley: University of California Press.

Wood, Hugh B. 1987. Nepal Diary. Tillamook, OR: American Nepal Education Foundation.

Zimmermann, Francis. 1987. The Jungle and the Aroma of Meats: An Ecological Theme in Hindu Medicine. Berkeley: University of California Press.

19

Demystifying Micro-Credit
The Grameen Bank, NGOs, and Neoliberalism in Bangladesh
Lamia Karim

While economic globalization refers to the removal of trade barriers and open markets, its effects on communities are variable, contingent, and locally constructed. This article is an interpretation of these variable, contingent, and local expressions of grassroots globalization through an ethnographic study of globalization and neoliberalism in rural Bangladesh. It examines how globalization and neoliberalism are brought to the grassroots—the most intimate sphere of the social, the home and women—through the modernist discourse of women's empowerment through micro-credit.

Focusing on the micro-credit policies of the 2006 Nobel Peace Prize winner, the Grameen Bank of Bangladesh, and three other leading non-governmental organizations in the country, I analyze the centrality of gender in the expansion of globalization and neoliberalism in Bangladesh.[1] I examine how Bangladeshi rural women's honor and shame are instrumentally appropriated by NGOs in the welfare of their capitalist interests. I analyze this relationship between rural women and NGOs by placing it within the political economy of shame, a concept I explain later.

Arjun Appadurai has defined grassroots globalization as:

> ... new forms of social mobilization that proceed independently of the actions of corporate capital and the nation-state system ... these social forms rely on strategies, visions, and horizons for globalization on behalf of the poor ... this kind of globalization strives for a democratic and autonomous standing in respect to the various forms by which global power seeks to further its dominions. (2001: 3)

The grassroots globalization I studied in Bangladesh is contrary to Appadurai's model. It works through and not against corporate capital, donors, state, NGOs, and members of civil society, and creates complex new maps of social interdependencies that are laden with the financial investments of multiple actors at the local, national, and global levels. Grassroots globalization weakens the sovereignty of the patriarchal home family, and replaces it with the sovereignty of the market through NGOs, contracts, courts, juridical subjects, and the remaking of subjects as a community police to safeguard their investments. The developmental NGO is the purveyor of this new economic sovereignty that is represented by corporate capital interests and local institutional interests (NGOs), and is an architect of neoliberalism within a modernist developmental discourse of poor women's empowerment through the market.

Neoliberalism as an ideology rests on the idea that human welfare is best served by the withdrawal of the state from welfarist policies (Harvey, 2005: 64). Extending this economic definition, Ong has termed neoliberalism as a rationality of governance stating that 'governing relies on calculative choices and techniques in the domain of citizenship and of governing'. It subjects citizens to act in accordance with the 'market principles of discipline, efficiency and competitiveness' (Ong, 2006: 4). Neoliberalism is about the subjection of targeted populations to certain rules that inform and regulate behavior. In many postcolonial countries with weak sovereignties, the notion of citizenship as a set of entitlements that are bound up with a nation-state that guarantees those rights, is lacking. In its place, we see the articulation of a postcolonial governance authorized by NGOs whose clients are subjected to act in accordance with the values of 'discipline, efficiency and competitiveness'. By postcolonial governance I refer to the subjection of targeted populations by non-state actors such as NGOs to new technologies of market-oriented disciplinary mechanisms. It also refers to governance by NGOs that have begun to act like a state with what Ong has termed as 'graduated sovereignties', and they seek to implement social engineering programs (population control, HIV/AIDS management, primary education, voter education, etc.) that was formerly in the domain of the state.

But neoliberalism and globalization have also created new pathways for rural people to access new routes of capital circulation and have facilitated new movements of migrant labor. In Bangladesh, micro-credit borrowers and their families have been networked into Appadurai's 'finanscapes' (Appadurai, 1996: 37). These new circulations of 'finanscapes' have brought new wealth, ideas, and social identities into rural spaces. Successful rural women are sometimes able to pool their loans together to send a male kin to the Middle East or Malaysia as migrant labor who, if all goes well, repays the investment at a high interest rate to them. While these opportunities are limited, they function in a similar way to the lotteries in the US. While the chances of 'making a windfall' are extremely rare, people begin to believe that they too can win.

In the analysis under consideration, neoliberalism and globalization operate at the grassroots through the micro-credit policies of NGOs. As providers of credit, jobs, and sustenance to a financially strapped poor rural population, NGOs in Bangladesh have tremendous power to regulate people's behavior, and subject them to NGO mandates and priorities. I make three arguments. Firstly, NGOs that work with micro-credit manipulate existing notions of Bangladeshi rural women's honor and shame in the furtherance of their capitalist goals, and instrumentally violate local norms of cohesion and community. I call this the *economy of shame*. Secondly, the work of microcredit has resulted in unanticipated neoliberal subjects, the female petty moneylender for example, that this article examines. Finally, I argue that the developmental NGO operates as a shadow state in Bangladesh, and is able to exercise tremendous control over the lives of the poor through a Gramscian notion of hegemony where their relationship is characterized by a 'combination of force and consent, which balance each other reciprocally, without force predominating excessively over consent' (Hoare and Nowell-Smith, 1971: 248). This enables the NGOs to neutralize dissenting voices in public spaces, a point I discuss at the conclusion of the article.

The research for this article was conducted over eighteen months (1998–9), and was based on a study of the Grameen Bank and three of the largest NGOs in the country. Each of these NGOs works with micro-credit, has millions of dollars in donor support, and millions of rural subscribers. These NGOs reach 80 percent of the rural people.[2] According to the Bangladesh NGO Affairs Bureau (NGOAB), during 1990 to 1998 the cumulative amount of foreign funds disbursed to NGOs stood at Taka 1,364,421,079 for 5096 NGO projects. In 1994–5, 20 percent of foreign funds were disbursed through the NGOs (Karim, 2001: 96). For western donors in Bangladesh the NGO sector is the preferred mode of developmental aid. The NGOs offer a streamlined and accountable system of aid delivery compared to the Bangladeshi state that is bureaucratic, corrupt, and inefficient, and is considered a 'failed' state by western aid agencies. The celebration of the neoliberal policies of the Grameen Bank has to be understood against this predicament of postcolonial governmentality.

GLOBALIZATION, NEOLIBERALISM, AND THE NGO AS A SHADOW STATE

Globalization has been theorized as a 'crisis in the sovereignty of the nation-state' with rapid movement of finance capital that lies outside the control of the state (Appadurai, 2001:4). I analyze globalization in a different context: the virtually absent state in a postcolonial country where the critical question is the emergence of a new sovereignty, the *NGO as a shadow state*. In terms of national development, many 'third world' countries are heavily dependent on western aid.[3] It is precisely the lack of economic sovereignty of third world countries that allows the International Monetary Fund (IMF), the World Bank, and Western industrialized nations and multinational corporations to exploit these countries and their populations for their corporate and political goals. This lack of economic sovereignty in developing countries gets exacerbated when NGOs with economic ties to western capital enter development, target poor people with much-needed services that the state fails to deliver, and link together economic, political, and social life through their programs. In the absence or a weakening of progressive social movements in many postcolonial countries[4], these NGOs are able to set themselves up as working with the 'poorest of the poor', and install themselves as *the* progressive voice in rural society. The NGO rhetoric of 'working for the poorest of the poor' does not occur in a vacuum. It occurs in those instances where the state has failed or has withdrawn from the welfare of its citizens, shifting that responsibility increasingly to private charities, corporations, and developmental NGOs. Consequently, NGOs that step in to take many of the services traditionally reserved for the state (education, healthcare, credit, employment)begin to act like a state. In Bangladesh, I found that villagers often referred to the NGO as *sarkar* or state (Scott, 2006).[5]

In the rural Bangladeshi economy, which is the focus of my analysis, the Grameen Bank and NGOs that were aided by western donors largely facilitated the process of globalization.[6] Through micro-credit operations, rural people and NGOs in Bangladesh have become mutually dependent, and rural people and multinational corporations have become connected for the first time. Through NGOs, micro-credit recipients have become consumers of products of multinational corporations such as finance capital, breeder chickens, cell phones, and as producers, they remain dependent on multinational corporations for physical inputs such as seeds, fertilizers and pesticides. But NGOs are not passive agents of capital. NGOs are also active producers of new subjectivities and social meanings for people through their various economic and social programs. Thus, the relationship between rural subjects and NGOs is contradictory and varied; they instrumentally exploit each other. However, the balance of power is with the NGOs. Yet very little ethnographic work[7] has been done to examine how this micro-credit model might intersect with local patriarchal norms and cultural practices, and result in behaviors that may not correspond to building social solidarity and goodwill among targeted populations (Goetz and Sengupta, 1996; Rahman, 1999 & 2001; Ahmad, 2007). Internal NGO staff and local and international consultants hired by NGOs and aid organizations do the bulk of the research on micro-credit NGOs in Bangladesh (Hashemi & Schuler, 1996; Counts, 1996; Bornstein, 1996; Khandaker, 1998; Todd, 1996a, 1996b are some examples).

MICRO-CREDIT AND THE POLITICAL ECONOMY OF SHAME

Before proceeding to an analysis of how globalization and neoliberalism operate in rural Bangladesh through micro-credit operations, I would like to first introduce the two terms I use to analyze the Grameen model: microcredit and the economy of shame.

Micro-credit

In development rhetoric, micro-credit is the extension of small loans to women for income-generating projects and has been eulogized as a magic bullet of poverty alleviation. However, according to Professor Yunus, the Grameen Bank model of micro-credit is not solely a matter of the extension of credit, it has a unique set of social objectives that it aims to implement through micro-credit policies.

- It promotes credit as a human right.
- It is aimed towards the poor, particularly poor women.
- It is based on 'trust', not on legal procedures and system.
- It is offered to create self-employment, income-generating activities and housing for the poor, as opposed to consumption.
- It was initiated as a challenge to conventional banking which rejected the poor by classifying them as 'not creditworthy'.
- It provides service on the door-step of the poor based on the principle that the people should not go to the bank, the bank should go to the people.
- It gives high priority to building social capital.[8]

If we replace the term credit with debt, we get the mediation of rural social relations through debt-related dependencies. In theoretical terms, debt ties the present and the future together. Debt is thus a regulator of social behavior, and present behavior determines future pay-offs. By replacing credit with debt and introducing the concepts of culture and the uncertainty of the market into the equation, we can ask some difficult questions of micro-credit practices of development. What happens to people in a face-to-face community when they are linked through relations of debt introduced by a modern banking system? What happens to the social position of women when they become the bearers of debt within the patriarchy of the home and the patriarchy of the modern NGO institution?

The Economy of Shame

The use of shaming as an instrument of social control of the poor, particularly of poor women, has a long history in rural Bangladesh. Women are the traditional custodians of family honor. The shaming of men through their women (mothers, wives, daughters) is a pre-existing social practice. In a face-to-face society, one's ability to maintain honor (the protection of one's good name, the honor of the womenfolk, and the patriline) structures one's social acceptability. To lose face is the ultimate mark of dishonor. Rural discourse is structured around notions of honor, and any trespassing behavior (a woman seen talking to a non-kin man, for example) is spoken of in terms of the protection of the honor code, i.e. our women do not do X because we are honorable people. For the poor, the discourse of honor is a symbolic covenant with God. It is a moral resource through which they view themselves as morally superior to rich and urban people.

As I illustrate in this article, the economy of shame refers to the appropriation of pre-existing forms of shaming by a modern institution, the NGO, which instrumentally deploys various forms of shaming in its own capitalist welfare, i.e. the recovery of loans. Shaming takes many forms in Bangladeshi rural society, from rude language to regulation of women's sexuality to disciplining of poor people through accusations of sexual infidelities resulting from public floggings, pouring pitch over bodies, tonsuring women's hair, hanging a garland of shoes around one's neck, to isolating one's family in the village, to publicly spitting on the person every time s/he walks by, to making adults hold their ears as a sign of their guilt in a public forum, to breaking apart a person's house to recover money, and so on. In this context, Grameen Bank's insistence of a no-collateral loan and repayment of loans at 98 percent takes on a different meaning (see Amartya Sen for a celebratory reading of Grameen Bank, 1999: 201). The honor and shame codes act as the collateral of these loans. It is the honor of the family that is at stake, and which the woman represents. If the woman gets publicly shamed, the family is dishonored. In a face-to-face society, men and their families try to maintain the sanctity of their family honor by observing the honor of their women.

NGOs IN BANGLADESH

Bangladesh, as an independent state, entered the global economy in 1971 when globalization and neoliberalism were dismantling the traditional welfare state in the West, and women-centric aid policies had become the norm for western aid agencies. After nine months of war against Pakistani forces, Bangladesh broke away from Pakistan on 16 December 1971 and declared itself an independent state. In 1947 when the British divided India into India and Pakistan, Bangladesh was the region known as East Pakistan. The West Pakistani leadership had paid little attention to the growth of its eastern province, which was ethnically Bengali and distinct from West Pakistanis. Bangladesh (former East Pakistan) was an internal colony of West Pakistan that provided raw materials (jute, tea, paper, etc.) to West Pakistani-controlled corporations. After the war in 1971, the already fragile infrastructure of Bangladesh was in chaos (Sisson and Rose, 1991; Umar, 2004). It was in this scenario that developmental NGOs stepped in as rural service providers.

NGOs began their work of war reconstruction and rehabilitation of refugees, occupying an infrastructural vacuum in the newly independent state. The developmental NGO sector soon capitalized on the women-in-development (WID) paradigm of the United Nations and western aid organizations. The Bangladeshi state, under military leadership, also capitalized on the WID paradigm to gain development dollars and legitimacy from western democracies.[9] The idea of women's participation in the economy was celebrated as a national goal, and developmental NGOs were given a free reign to grow and expand their rural outreach with western aid. The western aid organizations also preferred the NGO sector as their aid allies. It enabled them to bypass the bureaucracy and corruption of the Bangladeshi state,[10] and to directly reach targeted segments of the rural population (Karim, 2004). Over time, this developed into a lattice of dependent relationships between aid organizations, western capital, NGOs and the Bangladeshi state.

With the transition to democracy in Bangladesh in the 1990s, NGOs have moved into the political sphere. They have begun to use their borrowers as vote banks, urging them to cast votes for political candidates who represent an NGO-friendly platform.[11] NGOs, through their partnership with western aid agencies, USAID in particular, that emphasize 'good' governance programs, have reconstituted themselves as institutions for grassroots democratization. The space of the political, that is, what notions of politics can be conceptualized and authorized, is under construction through a diverse set of actors—national political parties, NGOs, clergy—all of whom are making claims on rural female subjects for their adherence. Neoliberalism and globalization have unhinged politics from the older left-identified politics with the vanguard political party as the catalyst of social justice, and have introduced a new politics of grassroots mobilization of the poor organized by the NGOs. Given the dominance of NGOs over rural populations, national political parties also seek the alliance of NGOs in order to win elections. Many NGOs have aggressively sponsored their female members for village-level local elections, posing a challenge to the rural patriarchal power structure through democratic means (Karim, 2001: 99, see also Cruikshank for a critique of empowerment, 1999: 68). After winning the 2006 Nobel Peace Prize, Professor Yunus (founder of the Grameen Bank) initially announced that he would start a new political party, a decision that he later withdrew.[12] In the unfolding scenario, politics and development have become connected in the architecture of globalization at the grassroots.

It can be said that NGOs are reterritorializing rural subjects as new subjects of a market-driven democratization, yet what remains amorphous is the nature of this reterritorialization. And as Ong has pointed out, 'Neoliberalism can also be conceptualized as a new relationship between government and knowledge through which governing activities are recast as non-political and nonideological problems that need technical solutions' (Ong, 2006: 3). It must be mentioned that, while NGOs can subject the poor to their will, they do not control the choices people make. For example, once empowered to vote, NGO female borrowers often cast the vote according to family preference.[13] While this grassroots mobilization unleashes new energies and potentials, and perhaps even challenges globalization at the grassroots, it remains inhibited by the financial imperatives of NGO lending institutions, i.e. the management of rural populations through micro-credit that tends to de-politicize political possibilities (Ferguson, 1994).

There are several critical factors that allow the NGOs to play such a decisive role in rural life in Bangladesh. Firstly, there is the virtual absence of the state in the rural economy. NGOs dominate the rural economy from rural credit to telecommunications to primary education.[14] Secondly, the NGOs provide two-thirds of the institutional credit in rural areas (Sobhan, 1997: 133). In Bangladesh, neither the government banks nor the traditional moneylenders loan to the very poor because they lack physical collateral. This financial dependency on the NGO has given them the power to act as patrons of the poor. They constitute a modern landlord with a global vision. Thirdly, the NGOs are a major source of employment in a country with limited job opportunities for its burgeoning young population. Young college graduates seek entry-level jobs with NGOs. NGOs are seen as the future—a promise of a better life and, for the better educated, an opportunity to go abroad for training. Fourthly, the NGOs have silenced dissent in the public sphere by inducting a large number of university professors and researchers as consultants in their various programs; public intellectuals who might otherwise have spoken out against the excess of NGOs. In fact, many university professors operate as fulltime NGO consultants and part-time teachers. This shift is legible in discourse. Researchers talk about NGO research as a job (*kaaj*) and not as research (*gobeshona*). Finally, the work of NGOs fragmented the left political parties from the 1970s onward when both groups struggled over the adherence of the poor. The resource-rich NGOs won. Thus many people—from the rural to the urban, from the illiterate to the highly educated—in Bangladesh are direct and indirect beneficiaries of NGO programs and policies.

THE GRAMEEN BANK MODEL OF MICRO-CREDIT

Grameen Bank (GB) has reversed conventional banking practice by removing the need for *collateral* and created a banking system based on mutual trust, accountability, participation, and creativity. GB provides credit to the poorest of the poor in rural Bangladesh, without any collateral. At GB, credit is a cost effective weapon to fight poverty and it serves as a catalyst in the overall development of socioeconomic conditions of the poor who have been kept outside the banking orbit on the ground that they are poor and hence not bankable.

The Grameen Bank (or Rural Bank) was started by a local economist; Professor Muhammad Yunus, in 1976. The Bank originally targeted rural men for its credit programs. In its early days, the Bank ran into difficulties in collecting money from men who would not allow themselves to be subjected to the Bank's strict rules. By the late 1970s, the Bank had appropriated the Women-in-Development (WID) paradigm of western aid agencies, and reinvented itself as a bank for poor women. In 1998, the Bank had been replicated in 54 countries and 94 percent of its borrowers were poor women.

Grameen Bank has made significant contributions to the practice of commercial banking. It has made credit available to the poor who were denied commercial loans due to a lack of physical collateral. It has demonstrated through its 98 percent rate of recovery that the poor are not defaulters, that the poor pay back their loans. It has taught women the importance of managing money, and keeping basic account of expenditures. Additionally, it has introduced some new forms of social identity among rural women, such as women's weekly meetings where women collect and discuss loan proposals, the creation of a space where women can speak without men dominating the discourse. Grameen women are required to say their and their husbands' names publicly (Bangladeshi rural women do not speak their husbands names), women are taught to sign their names on contracts, and the Sixteen

Decisions of the Grameen Bank focus on social engineering (Hashemi, Schuler & Riley, 1996: 649).

Professor Yunus advocates this liberal doctrine for poor women. In many of his speeches, he claimed that, not only is capitalism good for the poor, 'the poor are good for capitalism'.[15] Basing his claims on the 98 percent rate of return of his bank (a rate that rivals that of CitiBank), he argues that the poor are good investments for large banks, and the financial world should take notice of that fact. The chief contribution of the bank lies in proving to the development community that the poor are 'bankable', i.e. the poor repay their debt.

In my research, I found that micro-credit benefited several categories of women the most—the rural middle class, women with marketable skills, women whose husbands had marketable skills—or whose husbands had a regular employment and could thus pay the weekly installments—widows, divorced and abandoned women. In the majority of the cases, the husbands and male kin of the women used the loans. In most instances, their husbands were day laborers and this allowed them to repay the weekly installments on the loans.

The Grameen Bank model rests on the idea of the individual entrepreneur who, with the help of micro-credit, becomes self-employed, owns private property (the assets she builds with the loans), and sells her labor on the market. The out-of-the-home entrepreneur links seamlessly with the ideology of neoliberalism. She is an owner of petty capital. This production of the ownership ethic is against wage labor, overtime pay, retirement benefits and worker's compensation, i.e. against the very foundations of a welfare state.[16] Failure to succeed now rests solely with the individual and not with the cor-poration/NGO/state.[17] In this scenario, the state withdraws from the welfare of its citizens to the welfare of capital.

Interestingly, micro-credit policies have also shifted the discourse of poverty to a discourse of neoliberalism at the local level. Calling oneself poor[18] is now seen as pejorative in rural Bangladesh. Prior to the mass mediation of rural relations through credit, the poor felt a claim on the wealth of the rich because they were in a patron-client relationship. Thus in times of hardship, the poor could forage on the lands and ponds of the rich for sustenance. Similarly, the rural rich would make claims on the free labor and adherence of the poor in exchange. This traditional patron-client relationship has weakened, and has been replaced by a neoliberal discourse of self-help and individual responsibility.

While the Grameen Bank and NGOs claim that poor women are the beneficiaries of these loans, it is the husbands of the women and other male members who really use the loans. Bangladeshi women are primarily the carriers of NGO loans; they are not their end users. In my research, I found that men used 95 percent of the loans. Professor Yunus has conceded as much. Commenting on the long struggle of Grameen of loaning to women over their husbands, he says, 'Grameen has come a long way since then. Now Grameen lends money to husbands, but *only through the wives*. The principal borrower remains the wife' (Yunus and Jolis, 1998: 91; my emphasis). In my research area, rural men laughed when they were asked whether the money belonged to their wives. They pointedly remarked that 'since their wives belong to them, the money rightfully belongs to them'. Women also told me that, as a Bangladeshi woman, I should know that they would give the money to their husbands who labor outside the home.

NGO officers and researchers in Bangladesh connected with the microcredit industry are aware that the men control the use of the money, but in their public scripts they censor this vital information. This silencing in public scripts of who really uses the money occurs for two reasons. On one level, it fulfills the western aid mandate of targeting women in development. NGOs can show to their western donors that women are participating in loan meetings, and the loans are given in the names of women. On another level, NGOs seek out women because they are seen as docile subjects who can be subjected to their codes and more easily manipulated than men. In the latter instance, local patriarchal norms, the status of rural women, are manipulated by the NGOs in their advancement of their economic goals.

Rural kinship structures are an important pillar of micro-credit operations. Based on gender, status, and age differentiations, kin members have varying levels of obligations to each other. Into this set of existing obligatory kin relationships, the micro-credit NGO has inserted the notion of collective responsibility alongside individual loans. That is, the group is both the enforcer and the guarantor of loans to the NGO. These two structures—kin obligations and collective responsibilities—are toxically synergistic, and coupled together they work to operate within an economy of shame.

In my research area, an older woman (a widow) was returning home with her loan from the Grameen Bank. On the way, her nephew hailed her as 'aunt'. He said that he knew that she had just received a loan from the bank, and as her nephew he was making a claim on her money to fund his own business. As this woman explained, as the aunt and as a woman (further complicated by the fact that she was widow), she was obligated to give him the money. If she did not, there would be pressure from her family to do so. Thus, obligation to give to a male kin was considered by her family to be her responsibility, a higher good, and more important than her need of that money.[19]

Given the profitability of microcredit operations from the perspective of NGOs and the donor agencies (the loans of the poor are recovered), one finds too many NGOs with too much cash chasing too few creditworthy members in the rural economy. Consequently, almost every female NGO member has membership with multiple (seven to eight) NGOs. According to the Credit Development Forum in 1998 out of 1200 foreign-aided NGOs, 369 dealt specifically with credit. This has led to a routinization and simplification of NGO credit operations, from the earlier emphasis on social engineering to the newer role as credit provider. As a result women are now unwilling to spend time learning NGO rhetoric (the Grameen Bank's 16 Decisions, for example), and the loan officers are under pressure from headquarters to find additional creditworthy borrowers. In my research area, very few Grameen women knew of any of the 16 Decisions.[20] At the time of getting loans, women put down on paper various projects that they would undertake with the loans. However, because of the pressure on loan officers to recover money, officers seldom have the time to monitor what the borrowers do with the loans. As one borrower's husband said to me with a smile:

> We took a cow loan. Fifty percent will be spent to pay off old debts, and another
> fifty percent will be invested in moneylending. If the manager comes to see our cow,
> we can easily borrow one from the neighbors.

From the perspective of the credit NGOs, what mattered was the maintenance of high recovery rates and not the skills training of individual borrowers. In fact, the emphasis on expanding micro-credit operations had reproduced usury at multiple levels of rural society.

Similarly, the availability of NGO money has encouraged many rich clients to enter the micro-credit market.[21] In many instances, richer clients used poorer women as proxy members. That is, the rich client used the loan while the poor woman joined the NGO as a proxy member in exchange for a fee. If the rich client defaulted, it was still the poor proxy member who was held accountable by the NGO.

In analyzing the reasons why rural men allowed their women to become NGO members even though it brought their women in contact with non-kin men, one noticed a deep level of complicity between NGOs and rural men. Despite rural codes of honor/shame that dictated that women should not come in contact with non-kin men (and most NGOs, especially Grameen Bank, have male officers), rural men found it more useful to allow their women to join NGOs because they (rural men) work during the day. Poor men who lack physical collateral 'give' their women in membership to NGOs as economic reassurance. In reality, *the collateral that Grameen and all other NGOs extract from the poor is the Bangladeshi rural woman's honor and shame.* The poor give their honor embodied in their women to the NGOs in exchange for the loans. It is very important to note that *this* is the pivot on which the successes of the Grameen model of micro-credit hinges. However, rural men are ambivalent about the condition in which they find themselves. While they were more comfortable with micro-credit because their women could stay at home, they also felt vulnerable because home enterprises do not necessarily guarantee a fixed income at the end of the month which they can count on. Many rural men I spoke with said that they preferred jobs from NGOs that would offer them a guaranteed income. That is, given a choice between entrepreneurship with its associated risks and regular employment, most people I surveyed preferred the latter.

GROUP VERSUS INDIVIDUAL RESPONSIBILITY

Group responsibility for individual loans is a fundamental organizing principle of the micro-credit model. The Grameen Bank operates on this model.[22] Forty women form a Center, which is housed in a female member's house. The women elect a leader from the group who advocates the loan proposals in their weekly meetings. These forty women form eight smaller groups that include five women in each group. Each week, the women meet in the Center and hand over their weekly installments (*kisti* in Bengali) to the bank officer.

The loans, usually between $100 and $200, are given for a year on a fixed interest rate of 16 percent, that came to 32 percent in effective or actual interest (1999 figures). The borrowers paid the interest on the original principal through the life of the loan. That is, the interest paid was not adjusted as the principal was paid off. What the borrower actually ended up paying was much higher because these loans contained many hidden costs (entrance fees, cancellation fees, late fees, mandatory savings, and often product tie-ins with loans) that raised the rate to 50–60 percent.[23]

It should be borne in mind though, that this number is still much lower than the rate charged by the rural moneylender (120 percent). Thus, in a landscape of loans that the poor could actually access, the borrowers were better off paying 60 percent to the NGOs rather than 120 percent to the rural moneylender.

All these women were jointly held responsible for the repayment of individual loans. Thus each woman was responsible for the repayment of all the other loans in the Center. When a default occurred, the bank (or the NGO) withheld money from the other members, forcing them to either pay up or lose access to future loans. The bank tied individual responsibility to group responsibility, using that as a mechanism to (a) maintain tight fiscal control over repayments; (b) police women borrowers' financial conduct after they received a loan; and (c) enforce payment through collective punishment for individual defaults.

The bank monitored its members though tight fiscal control. This close surveillance of its women members[24] allowed the bank officers to forestall any impending default. It was the women borrowers who did the surveillance on behalf of the bank (or the NGO). Fearing potential defaults, women informed their managers about misuse of the loans by borrowers. This surveillance of conduct resulted in the daily strife that I witnessed in these group relations. Since these women and their families were linked together through loans, it was not only the women but also the community that had become part of this surveillance mechanism.

The surveillance of women already exists in rural Bangladesh, especially in the regulation of rural women's sexuality and comportment. The micro-credit NGO (the Grameen Bank and other NGOs) appropriated and routinized this form of surveillance as part of its credit operating structure. NGO managers routinely told their women clients: 'You are responsible for the loan and you have to make sure that no one defaults.' This transference of responsibility from the NGO to the women reduced the operating costs for the NGOs (they do not have to hire additional people to monitor the borrowers) and at the same time, it created a very effective policing system whereby rural people reported to the NGOs for fear of financial loss. Thus, poor women police other poor women, evicting poorer members from the group in fear of losing future income. NGO officers could also withdraw from taking any responsibility for actions that the community took to enforce payments.

The picture gets complicated when one realizes that the most widespread and profitable business from micro-credit is the practice of usury by women. Moneylending allows women to conduct business without leaving their homes. Women who do not possess marketable skills have opted for moneylending as a profitable alternative. Women adopt the norms of the traditional moneylender and loan money at 120 percent rate of return. This notion of 120 percent interest is a form of implicit social knowledge. Rural women do not make exact calculations on these loans. In their universe of social knowledge, two interest rates are known, the rate charged by the NGO and that by the rural moneylender. As rational economic agents, they opt for the higher number of the traditional moneylender. Usury creates a chain of dependencies that involves kin and non-kin alike, and ties multiple NGOs together. A loans to B who loans to C who loans to D, and so on. The failure on the part of a distant person on this chain has a ripple effect in rural society, affecting a sum much larger than one or two people or one or two NGOs.

During my research, I saw that credit-related strife amongst members and their families were routine occurrences. Women would march off together to scold the defaulting woman, shame her or her husband in a public place, and when she could not pay the full amount of the installment, go through her possessions and take away whatever they could sell off to recover the defaulted sum. In circumstances when the woman failed to pay the sum, which happened several times a month in the NGOs I studied, the group members would repossess the capital that the woman had built with her loans. This ranged from taking away her gold nose-ring (a symbol of marital status for rural women, and removing it symbolically marks the 'divorcing/widowing' of a woman) to cows and chicks to trees that had been planted to be sold as timber to collecting rice and grains that the family had accumulated as food, very often leaving the family with no food whatsoever. The women who committed these acts did so at the exhortations of NGO officers, but they also considered these acts to be 'protecting their investments', and the defaulting woman as someone who had 'broken faith with the community'. These acts were committed with the full knowledge of NGO officers, but the officers did not participate in these collective acts of aggression. Instead, they threatened to withhold future loans unless the defaulted money was recovered.

In instances where everything had been repossessed because of a large default, members would sell off the defaulting member's house. This is known as house-breaking (*ghar bhanga*) and has a long history in rural society. It is considered as the ultimate shame of dishonor in rural society. In other words, serious defaults led to homelessness of the families concerned. In my research area, house-breaking occurred several (six to seven) times, whereas smaller forms of public shaming occurred every week. There were several incidents of suicide committed by men who had been shamed by their inability to protect the honor of their families. But these instances were rare, and were often the result of multiple causes, such as flooding in low-lying areas. What is important to note though is how these pre-existing coercive norms, of house-breaking for example, have become institutionalized as part of the NGO technologies of loan recovery.

The NGOs also used the apparatuses of the state, such as the police and courts, to harass these poor women to pay up. NGOs often filed cases against individual women who would be taken into police custody and kept as criminals (*ashami*) until the family repaid the defaulted sum. In Bangladesh where discourses of shame and modesty predominate, if a woman is held in police custody overnight not only had she brought shame on her husband as a criminal, she had also lost her virtue. When loan recovery techniques became entangled in existing social attitudes toward women, women who came into their affinal homes through marriage were often isolated as 'outsiders', and blamed for bringing shame to their husbands and their families. I met with several of these women who were divorced by their husbands because they had 'disgraced' their families by going to jail.[25] Husbands blamed their wives for shaming them and their families, although the husbands were the beneficiaries of these loans. Thus, micro-credit loans and women borrowers do not operate outside of local patriarchy but within it.

The question of rural women's complicity and dissent are important facets of how this technology works in rural life. Women do try to increase the wealth of their family by monitoring other women. Bring a provider of loans secures the woman's status within the family as long as she can forestall defaults and not shame her family. Women also try to manipulate the NGOs by borrowing from multiple sources without letting their NGO managers know. To forestall overlapping, NGOs demand that their borrowers remain faithful to one institution. Women sometimes travel to neighboring villages to borrow from different NGOs. Women will make their loan officer wait for when they are unwilling to return the money. NGO association has given women some limited forms of practical freedom. Rural women have more reasons to be seen around town. They can take some time off from their housework. If one carefully analyzes these small acts of resistance, the poor women are firmly inside an interlocking system of debt where they are in debt to multiple NGOs, kin, fellow borrowers, and traditional moneylenders. The more they expand their circulation in these overlapping maps of credit, the more indebted they become.

With the spread of micro-credit operations in rural economy, NGO managers face tremendous pressure from NGO headquarters to operate smooth loan programs. Failure on their part to collect the money from the women borrowers results in the NGOs withholding money from their paychecks. Too many defaults in their area will result in their getting fired or never being promoted. Thus, NGO managers manipulate money from the women through cancellation and late fees that would form a safety net in the event of a default. These charges do not show up on paper, and could only be accessed by creating trust with the women.

The NGOs are fully cognizant of the negative consequences on women from their actions to recover the money.[26] Yet they are unwilling to replace the notion of collective contracts with individual contracts. Weakening the tight fiscal control of loan recovery would make them lose profit. When I mentioned some of my reservations to a manager of the Grameen Bank, she pointedly said: 'Why are you surprised? Grameen Bank is a business and not a charity.'

THE MAKING OF A NEOLIBERAL SUBJECTIVITY: THE FEMALE PETTY MONEYLENDER

Contrary to the claims of the Grameen Bank and other NGOs that they have reduced traditional moneylending through micro-credit NGOs, what we find instead is the reproduction of usury at multiple levels of society, and the normalization of that activity within a new group of actors: poor, Muslim women.[27] Through membership in NGO loan programs, the formerly asset-less poor have been able to accumulate some assets which now make them creditworthy in the estimation of the moneylender. Thus, the net of usury is cast much wider, bringing all sorts of formerly poor and assetless people inside its web. In my research area, the traditional moneylenders often boasted that their business was better due to NGO loans. The neoliberal subject that has emerged out of this encounter between micro-credit and rural social relations is the figure of the female petty moneylender.

Jahanara's Story

Moneylending is prevalent in villages that are close to markets, for the obvious reason that traders seek out the women borrowers for loans. In my research area, this village was Krishnonagar, which was located next to the main market of the town. In an informal survey of Krishnonagar, 100 households out of 230 NGO beneficiary households were engaged in moneylending.

As a result of the proximity to the market, the women of this village were visible in public spaces. Compared to women living in the interior villages, these women possessed a higher degree of physical mobility. Women in Krishnonagar had more access to non-kin men because of the location of their village, and it was acceptable for them to talk to non-kin men. NGO-related activities had added to that mobility and had created some new pathways for these women to interact with the larger community. Grameen Bank, BRAC, Proshika, and ASA offices were spread through the town, and access to these offices meant a trek through town. The women of Krishnonagar told me that they had access to the market prior to joining these NGOs. Many of them had to walk through the market to get to other places. As they pointed out, NGO membership did not necessarily make them into more 'mobile subjects', but it did give them more reasons to be seen around town without people necessarily casting aspersions on their moral character.

One morning in December 1998, I went with my research assistant in search of female petty moneylenders in Krishnonagar. I was told that Jahanara Begum was the most famous moneylender in this area. She had over 350,000 takas ($7446) invested in moneylending.[28] What did it mean, I had wondered, for a woman to have amassed so much money? How did she get to become such a successful moneylender?

Jahanara's husband operated a tea-shop with her money. Her husband was considered a 'weak' man by villagers because his wife was so successful. Jahanara had two sons and two daughters. Her eldest daughter had studied up to grade seven and she was training to be a moneylender. However, none of the younger children was enrolled in school. In her words, 'What can they do with an education? Better to learn moneylending at a young age.'

When we arrived, Jahanara came forward to meet us. She was dressed in a red sari and wore substantial amounts of gold on her person (nose ring, bangles, and a chain) for a rural person. A striking woman, Jahanara looked confident and well fed. She had already notified several of her neighbors that an elder sister from abroad was going to write about her in a book that would be read by many people, and soon a group of women gathered around us. They all look up to Jahanara, and soon it was clear that they were all in debt to her.

Jahanara invested her money in four categories: short-term business, small businesses in the market, middle-level farmers, and NGO borrowers. Of this, the majority of the money was invested in short-term business, usually the profits were repaid after three to six months. The money was lent to traders who would buy local produce such as paddy, betel leaves, jute, timber, and take them by boat to other parts of the country where they fetched higher prices. Then they returned with produce from other parts of the country to sell it in their local market. People consider it a safe form of investment. They do not lose the money unless the boat capsizes with the goods, which, from what I was told, was a rare event.

Jahanara's day was not typical for a rural woman. She did not stay at home to do housework. Most of her time was spent collecting money from traders. She also spent considerable time going to NGO meetings to pay her dues or to collect new loans. When I asked Jahanara about her success, she began to share this with me:

> I have also taken out loans in my daughter's name and in the names of other people. I am teaching my daughter my trade. I take loans out by proxy. I pay these women Tk. 100 (approx. $2) each for letting me take the loan. Now all the NGOs give me the highest loans possible. If they do not want to give me the kind of loan I want, I say to them, I will cross out my name and go elsewhere. There are so many NGOs, another NGO will give me money. (*Here she pauses and laughs.*) They need me more than I need them. They do not want me to leave. I am a good investment. I have money so I always pay my installments on time …

This is how Jahanara described her success:

> One has to run. If you sit around, nothing will happen. I go with the members to the NGO office when we have to get the loan. I get the money and leave. I don't stay in their office long. When I give money to NGO women borrowers, I have to be careful. These women are so needy. You cannot give them too much money; Tk. 1000 or 2000 [between $21 and $43] is about the maximum amount. If I give them too much money, then I have to walk around empty-handed later. They will not be able to pay back. I give them loans when they cannot pay their *kistis* or when there is an emergency …

At the end of our conversation, Jahanara said that she didn't think that other women could become like her. According to her,

> They do not understand anything except their husbands. If I gave my earnings to my husband, he would use it all up. And I just invest my money in business. In the beginning, I never thought of getting food, clothes for my children. I was very careful with my money. If you go to the homes of these women on the day they

get a loan from an NGO, you will find that for the next seven days they spend the money on fish and meat. My husband is also not like other men. He lets me have my way …

The following week, we met Jahanara at the Grameen Bank meeting. She was the Center leader of the Grameen Group in that village. Grameen Bank officers only collect the installments after everyone has assembled and paid up every single penny owed to Grameen. If any woman was missing (as usually happened when she did not have the money), then all the other women in the group had to wait. This coercive technique deployed by bank officers creates a lot of friction among the women as they were forced to remain at the Center instead of returning home and doing their housework.

At this meeting one woman called Kashai Bou (butcher's wife) was not present. Kashai Bou lived several villages away and the Grameen Bank officer took Jahanara as Center leader with him to collect the money from her. We went along with them. On the way to Kashai Bou's house, Jahanara proudly told us that she had broken many houses when members could not pay. 'We know when they cannot pay, so we take a carpenter with us to break the house.'

When I asked Jahanara, 'Why do you break the houses of kin?' Jahanara became indignant at first. Her initial comment was 'Why shouldn't we? They have breached their trust with us. If they cannot pay, then we will have to pay. Why should I pay for them?' Then she became quiet and said after a while:

> It is not good to break someone's house, but we are forced to do it. This is how we get loans from Grameen Bank and other NGOs. They put pressure on us to recover the money, then we all get together and force the defaulting member to give us the money. We don't care how we do it.

NEUTRALIZING DISSENT: POWER/KNOWLEDGE IN DEVELOPMENT

"The texts of development have always been avowedly strategic and tactical—promoting, licensing, and justifying certain interventions and practices, delegitimizing others … What do the texts of development not say? What do they suppress? Who do they silence—and why?" (Crush, 1995: 5).

Why is it that what I have written in these pages is not legible as a public discourse? The answer to that question is that the critiques are *silenced* in NGO-dominated research spaces. Knowledge is power, but power also legitimizes what counts as knowledge, and NGOs are powerful institutions in Bangladesh. The hagiographic transcripts of the Grameen Bank have to be apprehended at the crux of power/knowledge in the context of Bangladesh. In Bangladesh, there is only one academic English publishing house, called University Press Limited (UPL). The editor of UPL declined to publish Aminur Rahman's critical assessment of the Grameen Bank, *Women and Micro-Credit in Bangladesh* (1999), stating that a prominent economist had advised against its publication.[29] Interestingly, although Rahman's book was published by Westview Press in the US, his critique of the Grameen Bank lending practices was silenced in Bangladesh through the lack of alternative academic publishing institutions.

Similarly, in the absence of a responsible state or a progressive social movement, the rural poor have to rely on the goodwill of the NGOs.[30] Villagers critique NGOs with the qualifier that NGOs offer them services that they need, but that they want the terms of these loans to be more humane. NGO officials in their private scripts admit that development cannot take place solely through micro-credit but they censor this in their public scripts for fear of jeopardizing their jobs (Pereira, 1998). The fragmented political left continues to talk about this but since the 1990s they have lost legitimacy as a political voice. The role of feminists is complicated in this scenario because feminists find it more important to focus on other violent forms of aggression against women, such acid burnings and rape, and to keep a united NGO voice against the tyranny of the clergy.

The vernacular press is a rich source of these critiques but western donors and researchers do not access them. In NGO-dominated research spaces where donors and western researchers gather, the medium of communication is English and that precludes the majority of Bangladeshis who cannot communicate in English. In fact, the use of English in NGO research spaces is ostensibly to accommodate the western donors, but in reality it regulates who can be heard in these spaces.

On 22 August 1998 a conference was held in Dhaka entitled 'Yunusonomics', organized by a local professor. The intent of the conference was to offer micro-credit as the new panacea in development economics. The conference papers were presented in English. When the floor was opened for questions, the first speaker was an angry retired doctor who said that he had expected the discussion to be carried on in a language that was accessible to him. He added that he would speak his opinions in Bengali. He often went to his village and found that most people were becoming poorer after several years of membership with Grameen Bank. He had calculated the interest charged by Grameen to be over 50 percent. He asked, 'How could they claim that this was a new paradigm to be followed? How was this high interest helping the poor?' Yet not a single person among the speakers engaged with the doctor, an ordinary citizen who had come to the conference to engage in a dialogue. There were some donor representatives present at the conference but it was unclear if they understood what the doctor was saying. Thus, critique expressed in vernacular language is neutralized within NGO-dominated research spaces that are sustained by western agencies in the aid of their policies.

Finally, on a more significant level, for middle class Bangladeshis the Grameen Bank operates as a source of symbolic capital. For the first time, we, the people of Bangladesh—Henry Kissinger's 'bottomless basket'—have given a gift to the western development community. Now visitors, from former US President Bill and Senator Hillary Clinton to Queen Sophia of Spain, come to Bangladesh to study a development phenomenon. It is a source of tremendous national pride for many Bangladeshis, which makes it all the more difficult to critique the Grameen Bank, or for that critique to be taken seriously. In fact, speaking out against the Grameen Bank makes one into a 'traitor within'.[31] In this scenario, Grameen Bank's latest triumph in winning the 2006 Nobel Peace Prize, operates as a form of governmentality and authorizes what can be said about the Grameen Bank. In the absence of a robust social movement in Bangladesh, it makes it all the more difficult for a radical critique against micro-credit policies to be heard. The Nobel Peace Prize signals Bangladesh's arrival onto the modern landscape as equals with the West. Consequently, the Grameen Bank gains more power and authority both locally and globally by enmeshing profit with poor people's empowerment to create 'brave new worlds'.

NOTES

1. The other three NGOs are Bangladesh Rural Advancement Committee (BRAC), Proshika Human Development Forum, and Association for Social Advancement (ASA). All of these NGOs work with slight variations on the Grameen Bank model. They all have millions of subscribers, and cover more than eighty percent of the rural population. The Grameen Bank is officially registered as a bank under the Bangladesh Bank Ordinance (1983) but conceptually it is a non-governmental organization. Therefore, in my analysis, I treat it as such.
2. According to the websites of these NGOs: www.grameen.com, www.brac.net, www.asabd.org, www.proshika.org.
3. In Bangladesh, western aid organizations channel most of their aid through the NGO sector, which they helped to create in the 1970s. In 1997, the EU channeled 25% of its aid through the NGO sector.
4. This point will not necessarily hold for smaller NGOs in Latin American countries that have a long tradition of social movements.
5. James Scott (2006) analyzed the high modernist goals of 'well-intended' socialist engineering. NGOs, such as the Grameen Bank, also seek to bring about high modernist values, coupled with the incentives of a market-driven economy, to rural constituencies. To facilitate that, they also undertake information gathering on diet, health, education, and consumption, similar to the modern state.
6. Globalization and the need for cheap labor from 'third world' countries has resulted in the out-migration of rural people as labor overseas, first to the Middle East in the 1970s and 1980s, and to East Asian countries in the 1990s. It has led to remittances of wages, and a flow of ideas from Muslim societies. One of the consequences of this new networked society of Muslims is the increase in Islamic seminaries (madrassahs). It has increased wealth and brought communication technologies to rural areas (TV, cell phones, internet and Bollywood movies).
7. I maintain that ethnography yields very different conclusions from survey research and focus-group interviews, the methodological tools of development economists. Ethnography requires a sustained amount of time with a community, building their trust, and observing what people do as opposed to what people say they do when they are asked questions in a survey.
8. URL (accessed June 2007): http://www.grameen-info.org
9. During 1975–90, Bangladesh was under military dictatorship.
10. Transparency International (TI) routinely lists Bangladesh as one of the most corrupt countries in the world.
11. The development NGOs do not support the Jamaat-I-Islami and other Islamist parties which espouse a non-modernist role for women. If they sided with the Islamists, they would lose their western aid.
12. 'Prof. Yunus plans to form a political party in Bangladesh', 11 Feb. 2007. URL (accessed June 2007): http://muhammadyunus.org/content/view/83/1/lang,en/
13. Since the rural population is largely illiterate, voters are taught the symbols of different political parties (fish, a spring of wheat, the scales of justice, etc. that are the signs for various political parties) as identifiers of which political party they will vote for.
14. This topic is a paper in itself. But I do want to make the point that the NGO sector in Bangladesh signals a new kind of state formation for the 21st century, one that is a cross between private capital and welfarism.
15. URL (assessed June 2007): http://www.muhammadyunus.org/
16. From its inception Bangladesh was not a welfare state. I argue that countries like Bangladesh that came into being in the environment of globalization and neoliberalism, and are closely tied to western aid, can only be a proto-capitalist state.

17. In my research I found that NGO managers blamed the borrowers and their husbands for failures. For example, when 50% of breeder chickens died within a week of getting a loan and setting up operations, the NGO (BRAC in this instance) managers would speak of the failure as a fault of the 'poor, illiterate village women', and not as BRAC's fault in targeting people who didn't have the wherewithal (the training, the facilities, etc.) to run a chicken farm from a tin-shed in their house.

18. The NGO definition of poor is a family of four with less than 0.5 acre of arable land and living below the level of poverty in Bangladesh.

19. Giving to kin has a double bind. It is expected that kin members will intercede and prevent a potential default in order to save the honor of the family. However, if a serious default occurs, then the family usually sides with the defaulting male member and asks the woman to find other means (borrow at 120%) to pay off the loan.

20. The leading NGOs have model villages, usually close to the capital Dhaka, to showcase to international donors.

21. In my area, the local headmistress of a school, the wife of a lawyer, and wives of some of the richest merchants in town were members of micro-credit NGOs. NGOs prefer richer female members because they will not default. As high-status people in rural society, they can coerce poorer members to pay up. However, rich male members just do the opposite. When ASA began to target richer clients in my area, the collection became a problem with the rich clients threatening 'they will not pay back'. The situation was mediated by several prominent politicians, and finally, a payment schedule was worked out. Thus, local politicians became involved in NGO loan recovery.

22. All the NGOs I studied mimicked this basic structure, group responsibility of individual loans, strict recovery through weekly (ASA and Grameen) or biweekly meetings (BRAC) and monthly meetings (Proshika), and product tie-ins with loans (hybrid seeds with agricultural loans, breeder chickens for BRAC loanees).

23. At the time of my research, the Grameen Bank had decided to lower the payment schedule from fifty-two weeks to fifty weeks, which would mean an additional rise in the weekly amount (kisti) paid by the borrowers. For poor people, a weekly rise of a few takas (the unit of currency) is a tremendous hardship.

24. In development jargon this is euphemistically known as peer monitoring.

25. In my area, the NGO Proshika had filed 74 cases against its women members and many of them were taken into custody.

26. These incidents were happening in front of NGO officers. They would exhort the women to 'collect the money or else …' I brought several such incidents to the attention of NGO workers in my area, but they would dismiss my concerns by saying, 'These are the work of illiterate people. We (the NGO) do not encourage this. Did you see us present at the event?' Interestingly, officers in NGO headquarters in Dhaka get incensed if you report such incidents to them. I was literally thrown out of one of the leading NGO offices when I brought such activities to the attention of senior officials.

27. Moneylending in Bengal was traditionally handled by a caste of Hindu moneylenders. In some instances, Hindu widows often participated in small-time moneylending. With the creation of Pakistan in 1947, and with different waves of migration of Hindus from Bangladesh (formerly East Pakistan), Muslim male moneylenders have emerged. Often Muslims give up moneylending after performing the Hajj. However, the entrance of poor Muslim women into the institution of moneylending is a new phenomenon.

28. Calculated at Taka 47 (1998 rate) to 1 USD.

29. Personal communication to author by scholars from Bangladesh.

30. *Gonogebeshona* (People's Research) is a new concept developed by a professor of economics, Dr. Amisur Rahman of Bangladesh. It is a participatory form of research where the researcher and the targeted group work together to find solutions to problems. This research could offer an alternative to the existing model of top-down research conducted by highly paid consultants. For more information, consult the website: http://www.rib_bangladesh.org/.

31. During my research, local NGO researchers often reminded me that I was looking at the negative side of micro-credit. Instead, as a feminist scholar I should focus on the positive side of micro-credit such as rural women's ability to handle money, sign, and speak their names in public.

REFERENCES CITED

Ahmad, Q.K. (2007) Socio-economic and Indebtedness: Related Impact of Micro-credit in Bangladesh. Dhaka: University Press Ltd.

Appadurai, Arjun, (1996) 'Disjuncture and Difference in the Global Cultural Economy' in Modernity at Large: Cultural Dimensions of Globalization, pp. 47–67. Minneapolis, Minnesota: University of Minnesota Press.

Appadurai, Arjun (2001) 'Grassroots Globalization and the Research Imagination', in Arjun Appadurai (ed.) Globalization, pp. 1–21. Durham, NC: Duke University Press.

Bornstein, David (1996) The Price of a Dream. Dhaka: University Press Ltd.

Clinton, Bill (2007) Giving: How Each of us Can Change the World. Knopt: New York, 2007.

Counts, Alex (1996) Who Needs Credit? New Delhi: Research Press.

Credit Development Forum Annual Yearbook (1998) CDF Publications: Dhaka.

Cruikshank, Barbara (1999) The Will to Empower: Democratic Citizens and Other Subjects. Ithaca, NY: Cornell University Press.

Crush, Jonathan (1995) Imagining Development. New York and London: Routledge.

Ferguson, James (1994) The 'Anti-Politics' Machine: 'Development,' Depoliticization and Bureaucratic Power in Lesotho. Minnesota: University of Minnesota Press.

Goetz, Anne-Marie and Sengupta Rina (1996) 'Who Takes the Credit? Gender, Power and Control over Loan Use in Rural Credit Programs in Bangladesh', World Development 24(1): 45–64.

Harvey, David (2005) A Brief History of Neoliberalism. Oxford and New York: Oxford University Press.

Hashemi, Syed, Schuler, S. and Riley, A. (1996) 'Rural Credit Programs and Women's Empowerment in Bangladesh', World Development, 24(3): 635–653.

Hoare, Quintin, and Jeffrey Nowell-Smith (1971) Antonio Gramsci: Selections from the Prison Notebooks. New York: International Books.

Karim, Lamia (2001) 'Politics of the Poor: NGOs and Grass-roots Political Mobilization in Bangladesh', Political and Legal Anthropology Review 24(1): 97–107.

Karim, Lamia (2004) 'Democratizing Bangladesh: State, NGOs and Militant Islam', Cultural Dynamics 16(2–3): 219–318.

Khandaker, Shahidur (1998) Fighting Poverty with Micro-credit: Experience from Bangladesh. Dhaka: University Press Ltd.

Ong, Aihwa (2006) Neoliberalism as Exception: Mutations in Citizenship and Sovereignty. Durham, NC: Duke University Press.

Pereira, Jeffrey (1998) 'Those Who think Microcredit is the Only Key to Development are Making a Huge Mistake [Bengali]', Adhuna (Jan.-Mar.): 29–30.

Rahman, Aminur (1999) 'Micro-credit Initiatives for Equitable and Sustainable Development: Who Pays?', World Development, 27(1): 67–82.

Rahman, Aminur (2001) Women and Microcredit in Rural Bangladesh: An Anthropological Study of the Rhetoric and Realities of Grameen Bank Lending. Boulder, CO: Westview Press.

Scott, James (2006) 'Cities, People, Language', in Aradhana Sharma and Akhil Gupta (eds) Anthropology of the State, pp. 247–269. Malden, Ma and Oxford, UK: Wiley-Blackwell.

Sen, Amartya (1999) Development as Freedom. New York: Knopf.

Sisson, Richard and Leo E. Rose (1991) War and Secession: Pakistan, India and the Creation of Bangladesh. Berkeley, CA: University of California Press.

Sobhan, Rehman (1997) 'The Political Economy of Micro-Credit', in Geoffrey Wood and Iffath Sharif (eds) Who Needs Credit? Poverty and Finance in Bangladesh,pp. 131–41. Dhaka: University Press.

Todd, Helen (1996a) Women at the Center. Dhaka: University Press.

Todd, Helen (1996b) Cloning Grameen Bank: Replicating a Poverty Reduction Model in India, Nepal and Vietnam. London: Intermediate Technology Publications.

Umar, Badruddin (2004) The Emergence of Bangladesh: Class Struggles in East Pakistan (1947–1958). New York: Oxford University Press.

Yunus, Muhammad and Alan Jolis (1998) Banker to the Poor: Micro-Lending and the Battle Against World Poverty. Dhaka: University Press Ltd: Dhaka.

20

Commodity Animism and the Spirit of Brand-Name Capitalism

Anne Allison

The new issues around personal identity and material possessions in millennial Japan have even emerged in psychosomatic symptomatology. In the era that spawned the new wave of social "diseases" ("school refusal," social withdrawal, young criminals with good school records), Ohira Ken, a Japanese psychiatrist, noticed a new kind of patient visiting his office. Not really "sick" compared with his other patients, these people came in complaining of rather minor complications involving coworkers or family members. While none of these problems prevented these people from being socially functional, the patients were nonetheless inept in communicating with others. By contrast, all displayed amazing eloquence in talking volubly and assuredly about their material possessions. Calling this new type of patient "a person who talks about things *[mono no katari no hitobito]*" Ohira (1998) found their numbers proliferating in the 1990s and the syndrome itself a symptom of the times.

A typical case is that of a twenty-two-year-old woman who came to Ohira troubled by poor relations with her fellow workers, particularly one older woman. Extremely stylish herself, the woman (an OL, or office lady) expounded at length about her personal possessions: a wealth of brand-name goods that she recited in lists and genealogies of categories. When it came to the issue with her coworker, however, the patient was clueless except for saying that, unlike herself, the other woman had a poor feeling for material goods *(mono),* and there was tension between the two of them. The case of a twenty-five-year-old male office worker in an electric company was similar. Suffering from diarrhea at work, he found that what troubled him the most about his job was the cheap suit he had to wear because he could not afford anything better on his salary. Unable to establish good social relations or feel comfortable at work, the man spent much of his

Anne Allison, "Commodity Animism and the Spirit of Brand-name Capitalism," *Millennial Monsters: Japanese Toys and the Global Imagination*, pp. 86–92, 286–288. Copyright © 2006 by University of California Press. Reprinted with permission.

free time poring over consumer magazines with his wealthy girlfriend, picking out the goods they would like to buy. A third patient described herself, and the Japanese nation as a whole, entirely in terms of brand-name commodities: "We go to brand-name universities, enter brand-name companies, and wear brand-name goods. And this isn't just on the outside. On the inside, too, we're 'brand-name people' *[burando ningen]*" (Ohira 1998:51).

As Ohira points out, the *mono no katari no hitobito* is concerned with her place in the world and aims to elevate it by acquiring brand-name goods. Acquisition gives the person a sense of control, as does a propensity to classify everything. Life is managed by scrupulous cataloging: shoes, kitchen-ware, *meishi* (business cards), and phone friends. If something does not fit this pigeonholing, it either is gotten rid of or else provokes a problem—such as the difficulties experienced with real people, some of whom lack the passion for material goods of the *mono no katari no hitobito*. With the logic that buying and assembling goods will make one happy, things are used to "power up" and concretize the inner self. This mind-set is commonplace today in Japan, where a consuming public borrows the language of commodities to describe everything from personal identity and worth to companionship, intimacy, and interpersonal relationships. As Ohira notes, material wealth was the "Japanese dream" for postwar reconstruction. But the "treasures" of these earlier years (refrigerators, washing machines, color TVs) have long been realized, and the "dream" has nowhere else to go (1998:230–36). What Japan is now experiencing is a "pathology of abundance" (the title of his book on the subject, *Yutakasa no Seishinbyo),* generating the condition of "people who talk about things." Its symptoms are an intimacy with goods coupled with a deficit in interpersonal closeness.

As evidenced by the *mono no katari no hitobito* who seek out psychiatric assistance, this is not an altogether comfortable state. According to Ohira, these people do not enjoy being solitary and are actually seeking a way to communicate, albeit through the only language they can speak—that of material goods. Their dilemma echoes, if in reverse, the findings of the Ministry of Education about the "school refusers" who retreat to their homes not because they want to but because the outside world has no meaning or "space" for them. In both cases, the issue at hand is a variant of intimate alienation: alienation from a social world of people and labor (work and school), and intimacy formed with constructed realities (brand-name goods, video games) that are engaged while alone. Of course, "people who talk about things" move about in the world, whereas social shut-ins are marooned at home. But what does it say about millennial Japan that both these conditions not only proliferate today but are "pathologies" that blur into (or even constitute) the norm? And what does this suggest about the languages and conditions for "talking" these days, when children lock themselves in their rooms and adults communicate through material things?

In a 1987 study on consumer trends by Hakuhodo, the advertising agency, respondents were asked to draw their "dream house." Many did so by sketching single rooms or enclosed spaces that were obviously intended to be inhabited alone: images the researchers found to be "autistic" yet, notably, bright rather than dark. Seeing in this the contemporary mind-set— viewing the self as a "fenced-in paradise" and wanting to protect one's own space while not interfering with others—they have tracked how this trend was played out in consumer desires throughout the 1990s.

Strikingly, a high number of Japanese value goods that provide a sense of security, privacy, and warmth; both baths and cell phones, for example, are regarded as "private heavens" and "private resorts" (McCreery 2000:217–43). It is no wonder, perhaps, that Japan is the place that birthed the Walkman—Sony's mobile tape player that enables owners to stay plugged into their own aural worlds (of music/audio tapes/radio) literally wherever they go. Most of my fellow commuters on the trains I rode during my year in Japan were hooked up to such electronic devices: Walkmen, Palm Pilots, Game Boys, and cell phones (which, in many cases, now have multiple functions, from e-mail to digital cameras). The scene reflected what Raymond Williams (1975) has called "mobile privatization" and Kogawa Tetsuo (1984), speaking specifically about Japan, described as "electronic individualism." As Iain Chambers (1990) has noted about the Walkman, the cultural activity fostered is ambivalent, swaying between "autism and autonomy." And one wonders about the grammar of intimacy and alienation here: whether such dependence on private electronics/ dreams assuages or merely intensifies the atomism so deep-seated in millennial lifestyles.

According to the engineer who designed the PHS (personal handy phone system—a low-powered wireless phone technology developed in Japan) for Motorola in Japan, 85 percent of Japanese owners are personal users who carry their cell phones wherever they go and conceptualize them also as play devices, fashion wear, and companions. Since phones, in a manner of speaking, are so sutured to the body, *wearability* is a keyword for Japanese consumers, driving fashions that stress compactness and style, along with the latest in technology As Nakakawa states: "It's your own culture; you make it beautiful and users want to show this to others as well as to themselves" (*Nikkei Dezain* 1998:28). But what is private fashion here also translates into a communication device with which to maintain human connections. Kids these days have as many as three hundred names in their banks of cell-phone pals: up from the average of twenty-four held by the generation of "baby boomer juniors" (McCreery 2000:185).[1] This, in itself, can be a form of addiction, and the "friends" one calls on a cell phone may never be met in the flesh *(Nikkei Dezain* 1998:25). The line between communication and commodity, electronic individualism and *ningenkankei* (human relationships), is increasingly hard to discern.

This is also true of a fad that, blooming along with Japan's postwar prosperity in the 1970s, has peaked again (since 1997) in the millennial years of post-Bubble distress—a craving for "cuteness" as well as cute characters (Kitty-chan, Pikachu, Doraemon, Miffy) that adorn everything from backpacks, toy figures, and comic books to phone straps, key chains, and adult-targeted fashion. Emerging from the children's entertainment industry that, in the 1970s, produced toys out of mass-media characters (cartoons, comic books, television shows), the character business started taking off on its own when Sanrio came up with its Hello Kitty line in the 1970s. Bred, in this case, not from a media production but as an entire line of adorable consumer goods (stationery, hair clips, tea cups, lunch boxes, pajamas, umbrellas), the mouthless kitty cat triggered a fashion in both characters and cuteness (genetically referred to by the adjective *kawaii*, for cute). Although it was initially targeted to young girls *(shojo)*—and fostered by them in such fads as *hentai shojo moji* (a round, girlish form of handwriting)—cuteness exploded into a national obsession. In the 1980s, commercial businesses started adopting cute characters in promotional advertising. ANA airlines, for example, turned around a lagging ski campaign by employing the American character Snoopy, and JAL followed suit by using the character Popeye to target young women for tour packages. By the late 1980s, banks had adopted the practice of utilizing characters as a type of company logo and insignia on bankbooks (Dentsu 1999), and by the 1990s, personalizing cell phones with character straps (for adult men, the favorite is Doraemon, the blue robotic cat of the long-running *anime* and *manga* series) had become a common practice.

Character branding has become trendy, even fetishistic, in Japan today. In part, according to a book on the character business put out by the Japanese advertising agency Dentsu (1999), this is because cute characters are appropriated as symbols for personal, corporate, group, and national identity. The "essence" of character merchandising, Dentsu states, is that it "glues society at its root. A character accompanies the development of a group and becomes part of, and a symbol for, that identity." Characters, it continues, are a "device for self-realization" *(jikojitsugen)*. Certainly, the images of cute characters are as omnipresent today as animist spirits; indeed, I have a picture sitting in front of me of a *jizo* statue in the shape of Doraemon.[2] Besides commercial goods (hand towels, cooking pans, book bags, pencils), characters also embellish posters for public events or neighborhood fairs, show up on government notices or service announcements, and are stamped onto computers, Xerox machines, and even bulldozers. Cuteness is generally associated with childhood and childlike experiences: innocence, dependence, and freedom from the pressures of an adult world (though, as we have seen, the experience of childhood is quite different in reality). These are grafted from and onto the "play" of fantasy and dreams; the character of Doraemon, for example, whose fanciful concoctions such as the "door that goes anywhere" *(dokodemo doa)* keeps his own imagination open, as one adult fan put it, during the long days and nights he works in the unimaginative space of a *sarariman* (Fujimi 1998).

Speaking of the recent craze in character/cute goods, an advertising executive describes the relationships formed as both kinlike and (inter)personal. Whether a Kitty-chan key chain, Doraemon cell phone strap, or Pikachu backpack, these commodity spirits are "shadow families": constant and reliable companions that are soothing in these postindustrial times of nomadicism, orphanism, and stress. Someone else in the business states this more sharply: "Parents die, but characters remain forever" (Riri Furanki, cited in *Buren* 2000:15). Concurring, the authors of a recent book on the character business state that characters are the "lifeline of human relationships" in today's high-growth information society and serve as the totems, protectors *(omamori)*, and "utility symbols" of its citizens (Hashino and Miyashita 2001:4–5). With seeming pride, they label Japan a "character empire," noting that no country in the world has become as thoroughly inundated—both economically and culturally—with character merchandise as it has.

Yet another book (an anthology entitled *The Reasons Why 87 Percent of Japanese Like Characters*) links the vibrancy of the Japanese character business (one of the few successes in these recessionary times) to the unease of contemporary times. Pressured by bullying, academic hurdles, and economic instability, children find relief in characters that offer them a love at once absolute and personal ("they love you alone"; Aoyama and Bandai Kyarakuta Kenkyujo 2001:17). A psychiatrist calls this the "character therapy age," where characters relieve stress and also reflect the "inner self" (12–13). Chronicling the history of character trends in postwar Japan, he characterizes the present as an era where contemporary citizens "communicate" with character commodities. This is the "route" for relating to friends, and communication has now become the object of character consumption. Speaking of Sony's robotic dog, AIBO, the book concludes that such intimate play goods serve as friends and that these friends assume the role of pets (194).

As I argued in the introduction, the appeal of Japanese play goods can be characterized by two main qualities—polymorphous perversity and technoanimism—that help explain their cachet as the cutting edge of trendy" cool" on the marketplace of kids' entertainment today. This is fantasy-ware with a mass array of spirits and parts (techno-animism) that continually transform, come apart, and recombine in a variety of ways (polymorphous perversity). Further, such a logic of play has been packaged in forms that suit the tempo and lifestyle of these postindustrial times. Gameware is portable (making access convenient and continual) and adjustable for personal use (anything can be listened to on a Walkman), while the fantasy making conjures up playmates that "heal" the ills of materialism, all the while generating an addictive frenzy that literally buys into the same thing, of playing, wanting, and buying more and more commodified stuff. In this chapter I have laid out some of the socioeconomic factors and events that have shaped the national mood in Japan at this moment of the millennial crossover and can be traced not only in the "pathologies" of the era—Aum Shinrikyo, social shut-ins, criminal youth-but also in the trends in producing, accumulating, and bonding with "cute" play commodities that define the subject of this book.

As I have tried to suggest, there is a thin line between the "monstrous" behavior of children who, once "good," retreat into their rooms or act out in random violence and that of so-called normal kids who fetishistically consume brand-name goods and compulsively play with the fantasy monsters that are so popular in (and whose profits are so important to) the Japanese marketplace today. In the discourse surrounding both phenomena today in Japan, reference is made to the same set of conditions: a pressurized school system (of constant tests and rampant bullying), increasing amount of time spent alone, disconnection from others and the inability of Japanese these days to "communicate," and the transparency and superficiality of a materialist society. Keeping in mind these issues (and how Japanese play goods are situated contradictorily as both part of, and—imagined, imaginary—antidote to, millennial capitalism), I now move on to the specifics of four waves of made-in-Japan kids' play that became popular and profitable in the global marketplace in the 1990s. The first of these is the genre of live-action morphin team heroes that, beginning in Japan in 1973, took off as the *Mighty Morphin Power Rangers* on U.S. television screens in 1993.

NOTES

1. This is literal as well as figurative, as in the masterpieces mothers design in the *obento* they pack for children attending nursery school: nutritionally balanced multicourse feasts, all miniaturized and artistically stylized—food conducted with young *keitai* users in the late 1990s, have argued that Japanese youth tend to use their cell phones to maintain communication with no more than ten close friends, a pattern they refer to as "full-time intimate

community" (quoted in Matsuda 2005:30). For Japanese scholarship on *keitai* usage in English, see Ito, Okabe, and Matsuda 2005.

2. *Jizo* is a bodhisattva, an incarnation of the Buddha that has renounced Enlightenment in order to guide lesser beings through the stages and realms of creation. In Japan, *jizo* statues appear in Buddhist temples, typically in the form of a bald Buddhist monk with simple features.

REFERENCES CITED

Aoyama Rika and Bandai Kyarakutā Kenkyūjō. 2001. 87% no Nihonjin ga kyarakutā o tsukina riyū (Why 87% of Japanese like characters). Tokyo: Gakken.

Buren. 2000. "Kyarakutā no komyunikēshon pawā" (Character communication and power). 40, no. 3 (March): 9–19.

Chambers, Iain. 1990. "A Miniature History of the Walkman." In Iain Chambers, Border Dialogues: Journeys in Postmodernity, 1–4. London: Routledge.

Dentsū Kyarakutā Bijinesu Kenkyūkai. 1991. Kyarakutā bijinesu (Character business). Tokyo: Dentsū.

Fukimi Yukio. 1998. "Doraemon wa dare ka?" (Who is Doraemon?). Hato, January, 18–20.

Hashino Katsumi and Miyashita Makoto. 2001. Kyarakutā bijinesu shirarezaru senryaku (Strategies for expanding the character business). Tokyo: Seishun Shuppansha.

Ito, Mizuko, Daisuke Okabe, and Misa Marsuda. 2005. Personal, Portable, Pedestrian: Mobile Phones in Japanese Life. Cambridge, MA: MIT Press.

Kogawa Tetsuo. 1984. Nyū media no gyakusetsu (The paradox of new media). Tokyo: Shōbunsha.

Matsuda, Misa. 2005. "Mobile Communication and Selective Sociality." In Mizuko Ito, Daisuke Okabe, and Misa Matsuda, eds., Personal, Portable, Pedestrian: Mobile Phones in Japanese Life, 123–42. Cambridge, MA: MIT Press.

McCreery, John. 2000. Japanese Consumer Behavior: From Worker Bees to Wary Shoppers. Richmond, Surry, England: Curzon Press.

Nikkei Dezain. 1998. "Mienai kazoku" (The invisible family). 24–44.

Ōhira, Ken. 1998. Yutakasa no seishinbyō (The pathology of abundance). Tokyo: Iwanami Shinsho.

Williams, Raymond. 1975. Television: Technology and Cultural Form. New York: Schocken Books.

21

Almost Paradise

The Cultural Politics of Identity and Tourism in Samana, Dominican Republic

Kathleen Skoczen

They are offering a lot to buy property, if they offer me all the money in the world, I am not going to sell because I live here, I love it here and no one is going to take me (*sacarme*) from the (waterfront and throw me behind, it's the truth. They can offer me a million Canadian or American and they won't take me from here ... if the government dislocates me I will go, but because I have to, not for the money.

—[A Dominican living along the waterfront in Samaná, 2004]

No, I don't like it because everything here is only for the people from Samaná, the people born here. The foreigners come and invest their money, but they should not reap any benefits, nothing is for them (foreigners), the Samanese see this as stealing ... Everyone is a foreigner, only the people born here have rights—all of the world is a foreigner if you are not from here.

—[Capitaleña who had been living in Samaná for one year, responding to my query of how she liked life in Samaná, 2005]

They eat meat, while we eat bones.

—[Often heard sentiment in Samaná in reference to foreigner-owned businesses in Samaná]

Al pan pan y al vino vino.

—[Translated by a university student from Samaná as: If you're American you're American, if you're Dominican you're Dominican (there's no changing that), 2005]

Kathleen Skoczen, "Almost Paradise: The Cultural Politics of Identity and Tourism in Samana, Dominican Republic," *Journal of Latin American and Caribbean Anthropology*, pp. 141–167. Copyright © 2008 by American Anthropological Association. Reprinted with permission.

As these quotes suggest, people in Samaná in the northeast region of the Dominican Republic are in a struggle to control not only the public discourse surrounding who should benefit from tourism development, but also the tangible assets of the tourism infrastructure. This struggle came to a head in the late 1990s when a foreign owned company moved into the region, with the sanction of the national government, and attempted to usurp power, control, and economic benefits from locals. Local elites, the primary target of the takeover, felt they built the business (in this case day-long boat excursions to a beach) from the ground up and were seeing the fruits of their labor appropriated by a politically and economically stronger foreign entity. Claiming their Dominican identity and therefore, privilege, the boat owners organized strikes and protests to protect their control over the industry. On the other hand, local vendors (food and crafts) who had only ever minimally benefited economically from this activity, threatened to side with the international company and erode the veneer of solidarity.

Tourism has become the most important source of economic development in the Dominican Republic over the last two decades, primarily as a result of liberal economic policies and adherence to structural adjustment programs. As a country that was mired in economic stagnation, tourism is anticipated to solve economic woes, yet who benefits from tourism is a hotly debated issue in Samaná, itself often seen as distinct from the rest of the country based on a cultural heritage that includes a large settlement of African Americans. At times, in this country where many racial groups have settled Samaná was neglected if not isolated (Rodriguez Demorizi 1973). Now having the potential for developing beach resorts, large marinas, ecotourism, and cultural tourism the region has gained the attention of international tourism developers who are eager to reap the rewards of this undiscovered paradise. The anticipated boom in tourism, however, has been looming in the region since the era of the dictator Rafael Leonidas Trujillo Molina (1931–61), and has also attracted a large number of expatriates and local elites who have been waiting to realize the potential wealth that will come with the tourist boom. Finally, there is the majority of the population who are poor yet feel passionately about their ownership and rights to the region and its assets and are determined to lay claim to the profits when development finally arrives. This paper explores a case study where various factions struggle to gain control of the elusive benefits of tourism, and the cultural politics that surround these struggles. Cultural politics play an important role in staking a claim to the benefits and payoffs of the industry, on the one hand, and on the other, assigning blame when things are not going so well.

Tourism development has redefined the social and cultural landscape in the Dominican Republic over the last 20 years; positions and perspectives continue to shift, adjusting to an altered "situatedness" vis-à-vis understandings of history, politics, and global processes (Appadurai 1996; Gregory 2003). These transformations are complex and multilayered, affecting Samaná residents' conceptions of self, community, and nation, and in turn challenging identity, particularly surrounding relationships with other Samanese, the community and the state. Hutchins (2007) explores the "mutability" of physical bodies and cultural meanings' in the context of ecotourism in Ecuador's Upper Amazon "where local nature is reordered as global commodity, and local meanings are reinterpreted to better align with consumers' desires" (2007:76). Nonetheless, as he demonstrates convincingly, the cultural accommodation is not a simple or straightforward process, and native compliance has its limits. Here too, following Hutchins (2007), I recognize the distinction between identity politics and the politics of identity whereby the former can be seen as the appropriation of culture at the expense of native society. As Hill and Wilson have noted, this can contribute to "essentializing social identities by isolating them from their historical contexts and removing them from communities of real people" (Hutchins 2007:76) while the latter refers to local people resisting this redefinition and etching spaces where cultural identity can be protected and reasserted. In Samaná, residents find a need to appeal to, or at least newly promote aspects of their history, folklore, culture, and identity as a means of resisting complete redefinition by outsiders, be they Dominicans from the capital of Santo Domingo or foreigners from North America or Europe.

At the same time, the elites and even expatriates find themselves having to readjust cultural meanings to maintain their own positions of hierarchy and privilege in ways that may have been unimaginable only decades earlier. Elites, for example, have embraced a Eurocentric identity and heritage, distancing themselves from Dominicans of African descent; this case study suggests that elites may turn to their "Dominican-ness" and seek to form alliances with lower class, darker citizens when it gives them leverage against "the other," foreigners of non-Dominican citizenship. But foreigners, too, may be redefined as part of the Dominican community if this allows solidarity against "outsiders." Tourism development becomes a canvas on which identity politics and the politics of identity are played out, sometimes creating wedges between groups, other times drawing them together for redefinitions of "us" and "them" (Hutchins 2007).

A tourist economy, at once transnational but also rooted in "place," forces questions of identity on many levels. Identity is no longer seen as absolute, immutable or fixed in time or place (Rahier 1999). Instead identity is far more complicated, involving processes that might be fluid and subject to cooperation and compromise: "constructed through complex processes of relationality and representation; it is a process, not a thing, and it is constantly under negotiation" (Wade 1997:81; Rahier 1999). While "place" does not signify identity, identities are constructed in contexts, contexts that are mutable. Attention to these contexts allows us to gain a better understanding of the complex processes driving individuals to negotiate a piece of themselves that would be of vital concern. Thus, following Bisharat (1997), I argue that struggles over identity can also be, and frequently are, ultimately struggles over symbolic and material assets:

> statements about identity are virtually never idly made but are typically coded with implications for future action and sometimes with claims fielded with reference to some, not necessarily conscious, purpose. The negotiation of an identity is thus a step toward an end, not an end in itself; identity is always "identity for" something.

It follows that the social identity of an individual or group "for" one thing may shift and be transformed as it is constituted "for" something else. [1997:205]

As Bisharat points out, these struggles over identity can be "spatialized" in attempts to claim and control "place" (Bisharat 1997; Davila 2005). For Samaná residents working in the center or on the periphery of the encroaching tourist economy, transformations of space and place are ever more visible and urgent. Place is *thee* commodity in a tourist economy; political control over that place is negotiated through the production of identity in a cultural space, particularly as that identity plays a central role in political relationships and struggles (Hutchins 2007). In addition, more recently, emergent relationships with the state are both pressing and intimate as globalization filters down to local communities through new, novel, and sometimes invasive processes (Appadurai 1996; Trouillot 2001, 2003). In a post-Trujillo era, where his protégé, President Balaguer, held power for 12 consecutive years, the state had generally been, at its best, an abstract concept that held potential for improving daily life and, at its worst, was a series of corrupt officials who only periodically imposed themselves onto the local social landscape, thus only ever so slightly and temporarily inconveniencing the rhythm of daily life. With the growing power and imperative of international tourism, as well as mandates of neoliberal reforms, the local community is acquiring a transnational flavor, which is inviting an expanded and more intimate presence of the national government, thus presenting an ever more complex set of challenges for individuals and groups (Ferguson 1994). Yet, at the same time as the state imposes itself onto daily life, the limits of the state's power in the face of globalization is also being realized (Trouillot 2001). This ambiguity is often felt most tangibly in everyday practices by the recipients of "development" strategies.

Following Bourdieu (1977), tourism development in Samaná has given rise to a cultural field where a reorganization of relationships is creating spaces and opportunities for particular individuals and groups to experience and attempt to control the transformation of a cultural field. Examining individual and group agency in the Caribbean needs to be grounded in history, as these concerns are rooted in colonial relationships that have been forged over centuries of domination (Trouillot 1992). The heterogeneity of the Caribbean and its distinct communities needs to be contextualized to appreciate how and why particular groups end up competing or cooperating for power (Mintz 1974; Allahar 2002; Trouillot 2003).

TOURISM IN "ALMOST PARADISE"

Tourism in the Caribbean is a fiercely competitive industry, yet the Dominican Republic has significantly improved its participation in the last two decades: Fuller reports overnight visitors increased from 747,000 to 2.2 million between 1986 and 1997 (1999:6). In 1995 its market share in the region was 1.6 percent, yet by 2000 it rose to 2.2 percent with an average growth rate during these years of 12.8 percent, one of the highest in the region (WTO

2002). Nonetheless tourism is dominated by foreign interests that reap most of the profits while the host countries realize limited benefits and may even suffer (Gmelch 2003; Pattullo 2005). Few Caribbean countries have the power to resist or rearrange these business conditions, predicated, as they often are, on agreements with the International Monetary Fund and the hegemony of the United States (Deere 1990; Safa 1995; Raynolds 1998). The Dominican Republic only seriously focused its efforts on tourism development with Balaguer's return to power in 1986, following the IMF reforms of 1984. Between 1985 and 1994 the economic power of tourism doubled and it became the most important source of employment (Gregory 2003). Within a decade it became the largest tourist market in the Caribbean leaving behind a failing agriculture sector. Thus, the Dominican Republic has experienced major economic and social transitions (Raynolds 1998).

The peninsula, province, bay, and city of Samaná are found in the northeastern region of the Dominican Republic. Although it is cast as a newly discovered paradise, Samaná's tourist potential has been simmering for decades. Long admired for its natural beauty of coconut-covered mountains rising up from sandy inlets, the Samaná Basin is a United Nations biosphere reserve (see Fig. 1). During winter months North Atlantic hump-backed whales congregate to breed. Crossing the bay by boat, visitors visit Los Haitises National Park where pristine mangrove forests conceal caves where Taino Indians left hieroglyphs and petroglyphs. A small key sits in the center of the bay, a 15-minute boat ride from the town dock. Briefly renamed by Germans to Cayo Bacardi (after the rum company) as a promotional pitch, Cayo Levantado (Elevated Key) is the image of an island paradise with unspoiled beaches and the best snorkeling in the region, making it a magnet for day excursions (day-pax) and holding the potential for larger development in town. The bay, with its calm waters, has long been a respite of boaters who come to refuel and escape dangerous storms.

Although the peninsula offers many tourist attractions, its potential has never been fully realized. At times resistance to foreign developers has been significant, yet more important is the poor transportation, lack of infrastructure, and governmental and administrative mismanagement of local resources. A seventy-room hotel overlooking town, with satellite cottages, was built in the early 1960s but frequently was left empty or neglected by either the government, foreign management companies or, more frequently, because of contract disputes between the two. Recently it has been upgraded to a five star hotel with 350 rooms, but lacks the water to run its Jacuzzi tubs or newly installed toilets.

In concert with the 1992 quincentenary of Columbus' arrival to the "New World" the opening of a five star hotel, funded by a consortium of investors from Washington, DC, brought notoriety to the region. After a brief period of success, the hotel now caters to a "low-class trade" of all-inclusives. A small community of expatriates at the end of the peninsula is trying to establish a spin-off resort town as an alternative to the more commercialized boom they expect closer to the town of Samaná. Nonetheless, business in Samaná is slow and sporadic, except for the all-inclusive hotels and "day-pax" visitors.

Day-paxs are bussed in from outside resorts for daylong excursions year round to Cayo Levantado, Los Haitises, and in winter for whale watching. These visitors affect the local economy most directly through contracts for food and tours. Because of complaints over service, sanitary conditions, harassment by locals, and so forth, there is significant juggling of contracts. Garbage on Cayo has long been a problem and attracts hoards of flies that disrupt meals and tarnish the image of "paradise." The local cuisine is rarely appealing to foreigners' taste, giving expatriates, who have capitalized on the local specialties by adapting them and their presentations for a European pallet, an edge over local caterers, who are primarily poor women.[1] Vendors selling jewelry and souvenirs are predictably aggressive in a tight market where their alternatives for making money are all but nonexistent.

In the late 1990s there had been a decline in the once reliable business from boat travelers. Blamed for the decline are young men who, lacking steady employment, attempt to pick up odd jobs from boat owners. There has been a significant increase in crime since the early 1990s and it is assumed these young men are responsible. Referred to as *"tigres"* or *"buscones,"*[2] these young men have been important go-betweens for the boaters, many of whom have no Spanish-language skills, much less a familiarity with the local markets. As economic conditions have declined and the economy offers young men few prospects for employment (Safa 1995) they have become more aggressive. Unattended yachts and vulnerable expatriates become easy targets. Several of Samaná's business and community leaders with whom I spoke lamented the actions of these young men who they feel are "ruining business for everyone." The more aggressive these young men, the worse their reputation, the less likely lone tourists will venture off on their own, and a vicious cycle is established. It is far from clear, however, that the *tigres* are primarily responsible for the increase in crime: rarely are they implicated and charged with the most violent crimes, which are often found to be perpetrated by men from outside the area working alone or in groups.

The tourism market slowly increased throughout the 1990s in Samaná as the country overall saw an explosion in the number of tourists. New hotels opened, new projects are planned and at least started, and the region continues to move into a tourist economy. One company reported the growth in whale watching from 60 passengers on one boat in 1985 to 28,000 passengers on 32 vessels in 1998.[3] In 1997 the average number of passengers traveling on boats daily was 500, increasing significantly during the whale season and slowing to a trickle during off-season. The various actors, the conceptions and expectations of development and the clashing realities on the social landscape in Samaná need to be fully explored in order to better appreciate the transformations that have been unleashed with the growing tourist economy.

THE "SCAPES" OF SAMANÁ

Appadurai defines ethnoscapes as groups that are "no longer tightly territorialized, spatially bounded, historically unselfconscious, or culturally homogeneous" (1996:191). While recognizing that stable social relations are still in place in many localities, Appadurai, nonetheless, draws attention to the shifting context that results in the process of globalization. In a tourist haven, people with varying interests (hotel workers, hustlers, expatriates, developers, government officials, etc.) converge, bringing with them differing visions of the world. For the local population, encountering and interacting with different groups of people contributes to a redefinition of' "self" and "nation." Reality begins to look quite different, as does their imagination of possibilities for themselves and their children (Appadurai 1996). While the local population, struggling for daily survival, adapts to and attempts to control changing social and political identity,[4] these struggles are finding new and shifting contexts within which they are played out.

Through state intervention individuals and their communities are expected to adapt to the changing needs and desires of the latest development strategy (in this case tourism development), yet communities rarely have any say on the direction this development will take. In addition, while the state's role is to protect the interests of the population it is in serious conflict as it too needs to assuage developers, the international community and most importantly the IMF and World Bank (Safa 1995). While imposing tourism development (and other economic strategies, e.g., free trade zones) there are significant adjustments of relationships between the individual, community and the nation state, particularly as the necessities, agency, and ultimately control of the population becomes more closely tied to power from the state (Watts 1993; Ferguson 1994; Foucault 2006). Individuals are often in the ambiguous position of trying to manipulate such power or capture a piece of it (Appadurai 1996).

In Samaná (and elsewhere) these relationships are further confused as tourists and, more importantly, expatriates arrive and insert themselves into the social landscape, carrying their ideologies surrounding race, class, nation, development, and so forth, as they enter into intimate contact with the local population (Gregory 2003; Brennan 2004). As Gregory notes in reference to male sex tourists on the south shore of the Dominican Republic these interactions are often more about reifying the tourist's ideological construction of the world, and eliciting native compliance, than it is about the sexual relationship:

> Through the social practice of this form of hetero-normative masculinity ... these men collectively construct and naturalize ideologies of racial, class, ethnic, and sex/gender difference that both register and reinscribe the sociospatial hierarchies of the global economy. [2003:325–326]

In the context of globalization, tourism is available to a far wider range of individuals than it was in the past (Urry 1990), thus not only are the influences more varied, the range of intimacy has also expanded (Gregory 2003; Brennan 2004). Thus while Gregory is referring to a masculine discourse of hierarchy in the context of sex tourism, it is clear this hierarchy is played out in subtler forms in the everyday, mainstream practices of tourism.

Not to be overlooked, however, are the shifting positions and motivations of Samaná residents that also complicate and confuse such encounters (Bruner 2005). Individual histories and experiences frequently conform to emerging demands and necessities, particularly for those close to the center of tourism where the largest rewards are anticipated. Local understandings and perspectives are destabilized as influences beyond class, race, and ethnicity become pivotal for negotiating the changing social landscape. Transnationalism, for example, plays a more crucial role in cultural knowledge and symbolic capital as Dominicans are "on the move," increasingly participating in a circuitous process of migration (Deere 1990; Pessar 1997; Duany 2000). Many local residents have migrated for months and sometimes years to work outside the region, either in larger cities, the capital, other islands, or less frequently but more desirably, the United States or Europe. Thus, there are many complex and even contradictory understandings and images of reality that occupy the shared spaces of an emerging tourist community which itself is changing the very structure of the society.

The local community is inevitably affected by a larger national discourse, but its take on it is not predictable or consistent. Samaná is often observed as a distinct region of the Dominican Republic for historical reasons. Aiding this distinction has been a somewhat consistent movement of foreigners into and out of the region; most visibly are the visitors who travel on boats but stay for extended visits, and with much different aims, the missionaries who make yearly "pilgrimages." Adding to this changing cultural field are the returning or departing migrants, and the mass media (Sorensen 1997; Torres-Saillant 1998). The different perspectives with which the foreign is viewed and viewing and the ensuing reflection of "self" is complicated by the diversity of groups and interests. Collected and refracted images of the "other" and "self" contribute to the shifting "ideoscapes" within which locals operate (Appadurai 1996).

Conceptions of reality often clash in the intimate contact that is readily supplied in the interactions within the tourism industry. This intimacy is increasingly circumscribed and restricted to farther distances, placing tourists in tighter and tighter bubbles outside of local reach at the behest of the tourist industry as a "security" measure (Gmelch 2003). Of course, locals are highly ambivalent over this intimacy as well, some retreating and others ambiguously leaping in and out of the fray, while still others embrace this "space" which is at once a place in the world, but also, an imagined world (Appadurai 1996:33). The space created in tourist interactions is an intimate frontier, where locals are redefined and where they redefine "foreign" and "other," but where both are often based on biased and/or attenuated information. Denise Brennan explores this space in her work on "sexscapes" (1998:16) where Dominican sex workers encounter foreign clients in unique and unconventional liaisons, with expectations that are realized by few women. Likewise Steven Gregory demonstrates how complex these encounters can be: while showing how European and American men reassert their ideology of a global order with themselves at the apex, the agency of the Dominican women is not to be underestimated: "Women who do sex work ignore, parody, and disrupt these practices of homosociality as well as the attempts of male tourists to render them docile 'nonbeings'" (2003:344). Another example of borderless, unchecked, and haphazard cultural exchange is the dramatic increase in violence, both domestic and public. A prominent physician attributes the increases in crime in Samaná to the visibility and disproportionate distribution of wealth through tourism, the lack of opportunity and exposure to violent films. In Samaná there is an anxiety that has risen up around tourism development in the community. Even those who are at the center and are benefiting handsomely have voiced concern with the toll it is taking on Samaná "society." In the following paragraphs I would like to position the various actors in Samaná, by first unpacking some of the local ideology, then describing individuals and groups and how the different ideoscapes come together in problematic encounters.

The peninsula-province of Samaná is home to approximately 100,000 inhabitants who are primarily descended from Dominicans, Haitians, and U.S. African-Americans. There are also people of French, English, and Spanish ancestries in the area, and it is these heritages that are most commonly and publicly privileged despite genealogies of African origin (Sagas 2000). On a national level there is a systematic denial and discrimination against ancestries associated with Africa and Haiti—European ancestries are exalted, particularly at an official level (Davis 1987; Sorensen 1993; Sagas 2000). The reasons behind this institutionalized racism are based in complex historical events but encouraged by international racism.

Dominicans often deny the weight and significance of race. However, in Samaná, where the range of skin color varies considerably, where a majority are derived from African-Americans and Africans, and where African and Haitian ancestries are outright denied, race, particularly for those of dark skin, is as important as it is complex (Torres-Saillant 1998). There are two concepts that clarify this complex stance: pigmentocracy and *blanquiando* (whitening) (see Wade 1997; Sagás 2000). Sagás (2000) examines the "hegemonic ideology" of anti-Haitian, anti-African, and ultimately anti-black constructions in the Dominican Republic. Emphasizing that Dominican racism has its origins in the light-skinned elite, themselves often descendents of the Spanish colonizers, who create myths surrounding Spanish origins and identity, Sagas clarifies how economic and nationalistic interests are served by convincing Dominicans that Haitians are the source of their economic woes. This politically and economically divisive strategy has served the elite for centuries and gets played out in everyday politics whereby there is always someone of lesser status on whom to assign blame, thereby forfeiting any attempt at class or race solidarity (Torres-Saillant 1998).

According to Sagás (2000), there is a "pigmentocracy" in the Dominican Republic where the darkest skinned individuals, those most closely associated with Haiti, and by extension Africa, occupy the lowest end of the economic strata. Moving up the economic class system one finds a corresponding "lightening" in skin color. This cultural and political stratification of a coordinated race and class hierarchy in the Dominican Republic is supported by ideology surrounding race and "anti-*Haitianismo*" Torres-Saillant 1998). Perhaps to protect one's family from this discrimination, the notion of blanquiando, is the idea that you should "whiten" the family, thus the preference for daughters and sons to marry lighter skinned partners (Sagas 2000). This ideology was heavily influenced by Trujillo, a former dictator who ruled brutally for three decades and made it one of his goals to lighten or whiten the Dominican population

(Turits 2003; Martínez 2003). Nonetheless, as a social construct the "pigmentocracy" is easily transgressed in the interests of economics, thus someone can buy their way into a lighter skin category and conversely, light-skin does not guarantee a space at the table: there are many poor light-skinned Dominicans who nonetheless subscribe to the race ideology in hope of gaining an advantage at some unforeseen time in the future.[5]

Not all in Samaná accept this mainstream discourse, and in limited contexts some individuals, families and groups have taken to not only recognizing but exalting their African ancestry through what is often labeled Dominican Vùdú (Davis 1987). The ideology surrounding race, at least in some contexts, is highly contested, and it is here I find "ideoscapes" an important concept to clarify the myriad of understandings and perspectives that exist. While there are clearly competing ideologies surrounding race, there are also many individualistic understandings of race, which further inform an individual's position vis-à-vis the visitors or expatriates in the area. These understandings, particularly as they attend to notions of race, origin, and identity, are undergoing significant shifts and are becoming more central as exposure to foreigners increases. For example, North American notions of race and hierarchy are quite distinct from Dominican understandings. Locally, few people would consider themselves' "black" by North American definitions, and it is the contact with Europeans and North Americans that has brought these racial categories home for the local Dominican population in a way not experienced before. Locally the terminology of race is categorized by the terms *blanco* (white), *indio* (indian), *moreno* (dark-skinned) and *negro* (black). These categories not only refer to skin color but are complicated by hair texture, facial features, and other more obscure qualities, not least of which is wealth. These terms are employed officially, that is, on identification cards *(cedulas)* and in everyday practice, for example, nicknames *(apodos,* e.g. *Rubio, Moreno,* and *Negro).* Collapsing all Dominicans into black/white categories and ignoring local nuances can be outrageously offensive to lighter-skinned, upper-class Dominicans, and those aspiring to occupy these categories.

Another area where the notion of race, ethnicity, and identity is being reformulated is in the context of religion. Dominicans, primarily the poorer segments, unite with foreigners in the context of the Protestant-Evangelist movement, the fastest growing religion in this predominately Catholic country. The relationship with the United States is routinely reinforced as sister churches come south providing devotees with such irresistible spoils as new schools, churches, clothes, and other benefits, which may include cash. Not to be overlooked is the growing importance of forming wider alliances in a changing economic environment. The consensus in Samaná is that evangelists are hardworking and trustworthy and often there are unwritten rules of hiring only from this community.

The strict Protestant work ethic is conducive to a global economy based on capitalism and cheap wage labor. Evangelists are prohibited from participating in local politics, thus never confront the larger social structure; liberation will come through hard work and following the bible, which is filtered through a North American ideology. Any African heritage is denied and derogated in this context. The Evangelist Protestant church members explicitly denounce

Dominican Vùdú, claiming it is Satan worship. As some of these practitioners are revering African and Haitian Gods, the message is clear; African religious practices are evil and satanic.

Locals who work in and benefit from tourism reflect the class and race hierarchy. There is a small group of local "elites," primarily light-skinned or foreign whites who have benefited handsomely. This elite is found among (transport and whale watching) boat owners, restaurant owners and certain, usually European, shop owners. Less satisfied in the tourist industry are the majority of low-paid workers, generally darker-skinned who are economically disadvantaged. They find the hours grueling (six to seven-day work weeks), the wages insufficient and the tourists less than amiable. Low-level workers are usually happy to be employed (particularly in close proximity to their homes) but are, nonetheless, frustrated by barely tolerable working conditions, as my friend Bella described: "I work on Cayo, so I'm gone 12 hours a day. I leave when it is dark and I return when it is dark and I'm working 6 days a week right now, with one day off. How can you live like this?" Among the locals who are the most disenchanted and frustrated with tourism are local unemployed and underemployed individuals, accounting for a significant percentage of the population. The tigres/buscones mentioned above are an example of this populace.

High-level managerial employees maybe Dominicans from other regions of the country or foreigners. As mentioned above, there is an expatriate community yet few individuals actually maintain residence; that is, individual expatriates seem to come and go but nonetheless, there is always an expatriate "presence" in Samaná. The heterogeneity of this group is usually missed by the local population. Expatriates in Samaná range from young adults to octogenarians, from the very wealthy to the very poor, and include North Americans and Europeans. Overwhelmingly they are somehow connected with the tourist industry; many waiting to cash in on the large scale development that is assumed to be coming, although some have gotten old and died waiting. Yacht owners making a Caribbean tour were once central to the waxing and waning tourist industry, supporting the few restaurants and stores in town. Their significant absence has been a growing concern since 1998, both for its economic impact and the reflection on where the once sleepy town is heading. There is a palpable sense in town that tourism is an economic industry that should benefit the local community. There is resentment on both sides: natives are resentful that expatriates are capitalizing on the local potential they should be enjoying; and expatriates feel like they are doing all the hard work, doing it the "right way" but are never able to realize the benefits of their labor. Many expatriates leave frustrated and poor.

In Samaná, there are varying and contested ideas and experiences that create contexts for misunderstanding and conflict. While tourism is the primary development strategy of the country, the industry that will provide opportunities to lift people out of dire poverty, it is rarely these same people who realize any benefits. This happens for several pragmatic reasons, one obvious reason being the skewed expectations of the varying groups vis-a-vis each other: Dominicans are not schooled in the subservience expected of them, foreigners find paradise desanitized and filled with demanding natives, and expatriates are looking to strike gold under conditions over which they have little control or of which they have little/no knowledge. The answer to this conflict, almost universally, has been to place tourists into bubbles outside the reach of the local community, further "verticalizing" profits to fewer participants (Gmelch 2003; Pattullo 2005). This bubbling causes further resentment on the side of Dominicans and even expatriates, and further fear and misunderstanding on the side of tourists.

Reactions to the increasing transnational nature of the community and shifting scapes of Samaná are multifaceted. The following ethnographic case study highlights the complex cultural politics in a transnational context. In the rubric of Bourdieu (1977), the fields of race and class become the context where cultural and symbolic capital intersect, and where, following Trouillot (1992), the larger context constrains or allows individual agency. This case study highlights "the crucible of cultural politics where transnational influences have been reworked through grounded livelihood struggles" (Moore 2000:656). Tourism development becomes a cultural field where individuals can respond, resist or accommodate according to their interests, albeit in a context where the state is increasing its power and influence. The actors occupy very different spaces, but spaces that are highly fluid, shifting with context. Here challenges to and of "Dominican identity" are direct and specific.

"RIDE THE SURF": A SMALL TOWN IN A BIG WORLD

Eight boat owners participate in the Samaná Bay Boat Owners Association (Asociación de Barcos de la Bahia de Samaná, hereafter the Association), which enforces rules and regulations regarding transportation, fees, boat capacities, and so forth, surrounding the tourist industry.[6] The Dominican Navy generally monitors the actions of the boats and works closely with the Association. Another nonprofit organization, Center for the Conservation and Ecodevelopment of Samaná Bay and its Surroundings (CEBSE), also works closely with the Association. CEBSE has been in existence since 1991 and serves to increase community awareness regarding natural resources, promote sustainable and eco-tourist enterprises, and promote community development. There is a Cayo Levantado Vendors' Association which monitors the sale of foods, drinks, jewelry, clothes and crafts to tourists on the island. Generally these agencies work together. In the past, issues of garbage, sanitation of food preparation, harassment of tourists, organization of docking boats, and so forth, have been mediated through these organizations. Approximately 200 families belong to the Vendor's Association.

Cayo Levantado is featured in a rum commercial on German television and has thus become something of a shrine to German tourists, who are now the most numerous visitors to the region as a result. Sometime in 1996, a German company called "Ride the Surf" (RTS),[7] working out of its office in the United States, began to investigate Samaná as a site to expand their business, after "visiting all of the coastal regions of the country," according to their letter of introduction to the Boat Owners Association (letter from RTS to the Association, translation by author). This company already had an operation in the Bahamas and declared their intentions to expand into Samaná to offer water sports such as diving and submarining in "bobs," underwater scooters "of the newest technology." Describing their similar operation in or near a protected national park in the Bahamas, the company emphasized their concern for the natural environment. They also told the Association they had received a provisional license for six months from the Marina de Guerra (Dominican Navy). At a meeting the Association had with the company and reiterated in their letter, RTS confirmed that it would not infringe on the tourist markets of the Association, but would only be introducing a new activity into the area. By this time, however (as stated in their letter), they had already undertaken an "exhaustive cleaning" of the north beach on Cayo Levantado and begun the construction of two *muertos,* ten-ton moorings that would enable them to avoid dropping anchor directly onto the bay floor. Using river boats modified for water sports allowed them to essentially run a resort on the water; they brought the concept of all-inclusive for day-pax to a new level.

RTS quickly realized, however, that the real market in Samaná lay not in the limited diving possibilities, but in excursions to see whales and visit Los Haitises, and the transport to Cayo Levantado, all the while providing tour and catering services. Within six months, by April of 1997, RTS began transport to Cayo. The Association quickly organized to protest this invasion of their market, particularly considering the "irregular" conditions under which this German company received its license. The Association first wrote to all authorities possible, looking for support. Failing this they took their forum to the newspapers in November and December of 1997 and eventually turned to a strike to keep RTS off of Cayo on January 4, 1998 (the start of the tourist season).

RTS responded quickly and on January 7, 1998, sent a letter to the Association where their intentions were outlined in the proposal. RTS declared unilaterally that it would combine operations of the Association and RTS because it had "excellent marketing and sales capacity" and "specialized in the operation of marine transport." RTS also noted that most visitors to the area have "uncomfortable voyages," and by working together tourists could "enjoy whatever and all options that Samaná offers." A series of 19 "basic points" essentially dismantled the Association members' power, autonomy, and agency, handing this over to RTS who would redefine and control all aspects of tourism in the region. The Association members would in effect become subcontractors for RTS.

The final point of the agreement included the following statements: "Our interest is in securing the highest quantity of persons possible: our projections are to have approximately 2,000 persons a day. *With this agreement with the association we will manage the clients who visit Samaná no matter what excursion they take: 'Ride the Surf,' Isla Bacardi, Los Haitises or Whale Watching*" (Proposal of RTS to the Association, January 9, 1998). RTS apparently hoped that by outlining the potentially large profits the boat owners would overlook their loss of autonomy or control over their businesses, as well as forfeiting their roles in the marketing and promotion of their products. Despite their mention of a concern for the environment earlier in the proposal, their clear intentions were to increase business and, by appealing to that aspect of the Association, they assumed complete compliance.

Compliance, however, was not forthcoming from the Association. While they had to accept the presence of RTS in Samaná they wanted to control its encroachment onto the Association's territory. Their response was both formal and informal. Strikes were organized which limited or prevented access to the peninsula for all travelers, thus arousing national and even international interest on the eve of the tourist season. Strikes in the Dominican Republic are reminiscent of blockades as their purpose is to halt transportation upon which, of course, tourism hinges. Formally, a letter was quickly drawn up by the Association president and sent to the secretary of tourism directly addressing the terms of the proposal. In sum, the letter outlined the limited economic opportunities in the community, the monopoly RTS would have on the market, the lack of knowledge regarding the culture and history of the area, the ecological impact a huge increase in tourist traffic would have on the delicate ecosystem, and finally that this proposal would be serving foreign interests with no benefits for the community or region. Here they discussed the role of tourism development in aiding the local economy and community, stressing that a foreign company would be monopolizing an industry and resource the community had built from the ground up. A meeting was then called in February 1998 by the minister of tourism with the Association and RTS. RTS was then prohibited from entering Cayo and was directed to subcontract with the Association. The terms of subcontracting with members of the Association were still under negotiation, until RTS eventually took its operation elsewhere.

Other details surrounding this issue that worked in the community's favor, according to several informants, were the rumors of the company's involvement in a larger parent company who had a questionable reputation, the "irregular" conditions under which RTS obtained permission to operate, and the inside connections that the company had with an outgoing government. Many payments are suspected to change hands during negotiations for rights and contracts surrounding tourist development projects, frequently benefiting individuals rather than the community. Thus, in this case, a new administration would have had little left to gain from supporting RTS, while its image as a government for the people was enhanced by siding with the community. Despite the concern for the administration's image internationally as one of welcoming investment, it gave in to pressure from the community.

CULTURAL CAPITAL IN TOURIST DEVELOPMENT

Anthropology's concern for the "other" has been its hallmark, and in promoting this concern anthropology has also both mirrored and promoted a popular interest in foreign lands and peoples by the West, without the result scholars may have anticipated. The booming stock market in the 1990s and the ensuing foreign investment plays on popularly construed notions of the "other" living in places that are at once pristine and untouched while also inhabited by the not quite civilized native. These sweeping generalized views of foreign countries invite investors who are convinced they are providing a service for the local community while reaping substantial profits. The American representative of RTS told one boat owner: "Don't these people know we are going to help them? That we are good at this?" The boat owner's indignant reply demonstrated the transparency of the public transcript: "Why do you think it is alright for you to come down here and make money for your investors and pay off your debt, while Samaná gets nothing out of this? No one wants your help."

The actors of the Association who defended their right to maintain sovereignty over the industry they helped build deserve further scrutiny. The founders of the "whale watching" industry, which gave rise to commercial excursions to the National Park, were a Canadian expatriate and a Dominican national. The Dominican eventually left for the United States, leaving the Canadian behind to build the industry, which she did very successfully. So successfully in fact, that an ambitious and well-connected businessman (and aspiring boat owner) in the town quickly seized the opportunity to displace her, calling on her expatriate status versus his Dominican status (as his justification to exploit the natural resources for local or "native" advantage). When expatriates are visibly benefiting from the industry it is seen as being at the expense of natives. The discourse around tourism in Samaná recounts a long history where foreign entrepreneurs encounter insurmountable legal, logistical, and financial obstacles before they give up and leave. At times covert resistance turns into outright sabotage: I have documented several events in my field notes. While foreigners are targets and events are disturbing, more important is the discourse surrounding such incidences in both communities. The strong anti-foreign attitude is linked to who gets to profit from locally based enterprises. This bias has often been extended to Dominicans from other regions and countries (e.g., Dominicans from New York). This appears paradoxical: the area is economically depressed, yet attempts to integrate tourism into the local economy, because they were initiated by foreigners, were undermined or thwarted. This distinction of "us" versus "them" is taught at quite a young age.

In the summer of 2004, I attended an outing with a summer remedial reading program for elementary school students. Graduation was celebrated with a trip for the children and their families to spend the day on Cayo Levantado, sponsored by tourist businesses. An American expatriate was one of the teachers who attended the outing. Sitting with the group she witnessed a quarrel between one of the Dominican families and two children of Italian tourists. Lounging nearby I heard the end of the conflict and asked for details. She recounted the incident for me as follows:

> The Dominican boy was telling his dad about this crab that the Italian boy had caught and his father told him, "you go and take it" *(vengate macho, vengate grapo)* (encouraging him) … "you go and take the crab" encouraging him to go … and he apparently took it from the Italian boy … the Italian boy protested and was really upset … and here's the Dominican mother and father arguing and taunting and making fun of this little Italian boy who's no more than eight or nine.

After much ado the Italian boy's elder sister intervened with her fluent Spanish and convinced the parents to return the crab.

This incident is indicative of the hostility and resentment fostered through tourism in the region, where many necessities are siphoned from the needy to meet the demands of tourists. Infrastructure, like potable water, decent roads, electricity grids, are all set up for the foreign visitors, while most rural and urban areas do without. Moreover, expatriates all too often follow the model of privilege set by the local elite, whereby the majority of the population, poor and uneducated, is both exploited and at times outright abused by business owners.[8] Many Dominicans question expatriates' motivations for relocating to the region, especially as few are schooled in the cultural sensitivity and managerial skills that can assist them in their entrepreneurial adventures. Many expatriates in Samaná benefit from the power of their foreign currency and their skin color, and proceed to treat the lower classes in ways unimaginable back home (Brennan 1998; Gregory 2003). The antiforeigner discourse, not unexpectedly, is played out in various milieus. Relationships are often strained: marriages between expatriates and Dominicans in the region frequently end in divorce; the Dominican partner taking a Dominican lover is seen not only as natural and inevitable, but almost an obligation of the girlfriend or boyfriend to "take back what is ours" (c.f. Brennan 2004). The tendency to take advantage of foreigners who are perceived as naive and ripe for exploitation by locals who share emic understandings is also reported by Sorensen (1993).

The "local" businessman mentioned above who tried and briefly succeeded in taking over the whale-watching industry from the Canadian, using this same discourse to his advantage, is nonetheless a relative newcomer to the region. His father migrated to Samaná as a young man. Reportedly the father set up *colmados* (small neighborhood stores), liberally extended credit and then repossessed land when payment was not forthcoming. The narratives behind their rise to wealth and power were usually recounted as confirmation that the family used ruthless and underhanded methods. This family is now seen as native, a point emphasized by two family members, who have vowed never to leave or sell their property to "foreigners."[9] During the RTS negotiations, the Canadian played an important role in resisting the takeover. During this time, she noted, the Association included her as a local, a fact that she mentioned with irony. When does an outsider become native? Or in Bourdieu's language who defines cultural capital in Samaná? (Bourdieu 1977).

A wrinkle in negotiations between RTS and the Association occurred when the president of the Vendors' Association negotiated a deal with RTS without consulting or notifying the Association. This move compromised the arguments of the Association and weakened their bargaining power. While one member of the negotiating team declared that it was the current president merely having a show of power, it nonetheless complicated the situation significantly. Surprisingly, solidarity on the local level was highly fragile if not imaginary. While vendors struggle to etch out an existence, much larger profits (in U.S. currency) are realized by the boat owners. Thus the Association was "sandwiched" between the threat of control from a larger, more powerful foreign entity while being challenged from below by a less powerful, but pivotal organization. What was left for the Association to negotiate on both these levels was the appeal of the Association's Dominican-ness, its cultural capital, even as two of the eight members had questionable claims to this identity, one being Canadian and another from Spain.

Following Bourdieu (1977), this case study illustrates the transformation of a cultural field. Dominican-ness was presumed to be "inalienable cultural capital" that is, having value "above the values of the marketplace" (Webb *et al.* 2002:28) from the perspective of the Association. However, the Vendor's Association, made up of lower-class residents of the area, had long shared inalienable cultural capital in the values of loyalty and allegiance to their Dominican identity, yet here are willing to forgo this capital to embrace market assets. Hutchins identifies a similar agency among the Kichwa: "what Whitten calls 'the duality of power patterning,' through which a subordinate group can turn acquiescence to a more powerful institution … into a form of protest" (2007:83). While the Association made their cause public, the Vendor's protest was less visible, but perhaps more significant. In Samaná predictable and stable relationships are challenged in ever more unexpected milieus, redefining individual and group status and identity; old hierarchies are challenged, race and even status as "insider" versus "outsider" become ever more pliable to the demands of globalization and tourism development.

Local history suggests that there has been occasional conflict between various sectors of Dominican society, yet there has also been a privilege and loyalty enjoyed by Dominican elites that now, at least in Samaná, is beginning to erode as economic conditions continue to shift. Thus the movement away from cultural to material capital is a slow change in Samaná but one that may prevail. Ultimately the vendors did not win the higher-priced contract with RTS as the Association's resistance, by appealing locally and nationally to a cultural capital, was successful. However, as international and national businesses move into the area both Associations are finding their positions attenuated in their quest to define cultural capital.

Hutchins (2007) demonstrates that tourism development and the ensuing cultural politics not only creates but also plays on existing tensions within and between communities. Yet conversely, as we see here, it may also draw in unlikely alliances. In contrast to the Ecuadorian Amazon, where the "natives" are as much a commodity in tourism appeal as the "sacred places," Samaná natives have neither. It is the Samaná natives who must stake their claim to "place" in the Samaná context, a practice that is rife with contradiction and conflict, and may be a losing battle. As Hutchins points out, "place is not only a location where physical processes are carried out, it is also where possibilities are played out, and where agency and attitude are developed" (Hutchins 2007:88). Thus while the Kichwa in Ecuador may need to redefine "places" to conform to transnational demands, in Samaná individuals or groups are constantly needing to redefine themselves and bring the urgency of this definition to the table to affect agency and attitude; mutability may be Samanese only means of capturing power. The fluidity and instability of tourism development in Samaná is perhaps the only constant. As I write, the challenge to Samaná is growing in intensity. New hotels are being built, expansions of existing hotels are opening, Cayo is all but private. Local food vendors on Cayo, once as many as 45 were a mere 15 in 2007, selling a *tipico buffet* of local cuisine for $8, while Bahia Cruise sells an international buffet for $10. Transnational power continues to threaten Samaná yet there is no sense that Samanese are ready to give up their "weapons of the weak" (Scott 1990).

CONCLUSIONS

In this paper I have attempted to draw attention to globalization, emphasizing its influence through and on the international level (e.g., IMF policies), the national level (e.g., regulating tourism), and transnationalism (e.g., the changing "scapes" in Samaná) and the local-level struggles, often articulated through a discourse of identity, that are "simultaneously material and symbolic" (Bisharat 1997, Moore 2000:656). Tourism development, like other development projects, as Moore eloquently points out, "needs to be conceptualized not as a machine that secures fixed and determined outcomes but rather as a site of contestation, its boundaries carved out through the situated practices that constitute livelihood struggles" (2000:656). Tourism in the Caribbean is frequently developed in line with the Western imagination of paradise (Sheller 2003; Pattullo 2005). Isolated, "out of the way" places are targeted as potential hotspots, attracting both people and capital. Small towns in the path of major touristic development are being radically transformed to meet the needs of travelers and guests. Tourists bring the promise of jobs, economic development, and increased wealth and security to the local community, yet the increases in employment, wealth, and security are not evenly distributed. The visibility of inequality confronts people on a daily basis, yet, at the same time, it keeps alive the promise of prosperity. Several cultures come together in ways that are often circumscribed yet unpredictable, creating an imagination surrounding development and modernity. There is much at stake for Samaná residents in the newly constructed space of tourism development: cultural capital is being redefined and material concerns are becoming ever more urgent in a changing economy. Shifting ethnoscapes and ideoscapes converge on "place" since, as suggested earlier, it is both the attraction and commodity for sale in a tourism context.

Place, however, is not the only commodity, nor the only concern. I would argue it is not coincidental that Samaná in the late 1990s was the focus of intense interest from Dominican sociologists and tourism officials. The distinct identity of Samaná, Dominicans of dark-skinned African-American and Haitian descent, had long been a stigma and suspected reason for neglect of the region. In the field of tourism, marketing of the exotic began to shift values at a national level, this occurring at a time when concerns over identity are more liberally voiced, and selling Dominican culture is a key enticement in an extremely competitive tourist market. Subaltern definitions (e.g., embracing your African identity, practicing Dominican Vùdú, etc.), ironically, can assist in attracting tourism, putting the state in an ambiguous position as it has long tried to deny these aspects of Dominican-ness (Torres-Saillant 1998; Sagas 2000). Moreover, the sterilized identity of Dominican- ness promoted by the elite is directly challenged through tourism as locals are confronted with Western definitions of race and ethnicity which are all too often contrary to the official or public transcript (Scott 1990). Thus tourism produces shifting or new ideoscapes, while legitimizing some and undermining still others. Meanwhile changes in the ethnoscapes create further instability of and challenges to Dominican identity. This case study reminds us that the processes of disentangling individual and group interests with the concept of "identity" is always conditioned by both larger forces in the world (e.g., history, geo-politics, etc.) and local discourses and practices. Identity in Samaná has always been a multifaceted and complex process, situated in historical processes that are intended to destabilize issues of identity so that national political and economic interests might prevail (Mintz 1974). The current cultural politics of identity and tourism in Samaná suggest that this process is now more complex and challenging than ever before:

> It is important to point out that the transformation of a field, whether it is dramatic or gradual, does not occur in a consistent or homogeneous fashion. Certain sub-sections or even pockets of a field may embrace the transformation of the field much more quickly. As a result, that field is usually "traumatised" by fairly overt disagreements and agonistics, primarily over which part most truly represents or embodies the field and its values. [Webb *et al.* 2002:29-30]

Attention to the details of these struggles through ethnography, reveal both contemporary and historical processes that give us new insight into resistance and accommodation between the "powerful" and the "powerless," demonstrating the instability and fragility of such spaces.

NOTES

Research funding for this project was provided in part by a grant from a Rockefeller Foundation Humanities Fellowship and a Connecticut State University summer research grant. I thank four anonymous reviewers and particularly, Jean Muteba Rahier whose insightful and thoughtful comments allowed me to strengthen my theoretical analysis, thus significantly enhancing this article. I also thank Andrew Canessa and his assistant Lucy Glover for their very patient editorial assistance. Several colleagues have read, commented on, and significantly contributed to the development of this article including Ann Miles, Chaise LaDousa, Shubhra Gururani, Gretchen Herrmann, and Ann Schiller. In Samaná, I have received unlimited support from Kim Beddall, Mayra de la Cruz, Mario Jhonson, Jody, Dr. Fernandez, Dr. Caccivelli, the staff at CEBSE, particularly Patricia Lamelas, and countless other dear friends and helpful informants. An earlier version of this paper was presented at the International Union of Anthropological and Ethnological Sciences Conference in Florence, Italy in 2003.

1. This situation has transformed throughout the tourism development of the 1990s as local chefs have learned to adapt the buffet to European tastes, hygiene, and presentation.
2. The term *tigre* in the Dominican Republic has evolved from meaning a young, single male, street wise and manipulative, to someone involved in crime (hustling, drugs, robbery, etc.) and is identified by flashier, New York-style dress. In Samaná independent tour guides who race to greet itinerant travelers are called tigres and/or buscones, thus a less extreme interpretation than elsewhere in the Dominican Republic. One informant laughingly remarked that the *tigres* can get you anything from ice to a prostitute. (See, for a historical discussion, Derby 2000)
3. Personal communication with Kim Beddall, owner of Whale Samaná.
4. Quincentenary events in Samaná forced questions surrounding identity: a statue was constructed in a central location paying tribute to the Tainos, a Caribbean visiting theater troupe portrayed black slaves being brought to the Caribbean, and graffiti expressed discontent against "500 years of thievery."
5. See Sagás (2000) for a discussion of race and politics in the Dominican Republic.
6. The Asociación de Dueños de Barcos de la Bahia de Samaná Inc., is a non-profit organization set up by presidential decree dedicated to (1) the involvement of everyone who participates in marine transportation either commercially

or for touristic purposes and (2) with the intent to improve and develop marine transportation and activity in compliance with the norms and regulations of the navy to benefit the community of Samaná and the Dominican Republic.

7. A pseudonym.
8. Aside from the demanding work conditions is the key complaint that most workers are terminated at the end of the season.
9. The government has appropriated land along the waterfront in Samaná for development.

REFERENCES CITED

Allahar, Anton L. 2002. Race and Class in the Making of the Caribbean Political Culture. Transforming Anthropology 10(2): 13–29.

Appadurai, Arjun. 1996. Modernity at Large, Cultural Dimensions of Globalization. Minneapolis: University of Minnesota Press.

Bisharat, George E. 1997. Exile to Compatriot: Transformations in the Social Identity of Palestinian Refugees in the West Bank. In Culture, Power, Place, Explorations in Critical Anthropology. A. Gupta and J. Ferguson, eds. Pp. 203–233. Durham: Duke University Press.

Bourdieu, Pierre. 1977. Outline of a Theory of Practice. Cambridge, UK: Cambridge University Press.

Brennan, Denise. 1998. Everything is for Sale Here: Sex Tourism in Sosúa, The Dominican Republic. Ph.D. dissertation, Department of Anthropology, Yale University.

——2004. What's Love Got To Do With It?: Transnational Desires and Sex Tourism in The Dominican Republic. Durham: Duke University Press.

Bruner, Edward. 2005. Culture On Tour: Ethnographies of Travel. Chicago: University of Chicago Press.

Davila, Arlene. 2005. Barrios Dreams: Puerto Ricans, Latinos, and the Neoliberal City. Berkeley: University of California Press.

Davis, Marta Ellen. 1987. La Otra Ciencia: El Vodú Dominicano Como Religión Y Medicina Populares. Santo Domingo: Universidad Autónoma de Santo Domingo.

Derby, Lauren. 2000. The Dictator's Seduction, Gender and State Spectacle during the Trujillo Regime. Callaloo 23(3): 1112–1146.

Deere, Carmen Diana (coordinator). 1990. In the Shadows of the Sun, Caribbean Development Alternatives and U.S. Policy. Boulder: Westview Press.

Duany, Jorge. 2000. Nation on the Move: The Construction ofCultural Identities in Puerto Rico and the Diaspora. American Ethnologist 27(1): 5–30.

Ferguson, James. 1994. The Anti-Politics Machine: "Development," Depoliticization, and Bureaucratic Power in Lesotho. Minneapolis: University of Minnesota Press.

Foucault, Michel. 2006. Governmentality. In The Anthropology of the State. Aradhana Sharma and Akhil Gupta, eds. Pp. 131–143. Malden: Blackwell Publishing.

Fuller, Ann. 1999. Tourism Development in the Dominican Republic Growth, Costs, Benefits and Choices. Electronic document, http://kiskeya-alternative.org/publica/afuller/rd-tourism.html, accessed June 22, 2007.

Gmelch, George. 2003. Behind the Smile: The Working Lives of Caribbean Tourism. Bloomington: Indiana University Press.

Gregory, Stephen. 2003. Men in Paradise: Sex Tourism and the Political Economy of Masculinity. In Race, Nature, and the Politics of Difference. D. Moore, J. Kosek and A. Pandian, eds. Pp. 323–355. Durham: Duke University Press.

Hutchins, Frank. 2007 Footprints in the Forest: Ecotourism and Altered Meanings in Ecuador's Upper Amazon. Journal of Latin American and Caribbean Anthropology 12(1): 75–103.

Martinez, Samuel. 2003. Not a Cockfight: Rethinking Haitian-Dominican Relations. Latin American Perspectives 30(3): 80–101.

Mintz, Sidney W. 1974. Caribbean Transformations. Baltimore: Johns Hopkins University Press.

Moore, Donald S. 2000. The Crucible of Cultural Politics: Reworking "Development" in Zimbabwe's Eastern Highlands. American Ethnologist 26(3): 654–689.

Pattullo, Polly. 2005. Last Resorts: The Cost of Tourism in the Caribbean. London: Cassell and Latin American Bureau.

Pessar, Patricia, ed. 1997. Introduction: New Approaches to Caribbean Emigration and Return. In Caribbean Circuits: New Directions in the Study of Caribbean Migration. Pp. 1–11. New York: Center for Migration Studies.

Rahier, Jean Muteba, ed. 1999. Introduction. In Representations of Blackness and the Performance of Identities. Pp. 1–29. Westport: Bergin and Garvey.

Raynolds, Laura T. 1998. Harnessing Women's Work: Restructuring Agricultural and Industrial Labor Forces in the Dominican Republic. Economic Geography 74(2): 149–169.

Rodriguez, Demorizi, Emilio. 1973. Samaná, Pasado y Porvenir. Santo Domingo: Impreso en la Editora del Caribe.

Safa, Helen. 1995. The Myth of the Male Breadwinner: Women and Industrialization in the Caribbean. Boulder: Westview Press.

Sagás, Ernesto. 000. Race and Politics in the Dominican Republic. Gainesville: University Press of Florida.

Scott, James C. 1990. Domination and the Arts of Resistance: Hidden Transcripts. New Haven: Yale University Press.

Sheller, Mimi. 2003. Consuming the Caribbean: From Arawaks to Zombies. New York: Routledge.

Sorensen, Ninna Nyberg. 1993. Creole Culture, Dominican Identity. Folk 35: 17–34.

——1997. There Are No Indians in the Dominican Republic: The Cultural Construction of Dominican Identities. In Siting Culture. K. Fog Olwig and K. Hastrup, eds. Pp. 292–310. New York: Routledge Press.

Torres-Saillant, Silvio. 1998. The Tribulations of Blackness: Stages in Dominican Racial Identity. Latin American Perspectives 25(3): 126–146.

Turits, Richard Lee. 2003. A World Destroyed, A Nation Imposed: The 1937 Haitian Massacre in the Dominican Republic. Hispanic American Historical Review 82(3): 589–635.

Trouillot, Michel-Rolph. 1992. The Caribbean Region: An Open Frontier in Anthropological Theory. Annual Reviews in Anthropology 21: 19–42.

——2001 The Anthropology of the State in the Age of Globalization: Close Encounters of the Deceptive Kind. Current Anthropology 42(1): 125–138.

——2003. Global Transformations: Anthropology and the Modern World. New York: Palgrave Macmillan.

Urry, John. 1990. The Tourist Gaze: Leisure and Travel in Contemporary Societies. London: Sage Publications.

Wade, Peter. 1997. Race and Ethnicity in Latin America. London: Pluto Press.

Watts, Michael J. 1993. Development I: Power, Knowledge, Discursive Practice. Progress in Human Geography 17(2): 257–272. Webb, Jennifer, Tony Schirato and Geoff Danaher

——2002 Understanding Bourdieu. London: SAGE Publications.

WTO (World Tourism Organization). 2002 Tourism Market Trends: World Overview and Tourism Topics. Madrid: World Tourism Organization.

"Empty Cradles" and the Quiet Revolution

Demographic Discourse and Cultural Struggles of Gender, Race, and Class in Italy

Elizabeth Krause

The current record-low birthrate of Italian women has generated lively debate about the future of the nation. In Italy, the average number of children per woman has arrived at around 1.2, a level "likely the lowest ever documented in the history of humanity for a large-scale population," according to one Italian demographer (Golini *et al.* 1995:1; Instituto Nazionale di Statistico [ISTAT] 1996b). A paradox has arisen in the midst of Italians practicing what demographers claim is the lowest-ever national fertility level: as the rest of the world worries about overpopulation, Italy and many other European countries sound alarms about below-replacement fertility levels (Anagnost 1995; Bongaarts 1998; Sen 1997).[1] This article examines the social context related to the current demographic situation in Italy and has three objectives: (1) to expose the strategies demographers use to frame the birthrate in Italy as a "problem" and to argue that this exercise of scientific authority has powerful and hegemonic consequences in terms of producing demographic knowledge that extends beyond the field of demography; (2) to suggest that this knowledge is integral to a politics of cultural struggle that portrays men and, in particular, women as irrational family-makers; and (3) to argue that this instance of demographic science contributes to an alarmism that enables an "elite" sort of racism toward immigrant others.

I argue that Italian women's record-low fertility is not merely fact but fodder for a politics of cultural struggle related to the so-called quiet revolution. This terminology begs clarification. First, I use the term *cultural struggle* because I wish to draw attention to a politics situated in quotidian social life in which rules of "normalization" are defined and codified through discourse and practice. Indeed, cultural struggle is another way of talking about hegemony;[2] it is another way of talking about the way in which certain ideas and actions come to be considered normal and others as abnormal and even threatening to the reproduction of the social order. To this end, I aim to unveil how a society's commentary on a particular practice links to ideologies of gender, class, and race. Specific reproductive practices have resulted in a downward shift in aggregate births. The documentation of this reproductive pattern has created a discursive site, for the authoritative knowledge of demographers has made the birthrate "knowable" and subject to further commentary by the media and nonexperts experiencing the phenomenon in their own lives. Therefore, I show how using fertility decline as a discursive site yields insight into how relations of power are reproduced.

Second, I deploy the term *quiet revolution* to describe the process of rapid and comprehensive fertility decline that began in 19th-century Europe. It also refers to the more recent fertility declines of the 1970s-90s, and serves as a reminder of the processes of contestation underlying those declines. I first came across the term in a volume edited by historians Gillis, Tilly, and Levine who used it to underscore the "great social changes" directly related to the declining rates at which whole populations were producing children (1992:xii, 1). I expand on their work by extending the revolutionary dimension of the metaphor. What qualifies something as a revolution? Can there be such a thing as a quiet revolution? Eric Wolf's perhaps by-now forgotten insight from *Peasant Wars* offered an understanding of peasant rebellions as "parochial reactions to major social dislocations" (1969:265). A key characteristic of a revolution, for Wolf, was the way in which the spread of the market had "torn men up by their roots, and shaken them loose from the social relationships into which they were born" (1969:295).

Such major changes in the organization of the polity and economy resulted in imbalances that required people to seek new approaches to living. These adjustments were not merely functional but involved culturally informed negotiations within fields and relations of power. In northwestern Tuscany, where I spent 22 months conducting ethnographic and archival research, the onset of fertility decline dates back to the turn of the 20th century, and in part nu project sought to grasp how peasant workers there experienced fertility decline.[3] Piedmont, Liguria, and Tuscany were the regions in Italy "showing the earliest and most rapid decline," writes demographer Massimo Livi-Bacci (1977:68). Overall fertility by 1900-02 had declined 15 to 20 percent, and by 1910-12 marital fertility had dropped 25 percent in these regions (Livi-Bacci 1977:68). The large patriarchal sharecropping family that once dominated the social landscape of rural Tuscany was entering its final chapter as couples began to have far fewer children than their parents had and as those children increasingly sought ways of making a living that distanced them from the land and its nobility. I suggest, after Wolf, that they and their descendants were responding to an "overwhelming societal change" that involved a wholesale transformation from an economy centered around peasant sharecropping, artisan stone masonry, straw-hat weaving, and state-subsidized wet-nursing to one dominated by textiles and woolens connected to the eventual postwar boom and the nearby industrial district of Prato.[4]

I wish to show that although the quiet revolution began in a much earlier era and context of adjustment, its repercussions continue well into the present. The cultural politics of population are ongoing, and the knowledge demographers produce and, with the help of the media, circulate in society concretely informs ideologies related to gender, class, and race/ethnicity. My case demonstrates how demographic discourse depicts low fertility as "irrational" and thereby erases the real-life modifications that women and their partners, recognized or not, have made to altered material realities and shifting symbols related to class, gender, and even racial identities. Indeed, this genre of demographic knowledge production relies on a racial rationalization, which hides behind so-called objective concerns about social adjustments to shifting population structures. Current demographic science therefore breathes new life into the quiet revolution as it shifts the grounds for contesting the meaning and future of family making.

BROADENING THE CRITICAL FOCUS

This article participates in a movement of scholars seeking to create a critical field of population studies. Susan Greenhalgh's programmatic statement about constructing such a field advocates that we bring gender into the analysis, that we globalize our work by moving into national and transnational spaces, and that we broaden the critical focus by including analyses of population science itself (1995b:878). Demographic practices, like other habitual exercises of statecraft, have become so normalized as to be beyond the scope of questioning.[5] By unveiling key epistemologies of demographic practice, I put into question population-science strategies. I am convinced that the project I undertake here is a necessary one if we are to understand the dire consequences of knowledge production that masquerades as neutral science and hence as "truth." As Greenhalgh notes,

> until we tackle the task of critically examining the discourses and practices of the hegemonic disciplines of population, anthropological knowledges about population will remain subjugated ones in the national and transnational spaces where power becomes policy and begins to spread. [Greenhalgh 1995b:878]

The potential transformations of demographic knowledge into policy are numerous, ranging from pronatalist politics that narrowly define women by their reproductive capabilities, such as the Italian fascist demographic campaign of the 1920s and 1930s, to xenophobic anti-immigrant structures and sentiments, now rampant in Europe.

Demographic science in Italy, whether concerning the movement of populations, births, or deaths, must be understood within the broader European Union (EU) socioeconomic and political context as it moves toward a unified market, a process some critics have noted entails constructing a Fortress Europe (Martiniello and Kazim 1991). Despite its "hot" and "superstar" economy, Italy has been stigmatized in terms of its political instability and corruption as well as its lax immigration policies.[6] An early 1990s report for the Commission of the European Communities identified Italy as the worst of the Southern European countries, which were targeted as weak spots in the erection of "fortress Europe" because of their "virtually unrestricted and uncontrollable increase of *irregular migration*" (Werth 1991:1, 23). More recently, Italy's inclusion in the Monetary Union of Europe was doubtful. In 1996, EU finance ministers were skeptical of the Italian government's ability to lower its budget deficit, and the implication was that Italy was scrambling to get its "financial house in order" *(New York Times* 1996, quoted in Schneider 1998:7–8). The political and economic requirements necessary for fitting into the European Union, in more complex ways than I am able to delineate here, make demographic behaviors and policies not merely a national concern but a European concern. On the alleged occasion of the birth of the six billionth human in October 1999,[7] the authors of a national Italian research institute's study on its citizens' attitudes toward global population noted:

> Demographic events are no longer "private" phenomena; on the contrary, they involve every inhabitant of the earth not only in terms of everyday life (marriages, births, deaths, migrations, etc.) but in terms of the influence that everyone's behaviors has on global demographic dynamics and the future developments of our planet. [Palomba *et al.* 1999:1, my translation]

When did demographic events stop being "private"? The demographic campaigns of various nations of the 20th century suggest that nation-states and arts of statecraft have long ensured that life-cycle events were not private. They were, rather, "vital"—important business of the state. What has changed is the context in which population discourse now is taking place. I wish in this article to drive home the idea that what we believe to be individual reproductive choices are influenced in powerful ways by scientists who aggregate the outcomes of our intimate behaviors. Palomba (1991) suggests that she and other demographers are tuned into "global demographic dynamics," yet the way in which demographers frame Italy's low fertility as a grave "problem" suggests that demographers' thinking is still more deeply connected to national agendas and policies than it is to global ones.

THE "PROBLEM" OF LOW FERTILITY AND THE PARADOX OF "RATIONAL" REPRODUCTION

Demographic data, as social historian Silvana Patriarca notes, have long occupied "a fundamental role in the symptomatology of the national 'body'" (1998:79). In other words, the practice of generating statistics has provided a diagnostic tool for monitoring the social and economic well-being of the national body politic. This diagnostic role continues in the current demographic context. My analysis of authoritative and broadly cited texts written by well-known Italian demographers (see Table 1) reveals a systematic and consistent view of Italian women's fertility as a "problem."[8]

Demographers deploy a constellation of factors to create a view of low fertility as a problem. I argue their language indexes a type of modernity whose core logics have been turned upside down.[9] These core logics are anchored in an assumption of a certain type of procreation as "rational" behavior. As Jane and Peter Schneider point out, "Europeans appear in a great deal of early and classical population theory as paragons of rationality, their minds disciplining their bodies on behalf of long-range goals" (1996:5). These long-range goals were thought to be rational responses to Malthusian predictions about disastrous overpopulation and resource depletion. Demographer Ansley Coale used the well-known phrase "calculus of conscious choice" to refer to how Europeans had become "rational" in their intimate and private lives (Schneider and Schneider 1996:5). The dualism of modernization theory as applied to reproductive behavior historically connected the use of birth control "to a rational turn of mind," so that "traditional values" were opposed to "modern values." The traditional-modern dichotomy parallels that between "natural" and "controlled" fertility (Schneider and Schneider 1996:5; see also Coale and Watkins 1986; Greenhalgh 1996). Prolific reproducers were stigmatized as backwards, and in demographic parlance pejoratively described as "laggards."

The "*bassissima*," or super-low, fertility of Italians and other Europeans throws that old dichotomous irrational/backward versus rational/modern model into crisis, particularly for those scientists who keep track of such trends. Demographers assume that modern European populations are rational. This assumption draws on the laws of a linear, modernization model of social evolution. When populations exhibit patterns that do not fall within certain expectations, the scientists who track those patterns tend to interpret the irregularities as deriving from self-destructive behaviors that predictably will lead to population decline and imbalance rather than lasting equilibrium.

The record-low fertility rates have resulted in a bit of a crisis for demographers over the meaning of rationality: The measuring stick that demographers long used to mark "rational" reproductive behavior no longer has units that work for them. In the old scenario, it was enough to divide reproductive behavior into two halves: those who practiced "uncontrolled" or "natural"

Legend for Table 1

I identified ten key texts and then inventoried the authors' stances, evaluating them in terms of the degree to which they view the fertility rate as a problem. The findings are outlined in Table 1. The symbols used indicate the following:

-    −   neutral: the author's position is not obvious
- √− subtly present: the low fertility is a problem, but scientific narrative avoids language that frames it as such
- √   present: the low fertility is a problem, and scientific narrative clearly frames it as such
- √+ strongly present: the low fertility is a problem, scientific narrative reveals that the problem is serious through use of metaphors or indexical language

I did not use symbols for positions that framed the low fertility as *not* being a problem or as being a positive trend; I had developed such symbols but having not found any works that fell into this category, I eliminated them to avoid confusion. The first five references listed below derive from books; the second five from reports.

Table 1. Degree to which specific demographic texts portray Italian fertility as a problem.

Author, date, title	Textual evidence
1. √+ Golini (1991) Introduction to Palomba, *Crescita Zero* (Zero Growth)	a) "In developed countries the problem is to know if and how one can stop the long and rapid decline of fertility" (Golini 1991:vii). b) In both cases of the European community and Italy, it is a "problem of **knowledge** for understanding much better … the mechanisms that are at the base of procreative **behaviors** that push demographic tendencies on absolutely heterodox trajectories, which have never been documented in human history and which are very far from near zero population growth that good sense suggests" (Golini 1991:vii). c) "To judge how low this figure of births is, it is enough to consider that, if it were to remain constant for a long while, the Italian population would descend from 57.5 to 43–44 million (Golini 1991:viii). d) In the center-north one finds a "level of denatality never touched by another consistent population in the world" (Golini 1991:ix). e) "The median number of children per woman is between 0.9 and 1 in Emilia Romagna, in Friuli Venezia Giulia, when 2.05 children per woman would be necessary to insure a level of zero population growth. In other regions these indices are sensibly higher" (Golini 1991:ix). f) "In Italy few babies are born, so few in fact that only a few years ago an expert retained that such a level of denatality was 'impossible'" (Golini 1991:xii). g) "The new demographic behaviors in the nuptial and procreative field … brings to mind an Italian specificity demographically speaking not only for the negative records that we mark in the field of denatality or of aging of the population, but also for our own capacity to change without rupture, to adapt ourselves to the new conditions of social life without creating fractures with our history and our convictions" (Golini 1991:13).

Table 1. Degree to which specific demographic texts portray Italian fertility as a problem.

2. √–	Palomba (1991) *Crescita Zero*	Palomba's language itself is neutral; however, Golini's introductory essay (see above) frames low fertility as a serious and alarming problem and hence gives one the sense that the analyses that follow are designed as "solutions." In this light, Chapter 6, entitled "Italians and Demographic Policies," is a carefully constructed analysis of respondents' replies to questions about their views of state interventions designed to increase fertility (Palomba 1991).
3. √+	Golini (1994) *Tendenze demografiche e politiche per la popolazione* (Demographic tendencies and policies for the population)	"The Italian demographic tendencies are provoking in the population—quickly, but *silently*—a true and real 'mutation,' that has in itself the potential to unhinge the whole social and economic structure of the country" (Golini 1994:8).
4. √+	Livi-Bacci (1994) Introduction to Golini. *Tendenze demografiche e politiche per la popolazione*	"The topic of low fertility is perhaps the one that triggers the most emotional reactions. Whoever works on this topic is located in the worrisome position of the doctor faced with the case of an adolescent who refuses food. Are we dealing with a prolonged loss of appetite destined to disappear naturally or are we facing a case of anorexia? Are we talking about physiology or pathology?" (Livi-Bacci 1994:14). "Introduction: Gian Burrasca and the problem of children" (Volpi 1994:5).
5. √+	Volpi (1996) *Figli d'Italia* (Children of Italy)	"But the contradiction between words and facts could also reveal, how shall we say it? the guilty conscience (in the sense that the fewer children you have, the more you claim you desire them; the more the fertility rate of women declines, the more it creates a desire for them to be mothers) of a people—in this case, the Italians—for whom birth rate has undoubtedly sunk to the lowest level in the world" (Volpi 1996:31). "A grand problem remains to be examined . . . : that of the so-called age-stratified structure of the population. Let's begin, to explain ourselves, with the trend of genuine movement— or of the difference between births and deaths" (Volpi 1996:83).

Table 1. Degree to which specific demographic texts portray Italian fertility as a problem.

6. √–	ISTAT (1996) *Famiglia, abitazioni, servizi di pubblica utilità* (Family, housing, public transportation and services)	"The decline in fertility that has characterized the Nation in the last few years has led to, on the one hand, a decrease of couples with children and an increase of those without children; and on the other hand, a lessening of the number of couples with three or more children and a contemporaneous increase in the weight of couples with an only child" (ISTAT 1996:23).
7. √	ISTAT (1995) *Annuario statistico italiano 1994* (Annual Italian Statistics)	"In 1993, for the first time in the demographic history of post-unification Italy, except obviously for the war years of 1917 and 1918, the genuine balance (live births less deaths) had a negative result of more than 5,000 units, due to arriving at a new historical low in terms of births, equal to 538,000 (well 226,000 less than the preceding year) corresponding to a natality quotient of 9.3 per thousand inhabitants" (1995:55, cited in Volpi 1996:30).
8. √	Palomba, Menniti, Mussino, and Moors (1987) Attitudes Towards Demographic Trends and Population Policy	"In the last 20 to 30 years the Italian socio-demographic situation has changed in many respects. The fertility decline is undoubtedly one of the most important changes, with respect to both its demographic-economic consequences such as an aging population and the concomitant adjustments in the field of health care and social services, and to its sociocultural effects, such as changing attitudes toward marriage and children" (Palomba et al. 1987:3).
9. √	Golini, De Simoni, and Citoni (1995) *Tre scenari per il possibile sviluppo della popolazione delle regioni italiane al 2044* (Three scenarios for possible population development in Italian regions in 2044)	"None of the Italian scholars that work on population would have thought to imagine some thirty years ago that in the '90s the average number of children per woman in our Nation would have arrived at the level of around 1.2—the lowest in the world and likely the lowest ever documented in the history of humanity for a large-scale population (Golini et al. 1995:1).
10. √+	Lori, Golini, and Cantalini (1995) *Atlante dell'invecchiamento della popolazione* (Atlantas of the aging of the population)	"In the last decades all the attention and the effort of public opinion and political groups have turned toward the substantial economic and social transformations of the Nation, to the important political events—and to the fierce struggles that have accompanied them. We have been dealing with rapid and profound transformations that have radically modified, and in some cases unhinged, the entire structure of the whole society" (Lori et al. 1995:1).

fertility were labeled as "laggards" and viewed as backward and irrational; those who practiced "controlled" fertility were "leaders" and viewed as modern and rational.[10] So people who had small families (say, two or three children) were rational, and those who had large families (four, five, or more) were not there yet. Contemporary Italians control their fertility, and hence would be rational according to the old demographic transition theory rules.[11] But with the new zero population rules, their "*bassissima*," or super-low, fertility becomes a sign once again of "irrationality." So in a sense there has emerged a quite narrow range of reproductive -behavior that is considered "rational" if the discourses on the current fertility trends can stand as a guide.

Drawing on texts by well-known Italian demographers, I have identified and named three strategies that demographers commonly use to portray the low birthrate as so low as to be irrational. The most direct strategy, "Beyond Good Sense," is characterized by demographers' use of language that makes the reproductive practices underlying the trend appear irrational, self-destructive, and even immoral. A second strategy, the "Dangerous Heterodoxy" tactic, occurs when demographers use language that paints a picture of the trend as diverging from accepted doctrines or opinions. A third strategy, "Never-Before-Documented," occurs when the birthrate is described as so low as to be beyond imagination. The following examples draw from Table 1.

Beyond Good Sense. Note that Golini (Excerpt l.b) describes the current rate of reproduction as contrary to "a level which good sense suggests." He identifies Italian regions with very low birthrates and then describes as "sensibly higher" other regions where birthrates are well above those (Golini 1991 vii).

Dangerous Heterodoxy. The second strategy occurs where Golini describes demographic trends as being on "absolutely heterodox trajectories" (Excerpt 1.b). The accepted and desirable trajectory, by contrast, is zero population growth. Golini's description of Italian demographic tendencies as "provoking in the population … a true and real 'mutation'" (Excerpt 3) also reveals his view that the behavior is unorthodox. Furthermore, the metaphoric power of the word *mutation* conjures up images of cancer and other illnesses that threaten the well-being of an individual or a population. In another passage, Lori *et al.* (1995) describe the reproductive practices as having "radically modified, and in some cases unhinged, the entire structure of the whole society" (Excerpt 10). Again, the word choice of *unhinged* is anything but neutral; rather, it suggests something dangerous, something on the verge of collapsing.

Never-Before Documented. The third tactic is the most subtle yet pervasive strategy for depicting the low birthrate as a problem. We read of a "level of denatality never touched by another stable population" (Excerpt 1.d), of an expert who "maintained that such a level of denatality was 'impossible'" (Excerpt 1.f) "negative records" (Excerpt l.g), of a birthrate that has "sunk to the lowest level in the world" (Excerpt 6), of a "first time" phenomenon occurring only in times of war (Excerpt 7), and of a phenomenon beyond prediction (Excerpt 9):

> None of the Italian scholars that work on population would have thought to imagine some thirty years ago that in the '90s the average number of children per woman in our Nation would have arrived at the level of around 1.2—the lowest in the world

and likely the lowest ever documented in the history of humanity for a large-scale population. [Golini *et al.* 1995:1]

Rather than condemning Italian scholars for their inability to foresee the current population trend, this statement suggests that the national trend is so dramatic that it has taken even the most rational minds—those of scholars—by surprise.

"Loss of Appetite or Anorexia? ": A Demographer's Etiology of Very Low Fertility

The most blatant instance of current demographic discourse serving as a national sort of symptomatology—a reading of the signs of the national body's general health—can be found in Livi-Bacci's introduction (1994) to the important *Tendenze demografiche e politiche per la popolazione* (Demographic Tendencies and Policies for the Population), the third report on the Italian demographic situation, funded by the national population research institute (IRP). He describes demographers who work on the topic as being "in the worrisome position of the doctor faced with the case of an adolescent who refuses food" (Livi-Bacci 1994:14). This analogy epitomizes the "Beyond Good Sense" strategy. It frames reproductive activities of Italians as far from rational, for anorexia is considered neither reasonable nor sensible but rather a debilitating, self-destructive disorder, not unlike hysteria and insanity. It is also very much a gendered disorder.

In offering possible etiologies for this apparent deep-seated and self-destructive societal malady, Livi-Bacci offers two possibilities: the first he calls physiological (we might describe these factors as sociological), questioning whether the very low fertility is

> the consequence of the tiresome adjustment to a revolution that has brought millions of women into the workforce, of economic difficulty for the nuclear family faced with new and more demanding models of consumption, of education investments that are too long and expensive, of a complex lifestyle that weighs heavily due to inefficient social organization. [Livi-Bacci 1994:14]

If the cause for the loss of appetite, or very low fertility, is rooted in these types of factors, he argues, then "there is hope that social-political interventions can favor a demographic re-equilibrium with an upsurge in fertility. The list of possible interventions includes pronatalist measures" (Livi-Bacci 1994:14). In the second case there is "no hope" to reverse these "negative" trends, since they are the result of pathology: "It could also be that we are facing a hard 'refusal' of procreation that is rooted in a level of value choices beyond the influence of context and hence a true and real anorexia" (Livi-Bacci 1994:14, my translation).

This begs for pause. Who is engaging in a "hard refusal" to procreate if not women?[12] Without naming women, the language nevertheless most strongly indexes and implicates women, who ultimately are the sex/gender whose reproductive behaviors figure most centrally into demographers' calculations. (Men do not matter when it comes to calculations of fertility rates, since the biological parameters of getting pregnant, of gestating, of child-bearing, and of maternity are of such a different order of certainty than the biological parameters of inseminating and of paternity.[13]) Furthermore, we can infer the "hard refusers" are women since anorexia is a disorder typically associated with women and with infertile women at that. The implication, then, is that women, angst ridden and body obsessed, are rejecting the responsibility to refurbish the nation. At best, Italian women's family-making practices appear in demographers' accounts as a social ill to be fixed; at worse their behaviors appear as an irrational, even amoral, pathology beyond cure.

The way in which demographers have scientifically defined the current low birthrate as a problem serves as a moral guidepost for blaming women and has doubtlessly influenced Italian as well as global media representations of the trend. A *New York Times* article entitled "Population Implosion Worries a Graying Europe" frames low fertility as an "epidemic," one whose etiology can be located in women's "choosing work and education over having children" (Specter 1998). The article describes birthrates in many countries as being "in a rapid, sustained decline. Never before—except in times of plague, war and deep economic depression—have birthrates fallen so low, for so long." This popular press article participates in the "never-before documented" strategy that I identified above as a tactic demographers use to make reproductive patterns seem unthinkable, irrational, and dangerous. Plague, war, deep economic depression; these three phenomena are clearly disasters, and we can deduce that the article's central message is that, ultimately, women's "choice" to be productive rather than primarily reproductive is equivalent to a disaster on the order of plague, war, or deep economic depression. Easily overlooked are the important economic contributions that women have historically made to their families and regional economies. To reduce fertility decline to an epidemic like scenario in which women are portrayed as the major carriers is to deny the social and economic upheavals that dramatically transformed people's lives and their locations within kin, tribute, and capitalist modes of production.[14]

Furthermore, this portrayal of the "population problem" as a disaster complicates Palomba's suggestion that there is a global demographic dynamic at work. If global overpopulation were really the only issue—the birth of that 6 billionth human—then low' fertility rates like those of Italian women would be cause for celebration. The demographers, however, are not celebrating. Nor are the journalists who report on these trends. The global dynamics at play involve issues of political economy, for example, issues that get at the heart of economically wealthy and economically poor countries and those policymakers who decide when and whether immigrant workers should legitimately move between the cores and peripheries.

A JARRING MISFIT

Demographers and the media portray the low birthrate as a problem, but what does looking at the lived experiences of family-making reveal about the quiet revolution? In what unexpected ways does family-making create problems for those who live it? To speak of fertility decline primarily as a problem veils other struggles that have been playing out as demographic transitions have occurred. My ethnographic research in two textile and agricultural production communes in the Province of Prato during the latter 1990s leads me to conclude that there is a jarring misfit between the stories demographers are telling and the lives Italians have lived and are living.

In particular, struggles related to gendered aspects of identity have materialized as the patriarchal family hierarchy has toppled; struggles concerning class-based aspects of identity have emerged as new processes of class formation have taken hold; and struggles related to racial processes have come into a new light as migration patterns and policies have shifted. All of these struggles articulate in the context of global dynamics. They also recall the specter of history. For example, that many central Italians come from humble peasant or working-class backgrounds is particularly meaningful given that the economy of Prato has presented numerous people with the possibility of literally going from rags to riches. After all the thriving industrial district of Prato built on the city's 20th-century distinction as Italy's center of rag commerce: Old clothes and fabrics from all over the world were and still are regenerated into raw textile materials there. As the postwar economy boomed, many people had the chance to make money and, with it, acquire a new-moneyed identity. New strategies of family-making were a crucial aspect of this new consumer type of subjectivity

The remainder of this article draws on ethnographic fieldwork to examine how the current demographic situation plays out in terms of ideologies of gender, class, and ethnicity/race. It also considers how the prolific demographic concern about the low birthrate has shaped and continues to shape individual subjectivities and practices in powerful yet unexpected ways.[15]

The Three Pigs: A Local Theory

There are many "reasons" circulating in Italian society about why the birthrate is so low. One of my favorite local explanations comes from Carolina Morelli, a mother of three in her mid-fifties who was influential in local as well as regional politics. She and her husband managed the family sweater-finishing firm where I worked for about six months in 1996. One day while I was at her house, operating a machine to sew buttons on sweaters in the room designated for sweater work, she offered me her theory of why women used to have lots of babies and why they no longer do. Women, she said, were in the middle of three *maiali* (pigs): the priest, the *padrone* (landlord), and the husband. The priest wanted couples to have sex only for reproduction, to increase bodies tor his parish and souls for heaven; the padrone wanted lots of children because more arms meant a bigger harvest and a bigger share for him and his estate: and the husband wanted more people to order around. Now, nobody listens to the priest, the padrone no longer has peasants or title, and the husband views children as drains on his time and pocketbook.

Carolina's theory speaks to a perceived erosion of patriarchy. She views the trend toward small families as a positive one. The new generation so many Italians lament as egotistical for Carolina means independent-minded citizens who will not be so likely to fall for political movements like fascism. And her daughter will be able to work as an engineer. "*Figli programmati sono figli fortunate*' [Planned children are lucky children], she likes to say.[16]

Carolina's parable suggests that demographers' stories deny an important aspect of the quiet revolution: that it is a revolution, though often silently so, against patriarchy and the patriarchal structures of power that hierarchically ordered social relations for centuries. The shift in reproductive practices was in part rooted in a festering peasant protest among women and junior males against "the rigidity of the pecking-order in the family" (Becattini 1998:83). as well as powers of decision making and the availability of income "inconsistent with the distribution of workload, capacity, and responsibility" (Becattini 1986:908, my translation). In the area of central Italy where I worked, for example, women straw weavers comprised the leading force behind an industrializing countryside since they offered a cheap source of labor: the most extensive central Italian labor strikes of the 19th century involved these nonurban weavers working out of homes in the towns and hamlets lining the banks of the Arno River.[17] Nearly every household in a 1901 census contained at least one woman whose professional occupation was noted as *trecciaiola* (straw weaver).[18]

The One-Child Story of a Straw Weaver

Emilia, a straw weaver born in 1920 who worked from the time she was five years old, offered memories that revealed her connections to a global economy: she spoke of childhood speed-weaving games that tempted the winner with postcards sent from overseas emigrant relatives; she recalled for me the dramatic tale of a communist uncle who escaped Mussolini's regime by stowing away among straw-hat cargo destined for South America, where he became an importer of hats, many of which Emilia and her fellow women townsfolk produced. Deeply embedded in these memories were her postwar explanations about how she came to marry "late," at age 30 (in 1950), and how she came to have only one child. Her story offers insight into understanding a generation of women whose profound changes led them to put their own welfare before that of the patriarchal family. Emilia's strategy not to continue the peasant tradition of large families but to stop with her daughter was supported by her husband, who soon left the land for the factory. This shift in family making represents a cultural adjustment to tremendous social and economic changes, ones involving modernity and new definitions of and possibilities tor womanhood. These themes can be found in the following excerpt from a discussion I had with Emilia. In transcribing and analyzing this talk, I have drawn on linguistic anthropological methods (see, in particular, Ochs *et al.* 1996). I have retained the words in their original form because speakers of Italian will be able to hear the rural Tuscan dialect, one marked by cadences associated with a less-educated generation. I include my own talk in the transcription even though in the following passage it does not contribute to the content per se; however, the back-channel cues do reveal the research process in the final product.[19]

A key element of Emilia's narrative is the doctor's misdiagnosis of abdominal pain she was suffering as a young woman. At the time of the telling, her only child, Patricia, was three years old. Her discussion of the misdiagnosis—the doctor's mistaking the pain caused by a specific cyst for pain caused by general stress—offers insight into the cultural transformations in postwar central Italy. It reveals how hegemonic processes play out in the context of interpersonal relations between a rural peasant woman and an urban physician. In this case, the leading view of the urban, educated elite—embodied in the role of the doctor—was one that normalized the nuclear family as well as associated morality and health with this type of family making. By contrast, the hegemonic view pathologized the extended patriarchal family. The moment of pathos becomes apparent in the narrative when Emilia recalls the doctor's etiology of her illness. He suggested that her moving from a nuclear household to an extended family was the cause of her anxiety and cramps. He was thereby suggesting a psychological cause to her physical pain. Etiology here becomes ideology; the doctor, through his misrecognition of the cause of Emilia's pain, was expressing a leading idea related to family making. In particular, the story reveals how doctor-patient interactions can be opportunities for doctors to express hegemonic views of normal behavior, and, in turn, for patients to react to those views.

It is worth clarifying that Emilia's statement that the operation did not do her harm (Line 5) is a reference to a fear, at the time, that the intervention had left her infertile. In the hospital, she apparently had some rather catty roommates who insisted she had had a hysterectomy. Even though this was far from the truth, at the time she reassured herself that if the doctor had taken out everything it did not matter since she already had one child. She actually says "another child" (Line 5) but this is not a reference to a second child. It may be a colloquialism or an instance in which she imagines those never realized babies in the light of the doctor's gregarious comment (not reproduced here) that she "could have ten more children," a metaphorical way of saying her reproductive health was sound. Her story follows:

1.	Emilia:	La Patrizia l'aveva due anni e qualcosina.	Patricia, she was a little over two years old.
2.		Sicchè ebbi questa operazione.	And then I had this operation.
3.	Betsy:	Ahh.	Ohh.
4.	Emilia:	Però non mi dava noi(a)—	But it didn't really bother me—
5.		mi non noceva aveva un'altro bambino,	it didn't do me any harm since I had another child,
6.		mi disse il professore	the doctor said to me
7.		perchè non mi levarono niente a me	because he didn't remove anything from me
8.		soltanto questa ciste all' ovarie.	except for this ovarian cyst.
9.	Betsy:	Ah.	Oh.
10.	Emilia:	Eh! Sicchè mi disse il professore	See! So the doctor said to me,
11.		"Perchè?"	"Why?"
12.		quando gli chiesi io icchè gli aveva fatto.	when I asked him what he had done.
13.		Infatti penso l'aveva—	In fact I thought he had—

13.	Infatti penso l'aveva—	In fact I thought he had—
14.	La Patrizia due anni,	Patricia was two
15.	tr- tre!	th-three!
16.	quasi tre anni l'aveva.	almost three years old.
17.	Però io gl'era un pezzettino che mi sentio male	But it had been a while since I'd been feeling bad
18.	e mi si pigliava queste coliche.	and I was having these stomach pains.
19.	E non me l'aveva cono—	And he hadn't kno—
20.	non me l'avevano conosciuta.	and they hadn't recognized it.
21. Betsy:	Ah.	Oh.
22. Emilia:	Il dottore mi dicea	The doctor was like
23.	"Gli è un pò nervoso."	"You're a little nervous."
24.	Ero abituata io	I was used to [living]
25.	con la mi mamma	with my mother
26.	ei mi fratello e sola	and my brother only
27.	non- ripre—	I didn't—
28.	a ritrovarmi con la casa in dieci persone	to find myself in a household with ten people
29.	mi parea un po' di sopraccapo	it seemed like I was going to lose it
30.	e lo dicea a me	and he was like
31.	"era preso un pò di esaurimento nervoso."	"you're having a little nervous breakdown."
32. Betsy:	Ah	Oh.
33. Emilia:	Invece un'era vero.	But it wasn't true.
34.	Gli era il male avevo.	It was the illness I had.

It seems to me that Emilia recognizes the ideology at work beneath the surface of the doctor's misdiagnosis—though she would not use that terminology. Nevertheless, she appears to be telling me, in her peasant-worker approach to social analysis that this encounter was a normalization experience for her.[20] Urban Florentine elites in the postwar-era attached a stigma to large, extended rural families, and hence the doctor was in an opaque way chastising her for violating the established norm with regard to family making. The doctor, by locating the ultimate causal agent for her symptoms in the extended patriarchal family, was engaging in a modernist critique of this household structure; such a living arrangement is viewed here as a threat to one's sanity, to one's ability to exercise sound reason. In essence, the patriarchal extended family becomes the antithesis to modernity because being modern means being in control; once someone has "lost one's head" (*sopraccapo,* Line 29) one has lost control. This punch line, of sorts, directly relates to the larger point of Emilia's story: the misdiagnosis and its meaning.

The most significant "evaluation" clause occurs when Emilia interrupts the story's temporality to comment on the "so what" of the narrative (Labov 1972:366) at Line 20—"and they hadn't recognized it." The evaluation confirms that the point of the telling was indeed the misdiagnosis.

Furthermore, the sudden self-interruption (Line 19) signals the sideward glance: Bakhtin argues (1984:205) such moments occur when a speaker anticipates the response of the listener, and hence they often indicate ideological conflict. Note that between Lines 19 and 20 Emilia shifts in number from third-person singular to third-person plural, suggesting that not just one doctor but a worldview of men in white coats informs her memory of the misdiagnosis. The encounter between her and the medical establishment is a relation of power saturated with normalizing forces.

Later, when I asked Emilia to clarify why she did not have another child, her health problem emerged as only part of the story: in fact, she emphasized her good reproductive health and her generative capacity, citing the doctor's joking comment about having another "ten" children. Rather, the other part of her one-child story concerned important changes occurring in the social fabric of labor and its effect on kin modes of production. The sharecropping crisis resulted in major social dislocations particularly for the patriarchal family (Contini and Ravenni 1987). At one time daughters-in-law derived power from having numerous children, but this too was changing. As Emilia told me, her sister-in-law did not have any children and, nevertheless, her in-laws liked this other woman best of all. Emilia sensed little or no pressure to have more children. Her husband went along with his wife because the new family structure and the changing economy required and allowed it. Central to the experience of the quiet revolution was a shifting ideological process involving the breakdown of the patriarchal family and a related rise in individualism intertwined with a newly defined global market and reconfigured identities rooted in emergent class structures.

Postwar Class Formation and Risks of Stigma

In recent years, family-making practices of central Italians have been powerfully linked to social expectations about what has been seen as "necessary" for raising children and for seeking middle-class respectability (Schneider and Schneider 1996:273). An ideology of class and status combines with an ideology of gender to shape women's and men's decisions about the number of children to bring into their family. Social identities, as Henrietta Moore reminds, are constituted through "ideologies or 'naturalized' cultural conventions ... implicated in power structures and in the structuring of inequalities" (1994: 92). Allow me to offer two brief examples of identity formation related to emergent class structures.

The neighborhood where I lived during the first year of my fieldwork (October 1995-96) in a textile-production area of the Province of Prato was settled largely after World War II by former Tuscan peasants and Calabrian as well as Sicilian immigrants who had numerous siblings but few children themselves. This newly moneyed province is legendary for its variety of postwar consumer culture: former peasants and rag-wholesalers who came into money through the textile boom are known to have bought books by the kilo. As purchases of symbolic capital, these books would never be read. A fashion- and design-conscious sort of place, people joke that you live for your house rather than having a house to live in. Language teachers use words like *mania* (craziness).

fissazione (fixation), and *ossessione* (obsession) to describe how people, especially women, have a habit of always thinking about their house. It is also a place where certain material goods are said to distance those who possess them from *genterella* (low-class folk). Despite the strong tradition of leftist politics in central Italy, having few children is also important to the cultural play of transcending stigmas associated with poverty. That people speak openly about the relationship between family size, economic prosperity and image management serves as evidence that notions of modernity in demographic and development discourse are in wide, popular circulation.[21]

Carlotta was 38 when I met her, the mother of one child and part owner of a family sweater firm. Her husband, brother-in-law, and mother-in-law provided the key labor inside the firm; various stages of production were subcontracted to other small firms. The family lived in a graciously restored farmhouse; Carlotta, her husband, and daughter occupied one floor, and the widowed mother-in-law and her eldest, bachelor son the other. The *maglificio* (sweater firm) was located in one wing of the home. One day Carlotta and her mother-in-law spoke to me about their lives. Carlotta explained the pressure she felt to have everything—clothes, food, and house—in perfect order, and the ambivalence she and her husband felt concerning the possibility of having another child. A theme of social status and public displays of it emerged as 1 wrote up in my fieldnotes the conversation between Carlotta, her mother-in-law, and myself. This excerpt from my field notes begins with Carlotta speaking:

> "Everything has to be a name brand. Last year Alice (then gearing up to enter third grade) had a backpack that cost Lit 30,000 (US $18.00). All the kids looked at her, so this year I spent Lit 130,000 (US $78.00) and got her a Sailor Moon backpack, the type used in middle school. Otherwise you're looked upon as *genterella*."[22] a low-class or disrespectable person. "Ah," her mother-in-law chimed in, "they're all really *genterella*."
>
> "Of course they are," said Carlotta. "But everybody wants to cover it up, to show the next person up." [Field notes. 28 June 1997]

This passage suggests that Carlotta seeks to avoid a sense of social inferiority for herself as well as her daughter. Social status powerfully shapes Carlotta's sense of personal identity and self worth. With such an emphasis on the acquisition of expensive material goods, coupled with what I have elsewhere called a culture of responsibility in which a great deal of attention is placed on the details of laundering, ironing, clothing, feeding, healing, and educating, the thought of numerous children often seems beyond reach. It is worth noting that demographers' official surveys cite Italian women as those with the largest gap between children desired (an average of two) and those actually had (an average of one).

The stigma for having numerous (more than two) children is not merely imagined but lived, as revealed in the experience of another woman, who was pregnant with her third son at the time I interviewed her. Cinzia, then 36, had worked in a sweater factory until she had her first son. Afterward, she did part- time piecework or housecleaning. She experienced serious stigma with her third pregnancy. Friends, relatives and town acquaintances used words like "half-witted" and "idiot" as well as pitying phrases such as "Oh, that poor woman!" when they heard she was having a third *figliolo* (son).

Cinzia's talk about the stigma she endured was marked by frequent moments of hesitation, incoherence, and laughter—dysfluencies that emerged through fine-grained discourse analysis in a narrative describing others' reactions to her pregnancy. These dysfluent moments indicate the presence of a heteroglossic speech community in which "language, for the individual conscious-ness, lies on the borderline between oneself and the other" (Bakhtin 1981:293; see also Hill 1995). Reporting the harsh speech of her friends and relatives appears painful for Cinzia, as evidenced by the frequent presence of pauses (indicated below by " … "), elongated vowels (indicated by " = "), unfinished thoughts (indicated by " — "), and nervous laughter (indicated by " @ "):

Her explanation for why her friends might have been so concerned about the sex of the child reveals ideological conflict that we might recognize, after Gramsci, as contradictory consciousness (1971:333). Cinzia's self-reflective tendency allows her to see the unfairness embedded in a sex/gender system that elevates males to a status which prohibits them from doing housework, for housework is nothing more than "flinging air around," (Line 8). Yet her uncomfortable laughter would suggest that she is unable to rise above old habits and transform social reality and, in particular, gender relations. It is almost as though her laughter signals the multiple viewpoints she, by necessity, must hold in order to perpetuate the life she is living as a woman, wife, and expectant mother. In other passages, it became clear that the dominant ideology about controlled, "rational," small family making exercised its power directly on Cinzia's sense of social identity. Her personhood was thrown into crisis—"if I were a strong woman I wouldn't take it so hard," she told me. At times, she questioned whether she was indeed "half-witted"—a heavy burden to bear in a cultural context that places such a high premium on reason and on the appearance of rational reproductive behavior.

1.	Cinzia:	"Come farò con tre maschi?"	"How will I manage with three boys?"
2.		Dice: [. . .] "T- t'aurai da fa tanto,"	They go: [. . .] "Y- you'll have so much to do,"
3.		ma io passato i primi mesi	well I spent the first months
4.		ero un pò = o demoralizzata perchè dice,	I was a little = demoralized because they were like,
5.		"T'aurai da fa tanto con tre maschi.	"You'll have so much to do with three boys."
6.		Insomma perchè i maschi, l'omo qui praticamente—	Let's just say because boys, the man here practically—
7.		c'è sempre quello che i fare in casa della donna—	there's this idea that the stuff the woman does in the house—
8.		e l'omo gli ha altro che da buttare all'aria @	and the man has other stuff to do than fling air around @

Another Source of Postwar Stigma: Race

Stigma has its roots not only in class- and gender-based cultural struggles for respectability as key symbols of bourgeois rationality (Schneider and Schneider 1996), but also in shifting meanings of "race." People who became my friends told me painful stories about the racism they encountered when they first moved north from Calabria to Tuscany, in the 1960s, when the textile industry of Prato was booming, and the economy beckoned people to leave the countryside and the South to work in factories or artisan workshops. Elsewhere (Krause 1998), I have explored the much debated issue of whether one can call internal discrimination by Northern Italians against Southern Italians "racism" as opposed to "regional chauvinism." In both cases, somatic and cultural characteristics are fused and result in a type of "othering" that elevates the status and power of the "in" group. There has long been a biological basis to the type of discrimination practiced in Italy. Italian positivist scholars of criminology writing between 1880–1920 identified "race" as causal to the crime in Southern Italy (Gibson 1998), a glaring instance of biologism for which Gramsci took the positivists to task. Persistent economic differences between the North and the South, often referred to as the Southern Question, were framed as resulting from racial inferiority (Gibson 1998:100; Gramsci 1971:70–71). For northerners who did not accept that Italian unification resulted from a hegemonic process in which the North acted like an "octopus" enriching itself at the expense of the South, Gramsci scolded, "There only remained one explanation: the organic incapacity of the inhabitants, their barbarity, their biological inferiority" (1971:71).

One essential aspect of my fieldwork was my participation in community life as a parent of a first-grader in a local elementary school. The parents, mostly mothers of one or two children, congregated each afternoon in a courtyard outside the locked school until the bell rang, at which point the *bidella* (custodian) unlocked the doors. It was like floodgates had just been opened: black *grembiuli* (school smocks) with white collars and red bows blurred past as children burst into the schoolyard.

I always made an effort to arrive at least ten minutes before the bell rang to take part in the schoolyard talk. One day in March 1997, several mothers began speaking about the recent arrival of Albanians. "Tuscans are earning the Albanians on their backs," said one mother. She used the word *carico,* which means "load." She then switched her target to Southern Italians. "Things are so bad in parts of Calabria, the women still have to go and bring in water from outside," implying that the lack of infrastructure signified a backward place with backward people who prevent things from functioning. "These people don't really want to work. They're free-loaders, parasites."

A Sicilian friend of mine standing nearby took offense. She read into this woman's remarks a general anti-immigrant sentiment and began to defend herself and her husband, stressing how hard they both work since moving to Tuscany four years ago. "I'm allergic to dust and yet I still go and clean. I couldn't find any other work here, but I go every morning and clean other people's houses." As a southern Italian who had experienced racism, she was quick to note it.

A few days later, at the bar where I regularly had breakfast with a group of five mothers, the conversation turned to a comparison of new immigrants and gypsies. "At least the Albanians, the

Chinese, the Africans, they work. What do the gypsies do? All they do is rob. They freeload." To support her accusation, the woman drew on an experience from her extended family: she told us about a "gypsy kid" who attended her brother's child's school and complained that the gypsy parents did not pay taxes. She then implicated the gypsy population by invoking immoral reproductive practices. "All they do is bring children into the world and then they abandon them—throw them into the streets to beg and rob. ... All the gypsy women should be sterilized."

Demographic discourse was central to these daily moments of Othering. Anti-immigrant talk easily segued into anti-Southern Italian discourse and readily encompassed gypsies and perceptions of "reckless" parenting.[23] The migrations of southern peoples frequently blended into one another in the way they arose in social conversation, political rhetoric, and media reports. Discourse about populations also included strategic and often racialized evaluations of reproductive practices. These conversations led me to inquire into the racist associations that exist at an everyday discursive level.

The low Italian birthrate is frequently juxtaposed in popular media reports against the growing non-European immigrant population and easily becomes linked to fears about the demise of an Italian "race" and the disappearance of European culture.[24] What is the source of this alarm? Are only the media alarmist or can this sense of alarm also be detected in the reports and discourses of demographic science? My research suggests that the media and demographic science hold tremendous sway in shaping popular perceptions and sounding population-related alarms.[25]

DEMOGRAPHIC DISCOURSES, LOW FERTILITY, AND "ELITE" RACISM

The alarmist discourses of demographers, if not blatantly racist, enable racist ideological projects and hence help maintain hegemonic views toward immigrant "others." If we take ideologies to be "unified schemes or configurations developed to underwrite or manifest power" (Wolf 1999:4), then racist ideologies are those which rely on a type of power based on hierarchical fictions of race. In my view, race is a social construction; its consequences are no less real than if race were based purely on biological difference since the category is vacuous such that those in power can fill it with whatever is convenient (Goldberg 1993). Race "has been used as a legitimating ideological tool to suppress and exploit specific social groups and to deny them access to material and cultural resources, work, welfare services, housing, political rights, etc." remind Wodak and Reisigl (1999:176).[26] Relevant to my story about how a supposedly objective scientific endeavor enables racism is Teun van Dijk's observation that elite public discourse plays a primary role in reproducing racism. He argues that elites—the media, in particular, but also politicians, corporations, and academics—are key to reproducing racially-based social hierarchies (van Dijk 1993:31, 242-243, 257). The media clearly exercise substantial influence throughout Europe in shaping social outlooks and memories as well as in reproducing racist ideologies. Nevertheless, it is important to keep in mind that reporters, editors, and producers rely on "expert" sources for the information they disseminate.

Italian demographers' projections of subzero population growth, as frequently reported in the Italian media, contribute to fears and anxieties toward immigrants, who are seen as fulfilling alarmist demographic prophecies with regard to a future shortage of Italians in the labor force and the demise of an Italian "race." This emotion of fear was expressed by a former Labor Minister who called on Italians to produce more babies "to keep away armadas of immigrants from the southern shores of the Mediterranean" (Martiniello and Kazim 1991:88).[27] One does not have to look long or hard to detect negative associations between immigrants and the birthrates of Italians. Consider this headline, published in 1996, in a national daily:

Culle piu vuote, l'Italia cresce solo per l'apporto degli immigrati	More cradles empty. Italy grows only due to immigrant supply [La Nazione 1996:7][28]

The article set up a false cause-and-effect relationship, implying immigrants represent the only reason for population growth. The population, however, is also aging. Life expectancy has risen to 74 years for men and 80 for women. Worth noting is that the total foreign presence at that time equaled just over 2 percent of the Italian population. Official estimates from December 31, 1998 put the number of immigrants at 1,033,235 individuals holding a *permesso di soggiorno* (legal residency permit) plus about 250,000 "underground" people as compared to 57.8 million Italian citizens. As of January 1, 2000, the foreign resident population totaled 1,270,553, a 13.8 percent increase from the previous year (ISTAT 2000; Palanca 1999:15).

Alarmist language is one enabling device that helps perpetuate racist sentiments and practices. Such tones also characterize representations of the demo- graphic relationship between the country's low birthrate and its aging population. An article in July 1997 entitled "Italy? It Is Old and without Children," noted that in some regions of the center-north, the level of natality was below one child per couple *(La Stampa* 1997:17).[29] The report described Italy as having become "the oldest country in the world, a country of great-grandparents." Minister of Health Rosy Bindi said, "If the increase in the life span is a conquest, the low level of natality is a sign of lost civility or at least of tragic uneasiness" (quoted in *La Stampa* 1997:17).

The article did not explain why Bindi interpreted the low birthrate as an indicator of *incivilta* (barbarity), an ordeal of civility.[30] We can take a clue as to Bindi's spin on the matter from a national conference that received substantial media coverage. The motivation for looking to this report as a route of grasping the sense of tragedy evident in Bindi's perspective is that, as a public health official, her viewpoint is likely shaped by the expert number crunchers of the state, in other words, the demographers. And much of popular opinion about the demographic situation comes from the media's reportage on demographers' findings. The conference, "Population and Environment in Developed Countries," held in October 1996, was sponsored by CNR, the Italian national research council.[31] A newspaper reporter covering the event interviewed Italian demographer Antonio Golini, who used alarmist language as he discussed the "inescapable" progressive aging of the Italian population. He predicted some 400 *comuni* (counties) would be eliminated in the course of 34 years due to minimum population requirements. "The very low fertility of Italian women," Golini maintained, "assures a generational exchange that is well below 40 percent of that which would insure zero growth." He suggested that the only solution to the problem of a rapidly rising median age of the population is to increase fertility from "only 1.1 actual children per couple to 2." The journalist took Golini to task for making statements that always "wake up the ghost of Italian extinction." The reporter cited a non-Italian demographer's estimate of an ideal population for Italy of 21 million rather than 57 million to achieve optimal quality of life given available resources, and then asked, "Isn't it a little premature considering the problems of the survival of the earth?" Golini offered the following reply:[32]

> Effetivamente se abbiamo un'ottica mondiale non c'e nessun problema. Se la popo-lazione italiana cala in fretta arrivano gli immigrati e amen. Ma non possiamo fermarci a questo. Io studio la civiltà maya e come mi dispiace della sua comparsa mi può dispiacere che scompaia la cultura italiana o quella europea.

> Effectively if we have a global view there is no problem. If the Italian population declines quickly, the immigrants will arrive and amen. But we cannot stop at this. I study Mayan civilization and just as 1 regret their disappearance, I can regret it if the Italian or European culture were to disappear. [*L'Unità* 1996]

Golini implies that immigrants are not capable of carrying forth the Italian civilization. His discourse, as well as Bindi's, plays on social memory and indexes Italians as the bearers of a unique humanism. The implication is that certain genetic types (the ones that would lie in those empty cradles) are required to carry forth this civilizational legacy. This type of logic is what Angel-Ajani (2000:334), drawing on Malcomson (1995) and Gilroy (1991). has predicted: "A Euro-racial ideal may be created not only by legal means but through notions of cultural exclusivity that conflate race and nation to the point where racial others are deemed incompatible with European culture."[33] Although the media have a powerful role in perpetuating alarmist sentiments of in-compatibility, demographers, as the scientific authorities, occupy a crucial position in terms of constructing discourses to further the project of increasing the birthrate of Italian women.

Incentive programs (most of which are local) for augmenting the birthrate are meant to stimulate births of Italian nationals, not births to non-Europeans. For example, a pronatalist program proposed in May 1999 in Milan offered monthly payments of one million lire to residents, but only those who had lived in the city for at least 15 years. The article, without any evidence of actual immigrant birthrates, noted that "In the shadow of the Madonna shrine are *gli stranieri* (foreigners), who continue to procreate while the Milanese, due to choice or economic difficulty, seem always less enthusiastic to confront the prospect of having a family" *(La Repubblica* 1999). That the *stranieri* are described as in the shrine's shadow suggests they are not potential beneficiaries of the "blessings" of the madonna, in other words, a metaphoric reference to the local administration; this figure also plays on the presupposition that non- Europeans are also non-Catholic. The Left accused the proposal as being anti- constitutional and having a racist odor (1999).

There is, however, ambiguity in the current construction of Italianness. On the one hand, Southern Italians are counted along with Northern Italians to calculate national birthrates and to create a sense of an imagined community, of a homogeneous Italian "race."[34] On the other hand, demographic statistics, reported in the media, highlight differences between North and South. Consider this newspaper portrait of the nation following the release of national statistics:

> The changing Italy remains in fact tenaciously equal to itself in inequities, with a Mezzogiorno that chases after the North, which is by now aligned with the most advanced models of the industrialized West. From birthrates to occupation, from exports to consumption, the statistics seem to illustrate two different countries [*Il Sole 24 Ore* 1995]

Such divisions between the North and the South reverberate throughout xenophobic movements, such as the political rhetoric of the separatist party *Lega Nord* (Northern League) described by immigration scholars as among the "new political entrepreneurs of intolerance ... [who have] proved capable of exploiting the immigration issue in order to gain political support" (Pelrillo 1999:244). The League, at the beginning of the 1990s, argued that "the foreign invasion jeopardizes internal unity and the very identity of our people." A platform of superiority relied on old us-them dichotomies: "between natives and immigrants, between '*padani*' [northerners] and southern Italians" (quoted in Petrillo 1999:245). Xenophobic movements and, more subtly, national statistics echo the biological differences identified more than a century past in positivist criminologists' accounts.

CONCLUSIONS

I have moved this article between different levels of analysis, from the powerful constructions of knowledge undertaken by demographers, to media representations of this knowledge, and to the everyday experiences and perceptions of the subjects of demographic analysis: Italians and immigrants.

In Italy, demographers, politicians, and reporters have succeeded in making the body politic keenly aware of the low birthrate. Academic and state-sponsored elites deploy alarmist language and play on powerful metaphors—such as war on the one hand, loss of civil society on the other—to convince the public that the birthrate is too low. Magazine articles, cartoons, newspaper reports, books, and internet sites attest to the diffuse popular perception of Italy's self-consciousness about a demographic trend that has put "the two-child model into crisis," as the one-child family moves in as substitute (Menniti *et al.* 1997:239).

Demographic writings carry weight because of their authorship by demographers, who are *authorized* to speak scientifically about population.[35] The proliferation of demographic studies on the low birthrate is a type of knowledge production that serves as a sneaky sort of pronatalism; by not blatantly advocating specific measures to increase births, they avoid uncomfortable ties to the fascist demographic campaign of the 1920s and 1930s.[36] Framing the trend as an alarming problem nevertheless involves engaging in a politics of cultural struggle in which the concrete history of the quiet revolution is forgotten. The depiction of the birthrate as a problem denies rational agency especially to women and accuses them of failing their civilization. In addition, the prolific commentary about the low birthrate ensures that the quiet revolution is ongoing. In the context of a tightening European Union, and of Italy's change from a sending to a receiving country in terms of immigration, one can see how the official demographic project participates in the sort of war of position that Gramsci suggested occurs with hegemonic projects; an effort to raise consciousness aims to construct new grounds to stand on (Brackette Williams, personal communication 1994). I would like to suggest that the "problem" of the low birthrate and the "project" to remedy it are driven by nationalistic goals, ones that have become complicated and perhaps even more "urgent" against the backdrop of global movements of people into Italy as well as Italy's frontier location in Fortress Europe. Meanwhile, central Italians navigate the material conditions of a postwar context. Adjustments in family making are related to a newly defined global market economy, which has reconfigured identities rooted in articulations of gender, class, and race/ethnicity. The Italians living in central Italy and their non-European immigrant neighbors contend with a redefined context in which old and new forms of racism cross-fertilize. Prolific knowledge about the low birthrate and the persistent characterization of it as an alarming problem empower "racializing discourses" that contribute to the everyday re-production of racism.[37]

My analytic journey therefore suggests that demographers have embraced a "national" project of raising awareness among the population about key demographic trends and moving them to believe the birthrate is a problem with the goal of changing behavior. This tactic constitutes an effort to get the population to consent to a new hegemonic project of the state. This project, however, competes with another one: a hegemonic attitude toward family size that has led couples all over Europe to have small families.

In October 1998, I heard Bill Bradley remark in a speech to a U.S. oil industry association that by the year 2050, "white" Americans will be the minority. "It's demography. It's not ideology," he said, advocating a pluralistic society that "takes more and more people to higher ground." Later, I overheard an audience member make a tasteless, horrific comment: that there would be need for another holocaust. The remark reminded me of a central conviction: demography has a long and involved political history in terms of assisting in the management and control of populations. Our task, then, becomes to critically examine purportedly scientific demographic discourses with the goal of recognizing and exposing the ideological and political-hegemonic ends to which such demographic knowledge and claims may be put.[38] In this article I have tried to demonstrate how demographic discourses in Italy easily become fodder for anti- immigrant alarmism as well as for depicting women as irrational subjects who are not fulfilling their role as the ultimate reproducers of the nation. More work needs to be done on the silences that underpin the quiet revolution.

NOTES

This article traces its genesis to the "Racism as Culture" roundtable organized by Jane Hill for the Comparative Culture and Literary Studies Conference at the University of Arizona, February 27, 1998. Later incarnations were presented during the American Anthropological Association panel, "Toward a Critical Anthropology of Population," co-organized by David Kertzer and myself as an Executive Program Committee Invited Session on December 3, 1998 in Philadelphia; at a public talk at the University of Massachusetts, Amherst, Department of Anthropology, February 22, 2000; and at a public lecture to The Working Group on Anthropology and Population at Brown University on April 20, 2001. I am grateful to audience responses received in each of those public contexts and to comments by AAA discussants Susan Greenhalgh and Jane Schneider. I also value interactions with the AAA panel participants, with whom I shared a plan, which never materialized, to publish our collective articles together. My thanks extend to Hermann Rebel, Ana Alonso, Jane Hill. Susan Philips, and Mark Nichter for comments on earlier drafts of this article. This article has benefited enormously from the insights of anonymous reviewers for *Cultural Anthropology* and the journal's persistently attentive editor, Dan Segal. I am grateful for transcription and translation assistance from Antonella del Conte, Luciana Fellin, and Matilde Zampi; my understandings were also enriched by our conversations. Italian colleagues Massimo Bressan, anthropologist, and Giovanni Contini, oral historian, offered support and insights throughout the project, as did numerous other organic intellectuals from my field site. My appreciation goes out to Massimo Livi-Bacci, who graciously met with me and provided access to the statistics library at the Università degli Studi di Firenze, where many important Italian demography sources are held. The hard work of demographers informs my research even as I write critically about it. Research funds for ethnographic fieldwork (October 1995–August 1997 and June 1999) were provided by a Council for European Studies Pre-Dissertation Grant, a U.S. Fulbright Grant and Renewal, and a Final Project Fund Award from The University of Arizona (Krause 1999). This litany of acknowledgments aside, I accept full responsibility for any shortcomings with the caveat that any work is always in progress.

1. Contrary to popular usage, the demographic term *fertility* refers to the number of live births women on average have in a certain population. When demographers speak of declines in fertility, they do *not* mean increases in infertility or decreases in fecundity (the ability to have children) but, rather, declines in births.
2. My concept of hegemony draws heavily on Gramsci's notion (1971) as later developed by Rebel (1989), Roseberry (1994), B. Williams (1991), and R. Williams (1977).
3. I conducted doctoral field research from October 1995 to August 1997 with a follow-up visit during June 1999.
4. Giacomo Becattini, an economist well-known for the social flavor he lends to analyses of industrial development in Tuscany, particularly Prato's postwar industrial district, draws our attention to the "economic self-assertion by individuals" (Becattini 1998:83) that characterized people's entry into industry. On the one hand, small-scale, diffuse industry meant cheap labor; on the other, it meant that many more people could be their own bosses, but I would add only problematically so since the autonomy of individuals within a firm depended on their subject position. In his attempt to untie the "knotty" situation that led to economic development in Tuscany—against a moderate. 19th-century antidevelopment political leadership—Becattini views the *mezzadria* (sharecroppers) as crucial. He suggests that mounting tensions led to a "peasant protest, particularly by women and youth, not so much against the countryside itself as against the rigidity of the pecking-order in the family and against their close economic dependence on its older male members" (Becattini 1998:83). The powers of decision making and the availability of income were "inconsistent with the distribution of workload, capacity and responsibility" (Becattini 1986:908, my translation). Peasants, according to Becattini, began objecting to a social structure and ideology that permitted, even necessitated, an unfair distribution of duties and rights.
5. Everyday body ritual among Americans was made to appear unfamiliar and strange in Horace Miner's now classic Nacirema culture (Miner 1956). With a parallel objective, I wish to make us question the "naturalness" of statistical practices to see that they, too, are socially and historically constructed.
6. On the "hot" Italian economy, see Friedman 1997. Historian Paul Ginsborg writes, "By the late 1980s Italy claimed to have overtaken Britain, to become the fifth largest industrial nation of the Western world, after the United States, Japan. West Germany, and France. Giovanni Goria, then Treasury Minister, first made this claim in January 1987. It has been hotly disputed ever since" (1990:408). See also Italian Journal 1988 (1):31–48.
7. See http://pbs.org/sixbillion.
8. This article examines the following texts: Golini 1991, 1994; Golini *et al.* 1995; ISTAT 1995, 1996a; Livi-Bacci 1994; Lori *et al.* 1995; Palomba 1991; Palomba *et al.* 1987; Volpi 1996.1 located several of these sources at the Statistics

Library of the University di Firenze. Dr. Livi-Baoci graciously gave me permission to use the library in the Department of Statistics and provided me with the names of important Italian demographers whose work informed my research. I shared with Dr. Livi-Bacci the abstract of a paper entitled "Writing Against Demography" (Krause 1996). and hence made him aware of my critical sensibilities. We are both well aware of the difficult challenge of interdisciplinary work between demography and sociocultural anthropology though valiant attempts have been made recently (see edited volumes by Greenhalgh 1995; Kertzer and Fricke 1997). I am also aware that much of my knowledge about the structure of Italian society would not be possible without the statistically-grounded, hard work of demographers.

9. On indexicality, see in particular Ochs (1990) as well as Silverstein (1976) and Mertz (1985). Ochs' distinction between direct and indirect indexicality has been fruitfully developed by Hill (1999:683), who has applied it to her work on Mock Spanish. She suggests nonnative Spanish speakers' use of Mock Spanish directly indexes the speaker's "congenial persona"; however, indirectly the usage indexes pejorative aspects that are essentially racist and never acknowledged.

10. This language was common to the Princeton Fertility Project (see Coale and Watkins 1986). Such dichotomies between modern/rational and traditional/irrational appear in Livi-Bacci (1977:244, 257), which Schneider and Schneider have discussed (1991:891). Note the assumption of rationality in Livi-Bacci's description of the fertility of five villages in central Italy from the 17th to 19th centuries compared with Hutterite fertility in 1921–30: "The fertility of the five villages is sensibly lower than that of the Hutterites, but within the normal range found in the studies concerning populations of the 17th to 19th centuries, and still apparently untouched by voluntary control of fertility" (Livi-Bacci 1977:13). The Hutterites are the population whose known maximum fertility rates led it to be used in the Princeton Fertility Project; fertility of a given population was presented as a percentage of the Hutterites' since it was the highest on record (Livi-Bacci 1977:56). Furthermore, that demographers viewed "controlled" fertility as "rational" fertility is clear in statements such as the following: "Six children per woman are, undoubtedly, a heavy burden," (Livi-Bacci 1977:90). Looking back from how children in Italy in the 1970s or 1990s are reared, yes, six seems burdensome. But a 19th- century peasant woman in a rigid hierarchical system of patriarchy lived according to a different set of affective and caretaking relations, and six children meant something very different in the 1870s than it did in the 1970s (see Barbagli 1988:25; Saraceno 1996:145). Disciplinary frameworks can blind us from the logics of specific cultural systems.

11. These notions are based in linear evolutionary modernization models, as Greenhalgh (1995a:5–6) discusses. See also Greenhalgh's essay on the history of demographic science (1996).

12. When I delivered an earlier draft of this article at the University of Massachusetts in February 2000, I was blatantly pregnant and well into my 34th week of gestation. I interrupted the question, "Who is engaging in this hard refusal to procreate if not women?" with an under-the-breath "obviously not me." I felt then, as I do now, that this jocular moment broke some kind of tension related to a *perceived* discrepancy between discourse (what I was saying) and practice (what my body was showing). The scene played on the very critique of rationality I have tried to make throughout this article.

13. I have only ever seen female cohorts used to calculate standard demographic indicators, such as total fertility rate. This term refers to the average number of children born to a woman during her lifetime. See the glossary of the Population Reference Bureau or the 2000 World Population Data Sheet, http://www.prb.org.

14. See Wolf 1982, in particular chapter 3, in which he defines capitalist, tributary, and kin-ordered modes of production as the three modes that offer utility for revealing "the strategic relationships involved in the deployment of social labor by organized human pluralities" (1982:76).

15. After I wrote this, I came across Arturo Escobar's phrasing of a similar idea: "Foucault's work on the dynamics of discourse and power in representation of social reality, in particular, has been instrumental in unveiling the mechanisms by which a certain order of discourse produces permissible modes of being and thinking while disqualifying and even making others impossible" (Escobar 1995:5).

16. An interesting discussion of the policy implications of feminist and neo-Malthusian alliances can be found in Hodgson and Watkins (1997).

17. Pescarolo (1991:35) details the labor strikes of 1896.

18. Archivio del Comune di Carmignano, Censimento Generale della Popolazione del Regno D'Italia, Provincia di Firenze, Frazione di Poggio A Caiano, 1901.

19. This idea is expressed in Geertz's (1988:84) analysis of the shock waves that reverberated after the publication of Malinowski's diaries in 1967.

20. Taylor and Rebel (1981) offer an excellent discussion of peasant interpretations. Their detailed symbolic analysis of folk tales suggests the telling of tales were peasant women's responses to family disruption in the face of the state's drafting of their disinherited sons. See also Roseberry's (1989:27–28) discussion of their analysis.

21. Italians are highly aware of the declining birthrate and have been at least since the early 1980s. Results of a comparative survey conducted between 1983–84 in Italy and the Netherlands found that 93 percent of the Italians and 63 percent of the Dutch knew that the birthrate had been declining. The more aware a population was of declining birthrates, the more it viewed the trend negatively. The study's authors underscored this important difference: In Italy, about 2.5 times as many respondents evaluated the birth decline negatively; in the Netherlands, there was a very high percentage of

people (40 percent versus 10 percent in Italy) who were "indifferent to the problem." (Palomba *et al.* 1987:8). The findings were published by the Council of Europe and affiliated with the European Population Committee, whose stated goal is to "promote better understanding of demographic implications at all levels of political decision making."

22. The noun *gente* means people, and the suffix *-ella* indicates a negative, a lack. In this particular context, the word indexes material lack and likely points to a peasant past, a time in which commodities and education were scarce.

23. The so-called Southern Question, which in the 19th century was framed as a question of racial inferiority, has been a topic of discussion in Italy since the Italian nation was unified in 1861. As Gramsci noted.

24. The poverty of the Mezzogiorno was historically "inexplicable" for the popular masses in the North; they did not understand that the unity had not taken place on a basis of equality, but as hegemony of the North over the Mezzogiorno in a territorial version of the town-country relationship—in other words, that the North concretely was an "octopus" which enriched itself at the expense of the South, and that its economic-industrial increment was in direct proportion to the impoverishment of the economy and the agriculture of the South. [Gramsci 1971:70–71]

25. So, the Northerner reasoned, if the Southerners hadn't been able to improve their economic condition after liberation from the Bourbons, this meant the causes of poverty were to be found in some innate deficiencies. Continues Gramsci: "There only remained one explanation—the organic incapacity of the inhabitants, their barbarity, their biological inferiority" (1971:71). Nineteenth-century sociologists of positivism led credence to such biological-determinist popular positions with their scientific claims of truths. "Thus a polemic arose between North and South on the subject of race." Gramsci writes, "and about the superiority or inferiority of North and South" (Gramsci 1971:70–71).

26. Elsewhere (Krause 1998), I use a discourse-centered approach to analyze racism and compare in greater depth the "new" racism against non-European immigrants and "old" forms of racism against Southern Italians. I originally explored this theme in a 1995 seminar on "Language and Racism" with Jane Hill at the University of Arizona; see Hill 1993 and 1999. Recent works in English on Italian racism are Carter 1997, and Cole 1998. In Italian, see Palanca 1999. Gramsci (1971.70–71) discusses notions of "biological inferiority" and makes convincing links to 19th-century positivist sociology and the Southern question.

27. Public opinion about demographic events "is very much influenced" by daily newspapers and periodicals, according to Palomba and Righi (1993:10), authors of a booklet that examines media reportage of demographic trends.

28. Some scholars writing on racism in Europe have used the term neo-racism (see in particular Balibar 1991a, 1991b) to distinguish between old and new forms, the latter glossed as somehow more "polite" because of supposed grounding in cultural differences and relatively less vulgar discourse; other scholars, however, have sought to avoid using an old versus new distinction because they perceive no fundamental difference between the various forms of racism (Miles 1993). Sorting out the debates over old and new forms of racism is beyond the scope of this article.

29. Interview originally published in *L'Espresso,* July 1990.

30. For an overview of migration in Italy, see Petrillo 1999; di Maio 2001 offers a compassionate view of Italian immigrants through recent immigrant literature.

31. Thanks to Massimo Bressan, anthropologist and former director of IRIS, Istituto di Ricerche e Interventi Sociali. a social-economic research institute in Prato, for providing me with this article.

32. I first read this phrase in Cuddihy 1987.

33. The acronym stands for Consiglio nazionale delle ricerche.

34. *L'Unità,* October 29.1996. "Allarme dei demografi: a causa della natality sotto zero spariranno centinaia di cittadine italiane; Solo vecchi, via 400 paesi" and "Vecchi, pochi e spreconi" were the headlines for the articles on the population conference.

35. My thanks to Enoch Page for this reference.

36. The well-known phrase "imagined community" comes from Anderson (1991). There is by now a rich literature on the anthropology of ethnicity and the nation-state. The review essay by Alonso (1994) provides an excellent entry point.

37. In an essay exploring how knowledge is constructed in science, Joan Fujimura points out, "The stakes in the authoritarian battles are high" (1998:357). A fascinating case of the political use of statistics can be found in the language and culture struggles of the Basque country (Urla 1993). My critical reading of the way demographers represent populations has undeniably been shaped by Foucault (1972, 1978).

38. A great deal of scholarship has been produced on the fascist demographic campaign. See de Grazia 1992; Horn 1994; Krause 1994; Passerini 1987; Whitaker 2000.

39. In an effort to contribute to the "untangling of the complexity of racism." Hill (1999:681) suggests that we explore questions such as, "What are the different kinds of racializing discourses?" and "in what kinds of contexts" do they occur? I came across her questions as 1 was revising this article and was reconvinced by my own argument that demographic discourses now circulating in Italy and elsewhere in Europe, as well as in the United States, have powerful racializing effects. See the *New York Times* 1998.

40. This goal does not preclude collaborations that have recently been suggested between demographers and anthropologists (e.g., Hammel and Friou 1997; Kertzer 1997; Kertzer and Fricke 1997). It does, however, require that such collaborations allow for critical reflection.

REFERENCES CITED

Alonso, Ana Maria. 1994. The Politics of Space, Time and Substance: State Formation, Nationalism and Ethnicity. Annual Review of Anthropology 23:379–405.

Anagnost, Ann. 1995. A Surfeit of Bodies: Population and the Rationality of the State in Post-Mao China. In Conceiving the New World Order: The Global Politics of Reproduction. Faye D. Ginsburg and Rayna Rapp. eds. Pp. 22–41. Berkeley: University of California Press.

Anderson, Benedict. 1991. Imagined Communities: Reflections on the Origin and Spread of Nationalism. London: Verso.

Angel-Ajani, Asale. 2000. Italy's Racial Cauldron: Immigration. Criminalization and the Cultural Politics of Race. Cultural Dynamics 12(3):331–352.

Bakhtin, Mikhail. 1981. The Dialogic Imagination. Austin: University of Texas Press.

——1984. Discourse in Dostoevsky. In Theory and History of Literature, vol. 8. Problems of Dostoevsky's Poetics. Caryl Emerson, ed. Pp. 181–269. Minneapolis: University of Minnesota Press.

Balibar, Etienne. 1991a[1988] Is There a "Neo-Racism"? In Race, Nation, Class: Ambiguous Identities. Etienne Balibar and Immanuel Wallerstein, eds. Chris Turner, trans. Pp. 17–28. London: Verso.

——1991b Es Gibt Keinen Staat in Europa: Racism and Politics in Europe Today. New Left Review 186:5–19.

Barbagli, Marzio. 1988 Sotto lo stesso tetto: Mutamenti della famiglia in Italia dal XV al XX secolo. 2nd edition. Bologna: II Mulino.

Becattini, Giacomo. 1986 Riflessioni sullo sviluppo socio-economico della Toscana in questa dopo-guerra. In Storiad'Italia. Le Regioni dall'Unità ad Oggi. La Toscana. Pp. 901–926. Torino.

——1998 The Development of Light Industry in Tuscany: An Interpretation. In Regional Development in a Modern European Economy: The Case of Tuscany. Robert Leonardi and Raffaella Y. Nanetti, eds. Pp. 77–94. London: Pinter.

Bongaarts, John. 1998 Demographic Consequences of Declining Fertility. Science 282:419–420.

Carter, Donald Martin. 1997 States of Grace: Senegalese in Italy and the New European Immigration. Minneapolis: University of Minnesota Press.

Coale, Ansley J., and Susan C. Watkins. 1986 The Decline in Fertility in Europe. Princeton, NJ: Princeton University Press.

Cole, Jeffrey. 1998 The New Racism in Europe: A Sicilian Ethnography. Cambridge: Cambridge University Press.

Contini, Giovanni, and Gian Bruno Ravenni. 1987 Giovani, Scolarizzazione e Crisi della Mezzadria: San Gersolè (1920–1950). La Storia delle Famiglie attraverso i Diari Scolastici e le Fonti Orali. Annali dell'Istituto "Alcide Cervi" 9.145–170.

Cuddihy, John Murray. 1987 The Ordeal of Civility: Freud, Marx, Levi-Strauss and the Jewish Struggle with Modernity. Boston: Beacon Press.

de Grazia, Victoria. 1992 How Fascism Ruled Women: Italy 1922–1945. Berkeley: University of California Press.

di Maio, Alessandra. 2001 Immigration and National Literature: Italian Voices from Africa and the Diaspora. In The Mediterranean Passage: Migration and New Cultural Encounters in Southern Europe. Russell King, ed. Pp. 146–161. Liverpool: Liverpool University Press.

Escobar, Arturo. 1995 Encountering Development: The Making and Unmaking of the Third World. Princeton, NJ: Princeton University Press.

Foucault, Michel. 1972 The Discourse on Language. In The Archaeology of Knowledge. Pp. 215–238. New York: Pantheon Books.

——1978 The History of Sexuality, vol. 1. New York: Vintage Books.

Friedman, Thomas. 1997 The Hot Zones. New York Times, Feb. 12:A12.

Fujimura, Joan. 1998 Authorizing Knowledge in Science and Anthropology. American Anthropologist 100(2):347–360.

Geertz, Clifford. 1988 Works and Lives: The Anthropologist as Author. Stanford, CA: Stanford University Press.

Gibson, Mary. 1998 Biology or Environment: Race and Southern "Deviancy" in the Writings of Italian Criminologists, 1880-1920. In Italy's "Southern Question": Orientalism in One Country. Jane Schneider, ed. Pp. 99–115. Oxford: Berg.

Gillis, John R., Louise A. Tilly, and David Levine. eds.. 1992 The European Experience of Declining Fertility, 1850–1970: The Quiet Revolution. Cambridge: Blackwell.

Gilroy, Paul. 1991 Ain't No Black in the Union Jack: The Cultural Politics of Race and Nation. Chicago: University of Chicago Press.

Ginsborg, Paul. 1990 A History of Contemporary Italy. Society and Politics, 1943–1988. London: Penguin Books.

Goldberg, David Theo. 1993 The Social Formation of Racist Discourse. In Anatomy of Racism. David Theo Goldberg, ed. Pp. 295–318. Minneapolis: University of Minnesota Press.

Golini, Antonio. 1991 Introduction. In Crescita Zero. Rossella Palomba, ed. Pp. vii–xv. Scandicci (Firenze): La Nuova Italia.

——Prefazaione. In Tendenze demografiche e politiche per la popolazione. Terzo rapporto IRP sulla situazione demografica Italiana. Antonio Golini, ed. Pp. 7–12. Milan: II Mulino.

Golini, A., A. De Simoni, and F. Citoni, eds.. 1994 Tre scenari per il possibile sviluppo della popolazione delle regioni Italiane al 2044. Roma: Consiglio Nationale delle Ricerche, Istituto di Ricerche sulla Popolazione.

Gramsci, Antonio. 1971 Selections from the Prison Notebooks. New York: International Publishers.

Greenhalgh, Susan. 1995a Anthropology Theorizes Reproduction: Integrating Practice, Political Economic, and Feminist Perspectives. In Situating Fertility. Susan Greenhalgh, ed. Pp. 3–28. Cambridge: Cambridge University Press.

——1995b The Power in/of Population. Current Anthropology 36(5):875–878.

——The Social Construction of Population Science: An Intellectual. Institutional, and Political History of 20th-century Demography. Comparative Studies in Society and History 38:26–66.

Greenhalgh, Susan, ed. 1995 Situating Fertility: Anthropology and Demographic Inquiry. Cambridge: Cambridge University Press.

Hammel, E. A., and Diana S. Friou. 1997 Anthropology and Demography: Marriage, Liaison, or Encounter? In Anthropological Demography. David I. Kertzer and Tom Fricke, eds. Pp. 175–200. Chicago: University of Chicago Press.

Hill, Jane H..1993 Hasta la Vista, Baby: Anglo Spanish in the American Southwest. Critique of Anthropology 13:145–176.

——1995 The Voices of Don Gabriel: Responsibility and Self in a Modern Mexicano Narrative. In The Dialogic Emergence of Culture. Dennis Tedlock and Bruce Mannheim, eds. Pp. 97–147. Urbana: University of Illinois Press.

——1999 Language, Race, and White Public Space. American Anthropologist 100(3): 680-689.

Hodgson, Dennis, and Susan Cotts Watkins. 1997 Feminists and Neo-Malthusians: Past and Present Alliances. Population and Development Review 23(3):469–523.

Horn, David G. 1994 Social Bodies: Science, Reproduction, and Italian Modernity. Princeton, NJ: Princeton University Press.

II Sole 24 Ore. 1995 L'Annuario statistica 1995 scava negli aspetti più nascosti del paese; L'Istat vede un'Italia che non fa figli e sempre spaccata tra Nord e Sud. Section: Politica Italiana. Dec. 24.

Instituto Nazionale di Statistico. 1995 Annuario statistico italiano 1994.

——1996a Famiglia. abitazioni, servizi di pubblica utilita Indagini Multiscopo sulle fa- miglie Anni 1993–1994, Aspetti della vita quotidiana-111. Argomenti No. 6. Roma: lstituto Nazionale di Statistica.

——1996b Toscana: Informazioni Utili. Firenze: Emilcomp.

——2000 La popolazione straniera residente in Italia al 1° gennaio. Electronic document, http://www.istat.it/Anotizie/Aaltrein/statinbrev/strares.html, accessed June 2001.

Italian Journal. 1998 The Economist: a Survey of the Italian Economy 1:31–48

Kertzer, David I.. 1997 Qualitative and Quantitative Approaches to Historical Demography. Population and Development Review 23(4):839–846.

Kertzer, David I., and Tom Fricke. 1997 Toward an Anthropological Demography. In Anthropological Demography David I. Kertzer and Tom Fricke, eds. Pp. 1–35. Chicago: University of Chicago Press.

Krause, Elizabeth L. 1994 Forward vs. Reverse Gear: Politics of Proliferation and Resistance in the Italian Fascist State. Journal of Historical Sociology 7(3) 261–288.

——1996 Writing Against Demography: Anthropological Contributions to Understanding Fertility Decline in a Post-Mezzadrile Tuscan Economy. Paper Presented at the Italian Association for Ethno-Anthropological Science. (A.E.S.H.A.). University of Rome, La Sapienza, December 6, 1996.

——1998 Social Memory. Demographic Discourse and Shifting Whiteness in the "New" Racism of Italy. Paper presented at the Comparative Culture and Literary Studies. "Cultures in Conflict" conference. University of Arizona. Feb. 27–28, 1998.

——1999 Natalism and Nationalism: The Political Economy of Love. Labor and Low Fertility in Central Italy. Ph.D. dissertation. Department of Anthropology. The University of Arizona.

La Nazione. 1996 Culle più vuote. VItalia cresce solo per l'apporto degli immigrati. La Nazione, June 27: 7.

La Repubblica. 1999 Coppie milanesi, fate figli vi diamo un milione al mese. La Repubblica. May 5: 30.

La Stampa. 1997 Italia? Vecchia e senza bambini. Economia and Finanza. La Stampa. July 25: 17.

Labov, William. 1972 The Transformation of Experience in Narrative Syntax. In Language in the Inner City: Studies in the Black English Vernacular. Pp. 354–396. Philadelphia: University of Pennsylvania Press.

Livi-Bacci. Massimo. 1977 A History of Italian Fertility: During the Last Two Centuries Princeton. NJ. Princeton University Press.

——1994 lntroduzione. In Tendenze demografiche e politiche per la popolazione. Terzo rapporto IRP sulla situazione demografica italiana Antonio Golini. ed. Pp. 13–16. Milan: II Mulino.

Lori, Agostino, Antonio Golini, and Bruno Cantalini, eds. 1995 Atlante dell'invecchiamento della popolazione. Roma: Consiglio Nazionale delle Ricerche.

L'Unità. 1996 Allarme dei demografi: a causa della natality sotto zero spariranno centinaia di cittadine italiane; Solo vecchi, via 400 paesi; Vecchi, pochi e spreconi. October 29.

Malcomson, Scott. 1995 On European Union. Transitions 5(4):4–12.

Martiniello, Marco, and Paul Kazim. 1991 Italy: Two Perspectives. Racism Is No Paradise! Racism in Paradise? Race and Class 32(3):79–89.

Menniti, Adele, Rossella Palomba, and Linda Laura Sabbadini. 1997 Italy: Changing the Family from Within. In Family Life and Family Policies in Europe, vol. 1. Structures and Trends in the 1980s. Franz-Xaver Kaufmann. Anton Kuijsten, Hans-Joachim Schulze, and Klaus Peter Strohmeier, eds. Pp. 223–252 Oxford: Clarendon Press.

Mertz, Elizabeth. 1985 Beyond Symbolic Anthropology: Introducing Semiotic Mediation. In Semiotic Mediation: Sociocultural and Psychological Perspectives. Elizabeth Mertz and Richard Parmentier, eds. Pp. 1–19. Orlando, FL: Academic Press.

Miles, Robert. 1993 Racism after "Race Relations." London: Routledge.

Miner, Horace. 1956 Body Ritual among the Nacirema. In Applying Cultural Anthropology: An Introductory Reader. Aaron Podolefsky and Peter J. Brown, eds. Pp. 18–21. Mountain View, CA: Mayfield Publishing Co.

Moore, Henrietta L.. 1994 A Passion for Difference: Essays in Anthropology and Gender. Bloomington: Indiana University Press.

New York Times. 1996 North-South Divide in Italy, a Problem for Europe, Too. New York Times, November 15.

——1996 Hispanic Births in U.S. Reach Record High. New York Times, February 13.

Ochs, Elinor. 1990 Indexicality and Socialization. In Cultural Psychology. James Stigler, Richard A. Shweder, and Gilbert Herdt, eds. Pp. 287–308. Cambridge: Cambridge University Press.

Ochs, Elinor, Clotilde Pontecorvo, and Alessandra Fasulo. 1996 Socializing Taste. Ethnos 61(1–2):7–46.

Palanca, Vaifra. 1999 Guida al pianeta immigrazione. Manuali del Cittadino. Roma: Editori Riuniti.

Palomba, Rossella. 1991 Crescita Zero. Scandicci (Firenze): La Nuova Italia.

Palomba, Rossella, Adele Menniti, and Maura Misiti. 1999 6 Milliardi: Il Puntodi Vista degli Italiani. Consiglio nazionale delle Ricerche. Istituto di Ricerche Sulla Popolazione (IRP). Electronic document, http://www.irp.rm.cnr.it/comstamp/6miliardi.html, accessed December 8.

Palomba, R., A. Menniti, A. Mussino, and H. Moors. 1987 Attitudes Towards Demographic Trends and Population Policy. A Comparative Multi-Analysis of Survey Results from Italy and the Netherlands. Consiglio Nazionale delle Ricerche, Working Paper. Prepared for the European Population Conference, Finland, 1987.

Palomba, Rossella, and A. Righi. 1993 Information and Education in Demography. Netherlands: Council of Europe. Passerini, Luisa

——1987 Fascism in Popular Memory: The Cultural Experience of the Turin Working Class. Cambridge: Cambridge University Press.

Patriarca, Silvana. How Many Italies? Representing the South in Official Statistics. In Italy's "Southern Question": Orientalism in One Country. Jane Schneider, ed. Oxford: Berg.

Pescarolo, Alessandra. 1991 Lavoro, Protesta, Identity Le Trecciaiole fra Otto e Novecento. In 11 Proletariat Invisibile: La Manifattura della Paglia nella Toscana Mezzadrile (1820–1950). Alessandra Pescarolo and Gian Bruno Ravenni, eds. Pp. 23–121. Milano: Franco Angeli.

Petrillo, Agostino. Italy: Farewell to the "Bel Paese"? In The European Union and Migrant Labor. Gareth Dale and Mike Cole, eds. Pp. 231–262. Oxford: Berg.

Rebel, Hermann. 1989 Cultural Hegemony and Class Experience: A Critical Reading of Recent Ethnological-Historical Approaches (Part One). American Ethnologist 16 (1):117–136.

Roseberry, William. 1989 Balinese Cockfights and the Seduction of Anthropology. In Anthropologies and Histories: Essays in Culture, History and Political Economy. Pp. 17–29. New Brunswick, CT: Rutgers University Press.

1994 Hegemony and the Language of Contention. In Everyday Forms of State Formation: Revolution and the Negotiation of Rule in Modern Mexico. Gilbert Joseph and Daniel Nugent, eds. Pp. 355–366. Durham, NC: Duke University Press.

Saraceno, Chiara. 1990 Women, Family and the Law, 1750–1942. Journal of Family History 15(4): 427–442.

——1996 Sociologia della Famiglia. Bologna. Il Mulino.

Schneider, Jane C., and Peter T. Schneider. 1991 Sex and Respectability in an Age of Fertility Decline: A Sicilian Case Study. 1996 Social Science Medicine 33(8):885–895. 1996 Festival of the Poor: Fertility Decline and the Ideology of Class in Sicily: 1860–1980. Tucson: University of Arizona Press.

Schneider, Jane. 1998 Introduction: The Dynamics of Neo-orientalism in Italy (1848–1995). In Italy's "Southern Question": Orientalism in One Country. Jane Schneider, ed. Pp. 1–23. Oxford: Berg.

Sen, Amartya. 1997 Population: Delusion and Reality. In The Gender/Sexuality Reader: Culture, History, Political Economy. Roger N. Lancaster and Micaela di Leonardo, eds. Pp. 89–106. New York: Routledge.

Silverstein, Michael. 1976 Shifters, Linguistic Categories and Cultural Description. In Meaning in Anthropology. Keith Basso and Henry Selby, eds. Pp. 11–55. Albuquerque: University of New Mexico Press.

Specter, Michael. 1998 Population Implosion Worries a Graying Europe. New York Times, July 10: A1.

Taylor, Peter, and Hermann Rebel. 1981 Hessian Peasant Women, Their Families, and the Draft: A Socio-Historical Interpretation of Four Tales from the Grimm Collection. Journal of Family History 6:347–378.

Urla, Jacqueline. 1993 Cultural Politics in an Age of Statistics: Numbers, Nations, and the Making of Basque Identity. American Ethnologist 20(4):818–843.

van Dijk, Teun A. 1993 Elite Discourse and Racism. London: Sage Publications.

Volpi, Roberto. 1996 Figli d'Italia: Quanti, quali e come alle soglie del Duemila. Bagno A Ripoli (Firenze): La Nuova Italia.

Werth, Manfred. 1991 Immigration of Citizens from Third Countries into the Southern Member States of the EEC: A Comparative Survey of the Situation in Greece, Italy, Spain, and Portugal. Commission of the European Communities; Isoplan Institute for Development Research, Economic and Social Planning. Luxembourg Supplement 1/91.

Whitaker, Elizabeth Dixon. 2000 Measuring Mamma's Milk: Fascism and the Medicalization of Maternity in Italy. Ann Arbor: University of Michigan Press.

Williams, Brackette. 1991 Stains on My Name, War in My Veins: Guyana and the Politics of Cultural Struggle. Durham, NC: Duke University Press.

Williams, Raymond. 1977 Marxism and Language. New York: Oxford University Press.

Wodak, Ruth, and M. Reisigl. 1999 Discourse and Racism: European Perspectives. Annual Review of Anthropology 28:175–199.

Wolf, Eric R.. 1969 Peasant Wars of the 20th Century. New York: Harper Colophon Books.

——1982 Europe and the People without History. Berkeley: University of California Press.

——1999 Envisioning Power: Ideologies of Dominance and Crisis. Berkeley; University of California Press

23

The Camera's Positioning

Brides, Grooms, and Their Photographers in Taipei's Bridal Industry

Bonnie Adrian

A s four decades of martial law drew to a close in Taiwan of the mid-1980s, consumer society took off. Taiwan had become a rich country, and with the green light given by the Republic of China's government, Taiwan's large middle class began shifting its emphasis from production to consumption. Among the most visible beneficiaries of this process were bridal photography salons (*hunsha sheying gongsi*). By the mid-1990s, a bridal salon package was a virtually unavoidable wedding expense. From elite wedding banquets catered by celebrity chefs at the island's finest banquet facilities to workers' and farmers' wedding banquets held outdoors and served on Styrofoam plates, it was nearly impossible to find a bride who did not have the help of a bridal salon in orchestrating her display. Moreover, bridal salon packages were becoming increasingly ostentatious with each passing year.

In 1997 Taipei, a minimal bridal package included one poster-sized framed enlargement (at least 36 inches tall); a heavy wooden album of at least two dozen photographs 15 inches in height each; a small, informal album containing the proof copies of all the photographs ordered by the couple; and one box of "thank you" photo cards for banquet guests. In addition to the photographs, a bare-bones bridal package included an extensive, professional makeover for the bride and a simpler styling for the groom; the use of six different gowns during the photo shoot; and rental of three more gowns for the wedding banquet. The photographs depict couples as cosmopolitan elites, dressed in white, Western bridal gowns and colorful Hollywood-inspired eveningwear. Bridal salons also throw in the occasional "Chinese imperial" outfit—perhaps self-Orientalizing—and other "just-for-fun" costumes like Japanese kimono, "French court" attire, KMT military uniforms, and U.S. baseball jerseys (see Adrian 2003: 108–111). A minimal package such as this had a price tag of about US$1,000 in the mid-1990s, but the middle-class consumers I interviewed in Taipei proclaimed that a minimal package had become déclassé.

Upgraded packages including *two* framed enlargements—one 36 inches and one 48 inches high—and 30 to 40 images 18 or 20 inches in height for the album and package add-ons such as the use of brand-new gowns and photo shoot excursions outside of the studio to scenic parks and upscale urban consumer destinations were common. I attended several weddings in which the couple purchased more photographs than one album could contain, and, thus, two full albums of 50 to 75 images were on display. Middle class, urban grooms with whom I spoke indicated that US$1,600 was about the least a man could get away with spending on photographs of his bride. Taipei's most upscale salons claimed that US$4,000 was the average spent by their elite customers.

Conspicuous consumption and weddings are frequent bedfellows worldwide. Vassos Argyrou (1996), in his work on Greek Cypriots, argues that many modern weddings, because they involve couples who are already adults in every respect except for having attained marriage, have ceased to serve as meaningful rites of passage. Often bride and groom have already established adult economic and sexual status by the time of marriage, leaving the wedding to serve primarily as a "rite of distinction" whereby families display their social status by deploying symbols of high class standing and inviting wide networks of kin, neighbors, coworkers, and friends to see and enjoy the status display. East Asians have by no means cornered the market on lavish weddings, as Cele Otnes and Elizabeth Pleck's (2003) study of weddings in the United States confirms. Nevertheless, weddings have attracted the attention of anthropologists throughout the region for their competitive consumption and interweaving of old and new symbols and practices (see Adrian 2003; Edwards 1989; Gillette 1999; Goldstein-Gidoni 1997; Kendall 1996; Wolf 1972). Photography is only one of the newer forms of status display at weddings in Taiwan. Lush banquet meals, extravagant jewelry and gown ensembles, showy floral arrangements, name-brand engagement cakes (*xibin*), and costly bride-price (*pinjin*) and dowry (*jiazhuang*) transfers also partake of the logic of keeping up with the Wangs (see Adrian 2003: ch. 4).

Given the myriad ways in which wealth can be displayed and status exaggerated, one wonders why so many couples in Taiwan want albums of 25, 50, even 75 portraits of themselves. The albums rarely include images of anyone other than the bride and groom. No parents, siblings, relatives, or friends are included. These wedding participants and other banquet guests are often the subject of wedding day informal snapshots, but bridal albums consist of page after page of the bride posed alone and with her groom, interrupted only by the occasional shot of the groom alone. The use of multiple costumes, varied studio backdrops and props, and scenic or otherwise interesting location shots serve to break up the photographic monotony. Also important are the varied hair and makeup styles, facial expressions, and feelings the photographer captures to enhance monotonous photo albums. Ideally, photo albums portray the bride in multiple personae more beautiful and more variable than is the woman herself. Frequently, the manipulations of stylists and photographers produce images in which the now-beautiful bride is virtually unrecognizable, an accomplishment that is both idealized and the subject of much behind-the-scenes joking (Adrian 2003: 225–256). Many women I interviewed, in fact, anticipated that their portraits, although highly constructed, would in the future serve as memories of who they once were.

What in the subjective experience of brides and grooms renders portraiture a valuable means of status competition? Once the groom's credit card has been swiped, how do these individual women and men take up the appearance of generic Brides and Grooms? When I asked, most men and women in Taipei told me that women's love of physical beauty drives the bridal industry's near-universal popularity and that bridal industry workers—dress consultants, hair and makeup stylists, and photographers—transform everyday women and men into beautiful Brides and captivated Grooms through their labors. In other words, I was told the reason why these Taiwanese bridal practices exist is due to innate, natural qualities of *individual* women (as distinct from social conditioning) while the answer to the how question is wholly *social:* Beauty professionals make women beautiful for a price. I find these answers inadequate—unable to handle the range of views and behaviors I observed during a year of field research in and around Taipei's bridal industry. *Positioning* provides a conceptual apparatus for examining processes by which individual subjectivity and behavior are mediated or shaped by cultural models and social relations (see Holland and Leander this issue; Holland *et al.* 1998). Acts of positioning undertaken by kin, friends, and acquaintances and furthered by bridal salon workers combine to produce consumers of bridal services—Brides and Grooms—whose self-presentations in wedding displays are not only remarkably vast but also remarkably uniform. Taipei's bridal industry depends on positioning in two ways that I analyze in this case study. First, diffuse positioning processes take place before brides and grooms ever set foot in a bridal salon; experiences in peer groups and their families set them up to want, even need, the bridal industry's products. Later, positioning takes place inside bridal salons; saleswomen, hair and makeup stylists, photographers, and photographers' assistants work to mold their clients' thoughts and feelings while they paint their faces, shape their hair, and pose their bodies. I will begin with a story that illustrates issues at stake in the positioning processes that deliver women and men into the hands of bridal industry workers, whose work I describe later.

POSITIONED TO DESIRE BEAUTY

Fang-jin returned to Taipei after earning a master's degree in women's studies from a university in California. When I met her, she was working as a feminist activist, lobbying legislators on family law issues. As we left her office and walked across the elite National Taiwan University campus on a blistering hot day, I felt the sun stinging my skin. Normally, I walked under a parasol as do most women in Taipei, who do so to prevent tanning. Fair skin is the mark par excellence of beauty there. When I had first lived in Taipei as a Chinese language student, I used only sunscreen lotion for protection and walked about the city without a parasol, like men do. Women chided me at bus stops and cast puzzled looks at me on street corners. When I became a field researcher, I at last decided to stop alienating the women around me by refusing to take up a parasol, a basic accoutrement of feminine comportment. Now an anthropologist ever desperate to find people willing to talk to me, I bought a flowery umbrella and took to the streets. Enjoying the shade of a parasol, I discovered, was far superior to braving the sun armed only with sunscreen lotion—sticky and sweaty. Then came my appointment with Fang-jin. With skin much too dark by local standards of femininity, Fang-jin seemed to be making a political point as she brazenly walked around town without parasol: There is much more to being a woman than the cultivation of lovely fair skin. Or, I later wondered, could it be that she, like me, had changed her style of comportment depending on context (see Gal 1987)? I cannot know her intentions but I knew my own: I was too embarrassed to take out the flowery fold-up tucked away in my bag because Fang-jin, sweat beading on her brow, braved the sun like one of the guys. I very much wanted to take cover but did not for fear of disrupting the image I imagined Fang-jin held of me. We were two feminists, positioning one another. My subjective preferences and overt actions were not in line.

When we arrived at a shaded, open-air cafe in an alleyway crowded with motor scooters, we ordered iced drinks fashionable among young people: milk teas filled with tapioca balls served with wide diameter straws for simultaneous sipping and chewing. Telling Fang-jin of my bridal industry research, I asked for her views on why the enormous photographs are so popular as to be virtually universal. We talked about how bridal salon workers whiten women's faces with makeup and photographic lighting effects, how they use slivers of tape to create the appearance of double eyelids (*shuangyanpi*), and how they use all manner of artificial means to transform women's hair (see Adrian 2003: ch. 5 for detailed discussion of current and historical beauty practices related to weddings in Taiwan; Eugenia Kaw [1994] describes double eyelid preference and surgery among Asian Americans). After displaying the portraits at wedding banquets, couples typically hang the poster-sized enlargement above their bed where their future children will ask, "Who is that pretty auntie with Daddy?" The photographs, Fang-jin noted, are very artificial. But, she added, "When I get married, even I will want bridal photographs." Why? Because although Fang-jin lacked heartfelt desire for the highly artificial photographs in and of themselves, she felt it would be too embarrassing to have a wedding without the photographs. Specifically, Fang-jin worried that her friends would assume that her relationship with her future groom lacked romance. Marriage—its meaning, purpose, and practice—changed rapidly in post-war Taiwan such that today there is a wide generation gap (*daigou*) in views on courtship and matrimony. Parents and grandparents push for an older approach to marriage that is reflected in the wedding rites they organize for their children: marriage is the transfer of a woman from one family to another for the purpose of producing patrilineal heirs and securing a host for the woman's spirit in death (see Stockard 1989). Through their large, lavish, and loud bridal photographs, the younger generation protests their elders' views on marriage even while they respectfully submit to its logic (Adrian 2003: chs. 3–4). In other words, Fang-jin did not feel an inner desire for the beauty the photographs deliver, but the appearance of romance the photographs provide was enough to turn this cultural critic into a bridal salon consumer, coated in whitening makeup and bedecked with false eyelashes for the coveted Western-baby (*yangwawa*) look.

M. M. Bakhtin's (1981) theory of dialogic speech describes how individuals produce works that are neither purely individual nor purely social in origin. The author, whether of a literary work or of a simple utterance, draws upon a variety of existing "languages" and recombines or "orchestrates" them into an individual statement. In my walk with Fang-jin, both actors had available competing cultural models. We both knew that either tanned or fair skin could be considered "beautiful" and that different modes of comportment—walking with or without a parasol—could be considered either tacky or barbaric, depending on the social context. Moreover, both of these cultural models take the form not of speech but of embodied habits that, much of the time, seem to come naturally, examples of what Pierre Bourdieu (1984) calls "habitus." I read the social context—my interview with a young Taiwanese feminist educated in the United States—and made my choice: to sweat and burn for fear of alienating Fang-jin. In other words, the "orchestration" work that went in to my actions was social in two distinct respects. First, I chose between two cultural modes of comportment (and two opposing views of tanned skin). Second, I made my choice based on my reading of a specific social interaction and of what I hoped to gain from it. What was unusual in this situation was my self-consciousness about it. I certainly went on many other walks through town with other interviewees when I was not at all self-conscious about my comportment. That is, much of the time I did what came "naturally" as result of having spent more than two years in Taipei.

Later in my interaction with Fang-jin when I asked if she envisioned herself commissioning a bridal photography package in her future, she may have undertaken a mental process similar to the one I went through in my decision about how to walk to the cafe. Had Fang-jin given me the most common answer I heard—that of course she will expect a bridal photography package because it is important to have images commemorating a "girl's" youthful beauty—the cultural origins of her words would have been evident. Both the ideas of photographic commemoration and youthful beauty are very widespread and both, indeed, are relatively new to Taiwanese society. These are not the ideas of an individual untouched by her social context. However, in her answer Fang-jin drew on a competing but nevertheless cultural viewpoint developed between and among highly educated feminists: Taiwanese bridal photography's obsession with physical beauty demeans women but its preoccupation with romance is politically safe and even positive in a social context where the specter of arranged marriage persists. At the same time, Fang-jin was probably assessing her relationship to me. What were her expectations and hopes for future relations between us? Did she worry that I might conduct similar discussions with others in her circle of friends and repeat what she had said? Did she hope that I might assist her in networking among feminist scholars in the United States? Bakhtin's model suggests that both the social and the individual—structure and agency—exist in every utterance, dialogically.

(1)

(2)

(3)

(4)

Figures 1–4. These photographs appear in one couple's bridal album. A variety of costumes, background, props, and poses is important, but unless the photographer can coax the subjects into portraying different feelings, the photographs become repetitive leading couples to buy a reduced number of portraits. Photo credit: Wu Yong-jie, 2002.

Though Fang-jin's analysis of Taiwan's bridal photography phenomenon separates beauty and romance, in fact, romance and beauty are profoundly interwoven in bridal albums by the simple fact that grooms pay for them. Most young women told me that they desired gorgeous bridal photographs to "commemorate" (*jinian*) their youth so that they could, in the future, show the photographs to children and grandchildren who, young women imagined, would have difficulty believing that an old woman was once young and beautiful. Men, by contrast, often expressed the view that bridal photographs are overpriced and fake. "Then why buy them?" I asked. Because "women love beauty," I was told. "And, besides," a young groom-to-be added, "no woman would agree to marry me if I didn't!" Rightly so, women told me, what kind of woman would marry a man who refused to give her beautiful photographs? That men find the photographs a waste of their time and money is *precisely* the point. Part of what makes the photographs romantic is the fact that women are able to extract them from reluctant men. Only a man in love is willing to waste so much money to fulfill a woman's fantasy to be celebrity for a day, to look more like a fashion model than like herself. By indulging the bride, the groom admits to weakness. If he is not in love, he is at least desperate enough to get married that he can be made to cater to a woman's desires. It is his *sacrifice* that is romantic; everyone knows that the images of him fawning over her in the photo studio were a photographer's idea, not the groom's.

Scholars writing on romance in the United States have argued that both in romance fiction and in courtship, romance temporarily subverts gender status hierarchies. In Dorothy Holland and Margaret Eisenhart's (1990) research on college students, women gained prestige among peers when they received romantic niceties such as gifts, expensive dates, and thoughtful attention from men without having to provide commensurate compensation to suitors with the thing that boosted men's prestige in the peer system, sexual intimacy with few social or emotional demands. Fictional representations of romance turn on a similar logic, according to literary critic Janice Radway (1984). The male characters romance fiction readers in Radway's study liked best were those who at, novel's onset, were fiercely independent and, therefore, emotionally unavailable; whether deeply absorbed in career pursuits or interested only in womanizing, their favored male heroes began as highly masculine in their staunch independence from women, whom the heroes deemed relevant only as dehumanized objects of sexual conquest. The climax in romance fiction comes when the hero, at long last, sacrifices his masculine identity by making a grand, public profession of his desperate love for the heroine. By the end of the novel the hero has come to appreciate a woman not as a sexual object but as a person, a transformation that leaves him less independent than he was at the beginning of the story. He is softened, feminized by his admission of emotional attachment. His loss of face is her gain.

These and other scholars point out, however, that if romance is a period of female dominance and male subjugation, the problem with romance is its temporary nature. Women's efforts to gain prestige in the college peer system studied by Holland and Eisenhart tended to solidify the derailment of their educational and career goals. Romance novels, meanwhile, end at or before the wedding because marriage tends to reverse the power relations of romance where feminine values and styles of expression prevail (see Cancian 1986,1987). Even in the present era of improved educational and career opportunities for many U.S. women, numerous studies have documented that in dual wage earning families women perform most of the household and childcare labor, leaving employed mothers to work a second shift (e.g., Hochschild 1989). The ephemerality of romance is precisely what makes it so compelling in the movies; culturally sanctioned and celebrated moments of female transcendence and masculine subjugation are in short supply in real life (Snitow 1983).

In unaware agreement with these North American feminist critics is Song-xiu, a Taipei photographer in his late 40s who has married, divorced, and remarried; he has thus paid for and posed in bridal photographs twice. Song-xiu told me that before marriage, the man must court the woman's esteem and attention. After marriage, it is the woman must court the man. The verb I am translating here as "court"—*qiu*—also means to seek or beg. Song-xiu argued that a wedding marks the transition between two opposing states, during which time the woman loses status while the man gains. Bridal photographs, therefore, represent the woman's "last time" in the dominant position, and that is why they celebrate and exaggerate female superiority. The huge, extravagant photographs allow the bride to go out with a bang rather than a whimper. When a soon-to-be-bride shows her new photo album to friends and colleagues, the size, number, and quality of the photographs speak not only to her groom's buying power but also to her power to command his attention and resources.

Many men and women I met in Taipei spoke in essentializing terms of women's inherent love of looking pretty as the driving force behind Taiwan's bridal industry, but their views overlook the external forces that position women either to enjoy their transcendence in bridal photography or, at least, act as though they do. The dominant alternative to demanding a bridal package in this cultural system is for a woman to accept low status for herself.

Among the minority of young women I found who were willing to face the status implications of marriage without a bridal photography package, all but a few were prevented from doing so by family members and friends. In these cases, it was often not that the bride held herself in poor esteem but, rather, that her self-view was in conflict with the ultrafeminine, highly artificial Beautiful Bride image that bridal salon stylists and photographers impose upon women. For example, in one family I know, the bride-to-be was intensely focused on her career. Her future mother-in-law anticipated that the bride and groom were likely to fail to commission bridal salon services and took matters into her own hands—quite literally positioning the young woman as a consumer of bridal services. The groom's mother selected a bridal salon, chose a package, and paid for it herself. Later, she announced what she had done. As the bride was merely disinterested in, not opposed to posing for bridal photographs, there was little incentive for the couple to refuse the gift and upset the groom's mother. Although this bride was exceptional, similar positioning processes affect even brides who eagerly drag their reluctant grooms around town to shop for the best salon. If there is little choice in the matter, why not at least enjoy it?

Given the status system I have described, one must ask why grooms are disinterested in bridal photography. It stands to reason that grooms, too, have something to gain through the status enhancements on offer. If a groom finds a bride who does not demand costly bridal portraits, would this not suggest that he has acquired a low-status bride? Men in Taipei today can frequently be heard complaining that Taiwanese women have become too strong or fierce (*xiong*), thus harming men's chances at forming marriages to their advantage. In particular, women in Taiwan are hotly contesting married men's pursuit of extramarital sex, and some career women brazenly insist on men's help with household and child-care tasks. A few men claim to get around the problem of fierce Taiwanese women by looking offshore to neighboring poorer countries for wives, especially in the People's Republic China where Taiwanese men's economic clout and high status is said to attract economically disadvantaged Chinese women eager to play the part of the passive wife (cf. Constable 2003). One would imagine that such marriages afford men the opportunity to avoid the bridal photography practices from which they often distance themselves. Yet, Ming-song, a Taiwanese man who married a woman from the People's Republic, not only commissioned a bridal package at a salon in Taiwan, he even went so far as to purchase a bridal album significantly larger than those possessed by any of the Taiwanese couples in his circle of friends. When I joined Ming-song and his new bride in a post-wedding gathering of his friends, Ming-song surprised the group by bringing along his gigantic bridal album. (Female friends and coworkers expect brides to lug their albums around town for showings as soon as possible on completion, frequently well before the wedding. It is less common for grooms to do the same.) His excitement over the enormous bridal album was palpable. He talked animatedly about the various locations they visited for the photo shoot. His very average-looking bride looked stunningly beautiful in the highly retouched photographs. It seems possible that Ming-song indulged by purchasing an exceptionally large bridal package to make up for his bride's comparatively low symbolic capital amongst his friends and family in Taiwan. Ming-song—and, perhaps, every groom—has much to gain through the purchase of bridal photography packages. Why then is this practice construed as a female preoccupation that men merely tolerate?

GROOMS AND THE ARTS OF RESISTANCE

Attention to the positioning practices that take place in bridal salons suggests one answer. In my attempts to chat up grooms in bridal salons, I found them to be "aggressively nonchalant" (see Abu-Lughod 1990). Most I approached declared themselves unsuitable interviewees by saying "bridal photography is for women." Grooms prepare for photo shoots by bringing along reading materials in anticipation of boredom. One of the largest Taipei bridal shops even has a men's waiting room stocked with reading materials, vending machines, and a television.

Grooms' reluctant behavior during the process might be construed as "everyday acts of resistance" (Scott 1985) to the bridal industry that casts the bride as a celebrity star (*mingxing*) and treats the groom as just one among many props designed to enhance the bride's glamour. James Scott's (1985,1990) theory of resistance turns on notions of "on stage" and "off stage" behavior, a conceptual apparatus deployed by Erving Goffman to different ends (e.g., see Goffman 1973). Scott argues, for example, that landless Malaysian peasants—whose access to income-generating work was diminished by the mechanization of farm labor—behaved very differently on stage and off stage. On stage, the farm workers paid landowners respect. Off stage, they resorted to vandalism and petty theft to enact their real views of landowners' engagement of modern farming technology, which improved landowner profits at the expense of landless workers. In other words, onstage actors perform socially prescribed scripts. Off stage, actors express their true thoughts/feelings. In this light, it seems possible that grooms avail themselves of opportunities to move off stage during photo shoots because they dislike the subservient role they are expected to play when on stage, that of yet another prop to enhance the bride's appearance. Unable to protest these social arrangements and still procure a Taiwanese wife, grooms resort to foot-dragging. Note, however, that this line of analysis assumes that social actors' inner experiences are not themselves socially positioned—a point to which I will return shortly (see also Holland *et al.* 1998: ch. 7).

If a groom appears on stage with an attitude of strong disinterest in the photo studio, he risks embarrassing his bride and encountering her anger. Amidst laughter, photographers and their assistants enthusiastically told me stories of uncooperative grooms whose real-life behavior belied their on-stage performances of romance. One groom, for example, posed for only one round of shots with his bride, leaving the bride to pose alone for the rest of the day. Another groom agreed to attend the entire photo shoot but fell asleep in the waiting room during the bride's makeover and refused to be roused, creating the appearance that he had been out carousing the night before. Yet another groom played his role well enough, but circumstances beyond his control changed his on-stage performance: A former girlfriend encountered the couple and their photographer shooting photographs on an outdoor location shoot. Claiming to be pregnant with the groom's child, she attacked the couple and tore the wedding gown.

If a groom appears *too* enthusiastic, however, he compromises his masculinity—for he appears too willing to be bossed around by his bride or overly interested in the feminine pursuit of making beautiful, romantic photographs. Men whose enthusiasm for bridal photography becomes apparent to male friends and colleagues endure taunts such as, "You're showing off your album just like a woman. You must *really* be in love with her!" Even bridal photographers who observe unusually enthusiastic grooms may gently comment how odd such behavior is, implying—inadvertently perhaps—that the groom may want to reconsider his stance. Enthusiastic grooms are problematic; their overt interest in bridal photography reduces some of the romantic tension wherein the groom's participation ought to be a sacrifice made for the bride. If he enjoys it more than she does, his willingness to indulge the bride appears self-serving.

When grooms demonstrate just the right amount of resistance, they enhance the romance of producing bridal photographs. In this light, it is not clear that men's tendency to read the newspaper on studio sidelines is a move off stage, expressive of men's "true" subjective experience of bridal shoots untouched by cultural expectations. Photo studio dynamics position men to be moderately disinterested, a failure in either direction poses problems. Most men manage to strike the balance appropriately, perhaps precisely because subjective experience of bridal shoots and cultural expectations form a feedback loop in which expectations produce culturally-approved sentiments and these sentiments reinforce expectations (see Rebhun 1993, 1999: ch. 1).

EMOTION AND THE GAZE

Bridal photo shoots are considered to be unpleasant for men because the production process feminizes them. Stylists, though they spend fivefold more time making up brides, style grooms, too—applying foundation make-up, meticulous hair styling, and vast quantities of hair spray. Photographers also nudge grooms out of their everyday masculine positions by displacing them from behind the camera and casting its gaze upon them.

Photography is a popular male hobby in Taipei. Virtually every man and woman in Taipei can operate an automatic camera, but far more men than women own and operate specialized photographic equipment and participate in camera clubs (cf. Bourdieu 1990). Not coincidentally, women are one of hobbyists' favored photographic subjects. Photography is also a common courtship activity with romantic implications: The couple goes to a scenic park where the man takes photographs of the woman, usually posing alone against the scenery. The man, looking at her through his viewfinder, demonstrates his appreciation for the woman's beauty by showering her with his photographic attentions. His ability to create a beautiful image of her also reflects his innermost opinions about her. A mid-1990s Taiwan television commercial captured the cultural model that associates romance with photography well. A man takes photographs of his girlfriend on generic film and the resulting photographs are poor. The woman, angered by the photographs, throws them at him and turns her back. When he shoots a new set of photos of her on name-brand film, the results are beautiful and the woman embraces him lovingly in response. (These constructions of photography may sound familiar to non-Taiwanese readers because cultural ideas about photography are subject to transnational flows. Understandings and practices of photography in Taiwan are much influenced by Japanese and U.S. photographers as well as by multinational companies such as Kodak and Fuji, through their advertising and publications.)

In professional photo shoots where the quality of the resulting photographs makes or breaks the salon's profit margin, photographers strive to control not only what goes on behind the camera (lighting, exposure time, type of focus, film characteristics) but also everything that goes on in front of the camera. Photographers and their assistants must manipulate the subjects' bodies with intense attention to detail, making sure that every foot and hand is perfectly placed and taking care that the bride's earrings hang symmetrically and enough makeup covers her chest and neck to conceal the redness that develops with nervousness. Photographers must also focus the same kind of attention on manipulating the bride and groom's emotions. No amount of perfection in costuming and posing can make up for displeasing facial expressions by them. The same is certainly true for professional photo shoots in other cultural contexts. Comparing my own experience of wedding portrait photography in the United States to shoots I observed in Taiwan, a key difference is the amount of time spent on producing perfect portraits. The pace of the two hours I spent posing for wedding portraits that included the shuffling of many friends and family members in and out of the camera's gaze did not allow for the level of attention to detail that is common in Taiwan where shoots last all day. Moreover, because Taiwanese bridal albums typically do not picture anyone but bride and groom, the demand for a diversity of facial expressions is especially high there. Nevertheless, my description of photo shoots need not be read as exclusive to Taiwan.

Once a scene and pose are set up just right, the photographer talks to the bride and groom from behind his camera, cooing in gentle tones, *"Lovely,* you're beautiful, just beautiful. Groom, *smile* a little bit. Bride, look at the camera, look up a little bit, not too much! Relax a little. Perfect. Now don't you move! Perfect. Beautiful. One-two-three!" Photographers' talk is peppered with elements of baby talk—the tones more sing-songy, the pitch higher, the mood overly enthusiastic, commands softened with diminutives like "a little bit" (*yi dian*), word repetition, and sentences finished in softening "ah" sounds. This style of presentation is known as "sweet talk" (described as *hong hong de*), used especially for talking to small children or beloved pets. When spoken to an adult, sweet talk conveys a sense of intimacy and, sometimes, of hierarchical relations, for it evokes the image of a parent speaking to a child. Lovers often speak to one another this way in private settings, conveying intimacy and nurturing.

When I asked photographers about their propensity for sweet talk, they expressed instrumental motives. Most explicitly, the purpose is to direct the subject's pose from afar. The assistant has set up most of the pose, now assistant and photographer must be out of the way of the lens. Only bride and groom are left on stage, bright lights in their eyes, trying to hold their bodies in awkward poses without looking too stiff, trying to produce natural-looking facial expressions even while anticipating the flash of light to come and repressing the urge to blink. The photo shoot context renders the majority of brides and grooms nervous (*jinzhang*), especially at first (this itself is an example of the effect of social context on subjective experience). Photographers anticipate their nervousness and work to mitigate it. The photographer uses his or her voice to soothe them while directing their posing as if by remote control. The camera, perched on a large rolling stand, sits behind the lights, in the darkness of the studio. Because bride and groom have their eyes fixed on a designated object and cannot see the photographer's face clearly, the photographer's voice carries the weight of the interaction between them. Photographers explained to me that they must be careful not to sound too direct or harsh, which might make the couple feel inadequate and even more nervous. To avoid this, they sweet-talk their subjects.

Coaxing clients to behave rather unlike themselves (and still look "natural") requires a complex set of skills. Photographers use the word "communication" (*goutong*) as a gloss for the work they do in controlling and bringing out the subject's feelings, sometimes talking about their work as the management of emotion, though Arlie Hochschild (1983) might call this "the commercialization of human feeling." Most reported that they do so by focusing on the personal details offered by bride and groom during the preshoot meeting, honing in on public markers of identity to infer personality characteristics and forge common bonds with their clients to help them feel at ease in the studio. Photographers thus make references to their occupations or personal backgrounds to make them feel understood: "You're in public relations, you're not a shy person! Let's see you smile." Photographers also search for personal connections—a bride who works as a bank teller may be told that the photographer's sister, too, works for a bank. The pair, hence, has something in common to discuss: "Do you work in the bank's headquarters or a branch office? My sister works in a branch office and tells me that the pay there is disproportionately low in her bank. How about yours?" The photographer thus seeks to establish personal relations with clients from early in the day. Having demonstrated what appears to be a willingness to view clients as more than just clients, the photographer proceeds to work his or her way inward to call forth particular emotions. Depending on the desired mood for a group of photos, the photographer may try to make a woman feel glamorous, sophisticated, cute, or demure. Using words that connote the desired feeling and describing images for the couple to visualize as they pose, photographers work to photograph very different "feelings" (*ganjue*). (See Figures 1–4.[1])

Xiao-yu, a single bridal photographer in her early 30s, described an incident when her attempt to elicit emotion from a bride went too far. The bride was one of the very small minority who invite parents to pose in a few photos for the bridal album. As the bride and her mother were primped for the shoot, Xiao-yu talked about how sad it is to leave one's home at marriage. This photographer had hoped to show a bride and her mother's culturally honored sadness in some photographs. With the daughter dressed as a bride (perhaps beginning to feel the part and causing her mother to feel the part, too), both mother and daughter became more than a little sad. Not only did their tears create a dilemma for the makeup artist, but the bride also remained pensive for the rest of the shoot, even after her mother went home. The photographer had been *too* successful at positioning her subjects, so much that the photographs were so cheerless as to be unusable.

Figures 1–4. These photographs appear in one couple's bridal album. A variety of costumes, background, props, and poses is important, but unless the photographer can coax the subjects into portraying different feelings, the photographs become repetitive leading couples to buy a reduced number of portraits. Photo credit: Wu Yong-jie, 2002.

Photographers frequently complained to me of subjects who are so introverted (*neixiang*) that it is nearly impossible to get them to come out of their shells enough to look "natural" in poses and express feeling on their faces. It seems to me that the problem of shy subjects is actually a problem of the genre of photographs and the importance to studios of selling a great many photos. If a couple is reluctant to take up poses that are lively (*huopo*), sexy (*xinggan*), or cute (*ke-ai*), the photographer's repertoire of varied shots is diminished. Couples are not likely to buy more than their package's base number of photographs if all of their shots are similar in facial expression and pose, and photographers know that a cute pose with a deadpan facial expression will not sell. The most successful bridal photographers are not necessarily most talented at manipulating lights and camera but rather are those most adept at "positioning" brides and grooms—at evoking feeling states such as sophistication, tenderness, liveliness, sexiness, and cuteness in the photo studio.

In their positioning work, photographers strive to conceal the fact that this is, indeed, work. Most clients have little talent for what Hochschild (1983) describes as "surface acting." Photographers therefore work to direct their clients into states of "deep acting" as much as possible, positioning clients to express genuine, spontaneous feelings rather than acting them out self-consciously. The bride's makeup and hair transformations that accompany costume changes help to shift the mood for each round of shots, and the photographer furthers that process through speech and action. For example, if the bride has changed into a yellow, "cute" gown, the photographer may try to elicit feelings of cuteness by playfully volleying an inflated Japanese cartoon character back and forth in the studio. By acting childish to set the scene, the photographer hopes to create an inner experience of fun in the couple. Though he or she may shoot a few frames while they play, the primary intention is to evoke the right mood in them before posing them for a sellable shot. For contrast, if the bride changes into a straight, sexy gold lame gown, the photographer may speak to the couple in a calm, low voice and state that next round of shots will be "cool," suggesting mental images of aloofness from well-known music videos for the couple as they pose. Photographers thus self-consciously work to position their clients and mold their subjective experiences of the shoot.

POSITIONING FOR PROFIT

Bridal salon employees' ability to position clients and thus elicit the desired emotional expressions is crucial to generating profits because time, in this business, is money. The more costumes, stylings, and settings a photographer can shoot in one day, the more photographs are likely to sell. Few couples are willing to commit more than one day's time to posing for photographs, in part because most have to miss a day's paid work for the shoot as no Taipei bridal salon can stay in business by holding shoots only on weekends. Therefore, the speed with which the photographer and stylist can complete each set of photographs is critical. If one day's time does not produce enough quality photographs to complete the package ordered by the couple, not only will the couple be angry but the stylist, photographer, and assistants will also have to expend additional time on the couple when they could have moved on to another.

Most couples order more photographs than the number included in packages, moreover. These package add-ons result in improved salon profits and photographer commissions. The goal in many salons is for the photographer to produce nearly one hundred sellable shots during an eight-hour shoot such that there is enough variety to tempt couples to select 60 portraits for their albums. Extending the length of the workday to accommodate more shots is not practical. Couples typically arrive well before 7 a.m. to allow two to three hours for the initial makeover and hairstyling, and by 6 p.m. most couples are too exhausted to continue responding to photographers' efforts.

The pressure on photographers and stylists to work quickly is high, and the delimiting factor is their ability to manage clients. Photographers and their assistants develop routines: Certain poses go with certain backdrops and props. When clients make specific requests outside of the team's established repertoire, the process slows down considerably. Photographers rely on the salons' ability to position clients to experience feelings of respect and submission when in the midst of photographers. Photographers cannot wield authority that their clients do not give them without compromising the personal quality of the photographer-client relationship, which paves the way for clients' emotional responsiveness. Clients must feel photographers' authority inwardly and comply with photographers willingly, in subjectively experienced deference—not performative deference of the on-stage variety.

I observed, for example, a self-described "picky" bride by the name of Pei-ling request a set of photographs shot on a couch. The bridal salon's communication form sought her preferences for colors and feelings but not for specific details such as this. She had seen such a portrait in a friend's album made by one of Taipei's most exclusive bridal salons and wanted something similar for her own album despite her salon's pricey-but-not-quite-exclusive status. Most importantly, she was not inhibited and made her desires known. Her photographer, however, had not practiced this and knew it would be problematic. Given the construction of the bride as celebrity for the day, he had no choice but to comply. Jian-ming's first approach was to agree to shoot some photos on a couch later in the day, with the hope that Pei-ling would forget (or, at least, pretend to forget out of deference to the photographer whose lack of interest in her idea was fairly evident). She did not, and at one point in the midafternoon she requested that they take some couch photos right then. Jian-ming rolled an unattractive, old waiting-area couch on to the set and draped it in satin fabric. He tried setting it at various angles to the camera and seating the bride and groom on it, struggling to find the right angle and pose. After spending at least twenty minutes trying to find a satisfactory shot, he quickly took a few frames and declared that they were ready to move on. In the end, Pei-ling did not choose any of couch photographs, and her selection of photographs was probably reduced by at least ten images as a result of the wasted time. At other moments during the shoot, as well, Jian-ming's failure to render Pei-ling a compliant subject slowed him down. When I ran into him weeks later, Jian-ming confided that he felt his photographs of Pei-ling and her groom were not up to his usual standards. Pei-ling, too, was dissatisfied with the availability good of images for the final album. Her album was among the slimmest I encountered, comparatively low cost in marked contrast to other status markers associated with her wedding, such as the high-end engagement cakes distributed before the wedding, Tiffany jewelry, and famously expensive banquet hall. In my estimation, the inability of Jian-ming and his staff to position Pei-ling in the usual manner—rendering her deferential and compliant—was behind the bride and photographer's ultimate dissatisfaction. It is worth noting, however, that the groom was happy with the bridal photography package for, although Pei-ling viewed the album as inferior, the final bill was low in comparison to his other wedding expenses.

On the vast majority of shoots I observed, brides and grooms were extremely compliant, sometimes even puzzlingly so. For example, when photographers shoot black-and-white film, the backdrops they often select clash with the colors of bride's gown. A bride in pink might be posed against a backdrop of swirling brown and green. Rather than questioning the photographers' color choices, couples unaware of the use of black and white film will go along with the photographers' directives. Only later when they see the proofs in black and white will they comment that they had wondered why he chose such an ugly color combination. Similarly, most brides will permit stylists to use makeup techniques and colors they dislike. Why are brides—in their capacity of "celebrity for the day"—so remarkably passive?

Salon employees attempt to position customers as compliant as soon they have placed a deposit on the package. Saleswomen, the front line of the bridal salon team, initiate the positioning process. While saleswomen introduce themselves by personal name, they address photographers as *sheyingshi* (photography master, photographer), conveying the saleswomen's own deference to the photographer. When photographers enter the sales floor, saleswomen also point them out and talk up their talents, often soliciting photographers' opinions on nonphotographic matters such as the selection of a frame style. When saleswomen show their customers sample albums, they talk about the photographer who shot the album in ways that suggest reverence for the photographer's artistic capabilities by emphasizing the importance of the photography over other aspects of the albums that may be of even greater importance in contributing to the book's airs of sophistication. No matter how talented the photographer, sloppy graphics, poor quality of mounting work, and a cheap album cover make for a low prestige album. Once a couple has made a deposit on a bridal package, saleswomen further talk up the skill of the particular photographer assigned to their clients by showing off sample albums that he or she (is said to have) produced. (In fact, many salons purchase their sample albums from photographers not in their employ.) Stylists, too, defer to photographers' specific requests for makeup and styling changes. When clients occasionally fail to submit to stylists out of respect for their expertise, the stylist can fall back upon the photographer's authority. A bride who claims that a lipstick color is too dark, for example, may be told that the photographer has requested this, thereby forcing the bride to challenge the photographer's authority if she wants her lip color lightened.

The positioning work undertaken in bridal salons is often quite explicit on the employee's side though invisible to the client. Take gown selection, for example. Because brides need no less than six gowns for the photo shoot and three for the wedding day, the gown selection process can potentially occupy many hours of an employee's time. Saleswomen frequently double as dress consultants, and their ability to earn commissions is reduced by spending too much time with a bride on gown selection. At the same time, a saleswoman who leaves a bride feeling deserted or manipulated risks losing future referrals. One trick of the trade for hurrying brides through gown selection is as follows: The saleswoman urges the bride to select half a dozen gowns and then begin trying them on, "just for starters." As she tries them on, the saleswoman comments on ways in which particular gowns are flattering or not. After trying on the initial six gowns, the saleswoman may ask, "Which of these do you like the most?" The saleswoman then declares those gowns as chosen and promptly begins attaching reservation tickets to the gowns for the date in question. The bride may have meant only to indicate that those gowns were merely still in the running, but the saleswoman's statement forces the bride to challenge her to regain control over the selection process. Many find it easier to go along with the saleswoman's direction. Some brides, of course, wrest control of the process away. The self-described "picky" bride, Pei-ling, spent six hours one afternoon selecting gowns from the salon's collection of over two hundred. This same bride also got into a minor conflict with her stylist. From my point of view, all of her demands were reasonable, especially given the industry's motto of "once-in-a-lifetime" service and celebrity treatment. Nevertheless, bridal salon workers told me that they have to structure brides' and grooms' experiences in such a way that they are positioned to refrain from making special requests and becoming too involved in their own production process.

CONCLUSION

Amidst positioning processes taking place both inside and outside of bridal salons, Taiwanese bridal photography emerges. Even reluctant young women become eager consumers. Even shy couples strike lively poses. Even spend-thrifty grooms pay hefty bills. Agency exists in the process, of course. Couples make choices along the way—gowns with rounded neckline or V-shaped, painted or stained frame? These choices, like many in consumer society, distinguish amongst what are, at heart, minor microvariations (see Ewen and Ewen 1982). Taiwanese bridal salons are unusual among beauty industries, however, in that the consumer is not positioned as the agent of her own bodily transformation. Other studies of beauty industries, by contrast, point out that consumers learn to investigate their own bodies for defects—often with the help of beauty "experts"—and seek out treatments to correct perceived deficiencies. Scholars thus debate the nature of and significance of human agency in beauty pursuits (e.g., see Bordo 1993,1997; Davis 1995). The work of positioning in this Taipei beauty industry is focused on producing compliant, emotionally expressive clients who allow themselves to be transformed directly by the experts. The agency of brides is strongest before they enter the bridal salon, in the initial decision to consume bridal services.

In this context, where the only socially acceptable choice is to play the part of Beautiful Bride, what then of agency? To be sure, many women experience strong, heartfelt desire to play the role of Beautiful Bride constructed by the hands of stylists and photographers. The fact that the Beautiful Bride is seen as an artificial construction, a role one plays, makes this practice different from the disciplining of bodies common in other late capitalist beauty industries. In the positioning processes that take place outside of bridal salons—the events and conversations that collectively render marrying women as bridal service consumers—women need not see themselves as agents. There are quite a few Taiwanese bridal consumers who, like Fang-jin, say that they are *not* doing it for themselves but for no reason other than social acceptability. Interestingly, couples in Taiwan are apt to speak of marriage in much the same way: One takes on the burdens of marrying and raising a family not for desire but duty (see Adrian 2003: ch. 3). Jane Collier (1997) argues, of the transformation of a marriage in a Spanish village amidst the rapid expansion of a market economy where women and men replaced earlier notions of family duty with a new emphasis on individual desire, that liberation from duty was not so very liberating. In both time periods, individuals largely followed social conventions. In the earlier period they did so with the knowledge that they were, in essence, role-playing. As Collier puts it, "underneath" their performances of family duty, men and women were free to feel contempt for duty. In the later period, by contrast, individuals expected their subjective experience and behavior to be in line. In other words, they expected themselves to *want* to conform to social norms and experienced themselves as agents in their own courtship and marriage choices. Those who, subjectively, experienced internal resistance to complying with social norms now had to engage in self-work to cultivate socially appropriate desires. Though women like Fang-jin may feel somewhat put out by the command to take up the role of Beautiful Bride, they can at least enjoy the freedom of that inner space "underneath" social performance.

It is precisely the freedom of subjectivity possible in role playing that photographers strive to erase in the effort to elicit the most natural and beautiful poses: feelings that are evoked, not performed. Photographers need their subjects to experience the moods they wish to photograph, not merely play act them. Significantly, though, the photographer's demands on bride and groom to perform a romance model of marriage are temporary while the competing demands of the parents for the couple to engage in a family duty model of marriage are long-term. The intense photo studio positioning work that leaves little space for a bride to define her own image, then, liberates her even while it defines her momentarily. In this cultural practice, there is no ongoing command to selfhood, no expectation that one disciplines herself to social norms in Foucauldian fashion in which it is not enough to conform, it is also necessary to self-police in the belief that failure to conform to social standards is an *inner* failing (Bartky 1988). As Judith Butler (1990) might put it, self-conscious role playing or performativity has the potential to subvert "identity" by underscoring its constructed nature. Taipei women can and often do contract bridal services without necessarily and subjectively wanting them. One can buy the photographs without *buying into* them, to be in the world of bridal photography without being of it.

NOTES

Field research was funded by grants from the J. William Fulbright Foreign Scholarship Board and the American Council of Learned Societies/Chiang Ching-kuo Foundation Fellowship Selection Committee with funds provided by the Chiang Ching-kuo Foundation. A National Science Foundation Graduate Fellowship and a Mellon Dissertation Fellowship at Yale University provided funding for initial write-up of the research on which this article is based. Names and identifying markers have been changed to protect the privacy of the women and men among whom I conducted research and to whom I am most thankful. I wish also to thank Dottie Holland and Kevin Leander for their efforts in organizing the Positioning and Subjectivity session for the 2003 APA meetings and Don Brenneis, Dottie Holland, Sara Harkness, and an anonymous reviewer for thoughtful readings of and comments on earlier drafts of this article.

1. The couple and the photographer did not participate in my research except to offer their photographs for use in academic publications, with signed consent by all parties.

REFERENCES CITED

Abu-Lughod, Lila. 1990. Shifting Politics in Bedouin Love Poetry. In Language and the Politics of Emotion. Catherine Lutz and Lila Abu-Lughod, eds. Pp. 24–45. Cambridge: Cambridge University Press.

Adrian, Bonnie. 2003. Framing the Bride: Globalizing Beauty and Romance in Taiwan's Bridal Industry. Berkeley: University of California Press.

Argyrou, Vassos. 1996. Tradition and Modernity in the Mediterranean: The Wedding as Symbolic Struggle. New York: Cambridge University Press.

Bakhtin, M. M. 1981. The Dialogic Imagination. Caryl Emerson and Michael Holquist, trans. Austin: University of Texas Press.

Bartky, Sandra Lee.1988. Foucault, Femininity and the Modernization of Patriarchal Power. In Feminism and Foucault: Paths of Resistance. L. Quinby and I. Diamond, eds. Pp. 61–86. Boston: Northeastern University Press.

Bordo, Susan. 1993. Unbearable Weight: Feminism, Western Culture, and the Body. Berkeley: University of California Press.

———1997. Twilight Zones: The Hidden Life of Cultural Images from Plato to O. J. Berkeley: University of California Press.

Bourdieu, Pierre. 1984. Distinction. R. Nice, trans. Cambridge, MA: Harvard University Press. 1990 Photography: A Middle-Brow Art. Stanford: Stanford University Press.

Butler, Judith. 1990. Gender Trouble: Feminism and the Subversion of Identity. New York: Routledge.

Cancian, Francesca. 1986. The Feminization of Love. Signs 11(4):692–709.

———1987. Love in America. New York: Cambridge University Press.

Collier, Jane Fishburne. 1997. From Duty to Desire: Remaking the Family in a Spanish Village. Princeton: Princeton University Press.

Constable, Nicole. 2003. Romance on a Global Stage: Pen Pals, Virtual Ethnography, and "Mail Order" Marriages. Berkeley: University of California Press.

Davis, Kathy. 1995. Reshaping the Female Body: The Dilemma of Cosmetic Surgery. New York: Routledge.

Edwards, Walter. 1989. Modern Japan through Its Weddings. Stanford: Stanford University Press.

Ewen, Stuart, and Elizabeth Ewen. 1992[1982]. Channels of Desire: Mass Images and the Shaping of American Consciousness. Minneapolis: University of Minnesota Press.

Gal, Susan. 1987. Language and Political Economy. Annual Reviews in Anthropology 18:345–367.

Gillette, Maris. 1999. What's in a Dress? Brides in the Hui Quarter of Xi'an. In The Consumer Revolution in Urban China. D. Davis, ed. Pp. 80–106. Berkeley: University of California Press.

Goffman, Erving. 1973. The Presentation of Self in Everyday Life. Woodstock, NY: Overlook Press.

Goldstein-Gidoni. 1997. Packaged Japaneseness: Weddings, Business, and Brides. Honolulu: University of Hawai'i Press.

Hochschild, Arlie Russel. 1983. The Managed Heart: Commercialization of Human Feeling. Berkeley: University of California Press. 1989 The Second Shift. New York: Viking.

Holland, Dorothy, and Margaret Eisenhart. 1990. Educated in Romance: Women, Achievement, and College Culture. Chicago: University of Chicago Press.

Holland, Dorothy, William Lachicotte, and Debra Skinner. 1998. Identity and Agency in Cultural Worlds. Cambridge, MA: Harvard University Press.

Kaw, Eugenia. 1994. "Opening" Faces: The Politics of Cosmetic Surgery and Asian American Women. In Many Mirrors: Body Image and Social Relations. N. Sault, ed. Pp. 241–265. New Brunswick, NJ: Rutgers University Press.

Kendall, Laurel. 1996. Getting Married in Korea. Berkeley: University of California Press.

Otnes, Cele C., and Elizabeth H. Pleck. 2003. Cinderella Dreams: The Allure of the Lavish Wedding. Berkeley: University of California Press.

Radway, Janice. 1984. Reading the Romance: Women, Patriarchy, and Popular Literature. Chapel Hill: University of North Carolina Press.

Rebhun, L. A. 1993. Nerves and Emotional Play in Northeast Brazil. Medical Anthropology Quarterly 7(2):131–151.

——1999. The Heart Is Unknown Country: Love in the Changing Economy of Northeast Brazil. Stanford: Stanford University Press.

Said, Edward W. 1978. Orientalism. New York: Pantheon.

Scott, James C. 1985. Weapons of the Weak: Everyday Forms of Peasant Resistance. New Haven, CT: Yale University Press.

——1990. Domination and the Arts of Resistance: Hidden Transcripts. New Haven, CT: Yale University Press.

Snitow, Ann Barr. 1983. Mass-Market Romance: Pornography for Women Is Different. In Powers of Desire. A. Snitow et al., eds. Pp. 245–263. New York: Monthly Review Press.

Stockard, Janice 1989. Daughters of the Canton Delta: Marriage Patterns and Economic Strategies in South China, 1860–1930. Stanford: Stanford University Press.

Wolf, Margery. 1972. Women and the Family in Rural Taiwan. Stanford: Stanford University Press.

24

Gifts Intercepted
Biopolitics and Spirit Debt
Jean M. Langford

I was sitting with Lt. Somsy and an interpreter in a small, spare room at a community center in a U.S. city.[1] A tape recorder sat on the beige formica-topped table between us. The lieutenant was describing how he and his unit in the Royal Lao Army handled the bodies of those killed in combat during the wars of the 1960s and 1970s.

> We tried to get rid of the body, to hide it from the enemy. We took off the ID. If we had time, we buried the dead person. One thing we knew we should never do was steal anything from him. If I took anything for myself the spirit might harm me. There are many people who stole things from the dead and were shot and killed.

I was speaking with Lt. Somsy as part of hospital-sponsored research about the perspectives of Lao and Cambodian emigrants toward death. Like other conversations, this one eventually gravitated to a conjunction between violence and material relations with the dead. The lieutenant's memory of the directive not to steal from the dead presumes that the dead are enfolded into a material exchange with the living that is characterized by an expectation of gifts, a presumption of debt, and an acknowledgment of sacrifice. Deprived of the ceremonies that would inform him that he was dead, ask him not to trouble the living, and supply him with provisions for his journey, a dead soldier was already disoriented and apt to harass the living. If, in addition, he were robbed, he might extract the very lives of the thieves.

The demands of the dead continue to weigh on emigrants from Laos and Cambodia living in the United States, particularly as these demands are mediated by biopolitical institutions. As material engagement with the dead has become entangled with welfare rules and mortuary protocol, survivors are often unable to fulfill obligations to the dead, not because of the violence of war, but because of the structural violence enacted through lowered economic means

Jean M. Langford, "Gifts Intercepted: Biopolitics and Spirit Debt," *Cultural Anthropology*, vol. 24, no. 4, pp. 681–711. Copyright © 2009 by American Anthropological Association. Reprinted with permission.

and minority status in relation to institutions that regulate the disposition and mourning of the dead according to dominant U.S. assumptions about matter and spirit. While it is difficult anyway to settle debts with those who died violent deaths, it is harder still for those who owe their lives, as they say, to the benevolence of the dead. The difficulty is recast in political exile, as socially marginalized survivors are less able to define the terms through which they relate to communities of the dead.

The present essay grapples with the implications of the frequent conjunction in emigrants' stories between past violence and material engagement with the dead. The stories inspire a rethinking of the biopolitical management of death from the perspective of the reciprocity of living and dead. I argue that the biopolitical protocol of hospitals and funeral homes negates the social existence of the dead in ways that echo violations of the dead during wartime. I further suggest that institutionalized violations of the dead are informed not simply by sciences of sanitation and death causation, but by latent theological presumptions about matter and spirit that are largely Protestant in genealogy. The separation of matter and spirit that organizes the management of death from the sidelines is also manifest in dominant U.S. mourning practices that emphasize memorialization over material intimacy with the dead.

SOCIAL WORLDS OF THE DEAD

Much contemporary literature on mourning is driven by a psychodynamic narrative of the healing of historical trauma through a public discourse in which the dead are evoked through monuments and eulogy. If the dead in this narrative often serve as stand-ins for historical violence—the Holocaust, the Vietnam War, the AIDS epidemic, or the events of September 11, 2001—such that spectral relations are transformed from concrete exchanges to vague legacies, the dead in the stories told by Lao, Khmer, Hmong, and Kmhmu emigrants suggest another semiotic spin whereby certain historical events become signs of extraordinary violence toward the dead. Here the dead work less as symbols of injustice, than as tangible participants in violated socialities of living and dead. Arguably, the emphasis on memorialization of the dead as a means of addressing or redressing collective injustice is the liberal political elaboration of a dominant Protestant mourning style. On the one hand, cemetery conversations with the dead (Francis *et al.* 2005), letters to the dead posted in cyberspace (Gilbert 2006) or placed against the Vietnam memorial (Sturken 1997), and fundamentalist insistence on a literal resurrection of the body, all suggest a persistent material entanglement with the dead on the part of modern Christians. On the other hand, this entanglement is often manifestly refused within that part of a Christian ethos that is institutionalized in funeral discourse, psychologies of mourning, and public discourses of reconciling past violence, which all suggest that the value of interactions with the dead lies in the consolation of the living, rather than the comfort of the dead.

Perhaps precisely because of the material entanglements of modern Christianity, there is often a self-consciously therapeutic, symbolic, or sardonic cast to North American interactions with the dead. The point is not that these interactions are empty of genuine belief. After all, relations with the dead among Lao, Khmer, Hmong, and Kmhmu emigrants are equally complicated by skepticism. The point, rather, is that the messages and gifts to the dead in much U.S. mourning appear to be largely unhinged from an imagination of the material needs of the dead in an ongoing existence.[2] Such an imagination may also be denied within doctrinaire Theravada Buddhism and Christianized versions of ancestor worship, as I show below. Certainly it would be a mistake to consider Christian and Southeast Asian mourning practices as illustrations of representational and material engagements with the dead, respectively. However, I suggest that a certain insistence on the separation of matter and spirit at work both in the bioethics of hospitals and funeral homes, and in public discourse on honoring the memories of the dead, is a sign not of the secular banishment of religious sentiment from public institutions, but, rather, of the institutional enshrinement of a particular religious sensibility (cf. Keane 2007).

An inability to conceive of a material indebtedness to the dead may be integral to a biopolitical regime that is not only focused on the management of human life(Foucault 1990), but also based on a division of that life into materiality and spirit. Agamben has glossed the material aspect of human life referenced by European philosophy as "bare life," life that is stripped of social and political value (1998; cf. 2002). His analysis of the ways that institutionalized violence demarcates a category of "bare life" is powerful in grasping the gestures of social exclusion that affect refugees, racially marked minorities and those hovering at the edge of life and death. However, the stories I retell here resist interpretation through a theory of "bare life" in two ways. First, by conflating extreme violence with a desubjectification that reduces its victims to the status of living dead, the concept of "bare life" seems to preclude any sociality in the existences imagined for the dead. Second, in arguing, following Primo Levi, that those reduced to "bare life" are unable to testify to their own dehumanization (or death), Agamben forecloses the imagination of a communicative interface between living and dead (2002).

For Agamben, testimonies of violence register an internal contradiction by marking what is unspeakable, a lacuna at the heart of the subject's speech. An account of extreme violence inevitably bears witness to a time when the person could not articulate her suffering (2002:162). The testifying survivor is therefore in perpetual tension with her own "bare life" that is stripped of speech. The material relations with the dead that structure the stories of Southeast Asian emigrants sidestep this (im)possibility of testimony, replacing a focus on narration with a focus on bodily intervention. These stories suggest that a theory of "bare life" is inadequate to address the violations of a social community that embraces both living and dead as part of one material-spectral world, and that addresses the effects of violence less through testimonial memory than through physical encounters with the dead.

Finally, Agamben's critique of biopolitics, although insightful about the devaluation of the living, precludes the imagination of concrete socialities of living and dead, or the violation of those socialities. Yet emigrants' stories suggest that participation in such socialities affords powerful possibilities for apprehending the material reverberations of past violence in the present. For violence pursues the dead into their very afterlives, violating them in ways that do not simply terrorize the living or desecrate the corpse in a symbolic reference to future or past violations, but that materially wound and rend social worlds in the present. In his memoir of life under Pol Pot, Pin Yathay recalled his first experience of Khmer Rouge contempt for the dead. He and others were being transported to a work site packed tightly in trucks with no food or water. When two women died en route, the driver ordered their bodies to be dumped at the side of the road, over the weeping and protests of their families. "The idea of leaving them there by the roadside was unthinkable, sacrilegious. I thought: Now I must not hope any longer" (1987:73). Until then, Pin Yathay had struggled to perceive the cruelty of the Khmer Rouge as an excess of revolutionary fervor. It was the willingness to negate the dead as social beings that exposed the radical devaluation of both living and dead.

During political asylum in the United States, survivors of the covert war in Laos or the Khmer Rouge regime in Cambodia are no longer asked to dump bodies of friends and family members by the roadside. Violence in the United States is experienced largely as the structural violence of racial minoritization and economic hardship. As the sociality of the dead is forcibly translated, within the terms set by poverty and minority status, into the representational economies of medical and mortuary institutions, it is desacralized in ways that echo the desecrations of war and state terror. Wartime devaluation of the dead therefore finds an uncanny counterpart in autopsy labs, cemeteries, and crematoria where bodies are handled as inanimate matter with only an intermittent and symbolic relation to spirit. One of the sites where emigrants experience the violence of minoritization most acutely, therefore, is in institutional settings that effectively negate the social existence of the dead.

MATERIALITIES OF CARE

If not only the violence of war, but also biopolitical governance interrupts the sociality of living and dead, it does so, I suggest, less as a bastion of rational secularism interfering with religious values, than as the institutionalization of a particular afterlife imaginary. I recommend, therefore, that the economies of care from which wartime dead were excluded, be read less as cultural description than as eschatological and ethical possibility. Although the Theravada Buddhism of Lao and Khmer and the modern animism of Kmhmu and Hmong offer a dynamic range of eschatological possibilities, their death rites share a presupposition that the spirit tangibly receives the care given to the body. Once entangled, body and spirit remain contiguous, still participating in one another's substance.[3] Lao and Khmer supply the dead with ID cards and passports, placing jewelry in their mouths to enable them to bribe the immigration officers who police the border between hell and heaven. In Laos people sifted through the bones after cremation, keeping jewelry or teeth as good luck charms, a trace of the gift to the dead returned as a talisman for the living. In Cambodia, relatives gathered the bone fragments, purified them with coconut water, and placed them in an urn in the *wat* (Buddhist temple) to be cared for in an ongoing way.

Lt. Somsy remembered small houses for the dead built by Northern Lao and furnished with household goods: "In there you put pots and pans, and other things to ensure that the dead person has what he needs for everyday life." When I visited a Lao wat in a U.S. city in 2006, gifts for the dead were piled several feet deep along one wall (see Figure 1). "Let's say you have offered more than enough for the person to use," one man, Major Thao, explained. "Then the person will also reserve some things for you when you die." In the circulation of gifts, a surplus returns to the giver. During Boun Khao Padap Dinh (or, for Khmer, Phchum Ben), the annual feast for the dead during which spirits residing in hell are temporarily released, families bring household items such as cooking utensils and clothing to the wat and offer them to the monks. "It's for all spirits," Lt. Somsy said. "First for the closest relatives and then for any spirit who is starved out there, like a homeless person." The vagrant dead include those for whom full ceremonies were never performed, like Lao soldiers who died in battle or Khmer civilians dumped in mass graves under Pol Pot. As Major Thao reflected, "The spirit of someone who

FIGURE 1. Gifts for the dead at a Lao wat in the United States.

has died and has no relatives to do the ceremony, will wander around like a bird without any tree branches on which to perch."

Those who understand death practices strictly in accordance with Buddhist doctrine, philosophize that money is placed in the mouth not to bribe the border guards of the next world, but to demonstrate that no earthly possessions can be taken into death. They say that the coins that remain among the ashes after cremation are evidence that *boun* (Khmer: *bon*) or merit is the only gift that circulates between the living and the dead. Every ceremony for the dead produces boun, which is doubly offered to the dead and rebounded back to the living, as an investment in improved afterlives and future incarnations (cf. Keyes 1983:267). Richard Gombrich argues that the practice of transferring merit to the dead developed as a Buddhist accommodation of a prior practice of feeding the dead through the mediation of the monks. "Sensible Theravadin monks decided that food being visibly consumed by a monk could not possibly be eaten by someone else, so that, if people persisted in their habit of feeding dead relatives, the custom required reinterpretation. What the relatives were really getting was something else—merit" (Gombrich 1971:213–214).[4] Here Theravada ideology almost approaches the "semiotic ideology" of certain modern Christians (Keane 2007) wherein the difficulty of imagining spirits in need of nutrition necessitates a more symbolic reading of physical offerings. Note, however, that in the Theravada reasoning, the problem lies less in the inability of spirits to digest food, than in the inability of food to be ingested twice.

Furthermore, in defiance of the illogic detected by Gombrich's hypothetical monks, Lao and Khmer emigrants suggest that food and goods offered to monks are transformed into both merit and gifts consumed by the dead. The Khmer ceremony of *bangskaul*, performed at the funeral, at a ceremony 100 days after death, and then again at Phchum Ben, transfers the merit of the living to the dead, even while, through the very generosity of that gesture, it simultaneously produces more merit for the living.[5] Yet bangskaul transmits not only merit, but also matter, sending ethereal forms of food and money to the dead and leaving physical forms for the monks, while retaining a karmic residue—the good intention motivating the gift—as merit for the giver (cf. Klima 2002:269). The ambiguity of these gifts prompts reflection, but not necessarily logical foreclosure. As one Khmer woman mused, "According to Buddhist doctrine, when someone dies, there is nothing left—no soul, no spirit—so how can they [the deceased] accept something like that [objects such as stoves and refrigerators]? But we believe those dead souls are suffering and we need to help them" (Smith-Hefner 1999:61). An acute awareness of the distress of the dead overcomes any logical objections to material reciprocity.

For Hmong and Kmhmu, the flow of material assistance between living and dead is unmediated by a notion of merit. Hmong dress the deceased in the burial clothes that will identify him to the ancestors, placing a butchered rooster, bottle of alcohol, crossbow, and other provisions near the body. As the *Qhuab Ke* ("Showing the Way") is sung, directing the dead person back along Hmong migration routes to the place of birth, and then on to the place of the ancestors, rice wine is offered to sustain him on his way. He is continuously questioned as to whether he has received the gifts or arrived at particular destinations, his answers read through the position assumed by the *kuam* (two halves of a buffalo horn or piece of bamboo) when tossed onto the ground. "We give [the deceased] money to hire a boat to cross the river to his home," Mr. Vangay said. "We tell him to show his appreciation to the country where he's living now, to the water, and wood, and fire he used, before he leaves. He needs to say thank you for that." The spirit repays the landscape with "spirit money" (specially fashioned strips of paper) and incense offered to him by funeral guests. Some Hmong refer to a marketplace on the bridge between the world of the living and the spirit world, where the living and dead "trade, deal, and bargain with each other" (Tapp 1989:64).

Guests stay at the home of the deceased for several days, playing cards and gambling until early morning to "keep the family warm," as one man said. These gambling parties are, as Klima observed for Thai funerals, "the gift of camaraderie … company for the deceased spirit" (2002:251). If the deceased Hmong is a revered older man, the day before the burial is devoted to the settlement of debts to assure that he is not so poor in the next world that he demands assistance from living relatives by making them ill. On the night before the burial, messages are delivered from him through the *txiv xaiv*, the "father of words" (Symonds 2004:142–144), instructing the descendents to be kind to one another and to remember to feed the ancestors. "If you do not want to remain healthy and prosperous," one translation specifies, "it does not matter, but if you want to, you must give charity to your father by giving him three joss sticks, and three amounts of paper money. … You must take your father and bury him in a good place and then you will have a lot of children. They will live together as crowded as the bamboo clump" (Chindarsi 1976:156–157). An essential gift to the dead is the correct orientation of the gravesite, derived from geomantic principles,[6] and translated by some emigrants as the dead person's desire for a "good view."

On the day of burial, animals are given to the dead by an opposite-gender sibling of the deceased.[7] A song the night before informs the descendants: "Tomorrow morning the oxen and pigs will be killed for your father but your father can have only their souls, so you divide the meat and pork among the people who have come to help work in the mortuary rite" (Chindarsi 1976:156–157). The dual form of the gift is explicit here: the deceased receives the souls of the animals, while the mourners consume the flesh. Pao Chang, a funeral specialist, emphasized, "The meaning of the sacrifice is love … I'm your brother, you're my sister and we love each other. I'm not going to leave you alone even though you've died.' It is strong, strong support. This is a kindness, not a demand." Perhaps fending off anthropological or Christian interpretations of animist rites, he insists that gift exchanges with the dead are not rote cultural rules or self-interested transactions, but communications of love.

The dead continue to be offered food for several days following the burial. Some conjecture that by the fifth day the dead "may be able to find his own food" (Thao 1993:67). Hmong speak of a spirit of the deceased (*plig*) who travels to the land of the ancestors, another who remains with the body, and a third who is reborn (Johnson 1992:60; Lemoine 1996; Symonds 2004:20–21).[8] By directly referring to a spirit that remains with the corpse, Hmong afterlife lore formalizes a contiguity of body and spirit, which, for Khmer and Lao Buddhists, is simply ritually enacted. Mr. Vangay's family invited his dead father's spirit to the ceremony known as *xi plig* on the 13th day after the burial. He drove to the cemetery, picked up a handful of dirt, called the spirit, and brought the dirt home for an offering of chicken, water, and liquor. "We sat beside his father," Mrs. Vangay said, "beside the dirt." Here the intermingling of the soul with the soil of the grave enables both material closeness and reciprocity. During the *tso plig* to release the plig for rebirth, the deceased is again invited home and fed. "We offer food and liquor," Mrs. Vangay said, "and everyone cries." Her comment is a reminder, once again, that these feasts are not simply formal rites but enactments of love and grief.

Whereas even Christian converts butcher animals at such times, one Catholic leader, Mr. Lo, explained, "We just kill it for a celebration for the ones who are living. We do not believe that we give the animal to the dead person. In the Christian teachings you don't need to take anything with you. So we as Christians do not really feed our ancestors." Note that Mr. Lo's understanding of Christianity, like doctrinaire Theravada Buddhism, works against the possibility that the dead participate in a material gift exchange with the living. As Christian converts, most Kmhmu in the United States are also careful to dissociate themselves from material reciprocity with the dead. "We don't pray to ghosts," one man assured me. "We pray for the person to get into heaven. During the mass the priest names the things that people are offering. The diocese allows us to do that." Yet the hybridity of this practice is suggested by other accounts. "We know what kind of food our ancestor likes," one woman said, "so we buy that kind of food and offer it to him. If someone offers that and eats that, then the ancestor will receive it." The materiality of the gift to the dead still haunts this Christian offertory. Cheuang, a Kmhmu healer, whose conversion to Christianity did not prevent his conscientious pursuit of non-Christian rites, described the preparation of his mother's body after her death.

> We said, "Here's some money. Whatever you want, you take, and leave us what you don't want." We wrapped the coins in black and white cloth and put them in her hand. In one hand we put sticky rice, and in the other meat. We put other coins in her mouth for her to buy her way to *mìang róoy* [the spirit city]. If we put them in a pocket we'd worry that somebody would steal them. In her mouth we know they're safe.

His story signals again the concreteness of the gift, the return of part of the gift to the giver, and the care taken to avoid any interference in the exchange with the dead.[9] The heart of these rites is not memorialization, but material reciprocity.

It is tempting to imagine that the materiality of such relations with the dead is in tension with their emotional charge. The exchange with the dead referenced here, as Pao Chang emphasized, is rooted less in rational self-interest, than in persistent connection and love. However, a confessionalist witnessing or expressivist remembering is not what the dead primarily ask of that love (cf. Chakrabarty 2000:118–148; Foucault 1990). They ask instead that it be manifest in meticulous physical care. The dead are affected by the handling of their bodies and the conditions of their graves. They are hungry or thirsty, distressed at their nakedness, in need of cash and visas to cross the border to the ancestors. They require less the expression of feeling and the exercise of memory, than company, hospitality, food and cigarettes, a good view from their burial sites, stainless steel pots and pans. Yet this materiality of relations with the dead signals not a utilitarian connection, but a continuous flow of care.

Drawing Heidegger's and Bataille's thoughts on the gift into dialogue, Rebecca Comay (1990) writes of an indebtedness that is simultaneously an infinite gratitude (for time, for other beings, for being itself).[10] Comay suggests that this indebtedness marks a sociality prior to exchange and a responsibility prior to law. It is gratitude so profound in the face of generosity so extravagant, that no payback can be thought. Within the limits of European philosophy such an exuberant gift, and the infinite gratitude it provokes, is imagined as a gesture toward an immaterial abstraction, rather than as a moment of material exchange. Although the gift exchanges with the dead traced here hold some of the resonance of that radical Heideggerian gift, they simultaneously exhibit a gritty physical existence: mung beans, rice wine, the washing of the bones, or polishing of the urn. Jean-Luc Nancy and Richard Livingston (1991) note that for "Western" thinkers, the concept of sacrifice is "spiritualized" such that true sacrifice is necessarily figurative, rather than literal. They point out that philosophers from the Greeks through Bataille consider the more literal sacrifice practiced by peoples around the world a vulgar economism. Yet they observe:

> When someone says to his gods: "Here is the butter. Where are the gifts?" it may be that we do not know what he is saying, since we know nothing of the community in which he lives with his gods. ... We need to admit that what we consider as mercenary exchange ("here is the butter ...") sustained and gave meaning to billions of individual and collective existences, and we do not know how to think about what founds this gesture. (We can only guess, confusedly, that this barter in itself goes beyond barter.) [Nancy and Livingston 1991:26, 35]

For "gods," in this statement, we might substitute "the dead." The parenthetical caution that barter may go beyond barter is provocative but enigmatic. Must academics resign ourselves to the absolute foreignness of a more literal sacrifice imagined by "billions" of humans? Instead might we not recognize in the stories told by our neighbors other possibilities of *rapprochement* with the dead?[11]

These stories are not told in an innocence of a more figurative interchange between living and dead, but, rather, in the face of it; Southeast Asian emigrants are no strangers to the symbolic economies of modern Christianity, cosmopolitan Buddhism, or academic thought. But if a modern reason or Christian conversion tends to constrain the dead to a metaphorical existence where they are only symbols for the grief of the living, the dead themselves insist on a more bodily presence. Charles, a Khmer man in his forties, recalled that once, as a young man living in the Cambodian countryside with his family, he fell ill after a visit to the city.

Having tried several remedies to no effect, his mother consulted a *krou teay*, a fortune teller, who ascertained that Charles's dead great-grandmother was angry with him. "Her spirit was upset because I went away from her without letting her know. My mom did a ritual and the next day I got better. Maybe I should have gone to the grave and said, 'Grandma, I'm going to go away.'" He laughed. "I don't really believe in it, but it happened." His skeptical comment registers his journey not only away from the burial site where his grandmother lingered, but also toward a civil society swept clear of spirits, where relations with the dead are subject to a more symbolic status. With such a seismic shift in the terms of reality, his great-grandmother demanded of him not just sticky rice, cooked with mung beans and pork, presented at Phchum Ben, but an acknowledgment of her capacity to participate in impromptu (and not only pre-scribed) physical exchanges with the living. It is such exchanges that are evoked by survivors of war and state violence who speak of their indebtedness to the dead.

DEBTS TO THE DEAD

In his memoir of life under the Khmer Rouge the musician Daran Kravanh says, "I cannot tell you why or how I survived ... love and music and invisible hands, and something that comes out of the society of the living and the dead, for which there are no words" (LaFreniere 2000:3). In Kravanh's rumination, the debt to the dead emerges as a form of sociality, less a transaction to be completed, than a relationship to be cultivated. Even if no words can capture this sociality, stories offer glimpses and approximations, singular moments in the social interchange of living and dead. When Kravanh first heard his brother play a certain song, he watched his spirit drift out of his body "like steam rising from a bowl of rice." Long after his brother had died, when Kravanh was in trouble, he heard the song again and sensed his brother nearby, offering him protection.

With the destruction of the wats and the murder and forced defrocking of monks by the Khmer Rouge, the gift exchange with the dead was severely disrupted.[12] "When the Vietnamese took over," Sodoeung, a Khmer counselor, said, "people were supposed to look for their relatives' bodies and bones. But how could they look?" One young woman, like many others, had lost her entire family. "She didn't do any ceremony," Sodoeung recalled. Then one day her family sent a message through a neighbor's dream. "'If you don't go to the wat, we won't have any food or clothes to wear.' She didn't believe it, because she was one of the kids who grew up under the communists. Later on she got sick." Even as the Khmer Rouge officially nullified all responsibilities to the dead, their violence, like the violence of the relentless U.S. bombing campaigns that preceded it, inflated the debt, prompting the dead to request recompense through bodily forms of haunting.

In stories of war and terror the unsettled dead frequently intermingle with the landscape, as the ground where extreme violence occurred is reimagined. With so many sudden and untended deaths, Cambodian forests were teeming with restless spirits. There is still public discussion of whether to cremate the anonymous remains of those who were summarily piled in mass graves. Meanwhile unfinished ceremonies pull at emigrants in the United States. "They have regrets," Sodoeung said. "Every time they go to the wat they say, 'I wish I could find where my parents' grave is, or their ashes, so I could put them in the wat.'" Sodoeung's own grandmother's ashes were housed in a wat that was later converted to a torture site. "[The Khmer Rouge] took a lot of people to that wat to kill. They buried them there. People told me it was just like a ghost town. When you stepped you could feel that the ground was mushy. It was not really solid." In that place the restless dead made themselves known, not with dream appearances or slammed doors as in the United States, but with an unnerving tactility. The sponginess of the earth suggested the presence of dead who were beyond the reach of civility. Not having made the transition to benevolent ancestors, their abandonment was embodied in their still decaying bodies.[13] The disturbing possibility went unspoken that Sodoeung's grandmother's ashes were absorbed into this blood-soaked earth.

Yet it was also the dead submerged in the landscape or emerging from it, who offered a haphazard protection during war or state terror. Kravanh recalled childhood hours spent under a fruit tree where his grandfather was buried, listening for advice. "The voice I heard from him," he said, "was not a human voice but one of nature—of that place where my grandfather had returned" (LaFreniere 2000:10). At the 100-day ceremony, when the family brought food to the grave, a lizard crawled out from under the tree and ate a few morsels. Some years later, on the run in the forest, wounded from a fight with Khmer Rouge soldiers, Kravanh took consolation from a lizard that appeared in his path, telling his companions, "It is my grandfather come to help us" (LaFreniere 2000:68).

Charles's soldier brother sought protection from a spirit known simply as Yeimao (grandma). According to legend, she declared that she would only marry a man who could defeat her in combat. After many men died in the attempt, she herself eventually died, still chaste, on the mountain where she had lived. "Hundreds of people cross the mountain," Charles said, "and before they cross they buy some fruit and offer it to her spirit, so that they can pass safely. Otherwise they end up in a car accident or falling off the mountain." Charles's brother took a rock from the mountain. "He went down on his knees and asked for it. Now even a bullet can't hit him. During the war, people would shell him, his clothes would burn, be all ripped, and no bullet touched his body. He brought this rock when he visited, and showed me. It's black. It changes color according to the temperature." Again skepticism wavered in the face of the physicality of the rock and of his brother's survival. Human dead who take the form of animals or minerals, merging into and emerging from the landscape confound a biopolitical division of human beings into animality and spirit, biological and sociopolitical existence. Through such situational transmigration, the dead simultaneously exemplify, like rocks or animals, both intimate ordinariness and ontological alterity. They are both communicative and mute, but their (im)possible testimony is shaped less by a tension between inarticulateness and speech, than by bodily exchanges between human and nonhuman matter. The indebtedness to such dead extends to the entire nonhuman realm, as articulated in the Hmong funeral song in which the deceased is advised to compensate the landscape for water and wood with the spirit money given her by the living.

In addition to the rock, Charles's brother carried a human skull in his backpack. "That skull protects me," he told Charles. "When I sleep I just put the skull on a stick standing next to me. I tell it, 'Any harm that comes, please wake me up.'" "He's been in the army for ten years, fighting in combat," Charles marveled. "And he still survives."[14] During an escape from her work unit under the Khmer Rouge, Sodoeung also sought protection from human remains. "I saw a monk's body in a stupa, sitting close to the Buddha's foot. I slept next to the monk's body. By that time it was just bones. I didn't smell anything. I saw the Buddha's picture and the monk and they both are very gentle people. I thought they would protect me." Here the lack of odor works against the swampy muck of the killing fields, indicating the auspiciousness of the dead. The spirit's purity and merit is evidenced by the cleanliness of the bones. The homology of spirit and corpse evoke a tangible sense of protection.

Hmong and Kmhmu emigrants also speak of debts to and protection from the dead under conditions of violence and displacement. Mysterious death in sleep among Hmong and Lao men (common enough to have earned a diagnosis, Sudden Unexpected Nocturnal Death Syndrome, SUNDS) is associated with nightmares of a suffocating spirit who sits on the sleeper's chest. Hmong say that those who have been deserted by their ancestors are particularly vulnerable to such attack (Adler 1991:59). "[My brother and I] are susceptible," one man said, "because we didn't follow all of the mourning rituals we should have when our parents died. … We have lost contact with their spirits, and thus we are left with no one to protect us from evil spirits. … I had hoped flying so far in a plane to come to America would protect me, but it turns out spirits can follow even this far" (Tobin and Friedman 1983:444). Pao Chang told a story of a man who returned to Thailand to tend his father's grave.

> When he came home, his son got cancer. He had radiation treatment but was still ill. The family called the *txiv neeb* [shaman] even though they were Catholic. The txiv neeb diagnosed: "You people have been Christian for a long time. You haven't done *laig dab* [the feeding of the ancestors] for 30 years. And one of you went back and damaged your father's house. He's not happy so he's punishing you for it."

The family performed laig dab belatedly, but the son did not recover. When a U.S. physician suspected ancestor illness in a young Hmong woman suffering from severe headaches and nightmares about her deceased parents, she and her husband insisted, "We're Catholic; we went to Catholic school, we don't know about these things" (Putsch 1988). Nonetheless they agreed to consult Hmong elders, who traced the illness to the woman's failure to seek permission to marry from her dead parents. After a meal was hosted for the parents to request their blessing, the dreams and headaches ceased. In these stories, efforts to "assimilate" to more symbolic recognitions of the dead or to "reconcile" past violence are subverted by a physical haunting that initially goes unrecognized. The stories underscore what might be at stake in the shift to a more representational economy of relationships with the dead: the loss of a means to address the past as materially embodied in the present.

Derrida explored an inherent paradox of the gift, that in the very instant it is noticed by either giver or receiver, it is no longer a gift as such. The giver experiences self-satisfaction and the anticipation of a countergift, even as the receiver becomes aware of a debt. The "pure gift" Derrida writes, would be "aneconomic," outside of all calculations of benefit (1992; cf. 1995).[15] In exchange with the dead, however, there is never final certainty regarding who granted the survivor the gift of life, whether a gift to the dead was received, or whether the value of a gift exceeds or falls short of a prior gift traveling in the reverse direction. It is impossible to erase the risk of dangling and unclaimed gifts, unknowingly accepted gifts, and mysterious remainders of debt that, being beyond calculation, might be neither repaid nor repayable. Gifts offered to the dead, therefore, take on some of the exteriority of a "pure gift" in relation to political economy. The exchange quickly falls into darkness, unfolding in a time out of time, exaggerating the quality of incommensurability that is already inherent to the gift (cf. Comay 1990:67), the mystery of trading rice for survival.

Heidegger observed that the gift of time precedes any process of exchange, exceeding the "measured reciprocity of a debit-credit exchange" (Comay 1990:87). For the storytellers quoted above, the living receive their very lifetimes from the dead, through ancestral bloodlines, and through the permission of spirits for (re)birth.[16] Because a countergift of life (death) can only be deferred, but never finally avoided, all other gifts to the dead can be partly understood as postponements of that gift.[17] In such a gift cycle, the ethical necessity is less to give without expectation of return (already a given in exchanges with the dead) than to participate in an open-ended reciprocity. Klima suggests that the Derridean problem of the pure gift evaporates within a Buddhist economy of karma (2002:269). He asks, "What if the 'gift without exchange' already was the state of affairs? What if the practice of exchange were seen through different moral eyes, ones not so full of an unfulfilled desire for the absence of interest, hierarchy, asymmetry, or—and this is forceful—not haunted by the deep cosmological tradition of the 'evil' of money?" (Klima 2002:269).

It is arguable that Derrida himself located the problem of the pure gift in European ethics, linking the valorization of the gift to a Christianity marked by solitude, interiority, and a private contract with God (1995). Nonetheless, following Klima, I want to contemplate further the difference between what Derrida called the "terrestrial" and "celestial" economies of Christianity, and what Klima calls the material—spiritual exchange of Buddhism. In the Christian contract, God sacrifices himself to pay off human debts, but only for those who "believe," becoming investors or creditors of God, giving alms for the sake of a heavenly reward (Derrida 1995:114–115). In the Buddhist exchange, the living offer gifts not only to ancestors, but also to anonymous crowds of dead, including the hungry, derelict, and abandoned. In this gift cycle, as in the sacrifices theorized by Bataille (1989:43–49), gifts surpass mere productive utility, as the distinction between giving and receiving dissolves in the possibility of abundant, redoubling, perennially flowering gifts, or in the danger of gifts gone awry. The sociality of living and dead is infused with a generosity that is simultaneously a protective symbiosis. Perhaps the most extreme danger in this sociality lies in its institutional disavowal, in an official ostracism of the dead amounting to contempt for their gifts.

DISAVOWAL: FROM COVERT WARS TO DIASPORA

In the United States, the disavowal of the gifts of the dead is interwoven with the disavowal of the sacrifices of those who died or nearly died in the U.S.-sponsored wars and their aftermath in Laos and Cambodia. The sacrifices of Kmhmu, Lao, Khmer, and Hmong in the covert wars and their attendant theaters of operation have largely gone unrecognized. Their displacement and diaspora was a direct consequence of U.S. military involvement, which changed the field of regional politics with its capital and armies, as much as it altered the landscape with its bombing campaigns and defoliants.[18] After U.S. withdrawal, emigrants found themselves not only without compensation for their sacrifice, but also without governmental protection. As refugees they were quintessential figures of social exile, recognized citizens of no national community, with no political rights unless to humanitarian charity.

Of his time spent in a Thai refugee camp Lt. Phanha, a Kmhmu commander under the CIA in the covert war, said, "If they saw that someone's wife was beautiful they would kill him and abuse his wife. Probably whoever did it didn't actually get an order to do it but they did it anyway, because we were refugees. Who cares if you kill them?" But the sense of being dispensable, without being explicitly targeted, did not end with arrival in the United States. As one Lao man asked, "What good to come here, USA, if nobody knows my name? Is this not the same as the dead ones?" (quoted in Proudfoot 1990:112). Emigrants found themselves on the fringes of the social world, in a chronic experience of unrecoverable lives. They sometimes speak therefore, not just of their own debts to spirits, but of the U.S. government's debts to them. "They say the Americans 'lost' the war," one Lao commented, "but really we lost because everything we knew was destroyed. ... Really they have won because they haven't been made to pay the damage" (quoted in Proudfoot 1990:117). Those who fought in the covert war remember that the CIA promised to compensate them for loss of families and homes. Lt. Phanha voiced his bitterness that Kmhmu veterans are seldom recognized for the services they rendered to the United States. What refugees receive from the U.S. government is less recognition of their sacrifice, than minoritization and the humiliations of public assistance. The injury is often experienced less as a broken contract than as unreturned hospitality and social exclusion. "Why did the United States invite us here with promises," asked one Lao, "and then make us feel very low when we ask for these promises?" (Proudfoot 1990:162).

When such promissory notes are ignored, falling outside of a national accounting, they may still be called in by the dead. Klima counterposes those Thai deaths that enabled the ousting of a military dictatorship and the establishment of a neoliberal democracy, against those other Thai deaths that led to no regime change, but only to wandering and dissatisfied ghosts, reminders of the violence buried at the foundations of the liberal state, and the structural violence that still sustains it. The ghosts of the forgotten, Klima writes, watch "restlessly from the outside" (2002:86)—outside, that is, of the cycle of exchange in its politically sanctioned and patriotically legible versions. It is in a similar environment of unresolved debt that U.S. institutions of death have become one of the sites at which the continued devaluation of Lao and Cambodian emigrants is acutely felt. U.S. medical and mortuary settings become the end points of failed gift exchange and discounted sacrifice (cf. Ong 2003:91–121). The possibility that relatives have been permitted to die because of immigrant status or dependence on welfare evokes a bureaucratic "bad death" in which inadequately tended bodies are poised to become restless spirits. The perception of disregard extends to post mortem procedures that tamper dangerously with the afterlife of the deceased.

There is a pervasive concern, for instance, about the engagement of medicine in bodily dismemberment (cf. Scheper-Hughes 2000). When elderly Khmer hear that a baby has been born without lungs, they say she must be the reincarnation of someone whose lungs were removed in a funeral home. Among Lao, anxieties about organ removal in medical or mortuary contexts invoke stories of bad spirits who eat the internal organs of others, and among Khmer, they invoke stories of soldiers who ate the livers of their enemies (Hinton 2005). Remembered violations of the dead in a context of warfare or state terror still reverberate in manipulations of the dead in a context of medical science. Hmong suggest that dead who are missing body parts seek replacements from the bodies of the living. Even Christian Hmong are opposed to autopsy, insofar as it treats the dead as experimental objects. "People complain that the doctors just use [autopsy] to study the body," Mr. Lo said. "They are angry about it. They don't like to have the body cut." One Kmhmu woman working as a hospital janitor told her community that she disposed of buckets of livers, hearts, and intestines every day. To rob dead bodies of organs is to cut the dead out of a relation of care that would otherwise sustain both them and their survivors.

As if to compensate for possible violations to dead bodies, people organize elaborate funerals. Yet even these fail to shield the dead from institutional disregard. "Here, even though we have everything," Sodoeung said, "food, cars, VCRs, all hi-tech, material things, still something is not complete. We do a lot of big ceremonies and spend a lot of money, but people feel like they still need something else to add to it." When her father died, the family performed ceremonies at the wat, but her mother wanted to perform a ceremony at home as well. "She really wanted to do a big ceremony, because she loved my father so much," Sodoeung said. "People who live in housing projects don't have space inside the house. We had to do the ceremony outside." Fifteen monks chanted morning and evening, lining up with their bowls to receive food from the guests. "The neighbors called the police. That's what made [my mother] upset, when she saw the police come." The arrival of police cars, and the accompanying sense of embarrassment and harassment, cramped an event that was intended as a lavish act of generosity to the dead.

Before cremation, funeral home staff remove any coins placed in the mouth of the deceased. Later Khmer families argue about whether the spirit will have enough money. "Younger people think it's just symbolic," Sodoeung said. "'Just put it on and then take it off. He's not going to know.' But my mom said, 'No, if you take it off that means you've lied. You didn't do it honestly.'" Whereas those educated in the United States learn to understand the offerings to the dead as symbols, in accordance with Christian theology and anthropology,[19] their elders understand them as gifts that secure the comfort of the deceased and the prosperity of the family. Some funeral homes prevent the relatives from initiating the cremation. "We want to witness the cremation with our five senses, to touch the button, to see the burning," Major Thao said. "We want to see the body going in the oven, see the smoke going up. Otherwise we don't feel good." Without a sensory engagement with the corpse to concretize the continued relationship with the dead, ceremonies seem empty and incomplete.

Mrs. Sann repeatedly returned, in our conversations, to her sorrow and anxiety about the deaths of two of her daughters, one in Cambodia, another in the United States. Yet she was smiling and animated as she narrated the home video of her mother's second burial in Vietnam, playing on a small TV in her apartment. Asked about the white string that twined from the coffin through the line of monks and around a pile of food and gifts, she said, "It's the way of sending goods to the person." After the body was exhumed she helped to wash the bones. "In that village they say that if you are a good person then, when they do the second burial, no one will smell anything. Before we dug up my mom's remains, I prayed 'please don't let her have any odor.' And she didn't. There were no flies and the villagers were happy and spoke a lot about it." Later she articulated her fears about the daughter who died in the United States.

> I asked the person at the cemetery if we would be able to do a second burial and he said I would have to ask the welfare office. Now I'm feeling bad that I buried her. If I had known that I couldn't do a second burial, I would have cremated her. Back home, we had a house and land. For some people we built a little house outside. Every mealtime, we brought them rice and soup.

In the United States, it is difficult to extend sufficient hospitality to the dead.[20]

For Khmer, anxiety about bodily remains in the United States echoes ongoing regrets over the dislocation of the dead under the Khmer Rouge. "My friend's son was shot to death," Mrs. Sann recounted. "She put his bones inside the house. Every mealtime she would offer him a little food. My children were scared of the remains. ... Here, if you want to put the ashes in the temple, you have to know the monk. And it is difficult to build a *chedey* [stupa]." Sodoeung agreed:

> My mother didn't think the wat was a safe place for my father's ashes in case of fire. She didn't want to lose his ashes. When he died she said, "Oh, I wish there was a place to put the ashes." We said, "Do you want to bury him here?" and she said, "No, we'll take him home." Right now his ashes are in the wat. He told me to take

them home when I can and bury them over there, build a stupa for him. But my mom says not to take him because she'll feel lonely.

Again the connection between bodily remains and spiritual presence is acutely apparent. The inadequacies of wats in the United States are reminiscent of the destruction of wats in Cambodia. Diaspora stirs up the wartime dread that the dead will be permanently displaced.

Kmhmu and Hmong also commented on institutional protocol that interferes with care for the dead. John Prachitham recalled that the funeral home that handled his father's body allowed only a few people to visit him and only for 15 minutes. People brought their gifts for the dead to his home. When I asked whether the elders worried about his ability to receive the gifts at such a distance from his body, John answered with a characteristically Christian presumption of the split between matter and spirit: "No. We don't care where the body is. We just make offerings for the spirit." Nonetheless one woman negotiated with funeral home staff to be permitted to place rice in her dead husband's hand. "If you don't give him rice," she asked, "what is he going to eat?" And when Cheuang died of cancer, a friend placed gifts of coins and food in his hands, reciting the route to his ancestors. There was, however, a troubling incident during his funeral. Typically the coffin would have been opened just before burial, to allow mourners to see him once more, and to offer him a last chance to return to life. Cheuang himself had spoken to me a few years earlier about the importance of giving the dead an opportunity to revive: "We made an offering of money, rice, and candles, and said to the *róoy* [spirits], 'Tell me if this person is really dead or if he is going to come back.' People will come back or not." But the funeral home personnel refused to open Cheuang's coffin, foreclosing this bodily communication between living and dead.

As one Hmong man was dying, the family dressed him in the burial garments that would identify him to his ancestors. Mrs. Vangay said, "We told the morgue, 'After you clean him up you should put the clothes back on.' But they didn't do that. They wrapped him in plastic." At the funeral home the family replaced the plastic with burial garments, laboring to turn a depersonalized corpse back into a spirit's body. In Laos, Hmong calculated an auspicious day and location for the burial, but here they can seldom afford that luxury. "Back there," Mr. Vangay recalled, "the funeral doesn't take much money. We did the ceremony at home and prepared everything ourselves. Here everything takes money." Those whose gravesites are paid for by public assistance are often stacked in layers, resulting in a burial configuration that can spark a hierarchical conflict among the dead, provoking them to send sickness to the living. Such burial practices can prove as risky to the living as the slipshod burials of wartime.

"When you're there with the dead person," Major Thao emphasized, "doing the ceremonies with your own hands, you gain a lot of merit, more than you would by donating money." This insistence on bodily intimacy—to be close to the corpse, to perform rites "with your own hands" is unfamiliar to predominant U.S. conceptions of mourning, which rest on a deeply ingrained assumption that death is a rupturing of body and soul. One physician observed that a man had lingered near his mother for an hour and a half after she stopped breathing. He added that he was "amazed" it took the son so long to "let her die" (Kaufman 2005:109).

Hospital discipline appears to operate according to a hidden eschatological assumption that a dead body becomes almost instantaneously an empty shell.

In this way a particular version of Christian numinology organizes the institutional management of death from the margins. Unlike Lao *khwan*, Khmer *praloeng*, Kmhmu *hrmàal*, or Hmong *plig*, Christian souls are not known to leave the body during severe illness, shock, or fright. After death, however, if post mortem practices are any indication, these souls are thought to effect a swift departure, indifferent to the body left behind. Whereas many Southeast Asian words translated as soul are used also to refer to the "spirits" of various body parts, or of houses or plants,[21] the Christian soul is singular and exclusively human. Its immateriality enables medical and mortuary practices in which human bodies are treated for periods of time as hunks of flesh, even though at other moments (e.g., during a viewing) they are dressed up to represent the social person. The immediate separation of the spirit from the body allows little temporal scope for tangible gifts, denying the dead not only materiality, but also the elapse of time that is essential to reciprocity.

Engaging with the dead for these emigrants is less a problem of memory, than a problem of a past that materially interpenetrates the present, manifesting in mysterious illnesses, spongy gravesites, or the suffocating pressure of a spirit who kills a man in his sleep; as much as in eerie funeral songs of the Hmong *qeej* (reed pipes), paper inscribed with names of the dead and passed into monks' hands, rotten flesh washed from human bones, or the smoke of a cremation fire. Mourning involves ongoing relationships with dead who might at any moment intervene in everyday life, leading your son to get AIDS, or your friend to die suddenly in his sleep, or, then again, enabling your brother to survive a battle, or your daughter to have daughters of her own. In these stories the dead "testify" in bodily ways, eating food left for them, demanding new clothes, asserting a contemporaneous presence. They demand less to be remembered than to be re-membered, re-embodied in material practice. U.S. institutions of death intercept this embodiment, implicitly urging emigrants to relegate the dead to the past, replace bodily engagement with memorialization, and embrace symbolic economies of mourning.[22]

Douang speculated that because of ceremonial lapses, people earn less boun making offerings to the dead in the United States than they would in Laos. Anyway, Lt. Somsy reasoned, most Lao spirits surely make their way back to Asia. "There's nothing here for them, no place to be comfortable." Even as emigrants adapt their relations with the dead to U.S. protocol, the sense of incompleteness is an endless ellipsis, a vague but escalating debt. What is missing is not any specific gift, but, rather, an uninhibited enactment of the sociality of living and dead. The inadequacies of diasporic ceremonies arise less from unfinished exchange than from the tendency of modern institutional practice to implicitly deny the material presence of the dead, substituting a symbolic presence that should be satisfied with symbolic gifts. This substitution can have the effect of discounting the dead as social beings, evoking the desecrations of wartime.

In his account of burial during battle, Lt. Somsy said nothing about the bodies of those he himself had killed. Might they also harm him? Of his brother's harassment by the dead, Charles said, "He spent a lot of time in the jungle fighting, and he saw a lot of spirits. Ghosts would bother him at night. He would spend the night in his hammock hanging in a big tree and a spirit would make noise, or make the tree branch break." These spirits undoubtedly included not only comrades whose deaths he witnessed, but also enemy soldiers whose deaths he caused. Lt. Phanha told me, "In this life I know I'll suffer badly because of what I have done. I had to kill so many people. I don't think god will ever forgive me." Here he almost certainly referred to the Christian god he expected one day to worship, because whenever he spoke of the spirits who helped him tend rice fields, heal illness, or escape from prison camp, he referred to *róoy*, the Kmhmu word used for spirits ranging from paternal ancestral dead, *róoy* kàang, to spirits of the forest (*róoy pri* or *róoy patay*), to those who died violent deaths (*róoy he'ép*).[23] In speaking of forgiveness, he evoked Christianity, as if it promised (and yet might fail) to assume his debts to those he had killed.

Are "enemy" dead also enfolded into a reciprocity with the living then? Or are they deliberately excluded from it? When Lt. Somsy spoke of "hiding" the body of his comrade, he tacitly acknowledged the risk that the dead could become targets for desecration. Katherine Verdery writes of Serbs who machine-gunned the graves of Croatians in post-Yugoslavia (1999:107). Alexander Hinton retells a story of a group of Khmer Rouge soldiers who ate the liver of a man as punishment for stealing cassava from a collective food cache (2005:290–293). They intended, Hinton argues, to strip the man of his membership in the social community, while simultaneously absorbing his vitality.[24] Violation of bodies does more than refer to acts of violence; it reiterates them in mimetic acts of terror. The defaced body is not merely a political symbol, but a violent trace, bearing an intense potency to affect not only mourners, but also possibly perpetrators.

Violence to the dead appears to position them decisively outside a given community as those to whom nothing is owed, whose deaths are, in Agamben's terms, forbidden to be seen as sacrifice. For Agamben, a sacrificial victim retains his social value insofar as his death is consecrated through a relationship to a deity, or in the more modern and supposedly secular sacrifice, to a political cause. *Homo sacer* are those, by contrast, whose deaths are permitted, but not meaningful, those who are killable with utter impunity, but not sacrificable. Their dead bodies, purged of personhood, are available as objects for scientific experimentation, commodity extraction, or anonymous disposal. There is surely a difference between casual treatment of bodies as commodities, and intentional desecration, which implicitly recognizes, if only to theatrically negate, the body's sacredness for others. Shooting into gravesites or eating body parts suggests an attack on the social existence of the dead, while piling bodies into mass graves suggests the preclusion of such an existence altogether. Yet mass graves also tend toward ritual excess in their ability to terrorize and horrify.

As noted earlier, the concept of "bare life" is of little help in interpreting the devaluation of the dead. After calling for an investigation of the "practical and political mystery" of the European separation of body and soul, Agamben, in a rare consideration of the ontological status of the dead, revisits Aquinas's solution to the medieval confusion over the resurrection of the body. Severing materiality from spirit, Aquinas asserted that in the Christian paradise there would be no need of eat, drink, sex, or sleep (Agamben 2004:16–19). It is noteworthy that Agamben's compelling discussion, in *The Open*, of the split between matter and spirit at the root of European definitions of the human, is marked by the recurrent phrase "in our culture" (2004:16, 80, 92). With these words he delimits the salience of the matter—spirit dynamic he so carefully examines. But what is "our culture" in a world where U.S. operatives recruit Hmong and Lao to fight North Vietnamese in the jungles of Southeast Asia; where Khmer, Kmhmu, Lao, and Hmong receive education about U.S. culture in Thai refugee camps and cram for examinations for U.S. citizenship in U.S. housing projects; where Hmong grow vegetables to sell in public markets to urban middle-class whites; where Hmong and Kmhmu bury their dead in North American soil and Khmer and Lao burn their dead in U.S. crematoriums; and where everyone forcibly learns the theological lesson of the merely symbolic presence of the dead in U.S. funeral homes and hospitals?

In a meditation on humanity as a troubled counterpoint of animality and spirit, what space is left for imagining relations of living and dead in other terms? The radical separation of matter and spirit found necessary by Aquinas, and all but ineluctable by Agamben, is problematized if not absent within stories of dead who return as lizards to watch over their grandsons, or dead who are in need of clothes and cookware. In the world imagined by those stories, desecration of the dead cannot be simply understood as the treatment of the dead as debased matter devoid of spirit. The stories gesture to a simultaneously corporeal and spectral power of the dead.

For the very actions that radically devalue the dead have the effect of back- handedly acknowledging their uncanny power. Desacralization involves active ritual effort (machine-gunning the grave, carving out the liver), which, as Michael Taussig observed, may stir up "a strange surplus of negative energy … from within the defaced thing itself" (1999:1). Many survivors, including those who themselves dealt death, are wary of that spectral surplus. They sense that those whose deaths are denied a sacrificial dimension, are precisely those who return to haunt the living, defying their devaluation, seizing for themselves the mystical power released in their fetishization. Of a death by shooting during a skirmish between CIA-sponsored and Pathet Lao forces in a Kmhmu village, John Prachitham said, "One communist tried to move into our house for protection. He died right there. After this happened everybody moved away. Later the whole village took a rope and dragged him, because nobody wanted to grab him. Dying that way, he's a bad spirit." Ghost narratives make reiterative reference to a dangerous agency that is never dissolved, and may even be intensified through a violent or desacralized death. One way of understanding restless ghosts, Klima suggests, is as those whose sacrifice has not been recognized. "To be a ghost," he writes, "is to be marginal, to have no role to play in the economy of the living" (Klima 2002:163). Yet the exclusion of ghosts, as he also shows, can never be absolute as long as the dead retain the power to haunt from the margins, impressing their material presence on the living. When emigrants experience ancestor illness or nightmares of the dead, they register in their bodies the violation of the sociality of living and dead that characterizes death, not just in the U.S.-sponsored wars of Southeast Asia, but in U.S. morgues, funeral homes, and cemeteries.

Spectrality is a well-traveled metaphor in recent years, appearing in discussions of economy as a metaphor for commodities and speculative forms of value, or in discussions of historical memory as a metaphor for past injustices whose effects persist in the present. In the stories retold here, the spectral quality of the gifts received from or offered to the dead, although it may lend its power to each of these usages, is not itself metaphorical. The disregarded dead bodies in these narratives are not just the violated property of political citizens, but the material traces of dead who insist on active relationships with the living. At stake in the diasporic disruption of this material sociality of living and dead, are not only particular imaginations of afterlives, but also particular politics of grief. The stories suggest that the dead are not so easily consigned to the past and that calls for reconciliation or forgetting overlook the ways that past violence inhabits the present.

NOTES

Initial research for this essay was sponsored by the Cross-Cultural Health Care Program. Additional research and writing was supported by the University of Minnesota, the School for Advanced Research in the Human Experience (SAR), and the Salus Mundi Foundation. Special thanks to Hoon Song and Stuart McLean for provocative and inspired critique, to Sharon Kaylen for her poet's eye, and to Mike and Kim Fortun and anonymous reviewers for their editorial insight.

1. Speakers' names are pseudonyms.
2. See also Baudrillard's discussion of the modern erosion of exchange with the dead (1993:125–194).
3. Hertz notes that in some communities the state of the dead body is considered parallel to the fate of the soul (1960). Subsequent work interprets this connection as a symbolic one whereby the condition of the body works as a metaphor for the adjustments of both the spirit and the community to death (e.g., Bloch and Parry 1982; Metcalf and Huntington 1991).
4. Wrestling with the apparent contradiction between transference of merit and individual karma, Keyes concludes that for Theravadin Buddhists, merit is a form of "spiritual currency" that strengthens social community (1983:282–283).
5. For accounts of Phchum Ben celebrations in the United States see Douglas (2005:132–134) and Smith-Hefner (1999:58–59).
6. For accounts of Hmong geomancy see Julian (2004:38), Tapp (1989:86; see also 1988), Bliatout (1993), and Cooper *et al.* (1996).
7. The cow's soul serves to replace one of the souls of the deceased, which has been consumed by Ntxwj Nyoog, the Hmong spirit responsible for sickness and death (Quincy 1988:108).
8. Although these different "souls" are key to the complexities of mourning practice, many hesitate to identify them as taxonomic categories (Tapp 1989:87).
9. The importance of material care of the dead is referenced in a Kmhmu tale of two brothers, one of whom neglects his dead mother to his own detriment (Lindell *et al.* 1977–95, vol. 3:83–84).
10. Heidegger speaks of this indebtedness as "guilt" (1996:284), casting it in a distinctively Christian light.
11. See also Chakrabarty (1998) on the persistence of gods and spirits in modern practices.
12. For histories of Khmer Rouge policies toward Buddhist wats and monks see Boua (1991) and Harris (2005:157–189).
13. See also McLean's (2004:109–110) account of "hungry grass," a landscape haunted by the dead of the Irish potato famine.

14. See Harris on "occult" powers in use by the Cambodian military during the 1970s (2005:168).
15. This is an insight variously articulated by Bataille (1988:70), as well as Marx, Hegel, and Nietzsche (Comay 1990:66).
16. Khmer speak of spirit families to whom newborn children belong (Choulean 1986; Thompson 1996:18). Hmong speak of "spirit parents" (*txoov kab yeeb*) who are offered "spirit money" in gratitude or payment for a newborn child's spirit (Rice 2000).
17. Noting that the dead are the first group with whom humans entered into contract, Mauss commented, "Indeed, it is they who are the true owners of the things and possessions of this world" (1990:16).
18. On the war in Laos and its effects see Stuart-Fox (1997), Evans (1998), Ireson-Dolittle and Moreno-Black (2004), and Quincy (2000). On the war in Cambodia and the Khmer Rouge regime see Becker (1986), Chandler (2000), Kiernan (1996), and Jackson (1989).
19. See Asad for the genealogy of ritual as symbolic action (1988) and Keane (2007) on the semiotic ideology of Protestantism.
20. See Kalab (1994) for a related account of Khmer funerals in Paris.
21. On the spirits of body parts see Rajadhon (1946:124) and Chindarsi (1976:30). On praloeng, see Thompson (1996).
22. In a discussion of Japanese mediums, Marilyn Ivy suggests that it is the very slippage in the physical encounter with the dead (the way the voice of the dead speaking through the medium differs from the voice mourners remember) that facilitates an outpouring of grief (1995:180). Perhaps similar slippages in the material exchange with the dead in the stories told above—the dirt that is not quite the body, the dream image that is not quite the person, the coin that remains in the ashes—sustain an awareness of the absences in the present that reference the violence of the past. To interrupt these material encounters might be to foreclose mourning of both personal and collective loss.
23. For a description of various róoy, see Tayanin (1994:20–28).
24. See Hinton (2005:289–290) for the significance of the liver in Khmer conceptions of power.

REFERENCES CITED

Adler, Shelley R. 1991 Sudden Unexpected Nocturnal Death Syndrome among Hmong Immigrants: Examining the Role of the "Nightmare." Journal of American Folklore 104:54–71.
Agamben, Giorgio 1998 Homo Sacer: Sovereign Power and Bare Life. D. Heller-Roazen, trans. Palo Alto, CA: Stanford University Press.
—2002 Remnants of Auschwitz: The Witness and the Archive. D. Heller-Roazen, trans. New York: Zone.
—2004 The Open: Man and Animal. K. Attell, trans. Palo Alto, CA: Stanford University Press.
Asad, Talal 1988 Towards a Genealogy of the Concept of Ritual. In Vernacular Christianity: Essays in the Social Anthropology of Religion. W. James and D. H. Johnson, eds. Pp. 73–87. Oxford: Jaso.
Bataille, Georges 1988 [1967] The Accursed Share: An Essay on General Economy, vol. 1: Consumption. New York: Zone.
—1989 [1973] Theory of Religion. New York: Zone.
Baudrillard, Jean 1993 [1976] Symbolic Exchange and Death. I. H. Grant, trans. London: Sage.
Becker, Elizabeth 1986 When the War Was Over: Cambodia and the Khmer Rouge Revolution. New York: Public Affairs.
Benson, Peter 2008 El Campo: Faciality and Structural Violence in Farm Labor Camps. Cultural Anthropology 23(4):589–629.
Bliatout, Bruce Thowpaou 1993 Hmong Death Customs: Traditional and Acculturated. In Ethnic Variation in Death, Dying and Grief: Diversity in Universality. D. P. Irish, K. F. Lundquist, and V. J. Nelsen, eds. Pp. 79–100. Washington, DC: Taylor and Frances.
Bloch, Maurice, and Jonathan Parry 1982 Introduction: Death and the Regeneration of Life. In Death and the Regeneration of Life. M. Bloch and J. Parry, eds. Pp. 1–44. Cambridge: Cambridge University Press.
Boua, Chanthou 1991 Genocide of a Religious Group: Pol Pot and Cambodia's Buddhist Monks. In State Organized Terror: The Case of Violent Internal Repression. P. T. Bushnell, V. Shlapentokh, C. K. Vanderpool, and J. Sundram, eds. Pp. 227–240. Boulder, CO: Westview.
Boyarin, Jonathan 1994 Death and the Minyan. Cultural Anthropology 9(1):3–22.
Chakrabarty, Dipesh 1998 Minority Histories, Subaltern Pasts. Postcolonial Studies 1(1):15–29.
—2000 Provincializing Europe: Postcolonial Thought and Historical Difference. Princeton: Princeton University Press.
Chandler, David 2000 A History of Cambodia. Boulder, CO: Westview.
Chindarsi, Nusit 1976 The Religion of the Hmong Njua. Bangkok: Siam Society.
Choulean, Ang 1986 Les Etres Surnaturels dans la Religion Populaire Khmere. Paris: Cedoreck.

Comay, Rebecca 1990 Gifts without Presents: Economies of "Experience" in Bataille and Heidegger. Yale French Studies: On Bataille 78:66–89.

Cooper, Robert, Nicholas Tapp, Gary Yia Lee, and Gretel Schwoer-Kohl 1996 The Hmong. Bangkok: Artasia.

Derrida, Jacques 1992 Given Time: 1. Counterfeit Money. P. Kamuf, trans. Chicago: University of Chicago Press.

—1995 The Gift of Death. D. Wills, trans. Chicago: University of Chicago Press.

Desjarlais, Robert 2000 Echoes of a Yolmo Buddhist's Life, in Death. Cultural Anthropology 15(2):260–293.

Douglas, Thomas J. 2005 Changing Religious Practices among Cambodian Immigrants in Long Beach and Seattle. In Immigrant Faiths: Transforming Religious Life in America. K. I. Leonard, A. Stepick, M. A. Vasquez, and J. Holdaway, eds. Pp. 123–144. Walnut Creek, CA: AltaMira.

Evans, Grant 1998 The Politics of Ritual and Remembrance: Laos since 1975. Honolulu: University of Hawai'i Press.

Faier, Leiba 2008 Runaway Stories: The Underground Micromovements of Filipina Oyomesan in Rural Japan. Cultural Anthropology 23(4):630–659.

Foucault, Michel 1990 [1978] The History of Sexuality, vol. 1: An Introduction. R. Hurley, trans. New York: Vintage.

Francis, Doris, Leonie Kellaher, and Georgina Neophytou 2005 The Secret Cemetery. Oxford: Berg.

Gilbert, Sandra 2006 Death's Door: Modern Dying and the Ways We Grieve. New York: W.W. Norton.

Gombrich, Richard 1971 Merit-Transference in Sinhalese Buddhism: A Case Study of the Interaction between Doctrine and Practice. History of Religions 11:203–219.

Harris, Ian 2005 Cambodian Buddhism: History and Practice. Honolulu: University of Hawai'i Press.

Heidegger, Martin 1996 [1953] Being and Time: A Translation of Sein und Zeit. J. Stambaugh, trans. Albany: State University of New York Press. Hertz, Robert

—1960 [1907] A Contribution to the Study of the Collective Representation of Death. In Death and the Right Hand. Pp. 27–154. Glencoe, IL: Free Press.

Hinton, Alexander Laban 2005 Why Did They Kill? Cambodia in the Shadow of Genocide. Berkeley: University of California Press.

Ireson-Doolittle, Carol, and Geraldine Moreno-Black 2004 The Lao: Gender, Power, and Livelihood. Boulder, CO: Westview.

Ivy, Marilyn 1995 Discourses of the Vanishing: Modernity, Phantasm, Japan. Chicago: University of Chicago Press.

Jackson, Karl D., ed. 1989 Cambodia 1975–1978: Rendezvous with Death. Princeton: Princeton University Press.

Johnson, Charles, ed. 1992 Dab Neeg Hmoob. Myths, Legends and Folk Tales from the Hmong of Laos. Saint Paul, MN: Macalaster College Press.

Julian, Roberta 2004 Living Locally, Dreaming Globally: Transnational Cultural Imaginings and Practices in the Hmong Diaspora. In The Hmong of Australia: Culture and Diaspora. N. Tapp and G. Y. Lee, eds. Pp. 25–58. Canberra: Pandanus.

Kalab, Milada 1994 Cambodian Buddhist Monasteries in Paris: Continuing Tradition and Changing Patterns. In Cambodian Culture since 1975: Homeland and Exile. M. Ebihara, C. A. Mortland, and J. Ledgerwood, eds. Pp. 57–71. Ithaca, NY: Cornell University Press.

Kaufman, Sharon R. 2005 … And a Time to Die: How American Hospitals Shape the End of Life. Chicago: University of Chicago Press.

Keane, Webb 2007 Christian Moderns: Freedom and Fetish in the Mission Encounter. Berkeley: University of California Press.

Keyes, Charles F. 1983 Merit-Transference in the Kammic Theory of Popular Theravada Buddhism. In Karma: An Anthropological Inquiry. C. F. Keyes and E. V. Daniel, eds. Pp. 261–286. Berkeley: University of California Press.

Kiernan, Ben 1996 The Pol Pot Regime: Race, Power, and Genocide in Cambodia under the Khmer Rouge, 1975–1979. New Haven, CT: Yale University.

Klima, Alan 2002 The Funeral Casino: Meditation, Massacre, and Exchange with the Dead in Thailand. Princeton: Princeton University Press.

LaFreniere, Bree 2000 Music through the Dark: A Tale of Survival in Cambodia. Honolulu: University of Hawai'i Press.

Lemoine, Jacques 1996 The Constitution of a Hmong Shaman's Powers of Healing and Folk Culture. Shaman 4(1–2):143–165.

Lindell, Kristina, Jan-Ojvind Swahn, and Damrong Tayanin 1977–95 Folk Tales from Kammu. 5 vols. London: Curzon.

Mauss, Marcel 1990 The Gift: The Form and Reasons for Exchange in Archaic Societies. W. D. Halls, trans. New York: W. W. Norton.

McCallum, Cecilia 1999 Consuming Pity: The Production of Death among the Cashinahua. Cultural Anthropology 14(4):443–471.

McLean, Stuart 2004 The Event and Its Terrors: Ireland, Famine, Modernity. Palo Alto, CA: Stanford University Press.

Metcalf, Peter, and Richard Huntington 1991 Celebrations of Death: The Anthropology of Mortuary Ritual. Cambridge: Cambridge University Press.

Nancy, Jean-Luc, and Richard Livingston 1991 The Unsacrificeable. Yale French Studies: Literature and the Ethical Question 79:20–38.

Ong, Aihwa 2003 Buddha Is Hiding: Refugees, Citizenship, the New America. Berkeley: University of California Press.

Orta, Andrew 2002 Burying the Past: Locality, Lived History, and Death in an Aymara Ritual of Remembrance. Cultural Anthropology 17(4):471–511.

Proudfoot, Robert 1990 Even the Birds Don't Sound the Same Here: The Laotian Refugees' Search for Heart in American Culture. New York: Peter Lang.

Putsch, Robert W. 1988 Ghost Illness: A Cross-Cultural Experience with the Expression of a Non-Western Tradition in Clinical Practice. American Indian and Alaska Native Mental Health Research 2(2):6–26.

Quincy, Keith 1988 Hmong: History of a People. Cheney: Eastern Washington University Press.

—2000 Harvesting Pa Chay's Wheat: The Hmong and America's Secret War in Laos. Spokane: Eastern Washington University Press.

Rajadhon, Phra Anuman 1946 The Khwan and Its Ceremonies. Journal of the Siam Society 50(2):119–164.

Rice, Pranee Liamputtong 2000 Baby, Souls, Name and Health: Traditional Customs for a Newborn Infant among the Hmong in Melbourne. Early Human Development 57:189–203.

Scheper-Hughes, Nancy 2000 The Global Traffic in Human Organs. Current Anthropology 41(2):191–211.

Smith-Hefner, Nancy J. 1999 Khmer American: Identity and Moral Education in a Diasporic Community. Berkeley: University of California Press.

Stuart-Fox, Martin 1997 A History of Laos. Cambridge: Cambridge University Press.

Sturken, Marita 1997 Tangled Memories: The Vietnam War, the AIDS Epidemic, and the Politics of Remembering. Berkeley: University of California Press.

Symonds, Patricia V. 2004 Calling in the Soul: Gender and the Cycle of Life in a Hmong Village. Seattle: University of Washington Press.

Tapp, Nicholas 1988 Geomancy and Development: The Case of the White Hmong of North Thailand. Ethnos 53:228–238. Hmong Religion. Asian Folklore Studies 48(1):59–94.

Taussig, Michael 1999 Defacement: Public Secrecy and the Labor of the Negative. Palo Alto, CA: Stanford University Press.

Tayanin, Damrong 1994 Being Kammu: My Village, My Life. Ithaca, NY: Cornell Southeast Asia Program.

Thao, Phillipe Nompus 1993 Between Two Worlds: Hmong Ethnography, Spirituality and Ceremony for the Deceased. M.S. thesis, Department of Anthropology, Mankato State University.

Thompson, Ashley 1996 The Calling of the Souls: A Study of the Khmer Ritual Hau Bralin. Clayton, Victoria, Australia: Monash Asia Institute, Monash University.

Tobin, Joseph Jay, and Joan Friedman 1983 Spirits, Shamans, and Nightmare Death: Survivor Stress in a Hmong Refugee. American Journal of Orthopsychiatry 53(3):439–448.

Verdery, Katherine 1999 The Political Lives of Dead Bodies: Reburial and Postsocialist Change. New York: Columbia University Press.

Yathay, Pin 1987 Stay Alive, My Son. New York: Simon & Schuster.

25

A Witch Hunt in New Guinea
Anthropology on Trial
Michael Wesch

Recently, it has become increasingly common for anthropologists to note that witchcraft, often thought of as something "traditional," has not faded with the effects of modernization throughout the world. Contrary to some expectations, witchcraft has become an active conceptual field for locals to interpret and act in emerging fields of modernity (e.g., Comaroff and Comaroff 1993; Moore and Sanders 2001). While ethnographers the world over seek to understand how different local modernities are forming, locals themselves are using the paradigm of witchcraft to explain their own experiences of modernity, such as why they are poor, subservient, corrupt, dying of AIDS, or losing World Cup soccer matches. Witchcraft imageries are employed to explain why a development project did not work or why it *did* work for the neighboring town or district but not one's own. They commonly provide a framework to understand new inequalities of wealth and political power (e.g., Geschiere 1997; Niehaus 2001).

Unfortunately, witchcraft imageries are matched in pervasiveness by the persecution of accused witches. The World Health Organization (2002) recently estimated that 500 elderly women accused of witchcraft are killed each year in Tanzania alone. News reports from parts of India, Indonesia, Papua New Guinea, and other areas in Africa tell of similar scenarios. By way of comparison, most historians now estimate that approximately 40,000 accused witches were killed during the so-called witch craze in Europe from the 15th to the 17th centuries, at a rate of approximately 133 killings per year (Levack 1995). We look back on that era with a sense of horror. Yet we seem to look on our current era, in which the numbers I have presented suggest that the rate of persecution may be many times higher, with a sense of ambivalence. To what can we attribute this ambivalence? Why have there been no widespread calls to action? Commenting on this problem over 35 years ago, Mary Douglas noted this ironic double standard: "Dangerous in Europe, the same beliefs in Melanesia or Africa appeared to be tame, even domesticated; they served useful functions and were not expected to run amuck" (1970:xiii). Now enter the anthropologist into fieldwork situations where witchcraft-related violence does indeed seem to be running amok, and the quandaries of engagement I will be discussing in this article become readily apparent.

I was an unfortunate witness to the horrors of a witch hunt in central New Guinea.[1] Many of the dilemmas I faced were born from the situation itself. But in this article I would like to point out that these dilemmas were only magnified by my role as an anthropologist, in particular the paradoxes and dilemmas implicit in anthropological practice itself. They are dilemmas born within the roots of anthropology that seemed to grow around me as the witch hunt continued, until I felt trapped within a thick infestation of twisted vines of paradox and self-doubt. I locate the roots of my dilemmas within a classic trio of anthropology: cultural relativism, holism, and participant-observation. I locate the growing complexities of my dilemmas within the growing complexities of these terms: cultural relativism's transformation into what Michael Carrithers has recently labeled "radical cultural relativism … constant processes of cultural creation, destruction, hybridization, and diversification" (2005:441); the attendant transformation of holism from its association with "whole" (distinct) cultures to the imagined whole of vast and intricate global interconnections; as well as the transformation from Malinowski's relatively scientist participant-observation to an increasingly morally engaged observant participation (e.g., Scheper-Hughes 1995).

THE CLASSIC TRIO OF ANTHROPOLOGY: HOLISM, CULTURAL RELATIVISM, AND PARTICIPANT-OBSERVATION

Despite their recent transformations, cultural relativism, holism, and participant-observation remain key fundamental principles of cultural anthropology. Later in this article, I will argue that in its classic textbook form the trio inhibits moral action in fieldwork situations by promoting a value of scientific detachment. But while moral action in the field is inhibited, the three contribute to a classic story line promoting open-mindedness toward other ways of life and can show even the most exotic beliefs and practices as functional and meaningful within the local culture.

The best-selling introductory textbook in cultural anthropology defines holism as "a fundamental principle of anthropology, that the various parts of culture must be viewed in the broadest possible context in order to understand their interconnections and interdependence" (Haviland *et al.* 2005:14). Prior to the "crisis" in anthropology (Tyler 1987), holism often went hand in hand with varieties of functionalism and placed an emphasis on understanding cultures as distinct wholes. To understand one aspect of "a" culture, one needed to understand all of the other aspects of that particular culture as well.

This fundamental principle of anthropology is deeply wedded to another fundamental principle, cultural relativism. The textbook definition is "the thesis that one must suspend judgment of other peoples' practices in order to understand them in their own cultural terms" (Haviland *et al.* 2005:49). In other words, such practices should be approached holistically, "viewed in the broadest possible context in order to understand their interconnections and interdependence" with other aspects of the culture and that culture's particular web of meanings (Haviland *et al.* 2005:49). We are all well versed in the limitations of these two fundamental principles and the many transformations they have undertaken in recent decades. We no longer approach our fieldwork sites as if they contain within them an isolated and distinct "whole" culture. Nonetheless I would like to start with them in their "textbook definition" form in order to examine the implications for the third fundamental principle in our classic trio: participant-observation.

We owe the name of this third foundational principle to Bronislaw Malinowski. For Malinowski, participation was primarily a way to improve observation by stepping off the veranda to gain a better perspective, as he describes in the following:

> Soon after I had established myself I began to take part, in a way, in the village life … I had to learn how to behave, and to a certain extent, I acquired "the feeling" for native good and bad manners. With this, and with the capacity of enjoying their company and sharing some of their games and amusements, I began to feel that I was indeed in touch with the natives, and this is certainly the preliminary condition of being able to carry on successful field work. [1953:7–8]

Analyzing this mode of fieldwork in 1963, John Barnes noted that it was built on a model of the field as a scientific laboratory. People were studied as if "under the microscope" (Barnes 1963:123). The effects of the researcher on the field were ignored, and fieldworkers were expected to act in such a way as to minimize their effects on the local culture. The influences of outside groups such as missionaries, administrators, schools, and markets were seen as contaminants to be disregarded in the final analysis. Turning to questions of moral judgment in the field, Barnes notes that "under the microscope there could be no moral judgments. They had their code and we had ours, and the two never met" (1963:123).

In its classic form, the key trio rests on the notion of cultures as wholes that can be bracketed off from the rest of the world. Importantly, this notion entails another: the fieldworkers bracket themselves from the culture. Cultural relativism's call to "suspend judgment" asks the fieldworker to leave some part of the self behind when entering the field, to tread lightly and respect cultural practices rather than alter them, regardless of how they might work against the fieldworker's own personal or cultural values.

As such, personal accounts of fieldwork dilemmas were rare, even where there were intense social dramas including actual or alleged physical and mystical violence such as witchcraft. In Evans-Pritchard's (1937) classic work on the Azande we find only a few hints of the moral dilemmas he may have faced. We know from a relatively harmless example of a boy stubbing his toe and blaming witchcraft that Evans-Pritchard (1937:66) challenged their statements, but this is stated as a method for obtaining more information rather than a moral action.

Even the intimately personal account of Bowen's *Return to Laughter* echoes this sentiment. Caught up in dramas and trials of witchcraft accusations she relents, "I had come from one world to live in another. These two worlds judged by standards so greatly different that translation was often impossible" (1964:231). Her work transcends other studies of witchcraft by her contemporaries in many respects, yet maintains the sense of otherworldliness. The unnamed group she is studying is somewhere *out there,* and although they may reflect and refract elements of *us here,* they remain *other* through and through.

Although such notions of otherworldliness may have precluded moral interventions in the field, this same otherworldliness was foundational to the moral agenda implicit within the classic trio of holism, cultural relativism, and participant-observation. Mary Douglas notes that this perspective, which views the culture as an isolated whole, allowed colonial fieldworkers like Evans-Pritchard to argue that seemingly strange practices and beliefs such as those involving witchcraft actually *functioned* within a particular social and cultural system. "The responsibility to protect and to preach tolerance was widely echoed," she notes: "To show witchcraft beliefs as performing a constructive role in a functioning social system has been one way of carrying out this responsibility" (1970:xxiii).

The moral of the story that these three fundamental principles tell is one that is still worth telling, not least of all because it still informs anthropological practice. It tells us that if we are willing to suspend our judgments (cultural relativism), explore the issue firsthand (participant-observation), and try to understand a phenomenon's rich contexts and interconnections (holism), we can build our capacity for empathy, tolerance, and an appreciation of otherness. The following is the story as I tell it to my introductory students. It is entirely true, except for one looming asterisk, which makes up the remainder of this article.

Being *there* (in "another world") is where our story begins. When I first arrived in Papua New Guinea a large dance was planned to welcome my arrival. I could not wait to see the body paint, feathers, cassowary quills, and lizard-skin drums dancing before me in a rich display of visual symbolic play. As the dancers appeared wearing elaborate headdresses and body decorations, they did not disappoint me. But the dance itself was entirely incomprehensible. It was in constant motion, moving from place to place, circling in on itself, dissolving, moving again, denying me any chance at a good perspective. It was only much later in my fieldwork, when I actually *participated* in the dance, that I learned what was going on. Had I not participated in their dance I would never have known the little things that make the dance what it is—that one slides up and down rather than bounces; that one must keep the shoulders square and eyes focused forward; that it requires a perfectly cupped hand and a strong but not too strong wrist to make the drum really sing; and that all of this must be done among constant sexual innuendo, flirtation, and playfulness as women flock like birds to the men, holding their feathers and pulling their penis gourds. The only worthwhile perspective on this dance is from the inside, participating, and this I took as the metaphor for my fieldwork.

Many anthropologists tell a similar story. We tend to accentuate the story with tales of exotic foods or funny faux pas, all of which serve to further illustrate the sense of really *being there*. But beyond these surface elements, the story goes, we find ourselves becoming increasingly enmeshed in rich personal relationships. Oftentimes we are adopted into families and refer to our so-called key informants with terms like *brother, sister, mother,* and *father.*

As this is another cultural world, a more intensely challenging tale of cultural difference inevitably ensues. In my case, the challenges began when my good friend Kodenim became ill, his stomach swollen and distended. I remember sitting with him one day while he explained again that his stomach did not hurt all over but only in two places, as if an arrow had hit him near the center of the stomach and exited through his side. In fact, that was precisely what he suspected—that he had been shot with an invisible witchcraft arrow. I offered to take him to a hospital, but he insisted that he needed to stay in the village to deal with the witchcraft that he viewed as the root cause of his illness. If he could not find the perpetrator soon and ask him to retract the witchcraft, the witch would soon come to finish him off. In fact, Kodenim sometimes wondered if he had not already been killed and eaten and that the disfunctional body he now occupied was nothing but a poor imitation created by cannibal witches to disguise their nefarious activities.

The intro anthropology student inevitably thinks of this as bizarre and perhaps irrational at first, but it is nothing for which a little cultural relativism does not already have a reasonable answer. Invoking Evans-Pritchard's famous Azande rice barn example, it is not that Kodenim and other locals did not understand that there was something physically wrong with his body. It is that these (often biomedical) explanations do not address the socially relevant cause of why these particular physical problems had afflicted *his* body at that particular time.

As we follow the story of how Kodenim sought out this socially relevant cause, we find that beliefs in witchcraft may serve an important sociological function. To discover the witch, Kodenim and others in the community engaged in a careful analysis of Kodenim's past words and actions, revealing virtually all of his past wrongs and grievances. A close friend of Kodenim's (my "brother") made a mental list of all Kodenim's social problems and called for a community meeting. Over 100 people gathered around as my brother went through his list. One by one each social problem was revealed, discussed, and then healed through an exchange of gifts or kind words of repentance. Though there were many such social problems, the most convincing cause of witchcraft for virtually everybody present was the fact that Kodenim had stolen a pig from my "father." Kodenim had already paid compensation to my father, but there was concern that perhaps the compensation had not been enough. My father stood and gave a long, powerful speech about his multiple relationship ties to Kodenim and the support he had given Kodenim throughout his life in school and other endeavors. He ended with a simple, yet profound expression of solidarity, referring to Kodenim as one of his own, his son whom he could never harm. The meeting concluded with a group prayer and a mass washing of Kodenim. Everybody in the community that had ever had any form of conflict with Kodenim touched a bar of soap and prayed for his health. Kodenim sat in the middle of the village while one by one each member of the community came forward, scooped up a handful of water, and sprinkled it onto his body while stating words of hope and healing.

Unfortunately, Kodenim died soon after the washing. Though I was deeply saddened, I took comfort in the social healing that he inspired in his final days. Through his suffering, many of the hidden tensions from past wrongs and grievances that had been lurking just under the surface of village life had been brought before us all to be dealt with and reconciled. If ever there was a ritual that functioned in a classic Durkheimian way to build social solidarity, this was it. Kodenim was perhaps the greatest beneficiary. The ritual allowed him to make amends for all of his wrongs and accept the beautiful outpouring of love and reconciliation symbolized in the water flowing from the hands of those with whom he had lived his entire life.

After Kodenim died, his family came to my father asking for compensation. They claimed that even if my father had not been the witch, he should have been there to protect Kodenim from the witchcraft of others. Besides, people who had exchange relations with Kodenim would soon be arriving in the village asking for compensation themselves, and the family had none to give. My father once again denied any accusation of witchcraft but offered compensation for their loss nonetheless. Like all compensation payments, it was much larger than any one person could ever afford. It required massive coordination among a large network of people with whom my father had strong relations. As a member of my father's family, I also contributed. The large pile of gifts we gave to Kodenim's family would be shared widely, and those who shared in this bounty would one day make a return gift. The returned gift would be returned, and so on, reconnecting those strands of the intricate web of relations that had been torn when Kodenim passed away.

The value of holism and cultural relativism to find function and meaning in these events is clear. As for my participation in these events, it only further enveloped me in the local culture, holding the promise for better future insights while providing a nice little story that I might use later to establish my ethnographic authority of "being there." The story nicely illustrates the functional role of witchcraft beliefs and how those beliefs are grounded within a local worldview that is complete and coherent. It is a shining example of the power of holism, cultural relativism, and participant-observation that I can share with my students through a familiar formula: Start with something exotic, suspend our judgments with cultural relativism, invoke the holistic approach to show how it works and makes sense within the local cultural system, and finish it off with a touching vision of a village reunited.

*

Now for the asterisk. The culture is not an isolated whole that can be artificially set apart. The prayers are Christian, the soap is store-bought, and the community meeting was called a "safety meeting" and modeled after "safety meetings" held at a nearby multinational copper mine. More important, in the version of the story presented above, I have bracketed out and excluded a very important ambiguous figure: the *komiti* (Tok Pisin). The komiti is both a local man and an appointed government officer. He is one of many ambiguous symbols reminding me that "here" and "there" are intimately connected so as to bring the distinction itself into question. It was the komiti who acted as mediator throughout the ordeal. He led the prayer and dutifully recorded the number and value of each object exchanged. As the exchanges took place, he shouted anxiously about the importance of "community" and "population." He reminded those involved that government services only come to villages with large populations and finished by threatening that if they moved into separate villages he would stage an operation to burn their houses. He was referring to "Operation Clean and Sweep," a plan developed by local government officers, such as himself, designed to force people out of small semino-madic hamlets and into large permanent government-recognized villages. By the time Kodenim passed away, they had already begun the operation by burning several small hamlets—just the type of messiness that does not fit so nicely into an otherwise textbook example of the virtues of cultural relativism, holism, and participant-observation.

This kind of ambiguous and challenging situation is not new. Tucked away in Evans-Pritchard's classic on the Azande is a note that witchcraft accusations seemed to be on the rise since locals were asked to abandon their hamlets and move to larger roadside villages. Evans-Pritchard simply bracketed these effects in his overall analysis. As Mary Douglas pointed out in 1970, in order to support his analysis of the overall logic and functionality of Azande witchcraft beliefs, Evans-Pritchard "had to proceed as if the Azande study had no relevance to ourselves and our history" (1970:xxiii). To invoke Barnes's metaphor once again, he was looking down a one-way microscope into a different, disconnected world. But in that same article, published in 1963, Barnes notes that "the division between those under the microscope and those looking scientifically down the eye-piece has broken down. … [T]he group or institution being studied is now seen to be embedded in a network of social relations of which the observer is an integral if reluctant part" (1963:124).

Since this statement by Barnes, the classic trio of holism, cultural relativism, and participant-observation has been through a continual process of reinvention. In a recent discussion in the pages of *Current Anthropology*, Michael Carrithers builds on a comment by Marilyn Strathern to note that the new holism "refers not to some imagined societal whole but to the imagined whole (and actual infinity) of connections between one matter under scrutiny with another" (2005:455). In the same article, Carrithers writes about a "more radical cultural relativism," which is not dependent on a notion of static whole cultures but, instead, recognizes "constant processes of cultural creation, destruction, hybridization, and diversification at work" (2005:441).

Where we do not enter a new world, we also do not necessarily bracket ourselves. If we no longer draw a strict line between here and there, our moral responsibilities also expand. Recombining the classic trio in their new forms we find that we have a new sense of moral responsibility but must find a way to exercise this responsibility within complex cultural fields where multiple beliefs, values, and practices compete, conflate, and contradict one another.

How do we participate in these complex situations? And more specifically, how do we deal with complex moral dilemmas such as those that often come about through both physical and mystical violence associated with witchcraft? Witchcraft itself creates a unique dilemma, for it is an invisible realm populated by multiple imaginations working together to construct an intersubjective understanding of mystical interpersonal violence and conflict. Oftentimes, these multiple imaginations are not in agreement. Certainly, the imagination of the anthropologist is often the least in agreement, commonly not subscribing to witchcraft beliefs at all. All of this makes for an even more complex fieldwork situation. If the story I told before is a closed book with a clear moral, the following is a story still being written, sending me deeper and deeper into the paradoxes and contradictions at the core of anthropological practice.

The week before the safety meeting regarding Kodenim's family, operation teams had already been sent to distant hamlets to burn them and move the people into one of the main government villages. On the same day that Kodenim passed away, people in small hamlets launched virulent complaints that they could not move to the large villages because their enemies who lived there would work witchcraft on them and kill them.

The officers reasoned that if they were to make large and stable villages, they would need to eliminate witchcraft. Kodenim's death contributed to the sense of urgency. Within a week officials called for another "safety meeting" and announced their plan. They decided to gather up weak old women they suspected of witchcraft, charge them under the law, and then hold them as key witnesses, forcing them to list the names of the stronger and more covert witches in the area.

The first woman to face trial was a woman I called "auntie," my "mother's" sister. She was apprehended and charged under Village Courts Act 1988 Section 41 Subsection P, which prohibits "practicing or pretending to practice sorcery." A small boy had been ill, and, because of a complicated series of relational tensions extending back to her first failed marriage, she was the primary suspect. I arrived to the trial late, and she had already confessed. I cannot be certain what inspired her to confess, but it was apparent that she felt threatened by the officers around her. I hoped that whatever violence might have occurred before I arrived would not continue now that I was in the room with my video camera recording their every move. I was disappointed to find that some of my best friends had been involved in whatever had been transpiring.

After her confession, the officers asked her for the names of other witches with whom she was conspiring. Over and over again she tried to reclaim her innocence, but she only aggravated the officers, who were already certain of her guilt. To have empathy with the officers on this point is to recognize that they truly believed that their own lives and the lives of everybody in the community were under assault by cannibalistic witches like this woman sitting before them. They desperately wanted to know the names of other witches so they could protect themselves from this horrific threat, and they interpreted her pleas as nothing more than evasions and trickery. In frustration, one of the officers hit her with an open fist, slamming her head into the wall behind her. And there I was viewing the whole thing through a recording "microscope," not knowing if this was really happening in my world or if it were another world altogether. Frozen in contradictions, fear, and confusion, I did nothing.

Eventually she named names. From her list more were brought in. The convicted were forced to run two miles carrying a 30 lb stone over their heads while others gathered around to shame them. They were then put to work digging the standardized government road, wide with drainage ditches and, most importantly, straight. Straightness, orderliness, cleanliness—these were the rallying cries of Operation Clean and Sweep. Within three weeks, four had been convicted, and there were over 40 names on the list. Throughout this time, I did nothing but hide behind my recording microscope. But I was not hiding because I felt that they were in a world apart from me. I was hiding because I felt trapped within a whole new set of contradictions born from the emerging revisions to our classic trio and the contradictions between these revisions and their more classic forms.

I spent most of my time pacing, feeling crushed at the nexus of the paradoxes I was only then beginning to discover in the heart of anthropological practice. On one side pressed my respect for their local cultural beliefs inspired by my sense of cultural relativism; on the other pressed my desire to uphold basic individual human rights. Both were problematic in this multifaceted social field. The idea of one single set of "local cultural beliefs" was undermined by the multiple sets of beliefs and practices that coexisted and sometimes contradicted one another (such as those in the government, school, clinic, different churches, and others less formalized). The idea of "individual" human rights was undermined by local notions of self and personhood grounded primarily in a relational ontology that has little space for the Western judicial "individual."

The position of the government officers also perplexed me. These government officers were at the same time local people, themselves born into small hamlets in the area. Much has been written about how to negotiate the relationship between the culture and the administration. There is less guidance for understanding what to do when the culture *is* the administration. I found it telling that this seemingly small fact would have an impact on my action. If they were purely government officers from outside, I would have readily stood up to them—"speaking truth to power." If they had not been government officers at all, I would likely not have considered interfering at all—afraid I was simply "power" undermining a local "truth." Their ambiguous cultural and political position left me in an ambiguous moral and ethical position.

Of key importance to my dilemma was what Peter Geschiere (2002) has recently referred to as "the reality question." My moral decisions depended greatly on my own opinions about the possibilities of witchcraft. I had come to the field thinking I would be open to all local beliefs, including witchcraft. I was partially inspired by Rodney Needham's argument in which he calls attention to what to him seemed the strange fact of an "almost universal premise subscribed to by anthropologists, that witches do not really exist" (1978:27). There is in fact no way of knowing for sure whether or not some human beings have mystical powers allowing them to inflict harm on others from a distance or even to shoot them with invisible arrows, eat their flesh, and then stuff their skin with twigs and leaves to make the victim appear as if alive only to die soon thereafter, as witches are said to do in central New Guinea. Needham and many others after him sidestep the question by claiming that notions of witchcraft are simply social facts and there is no need to claim them to be true or false. Although this may be true for abstract theorizing and analysis, it is not true when making moral judgments in the field. If one truly believes that a person has shot, killed, and eaten another human being, one's moral response to that person will obviously be different than if one feels that the person could not possibly have done the deeds of which he or she is accused. Perhaps I was feeling the postmodernist guilt of imposing my Western power/knowledge, but in the early stages of the hunt I stalled on coming to any final conclusions on this matter.

My silence ultimately rested within my own culturally constructed notions of self. Anthropology—and the trio of cultural relativism, holism, and participant-observation—had transformed me into something resembling what psychiatrist Robert Jay Lifton (1970) has called "Protean man." Based on the Greek mythology of Proteus, Protean man is at home embracing multiple perspectives at once, modifying them at will, and then letting them all go only to re-embrace them again in a playful (and sometimes *seriously* playful) manner. In slightly different terms, Richard Rorty refers to the Protean man as an "ironist," someone who is "always aware that the terms in which they describe themselves are subject to change, always aware of the contingency and fragility of their final vocabularies, and thus of their selves" (1989:101). If there is one thing Protean man or the ironist finds difficult, it is committing to a single perspective among a plethora of options and then acting on it (Lifton 1970).

As I remained silently behind my recording microscope, the trials proceeded. The list grew, and so did the government officers' collective imagination. As in other witchcraft imageries throughout the world, the witches took shape as a perfect inversion of those hunting them (Jackson 1989). As such, former government leaders (*tultuls* and *luluais* from the days of the Australian colonial administration) were most suspect, as they were thought to be the heads of an "antigovernment" scheme to undermine the real government's every move by subverting all attempts of community development. As a former tultul, my father was emerging as the "king" of all witches.

My father had personally experienced and been an active participant in some of the most remarkable cultural transformations in the region. Over time he had developed a remarkable sense of humor about these changes, accompanied by an endless supply of self-deprecating one-liners about the new developments: the soap he mistook for the fat of a pig and tried to eat; the rice he was given to eat, which he did, uncooked. My arrival had supplied him with endless material. He often joked about my camera and the powers it must have. He knew better but enjoyed playing the role of the naive "primitive." As the trials continued and the fact that my father was destined to face trial seemed more imminent, one such joke seemed to shatter through my own naïveté. "My son," he said, "take my picture and show them all that I am not a witch." His effortless signature laugh let me know that he was joking, but I heard the subtext. As much as I might try to hide myself behind my recording microscope, this was my world too, and I was always involved. I suddenly realized that participation is not a choice.

Our only choice is how we participate. Silence is itself participation, and sometimes it speaks volumes we do not intend.

I turned red with the guilty realization that I may have in some ways been complicit in the events of the trials I so abhorred. If the list of witches was seen as a technology of revelation, might not my camera also be seen in a similar light? Did my presence and that of my camera help to legitimize what was taking place?

I became determined to transform myself and my camera. This would mean stepping out from behind the recording microscope and engaging the situation. The plethora of voices in the fragmented community had left me confused and silent. Now I found my voice through these same fragmentations. Instead of silence, I simply chose to support and work to magnify those voices and perspectives I found most advantageous to my goal of ending the hunt before the community completely disintegrated or somebody was seriously hurt or perhaps even killed. Ironically, the first voice I chose to support was the government officers' voice of the law. I went to every suspect on the list and briefed them on the law, reading to them sections of the national constitution that protect basic human rights and prohibit the use of threats or violence to force a confession. I had decided that if the law was to be used to prosecute suspected witches, the suspects should know a bit about the law before being put on trial. Word of my visits to these suspects traveled throughout the area, and it was made clear to the government officers that I and my camera were not in the courtroom to legitimize the trial but, rather, to ensure that it took place without improper incident.

Previously I had found the web of relations constraining. When somebody I referred to as a good friend or even "brother" interrogated or flogged somebody I called "auntie" I felt trapped between the competing demands of two important relationships. I now found this same web of relations liberating. I discovered a freedom to express myself beyond my constrained scientific observer status precisely because I was related. My vigilance and anger could be read relationally. If I protested the idea of witchcraft beliefs or challenged the legitimacy of a court ruling, it was because I was concerned for my auntie or my father; I was not acting outside the boundaries of what was locally acceptable. On the contrary, as I stepped out from behind my recording microscope and made such protests, I may have become acceptable for the first time since the witch hunt began. After all, what kind of son would I be if I did not protest?

Always the ironist, I found myself in a remarkably ironic position. Once dedicated to respecting an equality of worldviews and perspectives, I now found myself approaching government officers armed with a laptop computer that I used to show them the story of Salem and other witch hunts. I showed them articles from the Internet of witch killings throughout the world, proving that it is the witch hunters, not the witches, who face widespread disapproval by the media and authorities outside the local situation. I even showed them pictures of viruses and bacteria, to back up the recent talks given by clinic workers trying to promote biomedical explanations of sickness over witchcraft explanations.

Even as I became increasingly more public with my protests, I eventually came to recognize the limits of my power in changing the situation. There are well-founded concerns that as anthropologists we are often "studying down" and therefore hold a certain amount of power in our fieldwork situations. Such concerns had contributed to my original silence, and even as I started to engage I remained troubled by this. I soon discovered, though, that any power I may have thought I had was illusory. Though I was highly respected and considered knowledgeable about a great many subjects, witchcraft was not one of them. My protests that the acts of witchcraft under investigation were impossible were often met with laughter and almost complete disregard. After one of my protests, one man asked me if we had witchcraft like theirs in the United States. When I replied that we do not, a knowing look came upon his face as he turned to the others, who laughed as he explained, "That's why the white man is confused." Through it all, my attempts to impose my logic never made any changes in behavior, even when it was framed in support of other local voices.

The hunt had its own dynamics in which I played a remarkably minor role. Key to the dynamics was the simple fact that the list made its own enemies. The person listed invariably denied the accusation, and relatives came to his or her side to support the denial. As the list grew to over 70 names, nearly everybody had somebody on the list to defend, and the credibility of the list itself was called into question. On the morning of the last trial, there was a growing sense of outrage that the officers were continuing to hold such trials despite widespread public disapproval. As in previous trials, when the suspects inevitably confessed they were forced to run up and down the airstrip carrying heavy stones on their heads. But this time nobody was watching. Support for the witch hunt had subsided.

I sat on my veranda with friends as the convicted slowly made their way up and down the airstrip. The most elderly of them moved ever so slowly, aggravating the officers assigned to monitor her punishment. In frustration, one of the officers kicked her in the back to make her speed up. The force of his foot on her back combined with the weight of the stone on her head forced her back to buckle, and she collapsed to the ground. To this day, I only vaguely remember running from my veranda to her side. By the time I arrived a large crowd had gathered. I checked to see if she was okay. She was exhausted but otherwise fine. Seeing the stone beside her, I grew angry. I picked up the stone, marched it over to the edge of the airstrip, and launched it into a deep ravine—the moment so surreal that the yells of the officers seemed muffled, muted, and unreal. Before I could defend myself, I could hear the swell of voices from others rising up to defend me and protest the witch hunt. Some called for a broader recognition of human rights. Seventh Day Adventist leaders restated their claim for biomedical awareness. But the broadest, most widely held complaint about the witch hunt—one that I could never support or share and yet the one that ultimately ended the hunt altogether—was that the officers had failed in bringing in the "real" witches who were terrorizing their communities. The government consistently picked on weak old women, while the real witches (like my father) remained free and continued to kill and consume them. Protestors claimed that the government was ineffective at finding and bringing to justice the "real" witches because members of the government were themselves the most powerful witches and used the witch hunt as a ploy to divert attention away from their nefarious activities.

CONCLUSION

The witch hunt began as an effort to rid the area of witches so that people would feel safe moving to the large government villages. But the hunt only increased fears and fissions. It had an opposite effect to the one intended. People further divided into small hamlets, and the government villages nearly became ghost towns. In these villages, the people not only faced the tensions of living with more people than they were used to but, like me, also faced the tensions of competing and contradictory sets of beliefs and practices variously embodied in the government, clinic, and the different churches. The tensions among these contradictory beliefs and practices only exacerbated tensions throughout the community.

Perhaps my deep desire to participate encouraged me to identify with all of these different and contradictory beliefs and practices. As they turned on each other, I turned on myself. In the end, I wish I could offer a happy ending, but I remain fragmented—just like the community— and not unlike anthropology. The only solace I can offer is that it is a productive position to be in. Fragmentation is in another guise flexibility and openness. It is the proud claim of being incomplete and unfinished, accepting unresolved tensions and learning from them rather than explaining them away. In reconciling myself to the revised form of that fundamental trio of holism, cultural relativism, and participant-observation, I find myself embracing my ironist self and attempting to refashion it to create a Protean man flexible enough to have empathy for numerous competing and constantly changing perspectives, patient enough to pause long enough to see a broad range of implications, strong enough to act on what I believe to be right after I make these careful considerations, and finally, humble enough to accept that even this statement is perhaps too strong of a conclusion for what remains an open-ended unfinished story.

NOTE

I would like to extend a special thank you to all those who have listened to this story and helped me disentangle the multiple ethical dilemmas I have begun to describe here. In particular, I would like to thank Robert Welsch, Roy Wagner, Edie Turner, Ira Bashkow, Eve Danziger, Peter Metcalf, and Eric Midelfort for providing priceless support and feedback. This article was first presented as a paper at the 2005 American Anthropological Association meetings in the session "Witnessing Witchcraft: Quandaries of Engagement" and benefited greatly from the comments and general camaraderie that the session created among all participants. Funding for fieldwork was provided by a National Science Foundation Graduate Research Fellowship, Fulbright-Hayes International Dissertation Research Fellowship, and the University of Virginia, with special thanks also going to James Robins and the National Research Institute, with which I was affiliated during my fieldwork.

1.   Locations and names in this article have been altered or left ambiguous in an effort to maintain confidentiality.

REFERENCES CITED

Barnes, John A. 1963. Some Ethical Problems in Modern Fieldwork. British Journal of Sociology 14(2):118–133.
Bowen, Elenore Smith. 1964[1954]. Return to Laughter. New York: Anchor Books.
Carrithers, Michael. 2005. Anthropology as a Moral Science of Possibilities. Current Anthropology 46(3): 433–455.

Comaroff, Jean, and John Comaroff, eds. 1993. Modernity and Its Malcontents: Ritual and Power in Postcolonial Africa. Chicago: University of Chicago Press.

Douglas, Mary. 1970. Thirty Years after Witchcraft, Oracles, and Magic. In Witchcraft Confessions and Accusations. Mary Douglas, ed. Pp. xiii-xxxviii. London: Tavistock.

Evans-Pritchard, E. E. 1937. Witchcraft Oracles and Magic among the Azande. Oxford: Clarendon Press.

Geschiere, Peter. 1997. The Modernity of Witchcraft: Politics and the Occult in Postcolonial Africa. Charlottesville: University Press of Virginia.

——2002. Gruesome Rumours, the Reality Question, and Writing History. Journal of African History 43(3):499–501.

Haviland, William, Harald Prins, Dana Walrath, and Bunny McBride. 2005. Cultural Anthropology: The Human Challenge. 11th ed. Toronto: Thomson Wadsworth.

Jackson, Michael. 1989. Paths toward a Clearing: Radical Empiricism and Ethnographic Inquiry. Bloomington: Indiana University Press.

Levack, Brian. 1995. The Witch-Hunt in Early Modern Europe. 2nd ed. New York: Longman.

Lifton, Robert Jay. 1970. Boundaries: Psychological Man in Revolution. New York: Vintage Books.

Malinowski, Bronislaw. 1953 [1922]. Argonauts of the Western Pacific. New York: Dutton.

Moore, Henrietta, and Todd Sanders, eds. 2001. Magical Interpretations, Material Realities: Modernity, Witchcraft and the Occult in Postcolonial Africa. New York: Routledge.

Needham, Rodney. 1978. Primordial Characters. Charlottesville: University Press of Virginia.

Niehaus, Isak. 2001. Witchcraft, Power and Politics: Exploring the Occult in South African Lowveld. London: Pluto Press.

Rorty, Richard. 1989. Contingency, Irony, and Solidarity. Cambridge: Cambridge University Press.

Scheper-Hughes, Nancy. 1995. The Primacy of the Ethical: Propositions for a Militant Anthropology. Current Anthropology 36(3):409–420.

Tyler, Stephen. 1987. The Unspeakable: Discourse, Dialogue, and Rhetoric in the Postmodern World. Madison: University of Wisconsin Press.

World Health Organization. 2002. World Report on Violence and Health. Electronic document, http://www.who.int/violence_injury_prevention/violence/world_report/en, accessed February 23, 2007.

26

Recovering from Codependence in Japan

Amy Borovoy

W hen elements of one culture are appropriated by another, they can become the ful-
crum through which social actors identify issues, fissures, and contradictions within
dominant cultural cosmologies. In this article, I explore Japanese appropriations of American
popular psychology and how these appropriations provide a window for Japanese women into
unquestioned or unspeakable aspects of dominant constructions of gender, family, and social
cohesion. I focus specifically on the concept of codependence: the notion that mitigating or
taking responsibility for the social consequences of a substance abuser's habit functions to
sustain the addictive behavior itself. In the context of American popular psychology, the term
has come to define a personality profile. A codependent person is "one who has let another
person's behavior affect him or her" (Beattie 1987:31) and who is prone to caretaking, people-
pleasing, and "other-centeredness that results in abandonment of self" (Beattie 1987:32). A
codependent person is someone who, owing to a troubled or "dysfunctional" family environment, has lost his or her sense of self, and, as a result, enters into relationships that blur the
boundary between self and other (Beattie 1987:38). Beattie writes that codependents may
"find themselves saying yes when they mean no, doing things they don't really want to be doing, doing more than their fair share of the work" (1987:37). Codependents "may think and
feel responsible for other people, ... anticipate other people's needs ... [and] find themselves
attracted to needy people" (1987:37).

Since the early 1980s, American popular psychology has been entering Japan through
translated texts, such as *Women Who Love Too Much* (Norwood 1991), *Codependent No More*
(Beattie 1987), and *The Cinderella Complex* (Dowling 1990). Some of these texts circulate as
"hot copies" (in instances where the publisher is unable to procure translating rights) among
women who, like American women, are eager to believe that one can love someone else while

still drawing boundaries, that others' behavior should not be seen as a reflection of one's own self-worth, or that there is such a thing as a nurturing kind of detachment (in 12-step argot, "tough love"). In looking more closely at the Japanese context, however, it becomes clear that the concept is interpreted somewhat differently than in U.S. popular psychology, with very different social implications. On my first day at the Tokyo public mental health care center where I conducted field research (hereafter referred to as "the Center," as it was commonly called), a social worker explained to me that Japan is a "culture of codependence" (*kyōizon no bunka*). The chief psychiatrist, a writer of popular literature, was fond of saying that Japanese people are "addicted to human relationships." Among a prominent group of Tokyo specialists who share an epistemological framework, human relationships (*ningen kankei*) are described as the primary addiction, and substance abuse itself as the secondary, or instrumental, addiction.

The notion that Japan is a culture of codependence, despite its rhetorical excess, suggests the proximity between what are historically constituted as normal, healthy, even virtuous forms of interdependent social relationships, and what is, in the context of substance abuse treatment and discourse, increasingly constituted as unhealthy or codependent behavior. Japanese postwar cultural cosmologies, rooted in prewar discourses of "nation as family," describe a wide spectrum of power relations as benevolent forms of interdependence and indulgence, making it difficult to draw a sharp line between asymmetrical relationships that are compelling, mutualistic, and viewed as deeply Japanese, and systems of exploitation and structured inequalities. The notion of codependency provokes women to begin to forge such distinctions. In recovering from codependence, women must define the extremely fine line between interdependence (*amae*), which they see as a healthy and distinctively Japanese form of relationality, and codependence, which they come to construct as an unhealthy and destructive version of this relationality.

In considering how a medicalized concept such as codependence could provide a language for social criticism, I rely on notions of power, resistance, and practice that became central to anthropological theory in the 1980s (Bourdieu 1977; Foucault 1965, 1977, 1978; Gramsci 1971). These theories emphasize the ways in which the workings of power are diffuse, embodied, consensual, and thoroughly imbricated with the language and practice of everyday life. In particular, Gramsci's notion of hegemony draws attention to the extent to which all social systems rely on the lived experiences, discourses, and practices of everyday life that compel individuals to view even systems of inequality or oppression as acceptable and reasonable.[1]

Theories of resistance emerging in the 1980s emphasized the significance of every day practices, private acts, and discursive or symbolic contestations—shifting the focus from political confrontation, political mobilization, class consciousness, and other forms of protest that have historically served as the markers of social change in the context of Marxist and liberal social theories (see for example Abu-Lughod 1990; Comaroff 1985; de Certeau 1984; Diamond and Quinby 1988; Foucault 1980; Scott 1987a, 1987b).[2] In the conclusion to her study of Tshidi Zionism as a form of resistance to colonialism and capitalism in the South African borderland, Jean Comaroff writes:

If we confine our historical scrutiny to the zero-sum heroics of revolution successfully achieved, we discount the vast proportion of human social action which is played out, perforce, on a more humble scale. We also evade, by teleological reasoning, the real questions that remain as to what are the transformative motors of history. [1985:261]

In addition to pointing out the importance of everyday symbolic and discursive terrains of contestation, this literature suggests that resistance itself is socially constructed. This point is partially made by James Scott's notion of weapons of the weak: actors make use of the tools available to them in protesting injustice (Scott 1987b). In exploring the question of resistance and social criticism among middle-class Japanese housewives, I look at the ways in which resistance is both contained and shaped by dominant cultural forms and how some cultural domains become particularly salient terrains for social criticism. Practices of resistance, as Lila Abu-Lughod (1990) notes, are informative about structures of power. Through a study of the shifting consciousnesses of a group of Japanese women, I explore dominant postwar constructions of gender, family, and social collectivity (as these are linked) and the purview and limits of opposition to these discourses. I also ask why dominant discourses are compelling to Japanese citizens and what is their seductive power? Understanding why dominant discourses might be compelling (if simultaneously oppressive) is, I believe, crucial in determining both the limits and possibilities for social change.

In exploring the possibility of social change, anthropologists have tended to look for counterhegemonic discourses among marginalized groups, minorities, or radical factions who explicitly position themselves outside the cultural mainstream. In Japan, for example, the voices of feminist groups, artists, international filmmakers, and political reformists have garnered much international attention through translated texts. Many of these voices echo popular American accusations of Japan as parochial, conformist, and not fully modern. Ozawa Ichiro,[3] founder of the New Frontier Party, an alternative to the Liberal Democratic Party, argued in his widely selling, *Blueprint for a New Japan* (1994), that the Japanese state must give up its practices of economic regulation and social protection and allow Japan to become a "normal nation" (1994:93-100). The social critic Miyamoto Masao, a former bureaucrat and author of an expose, *Straightjacket Society* (1994), describes the conformity, rigidity, and pettiness of the Japanese bureaucracy. These critiques have been translated and have gained considerable attention in the mass media, perhaps because they confirm dominant American beliefs that Japan's problems stem from its failure to become more like the United States. Research on women's issues and Japanese feminism, too, has focused on Japanese feminism's most radical moments, chronicling women's participation in political demonstrations and legal reform—movements that were clearly influenced by European Marxist models of social change through upheaval or by liberal ideals of change through political mobilization (see for example Hane 1993; Molony 1980; Sievers 1983).

In contrast, the women I describe here encounter the Center and the discourse of codependence not to protest the system in which they live, but to seek help in relation to a particular problem. They are not aligned with international movements, nor do they explicitly position themselves outside of or in opposition to dominant cultural ideologies. They are largely middle-aged, middle-class housewives who ordinarily conceptualize themselves within the mainstream; yet, owing to unfortunate family problems, they confront a fundamental barrier to making dominant cultural assumptions work.[4] Nor are they women who would ordinarily seek out American therapies or countercultural discourse. Unlike most other forms of American culture, Alcoholics Anonymous (AA) is not actively exported or promoted by centralized organizations; there are no commercial, political, military, or national interests connected to its dispersion (Makela *et al.* 1996:29). Counselors and social workers at the Center, though disproportionately female, are not trained in feminist theory or Western forms of psychotherapy. They are civil servants who chose this profession because it avoids the obligatory overtime of private sector employment and offers more opportunities for advancement to women. By examining the responses not of those who explicitly resist or attack hegemonic frameworks but of those who are compelled to undertake a critique of normalcy from within, it is possible to peer into the spectrum of available social criticism contained within hegemonic cultural processes. As clients of the Center, women are pressed to reach beyond cultural truisms while continuing to function within the confines of mainstream Japanese society.[5]

In the first section of this article, I briefly examine how the concept of codependence—an American concept that embraces liberal individualism in its 1960s incarnation—enters Japan, engaging with historically shaped discourses of familiality and national culture. I argue that Japanese women who construct themselves as codependent are incited to define the boundary between interdependence and codependence—that is, between forms of interdependence and nurturance that are socially sanctioned and systematic power imbalances inhering in dominant postwar shifts in national identity. Next, I analyze women's gradually strengthening ability to articulate that boundary through shifts in their narrative voice and subversions of assumed economies of labor. I consider how alcohol is itself woven into the fabric of daily life in Japan, to the extent that questioning women's complicity in their husbands' alcoholism necessarily entails questioning a broader division of labor, indeed a social compact, that is tacitly sustained (even demanded) by a host of Japanese institutions. Finally, I consider how women's shifts in consciousness create spaces for social criticism. I suggest that conversations around codependence engage with central sources of tension in contemporary society and ideology. To the extent that women become sensitized to the darker sides of dominant constructions of family, they may be more likely to resist state and societal demands that work against them.

The notions of addiction and codependence strike at the heart of contemporary normative American conceptions of familial and love relationships as rooted in mutual independence (Giddens 1991, 1992). Initially, the concept of codependence, known as "co-alcoholism," was the insight of wives of American alcoholics who first convened in the 1950s and concluded that by intervening and protecting the alcoholic by lying to his boss, cleaning up his messes, paying unpaid bills, and otherwise compensating for his forfeit of responsibility, they inadvertently "enabled" the alcoholic to sustain his addictive and destructive behavior (Haaken 1993:329). The concept was subsequently redefined by professional psychotherapists as a psychodynamic maladjustment that causes particular behaviors. In other words, codependency does not result from engaging with substance abusers; rather, codependents choose substance abusers as associates. Beattie, author of the best-seller *Codependent No More* (1987), quotes Ellen, an Al-Anon member: "When I say I'm codependent, I don't mean I'm a little bit codependent. I mean I'm really codependent. I don't marry men who stop for a few beers after work. I marry men who won't work" (Beattie 1987:17).

U.S. codependency discourse is the legacy of humanistic and liberation psycho- therapies that flourished in the United States in the 1960s (Rice 1996). These therapies draw on dominant strands of American social thought that construct "freedom" as "being left alone by others … being free of arbitrary authority in work, family, and political life" (Bellah 1985:23). They take the "true self" to lie outside of society and thus construe the social shaping of identities as pathogenic.[6] In codependency discourse, socialization itself is discussed in terms of "shaming" and there appears to be an easy slippage between necessary socializing practices (such as parental discipline) and abuse (Rice 1996:205). According to Anne Wilson Schaef, a prominent theorizer of codependence, all addictions "are generated by our families and our schools, our churches, our political system, and our society as a whole" (Schaef in Rice 1996:185).[7] The result of the U.S. construction is that the language of codependence leaves little room for the conceptualization of healthy or necessary forms of interdependence that, though asymmetrical, unequal, and confining in some moments, must also comprise some part of social relationships and social participation. Rather, all social practices that compromise individual rights, autonomy, and absolute equality are regarded as problematic—with little means of explaining why individuals would voluntarily enter into such relations except through self-loathing, uncontrollable compulsion, or a troubled family background.[8] Janice Haaken articulates this tension:

> The codependence label becomes a broad conceptual container into which myriad life difficulties and internal and external pressures are placed. The message is compelling because it seems to provide both the therapists who draw on the codependence literature and the individuals who identify with the "disease" deliverance from the difficult task of separating out what is internal from what is external, and what is

healthy and emotionally useful from what is pathological and emotionally destructive in worrisome, conflictual, interpersonal relationships. [1990:405]

In the Japanese context, in contrast with American readings, codependent women are not seen as deviating from rational behavior through deep psychodynamic compulsions or lack of control, and there is little sense that the situation they find themselves in betrays a self-destructiveness on their part. From the standpoint of Japanese social dictates, codependent women are women who have made all the right decisions; women who are, in fact, supremely in control of themselves and their surroundings. While the notion that some people are more codependent than others exists on the periphery, neither group discussions nor educational materials focus on members' upbringing or family environments as causal explanations for codependence. Nor is there a sense that women have actively chosen alcoholic or otherwise troubled husbands. The focus of discussion is rather on the social expectations and belief systems that produce and even require codependent behavior. That is, codependence is read as socially rather than psychodynamically produced.

The definition of codependency in the American popular literature is peppered with pathologizing phrases: obsession, low self-worth, repression, denial, and so forth (Beattie 1987:37–44). But for Japanese women, the notion that codependent behavior, or the entanglement in complicated relationships of dependency and obligation, is the result of personal maladjustment is counterintuitive. In my experience, women arrived at the Center with a strong sense that they had been doing the best they could, and yet, despite this, they remained unable to better their situations. Many women told me that it took them a very long time to accept the concept of "enabling" and the idea that their own behavior might be counterproductive. For example, Fukuda-san, a client at the Center, told me over tea:[9]

> His relatives used to blame his drinking on me. "Just don't buy him sake! Don't give it to him! Just take it away!" they'd tell me. But frankly I could never imagine that *I* had done anything wrong. I had put myself out for my husband's every wish. I kept telling myself that at the time. I thought I was doing exactly what I was supposed to do: serve my husband [*otto ni tsukusu*], buy the sake, protect the family. But over the years of coming to the Center, I've begun to see that I too had some responsibility. I helped create the kind of relationship environment wherein he could drink [*nomu kankei o tsukutta*].

Popularized writings on addiction, too, exploit this proximity between codependent and socially sanctioned social relationships, using addiction theory and treatment as a ground for criticism of Japanese society more broadly. Dr. Saitō Satoru, the chief psychiatrist at the Center and an expert in addiction problems, has published a widely read series of books and public lectures, such as *Family Dependency Syndrome* (1989) and *The Darkness of Families* (1998), in which he presents Japanese society and its rigid regimes of work, school, and domestic support as the cause of a variety of addictions; he even goes so far as to use "addiction" as a metaphor for the social processes of Japanese late capitalism (Saitō 1989, 1998).[10] Led by Saitō, the field of addiction has attracted physicians, nurses, and social workers associated with community health care facilities who tend to be more socially progressive than physicians in lucrative private practices. Social workers at the Center felt Saitō's influence to the extent that they too saw the unhealthy dimensions of entrenched cultural practices; however, most did not go so far as to describe Japanese culture as "pathological." Instead, they encouraged women to find a middle ground between detached social criticism and functioning in community life.

GENDER, NURTURANCE, AND ARTICULATIONS OF NATIONAL CULTURE

To understand the fine line between socially sanctioned notions of family and what women at the Center come to view as codependence, it is necessary to consider the state's linking of women's nurturance with broader constructions of national identity and the collective good. Notions of family and community were central to both prewar and postwar national ideologies. Incipient conceptualizations of the modern Japanese nation-state in the Meiji period (1868–1912) specified the household (*ie*) as the smallest unit of the state; later, prewar government-issued tracts described the state itself as a "national family" (*kazoku kokka*)—with the emperor as the "father." Early constructions of "domesticity" were tied to this consolidation of national identity, and domesticity itself was regarded as a public project rather than as a space for the expression of private sentiment (Nolte and Hastings 1991:172–174)—even as women lost certain entitlements to inherit property or choose their marriage partners and were prohibited from voting or political mobilization. Meiji statesmen and intellectuals articulated the ideal of the "good wife and wise mother" (*ryōsai kenbo*): domestic work became valorized as skilled work and central to the project of instilling modern values in Japanese citizens (Nolte and Hastings 1991:171; Tamanoi 1991; Uno 1993a).[11]

The official household system was legally abolished in the wake of Japan's defeat in World War II, and authoritarian forms of state intervention into daily life were eschewed; however, women, as wives and mothers, continued to be central to public life and were active in promoting various state agendas of hygiene, nutrition, and savings (Garon 1997:179–195). The home came to be constructed as a satellite of Japanese corporate capitalism—a parallel sphere of activity, mutually integrated with the needs of capitalism, rather than as a safe haven from them (Gordon 1997).[12]

The family itself underwent great changes in the 1950s and 1960s. Birth rates declined rapidly in the 1950s (*Japan Statistical Yearbook* 1998:59), and child rearing became a focus of scientific study. By the 1960s, family in popular culture was portrayed as a distinctly mother-centric sphere. In popular movies on the family (*hōmu dorama*) of the 1950s and 1960s, mothers were portrayed as the managers of home life, a home life that increasingly centered on relationships between mothers and children. Fathers were portrayed as helpless and once removed from the family environment, consoled by family members when things went awry at work, but generally stubborn and insensitive to the needs of their wives and children (Sakamoto 1997:242). At this same time, men grew increasingly absent from the home, commuting longer distances to work and working longer hours in the push to regenerate the country (Gordon 2000:287; Vogel 1963:34-35). In contrast with the images of strength, discipline, and morality that characterized the prewar *ryōsai kenbo*, the image of the postwar housewife focuses on intimacy and devotion, the kind and gentle mother (*yasashii okaasan*). Dominant discourses on family emerging in the 1960s and 1970s invoke these shifting constructions of home. Takeo Doi's *The Anatomy of Dependence* (1973), discussed in the next section, emphasizes a closeness that is almost intuitive, and this idea is generalized to describe Japanese culture and the national polity more broadly. Prewar nationalism had centered on the patriarchal, hierarchical, multigenerational family with explicit ties to the state. Postwar discourses, while continuing to emphasize the centrality of family and vertical kinship ties, recoded these ties as maternalistic, interpersonal, intimate, and benevolent.

THE ANATOMY OF DEPENDENCE

A central concept in these postwar conversations was the notion of *amae* (dependence), the language through which contemporary women grappled with the concept of codependence. The notion of amae was elaborated by the psychoanalytic psychiatrist Doi in his text, *The Anatomy of Dependence*. Amae, often translated as "dependence" or "indulgence," refers to a desire to be loved passively and to presume on familiarity in order to behave in a self-indulgent manner (Doi 1973). The language of amae is everywhere present in Japan, and there is frequent slippage between the clinical concept of individual psychodynamic needs and cultural ethos. The concept of amae captured many aspects of postwar society and came to be used popularly to describe a society where individuals are looked after by their families, companies, and the state—in contrast with American competitive individualism.

Doi arrived at the notion of amae as elemental Japanese mentality while training as a psychiatrist in the United States. While in the United States, he was struck by the American privileging and reification of individual independence, which became the central problematic of his thought. In the first chapter of the book, Doi tells the following story:

The "please help yourself" that Americans use so often had a rather unpleasant ring in my ears before I became used to English conversation. The meaning, of course, is simply "please take what you want without hesitation," but literally translated it has somehow a flavor of "nobody else will help you," and I could not see how it came to be an expression of good will. The Japanese sensibility would demand that, in entertaining, a host should show sensitivity in detecting what was required and should himself "help" his guests. To leave a guest unfamiliar with the house to "help himself" would seem excessively lacking in consideration. This increased still further my feeling that Americans were a people who did not show the same consideration and sensitivity towards others as the Japanese. As a result, my early days in America, which would have been lonely at any rate, so far from home, were made lonelier still. [Doi 1973:13]

The Anatomy of Dependence draws on gendered metaphors of nurturance and familial intimacy to explicate Japanese social relations. Doi writes, "The psychological prototype of amae lies in the psychology of the infant in its relationship to its mother" (1973:74), and he speculates that the etymology of the word *amae* may be related to the children's word indicating a request for the breast or food, *uma-uma*" (1973:72). A mother holding the hand of a small child decorates the cover of both the English and Japanese paperbacks. In this respect, Doi's work is not critical of prewar synecdochic linkings of family and state.

Doi's research in the 1960s followed upon a decade of avid renunciation of Japan's immediate past among many progressive intellectuals (see Pyle 1996). This renunciation focused particularly on Meiji constructions of the family as household, depicting these constructions as a feudalistic form of loyalty in which the family was subsumed by the state, preventing individuals from forming "modern" subjectivities that could resist "social opinion and external authority" (Koschmann 1981–82; Sakuta 1986:2). Doi's research, as well as his credentials as a humanist—both a scientist and a Christian—offered the Japanese a language to talk about historical-cultural continuities in the context of postwar disavowal of the past and Japan's new status as a democracy under American patronage. The notion of amae rearticulates the nature of the ties that bind Japanese society together using the humanistic, universalizing language of Western psychology—specifically object relations theory and Freudian and Eriksonian theories of universal human development. In the postwar context, the notion of Japanese society as held together by mutual sensitivity, childlike innocence, and nurturance was more compelling than the notion of collective loyalty to a centralized state.[13]

The concept of amae suggests a world where social order is orchestrated and legitimized through intimate social relations rather than top-down commands: the presumption of mutualism, the notion of harmony through division of labor or benevolent hierarchy, trust through intimacy rather than contractuality, the pursuit of one's own ends through presuming on the good graces of others, and the notion that one need not look out for oneself but rather can trust to be looked after.

The notion of amae captured important institutional changes taking place in the postwar years of the 1960s and 1970s as the authority of the state and its constituent institutions was gradually reconstituted in ways compatible with Japan's postwar democracy. As authoritarian means of insuring social cohesion were eschewed, softer forms of suasion were institutionalized in schools and companies (Haley 1991; Hamilton and Sanders 1992; Rohlen 1989; Upham 1987). These forms often relied on gendered divisions of labor and the incorporation of gendered forms of nurturance into regimes of social order in public spheres. For example, in analyses of mothers, bar hostesses, and children's comics, Anne Allison (1991, 1994, 1996) has shown how the labor and discourses of motherhood and femininity frequently facilitate Japanese social order, "suturing" (in Allison's words) home and motherhood to regimes of productivity and discipline at work and at school (1996: xv). Allison's analysis of the Japanese lunch box (*obentō*) as "ideological state apparatus" vividly analyzes how a mother's love—as emblematized through the lunch she prepares for her child to consume at school—is used to impel the child to associate the constraining practices of classroom order, self-discipline, and punctuality with nurturance and unconditional love (1991).

This construction of the public in terms of the private makes social commentary and everyday resistance complicated and ambiguous processes. The realm of the personal becomes so encompassing that its political component becomes difficult to articulate. In this context, the notion of codependence raises issues and tensions for scrutiny that are ordinarily obscured. For example, where is the line between amae (an idealized conceptualization of social relations based on dominant constructions of family) and codependence (a set of behaviors that makes women complicit in an ultimately destructive and self-destructive pattern)? How do the asymmetries that Doi views as richly rewarding come to be exploitative? And how do they emerge from decisions that women undertake self-consciously?

One day, while sitting in a coffee shop after the meetings, several of the women who regularly attended the Center reflected on their experiences and the most trying times of their husbands' disease. Considering her dilemma, Hoshi-san carefully chose her words: "During my husband's worst stage, I felt like I was immersed in dirty lukewarm water. It was dirty—but I couldn't get out." In Japanese a "lukewarm water situation" (*nurumayu jōtai*) means a situation that, because of its moderate and comfortable climate, invites complacency, even contentment. Hoshi-san's image of "dirty" lukewarm water was a vivid metaphor of the situation these women found themselves in: a situation that was socially constructed as a warm, intimate family environment—with broader implications of a warm societal environment—yet one which was ultimately untenable and provided no legitimate means of escape. In the sections that follow, I explore the question of how women came to view their family situations as problematic.

ALCOHOL AND ALCOHOLISM IN DAILY LIFE

The notion of amae is played out in a number of social contexts in Japan with respect to issues of alcohol. Alcohol itself is woven into the fabric of Japanese society. There is little enforced government regulation of the legal drinking age or of advertising for alcohol; vending machines with beer, sake, and even whiskey are ubiquitous. Public drunkenness is tolerated, indulged, and even portrayed affectionately in popular culture as a vehicle for men to express their masculinity and true selves ("Let's Find out About ..." 1993). Companies regularly allocate funds for men's drinking after work; indeed, the intimacy and relaxation that occurs in these after-hours contexts are integral to constructions of work itself (Allison 1994). Furthermore, many physicians still routinely diagnose alcoholism as a liver dysfunction, and patients may be dismissed after a brief detoxification period in the hospital.[14]

Nonetheless, despite heavy drinking among men as an almost obligatory aspect of working life (Smith 1988) and despite absolute increases in alcohol consumption over the past decade, Japan continues to be a highly productive society with relatively high levels of social stability and low divorce rates. These facts are testimony to the many ways in which a shadow economy of women's labor as wives and mothers functions to prevent or mediate the destructive social consequences associated with drinking and drunkenness. (The shadow economy extends beyond the home. In after-hours districts, bar hostesses can be seen gently ushering drunken men into taxis; railway workers regularly pick men up off train platforms or wake them up so they do not miss their stops.)

In his study of drinking and alcoholism in Japan, Stephen Smith (1988) remarks that because the amount or frequency of alcohol consumed is not in itself considered a symptom of alcoholism, men's drinking is often diagnosed as a problem only when drunken behavior erupts into public conflict or disruption or when the functioning of the alcoholic declines to the point that it inhibits his ability to work—an obvious violation of constructions of gender, marriage, and social participation.[15] According to Smith, "Most patients who are diagnosed as alcoholics have come to that situation because of disturbances in their social relations. They eventually exceed the ability or desire of families to make excuses for them" (Smith 1988:185). This suggests the ways in which both men's drinking and women's prolonged management of their alcoholic husbands are normalized in Japanese society. Couples may go a long time in this condition without seeking help, since women's concealment and management of their husbands' behavior can still be construed as normal within dominant constructions of a healthy family. As one social worker told me, "Women often wait until the situation gets serious before they appear" *(omokunatte kara tōjō suru)*.[16]

Once, over tea, Fukuda-san described to me the period before her husband's diagnosis. When the problem began, her husband was a long-distance truck driver delivering coal. By 1980, he was addicted to alcohol but still working. Upon reaching his destination in Kyoto once, he passed out in his truck and was taken to a Kyoto hospital. He was treated for a liver problem for 10 days and then pronounced healthy. According to Fukuda-san, "Not one single person told him to stop drinking! The doctor said, 'If it's just a little, it shouldn't be a problem.' From my point of view, I thought the problem was that he worked too hard. Anyway, he was drinking beer on the way home." Although this crisis occurred in 1980, it was not until 10 years later that Fukuda-san gained a referral to the Center. Later, as she told the story of her husband's eventual diagnosis, Fukuda-san explained:

> In 1980, He started getting bad hangovers, and he'd take days off work. On Sundays, he'd start drinking in the morning, and on Mondays he wouldn't be able to get up. So other people would have to cover his work for him, and they stopped being able

to depend on him. The problem got worse and worse. And I was always the one who had to call up and say he wouldn't be coming in that day. I couldn't say he had a hangover, so I'd say, "He isn't feeling quite well today ..." At first they understood that [*sore de tsōjita*], but after a while they didn't. "He's hung-over no doubt!" they said to me once. ... He's your average overbearing husband [*teishu kanpaku*], which meant that if I said "Don't drink," he would. And if he said, "Go buy me some sake," I did. I thought to myself, "So this is what living hell is like" [*ikijigoku wa kō iu koto da na to omoimashita.*] I was the perfect service wife [*sewa nyōbō*], picking up after him, changing his clothes, pulling up his pants when he came out of the toilet half dressed.

Although the treatment program at the Center was designed as support for families of substance abusers, in keeping with their construction of their roles, most women initially sought counsel in order to have their husbands admitted to treatment, a continuance of the old paradigm of the "good wife" managing her husband. The diagnosis of their husbands' problems as "alcoholism"—an addictive disorder in which family relationships are implicated—was central to women's reconceptualization of the problem, as it shifted the kinds of questions they posed to themselves: once their husbands had been diagnosed with alcoholism, they could stop feeling that they were not being good enough wives and mothers and start asking whether they were being too good.

Once women began attending meetings, a pivotal conceptual shift occurred when they began to see their attendance not as a means to cure their husbands but instead to strengthen themselves. Several women who regularly attended the weekly family meetings told me that they initially resisted the idea of coming, since they saw it as merely one more thing they were being asked to do for their husbands. Yet after attending meetings, they came to see it as something they were doing "for themselves." Hoshi-san said that once her husband even thanked her for coming. She answered, "Don't thank me. I'm not going for your sake; I'm going for mine." Social workers who led the meetings, too, insisted that as long as women persisted in believing that they were coming to help their husbands or children, they had little hope of recovering (*kaifuku*). In fact, few men did recover from their alcoholism in the group I encountered, and treatment for families of alcoholics largely focused on how women could better cope with the problem.[17]

AT THE FAMILY MEETING

The Center offers a rare window into the lives of families wrestling with tensions within Japanese cultural ideologies. It is a site where private musings are narrativized and where intimate engagements are raised as public conversations. This transition, from a private sense that something is not right to a public articulation of an injustice, is emphasized in recent treatments of ideology and social change. While classical Marxian notions of resistance describe a "laying bare" of ideological manipulation (Williams 1977 in Dirks *et al*. 1994:593) or the unseating of a central locus of power, the focus on hegemonic forms of power has emphasized more partial shifts in consciousness: those moments when subjects become aware of disjunctures between the "world as hegemonically constituted" and the world as apprehended through lived, daily experiences (Comaroff and Comaroff 1991; Gramsci 1971:333).[18] The Comaroffs describe the emergent awareness of hegemonic processes as occurring within "the liminal space of human experience in which people discern acts and facts but cannot or do not order them into narrative descriptions or even into articulate conceptions of the world" (1991:29). The Comaroffs argue: "It is from this realm that silent signifiers and unmarked practices may rise to the level of explicit consciousness, of ideological assertion, and become the subject of overt political and social contestation—or from which they may recede into the hegemonic, to languish there unremarked for the time being" (1991:29). In the following sections, I explore the critical spaces made available to these women as they encountered discourses of addiction. I draw on narratives presented at weekly support groups (called "family meetings" [*kazoku miitingu*]) held at the Center for family members of substance abusers.[19]

NARRATIVE VOICES

Constructions of narrative voice and powers of articulation (*hatsugen ryoku*) were considered by social workers to be aspects of recovery. Recovery entailed learning to talk about oneself (*jibun o hanasu*): women who began their sentences with "my husband" or "my son" were regarded as not yet recovered—although Japanese housewives often identify themselves in their communities as "X's wife" or "Y's mother." One aspect of this process that was taken as central by clinicians was clarity in marking the subject of the sentence. Wives of alcoholics are known by clinicians to leave out their subjects, and Japanese language makes it possible to leave out the subject of a sentence and make oneself understood through context. Not specifying the subject or subjective pronoun of a sentence, however, was taken by clinicians to be a sign of attenuated personal boundaries. For example, Ōta-san, an elderly participant in the group whose adult son lived at home with her, said:

> *Ōta desu* [I'm Ōta].[20] I'm here for my son's drug addiction. [He was] admitted to the hospital two times this year. [If he] didn't like it then he would just leave; [he has] no appreciation for money. [He] comes home and doesn't do a thing. Doesn't talk with my husband. I have to really hold myself together or else.[21]

At one meeting, this same woman (Ōta-san) introduced herself in a way that caught the social workers' attention. Instead of repeating the conventional introduction, "I'm Ōta. I'm here because of my son's drug addiction," she elided the two sentences saying, "I'm drug addiction

Ōta" (*Yakubutsu no Ōta desu*), transforming her son's sickness into an adjectival phrase modifying herself, a grammatically correct construction in Japanese. The staff commented on the elision after the meeting, citing it as symbolic of how "attached and identified" she is with her son. Bachnik and Quinn (1994) and Wetzel (1994) have argued that the construction of language is intertwined with cultural constructions of self. Wetzel shows that Japanese sentence structure de-emphasizes the speaking subject as the fixed reference point of the sentence and that verbs are conjugated contextually, according to the relationship of the speaker to the interlocutor, rather than according to the personal pronoun itself, independent of its context. Language naturalizes the slippage in boundaries, making this slippage difficult to problematize explicitly. In placing themselves at the center of their narratives, and in clearly distinguishing the "I" of the sentence, women attempted to overwrite implicit cultural assumptions coded into daily life through language.

WOMEN'S INVISIBLE LABOR

Once women began attending meetings regularly and learned to talk about themselves, a central theme that emerged in their conversations was the invisibility of their daily work as housewives. They began to see this invisibility as one aspect of the behavior that had led them to be complicit in their husbands' drinking and destructiveness. While the program's intervention focuses on behavior around drinking, it incited women to consider their daily lives more broadly. For example, Fukuda-san, whom clinicians held up as a model of progress, told this story:

> Fukuda desu. I'm here because of my husband's alcoholism. At the moment, there is a plate of sweet bean cakes sitting on top of our table at home. Since my husband has stopped drinking, he enjoys sweets. But I'm always the one who brings home the sweets. I remember when he was still drinking, it was always I who devotedly bought his sake. These days I'm starting to think that I'm just repeating the same old pattern.

The narrative relates a moment of taking notice of the ways in which women's work is often unspoken, unseen, and unremunerated.[22] The asymmetry of household work itself, including interpersonal facilitation, was not a new realization for these women, but they began to pay particular attention to the fine line between assumed intimacy and being taken for granted. For example Hata-san said:

> After dinner my custom is to make tea and then take a cup upstairs. The other night after I made tea and said to my husband, "Tea is ready," he said, "Thanks" [*O sewa ni naru ne*]. I was shocked! Usually he just treats these services like air.

"Air" is a traditional metaphor for the idealized construction of marital intimacy, reflecting the notion that couples can understand each other without speaking, through a kind of telepathy (*ishin denshin*), and that their mutual affection and understanding need not be explicitly expressed except in times of crisis, just as one becomes conscious of the air one breathes only in times of physical crisis (Iwao 1991:6).

Following his anecdote of arriving in the United States and being told by his guests to "help himself," Doi elaborates the ways that Japanese family members simply understand one another, responding to one another's needs without having to be asked; in fact, he argues that to thank explicitly someone with whom one is intimate would be "too coldly formal" (Doi 1973:91).[23] In idealistic terms, households are supposed to function seamlessly. There is a rich lexicon to describe this quality: the notion that people simply understand one another without explicit communication (*ishin denshin*, separate hearts communicating as one) is often held up as testimony to Japanese homogeneity and cultural uniqueness in popular *Nihonjinron* (discourses on Japaneseness). Within a Japanese home, a housewife's work means anticipating family members' needs before they are articulated (*sakidōri, sakimawari*); this quality of pre-emptive attentiveness is highly valued in wives, mothers, and female employees. It is suggested in a number of Japanese expressions that describe the way one holds one's *ki* or animating spirit: *kizuku* (ki is ignited, connoting noticing and awareness), *kimawashi* (to circulate one's ki), and *kikubari* (to hand out one's ki).[24]

The concept implies a mutualism that does not require explicit negotiation, though it is most often women's own work that facilitates such smoothly functioning family relationships. The notion of intuitive or unspoken harmoniousness forecloses the possibility of renegotiating this division of labor, instead implying that intimate relationships are beyond the reach of explicit discussion.

Women who attended the meetings at the Center began to call attention to the work they were doing—sometimes by not doing it. At times these acts involved breaching the home's boundaries as a private space. At meetings, women recounted stories of being a "bad wife" (*akusai*): not waiting up for their husbands to return from work, getting "loose" with the housework, putting the same food out for dinner as they had for lunch, or buying inferior quality food if that was more convenient. Some women trained their children to say "thank you," or, instead of making everyone's lunch, left notes to indicate where the ingredients were to be found. In one instance, Fukuda-san recounted her own realization of the minute nature of the forms of attentiveness she had given up:

> On Sunday, my husband and I went to a Buddhist memorial service for a friend. Lunch was served and the couple sitting opposite us was related to the deceased. The wife cut and prepared all the food that appeared and fed it to her husband—even peeling the skin off the shrimp. "What the heck is she doing?" I thought to myself. "How odd!" But of course I realized I used to do the same kinds of things. Now I can appreciate how strange it is. Well, I don't do it for my husband anymore, but

now I'm doing it for the dog. We've had a dog for seven years, and I lovingly tear up his food in tiny pieces for him to eat. I suppose there is still a part of me that just needs to dote on someone. Occasionally I wonder if I'm casting a burden on the dog [laughter].

Shifts in the work women performed had broader repercussions beyond family dynamics, and women were often forced to confront neighbors and bosses who held them accountable for their husbands' behavior, even when they declined to intervene. Though women felt considerable pressure to conceal social conflict (thereby preventing social disruption from seeping into domains beyond the home), counselors advised women to stop hiding scenes created by drunken husbands. In his book, Dr. Saitō advises women to open the windows and curtains to let everyone hear a husband's yell and scream. For some women, this strategy appeared to grant relief in and of itself, and women reported deliberately opening the front door during a fight.

Such a strategy makes for provocative advice and widely-selling books. And while it allows sympathetic neighbors to show solidarity, it also carries the risk of damaging the family's reputation. Women who chose to let family turmoil seep into the public often found that theories of alcoholism and codependence were counterintuitive to neighbors, extended family, bosses, and others. Koike-san told this story:

> Koike desu. I'm here because my husband has alcoholism. ... The other day he began a drinking bout in the neighborhood and ended up crouched on the sidewalk unable to stand up. Two neighbors came by to inform me that he was there, but I told them, "Please just leave him until he realizes and picks himself up. He is an alcoholic, so that's the best thing to do." They looked at me very strangely. Later that day, one man brought him to the doorstep.

Many women who stood their ground had to face such uncomfortable situations. Through conversations at the meetings, women reminded each other that they were not at fault, should not feel embarrassed, and were not being irresponsible, callous, or selfish. They were counseled to deflect the criticisms of others (*ukenagasu*) and not dwell on them.

SPACES OF RESISTANCE

Many women took transgressive steps as they embraced the concept of codependence. At the same time, certain Al-Anon interventions were more easily incorporated into Japanese cultural practice than they perhaps are in the United States. Al-Anon tenets of recovery involve constructing boundaries, learning how to disengage, maintaining distance (*kyori o oku*), and recognize that "I am I, and my husband is my husband." For Japanese women, these concepts proved to be less transgressive than they may be in an American context, where marriage is historically constructed around the ideal of heterosexual love and romantic intimacy (D'Emilio and Freedman 1997).

Japanese kinship has historically emphasized vertical ties; marital intimacy was less privileged than the perpetuation of the family line (Befu 1966; Nakane 1967). These patterns have served the needs of industrial capitalism, and as gendered divisions of labor have grown increasingly polarized in the postwar period, middle-class women have cultivated their chief intimacies with their children and their social relations with other mothers, and men have cultivated social relationships in the context of work (Allison 1994; Rohlen 1974).

Thus, women at the Center felt relatively comfortable establishing distance from their husbands, poking fun at their husbands during meetings, and even expressing dislike and violent impulses toward them; a few established separate living spaces within the same home, which they described as their "separate residences" (*bekkyo*). The proximity of Al-Anon dictums with Japanese commonsense constructions of marriage is reflected in Koike-san's matter-of-fact statement at one meeting:

> When my husband was carried to the hospital in an ambulance one time, I felt entirely cool and composed. I'm not sure if that was on account of my studies here at the Center or simply that I dislike my husband.

The dark side of this division of labor is that for most Japanese women, it is simply not economically viable to leave a marriage and attempt to strike out on one's own. (This is exacerbated by the social stigma that persists regarding divorce.) The brighter side of this construction of marriage is that it has created a stable environment for housewives. Women's relationships with their husbands are only one aspect of their married life, and they derive social credentials and resources from being a housewife that are independent of their relationships to their husbands (see Borovoy 1998; Imamura 1987; Le Blanc 1999; Vogel 1988). Women need not fear divorce and poverty should their husbands "fall out of love" with them. Many women (even of younger generations) appear willing to trade off romantic constructions of marriage for this stability.[25] At one weekly meeting, the subject turned to the topic of saying "I love you" between husband and wife. Few women found the idea appealing, and some viewed it as a fatuous form of flattery.[26]

Thus women had incentives to continue to operate within the confines of their marriage. During my year attending the meetings, only one woman, Hoshi-san, separated from her husband, moving to a separate apartment and finding work as a part-time janitor in an office building. (Her husband continued to subsidize her.) Interestingly, divorce was not considered a successful outcome by counselors at the Center,[27] and Sano-San, the one client I encountered who did divorce her husband, reported on her feelings of loss and lack of structure. At our 1998 reunion, she said she felt like a "broken off chopstick" (*waribashi no ippon*). Even though she had taken the step of divorcing her alcoholic husband, Sano-san commented to me that she felt sorry seeing her now-married son doing chores around the house. "I can't bear to look," she said. While she understood that the couple was trying to cultivate "partnership," she retained the conventional view of a happy marriage as rooted in a division of labor.

CONCLUSION: SPACES OF SOCIAL CRITICISM

In the context of dominant American ideologies that fetishize individual rights and view freedom and self-cultivation as the liberation from social constraints, there is little language for conceptualizing the necessary compromises of self-determination that sociality entails; ambiguous relationships that contain evidence of both power asymmetries and complicity are readily classified as abusive or exploitative—an infringement of human rights. In contrast, the social compact that has emerged in various social contexts in postwar Japan (including the family and workplace) hinges on discourses and practices that encourage individuals to tolerate asymmetrical relationships of power in the belief that these are combined with benevolent forces of intimacy, mutualism, and protection. From the standpoint of Western social theories—particularly liberalism and liberal feminism, which politicize the personal through the language of rights and self-determination—it is not clear what resistance to such a social compact might entail.

The one of the most striking aspects of Japanese women's discussions of their daily lives—from the standpoint of those trained in liberal social theory—is the almost complete absence of reference to structured gender inequalities and the institutions that sustain them. Given the centrality of home and family in the production of social order and in narratives of national identity, it was logical that women's awakenings concerning asymmetries at home would reshape their experience of social life beyond the home. In fact, many stories women told in meetings (meetings gathered around the premise of how to cope with a family member's substance abuse) made no mention of families and instead focused on observations about everyday public life: learning to turn away door-to-door salesmen, to speak up when they were being made uncomfortable on the train, or to ask their employers their reason for pay cuts. Yet rarely did women's conversations turn to the issues of disparities in economic opportunity, expectations placed on women by the public school system and Japanese companies, or the conservative nature of the family court system.

The one woman who did conceptualize her plight as a political struggle for justice, Koike-san, had a significantly different background from the rest of the women: she was a long-standing member of a Marxist-influenced women's group, the New Housewives Association (*Shin Nihon Fujin no Kai*), concerned with women's labor issues. She eventually became disenchanted with the meetings and stopped attending. During my follow-up visit in 1998, Koike-san told me that she felt she was different from the other women, in particular because she was "poor" (as she put it) and living in public housing. (She had also been politically active as the head of the Residents Association, which lobbied the city for better services.) Her husband had died since I knew her in 1993, and he had not been working during his last years;

thus she received few pension benefits from his company or aid from the state. She described herself as "angry": "I've worked this hard … only to find that the women who are ultimately rewarded are the women who don't work and just marry rich men."

Because most women do not challenge gender oppression at the level of structured inequalities but rather persevere in working within the system, are their conversations and strategies evidence of "false consciousness"? On the contrary, I would suggest that the data collected in this study show how even thoughtful, articulate subjects—and subjects under considerable duress—question only certain aspects of dominant cultural ideologies while leaving others intact. The ideal outcome for most of the clients at the Center (from their own perspective and the staff's) was to be "good wives" when they chose to or when it seemed rewarding and to relinquish this duty when it was undermining. One of the stories the staff cited as an example of true recovery was this story of Fukuda-san's:

> This week I experienced something for the first time since I was born. At 2 a.m. my eyes popped open when I heard a BANG BANG sound like a pistol. I listened closely as I wondered what to do. It began to come closer. My son came down the stairs and yelled out 'Fire!!' and there turned out to be a fire just about 30 meters from our house.
>
> Two houses were completely burned to the ground. We went all out to take care of the three people whose houses had burned—I exhausted myself attending to them like I haven't in a longtime.
>
> Afterwards I thought that perhaps I'd inadvertently returned to my former "service" self. But then I realized that there is, after all, a place and time for going all out for people. I want to save that little part of me for times like this.
>
> It's funny, though, when I heard "It's a fire!" I remember waking my husband up, but after that I had no idea what happened to him. All I remember was standing outside cradling the dog, thinking to myself, "What should I do with the dog? Where can I put the dog?!" [Laughter]

The story—and the staff's enthusiasm about it—illustrates the cultural forces in place that continue to sanction the work of caretaking as important work and as women's work and that continue to see the idealistic rendering of amae as a worthwhile goal to pursue.

In the summer of 2000, I brought a translated version of an earlier draft of this article to Tokyo. One colleague who read it, Nishida-san, was a 45-year-old social worker at an elite, Western-influenced private hospital known for its progressive patient care. She is an extremely well-educated and thoughtful woman, a full-time professional with a family. She also places great value in women's work as wives and mothers and has been unsympathetic to Western-influenced academic feminism in Japan—the call to women to devalue work at home and to question the naturalness of women's roles as wives and mothers. Nishida found Fukuda-san's story extremely compelling and felt that to follow it with a discussion of exploitation of women in Japanese society (as I had done) was a mistake. She felt there was a disjuncture between the story and the analysis and that I hadn't captured the complexity of Fukuda-san's story or paid sufficient attention to her feelings. "When I read it, I really understood her feeling that even after going through so much, she still wanted to preserve that part of herself." What a discussion of "exploitation" is missing, she argued, is an appreciation of these women's audacity or head-strongness (*shibutosa*) and their flexibility.

> When I read these women's stories, I really think that they've gotten healthier over the 20 years that they've lived with their husbands without divorcing: supporting them, working part-time, telling their stories in ways that show off their triumphs. I think that's tremendously healthy! I think it's admirable. [*Watashi wa sugoku kenkō da to omoimasu. Rippa da to omoimasu.*]

Nishida's position may in part reflect a clinician's worldview, which sees functioning adeptly within social prescriptions as the definition of health. Yet Nishida is far more progressive than the countless voices in contemporary Japan (including physicians, mediators at family courts, and counselors—some women themselves) who encourage women to endure and persevere for the sake of the family or lament that women have been spoiled by Japan's postwar wealth and the conveniences of modernization to the point that they no longer know how to be proper wives and mothers. Nishida's view represents an entrenched view common even to many progressive factions in Japan; it sees value in more conservative constructions of family and questions the assumption that following the American example is necessarily the best path for Japanese women or for Japanese society more broadly.[28] Nishida's comments on this article lead back to the point made at the outset: that resistance itself is culturally constructed. To focus on the absence of familiar forms of feminism and discourses of gender inequality in women's narratives is to ignore shifts in consciousness that have important ramifications for social change in contemporary Japan.

While Japanese feminists have mobilized around equal opportunities in the workplace, as exemplified in the 1986 passage of the Equal Employment Opportunities Law (Gelb 1991; Mackie 1988), many prominent feminists have declined to follow the example of American second wave feminism, which promoted women's wage-earning capacity as the single most important marker of their liberation. Many grassroots and academic feminists, including Marxist feminists, such as Ueno Chizuko, have argued for a better life for the housewife—anticipating in many ways U.S. third wave feminism, which acknowledges that women can gain only limited ground as long as "dependency work" (Delaney 1998) continues to be undervalued. Ueno has argued that until men take up the work of raising children, caring for the elderly, and helping manage the home—what Ueno refers to as the "feminization of men"—women's entry into the work place can only mean their double exploitation (Ueno 1988:183).

The feminist scholar Asai Michiko (1990) has argued that the cultural apparatus that oppresses Japanese women is historically different from the one that oppresses Western women and demands different interventions. While Western radical and Marxist feminisms have pointed to heterosexual patriarchy as the foundation of gender inequality, Japanese women are in contrast oppressed by the powers and virtues associated with motherhood and femininity—what she calls the "fantasy of motherly nature" (*bosei gensō*). In her article, "Towards a Liberation from the Myth of the Modern Family," Asai argues that the image of the pure (*muku*), nurturing wife and mother at the center of the family obscures women's exploitation since "motherhood" eclipses "womanhood." This eliminates recourse to discourses of individual rights and equality by casting social relations in the language of dependency and nurturance; furthermore, it desexualizes women, painting them as pure and innocent (*junsui muku*) or as desireless (*muyoku*) maternal figures outside the purview of gender discrimination or violation, "able to turn the other way in the face of sexual oppression" (*sei ni yoru yoku atsu ni me o memuru koto go dekite*; Asai 1990:100).

In a context where the discourse of familial nurturance inflects not only women's private lives but also constructions of work, home, and society itself, conversations about codependence (and the range of behavior it includes) reach to the very heart of central social tensions. For women, the question of the fine line between amae and unhealthy, or systematically exploitative forms of intimacy is key to developing a social criticism. In Japan, state sponsored ideologies and structured inequalities may be perceived as legitimate precisely because they are able to exploit this fine conceptual line between nurturance and exploitation. The Japanese state is poised increasingly to delegate to women the tasks of compensating for Japan's shrinking welfare state—a task that is sure to grow greater with the aging of the populace, dwindling corporate safety nets, and increasing international economic competition (Buckley and Mackie 1986; Lock 1993a, 1993b). To the extent that women hone their awareness of the darker sides of cultural assumptions that underlie close communities, family values, and economic productivity, they will be better poised to resist this delegation of labor as the natural or obvious terrain of women's work.

NOTES

I would like to thank Tom Rohlen, Laura Nelson, and Jonathan Mor- duch for many conversations about the material and for reading earlier drafts. In addition to the three anonymous reviewers for American Ethnologist, I would like to thank Anne Allison, Harumi Befu, Judith Barker, Jane Collier, Carol Delaney, Charo D'Etcheverry, Joseph Dumit, Sheldon Garon, Sally Gibbons, Richard Gordon, Hitesh Hathi, Arthur Kleinman, Linda Mitte- ness, Joel Streicker, Renato Rosaldo, Claire Waters, Sylvia Yanagisako, and Tomiko Yoda for their contributions. Support for fieldwork was generously provided by IIE Fulbright, the National Science Foundation (Anthropological and Geographical Sciences #9209871), and the Stanford University Center for East Asian Studies grant for the study of women in Asia. The writing process was assisted by a grant from the Joint Committee on Japan Studies of the Social Science Research Council and the American Council of Learned Societies with funds provided by the Andrew W. Mellon Foundation and by a National Institute of Aging Postdoctoral Training Grant #T32AG0045, Linda S. Mitteness, Director.

1.   In his interpretation of Gramsci, Raymond Williams defines hegemony as "a set of meanings and values which as they are experienced as practices appear as reciprocally confirming" (1980:38). He writes:

     It thus constitutes a sense of reality for most people in the society, a sense of absolute because experienced reality beyond which it is very difficult for most members of the society to move, in most areas of their lives. It is, that is to say, in the strongest sense a 'culture,' but a culture which has also to be seen as the lived dominance and subordination of particular classes. [Williams 1977:110]

2. Exploring histories of peasant resistance in Malaysia and France, Scott argues that contrary to conventional views of peasant resistance as involving collective mobilization and "mass rage" (1987a:417), most instances of peasant resistance "require little or no planning, … often represent forms of individual self-help, and … typically avoid any *direct* symbolic confrontation with authority or with elite norms" (1987a:419–420, 1987b).

3. Japanese names are listed in customary fashion with surname first.

4. Predominantly, these were women born in the 1930s and 40s, the first two decades of the Showa era (1926–88) and were members of generational cohorts that have traversed two starkly contrasting cultural value systems within their own lifetimes: the prewar militarist- nationalist regime and the postwar American-mandated democracy. According to national surveys, these women, particularly those born in the 1930s, are thought to retain traditional value systems (see Lock 1993a:80–83).

5. Research for this project was conducted between 1992 and 1993 with a follow-up visit in 1998. The treatment program at the Center is for families of substance abusers, not substance abusers themselves. The program includes a six-week educational seminar on the nature of substance abuse as an illness and also on family systems models of treatment: the role of family dynamics in sustaining addictive behavior and strategies for subverting these dynamics. Women who complete the seminar may join a weekly support group known as the "family meeting." The Center is a designated training ground for nurses, doctors, and social workers from hospitals and community health care centers all over Japan. The major alcohol treatment facilities in Tokyo were founded by doctors and psychologists trained at the Center.

6. See, for example, Bellah 1985; Coles 1980; and Sennett 1976 for a critique of impoverished concepts of the social in American therapeutic discourse.

7. Given this construction, it is not surprising that one observer suggested that Co-dependents Anonymous may be the first "12-step program for everybody" (W. 1990:9 in Makela 1996:228).

8. The self-help concept that formed the basis of the AA conceptual apparatus emerged in the context of the Great Depression and New Deal; it recognized and grappled with the tensions in American social life between self-determination and public responsibility, and between rights and responsibilities (Delbanco and Delbanco 1995). In contrast, in his study of Co-dependents Anonymous (CoDA, a group that emerged in the 1980s for those who identify as codependent but are not necessarily involved with a substance abuser), Rice argues that in CoDA, "moral action is not understood in terms of a commitment that transcends the self-interest but, rather, in terms of a commitment to self-interest" (1996:163).

9. All clients' names appearing here are pseudonyms.

10. For example, Saitō describes Japanese parents as "addicted to the school system" (1989:61–62), and workaholism as "Japan's biggest addiction" (personal communication, April 30,1993).

11. Previously, farm families and middle-class urban families had not privileged domestic cleanliness, nor had domesticity or the work of childrearing been explicitly gendered (Tamanoi 1991; Uno 1993b:50–58).

12. After the war, women, as housewives, were quickly solicited in the project of economic productivity—to the extent that many prominent corporations initiated programs (with sponsorship from the prime minister) that aimed to train housewives to establish "bright," "cheerful," and "cultivated" homes (Orii 1973 in Gordon 1997:247) in order to allow men to "devote [themselves] to production free from anxiety" (Manejimento 1955 in Gordon 1997:247). The phenomenon was key to both the naturalization of gender roles and to what Andrew Gordon has called "the ascendance of the 'enterprise society'" in postwar Japan: "a society where meeting the needs of the corporation is 'naturally' understood to be social common sense and to be congruent with meeting the needs of all society's inhabitants" (1997:247).

13. In its articulation of public social relationships through the idiom of family, the text echoes prewar synecdochic linkings of family and state. Though the thrust of the book is not a political one, Doi casts both prewar and postwar Japanese social harmony, cooperation, and social cohesion—indeed he attributes them to the same sentiments—with a rosy, benevolent, even infantile hue rather than a critical one. He briefly addresses the problem of Japan's militarism and mass loyalty to the Emperor, arguing that the emperor system was a manifestation of underlying sentiments of amae among the Japanese people, but that these sentiments could not be made manifest until old-fashioned hierarchical ideologies of loyalty and duty to the emperor had been abolished (1973:61).

14. The term most commonly used for alcoholism, in both medical and popular realms, *arukōru chudoku*, translates literally as "alcohol poisoning" and does not connote the condition of chronic alcoholism. Within the past 15 years, however, some nurses, social workers, psychiatrists, and physicians have mobilized to foster greater public awareness of alcoholism as an addictive illness with its own particular phenomenology, renaming the illness *arukōru izonshō* (literally, "alcohol dependency syndrome"). Paradigms of alcohol addiction encourage women to abdicate responsibility sooner: the phenomenology of alcohol dependency syndrome requires that patients must want to recover and must initiate the course of treatment in order to be successful; family members are powerless to cure them.

15. Koike-san, whose husband had not worked for several years and who was supporting her family single-handedly, once described her initial perception of the problem. Her comments suggest her preoccupation with her husband's inability to work in a way that distracted her from the possibility of other problems:

> I suppose I just wasn't thoughtful enough about it. "How did my husband come to such astate?"—I didn't ask myself. All I knew was that he couldn't work like usual people. I figured he must have some defect in that regard. I didn't consult a psychiatrist; I never thought he was mentally ill. I just thought he didn't have the power to face adversity. All I knew was that I couldn't expect him to work normally. If only he could find work that suited him, I kept thinking.

16. Before the discourse of alcohol dependency syndrome (*arukōru izonshō*) emerged, alcoholism was treated similarly to a mental illness: families were encouraged to cope with the matter privately until this was no longer feasible, at which point patients were forcibly admitted to mental hospitals—largely as a custodial rather than therapeutic gesture (Munakata 1986; Smith 1988:186).

17. Of the 13 wives of alcoholics who attended meetings regularly over the course of the year, only two had husbands who had remained sober for at least a year; two more had husbands who were generally sober but occasionally "slipped." Upon a five-year follow-up, only one husband was completely sober. One had passed away.

18. See Comaroff and Comaroff (1991:19-27) for a useful interpretation of Gramsci's idea of "contradictory consciousness" (Gramsci 1971:333).

19. The treatment program attracted two groups of women: women married to alcoholics and mothers of teenage substance abusers. The teenagers were usually sniffing paint thinner, a highly destructive yet available product in Japan. The issues faced by the two groups were different though overlapping, and three times a month the groups met separately. In this article, I focus on women married to alcoholics, analyzing how shifting constructions of alcoholism were involved with women's own consciousness-raising.

20. At weekly meetings, each person introduced herself by stating her name and reason for coming—a ritual modeled after the AA format that requires members to state that they are alcoholics. Unlike AA and Al-Anon, Japanese meetings typically do not require anonymity (see Smith 1988 for a discussion of the differences).

21. I have put the subjects in brackets in the narrative. The Japanese narrative recorded in the meeting log was as follows: "*Nen ni nikkai no nyuin. Ki ni kuwanai to dete kite okane no mushin. Ie ni kaeru to nan mo hitotsu shinai. Shujin to hanashi o shinai. Watashi ga shikkari shinai to ikenai.*"

    The narratives taken from weekly meetings were recorded in writing by a staff member for recordkeeping purposes. I have translated these transcripts. The staff log was quite thorough, and, as I transcribed it, I included any details I remembered. The narratives, thus, are as close as possible to the verbatim narratives short of transcribing a tape-recording. Japanese speakers will notice that the narrative verb endings usually appear in written rather than verbal form.

22. I have also heard women refer to traditional Japanese housewives as transparent beings (*tōmei ningen*).

23. In *The Anatomy of Dependence*, Doi writes:

> It is precisely because the two are part of one whole that it is impossible that one of them should bow his head in thanks to the other. Any Japanese, I suspect, could understand this reasoning. … The more intimate the relationship the fewer the expressions of gratitude; between husband and wife or parent and child words of thanks are normally almost unknown. [1973:91]

24. As an American guest in traditionally-minded Japanese households, I found myself experiencing such service as a form of surveillance. Slippers were magically turned the other direction in between the time I entered a room and prepared to leave it. At meals, a good hostess monitors what guests' tastes are and whether the dishes they seem to prefer are in reach; she times the presentation of each course precisely and serves the rice (the final course) when she judges that everyone has had the right amount to drink.

25. One Japanese housewife, an audience member of a public symposium on alcoholism sponsored by the Center's research institute, commented that drunken husbands are "easier" than sober ones, as they come home late and only require being bathed and put to bed, making no demands for intimacy or sex.

26. On one occasion when Hata-san announced that her husband had told her that he loved her, a number of women responded:

> Koike desu. 20 years ago my husband told me that he loved me. I wasn't the least bit pleased [*Jitsu wa zen zen ureshikunakatta*]. It was so obviously just flattery [*kuchi saki*] that I actually got mad. I really didn't want to hear it.
>
> Ehara desu. I'm subjected to such flattery all the time. I come down in the morning, and I have no make up on. I'm wearing crummy old clothes—nothing special at all, and he'll say, "Gee you look so nice today" [*Kyō wa kirei desu ne*]. Then the next minute he'll say something like, 'Who needs you anyway, why don't you just return to your parents' home where you came from!" [*Omei nanka wa iranei kara jikka ni kaere!*] And then he'll actually ask me to do him a favor! [*Are kore shite kure to iu!*] Really, I think he's an imbecile [*baka*] sometimes. Just this morning he said I

looked nice in what I was wearing, and then the very next thing he said was, "Are you going out in public looking like that?" I felt very manipulated [*Zuibun furimawasareru to omotta*].

Koike desu [second round]. I wish I could be more like Hata-san and try to cultivate a kind of relationship with my husband and make conversation. But it's just too much of a nuisance.

Ehara desu [second round]. I'm not good either at making small conversation [*fafu kaiwa*]. My husband and I have so little in common—we think differently, we like different foods. Occasionally, he'll show some thanks or awareness for the things I do for him everyday and say "thank you" or something like that. But I can't bring myself to reply. I can't bring myself to be sincere [*Sunao ni narenai*].

27. While no-fault divorce is frequently touted as a triumph of women's liberation in the United States, the financial and other hardships involved for women are often minimized. In contrast, few middle-class Japanese women see divorce as a mark of independence or liberation. Japanese women are well aware of the considerable financial and other hardships that face divorced women and view divorce as the last recourse.

28. In fact, since my initial year of fieldwork, as the concept of codependence has taken root, a number of critics of the concept have emerged. Nishida was among them. She felt the concept was too rigid, applying a fixed label to those with more complicated and ambiguous problems. And while the social workers at the Center were quite conservative in the way they applied the concept (celebrating women's small accomplishments, not advocating divorce, etc.), Nishida told me that when she had referred clients to facilities where the concept is applied more stridently, the clients inevitably returned to the hospital. The categories just do not fit perfectly in the context of Japanese history. (Poking fun at 12-step argot, she told me, "In the Edo Period [1603–1867; the period leading up to Japan's modernization], parents' first impulse was to hit their kids, then discuss it; now those kids would be called 'adult children'!")

REFERENCES CITED

Abu-Lughod, Lila. 1990. The Romance of Resistance: Tracing Transformations of Power Through Bedouin Women. American Ethnologist 17(1):41–55.

Allison, Anne. 1991. Japanese Mothers and Obentos: The Lunch Box as State Ideological Apparatus. Anthropology Quarterly 64(4): 195–208.

1994. Nightwork: Sexuality, Pleasure, and Corporate Masculinity in a Tokyo Hostess Club. Chicago: University of Chicago Press. 1996 Permitted and Prohibited Desires. Boulder, CO: Westview Press.

Asai, Michiko. 1990. Kindai kazoku gensōkara no kaihō mezashite [Towards Liberation From Illusions of the Modern Family]. In Feminizumu Ronsō: 70 Nendai kara 90 Nendai e (Feminist Debates: From the 70s to the 90s]. Yumiko Ehara, ed. Pp. 87–117. Tokyo: Keisō Publishers.

Bachnik, Jane M., and Charles J. Quinn

1994. Situated Meaning: Inside and Outside in Japanese Self, Society, and Language. Princeton, NJ: Princeton University Press.

Beattie, Melody. 1987. Codependent No More: How to Stop Controlling Others and Start Caring for Yourself. New York: Harper Collins.

Befu, Harumi. 1966. Corporate Emphasis and Patterns of Descent in Japanese Family. In Japanese Culture: Its Development and Characteristics. Robert. J. Smith and Richard K. Beardsley, eds. Pp. 34–41. Chicago: Aldine Publishing Co.

Bellah, Robert. Habits of the Heart: Individualism and Commitment in American Life. Berkeley: University of California Press.

Borovoy, Amy. 1994. Good Wives and Mothers: The Production of Domesticity in a Global Economy. Ph.D. dissertation, Department of Anthropology, Stanford University.

——1998. Not a Doll's House: Public Uses of Domesticity in Japan. Department of East Asian Studies, Princeton University, unpublished manuscript.

Bourdieu, Pierre. 1977. Outline of a Theory of Practice. Richard Nice, trans. Cambridge: Cambridge University Press.

Buckley, Sandra, and Vera Mackie. Women in the New Japanese State. In Democracy in Contemporary Japan. Y. S. Gavan McCormack, ed. Pp. 173–185. New York: M. E. Sharpe.

Coles, Robert. 1980. Civility and Psychology. Daedalus (summer):! 32–141.

Comaroff, Jean. 1985. Body of Power Spirit of Resistance: The Culture and History of a South African People. Chicago: University of Chicago Press.

Comaroff, Jean, and John L. Comaroff. 1991. Of Revelation and Revolution: Christianity, Colonialism, and Consciousness in South Africa, vol. 1. Chicago: University of Chicago Press.

de Certeau, Michel. 1984. The Practice of Everyday Life. Steven F. Rendall, trans. Berkeley: University of California Press.

Delaney, Carol. 1998. Abraham On Trial: The Social Legacy of Biblical Myth. Princeton, NJ: Princeton University Press.

Delbanco, Andrew, and Thomas Delbanco. A.A. at the Crossroads. The New Yorker, March 20:49–63.

D'Emilio, John, and Estelle B. Freedman. 1997. Intimate Matters: A History of Sexuality in America. Chicago: University of Chicago Press.

Diamond, Irene, and Lee Quinby, eds. Feminism and Foucault: Reflections on Resistance. Boston: Northeastern University Press.

Dirks, Nicholas, Geoff Eley, and Sherry B. Ortner, eds. 1994. A Reader in Contemporary Social Theory. Princeton, Nj: Princeton University Press.

Doi, Takeo. 1973. The Anatomy of Dependence. New York: Kodansha International.

Dowling, Colette. 1990. The Cinderella Complex: Women's Hidden Fear of Independence. New York: Moss Market Paperbacks.

Foucault, Michel. 1965. Madness and Civilization. Richard Howard, trans. New York: Vintage.

——1977. Discipline and Punish. Alan Sheridan, trans. New York: Vintage.

——1978. The History of Sexuality Volume I: An Introduction. Robert Harley, trans. New York: Vintage.

——1980. Power/Knowledge: Selected Interviews and Other Writings 1972–1977. Colin Gordon, ed. Colin Gordon, Leo Marshall, John Mepham, and Kate Soper, trans. New York: Pantheon.

Garon, Sheldon. 1997. Molding Japanese Minds: The State in Everday Life. Princeton, NJ: Princeton University Press.

Gelb, Joyce. 1991. Tradition and Change in Japan: The Case of Equal Employment Opportunity Law. U.S.-Japan Women's Journal English Supplement 1:51–77.

Giddens, Anthony. 1991. Modernity and Self-Identity. Stanford, CA: Stanford University Press.

——1992. The Transformation of Intimacy. Stanford, CA: Stanford University Press.

Gordon, Andrew. 1977. Managing the Japanese Household: The New Life Movement in Postwar Japan. Social Politics (summer):245–283.

——2000. Society and Politics from Transwar through Postwar Japan. In Historical Perspectives on Contemporary East Asia. Merle Goldman and Andrew Gordon, eds. Pp. 287. Cambridge, MA: Harvard University Press.

Gramsci, Antonio. 1971. Selections from the Prison Notebooks. Quintin Hoare and Geoffrey Nowell Smith, trans. New York: International Publishers.

Haaken, Janice. 1990. A Critical Analysis of the Co-dependence Construct. Psychiatry 53:396–406.

——1993. From Al-Anon to ACOA: Codependence and the Reconstruction of Caregiving. Signs 18(2):321–345.

Haley, John Owen. 1991. Authority Without Power. New York: Oxford University Press.

Hamilton, V. Lee, and Joseph Sanders. 1992. Everyday Justice: Responsibility and the Individual in Japan and the United States. New Haven, CT: Yale University Press.

Hane, Mikiso. 1993. Reflections on the Way to the Gallows: Rebel Women in Prewar Japan. Berkeley: University of California Press.

Imamura, Anne. 1987. Urban Japanese Housewives: At Home and in the Community. Honolulu: University of Hawai'i Press.

Iwao, Sumiko. 1991. The Quiet Revolution: Japanese Women Today. The Japan Foundation Newsletter 19(3):1–9.

Japan Statistical Yearbook. 1988. Japan Statistical Yearbook (Nihon Tokei Kyokai). Tokyo: Mainichi Shinbunsha.

Koschmann, J. Victor. 1981-82. The Debate on Subjectivity in Postwar Japan: Foundations of Modernism as a Political Critique. Pacific Affairs 54(4):609–631.

LeBlanc, Robin. 1999. Bicycle Citizens: The Political World of the Japanese Housewife. Berkeley: University of California Press.

"Let's Find Out About …" 1993. Let's Find Out About [Soko ga shiritai …]. Tokyo Broadcasting System, January 26.

Lock, Margaret. 1993a. Encounters with Aging: Mythologies of Menopause in Japan and North America. Berkeley: University of California Press.

——1993b. Ideology, Female Midlife, and the Greying of Japan, journal of Japanese Studies 19(1):43–77.

Mackie, Vera. 1988. Feminist Politics in Japan. New Left Review 167:53–76.

Makela, Klaus. 1996. Alcohlics Anonymous as a Mutual-Help Movement. Madison: University of Wisconsin Press.

Manejimento. 1955. Katei ni chokketsu shita shinseikatsu undo (New Life Movement Ties Up Directly with Families) 14(9):20–21.

Miyamoto, Masao. 1994. Straightjacket Society: An Insider's Irreverent View of Bureaucratic Japan. New York: Kodansha International.

Molony, Kathleen Susan. 1980. One Woman Who Dared: Ichikawa Fusae and the Japanese Women's Suffrage Movement. Ph.D. dissertation, Department of History, University of Michigan.

Munakata, Tsunetsugu. 1986. Japanese Attitudes Toward Mental Health and Mental Health Care. In Japanese Culture and Behavior. Takie Sugiyama Lebra and William P. Lebra, eds. Pp. 369–378. Honolulu: University of Hawai'i Press.

Nakane, Chie. 1967. Kinship and Economic Organization in Rural Japan. London: Athlone Press.

Nolte, Sharon H., and Sally Ann Hastings. 1991. The Meiji State's Policy Towards Women, 1890–1910. In Recreating Japanese Women, 1600–1945. Gail L. Bernstein, ed. Pp. 151–175. Berkeley: University of California Press.

Norwood, Robin. 1991. Women Who Love Too Much: When You Keep Wishing and Hoping He'll Change. New York: Mass Market Paperback.

Orii, Hyūga. 1973. Rōmu kanri 20 nen (Twenty Years of Labor Management). Tokyo: Keizai Tōyo Shinpōsha.

Ōzawa, Ichirō. 1994. Blueprint for New Japan: The Rethinking of Nation. New York: Kodansha International.

Pyle, Kenneth
——1996. A World Historical Significance of Japan. In A Vision of a New Liberalism? Critical Essays on Murakami's Anticlassical Analysis. Kozo Yamamura, ed. Pp. 208–237. Stanford, CA: Stanford University Press.

Rice, John Steadman. 1996. A Disease of One's Own. New Brunswick, NJ: Transaction Publishers.

Rohlen, Thomas P.. 1974. For Harmony and Strength: Japanese White-Collar Organization in Anthropological Perspective. Berkeley: University of California Press.

——1989. Order in Japanese Society: Attachment, Authority, and Routine. Journal of Japanese Studies 15(1):1–40.

Saitō, Satoru. 1989. Kazoku izunsho [Family Addiction]. Tokyo: Seishin Publishers.

——1998. Kazoku no yami o saguru: Gendai no oyako kankei [Exploring the Darkness of Families: Contemporary Parent-Child Relations]. Tokyo: NHK.

Sakamoto, Kazue. 1997. Kazoku imeji no tanjō: Nihon eiga ni miru hōmu dorama no keisei (The Development of the Home Drama in Japanese Movies). Tokyo: Shinyōsha.

Sakuta, Keiichi. 1986. A Reconsideration of the Culture of Shame. Review of Japanese Culture and Society 1 (1):32–39.

Scott, James C.. 1987a. Resistance Without Protest and Without Organization: Peasant Opposition to the Islamic Zakat and the Christian Tithe. Comparative Study of Society and History 29(3):417–452.

——1987b. Weapons of the Weak: Everyday Forms of Peasant Resistance. New Haven, CT: Yale University Press.

Sennett, Richard. 1972. The Fall of Public Man. New York: W. W. Norton.

Sievers, Sharon L. 1983. Flowers in Salt: The Beginnings of Feminist Consciousness in Modern Japan. Stanford, CA: Stanford University Press.

Smith, Stephen. 1988. Drinking and Sobriety in Japan. Ph.D. dissertation, Department of Anthropology, Columbia University.

Tamanoi, Mariko Asano. 1991. Songs as Weapons: The Culture and History of Komori (Nursemaids) in Modern Japan. Journal of Japanese Studies 50(4):793–816.

Ueno, Chizuko. 1988. The Japanese Women's Movement: The Counter-values to Industrialism. In The Japanese Trajectory: Modernization and Beyond. Gavin McCormick and Yoshio Sugimoto, eds. Pp. 167–185. New York: Cambridge University Press.

Uno, Kathleen. 1993a. The Death of "Good Wife, Wise Mother"? In Postwar Japan as History. Andrew Gordon, ed. Pp. 293–324. Berkeley: University of California Press.

——1993b. One Day at a Time: Work and Domestic Activities of Urban Lower-Class Women in Early Twentieth Century Japan. In Japanese Women Working. Janet Hunter, ed. Pp. 37–68. New York: Routledge.

Upham, Frank. 1987. Law and Social Change in Postwar Japan. Cambridge, MA: Harvard University Press.

Vogel, Ezra. 1963. Japan's New Middle Class. Berkeley: University of California Press.

Vogel, Suzanne. 1988. Professional Housewife: The Career of Urban Middle Class Japanese Women. Cambridge: Institute for Independent Study, RadcliffeCollege.

W., Chuck. 1990. ACA vs. CoDA. Changes (May-June):9.

Wetzel, Patricia J. 1994. A Movable Self: The Linguistic Indexing of Uchi and Soto. In Situated Meanings: Inside and Outside in Japanese Self, Society, and Language. Jane M. Bachnik and Charles J. Quinn, Jr., eds. Pp. 73–87. Princeton, NJ: Princeton University Press.

Williams, Raymond. 1977. Marxism and Literature. New York: Oxford University Press.

——1980. Problems in Materialism and Culture. London: Verso.

27

Local Knowledge in the Environment-Development Discourse

Anja Nygren

In the past two decades, local knowledge systems have been the subject of increasing at-tention not only by anthropologists, but also by environmental researchers, biodiversity prospectors, development experts, businessmen and local people themselves. Local knowledge has been portrayed as a part of a romantic past, as the major obstacle to development, as a non-issue, as a panacea for dealing with the most pressing environmental problems, and as a critical component of a cultural alternative to modernization (Agrawal, 1995; Heyd, 1995).[1]

Conventionally, local knowledge has been represented as something in opposition to mod-ern knowledge. As remarked by Kloppenburg (1991: 527–8), a wide variety of analysts, from phenomenologist philosophers to contemporary anthropologists, have tried to illuminate the epistemological difference between local knowledge and scientific knowledge by elaborating a range of binary concepts: *la science du concrète/la science* (Lévi-Strauss, 1962), tacit knowledge/ scientific knowledge (Polanyi, 1966), folk knowledge/universal knowledge (Hunn, 1982), indigenous knowledge/Western knowledge (Posey, 1983; Warren *et al.*, 1995), and traditional knowledge/modern knowledge (Huber and Pedersen, 1997).

Characteristic of these dichotomies has been the view of local knowledge as practical, col-lective, and strongly rooted in place. According to Geertz (1983: 75), local knowledge forms a relatively organised body of thought based on immediacy of experience, while van der Ploeg (1993) speaks of the *art de la localité*, which is intimately linked to spatially specific practices. In this call for the location-specific, ethnoscientists have revealed sophisticated insights into indigenous knowledge systems and world-views. What has been rarely questioned in all this is

Anja Nygren, "Local Knowledge in the Environment-Development Discourse," *Critique of Anthropology*, vol. 19, no. 3, pp. 267–288. Copyright © 1999 by Sage Publications. Reprinted with permission.

the representation of local knowledges as monolithic and culturally bounded systems. As remarked by Moore (1996: 2–3), anthropologists have been happy to highlight the 'indigenous point of view' and to see the local people as producers of endogenous knowledge regarding natural resource management, cosmological theories and medical cures; however less attention has been paid to the contested and hybrid character of such knowledges. The concept that local people produce 'shared knowledge', which serves as a 'cultural totem' about 'how we know' (Cohen, 1993: 37), includes an implicit assumption of people living in closed communities and having unique ways of knowing.

Recent trends of post-structuralism and deconstructivism have challenged such ways of constructing the other. Many black and Third World scholars, postcolonial theorists and feminists have pointed out that the absolutist dichotomy 'either/or' that underpins Western philosophical thinking works in a discriminatory manner to structure representations of knowledges in specific contexts (Escobar, 1997; Haraway, 1989, 1996; Mohanty, 1991). It is based on a Cartesian model of the subject who knows and the object who is to be known. According to the post-structuralists, all knowledges are socially constructed, thus the focus of analysis should be on those processes that legitimize certain hierarchies of knowledge and power between local and global (scientific) knowledges.

The purpose in this article is to analyse the role of local knowledges in the current debate on environment and development by drawing on ethnographic research done among peasant colonists in Río San Juan, Nicaragua.[2] The two mainstream approaches—constructing local knowledge as a scapegoat for underdevelopment or as a panacea for sustainability—are critically examined. The study then aims to reconstruct an alternative view of situated knowledges which are simultaneously local and global. Such a perspective re-maps the fixed boundaries between rational and practical, and modern and traditional, that have characterized some of the main disputes in anthropology in its current crisis of representation (Nash, 1997). It also opens up a new field of ethnographic analysis in which the principal research problem is no longer the local knowledge systems as clearly separated 'there', but the hegemonic discourses that authorize essentialist representations of heterogeneous knowledges.

CONTEXT: MIGRANT PEASANTS AS DISEMBEDDED OTHERS

In 1996, I became interested in nature-based conflicts in a protected area buffer zone in Río San Juan, southeastern Nicaragua. This humid tropical forest area, located in the municipality of El Castillo, belongs to the buffer zone of the biological reserve of Indio-Maíz, established in 1990. Indio-Maíz has acquired a great international reputation as one of the most outstanding protected areas in Central America. It belongs within the category of strictly protected areas: the only activities permitted in the reserve are scientific investigation and wilderness protection.

The establishment of the reserve has many implications for the livelihood opportunities of the surrounding forest-edge communities. The buffer zone of Indio-Maíz covers 180,000 hectares of land and has some 10,000 inhabitants. It belongs to one of the most intensive agricultural frontiers in the country, with high rates of immigration and deforestation. To secure the support of the local population, the programmes working for the protection of Indio-Maíz are linked to compensatory rural development projects in the buffer zone. In 1994–8, there were 30 projects with a total budget of US$21 million under way in Río San Juan involving agricultural diversification, community forestry, ecotourism, environmental education, local organization and women in development, with financing from various international aid agencies and NGOs (Veracruz, 1995).

Until the 1950s, there were scattered hamlets of smallholders in this buffer zone.[3] These households cleared small patches of forest for crop production, and they also practised small-scale extraction of rubber, chicle and precious timber species. During the 1960–70s, a wave of new colonists entered the region. They were principally smallholders from Pacific areas who had lost their lands to cattle estates and cotton plantations. These people without land began to open up the Río San Juan forests to slash-and-burn agriculture.

The Nicaraguan civil war (1979–90) largely depopulated the region. Most of the people left as refugees for Costa Rica or they were evacuated to government-established settlements and cooperatives located in the more controllable regions. Since 1990, a considerable number of the refugees and internally displaced people have returned to their farms 'in the interior'. At the same time, the flow of new colonists entering the region has dramatically increased. There is a high degree of mobility; people come and go, and many of them move ever further into the hinterland. The great competition over resources promotes a high level of conflicts with varying degrees of violence (Utting, 1993: 147–50).

Most of the current inhabitants are peasant smallholders (*campesinos*), who cultivate basic crops by slash-and-burn agriculture and supplement their livelihood with small-scale forest extraction, logging and trading. Many of them also participate in two-step migration, which involves clearing land for pasture and then selling it to land speculators. A great many of these smallholders encounter a serious crisis of survival in a situation where access to free land has ceased, crop productivity is low and hierarchical forms of commercialization make it difficult for them to compete in national markets. The ongoing structural adjustment policies have only increased the economic hardships of many smallholders. All this has provoked a series of conflicts between the forest-edge communities, conservation agents and development projects under way in the region.

One of the main strands of my study concerned the everyday encounter between development experts and local population in this 'jungle', invaded by rural education campaigns. In such a politicized context, where interventions transcended the strict boundaries of time and space, I noted that the arguments of local knowledge as traditional knowledge, intimately linked to a particular place, transmitted from one generation to another, and going from 'practice to practice' (cf. van Beek, 1993; Berkes, 1993; Huber and Pedersen, 1997), could not explain the situationality of knowledges involved in these struggles of development and power. The categorical opposition between local and global could not illustrate the complex negotiation between diverse knowledges; rather, in order to understand the power of development discourses to tie local people into networks far beyond their control, it was necessary to analyse the local knowledges as highly situated ways of knowing, that have been subjected to multiple forms of domination and hybridization.

When explaining my research objectives, many anthropologists were amazed at my interest in studying the environmental knowledge of these 'forest encroachers', more or less contaminated by modernization. They really wondered whether it was worth studying the 'ethnoecology' of these peasant colonists, who had no autochthonous traditions. All this shows the powerful tendency within conventional anthropology to award high prestige to those who study 'intact cultures', while granting less attention to those interested in more complicated societies and their hybrid ways of knowing. As remarked by Nugent (1993: 40), in this discourse, non-indigenous peasants are still portrayed as incomplete others, too eroded by westernization to have that quality of 'pristine otherness' that would make them suitable for ethnographic research. All this means that in order to understand the complexity of migrant peasants' knowledge systems, we have to pay attention not only to the heterogeneity of their knowledges, but also to the situationality of anthropology and Western science, with their respective trends and marginalizations. In the following, the construction of local knowledge as a discrete form of knowledge, either inferior or superior to scientific knowledge, is analysed in the light of the environment-development struggles in Río San Juan. The analysis then progresses to an alternative view of these migrant peasants' knowledge systems as knowledges that are being reconfigured within the ongoing struggles over resources and representations.

LOCAL KNOWLEDGE AS NON-KNOWLEDGE

Traditionally, scientists and development experts have simply not wanted to see local forms of knowledge as having anything important to say. Scientific knowledge has been defined as a paradigm of knowledge, and the only epistemologically adequate one. This has resulted in a view of local knowledge as non-knowledge, that is based on irrationality and ignorance (Murdoch and Clark, 1994). Among the development experts working in Río San Juan, local knowledge was commonly seen as a constraint on progress and local settlers as confined by their traditional modes of thought. In one of the workshops held for training of the local people, a leading rural adviser[4] presented the following list of *-isms* which, according to him, obstructed the process of development in these jungle communities:

1. lack of will to change one's attitudes and customs (conformism)
2. lack of initiative to resolve one's problems (fatalism)
3. lack of responsibility; supposition that the government and development institutions should always help (parasitism)
4. magic traditions and beliefs (irrationalism)

5. lack of education (analphabetism)

Through such a representation, the local forest-edge communities were constructed as spaces of backwardness and their settlers as maladaptive parasites, imprisoned by their superstitions. They were rendered primitive and pre-scientific, and their capacity for progress was thought to depend on the intellectual skills of the rural advisers to unveil their ignorance and instruct them from the age of magic to the age of logic. The development agents were characterized as experts bringing civilization to barbarians, science to the superstitious, and well-being to those suffering from various lacks: lack of managerial skills, lack of sustainability, lack of environmental ethics and lack of long-term plans. To emphasize the difference between expert knowledge and local ways of knowing, the developers utilized a discourse that featured sharp contrasts: rational/magical, universal/particular, theoretical/practical and modern/traditional.

These dichotomies were powerful mind organizers, privileging one form of knowledge over another. Local knowledge was defined as knowledge of an out-of-the-way other, contrasted with progressive representatives of the expert world. This polarization served to elaborate the omniscience of experts as opposed to the ignorance of the rural poor, the enlightenment of 'us' from the obscurity of 'them', and the rationality of science from the irrationality of local knowledge. The criteria of what constituted knowledge and who was designated as qualified to know, were articulated by developers who spoke for the others who had been rendered voiceless.[5]

Such exclusion became clear in the conventional encounter between conservation authorities and local peasants in Río San Juan. Many conservation agents constructed local environmental knowledge in such a way as to suggest that, although the local people live in a rich tropical habitat, they are unaware of its ecological diversity and ignorant of how to take care of it. They were deemed to be colonists who know how to tame the jungle with the *machete* but who do not know how to conserve tropical biodiversity; only the conservation agents were considered to have the capacity to decide how this tropical landscape should be used. This argument of knowledge difference was then utilized to reinforce the conservation authorities' right to control the local resource users, who were argued to be in need of effective governance and guidance in order to achieve a 'modern' environmental consciousness.

Local settlers responded to these accusations by pointing out that the appeals for local people to change their attitudes toward nature have little relevance to the extent that the power to make a difference in local resource management is so unequally distributed. They also challenged the relevance of all this care for biodiversity by critically asking whom it was supposed to benefit. All this demonstrates how developers imposed particular representations upon local knowledges, while at the same time ignoring all the alternative conceptualizations. The everyday system of these slash-and-burn cultivators of classifying plants and soils as hot or cold was likewise judged as parochial.[6] Their practice of burning the land cleared from the forest, considered fresh (cold), until maize as a hot crop could be sown on it, was condemned simply by claiming that their traditional belief in 'hot' and 'cold' was nonsense. In the transfer of knowledge 'from experts to clients', the role of local knowledges as symbols of social identity and as signs by which the local people interpret their relationships with past, present and future, was ignored, while the interaction between developers and those-to-be-developed was constituted solely by the experts' categories.

There were also those development agents who utilized local knowledge as a strategy to achieve the desired change in these buffer zone communities. In various development projects, the rural advisers spoke of the need to respect local traditions, such as the conception of the moon controlling the vitality of the plants, the belief in the evil eye causing illnesses, and the classification of soil fertility by observing the colour of the soil. They carefully argued that there is no scientific proof of the rationality of these concepts, but in order to gain approval among the targeted local groups, one had to show respect for their beliefs. This meant paying lip service to local knowledge in order to achieve success in one's development programme.

Characteristic of this discourse was a powerful theme of rationality which judged local knowledges in terms of their appropriateness. The main idea was the involvement of local people and the incorporation of their knowledges into global strategies of sustainable development; the contribution of anthropology to this task was seen as one of providing ethnographic 'hints' to enable developers to distinguish valuable information from irrelevant drivel in these alien knowledge systems.[7] All this meant that local knowledge was legitimized only if it conformed to experts' principles of sustainability, having no right as knowledge per se.[8]

This conception emerged clearly in the discourse of biodiversity, in which local knowledges were often seen as under-used mines of information to be shared for the benefit of humanity at large. It was the bioprospectors who were the most eager speakers on behalf of local environmental knowledge, seen as a culturally and socially free 'human capital' to be harnessed in the service of biobusiness. Many of them considered the 'unimproved' genetic material—wild species and traditional varieties of crops grown by local people—as an 'open-access resource', and the knowledge of its potential use as the 'common heritage of all humans'. At the same time, they promoted maximum protection for modern medicines and crop varieties as a private property, and monetary compensation for scientists and corporations who manipulate folk varieties in their laboratories.[9]

In this situation, the local people themselves critically remarked that 'what you call bioprospecting, we call biopiracy'; in this way they called attention to the fact that the view of local knowledges as gems of information follows a familiar pattern of outsiders extracting raw materials. This new, intellectual imperialism misconstrues local knowledges as collective and 'out of history', and thus available for appropriation into scientific and developmentalist procedures. All this was cleverly pointed out by a local healer, don Sefarino, in saying that 'Every year scientists come here to take sacks of samples of our medicinal plants, and pads of notes on our healing practices, and after having grabbed all this information, they disappear and never give us any compensation.'

Such a view also assumed that the relevance of local knowledges could be verified only when subordinated to the conceptual apparatus of science. The capacity of local people to innovate, systematize and transfer knowledge was seen as limited, while scientific knowledge was considered rigorous and cumulative. There was little recognition of the fact that in practice science is 'achieved' in much the same way as other forms of knowledge—through social construction and negotiation—despite the tendency of many researchers to hide the acquisition of resources behind the presentation of scientific facts as reality 'reveals' itself. The staunch faith in objective science among the developers concealed the fact that what we call modern science is itself a historical product of continuous struggle not only to define science in a particular way, but also to exclude other ways of producing knowledge from that definition.[10]

LOCAL KNOWLEDGE AS A HOLISTIC WAY OF KNOWING

Today, there is an increasing number of environmentalists and alternative movement activists criticizing the hegemony of science and emphasizing the necessity of creating space for competing modes of knowledge. According to many of them, it is time to replace the reductionist framework of science with a methodology that draws its guidelines from non-Western traditions, based on holistic ways of knowing and ecologically evolved learning to live in equilibrium with nature.

This perception was fairly common among the environmentalists and alternative developmentalists working in Río San Juan. The matter was conceptualized as follows by one of the alternativists interested in rural empowerment in the buffer zone communities:

> Western science has for centuries oppressed rural people and their traditional knowledge. Instead of considering us as experts, we should admit that we are apprentices and have enormously to learn from the local people. They know their environment intimately and they have deep knowledge of the local ecosystems. You as anthropologist should help us in preserving this practical wisdom, totally different from scientific abstractions.

According to alternative developmentalists, local settlers were 'minimal disturbers of nature', and 'admirable scientists of the concrete' (Malkki, 1992: 29), genuinely unfolding the hidden innards of the local habitats. Their knowledges were portrayed as utilitarian, responding to precise everyday problems, in contrast to scientists' theoretical deliberations.

All this meant the resurgence of a new range of polarities, in which human knowledge was once again characterized as being composed of two opposing archetypes: Western science was constructed as reductionist and theoretical while non-Western knowledge was considered holistic and practical. These two knowledge systems were seen as highly segmented and occupying different cultural spaces, with little exchange of information between them. All this led to essentialist visions of local knowledges and romantic images of 'noble savages'. The non-industrial people were seen as paragons of ecological virtue, with scant attention paid to the existing diversity of environments, cultures and histories, and to the larger questions of knowledge and power. The image of rural communities possessing primordial environmental wisdom formed the basis of these radical environmentalists' critique that modernity per se was responsible for environmental destruction.[11]

All this was closely involved within global environmental discourses in which local knowledge is acquiring a strategic value in the environmentalists' humanist stance of defending disempowered people and not just protecting flora and fauna. This concerned especially the environmental knowledge of indigenous people. In recent years, the rainforest Indians and their environmental skills have become key symbols in transnational politics. These alliances between environmentalists and Indians are often founded on the assertion that native peoples' environmental knowledges are consistent with Western conservationist principles: The Indians are represented as 'guardians of forest', and as 'people dwelling in nature according to nature'. Such images ignore the complexity of indigenous knowledges and they also contradict the priorities of many native peoples who seek control over their resources by these alliances, while the environmentalists need Indians and their traditional knowledges in order to provide a 'human face' for their global strategies of sustainability. There is a risk that the Indians are approved as useful partners in these alliances only to the extent that they conform to Western images as 'authentic others' who demonstrate stewardship qualities toward nature (Conklin and Graham, 1995).

The peasant colonists have the bad luck of being relegated as evil others even by this discourse. When comparing the images of indigenous versus non-indigenous rainforest dwellers in the global environmental discourse, in the representations of the Indians there are precious tropical forests, rivers and mountains, huge trees with orchids and toucans, and delighted children with canoes and crossbows in the enchanted wilderness. This paradise, associated with ancient roots, time-tested lifeways and primordial mysticism, is in danger of being lost because of the terrible encroachment of non-Indian colonists, portrayed as unruly forest ravagers. There are representations of colonist families in their rustic huts and muddy patios, with pigs wandering here and there, men listening to the transistor radio and women caring for lean children with ragged clothes. All these images are based on a sharp dichotomy according to which tropical forest dwellers either are ecologically noble or they are not. The Indians are essentialized as peoples of simplicity, purity and environmental wisdom, while the non-Indian colonists are portrayed as rootless, corrupted and lacking environmental knowledge.[12]

Such a perception was implicitly constructed by one of the project leaders working for an international environmental movement in Nicaragua when explaining to me that:

> ... we prefer to work with indigenous people rather than with colonists, because the Indians have rich, accumulated knowledge of the rainforest and they still preserve their traditional practices of nature conservation. This offers us much more potentiality for global conservation, because they are more aware of our objectives.

According to him, the peasant colonists possess the 'mentality of pioneering' and the 'culture of mining', with no ethics of conservation. They were portrayed as 'malignant children of Malinche', haphazard meldings of Western and non-Western, and as 'vagabonds roving here and there'. When the Indians were associated with tropical flora and fauna as part of the overall spectacle of natural wilderness, the colonists, portrayed as 'men combating the forest', belonged to culture, spoiled by the evils of modernization.

These images dismissed local forest dwellers as social actors and the historical construction of their knowledges. There was no notion that both colonists and indigenes are 'people of the forest', although they have shaped the tropical landscape in different ways. Through categorical cultural representations, the power structures that mediate the struggle between competing knowledges and environmental ideologies were alienated. The forest-clearing activities of non-Indian colonists were attributed to their primordial 'land hunger', or to their cultural 'forest phobia', with no references to the wider contextual factors—such as agrarian policies, land tenure regimes and market forces—which have reinforced a land use pattern of forest conversion in most tropical forest areas.

Characteristic among the advocates of alternative knowledges was also an idealist assumption that it is possible to get rid of all forms of domination by simply replacing scientific hierarchies with alternative bottom-up approaches. Many of them insisted that their methodologies of 'thinking from below' successfully achieve an in-depth appreciation of the local life-worlds, and finally portray events 'as the natives find them'. In their perceptions, power came only from the top down, rather than operating in diverse social spaces. There was a tendency to portray local people as homogeneous, assume communication as unproblematic and overstate the practicability of everything that is 'local'. The opposition between us and them and here and there was taken as given; the main question was only how to establish mutual communication between the conceptually separated knowledge systems. All this meant little problematization of people's positions in the production of knowledge differences and little recognition of the political context in which alternative knowledges were being promoted.

Both of the above presented perspectives thus rely on the categorical alienation of local knowledge from universal knowledge. In scientific reductionism, local knowledge is seen as a resource of information to be interpreted by scientists; in the alternative 'noble savage' vision it is considered as a panacea for emancipation, without any notion that there is a danger of appropriating the vision of the less powerful while claiming to see from their positions (Haraway, 1996). In both cases, local knowledge is portrayed as essentially non-rational—either because of its pre-scientific and backward character, or because of its primordial wisdom. These two apparently opposed approaches then have a common structure of sustaining the discourse of otherness, in which local knowledge serves as a mirror image of scientific knowledge and local people are left without agency and reason. Both cases demonstrate that the representations are inevitably political, consequently a critical analysis of local knowledges requires more attention to be paid to the relationship of diverse knowledges and to those power structures affecting the dominance of particular knowledges.

Processes of Contestation and Reinterpretation

When trying to analyse the relationship of expert knowledges and local knowledges in the forest-edge communities of Río San Juan, any conception of local insights as objectively knowable phenomena occupying discrete spaces became implausible. In these communities of colonization, where contradictory discourses overlapped and discrepant meanings criss-crossed, all knowledges were made up of diverse elements and combined within a world of multiple actors. Any attempt to draw sharp boundaries around what counted and what did not count as 'authentic' local knowledge proved to be fruitless; rather, there was a need to start to grapple with heterogeneous and hybrid knowledges.[13]

It is in these 'places of unpredictability' that we must begin to reformulate our anthropological paradigms. The characterizations of local knowledges as internally uncontested systems arising from a communal commitment to consensus (Browder, 1995; Heyd, 1995) simply did not hold true in these communities composed of diverse social actors—peasant smallholders, land speculators, squatters, forest extractors, ambulatory traders, timber dealers and healers—with their politically fragmented and socially differentiated knowledges. These knowledges carried with them responsibilities and rights that applied differentially according to the social position, as well as complex hierarchies for determining the power to narrate history, to define tradition, and to make claims to knowledge and authority. Although most of the inhabitants were 'rural cultivators', they also worked as itinerant peons, forest extractors and loggers, moving wherever economic opportunities seemed available to them. The occupational and sectoral boundaries were thus fluid and blurred, resulting in complicated hierarchies. The communities were politically fragmented into Sandinistas versus Liberals (or ex-Sandinistas versus ex-Contras) and religiously into Catholics versus Protestants. When conversing with local people it was thus necessary to carefully consider which metaphors to use in each situation: for many Sandinistas the term 'cooperative' brought to mind the epoch when they were given all the necessities free of charge, while most of the Liberals associated the term with directed development with no possibilities for independent action.

These colonist settlers' knowledges were, therefore, caught up in a rivalry of tendencies, fractured by class, age, religious, political and gender differences. Strategic differences in the environmental knowledge of men and women could be noted, depending upon the type of activity, resource and location. The knowledge of timber products was considered a speciality of men, because of the perception of the forest as a dangerous place that remains outside the range of women's activities. The knowledge of cattle husbandry was also assigned to men because they, as heads of the house-hold, owned the cattle; women's knowledge of cattle husbandry was confined to milking, the task which was stereotyped as an ideal activity for women because of their 'natural handiness'. Housework, including poultry raising, was considered a women's duty, while the women's special prestige was associated with their gendered knowledge of domestic healing. From early childhood, girls were socialized to make *tortillas*, wash clothes, sweep the ground floor, tend chickens and fetch water from the river, while boys were taught to 'flutter' the *machete*, ride a mule, carry sacks and defend themselves physically. All this demonstrates the uneven distribution of local knowledge and how it links to people's power relations and gendered access to resources.

Even in the knowledge repertoire among the local healers, significant variation could be remarked as a result of such factors as age, gender, kinship, religion and personal experience. Different healers used different methods and there was great competition between healers, midwives and 'magicians' on the 'true' interpretation of illnesses. Each specialist guarded his/her own knowledge as a secret property, which would lose its power or be transformed into harmful sorcery if it became known to other healing specialists. Local knowledge existed in diverse versions which were not separable from the people's competitive roles and historically situated practices.

The knowledges of these migrant peasants were also closely linked to their complex social history, composed of dynamic articulations between various knowledge systems. Their agricultural knowledge included practices of traditional slash-and-burn agriculture mixed with modern agribusiness, pre-Columbian metaphors of the earth as a symbol of life mixed with postcolonial resistance to Western images of local people's affinity with nature, traditional concepts of soils as hot and cold, mixed with modern insights of soil mineralogy. Don Sefarino had constructed his healing practices from heterogeneous matrices: from his uncle who was an excellent healer, from the Catholic monks in Chontales, from the indigenous herbalists in the Atlantic Coast, when assisting in a rural health project financed by USAID, in the training courses organized by the Ministry of Health, when serving as a guide for foreign ethnopharmacologists and bioscientists, and when practising as a healer in the local communities. His medicinal knowledge consisted of a complex repertoire of native herbs and vines, cultivated medicinal plants and 'modern' medicine, with their discrepant epistemologies.

To point out this character of knowledge production as a process, local people themselves used the term *conocer* (to be acquainted with), instead of *saber* (knowing). When asked about their knowledge of non-timber forest products or cures for snakebite, the typical answer was: 'I'm acquainted with some of that, but not so much.' People reworked their knowledges in response to changing social and political contexts that were products of local and non-local processes. Concerning this, their knowledges could not be defined as purely utilitarian and as 'conforming more closely to description than to the powerful deductive explanations provided by science' (Clark and Murdoch, 1997: 43). These peasant colonists also innovated insights and identified goals; they analysed their actions, and created epistemologies. Their environmental knowledge in regard to the forest could not be seen as simple knowledge about useful forest products. It also included symbolic constructions of the forest as an uncultured space, something intact and wild that remained beyond human control. It was a source of unpredictable rains, thunder and storms, as well as a place of malevolent supernatural beings attacking lonely travellers. Behind the local conceptions of hot and cold, there was a whole epistemology of various oppositional forces that should be in proper relationship with each other to make the cosmic order possible. The systems of utilization and the systems of signification were, thus, intrinsically interwoven in these colonists' knowledge systems.

People also engaged in critical thinking and so attempted to change the conditions of their living in the political economy, where the complicated relations of knowledge and power produced hierarchical patterns of resource control. They criticized the power of developers to determine what pattern of resource utilization is good for them at the same time that they challenged the authority of *caciques*, as traditional powerholders, to control all the local resources. They questioned the principles of traditional medicine by deliberating whether getting wet in the afternoon when your body is 'hot' has anything to do with falling ill with rheumatism, at the same time as they deconstructed the omniscience of modern medicine by remarking that 'the doctors in the cities have no consciousness of hot and cold illnesses'. They declared that they do not believe in evil eye, although afterwards they told you many stories of persons who had lost their luck due to the sorcery of envious neighbours. They criticized local healers as 'impostors who live at the expense of the credulous', even while attending them regularly. By this kind of bargaining and critical deliberation people tried to rework their knowledges to fit ever-changing situations.[14]

In this light, the entire dichotomization of traditional knowledge as inherently opposed to modern (or postmodern) knowledge seemed arbitrary. Only by examining the continuity in change, traditionality in modernity, and situationality in hybridity could a more profound significance involved in the reconstruction of local knowledge be revealed. There was no monolithic modernity expanding, inexorably, into this jungle; rather, local and global were intrinsically mingled together, and ambivalent meanings created complicated local life-worlds.

Struggles Over Knowledge and Representation

From this perspective of situated knowledges, it became evident that also in the game between 'experts' and 'clients', the local settlers were actors constructing the other. They contested the symbolic subjugation of their knowledges by critically challenging the developers' expertise as 'some loose tips' (instructions, pieces of advice), changing chaotically according to the vicissitudes of development policies. They also questioned the progressive character of science by pointing out that in the cycle of different booms the developers' 'big promises' are never fulfilled. In regard to the current boom of 'natural products' and 'local environmental wisdom' they even felt that the developers were making them ridiculous. When the physicians only a decade ago condemned their use of wild plants as medicines, scientists now come to ask them to serve as guides to the reserve of Indio-Maíz in search for natural remedies. A local extractor, Don Ernesto, could not but laugh at the whole circus; he told amusingly how 'some *cheles*[15] are going to implement a project of rattan as an alternative non-timber forest product in the community of Buena Vista, although there is almost no rattan left in this region. And all this just because the experts have now realized that the tropical forests are more than timber.' By this story, Don Ernesto wanted to call attention to the ignorance of the developers who had no notion of the wider social and political context in which the 'utility' of local resources and local knowledges is continuously defined.

In this game of reconstruction, local people no longer identified themselves as authentic others, but as people who have for ages been mediated by globalization. The inevitable influence of modernization was recognized, as well as the existence of the 'new world', where their knowledges are characterized by alterity and hybridity. They were well aware that the intransigent dependency upon 'traditional' knowledge is a less efficient strategy to cope with globalization than a critical opening toward the present, including a selective engagement with current discourses of development. They clearly recognized that in a situation where bioprospectors define the value of their medicinal plants and rural advisers determine the reasonableness of their agricultural knowledge, any change in the current violence against the subject of knowledges requires struggle at different levels, from local to global.

In this regard, local settlers proved to be very clever in using the current phraseology of sustainability. When conversing with development experts, they carefully employed the cliches of environmental consciousness, local participation, and sound resource utilization. This confusing imitation of all the rhetoric of sustainability was a key to the reconstitution and redeployment of their knowledges. One of my key informants, Don Rufino, was well aware of the images salient in international environmental and development circles. He emphasized the value of the biological reserve of Indio-Maíz as the world's largest and last 'pharmacy', urging that it has to be studied by scientists before it vanishes. However, when talking with his neighbours, he merely wondered why the government did not give this 'reserve of idle land' to poor peasants who do not have a place where they can survive. He proudly told me about the native multi-purpose species, providing the necessary details to satisfy a foreign anthropologist interested in ethnoecology. He showed me the tree called *hombre grande* as an indispensable remedy against malaria, and the vine called *uña de gato* as the most promising cure against cancer, AIDS, and other 'modern' illnesses. When he himself felt any symptoms of malaria, however, he went to the nearest health centre to ask for malaria pills.

All this shows that these colonists were well aware of what anthropologists and environmentalists wanted them to do: go back to nature and live in thatched huts instead of concrete houses, preserve their traditional healing practices instead of using modern medicine, and conserve their forests for future generations instead of clearing them for agriculture. They were well acquainted with the expectations placed upon them by those who occupied high positions in regional, national and international development politics. In this situation, they reshaped their knowledges in order to fit better with the image of 'sound resource users', seen as a prerequisite for receiving benefits from the donors. At the same time, they eagerly stressed the systematic character of their knowledges, while disguising any aspect that could be associated with magic or primitivism. This was because they did not want to be confused with the 'savage Indians', whose knowledges they perceived as threatening witchcraft. When talking about their conception of the moon regulating the vitality of life, they carefully remarked that 'many scientists have been interested in the rationality of our practice of rooting up tubers in the waning moon'. They were strategically negotiating which aspects to emphasize or conceal in their knowledge repertoires, at the same time as they were reinterpreting the multiple meanings of sustainability.

All this challenges the alternative developmentalists' view that if both sides in the development process improve their communication, a major obstacle for development will be removed. Such a vision ignored the many reasons people may have for not wishing to communicate (Hobart, 1993: 11–12). In our daily conversations, people always insisted that they had no idea of the development projects going on in their communities, even those persons who regularly attended the projects' village meetings. By this rejection people wanted to imply that the developers are not trying to resolve their problems. Their reluctance to participate was not simply an indication of their passivity; it was also a strategic form of resistance against those planning for their future.

People also contested the role of clients thrust upon them by developers. When conversing with rural advisers they appreciated the improvements of their production systems by developers' expertise. In their heart of hearts, however, they felt a deep resentment towards any discourse of development. They themselves called this *hacer la guatuza*—'leaving a stranger in the lurch'—or as explained by Doña Ernestina: 'if you are a *chela* and you come here, people swear to you that they will participate and that everything is possible, and then they knife you in the back'. When a project implementing a campaign of agricultural diversification supplied pineapples to local settlers to be planted in their home gardens, people took dozens of pineapples, but instead of planting them, they either ate them or sold them in nearby communities. This was their way of criticizing the developers' ignorance of the vulnerability of local economy in relation to far-reaching global markets. All this demonstrates how people understand and misunderstand in strategic ways and how their knowledges are redefined in compliance, negotiation and resistance within the wider discourses of development and power.

The critical task of anthropology in this work of reconstruction is to search for fresh forms of knowledge and representation that identify difference without domination and diversity without totalization. Theoretically, this requires a new epistemological basis that recognizes the fluidity of boundaries and the partiality of entities, while emphasizing the multiplicity of voices and the diversity of visions. This struggle for a vision of contextualized knowledges is not just intellectual or 'academic', it also has enormous consequences for people's lives, for knowledge making and for political action, as can be noted when simply reflecting on the power that science, such as engineering, biotechnology and medicine, has today over people's bodies and life-worlds (Fujimura, 1997).

CONCLUSION

This study took a critical look at the conventional approaches categorizing local knowledge as opposed to universal knowledge. The epistemology of scientific rationalism, perceiving local knowledge as scapegoat for backwardness or as a raw material for scientists, was challenged. The alternative 'noble savage' approach, in which local knowledge is portrayed as holistic wisdom, was likewise deconstructed. The study emphasized the necessity of analysing local knowledges as heterogeneous ways of knowing that emerge out of a multidimensional reality in which diverse cultural, environmental, economic and socio-political factors intersect. All knowledges are derived from the interaction of multiple social actors, that are differentially empowered and move in a terrain characterized by contradictory, competitive and complementary relations.

All this makes it impossible to work with sharp boundaries between people's science and scientists' science. Local knowledge repertoires are a result of knowledge encounters in which local and global, and traditional and modern are intricately intermingled. A critical question is rather the relative status of the different components in these knowledge encounters. Would we expect to see the gradual marginalization of alternative knowledges, or can there be a symmetrical coexistence between these diverse forms of knowledge?

According to Turnbull (1991: 572), what is needed is 'to find ways to give a voice to local knowledges without smothering them in totalizing theories'. This requires spanning the all-encompassing divides and reorienting ourselves toward situated knowledges. Such a perspective offers interesting angles from which to analyse the existing heterogeneity of knowledges and the multiple ways by which the local knowledge systems become linked to global representations of knowledge and power. In today's highly interconnected world, local people find themselves tied into social, scientific and technical networks which extend far beyond their locality and, consequently, there is an increasing need to recognize the ongoing hybridization of their knowledges.

A strategy to empower local knowledges requires an understanding not only of the hegemonic discourses authorizing essentialist representations of knowledges, but also of the shifting and contested nature of local knowledges, which are themselves derived from discrepant epistemologies and practices. For us as anthropologists, this means we are called upon to pay greater heed to the interpretations of the people we study. It also demands that we welcome these alternative ways of conceptualization which now have no voice or which simply are not heard in contemporary scientific and developmentalist discourses. This at best offers us a much better understanding of marginalized people's struggles to reconfigure their knowledges and to reconstruct their life with meaning in today's networks of knowledge and power.

NOTES

This article draws on research financed by the Academy of Finland. I am grateful to the people of Río San Juan and to the many development institutions in Nicaragua that cooperated with my field research, as well as to Universidad Centroamericana which provided the logistical support during my field research. Karen Armstrong, Annelies Moors, Ulla

Vuorela and the three anonymous reviewers of *Critique of Anthropology* provided valuable comments on previous versions of this article. Of course, I remain solely responsible for any errors of fact or interpretation.

1. The terms 'local knowledge', 'indigenous knowledge', 'traditional knowledge' and 'ethnoscience' are used as synonyms here, although each has its drawbacks. 'Ethnoscience' has a competing meaning in linguistic anthropology, where it is limited to semantic analysis of folk taxonomies. 'Local knowledge' has a connotation that local people are only observing their immediate surroundings and that their knowledge has no wider application. 'Traditional knowledge' connotes a homogeneous system of thought, thus obscuring the fact that people everywhere constantly rework their knowledges. 'Indigenous knowledge' conceals the fact that all people, irrespective of whether they are indigenous to a given area, have developed complicated understandings of the world (De Walt, 1994; Sillitoe, 1998). A thorough semantic analysis of these terms is beyond the scope of this article.

2. The anthropological field research was carried out in Río San Juan in 1996–8. The primary information consists of tape-recorded interviews, informal meetings, daily conversations and participant observations involving local people, as well as numerous state agents, development experts, and environmental and social movement activists in 45 development institutions and NGOs. Except where explicitly stated, the presented information is based on my field material.

3. Two-thirds of the land in the department of Río San Juan belonged to the dictator Somoza and absentee land speculators. Most of these 'unoccupied' lands were nationalized during the Sandinista government (Rabella, 1995: 101–5).

4. Interestingly, only a day before, this rural adviser eagerly told me how he had participated in various courses of local empowerment.

5. For those criticizing the categorical distinction of us as knowers and them as to be known see Fabian (1990), Hobart (1996), Latour (1993) and Law and Whittaker (1988). For studies analysing the subjugation of local knowledges by a hegemonic discourse of expert knowledge see Escobar (1997), Hobart (1993) and Pigg (1996).

6. These metaphors of 'hot' and 'cold' form a network of meanings in everyday knowledge throughout Central America. They refer to plants, soils, bodily conditions, foods, illnesses and medicines. In this knowledge system, hot and cold are not transitory states of thermal quantities, but intrinsic qualities of each object; for example water considered as a cold element remains cold even when boiling. This classification system is a modified form of an ancient Greek humour pathology transmitted through Spain to the New World, where it combined with Mesoamerican traditions (Wilken, 1990). It is a dynamic system of classification in which people selectively mix diverse meanings together.

7. For recent studies, emphasizing the role of anthropology as one of promoting the potential contribution of indigenous knowledges to sustainable development see Forsyth (1996), Purcell (1998), Sillitoe (1998) and Warren *et al.* (1995).

8. This applies also to the famous *Agenda 21*. This global environmental strategy recognizes that indigenous peoples 'have developed over many generations a holistic traditional scientific knowledge of their lands, natural resources and environment', and then recommends the 'recognition of their values, traditional knowledge and resource management practices with a view to promoting environmentally sound and sustainable development' (UNCED, 1993: 227–8). According to the criticism expressed by many Third World experts, despite all the rhetoric on 'local knowledge', this environmental strategy appreciates the scientific knowledge of the West, and secures the political interests of the North, giving no space for alternative ways of making politics and representing knowledges. For more on this criticism, see Benton (1994) and Guha and Martínez-Allier (1997).

9. For detailed analyses of local knowledge and intellectual property rights concerning bioprospecting see Brush (1993), Brush and Stabinsky (1996) and Cleveland and Murray (1997).

10. For ethnographic laboratory studies that demonstrate how science attempts to decontextualize itself in order to make itself neutral see Knorr-Cetina (1995), Latour (1993), Shapin (1995) and Watson-Verran and Turnbull (1995). Such social studies of science have been criticized by Gross and Levitt (1994) and Sokal (1996), according to whom any argument about science as social practice is absurd and antiscientific. According to them, science as objective and systematic offers the best available methods for producing credible claims. For more on this epistemological controversy see Fujimura (1998) and Ross (1996).

11. The 'primitive environmental wisdom' continues to be an issue which provokes heated discussion in anthropology and the social sciences. For those proposing the superiority of non-Western knowledges because they represent a close affinity with nature see Hoffman (1997), Merchant (1992), Shiva (1989) and Warren (1990). For those criticizing the essentialist representation of non-Western peoples as 'nature conservationists' see Agrawal (1995), Bebbington (1993), Buege (1996), Colchester (1997), Guha and Martmez-Allier (1997), Headland (1997) and Milton (1996: 106–41).

12. For inspiring studies on representations of indigenous and non-indigenous people in the global imageries see Conklin and Graham (1995), Lutz and Collins (1993), Nugent (1993, 1997) and Ramos (1991).

13. For studies dismantling the dichotomies of local and global see Agrawal (1995), Descola and Palsson (1996), Haraway (1996), Moore (1996), Murdoch and Clark (1994) and Nader (1996). For studies on reconstruction and hybridization see Clark and Murdoch (1997), Gupta and Ferguson (1992), Jackson (1995) and Mitchell (1997).
14. In this respect, see the inspiring study by Pigg (1996) on the shifting character of 'traditional' belief systems in Nepal.
15. A pejorative appellation, referring to a person who is light-complexioned and foreign (North American or European).

REFERENCES CITED

Agrawal, Arun. 1995. 'Dismantling the Divide between Indigenous and Scientific Knowledge', Development and Change 26(3): 413–39.

Bebbington, Anthony. 1993. 'Modernization from Below: An Alternative Indigenous Development?', Economic Geography 69(3): 274–92.

Benton, Ted. 1994. 'Biology and Social Theory in the Environmental Debate', in M. Redclift and T. Benton (eds) Social Theory and Global Environment. London: Routledge.

Berkes, Fikret. 1993. 'Traditional Ecological Knowledge in Perspective', in J. Inglis (ed.) Traditional Ecological Knowledge: Concepts and Cases. Ottawa: International Development Research Centre.

Browder, John. 1995. 'Redemptive Communities: Indigenous Knowledge, Colonist Farming Systems, and Conservation of Tropical Forests', Agriculture and Human Values 12(1): 17–30.

Brush, Stephen. 1993. 'Indigenous Knowledge of Biological Resources and Intellectual Property Rights: The Role of Anthropology', American Anthropologist 95(3): 653–71.

Brush, Stephen and Doreen Stabinsky, eds. 1996. Valuing Local Knowledge: Indigenous People and Intellectual Property Rights. Washington, DC: Island Press.

Buege, Douglas. 1996. 'The Ecologically Noble Savage Revisited', Environmental Ethics 18(1): 71–88.

Clark, Judy and Jonathan Murdoch. 1997. 'Local Knowledge and the Precarious Extension of Scientific Networks: A Reflection of Three Case Studies', Sociologia Ruralis 37(1): 38–60.

Cleveland, David A. and Stephen C. Murray. 1997. 'The World's Crop Genetic Resources and the Rights of Indigenous Farmers', Current Anthropology 38(4): 477–515.

Cohen, Anthony. 1993. 'Segmentary Knowledge: A Whalsay Sketch', in M. Hobart (ed.) An Anthropological Critique of Development: The Growth of Ignorance. London: Routledge.

Colchester, Marcus. 1997. 'Salvaging Nature: Indigenous Peoples and Protected Areas', in K.B. Ghimire and M.P. Pimbert (eds) Social Change and Conservation. London: Earthscan.

Conklin, Beth and Laura Graham. 1995. 'The Shifting Middle Ground: Amazonian Indians and Eco-Politics', American Anthropologist 97(4): 695–710.

Descola, Philippe and Gisli Palsson. 1996. 'Introduction', in P. Descola and G. Palsson (eds) Nature and Society: Anthropological Perspectives. London: Routledge.

De Walt, Billie. 1994. 'Using Indigenous Knowledge to Improve Agriculture and Natural Resource Management', Human Organization 53(2): 123–31.

Escobar, Arturo. 1997. 'Anthropology and Development', International Social Science Journal 154: 497–515.

Fabian, Johannes. 1990. 'Presence and Representation: The Other and Anthropological Writing', Critical Inquiry 16: 753–72.

Forsyth, Timothy. 1996. 'Science, Myth and Knowledge: Testing Himalayan Environmental Degradation in Thailand', Geoforum 27(3): 375–92.

Fujimura, Joan H. 1998. 'Authorizing Knowledge in Science and Anthropology', American Anthropologist 100(2): 347–60.

Geertz, Clifford. 1983. Local Knowledge: Further Essays in Interpretive Anthropology. New York: Basic Books.

Gross, Paul and Norman Levitt. 1994. Higher Superstition: The Academic Left and its Quarrels with Science. Baltimore, MD: Johns Hopkins University Press.

Guha, Ramachandra and Juan Martmez-Allier. 1997. Varieties of Environmentalism: Essays North and South. London: Earthscan.

Gupta, Akhil and James Ferguson. 1992. 'Beyond "Culture": Space, Identity, and the Politics of Difference', Cultural Anthropology 7(1): 6–23.

Haraway, Donna. 1989. Primate Visions: Gender, Race, and Nature in the World of Modern Science. New York: Routledge.

Haraway, Donna. 1996. 'Situated Knowledges: The Science Question in Feminism and the Privilege of Partial Perspective', in J. Agnew, D. Livingstone and A. Rogers (eds) Human Geography: An Essential Geography. Oxford: Blackwell.

Headland, Thomas N. 1997. 'Revisionism in Ecological Anthropology', Current Anthropology 38(4): 605–30.

Heyd, Thomas. 1995. 'Indigenous Knowledge, Emancipation and Alienation', Knowledge and Policy 8(1): 63–73.

Hobart, Mark. 1993. 'Introduction: The Growth of Ignorance?', in M. Hobart (ed.) An Anthropological Critique of Development: The Growth of Ignorance. London: Routledge.

Hobart, Mark. 1996. 'As I Lay Laughing: Encountering Global Knowledge in Bali', in R. Fardon (ed.) Counterworks: Managing the Diversity of Knowledge. London: Routledge.

Hoffman, Thomas. 1997. 'Moving beyond Dualism: A Dialogue with Western European and American Indian Views of Spirituality, Nature, and Science', Social Science Journal 34(4): 447–60.

Huber, Toni and Poul Pedersen. 1997. 'Meteorological Knowledge and Environmental Ideas in Traditional and Modern Societies: The Case of Tibet', Journal of the Royal Anthropological Institute 3(3): 577–98.

Hunn, Eugene. 1982. 'The Utilitarian Factor in Folk Biological Classification', American Anthropologist 84(4): 830–47.

Jackson Jean E. 1995. 'Culture, Genuine and Spurious: The Politics of Indianness in the Vaupes, Colombia', American Ethnologist 22(1): 3–27.

Kloppenburg, Jack Jr. 1991. 'Social Theory and the De/Reconstruction of Agricultural Science: Local Knowledge for an Alternative Agriculture', Rural Sociology 56(4): 519–48.

Knorr-Cetina, Karen. 1995. 'Laboratory Studies: The Cultural Approach to the Study of Science', in S. Jasonoff et al. (eds) Handbook of Science and Technology Studies. London: Sage.

Latour, Bruno. 1993. We Have Never Been Modern. New York: Harvester Wheatsheaf.

Law, John and John Whittaker. 1988. 'On the Art of Representation: Notes on the Politics of Visualisation', in G. Fyfe and J. Law (eds) Picturing Power: Visual Depiction and Social Relations. Sociological Review Monograph 35. London: Routledge.

Lévi-Strauss, Claude. 1962. La Pensée sauvage. Paris: Plon.

Lutz, Catherine and Jane Collins. 1993. Reading National Geographic. Chicago, Il: University of Chicago Press.

Malkki, Liisa. 1992. 'National Geographic: The Rooting of Peoples and the Territorialization of National Identity among Scholars and Refugees', Cultural Anthropology 7(1): 24–44.

Merchant, Carolyn. 1992. Radical Ecology: The Search for a Livable World. New York: Routledge.

Milton, Kay. 1996. Environmentalism and Cultural Theory: Exploring the Role of Anthropology in Environmental Discourse. London: Routledge.

Mitchell, Katharyne. 1997. 'Different Diasporas and the Hype of Hybridity', Environment and Planning: Society and Space 15: 533–53.

Mohanty, Chandra. 1991. 'Under Western Eyes: Feminist Scholarship and Colonial Discourses', in C. Mohanty, A. Russo and L. Torres (eds) Third World Women and the Politics of Feminism. Bloomington: Indiana University Press.

Moore, Henrietta. 1996. 'The Changing Nature of Anthropological Knowledge: An Introduction', in H. Moore (ed.) The Future of Anthropological Knowledge. London: Routledge.

Murdoch, Jonathan and Judy Clark. 1994. 'Sustainable Knowledge', Geoforum 25(2): 115–32.

Nader, Laura. 1996. 'Anthropological Inquiry into Boundaries, Power, and Knowledge', in L. Nader (ed.) Naked Science: Anthropological Inquiry into Boundaries, Power, and Knowledge. London: Routledge.

Nash, June. 1997. 'When isms become wasms: Structural Functionalism, Marxism, Feminism and Postmodernism', Critique of Anthropology 17(1): 11–32.

Nugent, Stephen. 1993. Amazonian Caboclo Society: An Essay of Invisibility and Peasant Economy. Oxford: Berg.

Nugent, Stephen. 1997. 'The Coordinates of Identity in Amazonia: At Play in the Fields of Culture', Critique of Anthropology 17(1): 33–51.

Pigg, Stacy L. 1996. 'The Credible and the Credulous: The Question of "Villagers' Beliefs" in Nepal', Cultural Anthropology 11(2): 160–201.

Polanyi, Michael. 1966. The Tacit Dimension. New York: Doubleday and Co.

Posey, Darrell. 1983. 'Indigenous Ecological Knowledge and Development of Amazon', in E. Moran (ed.) The Dilemma of Amazon Development. Boulder, CO: Westview Press.

Purcell, Trevor. 1998. 'Indigenous Knowledge and Applied Anthropology: Questions of Definition and Direction', Human Organization 57(3): 258–72.

Rabella, Joaquim. 1995. Aproximación a la historia de Río San Juan. Managua: Sí-Internacional.

Ramos, Alcida R. 1991. 'A Hall of Mirrors: The Rhetoric of Indigenism in Brazil', Critique of Anthropology 11(2): 155–69.

Ross, Andrew, ed. 1996. Science Wars. Durham, NC: Duke University Press.

Shapin, Steven. 1995. 'Here and Everywhere: The Sociology of Scientific Knowledge', Annual Review of Sociology 21: 289–321.

Shiva, Vandana. 1989. Staying Alive: Women, Ecology and Development. London: Zed Books.

Sillitoe, Paul. 1998. 'The Development of Indigenous Knowledge: A New Applied Anthropology', Current Anthropology 39(2): 223–52.

Sokal, Alan D. 1996. 'A Physicist Experiments with Cultural Studies', Lingua Franca 6(4): 62–4.

Turnbull, David. 1991. 'Local Knowledge and "Absolute Standards": A Reply to Daly', Social Studies of Science 21(3): 571–3.

UNCED. 1993. Agenda 21: Programme of Action for Sustainable Development. New York: United Nations.

Utting, Peter. 1993. Trees, People and Power: Social Dimensions of Deforestation and Forest Protection in Central America. London: Earthscan.

Van Beek, Walter. 1993. 'Processes and Limitations of Dogon Agricultural Knowledge', in M. Hobart (ed.) An Anthropological Critique of Development: The Growth of Ignorance. London: Routledge.

Van der Ploeg, Jan. 1993. 'Potatoes and Knowledge', in M. Hobart (ed.) An Anthropological Critique of Development: The Growth of Ignorance. London: Routledge.

Veracruz, Carlos. 1995. Inventario de programas y proyectos existentes. Managua: MARENA.

Warren, Karen. 1990. 'The Power and the Promise of Ecological Feminism', Environmental Ethics 12(2): 125–46.

Warren, D. Michael, Jan Slikkerveer and David Brokhensa, eds. 1995. The Cultural Dimension of Development: Indigenous Knowledge Systems. London: Intermediate Technology Publications.

Watson-Verran, Helen and David Turnbull. 1995). 'Science and Other Indigenous Knowledge Systems', in S. Jasonoff et al. (eds) Handbook of Science and Technology Studies. London: Sage.

Wilken, Gene. 1990. Good Farmers: Traditional Agricultural Resource Management in Mexico and Central America. Berkeley: University of California Press.